The Complete

DEGREE COURSE
OFFERS 1994

AND HOW TO CHOOSE YOUR COURSE AT
UNIVERSITY AND COLLEGE

*The complete guide on
admission to all higher education courses*

by
BRIAN HEAP DA (MANC) ATD
Director: Higher Education Advice and Planning Service, Holborn College

T R O T M A N

This edition published in 1993 in Great Britain by
Trotman and Company Ltd
12 Hill Rise, Richmond, Surrey TW10 6UA

©Brian Heap and Trotman and Company Limited

British Library Cataloguing in Publication Data

A catalogue record for this book is available
from the British Library

ISBN 0-85660-166-7

LIST OF ADVERTISERS

CONTENTS

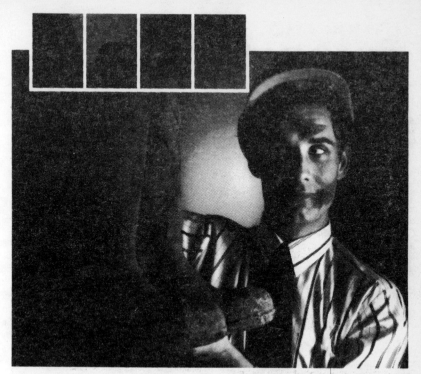

Accountants always wear suits

Or so they say. But that's without taking into account the variety of clients that you can expect to be involved with when you are training with the world's largest firm of accountants and management consultants.

That variety could take you, as part of an audit team, one hundred feet down a copper mine in Cornwall, or see you pulling on wellingtons with one of our major construction clients.

Predictable it won't be . . . although life at KPMG does have its certainties. For one thing you will be on the receiving end of one of the finest management training programmes. So, irrespective of the nature of your degree, if you enjoy a challenge and are determined to succeed, you can expect a future with real personal rewards with KPMG.

See how well one of our chartered accountants' suits would fit you – contact your careers adviser for details of opportunities for vacation work and future careers.

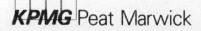 **KPMG** Peat Marwick

AUTHOR'S NOTES AND ACKNOWLEDGEMENTS

I gratefully acknowledge the efforts of university and college registrars, schools liaison staff, faculty and departmental heads and admissions tutors for their help in providing detailed information about their courses.

I should also like to thank the staff of the Universities Central Council on Admissions, the Polytechnics Central Admissions System (merged in 1993 to form a new single admissions agency for Higher Education, the Universities and Colleges Admissions Service (UCAS)), the Art and Design Admissions Registry and the Conference of Scottish Centrally-Funded Colleges for their help and assistance in providing me with up-to-date information. I am also grateful to Mr J Tarsh of the Economics Division of the Department for Education for providing statistical information on graduate employment and to the Careers Services of Anglia Polytechnic University, Bradford, Surrey, Teesside and York Universities for providing examples of careers entered by their graduates. I am also indebted to Robert Walls of the Royal Holloway, London, Mike Lumb of UMIST, staff at Imperial College, London, and of Hertfordshire and Portsmouth Universities for providing information on European placements, and also to Peter Spencer of the Leicestershire Careers Service for providing some information on BTEC offers. May I also thank those teachers and their pupils who have sent me interview reports and other information which has provided useful supplementary data for the book.

Every effort has been made to maintain absolute accuracy in course information and to ensure that the entire book is as up-to-date as possible. As the book goes to press, however, many changes are taking place in higher education so it is important for readers to check with prospectuses constantly before submitting their application.

It must be stressed that the positioning of the institutions in each of the subject tables published in this book must not be regarded as a reference to the quality of the course offered.

I also wish to thank the many readers who have written to me about the problems they have encountered in choosing courses and places to study. Such information adds to a valuable store of knowledge which can be passed on through the medium of the book, thus creating better understanding of mutual difficulties.

Finally, my thanks to Jane Heap of Putney High School for checking on course changes in all institutions and also to my wife Rita for her clerical help (and patience) through 24 years of publication.

Brian Heap
January 1993

Calling all 5th & 6th Formers

The Schools' Fair '93

The Business Design Centre, Islington, London

Wednesday 30th June 1993
Thursday 1st July 1993
Friday 2nd July 1993

** A date for your diary **

The Schools' Fair is targeted exclusively at the 16+ school leaver age group looking for long term career counselling, advice on Higher Education course choice and exciting opportunities in training and employment now and in the future, in both the UK and abroad.

* Exhibitors come from a wide range of educational, vocational and training institutions such as: Industry Groups, Major employers, Trade Associations, Government representatives, The Forces and Higher Education including Colleges and Universities from the UK, Europe and the United States of America.

* Over 100 **FREE** seminars covering Higher Education course choice and long term career advice.

* Career Clinic: **FREE** advice from the experts.

* ECCTIS 2000 - Search the ECCTIS database for the course that's right for you.

School party and individual visitors welcome. Entry free. For information and pre-registering details please write to:

Tricia Neill
News International Exhibitions Ltd
PO Box 495
Virginia Street
London E1 9XY

ABOUT THIS BOOK

Choosing a career or course of study is not easy. There is much that applicants need to know to make decisions that are right for them as individuals, and each year school and college leavers spend a great deal of time exploring various options. One option is higher education, but entry to degree and diploma courses is highly competitive. Applicants need good advice on how to choose their courses and up-to-date information about selection policies and institutions to help them secure a place.

Unfortunately, despite the mass of information available in prospectuses, some of which is confusing, the quality of advice and information varies considerably with the result that many applicants do not know enough about higher education to make informed choices. For the last 23 years *The Complete Degree Course Offers* has aimed to help school and college leavers to choose their degree courses and to provide the most up-to-date and comprehensive information obtained from official sources about entry to higher education. Its aim is to educate – not simply to provide basic facts and figures. By identifying and presenting the key elements of the selection process and other, essential facts, the book is intended to help the applicant gain a place in higher education at a time when there is unprecedented demand for them.

While there is competition between candidates for most courses, applicants should be aware that every institution, from the smallest to the largest, is competing to get the best students. To this end, subject departments are constantly reviewing their courses to make them more attractive. To help potential applicants in their decision-making we have asked institutions to highlight important features of their courses, to advise on their views on a 'gap year' and to provide information on study opportunities abroad. All this information is provided under the appropriate subject tables in Chapter 6.

When referring to the subject tables in Chapter 6, readers are reminded that the grades shown are not always the standard offers made because these may vary, depending on the academic and personal qualities of the applicant. **The offers listed relate to current policies and in most cases to those which will apply to next year's applicants.**

The Complete Degree Course Offers lists:

- institutions demanding actual grades, and those accepting equivalent points scores, after A-levels

- institutions likely to accept applicants who marginally fail their offers

- subject information

- course highlights

- opportunities for study and work experience abroad and advice for students

- advice on taking a gap year

- advice on what to do after A-level results are published

- advice for overseas and mature applicants

- examples of questions faced by applicants at interview

- offers to applicants with Scottish Certificate of Education, BTEC and Irish qualifications and the International and European Baccalaureates

- new graduates' destinations.

The information in *The Complete Degree Course Offers* is updated each year from over 6000 questionnaires returned by admissions tutors. The information is collated between November and January of each academic year (for publication in the spring) at a time when admissions tutors are able to forecast offers, admissions policies and details of new courses for the next application cycle starting in September.

The Complete Degree Course Offers 1994 therefore once more provides in a single volume the most up-to-date and complete survey of selection information and advice on how to choose courses for higher education for applicants at a time when they need it most.

Important note During 1992 polytechnics were permitted to call themselves universities and therefore many name changes took place. However, despite these name changes there is no indication as yet that the course information and selection policies or offers will change. **It is vital, however, that readers always check prospectuses carefully and contact the Admissions Offices of their chosen institutions if they have any queries.**

Brian Heap
January 1993

1   YOUR FIRST DECISIONS

HIGHER EDUCATION OR NOT?

Why do you want to go on to higher education? If you are taking A/AS- level or other examinations next year this is an important question to ask. Higher education is but one of two options you have. The other is employment, and perhaps it is important to note that higher education is not necessarily the best option for everyone. It is, however, one which is appropriate for many and therefore should not be rejected lightly. Higher education will not only open many doors and give you opportunities for work and leisure which would never be possible in a nine-to-five job, but it leads very often and quite accidentally into careers you have never previously considered.

Most courses in higher education lead to a degree or a diploma and, for either, you will have to make a subject choice. This can be difficult because the established universities alone offer over 2000 courses. When choosing you have two main options:

Choosing a course similar or the same as one (or more) of your A-level subjects or related to an interest outside the school curriculum eg, Anthropology, American Studies, Archaeology.

Choosing a course in preparation for a future career eg Medicine, Engineering.

CHOOSING YOUR COURSE

Degree/Diploma Course Choice by A-level Subject

The A-level subject choice is a reasonably safe option. You are already familiar with the subject and what it involves and you can possibly look forward to studying it to a much greater depth over the next few years. If the long term career prospects concern you, don't worry - a degree course isn't necessarily a training for a job. If you are taking science subjects these can naturally lead on to a range of scientific careers although many scientists follow non science careers such as law, and accountancy. If you are taking arts or social science subjects remember that the training for most non scientific careers can start once you have got your degree. (Information on graduate employment is given in many of the subject tables in Chapter 6.)

But let's go a stage further:

A-level subjects do not stand on their own, in isolation. Each subject you are taking is one of a much larger family. Each school subject has many similarities with subjects studied in degree and diploma courses which you might not have ever considered. So before you decide finally on taking an A-level subject to degree level read through the following tables. Here you will find some examples of degree courses with similarities to the A-level subjects you might be taking. (This list is also useful if you have to consider alternative courses after the A-level results are published!)

Ancient History: Archaeology, Biblical Studies, Classics and Classical Civilisation, Greek, Latin, Middle and Near Eastern Studies.

Art: Archaeology, Architecture, Communications Studies, Fine Art, Graphic Communication, History of Art, Landscape Studies, Media Studies, Photographic Art, Textile Design, Town and Country Planning, Typography.

Biology: Agricultural Sciences, Anatomy, Biochemistry, Biological Sciences, Botany, Dentistry, Dietetics, Ecology, Fishery Science, Food Science, Forestry, Health and Life Sciences, Horticulture, Human Sciences, Life Sciences, Marine Biology, Medicine, Microbiology, Nursing Studies, Nutrition, Oceanography, Occupational Therapy, Ophthalmic Optics (Optometry), Pharmacy, Physiology, Psychology, Speech Science (Therapy), Teaching, Veterinary Science, Wood Science, Zoology.

British Government and Politics: Government, Industrial Relations, International Politics, Law, Politics, Public Administration, Social Studies, Strategic Studies.

Chemistry: Agricultural Sciences, Animal Sciences, Bacteriology, Biochemistry, Biological Studies, Biotechnology, Botany, Brewing, Chemical Engineering, Chemical Physics, Colour Chemistry, Dentistry, Dietetics, Earth Sciences, Food Science and Technology, Fuel and Energy Science, Genetics, Geochemistry, Geology, Glass Technology, Human Sciences, Materials Science, Marine Biology, Medicine, Microbiology, Natural Sciences, Paper Science, Pharmacology, Pharmacy, Physiology, Polymer Sciences, Teaching, Textile Chemistry, Veterinary Science, Zoology.

Domestic Science: Dietetics, Health and Life Sciences, Hotel and Catering and Institutional Management, Marketing, Nursing Studies, Nutrition.

Economics: Accountancy, Administration, Business Economics, Business Studies, Estate Management, Operational Research, Politics, Quantity Surveying, Social Studies, Statistics.

English: Drama, English, Journalism, Librarianship.

Geography: Earth Sciences, Environmental Science, Estate Management, Forestry, Geography, Geology, Land Economy, Meteorology, Oceanography, Town Planning, Urban Studies.

Geology: Earth Sciences, Geography, Geophysics, Mineral Sciences, Minerals Surveying, Mining, Oceanography, Petroleum Geology, Soil Science, Surveying.

History: American Studies, International Relations, Law, Religious Studies.

Religious Studies: Archaeology, Anthropology, Divinity, Social Administration.

Languages: Apart from French, it is not usually necessary to have completed an A-level language course before studying many language courses offered at degree level eg, Chinese, Japanese, Scandinavian Studies.

Mathematics: Accountancy, Actuarial Mathematics, Aeronautical Engineering, Astrophysics, Building Science and Technology, Business Management, Chemical Engineering, Civil Engineering, Computational Science, Computer Systems Engineering, Control Systems, Cybernetics, Economics, Electrical/Electronic Technology, Engineering

Science, Ergonomics, Geophysics, Management Science, Materials Science and Technology, Mechanical Engineering, Metallurgy, Meteorology, Mining Engineering, Naval Architecture, Nuclear Engineering, Operational Research, Physics, Quantity Surveying, Statistics, Systems Analysis, Teaching, Telecommunications Engineering, Textile Engineering.

Physics: Aeronautical Engineering, Architecture, Astronomy, Astrophysics, Automotive Engineering, Biomedical Engineering, Biophysics, Building Science and Technology, Chemical Engineering, Civil Engineering, Communications Engineering, Computer Science, Cybernetics, Electrical/Electronic Engineering, Engineering Science, Ergonomics, Geophysics, Glass Science and Technology, Instrument Physics, Materials Science, Marine Engineering, Mechanical Engineering, Meteorology, Mineral Sciences and Technology, Naval Architecture, Oceanography, Ophthalmic Optics (Optometry), Teaching, Telecommunications Engineering, Textile Physics.

Degree/Diploma Course Choice by Career

Even though you may have set your mind on one career it is important to remember that other careers exist which sometimes are very similar. The following lists give examples of degree courses which can be considered under career headings.

Accountancy: Actuarial Science, Banking, Business Studies, Economics, Management Science.

Actuarial Science: Accountancy, Banking, Insurance.

Agriculture: Agricultural Engineering, Agricultural Surveying, Animal Sciences, Environmental Science, Estate Management, Forestry, Horticulture, Surveying.

Animal Sciences: Agricultural Sciences, Biological Sciences, Veterinary Science, Zoology.

Archaeology: Anthropology, History of Art and Architecture.

Architecture: Building, Civil Engineering, Landscape Architecture, Quantity Surveying, Surveying, Town and Country Planning.

Art: Advertising, Architecture, Art Teaching, Industrial Design, Landscape Architecture, Three Dimensional Design.

Astronomy: Astrophysics, Mathematics, Physics.

Audiology: Nursing, Teaching the Deaf.

Banking/Insurance: Accountancy, Business Studies, Economics.

Biological Sciences/Biology: Agricultural Sciences, Biochemistry, Botany, Ecology, Environmental Health, Environmental Science, Genetics, Medicine, Microbiology, Pharmacy, Teaching.

Book Publishing: Advertising, Business Studies, Printing, Typographical Communication.

Brewing: Biochemistry, Chemistry, Food Science.

Broadcasting: Film and TV Studies, Journalism, Media Studies.

Building: Architecture, Building Surveying, Civil Engineering, Estate Management, General Practice Surveying, Land Surveying, Quantity Surveying.

Business Studies: Accountancy, Advertising, Banking, Economics, Hospitality Management, Housing Management, Industrial Relations, Insurance, Marketing, Operational Research, Public Relations, Transport Management, Tourism.

Cartography: Geography, Land Surveying.

Catering Science: Dietetics, Food Science, Home Economics, Hotel Management, Nutrition.

Ceramics: Materials Science and Metallurgy, Physics.

Chemistry: Agricultural Science, Biochemistry, Botany, Ceramics, Chemical Engineering, Colour Chemistry, Geochemistry, Pharmacology, Pharmacy, Teaching. All Technologies eg Dairy, Food, Paper, Plastics, Materials.

Computer Studies: Business Studies, Electronic Engineering, Mathematics, Microelectronics, Physics, Telecommunications.

Construction: Building, Civil Engineering, Construction Engineering and Management, Structural Engineering.

Dance: Drama, Movement Studies, Physical Education, Theatre Studies.

Dentistry: Biochemistry, Medicine, Nursing, Pharmacy.

Drama: Dance, Movement Studies, Teaching, Theatre Management.

Education: Psychology, Social Work, Speech Therapy, Youth and Community Work.

Engineering: Engineering (eg Chemical, Civil, Computing, Control, Electrical, Environmental, Food Process, Geology and Geotechnics, Manufacturing, Mechanical, Microelectrics, Nuclear, Product Design, Software, Telecommunications), Mathematics, Physics.

Estate Management: Building, Civil Engineering, Economics, Forestry, Housing Studies, Town and Country Planning.

Fishery Science: Biological Sciences, Maritime Studies.

Food and Accommodation Studies: Dietetics, Home Economics, Hotel and Institutional Management, Housing Management, Nutrition.

Food Science and Technology: Biochemistry, Brewing, Chemistry, Dietetics, Home Economics, Nutrition.

Forestry: Biological Sciences, Botany, Ecology, Environmental Science, Wood Science.

Furniture Design: Furniture Production, History of Art and Design, Three Dimensional Design, Timber Technology.

Geology: Chemistry, Earth Sciences, Engineering (Civil, Mining), Environmental Science, Geochemistry, Geography, Land Surveying, Quarrying.

Graphic Design: Advertising, Photography, Printing.

Health and Safety: Environmental Health, Nursery Nursing. (See also **Medicine**.)

Home Economics: Dietetics, Environmental Health, Food Science, Food Technology, Hotel Management, Housing Management, Housing Studies, Institutional Management, Nutrition.

Horticulture: Agriculture, Botany, Landscape Architecture.

Hotel and Catering Administration: Food Science, Food Technology, Institutional Management, Travel and Tourism. (See also **Home Economics**.)

Housing: Architecture, General Practice Surveying, Social Administration, Town and Country Planning.

Law: Business Studies, International History, Land Management.

Leisure and Recreational Studies: Dance, Drama, Music, Movement Studies, Physical Education, Theatre Studies, Travel and Tourism.

Librarianship: Information Sciences, Publishing.

Maritime Studies: Marine Engineering, Nautical Studies, Naval Architecture, Oceanography, Offshore Engineering.

Marketing: Business Studies, Operational Research, Printing and Packaging, Travel and Tourism.

Materials Science/Metallurgy: Chemistry, Engineering, Glass Science and Technology, Materials Technology, Mineral Exploitation, Physics, Polymer Science.

Mathematics: Accountancy, Actuarial Science, Banking, Business Studies, Computer Studies, Economics, Engineering, Operational Research, Physics, Quantity Surveying, Teaching.

Medicine: Anatomy, Biochemistry, Biological Sciences, Dentistry, Human Physiology, Medical Laboratory Sciences, Nursing, Occupational Therapy, Orthoptics, Pharmacology, Pharmacy, Physiotherapy, Radiography, Speech Therapy, Social Sciences.

Micro-electronics: Computer Studies, Electrical/Electronic Engineering.

Mineral Processing: Chemistry, Earth Sciences, Chemical Engineering, Environmental Sciences, Geology, Mining Engineering, Soil Science.

Music: Drama, Performance Arts, Theatre Studies.

Nautical Studies: Marine Engineering, Naval Architecture, Oceanography, Offshore Engineering.

Naval Architecture: Maritime Studies, Marine Engineering, Offshore Engineering.

Nursing: Anatomy, Applied Biology, Biochemistry, Biological Sciences, Biology, Dentistry, Education, Environmental Health and Community Studies, Human Biology, Medicine, Occupational Therapy, Orthoptics, Physiotherapy, Psychology, Podiatry, Radiography, Social Administration, Speech Therapy. (See also **Medicine**.)

Nutrition: Food Science and Technology, Home Economics, Nursing.

Occupational Therapy: Art, Nursing, Orthoptics, Physiotherapy, Psychology, Speech Therapy.

Optometry (Ophthalmic Optics): Applied Physics, Orthoptics, Physics.

Packaging: Graphic Design, Printing.

Photography/Film/TV: Communication Studies (some courses), Documentary Communications, Graphic Art, Media Studies.

Physical Education: Leisure and Recreation Management, Sport and Recreational Studies, Sports Science.

Physiotherapy: Nursing, Orthoptics, Physical Education.

Physics: Applied Physics, Astronomy, Astrophysics, Education, Engineering (Civil, Electrical, Mechanical), Medical Instrumentation, Ophthalmic Optics (Optometry).

Polymer Science: Applied Chemistry, Chemistry, Materials Science.

Printing: Advertising, Graphic Design, Typographic Design and Communication.

Production Technology: Engineering (Mechanical, Manufacturing), Materials Science.

Property and Valuation Management: Architecture, Estate Management, Quantity Surveying, Urban Land Economics.

Psychology: Applied Social Studies, Occupational Therapy, Psychology (Clinical, Developmental, Educational, Experiential, Occupational, Social), Social Work.

Public Administration: Applied Social Social Studies, Business Studies, Social Administration, Youth and Community Work.

Quantity Surveying: Architecture, Building, Civil Engineering, Surveying (Building, Land and Valuation).

Radiography: Audiology, Biological Sciences, Medical Photography, Nursing, Orthoptics, Photography, Physiotherapy.

Secretarial Studies: Bi-lingual Secretarial Studies, Business Studies.

Silversmithing/Jewellery: Three Dimensional Design.

Social Science/Social Studies: Anthropology, Journalism, Politics and Government, Public Administration, Religious Studies, Social Administration, Sociology, Town and Country Planning, Youth and Community Work.

Speech Therapy: Audiology, Education (Handicapped Children), Nursing, Occupational Therapy, Psychology, Radiography.

Statistics: Business Studies, Economics, Mathematics, Operational Research.

Textile Design: Art, Clothing Studies, Fashion Buying, Fashion Design, Textile Management.

Theatre Design: Drama, Interior Design, Leisure and Recreational Studies, Theatre Management, Theatre Studies.

Three Dimensional Design: Architecture, Industrial Design, Interior Design, Theatre Design.

Timber Technology: Forestry, Furniture Production, Wood Science.

Town and Country Planning: Architecture, Environmental Science, Estate Management, Geography, Leisure and Recreational Management, Planning Studies, Statistics, Transport management.

Transport: Business Studies, Town and Country Planning.

Typography and Graphic communication: Graphic Design, Packaging, Printing, Publishing.

Veterinary Science: Agricultural Sciences, Agriculture, Animal Sciences, Medicine, Pharmacology, Pharmacy, Zoology.

Courses in the same subject at different universities and colleges can vary considerably. In almost every course, the options offered include some which reflect the research interests of individual members of staff. In some courses subsidiary subjects are available as minor courses alongside a single honours course. In an increasing number of courses these additional subjects include a European language, the importance of which cannot be over-emphasised with the arrival of the Single European Market.

GENERAL AND COURSE REQUIREMENTS

Choosing a subject to study for a degree or diploma is not quite the same as the choice of A-level subjects which you made two or three years ago. There are additional factors to consider which relate to the way in which each institution selects applicants, and the standards of entry set by various departments. Once you have chosen a subject, therefore, you cannot assume that you will be qualified to study it at every institution and you must check the **general requirements** of the university concerned.

Difficulties in meeting the general requirements often arise from three subjects: English, a modern language, and mathematics or a science subject. Some universities insist on grade C or above in GCSE in these subjects, irrespective of the course you want to follow.

After checking the general requirements, the next step is to check the **course requirements** for your chosen institutions. These can also vary: for example, for Architecture, Bath University requires English language, Glasgow University requires English language or English literature, and Edinburgh University asks for physics but will accept chemistry as an alternative. (All details of the general and course requirements are found in prospectuses - see **Booklist** for details.)

Not all applicants for places on degree courses in tJOINhe United Kingdom offer A/AS-levels. Some candidates offer Scottish or Irish qualifications, others offer BTEC qualifications, the International and European Baccalaureates, Scholastic Aptitude Tests (SAT) and Achievement and Advanced Placements Test (APT) and from 1993 increasing numbers of UK applicants will offer General National Vocational Qualifications (GNVQs). If you are offering any of these qualifications check with the institution concerned that your qualifications will meet the general and course requirements **before** you apply.

COURSE TYPES AND DIFFERENCES

Once over the hurdle of the general and course requirements, you will need to decide on the type of course you want to follow. For example, subjects might be offered as a single-subject course (a *single honours* degree), or as a two-subject course (a *joint honours* degree) or as one of two, three or four subjects (a *combined honours* degree).

When choosing your course, it is important to remember that one course is not better than another - it is just different. The best course for you is the one which best suits **you**. The same approach also applies to the institutions you choose. Each will differ a great deal, for example in their location (town or deep in the countryside), in the facilities they offer, in the ways they organise their courses and their teaching.

Differences between all courses in the same subject at the different institutions are described in *How to Choose Your Degree Course* (see **Booklist**.)

After provisionally choosing your courses read the prospectuses again carefully to be sure that you understand what is included during the three, four or more years of study for each. Each institution varies in its course content even though the course titles may be the same. Courses differ in several ways, for example, in their:

● subject options (minor courses of study alongside the main subject)

● methods of assessment (eg unseen examinations, continuous assessment, project work, dissertations)

● contact time with tutors

● lectures

● practicals

● library and laboratory facilities

● amount of free study time available.

These are useful points of comparison between courses in different institutions when you are making final course choices. Once you have done that, you can then move on to finding out about how to apply for courses (Chapter 3) and to decide on where you want to study (Chapter 2).

2   WHERE TO STUDY ?

Choosing where to study means different things to different people although since the main objective of higher education is to obtain your degree or diploma, your course choice must take priority. You have three, four or five years of study ahead of you and you need to choose a subject which is going to keep you interested. Motivation, therefore, is the most important factor and it is well worth realising that every year a large number of students drop out of their chosen course – often at the end of the first term – because the course is very different from what they expected.

It is estimated that about twelve per cent of students drop out each year– it could be even higher – but institutions are naturally cautious about publishing such information as this will reflect on their reputations. Each university or college is out to attract as many applicants as possible because the more applications they receive, the better the chance of receiving a high proportion of good candidates, who naturally have the first choice of places.

Another contributory cause for students' unhappiness or drop-out rates is insufficient knowledge about the location of the universities and colleges they select. Many applicants have little idea of where those institutions are or what their environment is really like and the discovery on arrival can unsettle even the well-motivated ones!

Most applicants look for places or courses with good reputations but they should be very cautious about jumping to conclusions. The word 'reputation' suggests that one place or a specific course is better than another. It is true that some universities such as Oxford or Cambridge or London are 'well known', but that is no criterion of quality. Many applicants are concerned as to what employers think about their chosen university or college but it is likely that most employers are more concerned with the quality of applicant and not necessarily with his or her place of study. Similarly the quality of teaching is often regarded as important – which it is – although it is dangerous to assume that the most popular institutions have the best teachers! (A recent survey listed universities which were rated best for teaching – but this referred to the number of applicants they had recruited – not the ability of their lecturers to teach their subjects!)

Research is also an important feature of any department, although applicants should realise that such advanced studies will not affect them greatly during their undergraduate years.

The main objective in choosing the right place, however, is for applicants to try to identify the character of each institution in which they are interested. This 'character' is a mix of factors which will determine whether or not it will prove to be an equitable place to study. Where is it located; how far or near from home? What courses are on offer and how are studies organised? How many students are there? How good are the study facilities – libraries, laboratories, teaching equipment? Finally, what does the Students' Union offer in the way of leisure activities?

The best way to choose what and where to study is to start by reading prospectuses which provide detailed information about all aspects of courses and facilities for students in universities and colleges. Readers wanting to compare institutions and courses are advised to refer to *How to Choose Your Degree Course* (see **Booklist**) which provides information in individual subject areas and enables useful comparisons to be made between institutions offering the same course subjects.

After reading the prospectuses, visit some of the institutions which interest you. Many have 'Open Days' and the dates of these are available from sixth form tutors, careers advisers and direct from the institutions concerned. Alternatively, applicants may write directly to the university or college and make arrangements for a personal visit.

The following descriptions of each of the main higher education institutions - in alphabetical order - are intended to give you a preliminary taster of the character and popularity of the universities and colleges offering degree and diploma courses.

NB In some of the descriptions which follow, reference is made to modular courses and to credit accumulation and transfer (CATS).

The aim of modular courses is to provide greater flexibility and choice for students. By following specified 'pathways' of subject groupings, and choosing modules within them, students can develop their own distinctive degree courses, with the help and approval of their course tutors.

Credit accumulation and transfer (CATS) is a mechanism by which students can gain 'credits' for modules or units of study in which they have been assessed and which can be accumulated towards certificate, diploma, first degree or postgraduate awards in higher education, with 120 credits awarded for each notional year of study. Therefore, for a three-year degree students will need to earn 360 credits at levels 1-3 (each level equating notionally to the first, second and third years of the full-time course). Credit accumulation schemes operate within many universities and colleges and enable students to tailor degree programmes to meet their own requirements. Credit accumulation and transfer schemes operate between particular universities and colleges and allow students to transfer credits gained at one to another.

DIRECTORY OF UNIVERSITIES AND COLLEGES OF HIGHER EDUCATION

Aberdeen (Univ) The University offers a three, four or five year degree programme. Students taking the BSc or MA courses have considerable flexibility in the choice of subjects to study. All courses except medicine are fully modularised. Courses worth noting are those in Human Resource Management, Petroleum Geology, Tropical Environmental Science, Forestry and Aquaculture. Entry is on faculty basis for most subjects. There are 6500 full-time first-degree students (70% Scottish). The University's main teaching buildings and student accommodation are closely grouped in Old Aberdeen. University accommodation is available for half the student population. *(The University of Aberdeen, Regent Walk, Aberdeen AB9 1FX, Scotland. Tel 0224 273504.)*

Aberystwyth (Univ) See under **Wales (Univ)**

Anglia (Poly Univ) All Anglia degree courses come within the Credit Accumulation and Modular Scheme (CAMS). There are some single honours courses (BA and BSc) but the majority are combined courses, with some HND courses. The institution has four main sites in Cambridge, Chelmsford, Brentwood and Danbury Park, the majority of courses being based in Cambridge. *(Anglia Polytechnic University, Cambridge Campus: East Road, Cambridge CB1 1PT. Tel 0223 63271; or Chelmsford Campus: Victoria Road South, Chelmsford, Essex CM1 1LL. Tel 0245 493131.)*

Architectural Association (School of Architecture) The School offers RIBA Parts I and II and the AA Diploma and has an international reputation. It is situated in Georgian houses in the centre of London. There are approximately 260 fee-paying students. *(Architectural Association School, 34 Bedford Square, London WC1B 3AS. Tel 071 636 0974.)* (Direct application)

Aston (Univ) Single, Joint and Combined honours degree courses in three faculties: engineering with applied science; life and health sciences; modern languages and management; also one of the most up-to-date Ophthalmic Optics departments. Two-thirds of students are on sandwich degree programmes. Forty-acre green city-centre campus in Birmingham with many new buildings. 3600 students, with accommodation for 65% (majority on campus). Excellent sports facilities. *(Aston University, Aston Triangle, Birmingham B4 7ET. Tel 021 359 6313.)*

Bangor Normal (CHE) Courses in Administration and Communication (competence in Welsh required) and Planning, but mainly BEd teaching courses in the 3-8 or 7-12 age ranges. The College is situated in a residential area of Bangor with 400 students. *(Bangor Normal College, Bangor, Gwynedd, North Wales LL57 2PX. Tel 0248 370171.)*

Bangor (Univ) See under **Wales (Univ)**

Bath (CHE) Combined Studies courses (BA or BSc) are offered (Japanese can be studied for one year) and also BEd teaching courses for Primary and Secondary age ranges. The BA Music and BSc Home Economics courses have a long tradition of excellence. The College is situated on two sites, one mile and four miles respectively from the city centre. 2130 students. *(Bath College of Higher Education, Newton Park, Bath BA2 9BN. Tel 0225 873701.)*

Bath (Univ) A mainly technological university but with strong modern languages/ European Studies departments. Many sandwich courses are offered. It is a very popular University located on campus site overlooking the city. There are 4000 students; 60% of first years accommodated on or near campus. Sports facilities next to campus. This University was rated first out of ten in a recent nation survey for graduate employment in 1991. *(The University of Bath, Claverton Down, Bath BA2 7AY. Tel 0225 826826.)*

Bedford (CHE) (Merger from 1 April 1993 with De Montfort University, Leicester). A modular scheme operates leading to BA or BSc, students choosing one or two pathways. There is also a BEd Primary teaching course and a long-established BEd Physical Education course. There are 750 students in the College located in pleasant surroundings. *(Bedford College of Higher Education, 37 Lansdowne Road, Bedford MK40 2BZ. Tel 0234 351966.)*

Belfast (Univ) Subjects are studied in one of nine faculties. Various degree programmes are offered - Single, Joint, Major/Minor (2 subjects in 65/35 patterns), Integrated (2 related subjects) and Combined degrees (3 subjects). The University is located to the south of city. There are 8400 students, about 50% live at home, and 29% in University accommodation. *(The University of Belfast, University Road, Belfast BT7 1NN, Northern Ireland. Tel 0232 245133.)*

Birmingham (Univ) A large university (10,000 students) with a wide selection of courses including the very popular Media Studies, Sports Studies and Sports Science. There is also a General Honours degree enabling students to make a choice of subjects as well as a large Combined Honours programme. It also validates the degrees of Newman & Westhill

ARCHITECTURAL ASSOCIATION
SCHOOL OF ARCHITECTURE
34–36 Bedford Square, London WC1B 3ES
Tel: 071-636 0974 Fax: 071-414 0782

The Architectural Association School of Architecture is the largest and only independent school of architecture in the UK. Visiting lecturers, teaching staff and students reflect the international character of the School.

The AA is not part of the UCAS process and entry for the 5-year RIBA course is by portfolio interview. Entry requirements comply with those of the RIBA.

Courses include:

● *5-year RIBA-recognised course in architecture leading to RIBA Parts 1 and 2 and the AA Diploma.*

● *1-year Foundation Course.*

● *1-year post-graduate courses leading to AA Graduate Diploma in Environment and Energy Studies, History and Theory, and Housing Studies.*

● *1-year Graduate Design Course.*

Application forms and further information may be obtained from the above address.

College, Birmingham. The University is located at Edgbaston, 2½ miles from city. *(The University of Birmingham, PO Box 363, Birmingham B15 2TT. Tel 021 414 3344.)*

Bishop Grosseteste (CHE) The College offers four-year BEd (Hons) courses awarded by the University of Hull for teaching in the 3–11 age range. All students spend their second year at the University. PGCE courses are also offered. There are 630 students with accommodation for all first years. The College is located on an open site 5 minutes from the city centre. *(Bishop Grosseteste College, Newport, Lincoln LN1 3DY. Tel 0522 527347.)*

Bolton (IHE) In addition to History, Literature, Psychology, Philosophy and a wide range of Engineering courses, the Institute offers a Combined Studies modular degree programme including Business Studies and HND courses. There are 2200 full-time and sandwich students. It is located on three campuses close to the city centre. *(Bolton Institute of Higher Education, Deane Road, Bolton BL3 5AB. Tel 0204 28851.)*

Bournemouth (Univ) There are two sites, the main campus being about 2 miles from the city centre. Courses have a marked vocational emphasis eg Marketing, Public Relations, Hotel Management, Nursing and Tourism Studies. There are approximately 7000 students.

Franchised courses: HND Business and Finance courses and Hotel Catering and Institutional Management courses are also offered at the Isle of Wight (CAT), Salisbury (CT), or Yeovil College. *(Bournemouth University, Dorset House, Talbot Campus, Fern Barrow, Dorset BH12 5BB. Tel 0202 595448.)*

Bradford (Univ) Some 6000 students are divided between engineering, natural and applied sciences and social sciences faculties. Several sandwich courses are offered (including Pharmacy). Bradford is popular for Management Studies, European Studies, Modern Languages and Applied Social Studies. It also validates the degrees of Bradford & Ilkley (CmC). The University is located on a city-centre site and 38% of students are housed in University accommodation. *(The University, Bradford, West Yorkshire BD7 1DP. Tel 0274 733466.)*

Bradford & Ilkley (CmC) Several Community Studies courses are offered and BEd courses for nursery and primary age ranges leading to Bradford University degrees. There are also a DipHE and an HND course in Business with language options. This is a very large college with 3600 full-time students. *(Bradford and Ilkley Community College, Great Horton Road, Bradford, West Yorkshire BD7 1AY. Tel 0274 733466.)*

Bretton Hall (CHE) This is a college particularly well known for its excellent Drama, Theatre and Art courses in addition to which Leeds University degrees are also offered in English, Dance, Music, Fashion and BEd teaching courses in the 3-8, 5-11 and 8-13 age ranges. It is located in 250 acres of very attractive parkland. There are approximately 1200 students. *(Bretton Hall College, West Bretton, Wakefield, West Yorkshire WF4 4LG. Tel 0924 830261.)*

Brighton (Univ) It is located on four sites, including one at Eastbourne for Sports Science, Hotel and Catering, Teaching and Podiatry. The six faculties offer degree and HND courses in Art, Design, Business, Education, Sport and Leisure, Engineering and Environmental Studies, Health and Information Technology. There are approximately 6500 students.
Franchised courses: HND courses in Engineering, Applied Biology and Hotel Catering and Institutional Management are offered in conjunction with the following colleges: Brighton (CT), Chichester (CT), Crawley (CT), Hastings (CAT), Northbrook (CDT). *(University of Brighton, Lewes Road, Brighton BN2 4AT. Tel 0273 600900.)*

Bristol (Univ) This is an extremely popular university with a population of 8300 students. There are six faculties: arts, science, medicine, engineering, law and social sciences. 44% of students in University accommodation. Highly rated for research. *(The University of Bristol, Senate House, Bristol BS8 1TH. Tel 0272 303030.)*

Bristol UWE This is a very popular institution located on five sites with approximately 6700 students. Degree and HND courses are offered. Courses include Languages, Architecture, Hotel and Tourism Studies, Education, Engineering; there is also a modular science scheme.
Franchised courses: One year of the BA courses in Economics, Politics, Social Science and Sociology are also offered at the franchise centres at Bridgwater College and Chippenham TC. HND courses with an agricultural bias are offered at Cannington College (see Ch 6). *(University of the West of England, Bristol, Coldharbour Lane, Frenchay, Bristol BS16 1QY. Tel 0272 656261 - Admissions 0272 763809.)*

Brunel (Univ) There are two campuses some 15 miles west of London. Faculties of technology, mathematics and science and social science at Uxbridge and the faculty of education and design at Runnymede. Teaching is based on four-year 'thin sandwich' courses, with periods of academic study integrated with industrial and professional training leading to high graduate employment. Approximately 3000 students, accommodation for about 1700. This University was in the top ten in graduate employment tables in 1991. *(Brunel, The University of West London, Uxbridge, Middlesex UB8 3PH. Tel 0895 274000.)*

Buckingham (Univ) This is an independent (fee-paying) university in restored historic buildings on edge of Buckingham. There are 750 students from over 70 countries. Degrees are taken in only two years. *(The University of Buckingham, Hunter Street, Buckingham MK18 1EG. Tel 0280 814080.)*

Buckinghamshire (CHE) The College (an associate college of Brunel University) offers several first degree and HND courses and should be considered by those interested in European and International Business Studies, Office Management, Furniture Production and Timber Technology (now called Forest Products Technology). There are 2000 full-time students on three campuses. *(Buckinghamshire College, Queen Alexandra Road, High Wycombe, Buckinghamshire HP11 2JZ. Tel 0494 522141.)*

Camborne (School of Mines) (Now part of Exeter University) Degree courses are offered in Minerals and Mining Engineering and Geology at both degree and HND levels. There are 125 students in this specialist college close to the Cornish coast. Applications are submitted through Exeter University. *(Camborne School of Mines, Trevenson, Pool, Redruth, Cornwall TR15 3SE. Tel 0209 714866.)*

Cambridge (Univ) Founded in 13th century. 13,500 students, about 37.6% women. Highly rated for research. Thirty-one colleges dominate the town of 100,000 people. Twenty faculties offering a wide range of subjects. Students admitted to colleges, not to the university. Library of 3,000,000 volumes as well as faculty and departmental libraries. Most students live in colleges or college lodgings. Over 300 societies, and excellent sports facilities. There are three colleges which admit women only (Lucy Cavendish - mature women, New Hall and Newnham) and 25 which admit both men and women undergraduates. These are Christ's, Churchill, Clare, Corpus Christi, Downing, Emmanuel, Fitzwilliam, Girton, Gonville & Caius, Homerton (BEd only), Jesus, King's, Magdalene, Pembroke, Peterhouse, Queens', Robinson, St Catharine's, St Edmund's (graduates and mature undergraduates), St John's, Selwyn, Sidney Sussex, Trinity, Trinity Hall and Wolfson (graduates and mature undergraduates). *(Enquiries should be addressed to the Tutor for Admissions,........College, Cambridge, or to Cambridge Intercollegiate Applications Office, Tennis Court Road, Cambridge CB2 1QJ. Tel 0223 333308.)*

Canterbury Christ Church (CHE) BA and BSc two-subject courses are offered, a BEd course covering 3-8, 5-8 and 7-12 age ranges and also courses in Diagnostic Radiography, Nursing and Occupational Therapy. Situated in Canterbury, there are 1700 full-time students on degree courses validated by Kent University.
Franchised courses: The DipHE/BA courses in Informal and Community Education are taught at YMCA College, Walthamstow, London. The HND Software Engineering and the BSc Extended Science courses are organised in collaboration with Canterbury College and Thanet (TC) (see Ch 6). *(Canterbury Christ Church College of Higher Education, North Holmes Road, Canterbury, Kent CT1 1QU. Tel 0227 762444.)*

Cardiff (IHE) The Institute offers a varied range of degree courses including European Administration, Nutrition and Dietetics, Speech Therapy, Environmental Health and Art Education Studies; also HND courses. It is located in six centres within this attractive capital city and has 3500 full-time and 3000 part-time students. *(Cardiff Institute of Higher Education, PO Box 377, Llandaff Centre, Western Avenue, Cardiff CF5 2SG. Tel 0222 551111.)*

Cardiff (Univ) See under **Wales (Univ)**

Central England (Univ) A wide range of degree and some HND courses are available including BEd courses for Primary Teaching and Music. The institution also offers Speech and Language Pathology and Nursing. There are 8050 students. The main campus 2 miles from the city with other campuses for art, music and teacher training.
Franchised courses: Extended Engineering BEng Foundation Year courses franchised to Dudley College, East Birmingham College, Handsworth College, Sandwell College, Stourbridge College, Sutton Coldfield College. *(University of Central England in Birmingham, Perry Bar, Birmingham B42 2SU. Tel 021 331 5000.)*

Central Lancashire (Univ) 6100 students following a range of courses on a single town-centre site to degree and HND levels. There is a very extensive combined honours programme.
Franchised courses: BA and HND Hotel courses are organised in conjunction with Blackpool and Fylde College, HND courses in Forestry and Environmental Land Management at Cumbria (CAgF) and Rural Land Management at Lancashire (CAg). *(The University of Central Lancashire, Preston PR1 2TQ. Tel 0772 892000.)*

Charlotte Mason (CEd) Small college located in the heart of the Lake District offering a BEd degree of Lancaster University leading to teaching in the 3-12 age range. There are approximately 1000 students. *(Charlotte Mason College of Education, Ambleside, Cumbria LA22 9BB. Tel 05394 33066.)*

Cheltenham & Glos (CHE) An extensive modular scheme operates at the College leading to BA and BSc degrees. The BEd course leads to teaching in the early and later primary age ranges and for secondary Maths, PE and Religious Studies. HND courses are also offered. The College is located on five sites in Cheltenham, a town with an attractive natural environment, historic buildings and a lively cultural background. There is a student population of 3000.
Franchised courses: HND Building and Engineering Design courses are offered by Gloucestershire College of Arts and Technology. *(Cheltenham and Gloucester College of Higher Education, The Park, Cheltenham, Gloucestershire GL50 2RH. Tel 0242 532824.)*

Chester (CHE) Combined subject courses, a BEd degree covering the 3-11 age range and a unique Health and Community Studies course are offered. The College has 2300 full-time students on BA, BSc and BEd degree courses of Liverpool University. *(Chester College, Cheyney Road, Chester CH1 4BJ. Tel 0244 375444.)*

City (Univ) The university was established in 1894 and granted its Royal Charter in 1966. It is based on a small campus site by the City of London. There are 5500 students and it is strong in Engineering, Business Management and medically-related disciplines. Accommodation for 1000 students. *(The City University, Northampton Square, London EC1V 0HB. Tel 071 477 8000.)*

Colchester (Inst) This is a small college offering a BA in Music (and a graduate Diploma in Music) and an HND course in Hotel, Catering and Institutional Management with direct entry to year 2 for those with a BTEC HND in Catering. *(Colchester Institute, Sheepen Road, Colchester CO3 3LL. Tel 0206 761660.)*

Coventry (Univ) This is a modern, purpose-built institution on a central site in Coventry with 7000 students many of whom are part-time and mature, A very large number of courses are offered leading to degree and HND awards.
Franchised courses: Courses in Equine Studies and Horse Studies are offered in conjunction with Warwickshire (CAg), and Performing Arts courses at Coventry Centre for the

Performing Arts or for DipHE courses at South Warwickshire College (Stratford) (see Ch 6). *(Coventry University, Priory Street, Coventry CV1 5FB. Tel 0203 631313.)*

Cranfield (IT) Technological university with 2000 students, mainly postgraduate. Two faculties offering undergraduate courses (see below). *(Cranfield Institute of Technology, Bedford MK43 0AL. Tel 0234 750111.)*

Cranfield (Silsoe) Faculty of Agricultural Engineering, Food Production and Rural Land Use. *(Silsoe College, Bedford MK45 4DT. Tel 0525 860428.)*

Cranfield (Shrivenham) This faculty of Cranfield includes schools of electrical engineering and science, mechanical, materials and civil engineering and defence management. *(The Royal Military College of Science, Shrivenham, Swindon, Wiltshire SN6 8LA. Tel 0793 785400/1.)*

Crewe & Alsager (CHE) A flexible range of studies is possible in Creative Arts, Humanities, Combined Studies and Independent Studies; there are also BEd courses covering all age ranges, DipHE and HND courses. Teaching is on two country campuses with 2000 approx. full-time students. *(Crewe and Alsager College of Higher Education, Crewe Road, Crewe, Cheshire CW1 1DU. Tel 0270 500661.)*

Dartington (CA) 373 students are following courses in Music, Theatre and Visual Performance on a rural campus on the edge of Dartmoor. *(Dartington College of Arts, Totnes, Devon TQ9 6EJ. Tel 0803 863234.)*

De Montfort (Univ) 9300 students at Leicester and at Milton Keynes studying degree and HND courses. It is also expected to merge with Bedford (CHE) and Lincolnshire (CAD). 21 halls of residence.

Franchised courses: The first year of some degree courses and HND courses can be taken at the following colleges and students may opt to choose their study location: Barnfield College (Luton), Boston College, Derby Tertiary College, Henley College (Coventry), Loughborough College, North Lincolnshire College (Lincoln), Northampton College, Peterborough Regional College and Trensham College (Kettering), Bedford College, Charles Keene College (Leicester), Milton Keynes (CFE), Broxtowe College (Nottingham) (see Ch 6). *(De Montfort University, PO Box 143, Leicester LE1 9BH. Tel 0533 551551.)*

Derby (Univ) This is a large institution offering a modular degree scheme covering 40 subjects. In addition there is a range of specialist degrees in such varied subjects as Biological Imaging, Nursing, Midwifery, Radiography, Occupational Therapy, Podiatry, Textile Design and Business Studies. 2500 students follow these courses on three campuses.

Franchised courses: HND courses in Engineering and Hotel Catering and Institutional Management are held in conjunction with Newark and Sherwood College and High Peak College, Buxton, respectively (see Ch 6). *(University of Derby, Kedleston Road, Derby DE3 1GB. Tel 0332 47181.)*

Doncaster (Coll) Range of HND courses and a Leeds University BEng in Quarry and Road Surfacing Engineering. 2200 full-time students. *(Doncaster College, Waterdale, Doncaster DN1 3EX. Tel 0302 322122.)*

Dundee (Univ) The University is located on a city-centre precinct site. There are 4200 students (57% Scottish). Accommodation is available for about half the student population. Entry to courses is on a faculty basis for most subjects. Thus application for any one subject can also give entry to other subjects for which the applicant is qualified. *(The University, Dundee DD1 4HN, Scotland. Tel 0382 23181 - Admissions: ext. 4028.)*

Durham-Tees (Coll) The College was designated in October 1991 and is located at Stockton-on-Tees. The first 240 students were admitted in October 1992 to courses in European Studies, Environmental Management, Enviromental Technology and Human Sciences; degrees are validated jointly by Durham and Teesside universities. *(The Admissions Officer, Joint University College on Teesside, Durham-Tees College, Old Shire Hall, Durham DH1 3HP. Tel 0642 618020.)*

Durham (Univ) This is an extremely popular university (ie, usually high offers for popular subjects) with buildings throughout the city. Students are admitted to 12 colleges. There are seven subject faculties, 5600 students, all of whom can be accommodated within Colleges although 15% (approx.) live out. There are 12 colleges and one society admitting undergraduates. Colleges for men: Grey, Hatfield, St Chads, University. College for women: St Mary's. Mixed colleges: Collingwood, St Aidan's, St Cuthbert's, St Hild/St Bede, St John's, Trevelyan, Van Mildert. This University was in the top ten in graduate employment tables in 1991. *(The University of Durham, Old Shire Hall, Durham DH1 3HP. Tel 091 374 2000.)*

East Anglia (Univ) The University is on a campus site two miles from Norwich. There are 11 schools of study and 4600 students of whom 60% are in university accommodation. Highly rated for research. *(The University of East Anglia, Norwich NR4 7TJ. Tel 0603 56161.)*

East London (Univ) The student population of 5550 (full-time and sandwich) follow courses on two precincts in Dagenham and Stratford. In addition to many single honours courses, 26 subjects are offered on two-subject degree courses. HND courses are also offered. *(The University of East London, Romford Road, London E15 4LZ. Tel 081 590 7722.)*

Edge Hill (CHE) BA and BSc courses are offered in a range of subjects which includes Communication and Information Media, Field Biology and Habitat Management, English, Geography and Management Studies. There is a student population of 2500 on a large, attractive rural campus. *(Edge Hill College of Higher Education, St Helen's Road, Ormskirk, Lancashire L39 4QP. Tel 0695 575171.)*

Edinburgh (Univ) This is a very popular university with eight subject faculties, seven of which (Arts, Divinity, Law, Medicine, Music, Social Science and Veterinary Medicine) are on city-centre sites and one, the science faculty (which includes Agriculture and Engineering), some 2 miles from the city centre. Highly rated for research. Admission is to a faculty, not to a subject department (Faculty of Science admits to subject groups), and transfer between subjects is usually possible. In addition to faculty and departmental libraries, there is a central library. 11,300 students (over 50% Scottish), with university accommodation for 4660. *(The University, Old College, South Bridge, Edinburgh EH8 9YL, Scotland. Tel 031 650 1000.)*

Essex (Univ) The University was established in 1964, two miles east of Colchester. There are 3600 students (14% from overseas). Five schools of study cover Comparative Studies, Social Sciences, Law, Mathematical, Science and Engineering. Highly rated for research. Sports facilities on campus. *(The University of Essex, Wivenhoe Park, Colchester CO4 3SQ. Tel 0206 873666.)*

Exeter (Univ) A very popular university on a wooded hillside site one mile from city centre. There are six subject faculties. 6000 students, 54% living in halls or flats. This University was in the top ten in graduate employment tables in 1991; it also validates the degrees of St Loye's School of Occupational Therapy and the College of St Mark & St John, Plymouth. *(The University, Northcote House, The Queen's Drive, Exeter, Devon EX4 4QJ. Tel 0392 263263.)*

Glamorgan (Univ) It is based on one site and has a student population of 4800 full-time and sandwich students. Degree, diploma and HND courses are offered across a wide range of subjects. *(The University of Glamorgan, Pontypridd, Mid-Glamorgan CF37 1DL. Tel 0443 480480.)*

Glasgow (Univ) The University is on a 14-acre site one mile from city centre. There are eight subject faculties and a wide range of subjects. Highly rated for research. 12,000 full-time students (80% Scottish; 50% live at home). *(The University, Glasgow G12 8QQ, Scotland. Tel 041 339 8855.)*

Glasgow Caledonian (Univ) Formed from the merger of Glasgow Polytechnic with Queen's College, Glasgow. It is one of the largest institutions in Scotland offering degree, diploma and the final examinations of professional bodies. The University's main site is on a modern purpose-built campus close to the city centre. Total student population is approx 9000 (3500 part-time; 75% Scottish). *(Glasgow Caledonian University, 70 Cowcaddens Road, Glasgow G4 0BA. Tel 041 331 3000.)*

Greenwich (Univ) It is based on seven sites in East London and has over 6500 students following full-time and sandwich courses, degree and HND courses. Associated colleges are located at Bromley, Hadlow and Tonbridge.
Franchised courses: A small number of degree and HND courses are organised in conjunction with the following colleges: Hadlow (CAg), West Kent College (Tonbridge), Bromley (CT).*(The University of Greenwich, Wellington Street, London SE18 6PF. Tel 081 316 8590.)*

Guildhall London (Univ) It is based on six sites in London and has a student population of 6791. In addition to a wide range of single honours and HND courses there is a comprehensive modular scheme in operation allowing for a flexible subject choice. *(London Guildhall University, India House, 139 Minories, London EC3N 2EY. Tel 071 320 1000.)*

Gwent (CHE) A large college in South Wales with 6000 Full-time and part-time students following courses in Art and Design, Education, Management and Technology. There are also some HND courses. *(Gwent College of Higher Education, College Crescent, Caerleon, Newport, Gwent NP6 1XJ. Tel 0633 432432.)*

Heriot-Watt (Univ) Founded in 1966; situated 6½ miles west of central Edinburgh on an attractive 370-acre site of wooded parkland around a small loch. There are five subject faculties: Science, Engineering, Economic and Social Studies and (in conjunction with Edinburgh College of Art) Environmental Studies and Art and Design with 5300 students in total (approx. 60% Scottish). *(Heriot-Watt University, Riccarton, Edinburgh EH14 4AS, Scotland. Tel 031 449 5111.)*

Hertfordshire (Univ) There are four sites with 9500 students; six schools of study cover Art and Design, Business, Engineering, Health and Human Sciences, Humanities and Education, Information Services, Natural Sciences. HND courses are also offered.
Franchised courses: Some BA, BSc, BEng and HND courses are held in conjunction with the following colleges: Oaklands College (St Albans), West Herts College (Watford), North Hertfordshire College (Stevenage). *(University of Hertfordshire, College Lane, Hatfield, Herts AL10 9AB. Tel 0707 279000.)*

Holborn (Coll) An independent college and an Associate College of Wolverhampton University. It offers full-time degree courses in Law (LLB) in conjunction with the University and also Law and Management degree courses LLB and BSc (Econ) London External. Mandatory grant of £675 available for courses. *(Holborn College, 200 Greyhound Road, London W14 9RY. Tel 071 385 3377.)*

Homerton (Coll) This is an approved society of Cambridge University with 690 students. It offers the Bachelor of Education degree awarded by the University. *(Homerton College, Hills Road, Cambridge. Tel 0223 245931.)*

Huddersfield (Univ) 5800 students based on two sites in and near Huddersfield. Degree courses are offered in Arts, Business Studies, Architecture, Education, Engineering, Science and Law. HND courses are also offered. *(The University of Huddersfield, Queensgate, Huddersfield HD1 3DH. Tel 0484 422288.)*

Hull (Univ) This popular university is based on a compact precinct two miles north of Hull. A wide range of subjects is available, divided between four faculties. 6000 students with accommodation for 70%. The University validates the degrees of Bishop Grosseteste College, Lincoln. *(The University, Hull, North Humberside HU6 7RX. Tel 0482 46311.)*

Humberside (Univ) 8000 students on two sites in Hull and Grimsby. Degree, DipHE and HND courses are offered in a wide range of subjects.
Franchised courses: BA courses in Combined Studies, Social Science and Contemporary Studies may also be studied at North Lindsey College (Scunthorpe) and European Administration at York (CAT). Some HND courses are only available at Bishop Burton (CAg) (Beverley) or at Grimsby (CTA). Other HND courses may be studied at Beverley (CFE) or Scarborough (TC). *(The University of Humberside, Cottingham Road, Hull HU6 7RT. Tel 0482 445005.)*

Keele (Univ) The University is located on a very attractive open-country campus near the Potteries. About half the students take the 4-year course, including the Foundation course after which over half change their original course options. Most of the 3000 students read two honours subjects. Campus accommodation for 90% of students. *(The University of Keele, Staffordshire ST5 5BG. Tel 0782 621111.)*

Kent (Univ) The University is located on a 300-acre campus overlooking Canterbury. Wide range of academic subjects. 5000 students; 40% live in one of four colleges, 60% live out. *(The University of Kent at Canterbury, Canterbury, Kent CT2 7NZ. Tel 0227 764000.)*

King Alfred's (CHE) The college is located on a campus site where 1250 students follow BEd, BA and diploma courses. *(King Alfred's College, Sparkford Road, Winchester, Hampshire SO22 4NR. Tel 0962 841515)*

Kingston (Univ) There are 6700 students on four sites in and around Kingston. Courses are offered in Architecture, Arts subjects, Engineering, Science, Education and a range of vocational studies to degree and HND levels.
Franchised courses: The BEng course in Civil Engineering may be studied at Kingston or at Hastings (CAT). Extended Science courses may be followed at East Surrey College, Hammersmith and West London College, Hounslow Borough College, Kingston (CFE), Merton College, South Thames College, Strode's College (see Ch 6). *(Kingston University, Penrhyn Road, Kingston upon Thames, Surrey KT1 2EE. Tel 081 547 2000.)*

Lancaster (Univ) A 200-acre campus site with spectacular views, south of Lancaster. Wide range of subjects available in single or combined (two or three) subject schemes. 5300 students, 50% housed in colleges on the campus. The University also validates the degrees of Charlotte Mason College, Ambleside, Edge Hill College, Ormskirk and S Martin's College, Lancaster. *(Lancaster University, University House, Lancaster LA1 4YW. Tel 0524 65201.)*

La Sainte Union (CHE) The College offers Southampton University degrees in Education, Combined Hons (BA), Podiatry and Theology. *(La Sainte Union College of Higher Education, The Avenue, Southampton, Hampshire SO9 5HB. Tel 0703 228761.)*

Leeds Met (Univ) 7700 students on two campuses in Leeds and Headingley. Almost all courses are vocational and lead to degree or in some cases HND status.
Franchised courses: Franchise arrangements exist with BA courses in Business Administration, and Combined and Community Studies at Barnsley (CAT)/Harrogate (CAT) and Huddersfield (TC)/Wakefield District College respectively. Some HND courses are also offered at Airedale and Wharfedale College and Walsall (CAT) (see Ch 6). *(Leeds Metropolitan University, Calverley Street, Leeds LS1 3HE. Tel 0532 832600.)*

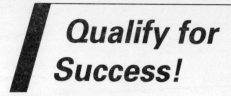

Leeds (Univ) An increasingly popular civic university on compact site just north of the city centre. Very wide range of subjects taught including a very large number of Arts and Science combinations. The University also validates the degrees of Bretton Hall College, Doncaster College, North Riding College, Pinderfields College of Physiotherapy, the College of Ripon & York St John and Trinity & All Saints College. *(The University of Leeds, Leeds LS2 9JT. Tel 0532 333993.)*

Leicester (Univ) The University is on a compact site with modern buildings one mile south of the city. 6000 students with accommodation for 70%, 1300 on an attractive site three miles from the University. *(The University of Leicester, University Road, Leicester LE1 7RH. Tel 0533 522522.)*

Liverpool (IHE) There are 2500 students on three campuses studying BA, BSc and BEd courses validated by Liverpool University. *(Liverpool Institute of Higher Education PO Box 6, Stand Park Road, Childwall, Liverpool L16 9JD. Tel 051 737 3000.)*

Liverpool John Moores (Univ) 8700 students following a range of degree and HND courses on four sites. A major feature is the integrated credit scheme offering students the opportunity to plan their own programme of study.
Franchised courses: Several degree and HND courses are offered in conjunction with the following colleges where students can take the first year of the course: City of Liverpool (CmC), Wirral Metropolitan College, South Cheshire College (Crewe), Knowsley (CmC), Southport College, St Helens (CmC) (see Ch 6). *(Liverpool John Moores University, 70 Mount Pleasant, Liverpool L3 5UX. Tel 051 207 3581.)*

Liverpool (Univ) Large urban university on an 85-acre compact site close to city centre. Wide range of subjects over seven faculties. 8700 students, with accommodation guaranteed for all first year students. This University was in the top ten in graduate employment tables in 1991. The University validates the degrees of Chester College and Liverpool Institute of Higher Education. *(The University of Liverpool, PO Box 147, Liverpool L69 3BX. Tel 051 794 2000.)*

London (Univ) - Birkbeck Degree courses are offered for 3700 mature part-time students. Evening teaching. A-level offers for places not made. *(Birkbeck College, Malet Street, London WC1E 7HX. Tel 071 631 6561.)*

London (Univ) - Courtauld Institute of Art There are 200 students specialising in the History of European Art. *(The Courtauld Institute of Art, Somerset House, Strand, London WC2R 0RN. Tel 071 873 2645.)*

London (Univ) - Goldsmiths' College College based at New Cross, 15-minute rail link with Charing Cross. 3000 students; 1200 students are in college halls and houses. BA and BSc courses are offered in Arts, Social Sciences, Mathematics and Education. *(Goldsmiths' College, Lewisham Way, London SE14 6NW. Tel 081 692 7171.)*

London (Univ) - Heythrop College Small college specialising in Theology and Philosophy with extensive tutorial teaching, with one of the largest theological libraries in the country. Situated near Oxford Circus; 190 students (including 46 postgraduates), with accommodation in inter-collegiate halls. *(Heythrop College, 11-13 Cavendish Square, London W1M 0AN. Tel 071 580 6941.)*

London (Univ) - Imperial College of Science, Technology and Medicine It is based on a precinct site in South Kensington; a leading college of Science and Technology and now including St Mary's Hospital Medical School with subject areas including Engineering, Sciences, Mining and Metallurgy. Highly rated for research. 5200 students. *(Imperial College of Science and Technology, South Kensington, London SW7 2AZ. Tel 071 589 5111.)*

London (Univ) - Jews College This college offers one degree course in Jewish Studies. The degrees are validated by London University Imperial College. *(Jews College, Albert Road, London NW4 2SJ. Tel 081 203 6427.)*

London (Univ) - King's College A central London location with 6900 students. Humanities, Science, Engineering, Education and Law courses are offered. *(King's College, Strand, London WC2R 2LS. Tel 071 836 5454.)*

London (Univ) - Queen Mary and Westfield College Campus-based college centrally located near the City and Docklands. 6000 students in seven faculties of Arts, Social Studies, Informatics and Mathematical Sciences, Engineering, Law and Physical and Biological Sciences. Popular course-unit system. Wide range of accommodation including on-campus residences, and halls in suburban South Woodford. *(Queen Mary College, Mile End Road, London E1 4NS. Tel 071 975 5555.)*

London (Univ) - Royal Holloway The only London University college on a country campus site. Close to Windsor and one hour from central London. Faculties of Science, Arts and Music. 3100 students of whom a high proportion can be accommodated in college. *(Royal Holloway, Egham Hill, Egham, Surrey TW20 0EX. Tel 0784 434455.)*

London (Univ) - Royal Veterinary College Pre-clinical and para-clinical work takes place at Camden Town; clinical work is done on a 470-acre site at Potters Bar, Middlesex. 380 students. *(Royal Veterinary College, Royal College Street, London NW1 0TU. Tel 071 387 2898.)*

London (Univ) - School of Economics and Political Science (LSE) The leading institution for courses in Social Studies in the UK, perhaps in the world. It is located in central London with a student population of 4000. *(London School of Economics and Political Science, Houghton Street, Aldwych, London WC2A 2AE. Tel 071 405 7686.)*

London (Univ) - School of Oriental and African Studies (SOAS) 1800 students specialise in Oriental and African languages and other studies. *(The School of Oriental and African Studies, Thornhaugh Street, Russell Square, London WC1M 0XG. Tel 071 637 2388.)*

London (Univ) - School of Pharmacy There are 350 students specialising in Pharmacy. *(The School of Pharmacy, 29-39 Brunswick Square, London WC1N 1AX. Tel 071 753 5800.)*

London (Univ) - School of Slavonic and East European Studies (SSEES) The School has a student population of 380 with degree courses leading to East European languages and history. *(The School of Slavonic and East European Studies, Malet Street, London WC1E 7HU. Tel 071 637 4934.)*

London (Univ) - University College There is a student body of 8000 with six faculties and 43 departments offering a wide range of courses. *(University College, Gower Street, London WC1E 6BT. Tel 071 387 7050.)*

London (Univ) - Wye College It is located five miles from Ashford and 60 miles from London and specialises in science subjects with honours courses in Agriculture and Horticulture. 650 students. Accommodation for 65% of the students. *(Wye College, Wye, Ashford, Kent TN25 5AH. Tel 0233 812401.)*

London Medical and Dental Schools:

Charing Cross and Westminster Medical School 850 students. St Dunstan's Road, London W6 8RP. Tel 081 846 7202.

King's College Hospital School of Medicine and Dentistry 840 students. Bessemer Road, London SE5 9PJ. Tel 071 274 6222; Dental School tel 071 326 3079.

London Hospital Medical College (Dentistry and Medicine) 1000 students. Turner Street, London E1 2AD. Tel 071 377 7611.

Royal Free Hospital School of Medicine 550 students. Rowland Hill Street, London NW3 2PF. Tel 071 794 0500.

St Bartholomew's Hospital Medical College (Dentistry and Medicine) 560 students. West Smithfield, London EC1A 7BE. Tel 071 601 8834.

St George's Hospital Medical School 770 students. Cranmer Terrace, Tooting, London SW17 0RE. Tel 081 672 9944.

St Mary's Hospital Medical School 570 students. Norfolk Place, Paddington, London W2 1PG. Tel 071 723 1252.

United Medical and Dental Schools of Guy's and St Thomas's Hospitals (Dentistry and Medicine) 1400 students. There are two sites: Guy's Campus, London Bridge, London SE1 9RT; St Thomas's Campus, Lambeth Palace Road, London SE1 7EH. Tel 071 922 8013. Enquiries to St Thomas's Campus only.

University College and Middlesex School of Medicine, University College London 1000 students (inc. Dentistry students). Gower Street, London WC1 6JJ. Tel 071 387 7050.

Student accommodation in medical schools is limited, but University of London inter-collegiate halls of residence are also available.

Loughborough (Univ) The University was established on a campus to the west of the town and offers a wide range of degree and sandwich courses. There are 5700 students with a high proportion (3500) living in the student village. *(University of Technology, Loughborough, Leicester LE11 3TU. Tel 0509 263171.)*

Luton (CHE) The College offers degree combined science, professional and diploma courses and a large number of HND courses. *(Luton College of Higher Education, Park Square, Luton, Bedfordshire LU1 3JU. Tel 0582 34111.)*

Manchester Met (Univ) It is based on six sites in and around the city. There are 13000 students following BA, BEd, BSc, BEng, LLB and HND courses. There is also a programme of Combined Studies in Science. *(Manchester Metropolitan University, All Saints, Manchester M15 6BH. Tel 061 247 2000.)*

Manchester (Univ) A large civic university with 12,600 approx. students. A very wide range of BA, BA (Econ), BSc, BEng, LLB and other degree courses are offered. *(The University of Manchester, Manchester M13 9PL. Tel 061 275 2000.)*

Manchester - The University of Manchester Institute of Science and Technology (UMIST): City centre location. One faculty of 20 departments, scientific and technological, but with an extensive Management Sciences programme. 5000 students, 33% sharing residences with the main University body. *(The University of Manchester Institute of Science and Technology, Manchester M60 1QD. Tel 061 236 3311.)*

Matthew Boulton (CFHE) Two courses are offered; one degree course (Podiatric Medicine) and one HND course (Business Studies). *(Matthew Boulton College of Further and Higher Education, Sherlock Street, Birmingham B5 7DB. Tel 021 446 4545.)*

Middlesex (Univ) It is based on seven sites in north London and Middlesex with a student population of 7900. There is an extensive modular degree programme.
Franchised courses: Writtle (CAg) offers the BEng course in Mechanical Engineering with the University (see Ch 6). *(Middlesex University, Bramley Road, Oakwood, London N14 4XS. Tel 081 368 1299.)*

Napier (Univ) The University has seven teaching sites situated to the south and west of the city centre. It offers a wide range of vocational courses including thick and thin sandwich courses. It has a student population of 9100. *(Napier University of Edinburgh, 219 Colinton Road, Edinburgh EH14 1DJ. Tel 031 444 2266.)*

Nene (CHE) An Associate College of Leicester University, the College offers a range of BA, BSc, BEd and HND courses in mainly vocational subjects. A flexible BA subject scheme is also available.
Franchised courses: One year of the English, History, Psychology and Sociology courses can be studied at Peterborough Regional College (see Ch 6). *(Nene College, Moulton Park, Northampton NN2 7AL. Tel 0604 735500.)*

New College, Durham The College offers a degree course in Podiatry and an HND course in Business Studies with 12 specialist options. *(New College, Framwellgate Moor Centre, Durham DH1 5ES. Tel 091 386 2421.)*

Newcastle (Univ) An increasingly popular university, it is located in a precinct in the centre of the city. There are a variety of courses covering Arts, Modern Languages, Social and Environmental Science, Engineering Science, Medicine, Dentistry, Law and Agriculture. Over 9000 students, 46% housed by the University. *(The University of Newcastle upon Tyne, 6 Kensington Terrace, Newcastle upon Tyne NE1 7RU. Tel 091 222 6000.)*

Newman & Westhill (CHE) The Colleges offer BEd courses in the nursery, lower primary and upper primary age ranges. Also a BTheol course. Courses are validated by Birmingham University. *(Newman College, Genners Lane, Bartley Green, Birmingham B32 3NT. Tel 021 476 1181; Westhill College, Weoley Park Road, Selly Oak, Birmingham B29 6LL. Tel 021 472 7245.)*

North Cheshire (CHE) The College offers four degree courses and one HND course relating to Business Studies, Leisure and Media Studies. *(North Cheshire College, Padgate Campus, Fearnhead, Warrington WA2 0DB. Tel 0925 814343.)*

North East Surrey (CT) A modular Biological Science degree programme is offered along with DipHE and HND courses. *(North East Surrey College of Technology, Reigate Road, Ewell, Epsom, Surrey KT17 3DS. Tel 081 394 1731.)*

North East Wales (IHE) 4500 full-time students following BA, BSc, BEng, BEd, Nursing courses and HND courses.
Franchised courses: Several BSc and BEng courses are offered in conjunction with Bangor, Cardiff, Liverpool, Manchester, Salford, UMIST (see Ch 6). *(North East Wales Institute of Higher Education Cartrefle, Mold Road, Wrexham, Clwyd LL11 2AW. Tel 0978 290666.)*

North London (Univ) There are 5300 full-time and sandwich students on three sites in Camden, Islington and Central London. Degree and HND courses are offered including flexible Humanities and Science courses. *(The University of North London, Holloway Road, London N7 8DB. Tel 071 607 2789.)*

North Riding (Coll) The College offers BA and BSc degree courses with Qualified Teacher Status validated by Leeds University. *(North Riding College, Filey Road, Scarborough, North Yorkshire YO11 3AZ. Tel 0723 362392.)*

Northumbria (Univ) An increasingly popular institution on two sites with a student population of over 8000 (full- and part-time). A large number of degree courses are offered including two-subject language combinations. The International Business Studies course is offered at either the Newcastle or Carlisle campuses. There is also a programme of HND courses. *(The University of Northumbria at Newcastle, Ellison Place, Newcastle upon Tyne NE1 8ST. Tel 091 232 6002.)*

Nottingham Trent (Univ) This popular institution has 9400 full-time and sandwich students. A very wide range of courses is offered including a number with links in Europe.
Franchised courses: HND courses in Horse Studies can be taken at Lincolnshire (CAg) or Brackenhurst College (see Ch 6). *(Nottingham Trent University, Burton Street, Nottingham NG1 4BU. Tel 0602 418418.)*

Nottingham (Univ) A very popular university on a campus site in parkland west of the city. Large number of courses. 8300 student population. Thirteen halls of residence catering for 3600 students. This University was in the top ten in graduate employment tables in 1991. *(The University of Nottingham, University Park, Nottingham NG7 2RD. Tel 0602 484848.)*

Oxford Brookes (Univ) A very popular institution with 5600 students based on two sites. It is perhaps best known for its extensive modular course with a wide range of two-subject degree courses. *(Oxford Brookes University, Headington, Oxford OX3 0BP. Tel 0865 741111.)*

Oxford (Univ) Dating from 12th century. 35 colleges admitting students (14,700): seven for graduates, one for women (graduates or undergraduates), and 27 mixed. Sixteen faculties offering a wide range of courses. Highly rated for research. Library (the Bodleian) of over seven million books and 60,000 manuscripts. Of 13,800 students only 2100 have to live out. (M)=Men only; (W)=Women only. All other colleges are mixed. **Group 1:** Brasenose, Christ Church, Jesus, Lincoln, Magdalen, Merton, Oriel, St Hilda's (W), Somerville; **Group 2:** Balliol, Exeter, Keble, Pembroke, St Anne's, St Edmund Hall, St John's, St Peter's, Wadham; **Group 3:** Corpus Christi, Hertford, Lady Margaret Hall, New College, Queen's, St Catherine's, St Hugh's, Trinity, University, Worcester. Private Halls: Campion Hall (M), St Benet's Hall (M), Mansfield, Regent's Park, Greyfriars (M). This University was rated second out of ten for graduate employment in 1991. The University validates the degrees of Westminster College, Oxford. (Enquiries should be addressed to *The Tutor for......Admissions, ...College, Oxford.* **Or** *The Oxford Colleges Admissions Office, University Offices, Wellington Square, Oxford OX1 2JD. Tel 0865 270207.)*

Paisley (Univ) The University occupies a 20-acre campus in the centre of Paisley, seven miles west of Glasgow. It concentrates on diploma, first degree and postgraduate work in Technology, Science, Engineering, Computing, surveying, Business Management and Social Studies. There is a student population of 3500. *(Paisley University, High Street, Paisley, Renfrewshire PA1 2BE. Tel 041 848 3000.)*

Plymouth (Univ) There are over 8000 students based on four sites - the largest higher education institution in the region. A large number of degree and HND courses are offered with a unique selection of Marine Studies courses.
Franchised courses: The Extended Engineering course is also offered with Cornwall College (Redruth) and Somerset (CAT) (Taunton). Students may choose their venue. The Extended Science course is also offered at Redruth. DipHe Nursing and Social Work courses are offered in association with South West College of Health Studies (Truro and Plymouth) and with East Devon College (Tiverton). All agriculture courses are offered at Seale Hayne (CAg) (Newton Abbot) and other franchised HND courses are offered at Plymouth (CFE), South Devon (CAT) (Torquay) and at Redruth, Tiverton and Taunton (above) (see Ch 6). *(University of Plymouth, Drake Circus, Plymouth PL4 8AA. Tel 0752 600600.)*

Portsmouth (Univ) There are 7100 students based on two sites with Faculties of Environment Studies, Engineering (with Extended Engineering courses with a foundation year), Humanities and Social Scinces and a Business School. Degree and HND courses are offered. *(The University of Portsmouth, Museum Road, Portsmouth PO1 2QQ. Tel 0705 827681.)*

Reading (Univ) The University is situated on a large parkland site south of the town with five faculties offering a wide range of degree courses. There are 7600 students, 3600 in residence. *(The University of Reading, PO Box 217 Reading, Berkshire RG6 2AH. Tel 0734 875123.)*

Ripon and York St John (CHE) The College offers Leeds University degrees in a very wide range of subjects. *(College of Ripon and York St John, Lord Mayor's Walk, York YO3 7EX. Tel 0904 656771.)*

Robert Gordon (Univ) The University comprises 13 Schools and a Centre for the Professions Allied to Medicine. It is located on eight sites throughout the city and has a student population of 6200. *(Robert Gordon University, Schoolhill, Aberdeen AB9 1FR. Tel 0224 633611.)*

Roehampton (IHE) The Institute offers Surrey University single and joint honours degrees across four colleges - Southlands, Whitelands, Digby Stuart and Froebel Institute. *(Roehampton Institute, Roehampton Lane, London SW15 5PU. Tel 081 878 8117.)*

St Andrews (Univ) This popular university dates back to 1413 and is relatively small in size. There are 4000 students (68% in student accommodation) and 40% are Scottish. This University was in the top ten in graduate employment tables in 1991. *(The University of St Andrews, College Gate, St Andrews, Fife KY16 9AJ. Tel 0334 76161.)*

St David's (Univ) See under **Wales (Univ)**

St Mark and St John (CHE) Offers BEd and BA courses in teaching subjects and combined courses. Degrees are validated by Exeter University. *(St Mark and St John College, Derriford Road, Plymouth PL6 8BH. Tel 0752 777188.)*

S Martin's (CHE) The College offers a very large number of Lancaster University BA joint honours courses. BA, BSc and Primary Teaching courses are also offered and single honours courses in Radiography, Nursing and Community Studies. There are 2600 students. *(S Martin's College, Lancaster LA1 3JD. Tel 0524 63446.)*

St Mary's (CHE) The college offers Teaching and Combined BA/BSc courses awarded by Surrey University. *(St Mary's College, Strawberry Hill, Twickenham, Middlesex TW1 4SX. Tel 081 892 0051.)*

Salford (Univ) The University is on a pleasant campus site. There are 4200 students (approx.) following BA, BSc and BEng courses many of which offer sandwich periods in industry and commerce. *(The University of Salford, Salford M5 4WT. Tel 061 745 5000.)*

Salford (Univ Coll) (Formerly **Salford College of Technology**) The College offers a wide range of degree, diploma and HND courses leading to professional qualifications. *Franchised courses:* The course in Professional Sound and Video Technology is offered in association with Sandwell (CHE). Courses in Applied Chemistry, Computer Science and

Prosthetics and Orthoptics are offered in association with Salford University (see Ch 6). *(Salford University College, Frederick Road, Salford M6 6PU. Tel 061 736 6541.)*

Sheffield (Univ) This is a large city university, two main sites with a wide range of single and dual honours courses. 9400 students, 44% are in university accommodation. *(The University of Sheffield, Western Bank, Sheffield S10 2TN. Tel 0742 768555. Medical School tel 0742 766222.)*

Sheffield Hallam (Univ) There are four sites and 9600 students. The University offers a very wide range of single honours courses and a good selection on HND courses. *(Sheffield Hallam University, Pond Street, Sheffield S1 1WB. Tel 0742 720911.)*

Southampton (IHE) The Institute offers BA, BEng, BSc and LLB courses validated by Southampton University; 16 HND courses are also offered. There are 2000 full-time and 11,000 part-time students.
Franchised courses: The HND course in Business and Finance (Agriculture) is held in conjunction with Sparsholt (CAg) (see Ch 6). *(Southampton Institute of Higher Education, East Park Terrace, Southampton SO9 4WW. Tel 0703 229381.)*

Southampton (Univ) It is based on a landscaped site close to the city centre. BA, BSc, LLB and BEng courses in a wide range of subjects are available. 7300 students, 48% in nearby university accommodation (inc. 20 in a purpose-built hall for the disabled). The University validates the degrees of King Alfred's College, La Sainte Union College, West Sussex Institute of Higher Education and Winchester School of Art. *(The University of Southampton, Highfield, Southampton SO9 5NH. Tel 0703 595000.)*

South Bank (Univ) There are 5800 students based on five sites, the main campus being Southwark. BA, BEd, BEng, BSc,LLB and HND courses are offered. There are also 12 franchised courses at colleges in the London area and also in Kent and Surrey.
Franchised courses: Foundation courses are offered at the following colleges: Guildford, Holborn, Lewisham, Mid-Kent, North East Surrey, South Bank, South London, South Thames, Southwark, Vauxhall, Waltham Forest and Westminster (see Ch 6). *(South Bank University, Borough Road, London SE1 0AA. Tel 071 928 8989.)*

South Devon (CAT) 2900 students follow two degree courses in Hospitality Management and Social Science along with several HND courses. *(South Devon College of Arts and Technology, Newton Road, Torquay, Devon. Tel 0803 213242.)*

Staffordshire (Univ) There are 6200 students on sites in Stafford and Stoke-on-Trent. Degree and HND courses are offered including an extensive BSc Applied Science programme.
Franchised courses: BSc courses in Quantity and Valuation Surveying are held in conjunction with Stoke-on-Trent College (see Ch 6). *(Staffordshire University, College Road, Stoke-on-Trent ST4 2DE. Tel 0785 52331.)*

Stirling (Univ) The University is located on a large, scenic campus site 2 miles north of the town. Courses relate to Management and Social Sciences, Arts, Sciences and Education. There are 3300 full-time students with housing for 2000 on-campus. Emphasis is on breadth and flexibility of degree programmes, organised around an academic session of two 15-week semesters. *(The University of Stirling, Stirling FK9 4LA, Scotland. Tel 0786 73171.)*

Strathclyde (Univ) The University is situated on a city-centre site, and is strong in Science, Technology and Business. There are 8300 students, 55% living at home, thus a high proportion of others can be housed by the University. _(The University of Strathclyde, 16 Richmond Street, Glasgow G1 1XQ, Scotland. Tel 041 553 4170.)_

Suffolk (CFHE) A small number of BA and BSc combined studies courses are offered along with DipHE and HND courses. _(Suffolk College, Rope Walk, Ipswich, Suffolk. Tel 0473 255885.)_

Sunderland (Univ) There are 5400 students based on two sites. In addition to a range of single honours courses a modular credit scheme is also offered. _(University of Sunderland, Ryhope Road, Sunderland, Tyne and Wear SR2 7EE. Tel 091 515 2000.)_

Surrey (Univ) The University is in Guildford on a hill site next to the Cathedral. Bias towards Science and Technology, but good choice of alternative subjects. 3900 students, 56% housed in University accommodation. This University was in the top ten in graduate employment tables in 1991. The University validates the degrees of Roehampton Institute of Higher Education and St Mary's College. _(The University of Surrey, Guildford, Surrey GU2 5XH. Tel 0483 300800.)_

Sussex (Univ) It is on a campus site north of Brighton. There is a wide range of courses organised in schools of studies. 4900 students; 1850 living on the campus. This University was in the top ten in graduate employment tables in 1991. _(The University of Sussex, Sussex House, Falmer, Brighton BN1 9RH. Tel 0273 678416.)_

36

Swansea (IHE) The Institute offers a range of courses covering BA, BSc, BEng and LLB degrees and HND courses. *(Swansea Institute of Higher Education, Townhill Road, Swansea SA2 0UT. Tel 0792 203482.)*

Swansea (Univ) See under **Wales (Univ)**

Teesside (Univ) There are 5000 students based on two sites. The institution is noted for its wide range of modular schemes allowing maximum flexibility for students in choosing subject combinations.
Franchised courses: Several HND courses are held in conjunction with Longlands (CFE), Kirkby Hall College, Northumberland and local further education colleges (see Ch 6). *(The University of Teesside, Borough Road, Middlesbrough, Cleveland TS1 3BA. Tel 0642 218121.)*

Thames Valley London (Univ) Degree and HND courses are offered at Ealing and Slough including an extensive range of applied language studies leading to BA degrees.
Franchised courses: Music degree courses are offered in conjunction with the London College of Music (Ealing) (see Ch 6). *(Thames Valley London University, St Mary's Road, London W5 5RF. Tel 081 579 5000.)*

Trinity & All Saints (CHE) The College offers a wide range of two-subject and teacher training courses leading to Leeds University degrees. There are 1570 full-time students. *(Trinity and All Saints' College, Brownberrie Lane, Horsforth, Leeds LS18 5HD. Tel 0532 584341.)*

Trinity Carmarthen (CHE) BEd and BA courses in Humanities are offered in this college with 1130 full-time students. *(Trinity College, Carmarthen, Dyfed, South Wales SA31 3EP. Tel 0267 237971.)*

Ulster (Univ) There are four campuses - Jordanstown, Belfast, Coleraine and Londonderry and 9100 students. An extensive range of courses is offered in the Faculties of Business, Education, Humanities, Science and Technology and Social and Health Sciences. *(The University of Ulster, Coleraine, County Londonderry BT52 1SA, Northern Ireland. Tel 0265 44141.)*

Wales (Univ) - Aberystwyth It is located on a large hill site overlooking the town. There is a wide range of subjects offered as single or joint courses. 3600 students with 66% in university accommodation. There is also the College of Librarianship on nearby campus offering a wide range of joint programmes. 400 students. Accommodation for 200. *(The University of Wales, PO Box 2, Aberystwyth, Dyfed SY23 2AX. Tel 0970 622021.)*

Wales (Univ) - Bangor Situated in a small city in an area of outstanding natural beauty between the mountains of Snowdonia and the shores of the Menai Strait. A wide range of courses is offered in Arts, Science (including Agriculture, Forestry and Wood Science, Marine Biology and Oceanography), Music and Theology. 3500 students with 49% in University accommodation. *(The University College of North Wales, Bangor, Gwynedd LL57 2DG. Tel 0248 351151.)*

Wales (Univ) - Cardiff There are 8700 students following an extensive range of single and joint courses. This elegant university is located close to the city centre. *(The University of Wales College of Cardiff, PO Box 68, Cardiff CF1 3XA. Tel 0222 874412.)*

Wales (Univ) - St David's The College buildings occupy a large area of the small country town. Degree courses are mainly in the faculty of arts. 950 students, 25% from Wales. Large proportion of students (80%) in university accommodation. This is a small university but has a strong community spirit. *(St David's University College, Lampeter, Dyfed SA48 7ED. Tel 0570 422351.)*

Wales (Univ) - Swansea It is situated on a campus site west of the city. Courses are offered in Arts, Science, Technology and Social Sciences. There are 5300 students with accommodation for 53%. *(University College of Swansea, Singleton Park, Swansea SA2 8PP. Tel 0792 205678.)*

Wales (Univ) College of Medicine (UWCM) The College shares a 53-acre parkland site in Cardiff with University Hospital. There are 900 medical, dental and nursing students (40% Welsh) with accommodation for about 300. The College validates the degrees awarded by the Institute of Health Care Studies. *(The University of Wales College of Medicine, Heath Park, Cardiff CF4 4XN. Tel 0222 747747.)*

Wales (Univ) Institute of Health Care Studies Courses are offered in Physiotherapy, Radiography and Occupational Therapy. *(Institute of Health Care Studies, University Hospital of Wales, Heath Park, Cardiff CF4 4XW. Tel 0222 747747.)*

Warwick (Univ) The University was founded in 1964 on a large campus site outside Coventry. Social science, arts and science subjects are offered to 6900 students. There is accommodation for 3175 on campus. Highly rated for research.
Franchised courses: The University has also organised a Higher Education Foundation Programme (HEFP), a one-year preparatory course for international students aiming for

entry to Bachelor degree courses in the UK. The courses are offered in Social Science, Business Studies, Law, Science and Engineering and Paramedical Studies at three colleges of technology. (See under subject headings in Ch 6 for further details.) *(The University of Warwick, Coventry CV4 7AL. Tel 0203 523523.)*

West Herts (Coll) One degree course in Graphic Media Studies is offered in the specialised area of Printing and Packaging. There are also a few HND courses. *(West Hertfordshire College, Hempstead Road, Watford, Hertfordshire WD1 3EZ. Tel 0923 57500.)*

West London (IHE) The Associate College of Brunel University offers BA, BSc and BEd courses on integrated degree schemes. There are 2750 students on two campuses to the west of London. *(West London Institute of Higher Education, 300 St Margarets Road, Twickenham, Middlesex TW1 1FT. Tel 081 891 0121.)*

Westminster (CHE) This Methodist foundation has a long tradition of teacher training courses validated by Oxford University. There are 750 students. *(Westminster College, North Hinksey, Oxford OX2 9AT. Tel 0865 247644.)*

Westminster (Univ) It has 14 sites throughout London and a population of 4000 students. It offers a wide range of courses including seven languages in combination groups and Film, Video and Photographic Arts. HND courses are also offered.
Franchised courses: The Speech and Drama degree course is offered in conjunction with the Central School of Speech and Drama (see Ch 6). *(University of Westminster, 309 Regent Street, London W1R 8AL. Tel 071 911 5000.)*

West Sussex (IHE) The Institute offers BA, BEd and BSc courses validated by Southampton University. There are 1900 students based on two sites at Bognor Regis and Chichester. *(West Sussex Institute of Higher Education, Upper Bognor Road, Bognor Regis, West Sussex PO21 1HR. Tel 0243 865581.)*

Wolverhampton (Univ) There are five campuses with a population of 7100 full-time and sandwich students. BA, BEd, BSc, BEng, LLB degrees are offered and there are also some HND courses. There is also an extensive modular degree scheme giving maximum flexibility to students.
Franchised courses: Degree courses in Law are also offered by Holborn College (London) and for the first year in Applied Science at Wulfrun (CFE) Wolverhampton (see Ch 6). *(The University of Wolverhampton, Wulfruna Street, Wolverhampton WV1 1SB. Tel 0902 321000.)*

Worcester (CHE) The College offers a range of degree courses including Education and single and Combined Studies. There are 1700 full-time students. *(Worcester College of Higher Education, Henwick Grove, Worcester WR2 6AJ. Tel 0905 748080.)*

York (Univ) The University, founded in 1963, is situated on a beautiful campus east of the city. Arts, natural sciences and social science courses are offered to the 4300 students, each being a member of a college. Majority live in college for first year. *(The University of York, Heslington, York YO1 5DD. Tel 0904 430000.)*

COLLEGES OF AGRICULTURE OFFERING ADVANCED COURSES (Many students are part-time).

Askham Bryan College of Agriculture and Horticulture Askham Bryan, York YO2 3PR. Tel 0904 702121.

A new freedom of choice in higher education.

If you're looking for a place in higher education, you might feel spoilt for choice this year.

At the University of Wolverhampton – formerly Wolverhampton Polytechnic – choice is precisely what we specialise in. For example, we have one of the most comprehensive modular degree schemes in the country, offering students thousands of possible study options.

With our expert help, you can more or less design your own degree programme from a "menu" of over 60 subjects. So, if you want to combine Computing and Law, Sociology and Mathematics, Russian and Engineering – you can. Of course, our commitment to choice allows you to specialise as well.

The Modular Degree Scheme is just one of the initiatives that has earned the University of Wolverhampton a reputation for flexibility and innovation. Making it one of the fastest-growing universities in the Midlands.

For more information about our distinctive higher education service, call (0902) 321000 for our latest Prospectus.

Or for friendly and confidential advice and counselling on your higher education needs, call or pop into our unique Higher Education Shop, 62-68 Lichfield Street, Wolverhampton, WV1 1SB. Open weekdays 10am to 4pm (closing at lunch between 1pm and 2pm). Telephone (0902) 321032.

UNIVERSITY OF WOLVERHAMPTON

TRINITY COLLEGE CARMARTHEN

Principal: D Clive Jones-Davies, OBE.,JP.,MA.,MPhil.,FRSA

The College offers the following courses:

* **B.Ed. (Honours)** - primary

* **B.Ed. Bilingual (Honours)** - primary

  English, Welsh, Mathematics, History, Geography,
  Music, Science and the Environment, Physical Education,
  Religious Education, Art, Craft and Design, Technology.

* **B.Ed. (Honours)** - secondary
  Major field - Welsh

  Second subjects - French, History, Mathematics,
                     Music, Geography, Religious
                     Education, Education,
                     Information Technology.

* **B.A. Humanities (Honours)**

  English/ Welsh, History, Religious Studies
  Theatre Studies, Welsh Studies, Archaeology

* **B.A. Studies in the Rural Environment (Honours)**

  Geography, Geology, Ecology, Conservation
  Information Systems Management, Pollution Studies etc.

* **Postgraduate Certificate in Education** - primary;
  Secondary for Religious Education only

For additional information, please contact
The Registrar
Trinity College, Carmarthen
Dyfed, SA31 3EP
(0267) 237971/2/3

Harper Adams Agricultural College Newport, Shropshire TF10 8NB. Tel 0952 820820. Several courses are held in conjunction with the following institutions: Keele, Central England and Staffordshire Universities, Pershore (CHort) and Cheshire and Staffordshire Colleges of Agriculture.

Lancashire College of Agriculture and Horticulture Myerscough Hall, Bilsborrow, Preston, Lancs PR3 0RY. Tel 0995 40611.

Lincolnshire College of Agriculture and Horticulture Caythorpe Court, Caythorpe, Grantham, Lincolnshire NG32 3EI

Merrist Wood College of Agriculture & Horticulture Worplesden, Guildford, Surrey GU3 3PE. Tel 0483 232424.

Pershore College of Horticulture Avonbank, Pershore, Worcestershire WR10 3JP. Tel 0386 552443.

Royal Agricultural College Cirencester, Gloucestershire GL2 6JS. Tel 0285 2531.

Seale Hayne Agricultural College Newton Abbott, Devon TQ12 6NQ. Tel 0626 52323. (Merged with **Plymouth University.**)

Shuttleworth Agricultural College Biggleswade, Bedfordshire SG18 9DX. Tel 076 727 441.

Welsh Agricultural College Aberystwyth, Dyfed SY23 3 AL. Tel 0970 624471.

Writtle Agricultural College Chelmsford, Essex CM1 3RR. Tel 0245 420705. The BSc Horticulture is offered in conjunction with Hertfordshire University and the Rural Resource Development course with Anglia (Polytechnic University).

COLLEGES OF ART

Berkshire College of Art and Design Kings Road, Reading, Berkshire SL6 6DF. Tel 0628 24302.

Camberwell School of Art and Crafts Peckham Road, London SE5 8UF. Tel 071 703 0987. (**The London Institute.**)

Canterbury College of Art (now merged with **Maidstone College of Art and Design** to form the **Kent Institute of Art and design** – see below). Tel 0227 69371.

Central School of Art and Design Southampton Row, London WC1B 4AP. Tel 071 405 1825. (**The London Institute.**)

Chelsea School of Art Manresa Road, London SW3 6LS. Tel 071 351 3844. (**The London Institute.**)

Chesterfield College of Technology and Arts Sheffield Road, Chesterfield, Derbyshire S41 7NG. Tel 0246 31212.

Cleveland College of Art and Design Green Lane, Linthorpe, Middlesbrough, Cleveland TS5 7RJ. Tel 0642 821441.

Cumbria College of Art and Design Brampton Road, Carlisle CA3 9AV. Tel 0228 25333.

Dartington College of Arts Totnes, Devon TQ9 6EJ. Tel 0803 862224.

Dewsbury College Halifax Road, Dewsbury, West Yorkshire WF13 2AS. Tel 0924 465916.

Epsom School of Art and Design Ashley Road, Epsom, Surrey KT18 5BE. Tel 03727 28811.

Exeter College of Art and Design East Richards Road North, Exeter EX2 6AS. Tel 0392 77977. (Now merged with **Plymouth University**.)

Falmouth School of Art Wood Lane, Falmouth, Cornwall TR11 4RA. Tel 0326 211077.

Hertfordshire College of Art and Design (now a Faculty of the University of Hertfordshire) 7 Hatfield Road, St Albans, Hertfordshire AL1 3RS. Tel 0727 64414.

Kent Institute of Art and Design Oakwood Road, Maidstone, Kent ME16 8AG. Tel 0622 757286.

Kidderminster College Hoo Road, Kidderminster, Worcestershire DY10 1LX. Tel 0562 820811.

Lincolnshire College of Art and Design Lindum Road, Lincoln LN2 1PF. Tel 0522 512912.

London College of Printing Elephant and Castle, London SE1 6SB. Tel 071 735 8484. **(The London Institute)**

Loughborough College of Art and Design Radmoor, Loughborough, Leicestershire LE11 3BT. Tel 0509 261515.

Matthew Boulton College Sherlock Street, Birmingham B5 7DB. Tel 021 446 4545.

Norfolk Institute of Art and Design St George's Street, Norwich NR3 1BB. Tel 0603 610561.

North East Worcestershire College Bromsgrove Campus, School Drive, Bromsgrove, Worcestershire B60 1PQ. Tel 0527 79500.

Plymouth College of Art and Design Tavistock Place, Plymouth. Tel 0752 221312.

Portsmouth College of Art, Design and Further Education Winston Churchill Avenue, Portsmouth PO1 2DJ. Tel 0705 826435.

Ravensbourne College of Design and Communication Walden Road, Chislehurst, Kent BR7 5SN. Tel 081 468 7071.

Royal Academy Schools (Royal Academy of Arts) Piccadilly, London W1V 0DS. Tel 071 734 9052.

Royal College of Art Kensington Gore, London SW7 2EV. Tel 071 584 5020. Royal Charter.

St Martin's School of Art 107 Charing Cross Road, London WC2H 0DU. Tel 071 437 0611. **(The London Institute.)**

Salisbury College of Art and Design Southampton Road, Salisbury, Wiltshire SP1 2LW. Tel 0772 26122.

Slade School of Fine Art University College, Gower Street, London WC1E 6BT. Tel 071 387 7050.

Stourbridge College of Technology and Art Hagley Road, Old Swinford, Stourbridge, West Midlands DY8 1LY. Tel 0384 378531.

West Surrey College of Art The Hart, Farnham, Surrey GU9 7DS. Tel 0252 722441.

Wimbledon School of Art Merton Hall Road, Wimbledon, London SW19 3QR. Tel 081 540 0231.

Winchester School of Art Park Avenue, Winchester, Hampshire SO23 8DL. Tel 0962 842500.

COLLEGES OF DRAMA, MUSIC AND SPEECH

Arts Educational Schools Drama Department, Cone Ripman House, 14 Bath Road, London W4 1LY. Tel 081 994 9366.

Birmingham Conservatoire Paradise Circus, Birmingham B3 3HG. Tel 021 359 6721.

Birmingham School of Speech Training and Dramatic Art 45 Church Street, Edgbaston, Birmingham B15 3SW. Tel 021 454 3424.

Bristol Vic Theatre School 1/2 Downside Road, Clifton, Bristol BS8 2XF. Tel 0272 733533.

Central School of Speech and Drama Embassy Theatre, Eton Avenue, London NW3 3HY. Tel 071 722 8183.

City of Leeds College of Music Cookridge Street, Leeds LS2 8BH. Tel 0532 452069.

Cleveland College of Art and Design Green Lane, Linthorpe, Middlesbrough, Cleveland TS5 7RJ. Tel 0642 821441.

Dartington College of Arts Totnes, Devon TQ9 6EJ. Tel 0803 862224.

Drama Centre, London 176 Prince of Wales Road, London NW5 3PT. Tel 071 267 1177.

East 15 Acting School Hatfields, Rectory Lane, Loughton, Essex IG10 3RU. Tel 081 508 5983

Guildford School of Acting and Dance 20 Buryfields, Guildford, Surrey GU2 5AZ. Tel 0483 60701

Guildhall School of Music and Drama Silk Street, Barbican, London EC2Y 8DT. Tel 071 628 2571.

Laban Centre for Movement and Dance at University of London Goldsmiths' College, New Cross, London SE14 6NW. Tel 081 692 4070.

London Academy of Music and Dramatic Art Tower House, 226 Cromwell Road, London SW5 0SR. Tel 071 373 9883.

London College of Music 47 Great Marlborough Street, London W1V 2AS. Tel 071 437 6120.

Manchester Metropolitan University, School of Theatre Capitol Building, School Lane, Didsbury, Manchester M20 0HT. Tel 061 434 3331.

Mountain Theatre School 104 Crouch Hill, London N8. Tel 081 340 5885.

National Hospitals College of Speech Science 59 Portland Place, London W1N 3AJ. Tel 071 636 1433. (**London University.**)

Rose Bruford College of Speech and Drama Sidcup, Kent DA15 9DF. Tel 081 300 3024.

Royal Academy of Dramatic Art 62 Gower Street, London WC1E 6ED. Tel 071 636 7076.

Royal Academy of Music Marylebone Road, London NW1 5AT. Tel 071 935 5461.

Royal College of Music Prince Consort Road, London SW7 2BS. Tel 071 589 3643.

Royal Northern College of Music 124 Oxford Road, Manchester M13 9RD. Tel 061 273 6283.

Trinity College of Music Mandeville Place, London W1M 6AQ. Tel 071 935 5773.

Webber Douglas Academy of Dramatic Art 30-36 Clareville Street, London SW7 5AP. Tel 071 370 4154.

Welsh College of Music and Drama Cathays Park, Cardiff CF1 3ER. Tel 0222 342854.

SCHOOLS OF CHIROPODY, OCCUPATIONAL THERAPY, PHYSIOTHERAPY AND RADIOGRAPHY

Contact the professional bodies listed below for names and addresses of schools offering courses in the appropriate fields, and for information relating to applications.

The Institute of Chiropodists 133 Oxford Street, London W1. Tel 071 439 8436.

The Society of Chiropodists 8 Wimpole Street, London W1H 3PE. Tel 071 486 3381.

The British Association of Occupational Therapists 20 Rede Place, London W2 4TU. Tel 071 229 9738.

The Chartered Society of Physiotherapy 14 Bedford Row, London WC1R 4ED. Tel 071 242 1941.

The Society of Radiographers 14 Upper Wimpole Street, London W1M 8BN. Tel 071 935 5726.

OTHER COLLEGES IN ENGLAND AND WALES

The following Colleges appear under various subject headings in the Tables in Chapter 6. Direct application is made to these Colleges.

Avon & Gloucestershire College of Health Glenside, Blackberry Hill, Stapleton, Bristol BS16 1DD. Tel 0272 585655.

Blackpool and Fylde College Ashfield Road, Bispham, Blackpool, Lancashire FY2 0HB. Tel 0253 52352.

City College (Liverpool) Myrtle Street, Liverpool L1 7DN. Tel 051 708 0423.

Eastbourne College of Food and Fashion 1 Silverdale Road, Eastbourne

Jacob Kramer (Coll) Blenheim Walk, Leeds LS2 9AQ. Tel 0532 433848)

Kilburn Polytechnic (not in the UCAS scheme) Priory Park Road, Kilburn, London NW6 1YB. Tel 071 328 8241.

Llandrillo Technical College Llandudno Road, Rhos-on-Sea, Colwyn Bay LL28 4HZ. Tel 0492 46666.

London Bible College Green Lane, Northwood, Middlesex. Tel 081 652 6061.

London College of Fashion 20 John Princes Street, London W1M 9HE. Tel 071 629 9401. (The **London Institute**.)

London College of Printing and Distributive Trades Elephant and Castle, London SE1 6SB. Tel 071 735 8484.

New College Framwellgate Moor, Durham DH1 5ES. Tel 091 386 2421.

Northumberland College of Arts College Road, Ashington, Northumberland NE63 9RG. Tel 0670 813248.

Norton College Dyche Lane, Sheffield S8 8BR. Tel 0742 372741.

Stockport College of Technology Wellington Road South, Stockport, Cheshire SK1 3 UQ. Tel 061 480 7331.

Stoke-on-Trent Technical College Moorland Road, Burslem, Stoke-on-Trent, Staffordshire ST6 1JT. Tel 0782 821222.

Westminster College Vincent Square, London SW1 2PD. Tel 081 828 1222.

COLLEGES FOR THE ARMED SERVICES

Cranwell Royal Air Force College Sleaford, Lincolnshire NG34 8HB. Tel 0400 61201.

Dartmouth Britannia Royal Naval College Dartmouth, Devon. Student enquiries to: The Officer Entry Section, Old Admiralty Building, London SW1A 2BE.

Manadon Royal Naval Engineering College Plymouth PL5 3AQ. Tel 0752 553740 ext. 213.

Sandhurst Royal Military Academy Camberley, Surrey GU15 4OQ. Tel 0276 63344.

Shrivenham Royal Military College of Science (a faculty of the **Cranfield Institute of Technology**) Swindon SN6 8LA. Tel 0793 782551.

HIGHER EDUCATION INSTITUTIONS IN SCOTLAND (other than Universities)

Below is a list of the major Scottish institutions.

CENTRAL INSTITUTIONS

Queen Margaret College 36 Clerwood Terrace, Edinburgh EH12 8TS. Tel 031 339 8111.

Scottish College of Textiles (associated with Heriot-Watt University) Netherdale, Galashiels, Selkirk TD1 3HF. Tel 0896 3351.

Dundee Institute of Technology 40 Bell Street, Dundee DD1 1HJ. Tel 0382 308000.

COLLEGES OF ART, MUSIC AND DRAMA

Duncan of Jordanstone College of Art Perth Road, Dundee DD1 4HT. Tel 0382 23261.

Edinburgh College of Art Lauriston Place, Edinburgh EH3 9DF. Tel 031 229 9311.

Glasgow School of Art 167 Renfrew Street, Glasgow G3 6RQ. Tel 041 332 9797.

Queen Margaret College, School of Drama 36 Clerwood Terrace, Edinburgh EH12 8TS. Tel 031 339 8111.

Royal Scottish Academy of Music and Drama 100 Renfrew Street, Glasgow G2 3DB. Tel 041 332 4101.

INSTITUTIONS OFFERING TEACHER TRAINING ONLY

Craigie Faculty of Education, Paisley University Ayr KA8 0SR. Tel 0292 260321.

St Andrew's College of Education Duntocher Road, Bearsden, Glasgow G61 4QA. Tel 041 943 1424.

INSTITUTIONS OFFERING TEACHER TRAINING AND OTHER COURSES

Jordanhill Faculty of Education, Strathclyde University Southbrae Drive, Glasgow G13 1PP. Tel 041 959 1232.

Moray House Institute of Education, Heriot-Watt University Holyrood Road, Edinburgh EH8 8AQ. Tel 031 556 8455.

Northern College of Education Dundee Campus, Gardyne Road, Broughty Ferry, Dundee DD5 1NY. Tel 0382 453433.

Northern College of Education Aberdeen Campus, Hilton Place, Aberdeen AB9 1FA. Tel 0224 283500.

COLLEGES OF TECHNOLOGY AND HIGHER EDUCATION

Aberdeen College of Commerce Holburn Street, Aberdeen AB9 2YT. Tel 0224 572811.

Anniesland College Hatfield Drive, Glasgow G12 0YE. Tel 041 357 3969.

Ayr College Dam Park, Ayr KA8 0EU. Tel 0292 265185.

Angus Technical College Keptie Road, Arbroath, Angus DD11 3EA. Tel 0241 72056.

Banff and Buchan College Argyll Road, Fraserburgh, Aberdeenshire AB4 5RF. Tel 0346 25777.

Bell College of Technology Almada Street, Hamilton, Lanarkshire ML3 0JB. Tel 0698 283100.

Borden College Melrose Road, Galasheils, Selkirkshire TD1 2AF. Tel 0896 57755.

Cardonald College 690 Mosspark Drive, Glasgow G52 3AY. Tel 041 883 6157.

Clackmannan College Branshill Road, Alloa FK10 3BT. Tel 0259 215121.

Clydebank College Kilbowie Road, Clydebank, Dunbartonshire G81 2AA. Tel 041 952 7771.

Dumfries and Galloway College Heathhall, Dumfries DG1 3OZ. Tel 0387 61261.

Dundee College of Further Education 30 Constitution Road, Dundee DD3 6TB. Tel 0382 29151.

Falkirk College of Technology Grangemouth Road, Falkirk, Stirlingshire FK2 9AD. Tel 0324 24981.

Glasgow College of Building and Printing 60 North Hanover Street, Glasgow G1 2BP. Tel 041 332 9969.

Glasgow College of Food Technology 230 Cathedral Street, Glasgow G1 2TG. Tel 041 552 3751.

Glasgow Nautical College 21 Thistle Street, Glasgow G5 9XB. Tel 041 429 3201.

Inverness College Longman Road, Inverness IV1 1SA. Tel 0463 236681.

James Watt College Finnart Street, Greenock, Renfrewshire PA16 8HF. Tel 0475 24433.

Kilmarnock College Holehouse Road, Kilmarnock, Ayrshire KA3 7AT. Tel 0563 23501.

Kirkcaldy College St Brycedale Avenue, Kirkcaldy KY1 1EX. Tel 0592 268591.

Lews Castle College Stornoway, Isle of Lewis PA86 0XR. Tel 0851 3311.

Moray College Hay Street, Elgin, Morayshire IV30 2NN. Tel 0343 3425.

Perth College Brahan Estate, Crieff Road, Perth PH1 2NX. Tel 0738 27044.

Reid Kerr College Renfrew Road, Paisley PA3 4DR. Tel 041 889 4225.

Scottish Agricultural College - Aberdeen King Street, Aberdeen AB9 1UD. Tel 0224 40291.

Scottish Agricultural College - Auchincruive Auchincruive, Ayrshire KA6 5HW. Tel 0292 520331.

Scottish Agricultural College - Edinburgh West Mains Road, Edinburgh EH9 3JG. Tel 031 667 1041.

3 APPLICATIONS AND SELECTION

For entry to higher education in the United Kingdom in 1994, there are two main application routes into degree courses. These routes cover applications for:

- Courses in universities and colleges and institutes of higher education, in their affiliated colleges and institutes of higher education - through **UCAS** (the Universities and Colleges Admissions Service).

- Art and design courses in some universities and colleges of higher education - through **ADAR** (Art and Design Admissions Registry).

UCAS APPLICATIONS TO UNIVERSITY AND COLLEGE COURSES

The Universities and Colleges Admissions Service (UCAS) deals with applications for admission to all full-time and sandwich first degree, Diploma of Higher Education and Higher National Diploma courses in all United Kingdom universities (except the Open University) and colleges and institutes of higher education.

The UCAS procedures are designed to give applicants freedom to make responsible choices of course and institution, while giving universities and colleges freedom to select their own students, using whatever criteria and selection methods they favour. UCAS does not recruit on behalf of universities and colleges, nor does it advise applicants on their choice of courses. Academic considerations are the concern of applicants, in conjunction with their careers teachers, parents, other advisers and the universities and colleges themselves.

Entry requirements

Before applying to universities and colleges, applicants should check that by the time they plan to start their course they will have the required qualifications. Details of entry requirements are available direct from the universities and colleges.

Applicants will need to fulfil:

(i) the **general** entry requirements for degree or DipHE or HND courses

(ii) any **specific** requirements to enter a particular course; for instance study of a specified subject at A- or AS-level, GCSE or BTEC qualifications. The course requirements are set out in prospectuses.

All potential applicants should ask the advice of teachers, careers officers, training officers and university and college advisers before submitting their application.

The application process

Details of application procedures are set out in the UCAS *Handbook* which is available with the UCAS application form and acknowledgement card from schools, colleges and careers offices during the summer before the year of entry. Other applicants can obtain the

Handbook, form and card direct from UCAS, PO Box 67, Cheltenham, Glos GL50 3SF, sending a self-addressed label with their request.

Applications for places should be submitted between 1 September and 15 December (or between 1 September and 15 October if you are including Oxford or Cambridge in your university choices) in the year before taking A/AS-levels. You should send in your UCAS form as soon as possible after 1 September. Although UCAS forwards applications received after 16 December to the universities or colleges concerned, institutions' admissions tutors will only consider them at their discretion.

The normal procedure is as follows:

1   You complete your UCAS application form in black ink and hand it with your fee to your educational referee.

2   The referee completes the confidential report and sends your form and fee to UCAS which then records your details.

3   UCAS acknowledges receipt of your form and sends you a personal application number.

4   UCAS sends reduced-size copies of your form to the universities/ colleges you have named on the form.

5   Each university/college considers your application and subsequently informs UCAS of its decision. (Applicants may hear unofficially from the institutions.)

6   UCAS notifies applicants of the institutions' decisions.

7   You reply through UCAS to any offers made by the universities/ colleges.

You do not have to reply to any university/college offers until you have received your last decision. If you know before then that you definitely want to accept firmly one of the offers, you can do so. However, it is not advisable to accept firmly an offer until you are **absolutely** sure that this is the university/college you want to commit yourself to attending.

You may decline any offer you receive before you have received all your decisions in the UCAS scheme. However, you cannot change your mind later and accept that offer.

If you have received more than one university/college offer, UCAS will send you - with your last decision - a statement of all your decisions in the scheme, a reply slip and an explanatory leaflet.

You will be asked to reply to your offers within 14 days of receiving the statement of decisions, but there will be a dispensation for you to delay replying to your offers if you have yet to attend an open day or group visit at one or more of the universities/ colleges concerned. You will not lose the offers made to you provided that your replies are received by UCAS by 15 May, but you should reply quickly after your visit(s).

If you have accepted firmly a conditional offer (CF) you can also hold one additional offer (either conditional or unconditional) as an insurance (CI or UI). Normally the insurance offer would be one which specifies lower grades. A typical A-level applicant's record might read as follows:

Conditional offer - Firmly accepted (CF) - Grades BBC
Conditional offer - Insurance (CI) - Grades BCC

If your results are not as good as you had hoped and you cannot meet the offer of the university/college you have firmly accepted but can fulfil the conditions of the insurance offer, you are committed togoing to the insurance institution for the specified course.

If you do not inform UCAS of your acceptance of a firm offer and (if appropriate) an insurance offer, it will not be possible to hold the offers open and they will be declined by UCAS on your behalf.

If you leave any boxes blank on the statement of decisions reply slip, UCAS will treat the offers concerned as declined and you will lose them. For example, if you have entered your firm acceptance but have not entered an insurance, UCAS will decline all your other offers, and you will lose the opportunity to hold an insurance offer.

Once you have replied to your offers, UCAS will send you a final statement of your replies and all the decisions made.

UCAS does not make decisions: it sends to you the decisions of the universities/colleges to which you have replied. It cannot change an institution's decision. If you need advice or more information, write direct to the institution.

8   (The institutions note all replies.)

9   The UCAS Clearing scheme operates from late August and throughout September. Its purpose is to try to match applicants without an offer with suitable courses where there are vacancies. Vacancy information is available via a number of network systems eg, ECCTIS and Campus 2000 as well as *The Independent* and *The Independent on Sunday* newspapers. Details of these services and any other sources of vacancy information are given in a leaflet sent to all applicants when they become eligible for Clearing.

UCAS Timetable

I September .... UCAS begins accepting applications.

15 October .... Deadline for applications (including Oxford or Cambridge) to reach UCAS.

15 December .... Deadline for all other applications to reach UCAS.

16 Dec onwards .... Late applications distributed by UCAS to up to eight choices of university/college, but institutions will consider these at their discretion.

Late July/Early September .... Confirmation of offers. UCAS tells you whether or not universities/colleges have confirmed conditional offers. If you are unsuccessful or received no offers earlier in the year, you will be sent Clearing instructions automatically. Send your completed Clearing Entry Form to UCAS as soon as possible if you want to use Clearing (see page 65).

Throughout September .... Remaining university/college places filled through Clearing (see page 65).

PLEASE NOTE:

- You are not required to reply to any university/college offers until you have received your last decision.

- Do not send a firm acceptance to more than one offer.

- Do not try to alter a firm acceptance.

- Send a withdrawal slip to UCAS at once if you decide not to go to university/college this year.

- Remember to tell the institutions and UCAS if you either change your address, change your examination board, subjects or arrangements.

The Application Form

Two important aspects of the UCAS application form concern Sections 3 and 9. In Section 3 all your university/college choices (up to eight choices) are to be listed in the order in which they are listed in the *UCAS Handbook*.

A brief glance at the subject tables in Chapter 6 will give you some idea of the popularity of various courses. In principle, institutions like to get the best applicants available, so if there are large numbers of applicants the offers made will be high. For Medicine, offers in terms of A-level grades usually reach BBB, and for Veterinary Science AAB. Conversely, for the less popular subjects such as Classical Studies or Mining Engineering, the offers are much lower - down to CC and even CD.

Similarly some institutions are more popular (not better) than others. Again, this popularity can be judged easily in the tables in Chapter 6 the higher the offer, the more popular the institution. In general terms, 'popular' universities are usually those located in attractive towns or cities such as Exeter, Warwick, Bath, Plymouth, Coventry or York. Other institutions have established a 'reputation' as a well-known university, for example, such as Oxford, Cambridge and Durham. Conversely, and unfortunately, some universities have confused applicants with unfamiliar names and no identity as to their location, such as De Montfort (situated in Leicester, Milton Keynes, Lincoln and Bedford) Heriot-Watt and Royal Holloway College, the former outside Edinburgh, the latter near Windsor. More applicants would obviously apply to these excellent institutions if their knowledge of geography was more extensive!

Thus the general rule for institution choice must be to regard them as not better than the next, but different. Often your choice will often be dictated by **location** - town, city, rural or by **size** - large or small - or by **distance** from home - or by **travel** factors, particularly the ease or difficulty of reaching the university or college by public transport. Finally, of course the major consideration is the offer you are likely to achieve, and the grades projected by your teachers on your reference.

When you have chosen your courses and your institutions, look again at the offers you expect to receive. It is most important to maximise your chances of a place by choosing institutions which might make you a range of offers. You can hold only two offers and naturally it is preferable for one to be lower than the other in case you do not achieve the A-level grades for your first choice of university or college.

The other Section of the UCAS form which deserves a lot of careful thought is Section 9 *(Further Information)*. How innocuous that sounds yet it is the only part of the form where you can put in a personal bid for a place! In short, you are asked to give relevant background information about yourself, your interests, your choice of course and career.

This means thinking back to the various activities in which you have been involved in the last three or four years. Get your parents and other members of the family to help - it is easy to forget something quite important. You might consider planning out this section in a series of sub-sections - and if you have a lot to say, be brief. The sub-sections can include:

School activities Are you a prefect, chairperson or treasurer of a society? Are you involved in supervisory duties of any kind? Are you in a school team? Which team? For how long? (Remember, teams mean any team: sports, chess, bridge, even business.)

Intellectual activities Have you attended any field or lecture courses in your main subjects? Where? When? Have you taken part in any school visits? Do you play in the school orchestra or have you taken part in a school drama production - on or off stage? Do you visit the theatre, art galleries or concerts?

Out-of-school activities This category might cover many of the topics above, but it could also include any community work you do, the scouts and guides, Duke of Edinburgh Awards, youth-hostelling, fell-walking etc. The countries you have visited might also be mentioned - for example, any exchange visits with friends living abroad.

Work experience Details of part-time, holiday or Saturday jobs could be included here, particularly if they have some connection with your chosen course. Some applicants plan ahead and arrange to visit firms and discuss career interests with various people who already work in the chosen field. For some careers such as veterinary science, work experience is virtually essential, and it certainly helps in Medicine, Architecture, Law and other popular courses.

Finally, plan your UCAS form carefully. Get a photocopy to use as a trial form and take a photocopy of your completed form to keep by you for reference when you are called for interview. Almost certainly you will be asked questions about what you have written. Remember also to write legibly. Your form will be reproduced and copies sent out to each university/college you have listed. As these copies will only be about two-thirds the size of the original it is important to present your information so that it can be read easily - type if necessary.

Admissions tutors always stress the importance of the confidential report written by your head teacher or form tutors. Most schools and colleges will make some effort to find out why you want to apply for a particular course, but if they do not ask do not take it for granted that they will know! Consequently, although you have the opportunity to write about your interests on the form, it is still a good idea to tell your teachers about them. Also, if you have to work at home under adverse conditions or if you suffer from any medical problem your teachers must be told as these points should be mentioned.

Deferred entry

Although application is usually made in the autumn of the year preceding the proposed year of entry, admissions tutors may be prepared to consider an application made two years before entry, so that the applicant can perhaps gain work experience or spend a period abroad. Policy on deferred entry may differ from department to department, and applicants should consult the Gap Year section of the tables in Chapter 6, prospectuses, or admissions staff at the institutions themselves before making an application for deferred entry. (It is important to check with the admissions tutor that a deferred entry application will receive the same consideration as a normal application.)

APPLICATIONS TO ART AND DESIGN COURSES THROUGH ADAR

Applications must be made on the official application/registration forms issued only by the Art and Design Admissions Registry (ADAR), Penn House, 9 Broad Street, Hereford HR4 9AP. Requests for forms should be made to the Registry before 31 January each year, but late applications can be considered up to the beginning of the session.

Colleges start interviewing applicants from 1 April but request portfolios before this date. Offers to first-choice applicants are normally made in early May. By mid-June ADAR normally send unplaced candidates a list of colleges which still have vacancies.

The great majority of successful applicants come from a preparatory full-time course in art and design such as the Foundation Course in Art and Design or the BTEC National Diploma in General Art and Design. These diagnostic courses provide a breadth of experience, an informed approach to specialisation and encourage self-motivation. They provide the usual entry route to Art and Design courses in higher education, as only a very small number of applicants are accepted direct from school.

ADMISSION TO CAMBRIDGE UNIVERSITY

The only major difference between the Cambridge admissions process and the normal UCAS arrangements is the date by which applications must be submitted. To allow early decisions for the benefit of other universities, the UCAS form and a Preliminary Application Form (PAF) must be submitted by October 15 at the latest: the UCAS form to Cheltenham and the PAF to Cambridge. This allows some interviewing to start in September, although the main batch of interviews takes place in December. Applicants who have already completed their education and who apply early enough to be interviewed in September or early October receive in late October either a firm offer, or a rejection, or a notification that a decision will be reached in January. Those still in education receive in January either an offer conditional upon certain grades in examinations to be taken the following summer, or a rejection.

Conditional offers are made on the basis of school reports and interviews. The conditions set are grades to be obtained in school-leaving examinations such as A-levels, Scottish Certificate of Sixth Year Studies or International Baccalaureate. Offers made by some

Cambridge University colleges will also include one or two specified grades either in S-papers (for A-level candidates only), or in Sixth Term Examination Papers (STEP).

Sixth Term Examination Papers are conducted by the Oxford and Cambridge Schools Examination Board using setting, marking and moderating procedures paralleling those employed for A-levels. Entry is open to all candidates, whatever their GCSE or other examination board. The published syllabuses for the various papers, available from the Board, are based on the common core A-level syllabuses, and so STEP is equally accessible to candidates taking A-levels set by any board, including those through which no S-papers are presently available.

The purpose of STEP is to assess academic potential in ways not always possible with other school-leaving examinations and to discriminate more finely amongst Cambridge candidates, nearly all of whom will do well in public examinations. If required, scripts are available to the colleges to assist them in making final selections among candidates who have narrowly failed to meet the grades set.

Sixth Term Examination Papers will take place in 1993 on Thursday 1 and Friday 2 July. Information on STEP may be obtained from the STEP office, Purbeck House, Purbeck Road, Cambridge CB1 2PU (Tel 0223 411211).

A syllabus booklet is available, price £1. Papers set in 1989, 1990, 1991 and 1992 are also available, price 50p each. Papers are set in Biology, Chemistry, Economics, English Literature, French, Further Mathematics A, Further Mathematics B, General Studies, Geography, Geology, German, Greek, History, Italian, Latin, Mathematics, Music, Physics, Religious Studies, Russian, Spanish. A Mathematics Formula booklet at 50p and a Physics Formulae sheet at 25p are also available from the STEP Office.

College Policies

All colleges which admit ordinary undergraduates will use the selection procedures described above. There will, however, be some minor variations in policy between the various colleges, and within each college also between subjects. Further information about the policies of any particular college can be found in the Cambridge Prospectus and may also be obtained from the Admissions Tutor of the college concerned.

No college operates a quota system for any subject except Medicine and Veterinary Medicine, where there are strict quotas for the whole University, from which places are allocated to each college.

Full details of the admissions procedures are contained in the *Cambridge Admissions Prospectus 1994-95* published in March 1993. Schools on the UCAS mailing list are invited to order copies in bulk from: Cambridge Intercollegiate Applications Office, Kellet Lodge, Tennis Court Road, Cambridge CB2 1QJ. Individuals can obtain copies from the same address or from the Admissions Officer of any Cambridge College.

ADMISSION TO OXFORD UNIVERSITY

Admission to Oxford is carried out on a college, and not a departmental, basis. There are no separate or specific standards required for each department apart from Medicine. Candidates may name up to three colleges but, if they prefer, may put in an open application. They will then be allocated a choice of college through a computer programme which takes account of their subject preferences (and sex, in the case of the two women-only colleges).

There are two methods of entry to Oxford, both of which take into account past academic record, school reference and interview. Mode E, which is only open to pre A-level candidates, also includes the written entrance examination. Offers through this mode are not conditional on any A-level results or further examination beyond the satisfaction of the University's matriculation requirements, which include two A-level passes at grade E or higher. Mode N does not involve the written examination. Post A-level offers are based on A-levels already held and are unconditional. Pre A-level candidates successful through mode N are given a conditional offer based on their A-level grades.

All colleges are prepared to consider applicants through either mode, and with a variety of qualifications (including Scottish qualifications, EB, IB etc). There are no predetermined quotas or proportions for admission; success rates by either mode E or mode N are almost identical. All applications should be submitted by the same date - 15 October 1993 for entry in October 1994 or later.

ENTRY TO SCOTTISH UNIVERSITIES

Applications for the 12 Scottish universities are made through UCAS. Many of the Scottish universities retain many traditional features which, in a number of important respects, distinguish them from their English counterparts. For many applicants they offer some notable advantages - the 'open' structure of most degree courses (for example, for BA, MA and BSc), the flexibility of course choice, the setting of standard going-rates in terms of A-level and SCE grades for entry to many courses within the same faculty-grouping. For some areas of study, such as Medicine, Law or Divinity, and in others such as Accountancy or Engineering (if maximum exemption is to be gained from professional examinations) there is little or no choice of curriculum. For other courses there is wide choice. For example, students in the faculties of Arts, Science and Social Sciences generally choose three or four subjects in their first year from a wide range of possible courses: they will probably (but not necessarily) include the subject specified in the course code returned in the UCAS form but the selected courses will usually extend over several distinct study areas (for example, English, History, Economics, Physics, Computing, Chemistry, Zoology). In Scotland students generally are not admitted into Honours until the end of the second year - only then do they decide which of their chosen subjects (or those into which they may lead, eg Cultural History, Genetics, Pharmacology) will be selected for specialist study. Thus students can try one or two years in both known and previously unknown areas of study, testing out their enthusiasm and abilities in the various subjects before deciding which Honours group to enter. Therefore, they are not committed by a statement made at the time of application, some three years earlier. It should be noted that some subjects within a faculty (eg Film and TV Studies at Glasgow) are very popular, and that students cannot be guaranteed a place on any such Honours course at the time of entry to university.

It is sometimes possible for GCE A/AS-level applicants with particularly good grades in appropriate subjects to obtain exemption from all or part of their first-year curricula, but in doingso they lose most of the opportunities for course-change and the flexibility of course-choice outlined above. Such exemptions are widely available within the pure and applied sciences; they are rather less frequently offered in arts and social sciences; and never in Medicine, Law or Divinity. Usually, however, applicants with good A-level passes who could ask for exemption decide to keep the advantages of the full four-year degree programme.

Such flexibility in course choice is only possible because, in most Scottish universities, the traditional system of faculty entry has been maintained through which an applicant is admitted to a faculty rather than to a particular department, to a grouping of related subjects rather than to the study of one subject alone. While admission to the faculties of Medicine, Divinity or Law is similar to that in an English university department, where paramount importance is attached to the particular course-code specified in the UCAS form, that course-code is of much less significance in applications to the faculties of Arts or Social Sciences or Science. Here candidates are required to meet the faculty's entry standard, and only after meeting their advisers of studies at the beginning of the first term do they finally select their initial courses within that faculty. While in the English departmental entry system it is the department through its selector which chooses the student it will teach, in Scotland – once they have met the faculty entry standard – it is the students who then choose the three or four departments in that faculty in which they will study: they are then potential Honours students in each of the selected study areas.

In Scotland there are, on the whole, very few restrictions on entry laid down by departments to their first year classes. While in a few subjects, eg French or Mathematics, it is usually necessary for students to hold good SCE Higher or GCE A-level passes, course requirements are kept to a minimum. It is not necessary, for example, to have prior qualifications in history or geography or economics, or in the less familiar languages to study them at university, or to have previously studied biology to enter first year studies in the range of biological subjects. Flexibility of course choice is assured by another distinctive Scottish feature: except in a few instances, no restrictions are placed on the numbers of students attending particular first-year or second-year classes in universities which admit by faculty into Arts and Social Sciences and Science courses. This traditional structure is to be found in the four ancient universities (St Andrews, Glasgow, Aberdeen and Edinburgh), in Arts, Social Science and Science at Dundee, and in Arts, Social Studies, in the Business School and (with some limitations) in Science at Strathclyde. In Stirling admission is made on a yet wider basis, to the University as a whole, across all subject areas.

Another distinctive feature of the Scottish system, followed by all universities, is the policy of declaring and adhering to a specified entry standard or 'going-rate' in all departments within a faculty or in a wide grouping of related subjects in a faculty or, where departmental entry is followed, in all courses in that department. All applicants for the same course or for the same area of studies are asked to obtain the same levels of pass. Interviews are seldom held: hence decisions regarding offers of admission are made on the basis of the UCAS application form alone – from the academic profile given there, from the predictions of performance and other qualitative comments in the school report, from the indications given by the candidates of their interests and aspirations. Most of the Scottish universities publish in their prospectuses and in the *Scottish Universities Entrance Guide* prepared by the Scottish Universities Council on Entrance, their expected going-rates for entry in the next round of admissions. Those which do not, issue later their own leaflets which detail the expected entry standards for their various courses. Further and, if needed, updated information can always be obtained from the universities' schools liaison officers.

CONVERSION TABLE FOR SCOTTISH APPLICANTS TO UNIVERSITIES OUTSIDE SCOTLAND

Throughout the tables in Chapter 6 some university departments have provided information of requirements in terms of the Scottish Certificate of Education Higher Grades. As mentioned in Chapter 1, Scottish applicants for places at English institutions are advised to pay particular attention to entry requirements published in prospectuses. In cases of difficulty they should write to the Registrar, or departmental head of the subject concerned giving details of the subjects they have and are taking in the SCE.

It is difficult to make direct comparisons between GCE A-level and SCE offers but the following pointers, provided by the Scottish Examination Board, may act as guidelines:

(1) SCE Higher grades of A and B are equivalent to GCE A-level passes grades A to E.

(2) Three SCE Higher passes are equivalent to two GCE A-level passes.

(3) Four SCE Higher passes are equivalent to three GCE A-level passes.

GENERAL SELECTION POLICIES

Selection procedures of institutions vary only slightly since all applicants are viewed largely on academic potential. In each case, departmental admissions tutors are responsible for selecting candidates. The outline which follows provides information on the way in which candidates are selected for university courses, but it is also relevant for all other degree and diploma courses.

Each year applicants for degree course places are selected on the basis of three main considerations: A/AS-level performance or potential (for applicants who have still to take A-level examinations), the school/college report on the applicant, an interview at the discretion of the institution concerned. There is little doubt that academic achievement and promise is the most important factor, although other subsidiary factors may be taken into consideration, such as:

● Pass grades obtained at GCSE examinations and the range of subjects studied.

● Academic record of applicant throughout his or her school career, especially up to A/AS-level.

● Suitability for the course of the applicant's A/AS-level subjects.

● Time taken to obtain passes at GCSE and A-level.

● Forecast of A/AS-level performance at school, and headteacher's report.

● Results obtained at the A/AS-level examinations (and from 1994 level 3 GNVQs). (Other acceptable qualifications include BTEC, the International and European Baccalaureates, Scottish Highers and Open University credits.)

● Applicant's intellectual development; evidence of ability and motivation to follow chosen course.

● Applicant's range of interests, both in and out of school; aspects of character and personality.

● Vocational interests, knowledge and experience, particularly of applicants choosing vocational courses.

- General Studies A-level which may or may not be acceptable by the department concerned. Applicants should confirm this point with admissions tutors.

Since some courses and institutions are more popular than others, admissions tutors have to adopt selection policies to suit their own subject areas. Details of individual selection policies appear in each of the subject tables throughout the book.

INTERVIEWS

Not all applicants are interviewed but even if you are not called you should make an effort to visit your chosen universities and/or colleges before you accept the offer.

Interviews may be arranged simply to give you a chance to see the institution and the department and to meet the staff and students. Alternatively, interviews may be an important part of the selection procedure. If they are, you need to prepare yourself well.

Most interviews last approximately 20-30 minutes and you may be interviewed by more than one person. For practical subjects such as Music and Drama almost certainly you will be asked to perform and, for artistic subjects, to take examples of your work. For some courses you may have a written or other test in your interview (institutions setting tests are shown in each table in Chapter 6 under 'Selection Interviews').

How best can you prepare yourself?

Firstly, as one applicant advised 'Go to the interview - at least you'll see the place'.

Secondly, on the question of dress, try to turn up looking smart (it may not matter, but it can't be wrong). Two previous applicants were more specific: 'Dress smartly but sensibly so you are comfortable for travelling and walking round the campus'.

More general advice was also important:

'Prepare well - interviewers are never impressed by applicants who only sit there with no willingness to take part.'

'Read up the prospectus and course details. Know how their course differs from any other you have applied for and be able to say why you prefer theirs.'

'They always ask if you have any questions to ask them - prepare some!'

This may seem difficult but here are some suggestions:

Admissions policy What A-levels are particularly relevant to the course? What grades are normally offered?

Assessment How is your course assessed? How many exams are there in each year? Can you re-sit exams if you fail? Is there any continuous assessment? How many people fail in the first year?

Course content Is the course biased towards any particular aspect of study? Do you have to do any subsidiary subjects? If so, what subjects are offered? Is field work a compulsory part of the course? If so, what sources of financial aid are available? How many optional courses are there? Do you need any specific qualifications to take various options? Are any parts of the course taken in other departments? If so, which parts and what liaison and co-ordination is there between departments?

Teaching methods What proportion of time will be spent in lectures, seminars, tutorials and practical classes? Do the lecturers mind being asked questions from the audience? Are there opportunities to consult members of staff if you want extra help with any course work?

General What are staff/student relations like? Do students take any part in decision-making within the department? Is there a staff/student committee? What, if any, are the problems which students encounter on the course? What jobs do graduates obtain? What does the department think of people who have a year off before they start the course? What special facilities are there in the department ie, library, coffee bar, photocopying facilities etc? Is there much contact between students in the different years?

Accommodation How much accommodation is actually within the university or college? What are the different types of accommodation? What is the best method of applying for accommodation? What are the costs of different types of accommodation?

These are only a few suggestions and other queries may come to mind during the interview which, above all, should be a two-way flow of information.

It is also important to keep a copy of your UCAS form (especially the interests section) since your interview will probably start with a question about something you have written.

Interviewers will usually want to know why you have chosen the subject and why you have chosen their particular institution. They will want to see how well-motivated you are, how much trouble you have taken in choosing your subject, how much you know about your subject, what books you have read about it. If you have chosen a vocational course they will want to find out how much you know about the career it leads to, and whether you have visited any places of work or had any work experience? If your chosen subject is also an A-level subject you will be asked about your course and the parts of the course you like the most.

Try to relax. For some people interviews can be an ordeal – most interviewers know this and will make allowances. The following extract from the Oxford prospectus will give you some idea of what admissions tutors look for:

'Interviews serve various purposes, and no two groups of tutors will conduct them in the same way or give them exactly the same weight. Most tutors wish to discover whether a candidate has done more than absorb passively what he/she has been taught. They try, sometimes by discussing the written papers from the entrance examinations, if taken, or the short written tests given just before the interview for some mode N candidates, and sometimes by raising general topics, to ascertain the nature and strength of candidates' intellectual interests and their capacity for independent development. They are also likely to ask about applicants' other interests outside their school curriculum. This is partly because between two candidates of equal academic merit, preference will be given to the one who has the livelier interests or activities, and partly because it is easier to learn about candidates when they talk on what interests them most.'

'Interviews are in no sense hostile interrogations. Those candidates who show themselves to be honest, thoughtful and unpretentious will be regarded more favourably than those who try to impress or take the view that it is safest to say as little as possible. We do not expect candidates to be invariably mature and judicious. Generally, interviews for candidates applying through mode N are likely to be more stringent and more like an oral examination than those for candidates applying through mode E.'

But how have some applicants reacted to their interviews? These were their reactions. Firstly - before the interview - they advise:

'Arrive early.'
'Take something to read; killing time was the hardest, particularly if you have to stay the night.'

Secondly - about the interview - they said:

'Not so much of an interview - more of a one-to-one!'
'Not so much of an interview - more of a Spanish inquisition!'
'Speak confidently and firmly.'
'It's an opportunity for you to learn as much about them as vice-versa.'
'Try to keep the conversation going all the time - long periods of strained nervous silence don't convey a good impression.'
'If it's very relaxed he may be lulling you into a sense of false security.'
'"I don't know" is better than "Umm".'
'Be honest: self-confidence is fine, arrogance is fatal.'
'Try to start talking early on - it gets progressively more difficult when the questions get harder.'
'If you don't know the answer, don't try to bluff: they will lead you into deeper water; they're no fools.'

Thirdly - about the interviewers - they said:

'He was more scared than I was.'
'Watch out for the door-to-door salesmen who will try and sell you their course.'
'He was quite bad-tempered and kept interrupting my answers.'
'He seemed considerably fed-up and bored with the whole interview and yawned all the way through.'
'They were confusing and a little hostile but really only looking for reactions.'
'I write in the italic script and he wanted to know if I was having an emotional relationship with my pen!'
'The questions were so long-winded that by the time he had finished I'd forgotten what he'd asked me.'
'The interviewers were too alert - they picked up things which I really didn't want to be questioned on.'
'Keep the interviewer talking - then she won't have time to ask any questions.'
'He was really ace - really friendly and willing to talk about anything. In fact that's all I had to do - mention a topic and he kept talking for most of the interview.'
'Disgusting, fake, sarcastic, annoying and very unsure of themselves. This was supposed to be one of the best universities. My questions were constantly evaded quite skilfully by the interviewer who was trying to sell the university. I didn't get a proper interview - just a pathetic lecture.'

And finally, if you have the nerve........!

'Project yourself, burst forth with confidence and bubble with vivacity. Interviewers are impressed with this. It worked for me anyway - but go easy on the Newcastle Brown Ale!'

Now turn to the main subject tables in Chapter 6 where you will find a list of questions which have been asked in recent years and which you might prepare for. If you are called for interview read through many of the interview questions from different subject areas. This will give you the 'flavour' of an interview and the different approaches among admissions tutors.

WHAT IS AN OFFER?

Before you send in your application:

CHECK that you have passes at Grade C or higher in the GCSE subjects required for the course at the institutions to which you are applying. FAILURE TO HAVE THE RIGHT GCSE SUBJECTS OR THE RIGHT NUMBER OF GRADE C PASSES IN THE GCSE WILL RESULT IN A REJECTION.

CHECK that you are taking (or have taken) the required A-level subjects stipulated for the course at the institution to which you are applying. FAILURE TO BE TAKING OR HAVE TAKEN THE RIGHT A-LEVELS WILL ALSO RESULT IN A REJECTION.

CHECK that the A-levels you are taking will be accepted for the course for which you are applying. Some subjects and institutions do not stipulate any specific A-levels, only that you are required to offer two or three A-levels. NOT ALL A-LEVELS, HOWEVER, CARRY THE SAME WEIGHT. This is often one of the HIDDEN policies adopted by some admissions tutors. Traditional academic A-level subjects are always accepted eg, maths, physics, chemistry, biology, geography, history, languages, religious studies, economics. Some subjects, however, are more vocational and some admissions tutors may not regard them as being sufficiently academic for the purposes of their courses eg, art, music, theatre studies, law. Sometimes you will find a list of acceptable GCSE and A-level subjects printed in the prospectus, if not telephone the admissions tutor before you submit your application to check if your combination is acceptable.

Offers

Remember, an admissions tutor's job often is to decide whom to reject - and on what basis. If he or she has 1000 applications for 50 places on the course then they will look carefully at all aspects of each application and are likely to raise their demands in terms of GCSE results and projected or achieved A-level results to try to reduce the number of applicants to be considered. If there are very few applicants then he/she will need to introduce a more flexible policy and lower their demands to attract applicants (see below).

Offers may be made by way of A-level grades (eg BCC or CCC or DD) or points (eg 16 points):

Grades: An offer made in terms of grades means that you will obtain your place if you can achieve the right A/AS-level grades. For some courses (eg French, history, geography) you may be asked, for example, for a Grade B in your chosen degree subject and two Cs in your other two A-level subjects. If you are made a graded offer, check with the admissions tutor if he or she will accept the same points score (see below).

Points: Many new universities and colleges make offers in points for the A/AS-level subjects you are taking. If you receive a points offer check with the admissions tutor if he or she will accept AS-level points, if you are offering subjects at this level.

A-level points:			AS-level points:		
grade A	=	10 pts	grade A	=	5 pts
grade B	=	8 pts	grade B	=	4 pts
grade C	=	6 pts	grade C	=	3 pts
grade D	=	4 pts	grade D	=	2 pts
grade E	=	2 pts	grade E	=	1 pt

The subject tables in Chapter 6 provide lists of the offers which are made by the various institutions offering the subject. These offers and any published offers (eg in prospectuses) must be regarded as guidelines.

An offer may mean:

(i)   The offer for the course is made only to applicants capable of getting higher grades (see below). (This is not always explained by admissions tutors!)

(ii)   The offer made to applicants capable of achieving those grades.

(iii)   An offer which compares favourably with offers made by other institutions competing for applicants! In many cases the less popular institutions and those offering less popular subjects will be prepared to make offers to applicants lower than those published. This happens often after the A-level results are published.

Just because your school reference states that you are expected to get grades of BBC for example, it does not mean that you automatically will receive an offer from every university and college making that offer. Some applicants are capable of getting grades higher than the stated offer and yet receive rejections!

Whilst very low offers often means that there is a shortage of applicants for a course, some popular institutions will make EE offers for a very popular course. This means that you are so outstanding that they want you to accept a place on their course instead of any other course for which you have applied. (NB: All institutions within the UCAS scheme receive regular print-outs showing what offers other institutions are making to you.)

Hidden Policies

The number and quality of applications for places may vary each year. Because of this admissions tutors will prefer not to publish exactly how or why they reject some applicants. Here are some of their considerations:

(a)   Which GCSE subjects have you taken? Are they a good spread of subjects?

(b)   What grades did you achieve in the GCSE? Did you have a good spread of reasonable grades or were the results patchy? For some courses such as Business Studies, some admissions tutors may reject anyone who obtained only a Grade C result. Other institutions may even decide on a minimum number of Grade As or As and Bs in GCSE for students applying for very popular courses.

(c) How many times did you need to repeat an examination to achieve the pass grade? This also applies to A-level subjects where it is often considered easier to pass subjects taken one at a time, rather than all at the same sitting (a common requirement).

(d) If you are an overseas student (who has to pay tuition fees for a course) admission conditions may be relaxed slightly. It should be noted, however, that any student from an EC country can apply through UCCA and receive free tuition in any UK university or college. No quota system of these students applies except for in Medicine (when students from countries offering a medical education cannot normally be considered).

(e) Section 9 'Further Information' on the UCAS form is very important. If you are applying for a vocational course in particular (for example, Law, Architecture, Medicine, Pharmacy, Dentistry, Business courses) evidence of practical experience is important. This experience may be in the form of work shadowing or actual work experience and full details should be given in this section of the form. In the case of non-vocational subjects, such as English, History, Geography, any evidence of study outside your A-level syllabus is important, as for example, vacation study, field study courses.

WHAT TO DO ON RESULTS DAY - AND AFTER!

BE AT HOME! Do not arrange to be away when your A/AS-level and other results are published. If you do not achieve the grades you require, you will need to follow a new course of action and to make new decisions which could affect your life during the next few years. Do not expect others to make these decisions for you.

If you achieve the grades or points which have been offered you will receive confirmation that you have a place. This confirmation may take a few days to reach you. Once your place is confirmed then contact the accommodation office at the university or college and inform them that you will need a place in a hall of residence etc.

If you achieve grades much higher than the offer you have received and you are already holding one or two places, you are not entitled to ignore these offers and to try for a place at another university or college. If, however you definitely have decided to change courses, advise the university or college immediately.

If your grades are higher than you expected and you are not holding any offers you can telephone the admissions tutor at the universities and colleges which rejected you and request that they might reconsider you.

If you miss your offers by one or two points, then telephone the universities and colleges to see if they can still offer you a place. ALWAYS HAVE YOUR UCAS REFERENCE NUMBER AVAILABLE WHEN YOU CALL. Their decisions may take a few days. You should check the universities and colleges in your order of preference. Your first choice must reject you before you contact your second choice.

If you have not applied then you can apply through the Clearing Scheme in September. Check the tables in Chapter 6 to identify which institutions normally make offers matching your results, then telephone the institution to see if they have any vacancies before completing your Clearing form.

If you learn finally that you do not have a place then you will automatically receive a Clearing form to enable you to reapply. Before you complete this form follow the instructions above.

If an institution has vacancies it will ask you for your grades. If they can consider you they will tell you and place you in the Q procedure which means that they will ask UCAS for a copy of your form to consider your application. You can only be 'Q'ed' by one institution at a time. If it can accept you, you will be advised on how to complete your Clearing form.

If you have to reapply for a place:

(a) Check the vacancies report for 1992 in Chapter 6 and in the tables. The vacancy situation probably will be very similar this year.

(b) Check the vacancies in the national press and through your local careers office. If vacancies occur in your subject, double check with the university and college that these vacancies have not been taken.

REMEMBER - There are many thousands of students just like you. Admissions tutors have a mammoth task checking how many students will be taking up their places since not all students whose grades match their offers decide to take up their places!

IF YOU HAVE AN OFFER AND HAVE THE RIGHT GRADES BUT ARE NOT ACCEPTING THAT OR AN ALTERNATIVE PLACE - TELL THE UNIVERSITY OR COLLEGE. Someone else is waiting for your place!

You may have to make many telephone calls to institutions before you are successful. It may even be late September before you know you have a place so BE PATIENT AND STAY CALM!

OVERSEAS APPLICANTS

The choice of a subject to study (from over 14,000 degree courses) and of a place for study (from over 220 institutions) is a major task for students living in the United Kingdom. For overseas applicants it is even greater and the decisions which have to be made need much careful planning, preferably beginning two years before the starting date of the course.

Choosing the subject may well be easy for applicants with a particular career in mind (for example, law, business, medicine, engineering) but for those who are undecided about their careers, it is worth remembering that over 50 per cent of students at UK universities start their degree courses without making career choices. They are studying subjects such as History, Geography, English and languages and will eventually go into a wide range of careers from accountancy and management training to banking, retailing, advertising, social work, journalism. To help you choose course subjects which are right for you, you will need to read carefully through this book, through its companion volume *How to Choose Your Degree Course* (see **Booklist**) and to browse through the prospectuses of the institutions (see **Chapter 2** for their addresses). You will also need to consult the reference books listed in this chapter and the **Booklist** and to talk to your parents, teachers and other advisers. After this you will have a much clearer idea of the subject and type of course you want to follow.

But many higher education institutions offer the same subjects, so the next decision you have to make is **where** to study. Do you want to study in a city, in a large town, in a small town or out in the country? Do you prefer a campus university with lecture theatres, libraries, laboratories, accommodation, sports facilities and shops on the same site? (Lancaster, Keele, Bath, Loughborough and Surrey are examples of campus universities.)

Accommodation is an important consideration in deciding where you would like to study and there are various possibilities. Do you prefer to live in university or college accommodation which may be 'on campus', close to your study facilities, or in the larger cities which may be some distance away ? Do you want to cook your own meals or do you want them cooked for you ? Would you prefer to 'live out' with a family or to live on your own? Whatever your decisions, contact your preferred institutions as soon as possible, and obtain all the information you need before submitting a formal application.

Another point you may want to consider is the proportion of overseas students at the institution or on the course of your choice. Some institutions have a large intake of overseas students each year, particularly East Anglia and Sheffield Universities; Newcastle University has an overseas student population of 20%; over 100 countries are represented by overseas students at Leeds University in the current academic year, and at Keele University there is a thriving overseas student population. Bath (CHE) offers a programme in Comparative International Studies for Japanese students which covers English language, cultural and social activities.

Another reason for making early contact with your preferred institution is to check their requirements for your chosen subject and their selection policies for overseas applicants. For example, for all Art and some Architecture courses you will have to present a portfolio of work or a box of slides. For Music courses your application will usually have to be accompanied by a tape recording you have made of your playing or singing, and in many cases a personal audition will be necessary. Attendance at an interview in this country is compulsory for some universities and some courses. At other institutions the interview may take place either in the UK or with a college representative in your own country.

The ability to speak and write good English is essential and many institutions require evidence of competence - for some you may have to send examples of your written work. At many institutions English classes are constantly available for example, Bangor, Cranfield, Leeds, Surrey, London (Royal Holloway), East Anglia universities and Holborn College. Pre-entry language courses are offered by Brighton, Bath, Liverpool and Loughborough, Sheffield Hallam, Coventry and De Montfort universities. Access and Foundation courses are also offered by many institutions covering English language and other subjects.

All higher education institutions in the United Kingdom have an overseas student adviser who can advise you on all these points as they relate to their own institution. They can also advise you on other factors you need to consider, such as passports, visas, entry certificates, evidence of financial support, medical certificates and medical insurance. These are very important and have to be thought about at the same time as choosing your course and institutions.

Finally, an excellent source of help, information and advice is your local office of the British Council. Their advisers can provide information on many of these points, or put you in touch with those who can, and they can also help with information on fees, scholarship schemes and arrangements for English language tuition. If you have difficulty in finding the address of your local British Council office, get in touch with the British Council at 10 Spring Gardens, London SW1A 2BN.

MATURE APPLICANTS

In the last five years there has been a massive expansion in the numbers of mature students in higher education. Many universities and colleges of higher education are keen to welcome them and increasingly provide more flexible courses to help older students fit study into working and family life.

What opportunities exist for the mature student? Firstly, there are full-time degree and diploma courses in universities and colleges and institutes of higher education, with the possibility of grants from the local authority in many cases. But because of family commitments coupled with the loss of income, this isn't the most popular alternative. The most popular alternative is part-time study, and while entry is often governed by the qualifications already held, institutions (particularly the new universities and colleges of higher education) are becoming more flexible in their admissions policies and in taking students with non-standard qualifications, giving credit for prior certificated or experiential learning.

For full-time courses applicants should always write initially to the registrar of the college or university, indicating the proposed course of study and giving a brief resumé of their educational background and experience, including all qualifications with subjects, grades and dates. Obsolete qualifications or past school examinations may be acceptable as an equivalent to O- or A-levels etc, particularly for teacher-training courses. In almost all cases applicants will be interviewed and given individual consideration. An early interview is important, since some mature students need a year of preparatory study to meet the course entry requirements, which also enables them to start the degree course with confidence.

Most institutions regard 21 as the minimum age for a mature student but the maximum varies - there is a 68 year-old student of Theology at one university! Age limits, however, may be set in some subject areas. For example, the maximum age for teaching courses would probably be about 45, and for Medicine and Dentistry, about 30. Admissions tutors for social work courses have taken students up to the age of 50, but those for engineering courses might not consider applicants over 40.

If entry requirements to part-time study are an obstacle, intending students should approach their local careers service for information on Access, Open College, Gateway or Second Chance courses. These courses are fast-growing in number and popularity, offering adults an alternative route into higher education other than A-levels.

These courses are usually developed jointly by colleges of further education and the local higher education institution. For example, in the north of England, the North West Open College offers courses in 18 centres in the region. There are a number of Open College consortia elsewhere.

For those planning to follow a part-time course of study it is important to recognise possible problems which can have social and family implications. Working for a degree means a commitment to a specific day or evening each week - over several years. For the mother or housewife in particular there are problems associated with keeping everyone at home happy. As one student housewife remarked 'It's not only a question of trying to get the domestic jobs done, but it's also getting the family to realise that there are times when they cannot have priority'. There are essays to write, exams to be prepared for and deadlines to be met. Other problems may involve coping with family illnesses and the likelihood that the mature student of 40 plus will have elderly parents with accompanying short- or long-term illnesses. The location of the course may also cause problems requiring periods of travel to and from home.

So in a nutshell you need stamina, fitness, a sense of humour and the support of your family. But, as another student said, there are compensations. 'Achievement against all the odds - to be with like-minded people exploring new ideas and, above all, the opportunity to fulfil the 'me' side of the equation'.

In the subject tables in Chapter 6 details are given concerning entry to various courses for mature students. Information is also available in *Access to Higher Education - Courses Directory* from ECCTIS (see **Booklist**) and in prospectuses. More general information about degree courses for mature students can be obtained from the Open University, Milton Keynes MK7 6DH and NIACE (National Institute of Adult Continuing Education), 19b de Montfort Street, Leicester LE1 7GE.

4 OVERSEAS STUDY AND WORK OPPORTUNITIES

WORK EXPERIENCE AND STUDY ABROAD

The importance of international trade, particularly with countries on the European mainland, is now a well-established fact. In preparation for the expansion of the trade opportunities young people should be made aware of the importance of proficiency in at least one European language.

Higher education institutions have become increasingly alive to these developments and are now rapidly forging educational, industrial and commercial links abroad. For modern language students, study abroad has been a common feature of many courses for many years, but now we are seeing the same arrangements applying to non-language courses, particularly for vocational students.

In the tables of Chapter 6, information is given, where available, of courses in institutions which offer students opportunities to study or work abroad during their degree programme. The time spent on work experience varies from six months to a full year, and provides students with an insight into their chosen careers and an experience of working outside the United Kingdom. It also gives employers an opportunity to observe the student's working abilities and potential over a period of time, to enable them to decide on whether or not to offer full-time employment to the student at the end of the course.

Finance, however, can be a problem for those spending time abroad. If you are on an LEA grant you will get support for your time abroad, provided it was included in your original application. However, the total cost of a year abroad (particularly in the USA) can be greater than that of staying at home, and some extra finance may be needed.

There are a few scholarships or special grants available for students studying abroad. However, educational awards and scholarships may be available through Rotary Clubs in Great Britain and Ireland. Students should contact their local Rotary Club to determine what awards or other arrangements might be available.

EUROPEAN STUDY OPPORTUNITIES

Under the European Community Action Scheme for the Mobility of University Students (ERASMUS) grants are available for students who want to spend between three months and a year of their degree/diploma course in an EC state other than their own. ERASMUS also gives financial support to higher education institutions to establish inter-university co-operation programmes (ICPs) and many students studying under the scheme do so as part of their 'university's' (Brussels' terminology for all higher education institutions) ICP arrangements.

ERASMUS operates a scheme - the European Community Credit Transfer Scheme (ECTS) - which enables institutions to give students credits for the study they have completed. ECTS also provides a quick and objective way of assessing students' academic performance and level of achievement so that they can enter at the most appropriate level of a course.

Credits are awarded on the basis of 60 per academic year, 30 for a half-year, 20 for a three-month term. ECTS started in the academic year 1989/90 and, as a pilot scheme, is expected to run for six years. Currently it covers five subjects - Business Administration, Mechanical Engineering, Chemistry, History and Medicine, and recently it has been expanded to include EFTA countries. In addition to this scheme, opportunities for study in Eastern Europe are possible through TEMPUS and details of both are obtainable from the European Officer in higher education institutions. A number of institutions have also made direct contacts with firms in Europe for their sandwich students, which again could be valuable experience for future employment.

The opportunity to spend time studying or working on the European mainland, however, is not a decision to be taken lightly, no matter how attractive the prospect may seem initially. Robert Walls, the Schools and International Liaison Officer at London Royal Holloway, describes some of the opportunities and some of the problems:

'For many years students of modern languages have spent part of their degree courses - usually the entire third year - living in a country where the native language is the one which the students are attempting to master. In addition to improving radically their ability to communicate in that language, students also benefit in a great variety of other ways. A year in a different culture may be stressful at times, but in dealing with those stresses students almost always grow in confidence and maturity and in their ability to deal with people who have a different background from themselves.

In recent years it has become possible for students who are not taking a foreign language as their primary course to benefit from a similar experience via a variety of programmes which have been set up to encourage mobility within Europe. Students do not need to concern themselves too much about the fine detail of these schemes, which are known by a variety of names such as ERASMUS, TEMPUS and LINGUA, but if you are interested in spending part of your degree course in a European country it is important to get an accurate impression of your chances before committing yourself to a particular course which enables you to do so.

Most schemes available to students who are taking courses other than languages involve student exchanges. From the point of view of British students it is a great advantage that vast numbers of young people from the European mainland perceive the ability to speak English well as a key requirement for future success. Until recently very few British students regarded the ability to communicate in European languages - French, German or Spanish - in the same light, so that there have been many young mainlanders beating at the gates of British higher education while, apart from the linguists, their British counterparts were content to remain monoglot and monocultured.

All this is changing rapidly. The approach of European economic unity and the possible move to political union seems to have fired a significant minority of young Britons with the desire to gain experiences on the mainland during their degree courses.'

HOW TO MAXIMISE YOUR CHANCES OF A SUCCESSFUL EUROPEAN EXPERIENCE

1   Get as much information as you can on European links before you apply. Before completing your UCAS form ask institutions you are considering for information on their links with Europe. Try to get hard infor mation. Don't be content with vague generalisations about 'excellent contacts'. What percentage of students are in Europe this year? What departments are they from? Which countries are they in? What are they doing there?

2   Keep your European ambitions in mind when you are going through the selection process and particularly if you are offered places on courses, when you may have to decide how important a part these ambitions play in your decision-making.

3   Learn the language, particularly if you are going to France, Germany, Italy or Spain. Even if you intend to go to countries such as Holland or Denmark, where many courses are taught in English, it will make life easier and impress your hosts, as well as adding to your education, if you know at least a little of the language.

To give you a more precise idea of what might be available, and some notion of the mechanics of the process, included below are statements from some institutions with European links.

PORTSMOUTH UNIVERSITY

Portsmouth has links with a wide variety of European universities. Geography students go to France and Italy, physicists to universities in Greece and Spain as well as some who work for the Philips company in Eindhoven. All science students at Portsmouth can take a language as part of their degree course and increasing numbers of students are choosing to do so.

The largest single group of Portsmouth students who spend part of their courses in Europe are those taking the European Business degree, who are scattered throughout a wide variety of European countries.

Students taking any degree can also work for a European Diploma in Business Management. This is an additional year for non-business students and includes a three-month placement in industry.

The University's Schools Liaison officer, Brian Henderson, notes that there is a 'recent boom in the number of British students who want to go to Europe for part of their course but, for the moment, it is still not very competitive. Most students who want to go can do so'.

UNIVERSITY OF HERTFORDSHIRE

The University has a good claim to be something of a pioneer in sending students, who are not linguists, to Europe for part of their courses. For example, the BEng in Manufacturing Systems Engineering has included European placements for around 20 years. This is a rather unusual course in that students are not required to have any foreign language qualification and indeed most do not have this, although they will study a language during their first two years of the course. Students will then spend a minimum of three months in a French or German-speaking country.

There are many other courses where a language qualification is not required but where students will be prepared by taking a language module which consists of two or three hours of teaching each week for two years.

The BA in European Business Studies includes a one-year placement abroad which consists of a semester (half an academic year) in an academic institution and a semester working for, and being paid by, an employer in Germany, France or Spain.

Brian Clarke, the University's Head of European Relations, is confident that the numbers studying in Europe would continue to grow. 'Manufacturing Systems, for example, attracts students who realise that the engineering industry is becoming much more European. This will be reinforced by the National Curriculum in schools which will mean more students will arrive at the University with a language qualification. It is important to provide students with the knowledge and skills they will require in professional life. In the near future this will mean that they will need to be mobile within Europe, confident in dealing with other Europeans and knowledgeable on such matters as the impact of Europe on such areas as industrial standards.'

IMPERIAL COLLEGE, LONDON

Imperial College does not offer language degrees and does not have large numbers of students in Europe - about 50 in a typical recent year. This number is now likely to increase rapidly. Most students going to Europe are studying Chemical Engineering, Chemistry or Physics but European experience is possible in any subject, usually in France or Germany, though a handful go to Spain or Italy. To be considered for this, students are normally required to have at least a grade C in a language at GCSE. They then take a formal course to improve their language in general and to give them the necessary technical vocabulary.

For the last two years Imperial has offered courses such as Chemistry or Civil Engineering with a year in Europe and students selected are guaranteed European experience as part of a four-year degree. For the European year they receive their normal LEA grant, together with a small amount of supplementary funding.

Other students go on ERASMUS programmes which vary from three to 12 months.

Schools Liaison Officer, Terry Whodcote, believes that during the time abroad there is usually less pressure academically (apart from that caused by language problems) than is typical at Imperial, but he goes on to say: 'The experience has to be 100 per cent a good thing. We get highly motivated students who gain a great deal from their time in Europe'.

ROYAL HOLLOWAY LONDON

In a total student population of about 3800 in 1992/3 about 120 were in Europe (another 15 or so will be in the USA, Canada or Japan). The vast majority will be studying a modern language as at least 50 per cent of their course, but there is a rapidly growing minority who are taking degrees in subjects as widely varying as Physics, Biochemistry, History and Music.

Dr Geoffrey Chew, of the Music Department, has been involved in setting up an Inter-University Co-operation Programme (ICP) through ERASMUS, which involves universities in Berlin, Cork, Durham, Ferrar, Ghent, Lancaster, Leuven, Lisbon, Paris, Pavia,

Pisa, Poitiers and Utrecht. He points out that 'at the very least this gives students access to a vast range of additional courses in the subject. Effectively, one is drawing on the staff of an entire European network rather than just those of one college or university'.

Asked to give advice which might be useful to all students considering spending time in Europe, Dr Chew said 'It is virtually essential for students going to Germany or France to have a GCSE in the language, or the equivalent, for them to gain any benefit. There are specific short courses for ERASMUS students offered at various universities. Our students can take French, German or Italian here, and for Dutch, for example, they can go to University College.

All institutions will help students to find accommodation and where the cost is higher than here, for example - in Berlin, Paris or Rome - ERASMUS will pay the difference.

At the moment it is not particularly competitive for British students to find a course in Europe. The indications are that it may become more difficult even though many of us are busy increasing the number of opportunities available.'

Royal Holloway London's newly established Centre for Management Studies aims to allow 25 per cent of its students to spend part of their courses abroad, in Europe, the USA, Canada or Japan. This involves three types of experience: some students will spend one year at a Business School, others will spend half the year at a Business School and half in a job, while the rest will work for a company for the entire year.

John Triggs, who is responsible for the overseas placements in the Centre, says that: 'The key is language skills which must be good enough to allow fairly easy communication. We are getting more and more students who are prepared to devote the time and energy to achieving this level. Students can see that a language, combined with European experience, will give them a great advantage in the world of employment.

Living and studying in a foreign country is not all plain sailing. Some time ago I met a student from Florence who had decided to study at a Belgian university (for the less-than-serious reason that he had met a student from there while on holiday in Nice). Without understanding what was involved, he arrived in Belgium with only the name and telephone number of the professor in charge of the exchange 'scheme'. He spoke very little French. He was not expected and had trouble finding somewhere to live.

"I managed to communicate with my professor by using English at first. I was allowed to invent a project as I could not cope with being taught in French. Only by the great good will of the Belgian staff was I able to succeed and, after much discussion, get credit for the time in Belgium. It was terrible at first but I think it did me far more good than if I had slotted into a smooth-running and well-tested scheme.'"

Engineering and science courses with a European language are becoming increasingly popular and are offered by the University of Manchester Institute of Science and Technology (UMIST) as well as many other institutions. UMIST offers such subjects as Biochemistry, Chemical Engineering, Chemistry, Computer Science, Paper Science, Physics and Textiles all combined with French or German and for some courses, Italian and Portuguese. For each of these courses a language qualification in GCSE is acceptable, although for other courses involving Computational Linguistics, International Management and Mathematics an A-level in French or German is necessary.

UMIST's experience with students abroad is extensive and Dr Michael Lumb, the Schools and Colleges Liaison Officer offers some more advice to would-be students:

'Many young people are looking for higher education courses which combine science or engineering with a year studying or working in industry in Europe. Some years ago these courses may have been regarded as a gimmick, but today there is considerable interest by the most able students who can cope with the rigours of a science or engineering degree course and yet study a foreign language in detail. The employment opportunities of these bilingual technologists must be enhanced and, on educational grounds, living abroad for a year must be beneficial. As most engineers or scientists are unlikely to take an A-level in a language alongside their physics, mathematics or chemistry A-levels, the language entry requirements are usually a grade B at GCSE or GCE O-level, and language communication skills are usually taught during the first two years of the degree course with a language examination at the end of the second year. This is the model adopted for example at UMIST, Manchester.

However, students going to live abroad must bear in mind that the transition from the familiar cosy student life in the UK to the unfamiliar, culturally different life in a European country can present problems. Whether you are in industry or a student abroad, the first few weeks can be frustrating. Being in an unknown environment you will not know how, why, what and when things are done. Being away from friends and family will create loneliness; you may end up talking to people you would never dream of talking to back home! It is important that you join local sports, social clubs or student societies so that you can get to know people of your own age rather than spend many a boring or lonely evening at home. If you are employed by a large company then they usually have excellent facilities for foreign employees. Another way to meet people and earn some extra money is to offer to teach English, but be warned - it is best to make contacts through friends and colleagues rather than advertise in the local press. Whilst you are abroad, do make the most of travel opportunities: the rail network in Europe is excellent and the trains do run on time!

Students contemplating going abroad should make sure that they have the necessary documents to live in a foreign country for an extended period of time. Obviously you must have an up-to-date passport and form E111 obtainable for social security and health care (this differs from the normal E111 obtainable from post offices for short trips abroad and application should be made direct to the overseas branch of the Department of Social Security (DSS) in Newcastle-Upon-Tyne). It is also worthwhile taking a dozen or so photographs of yourself for administrative purposes and photocopies of your passport, form E111 and your birth certificate (suitably endorsed in French/German or other European language). In France you will require a *Carte de Sejour* which you can obtain from your place of study or employment; in addition you will require a student card and proof of residence (accommodation).

Even though you will be abroad for a year, you must inform your Local Education Authority (LEA) about the dates of terms or period of employment. This is important, not only for your registered university to receive fees but you will find that your grant will increase for the period abroad. Also bear in mind that if you are taking an intensive language course prior to attending a university or being in employment, you need to let your LEA also know these dates. On other money matters you may find that additional funds (small) may come via the ERASMUS programme. Obviously, open a bank account local to your place of residence so that funds can easily be transferred from the UK.

Accommodation arrangements differ in Europe. Unlike the UK, higher education institutions on the continent do not accommodate a large proportion of their students in halls of residence, although ERASMUS students do have some priority. It is more difficult to find large unfurnished flats for groups of students, and finding and transporting furniture creates obvious difficulties. However, it is quite common to find furnished studio (bed-sit) type accommodation or lodgings. For those students working abroad in industry, most companies will have suitable rented accommodation available.

In conclusion, the opportunities of studying or working abroad present an exciting and worthwhile opportunity in character and career development and most students completing these Engineering or Science with a European language degree courses will emerge as the employable technocrats of a modern Europe.'

OVERSEAS STUDY AND WORK CHECKLIST

Before you apply for a course:

1   Check the tables in Chapter 6 for lists of study and work opportunities abroad - subject by subject - at institutions of higher education.

2   Check individual prospectuses for further information and subject entry requirements.

3   When you have decided on your subject area, get 'hard' information from admissions tutors about specific courses and opportunities.

4   Give top priority to learning the language, not only on an A-level course, but also by way of vacation courses and by spending time abroad.

Before you go abroad to study or work:

5   Check which documents you need to study, work or live abroad, eg form E111 for social security or health care.

6   Take about 12 photographs of yourself - you may need these for passport or administrative purposes, student cards etc. A photocopy of your birth certificate would be useful and proof of residence (accommodation) will be needed.

7   Inform your LEA about the dates of your residence abroad in order to take advantage of any increase in grant.

8   Contact your local RotaryClub to ascertain if any educational awards are possible.

9   If possible, arrange your accommodation; if not, find names of useful contacts to approach on arrival.

When you arrive:

10 Let your university or firm know that you have arrived and find out further instructions.

11 Get in touch with your accommodation contacts and arrange for somewhere to live.

12 Open a bank account so that money can be easily transferred.

13 Sort out your health care arrangements as soon as possible.

14 Join sports and social clubs organised by your firm or university or in the locality in which you live.

Enjoy your time abroad, it's a wonderful opportunity!

5 HOW TO READ THE TABLES

The subject tables in Chapter 6 list degree subjects on offer in universities, colleges and institutes of higher education and specialist colleges in the United Kingdom. The names of degree courses vary widely, even in the same subject area, so if you have any problems locating your chosen course CHECK THE INDEX. Details of joint courses - for example, French and German - will appear in either subject table but not necessarily in both.

The tables are designed to provide you with information on how to choose your course, how applicants are selected, with some of the important points to consider after the A-level results are published, about gap years and graduate employment. This information has been provided by admissions tutors and will be of help to applicants submitting UCAS applications in 1993 for entry in 1994. **It must not be assumed that the offers and policies will apply to courses commencing in 1995 or thereafter.**

When selecting a degree course it is important to try to judge what grades at A-level you are capable of achieving and to compare them with the offers made. Even though you might be capable of achieving the right grades, there is no guarantee that you will be offered a place (see Chapter 3 - What is an Offer?). Entry to degree courses is competitive and admissions tutors will consider other factors as well as your academic background.

Note: Except for the list of offers, the information in each table refers to Single Honours main subject courses and not to Joint courses, unless otherwise stated.

Each table is planned to provide the following information:

The title of the subject and the special subject requirements: The requirements of each course may vary but the information provided is a guide to the subjects required at GCSE and A-level. It should be noted that two AS-level passes are regarded as equivalent to one A-level pass. CHECK THE PROSPECTUSES before submitting your application. Remember - some universities stipulate **General Requirements** which apply to all courses offered in both science and arts subjects.

Institutions and offers:

Under each subject heading, details are given of the A-level offers made for each course at every university and college. A typical layout includes: (a) Name of institution; (b) Usual A-level offer; (c) Abbreviated title of the course (see UCAS handbook); (d) Number of AS-level subjects in excess of 2 AS-levels.

(a) **Name of Institution:** Universities and colleges offering degree courses are listed in order of level of offers.

(b) **Usual A-level offer:** Offers are made in terms of GCE A-level grades or points. For applicants offering A-levels only, points are allocated as follows:
Grade A = 10 pts, B = 8 pts, C = 6 pts, D = 4 pts, E = 2 pts.

For applicants taking A-levels and AS-levels, each A-level subject is equivalent to 2 units and each AS-level equivalent to one unit. Points are thus allocated as follows:
A-levels Grade A = 5 + 5 pts, B = 4 + 4 pts, C = 3 + 3 pts, D = 2 + 2 pts, E = 1 + 1 pt;
AS-level Grade A = 5 pts, B = 4 pts, C = 3 pts, D = 2 pts, E = 1 pt.
The final points score is calculated by the aggregation of the best six exam units eg, A-level Grade of BCD and AS-level Grade B would equal 20 pts ie, Grade B = **4** **+ 4** pts, Grade C = **3 + 3** pts, Grade D = **2 + 2** pts, AS-level Grade B = **4** pts.

(c) **Course title:** The abbreviated title of the course. Refer to the UCAS handbook. Some courses are shown as awaiting validation. Students MUST check that these courses will run before applying.

(d) **AS-level subjects:** This is a general guide on the maximum number of AS-level subjects in excess of two AS-level subjects acceptable as a **course requirement**. (All institutions will now accept at least two AS- levels for most subject areas.)

(e) **BTEC offers:** These are tailored to individual applicants: **they are not standard offers**. Offers may vary depending on the BTEC papers taken. They are shown in brackets after the AS-level offer eg, 3M (three merits), 2D + 2M (two distinctions plus 2 merits). In some examples, different offers are shown in separate brackets. Applicants should check if certain subjects are required to be taken within the BTEC scheme for the chosen course.

The BTEC award is made to students following courses in specific career areas. Within each course, subject units are taken at levels I, II or III depending on the importance of each unit. Awards are then made against three grades of achievement: Distinction (D); Merit (M); Pass (P).

As with GCSE and A-level requirements, universities and colleges will consider AS-levels as part of of both the **general** and the **course requirements**. For the **general requirements** universities will usually accept two AS-levels in place of a third A-level. Colleges will often accept four AS-levels in lieu of two A-level subjects. The same applies in many cases to the **course requirements** but certain complementary AS-level (science) subjects may be stipulated for some science courses.

AS-level passes are graded A-E with grade standards relating to the corresponding A-level grades. Few institutions have made decisions on the grades required.

THE OFFERS MADE FOR CANDIDATES TAKING 2 A-LEVELS AND 2 AS-LEVELS OR 1 A-LEVEL AND 2 OR 3 AS-LEVELS WILL NORMALLY EQUATE TO THE POINTS TOTAL OF THE NORMAL 3 A-LEVEL OR 2 A-LEVEL OFFER.

Offers are expressed in terms of A/AS-level grades and may vary between candidates, or alternatively the same offer may be made to all suitable applicants. In some cases you will be asked to get specific grades for the subjects you are taking: for example, if you are applying for French the offer might be for BCC or BC with the grade B in French. If you are taking three A-level subjects usually you will get a three grade offer. Alternatively two A-level candidates will receive an offer with two grades but check that the course for which you are applying does not require three A-levels. In rare cases some universities make EE offers. This means that they regard you as a very strong candidate and they are anxious to have you on their course! It is useful to remember that for many courses, institutions may be prepared to accept slightly lower grades after the A-level results are published.

Examples: The offers shown in the tables therefore appear for example, as:

(a) BCC/BC This refers to offers made to applicants offering three and two A-levels respectively.

(b) BCC-CCD/BC-CD This refers to a range of offers made to three and two A-level candidates respectively. In this range of offers, the standard offer would be CCC or CC, with the lower offer made to a strong candidate or for one who interviewed well.

(c) For joint courses or combined courses the offers are usually determined by the subject in the combination of two subjects which has the highest offer. For example, if an offer for Economics is BCC and the offer for Law is BBB, the offer for a joint course in Economics and Law would therefore stand at BBB. Entries for joint or combined courses may appear under both subject headings throughout the tables.

Some very popular universities may make low offers to applicants of outstanding ability.

The offers made by universities and colleges are dictated by the popularity of either the institution or the subject - or both. *An offer is not a guarantee of a place for all applicants who can achieve the grades.* NB Very popular institutions/subject areas may only make offers to applicants capable of achieving grades much higher than the level of the offer shown. Average and less popular institutions may publish an artificially high offer to try to achieve status parity with other institutions and in August accept lower grades.

Offers are always governed by the number of applicants and are not in any way related to the quality of a course. The quality of a course is extremely difficult, if not impossible, to assess and reputation is also a most unreliable measure of quality since staff and course changes are constantly taking place. Many students applying for university also apply for college places as an insurance against failing to achieve the right grades for university, although an increasing number are now university or college-only applicants. Many degree course applicants also apply for Higher National Diploma courses which creates difficulties for admissions tutors. There is considerable variation in the levels of offers for Foundation, Certificate and Diploma courses. After the A-level results are published, applicants are advised to contact institutions since offers may be reduced significantly.

Offers for Foundation, Certificate and Diploma courses:

Below the list of offers for degree courses, information is provided on offers made for courses leading to the Diploma of Higher Education, BTEC Higher National Diploma and SCOTVEC Higher Diploma with an indication of the points scores required. Applicants for Scottish universities should also refer to Chapter 3.

Franchised degree and HND courses:

These are franchised courses in which students will study (usually for the first year) at local colleges franchised by the validating (degree awarding) university.

Offers for Foundation, Certificate and Diploma courses:

There is considerable variation in the levels of offers for Foundation, Certificate and Diploma courses. After the A-level results are published, applicants are advised to contact institutions since offers may be reduced significantly.

Alternative offers:

EB offers: These are offers made to students taking the European Baccalaureate examination.

IB offers: The International Baccalaureate (IB) provides an internationally recognised pre-university curriculum and qualification. The IB Diploma is gained by external examination, following two years of study in the final years of secondary education. In the United Kingdom the IB Diploma provides a well regarded alternative to A-levels as an entry qualification to all British universities and institutions of higher education.

This two-year curriculum is intended to provide an appropriate educational training and qualification for students aiming for higher education. IB students are required to study six subjects, three at Higher Level and three at Subsidiary Level. These subjects should include the student's first language, a second foreign language, a subject from the humanities, the sciences, mathematics and a sixth subject which may allow for further specialisation or a choice from the creative arts.

Additional, essential aspects of the curriculum include the distinctive, inter-disciplinary course on the Theory of Knowledge, a 4000 word extended essay on a subject chosen by the candidate, and an opportunity to participate in experiential learning through the CAS (Creativity, Action, Service) component, where the emphasis may well be on the benefit of providing for the needs of others.

Assessment of all aspects of the IB curriculum is conducted both during and at the conclusion of the two year programme. All subjects at both Higher and Subsidiary levels are marked on a 1-7 scale with up to 20% of the marks in a given subject awarded upon the basis of internal assessment. All students require 24 points to qualify for the Diploma from a maximum of 45 points.

Irish offers: These are offers made to students taking the Irish Leaving Certificate.

SCE offers: These are offers made to students taking the Scottish Certificate of Education. Equivalent scores to published offers are acceptable usually.

Scottish applicants for English institutions should note that many admissions tutors in English universities and colleges have not received applications in recent years from candidates taking the SCE examination. Scottish applicants are therefore advised to contact admissions staff regarding offers, before submitting applications. The table below will provide a general comparison between A-level offers and average SCE offers:

AAA = SCE AAAAA;	**AAB** = SCE AAAAB;	**ABB** = SCE AAABB;
BBB-BBC = SCE AABB-ABBBB;	**BCC** = SCE BBBBB;	**CCC-CDD** = SCE ABBB-BBBB;
DDD-DEE = SCE BBCC-BCC;	**EEE-EE** = SCE CCC.	

Overseas applicants:

General information for overseas applicants is provided when available.

CHOOSING YOUR COURSE.

This section gives advice on courses and their content. In a number of cases advice is given on alternative courses which should be considered. This section should be read in conjunction with Chapter 1 and with **Admissions Tutors' advice** in each table.

Subject information:

Advice on the subject content and the priorities to be considered when choosing courses and similar alternative courses.

Course highlights:

All institutions aim to maintain a high standard of scholarship and teaching. However, courses offered by many universities are similar in content. This section identifies some of the differences which exist, such as bias, options, flexibility etc, and which might be of special interest to potential applicants. It is important to read this section in conjunction with prospectuses of institutions offering the listed courses.

Study opportunities abroad:

In recent years new initiatives have been introduced to enable undergraduates to study abroad. for example, the ERASMUS scheme gives students opportunities to take part of their course in a European 'university'. Details of the ERASMUS scheme are given in Chapter 4. Institutions involved in ERASMUS links are indicated (E). This section of the tables lists educational courses in which students attend a university or similar institution abroad for up to one year (see **Key to Countries** on page 88 for abbreviations of countries used in this table).

Work opportunities abroad:

There are now many subjects in which work placements abroad are an integral part of the course. These are often arranged by staff, although students also make their own arrangements when possible. Links with European countries are particularly important in view of the future of the European Community. This section lists work experience links in which students are attached to industrial, commercial and administrative organisations abroad. (Refer to **Key to Countries** on page 88 for abbreviations used in this section.)

NB If you are planning to study or work abroad during your course, it is important to consider the following points:

(a) the courses listed in the **Study Opportunities Abroad and Work Oppor tunities Abroad** sections of the tables are essentially for students who do not have a language at A-level, although in many cases some proficiency at GCSE level would be helpful. In some instances good grades in these examinations may be required.

(b)   these courses are expensive and opportunities will not necessarily be available for all students who want to travel and work abroad. Competition among students for an overseas placing could be fierce and may often depend on the academic ability they show during their course.

(c)   new developments are constantly taking place and these lists should not be assumed to be complete.

ADMISSIONS INFORMATION

Number of applicants per place (approx):

These figures show the approximate number of applicants initially applying for each place before any offers are made. It should be noted that any given number of applicants represents candidates who have also applied for other university and college courses.

Attitudes towards EC students and overseas students:

Details are provided on these applications in the **Medicine** table only.

General Studies acceptable:

Institutions which will accept an A-level pass in General Studies as one of the three grades of an offer or as one of two grades of an offer (indicated by (2)).

Selection interviews:

Institutions are listed which normally use the interview as part of their selection procedure. If oral or written tests are set at interview they are indicated (T).

Offers to applicants repeating A-levels:

This section gives details as to whether offers to repeating applicants may be **higher**, **possibly higher** or the **same** as those offers made to first time applicants for single honours. It should be noted, however, that circumstances may differ between candidates. Some will be repeating the same subjects taken in the previous year, while others may be taking different subjects. Offers will also be dictated by the level of grades achieved at the first sitting of the A-level examinations.

Admissions Tutors' advice:

Information concerning selection policies.

Examples of interview questions:

These are examples of some of the interview questions faced by applicants during recent years.

GAP YEAR ADVICE

Institutions accepting a Gap Year:

Names are listed of those institutions which have indicated that they will accept students wishing to take a gap year. In some cases additional information is provided.

Institutions willing to defer entry after A-levels:

These institutions will allow you to defer your entry until 1995 even though you originally applied to start your course in 1994.

AFTER A-LEVELS ADVICE

Institutions which may accept the same points score after A-levels:

Some A-level candidates may not achieve the actual A-level grades of the offer made to them, yet obtain grades with an equivalent points score (see above). The institutions listed in this section usually accept a points score equivalent to the original offer made after the publication of A-level results. (**NB** With the demand for places at present, some of the institutions listed may change their policies after the A-level results are known. Check with admissions tutors at the time of interview or when an offer is made to you.)

Institutions demanding the actual grades offered after A-levels:

The grades of offer made by the institution listed usually must be achieved by the applicant before the offer of a place can be confirmed. The higher the offer made, the more likely it is that the actual grades will be required.

Institutions which may accept under-achieving applicants after A-levels:

Some universities and colleges are able to accept applicants whose A-level grades are marginally lower than the offers originally made to them after the publication of A-levels. Applicants searching for a place are recommended to contact these institutions first.

Institutions with vacancies in Aug/Sept 1992:

Details are given of universities which had vacancies after A-levels in 1992 with the points scores required. The institutions listed indicated that they had vacancies or anticipated vacancies after A-levels in 1992. If you are not holding offers in May, you could contact these institutions since vacancies in the same subjects occur each year. Many other institutions declare vacancies but only in the week following the publication of the A-level results. If you have not obtained a place after A-levels then you should contact these universities and colleges in the first instance.

ADVICE FOR MATURE STUDENTS

General information for mature students is given for specific subject areas. Institutional information and advice is provided when available. Entry requirements will vary depending on the popularity of the institution or the subject area. Some institutions may demand A-levels, OU credits, Access courses or Return to Study courses. This particularly applies to scientific or technological courses, although work experience can also count towards acceptance. In all cases motivation and the ability to study over a period of time are regarded as highly important.

GRADUATE EMPLOYMENT

New Graduates' destinations (percentages) 1991:

The Department for Education has provided *The Complete Degree Course Offers* with statistics showing the first destinations of graduates from UK universities, polytechnics and colleges in 1991. The first destination results were calculated by the Economics Division of the DFE. These are listed in the appropriate subject table in Chapter 6. It should be noted that statistics are not necessarily available for all subject areas. Similarly, because of the nature of subjects offered and subject groupings, the availability of information between the university, polytechnic and college sectors also varies. For further information contact J Tarsh, DFE, Sanctury Buildings, Great Smith Street, London SW1P 3BT. (The author wishes to thank Mr Tarsh for allowing this information to be published.)

The tables provided show information under the following headings:

Permanent employment: The figures represent the percentage of graduates entering the labour force whose employment will be for a minimum of three months. Graduates entering employment overseas (usually averaging 6% - language graduates 21% approx) are included in these figures. Not included in these statistics are graduates who are in short-term employment.

Unemployment: This figure does not include statistics for those in short term unemployment lasting less than three months.

Further studies (all types): These figures give the percentage of all graduates entering further academic study, training as part of their work or courses leading to alternative careers.

Main career destinations (approx): Details are given which aim to provide **general guidance** on the specific career areas which graduates have entered. These are averages across universities, polytechnics and colleges. Variations sometimes occur in specific vocational subject areas, particularly when sandwich placements with firms lead to employment. For example, in Biological Sciences, 60% of polytechnic students entered subject-related work compared with (on average) 35% university students. Similarly 96% of college students aiming for education enter employment compared with 88% of university students.

Some examples of subject-related graduate employment also appear under some subject headings. This information has been kindly provided for readers by the careers services of Anglia Polytechnic University, and the universities of Bradford, Surrey, Teesside and York.

Employers' attitudes towards various universities are of constant interest to students and parents. Information on this subject, however, is extremely limited since little research has been attempted. It must be stressed that employers will not assume automatically that any one university will produce the best employees, since many employers may choose graduates from one institution only because the course is relevant to their type of work.

PIP research (below) however, has made an initial attempt to seek employers' views on the merits of institutions from which they recruit graduates, the results of which may be of interest to the reader.

Performance Indicator Project (PIP):

The following institutions are perceived as being above average in producing graduates for employment:
PIP is an independent statistical service for higher education. The survey to which this book refers is an annual enquiry of major recruiters of graduates of their views of which institutions are perceived as above or below average in producing suitably qualified students.

The institutions nominated by employers are then allocated perception points by a system which reflects employers' extent of recruitment and stated preference ranking. (In the tables in this book institutions are listed alphabetically.)

Inclusion in, or omission from, the listings in this publication implies no more than that some recruiters state their opinion of educational institutions and that these opinions might have some influence on graduates' eventual employment chances.

The findings are designed primarily for those in the institutions, but schools, colleges and careers services interested in the survey findings and methods should contact the project officer **in writing** for an application form at the following address: *Performance Indicator Project, c/o Department of Economics and Public Administration, Nottingham Trent University, Burton Street, Nottingham NG1 4BU.*

INSTITUTIONAL ABBREVIATIONS USED IN THE TABLES

Ch/Cross	-	Charing Cross and Westminster Hospital
Cons	-	Conservatoire (Birmingham)
Court	-	Courtauld Institute (London)
CSM	-	Camborne School of Mines (Exeter)
Gold	-	Goldsmiths' College (London)
Hom	-	Homerton College (Cambridge)
Hey	-	Heythrop College (London)
HSMD	-	Hospital School of Medicine and Dentistry (London)
Imp	-	Imperial College (London)
King's	-	King's College (London)
LSE	-	School of Economics and Political Science (London)
QM	-	Queen Margaret College (Edinburgh)
QMW	-	Queen Mary and Westfield College (London)
RAC	-	Royal Agricultural College (Cirencester)
RAcMus	-	Royal Academy of Music
RCMus	-	Royal College of Music
RH	-	Royal Holloway College (London)
RMCS	-	Royal Military College of Science
RNCM	-	Royal Northern College of Music
RNEC	-	Royal Navy Engineering College
RSAMD	-	Royal Scottish Academy of Music and Drama
SAC	-	Scottish Agricultural College sites: (Ab) Aberdeen, (Au) Auchincruive, (Ed) Edinburgh
SOAS	-	School of Oriental and Asian Studies (London)

SSEES	–	School of Slavonic and East European Studies (London)
TrCMus	–	Trinity College of Music
UC	–	University College (London & Salford)
UMDS	–	United Medical Schools of Guy's and St Thomas's (London)
UMIST	–	University of Manchester Institute of Science and Technology
UWCM	–	University of Wales College of Medicine (Cardiff)

OTHER ABBREVIATIONS USED IN THE TABLES

AS	–	Advanced Supplementary level
BTEC	–	Business and Technology Education Council National Certificates and Diplomas
C	–	College (Graduate employment details)
CA	–	College of Art
CAg	–	College of Agriculture
CAgF	–	College of Agriculture and Forestry
CAT	–	College of Advanced Technology *or* Arts and Technology
CB	–	College of Building
CC	–	College of Commerce
CD	–	College of Design
CDC	–	College of Design and Communication
CDT	–	College of Design and Technology
CE	–	College of Education
CF	–	College of Food
CFash	–	College of Fashion
CFE	–	College of Further Education
CHE	–	College of Higher Education
CHFE	–	College of Higher and Further Education
CHort	–	College of Horticulture
CMus	–	College of Music
Coll	–	College
Comb	–	Combined Studies degree courses
CP	–	College of Printing
CSYS	–	Certificate of Sixth Year Studies
CT	–	College of Technology
CTA	–	College of Technology and Arts
CText	–	College of Textiles
C	–	College (Graduate employment details)
D(s)	–	Distinction(s) in BTEC or preceded by the number required
Des Tech	–	Design and Technology
Dip	–	Diploma
Dist	–	Distinction
EB	–	European Baccalaureate
GCE	–	General Certificate of Education
GCSE	–	General Certificate of Secondary Education
gen stds	–	General Studies
Highers (H)	–	International Baccalaureate Higher Level Examination
HMC	–	Hospital Medical College
HMS	–	Hospital Medical School
HND	–	Higher National Diploma
IAD	–	Institute of Art and Design
IB	–	International Baccalaureate

IHCS	-	Institute of Health Care Studies
IHE	-	Institute of Higher Education
Int St	-	Integrated Studies degree courses
IT	-	Institute of Technology
JMB	-	Northern Universities' Joint Matriculation Board
M(s)	-	Merit(s) in BTEC or preceded by the number required
N/A	-	Not applicable
P	-	Polytechnic (Graduate employment details)
P(s)	-	Pass(es) in BTEC or preceded by the number required
Poly	-	Polytechnic
SA	-	School of Art
SAD	-	School of Art and Design
SCE	-	Scottish Certificate of Education
SM	-	School of Medicine
SOT	-	School of Occupational Therapy
SP	-	School of Physiotherapy
SPhm	-	School of Pharmacy
Subsids (S)	-	International Baccalaureate Subsidiary Level Examination
T	-	Test (at interview)
TC	-	Technical College
U	-	University (Graduate employment details)
Univ	-	University

Key to Countries

AB	- Abroad	FR	- France	NZ	- New Zealand
AF	- Africa	G	- Germany	P	- Portugal
AL	- Algeria	GR	- Greece	PA	- Pakistan
AU	- Austria	HG	- Hungary	PH	- Phillipines
AUS	- Australia	HK	- Hong Kong	PL	- Poland
B	- Belgium	IC	- Iceland	S	- Singapore
BR	- Brunei	IN	- India	SA	- South Africa
BUL	- Bulgaria	IT	- Italy	SL	- Sierra Leone
BZ	- Brazil	IRE	- Ireland	SLC	- Saint Lucia
C	- Cyprus	IS	- Israel	SP	- Spain
CAM	- Cameroon	J	- Jersey	SPA	- Spanish America
CAN	- Canada	JAP	- Japan	SW	- Sweden
CIS	- Confederation of	K	- Kenya	SWZ	- Swaziland
	Independent	LA	- Latin America	SZ	- Switzerland
	States	LUX	- Luxembourg	T	- Tibet
COL	- Colombia	M	- Malta	TU	- Tunisia
CZ	- Czechoslovakia	ME	- Middle East	TY	- Turkey
D	- Denmark	MEX	- Mexico	USA	- United States of
(E)	- ERASMUS	ML	- Maldive Islands		America
EG	- Egypt	N	- Norway	WI	- West Indies
EUR	- Europe	NI	- Nigeria	Y	- Yugoslavia
FE	- Far East	NAM	- Namibia	Z	- Zimbabwe
FN	- Finland	NL	- Netherlands		

6   THE SUBJECT TABLES

ACCOUNTANCY/ACCOUNTING

Special subject requirements: A-level mathematics often 'required' or 'preferred'. GCSE (grades A-C) mathematics essential.

NB Institutions may raise or lower the level of published offers depending either on the quality or otherwise of individual applications or the numbers of applications received; grades/points offered may be adjusted downwards after A-level results. The level of an offer is not indicative of the quality of a course.

26 pts. **Bath** – ABB/ABC (Bus/Admin)
Edinburgh – ABB (Com/Acc; Law/Acc)
24 pts. **Aberystwyth** – BBB-BBC/AB (Acctg) (BTEC 3D+3M)
Aston – BBB-BBC (Man/Admin)
Belfast – BBB-BBC (Acc Fin)
Bristol – ABC-BBC/BB (Econ/Accy)
East Anglia – BBB-BBC (Acc; Comp Acc; Acc/Eur) (BTEC 3D+M)
Exeter – BBB/AB (Accy) (4 AS) (BTEC Ms)
Loughborough – BBB-BBC/AB (Fin/Man) (BTEC 3D+4M)
Newcastle – BBB/AB (Acct Law) (BTEC 4D)
Nottingham – BBB-BBC/BB-BC (Ind Ec/Acc; Acc)
Reading – BBB (Acc/Econ)
Sheffield – BBB/AB (Accg; Dual Schools courses – see also **20 pts**) (BTEC 2D+M + B in GCSE maths)
Ulster – BBB-BBC/AB (Acc)
Warwick – BBB (Accy/Fin) (or BBB in 2 As and 2 AS or BB in 2 AS + CC in 1 A + 1 AS)
22 pts. **Aberdeen** – BBC (Acc courses)
Aberystwyth – BBC-BCC/AB-BB (BSc Econ; Acc/Wels) (BTEC 3D+3M)
Bangor – BBC (Euro F Man; Euro Int Man) (4 AS)
Birmingham – BBC (Com Acc; Com Acc/Fr) (D in all subjects) (BTEC D in all subjects)
Cardiff – BBC (Acc; Acc/Econ; Acc/Man) (BTEC 5D+2M)
City – BBC-CCC (Econ Acy)
Edinburgh – BBC (Acc – BCom/MA)
Essex – BBC/AB (A Fin M) (BTEC 3D+Ms)
Glasgow – BBC (Acc Comm)
Heriot-Watt – BBC (All courses)
Hull – BBC (Acct; Econ/Acct) (6 AS) (BTEC D+M)
Kent – BBC/AB (Acc courses)
Lancaster – BBC (All courses) (BTEC mainly Ds)
Leeds – BBC/AB (Acc/Fin; Acc/Dat Pro; Acc/Comp; Acc/OR)
Liverpool – BBC-BCC/BC (Acc)
Manchester – 22 pts approx (Acct)
Newcastle – BBC/AB (Acct/Fin; Econ/Acc) (BTEC 4D)
Salford – BBC (Fin/Acc) (BTEC Ds)
Stirling – BBC (Acc – BAcc)
Strathclyde – BBC/AB (1st yr entry) BBB (2nd yr entry) (Acc; Fin)
Southampton – BBC (All courses)
20 pts. **Bangor** – 20-18 pts (Acc Fin) (4 AS) (BTEC 3D+3M)
Dundee – BCC (inc maths) (Accy – BAcc)
Liverpool – BCC/BB (Acc/Comp)
Oxford Brookes – BCC/BB (Acc/Fin)
Sheffield – BCC/AB (Accg/Comp; Accg/Maths)
Stirling – BCC-CCC (Acc – BA)
18 pts. **Brighton** – 18-16 pts (Acc/Fin; Acc/Law; Int Acc/Fin)(BTEC 5/4D+Ms)
Bristol UWE – CCC/BB (Acc/Fin) (BTEC 3D)
Buckingham – 18-16 pts (Acc/Fin Man; Acc/Econ) (BTEC Ds+Ms)

Accountants always wear suits

Or so they say. But that's without taking into account the variety of clients that you can expect to be involved with when you are training with the world's largest firm of accountants and management consultants.

That variety could take you, as part of an audit team, one hundred feet down a copper mine in Cornwall, or see you pulling on wellingtons with one of our major construction clients.

Predictable it won't be . . . although life at KPMG does have its certainties. For one thing you will be on the receiving end of one of the finest management training programmes. So, irrespective of the nature of your degree, if you enjoy a challenge and are determined to succeed, you can expect a future with real personal rewards with KPMG.

See how well one of our chartered accountants' suits would fit you – contact your careers adviser for details of opportunities for vacation work and future careers.

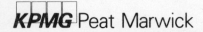

KPMG Peat Marwick

Central England - 18 pts (Acc) (4 AS) (BTEC 4D)
Kingston - CCC (Acc/Law)
Napier - CCC/BB (Acc) (4 AS)
Oxford Brookes - CCC/AB (Acc) (4 AS)
Sheffield Hallam - 18-14 pts (Acc/Man) (6 AS)
16 pts. **Bournemouth** - 16 pts (Accounting; Fin Serv) (4 AS) (BTEC 3D+Ms)
Glasgow Caledonian - CCD/DD
Guildhall London - CCD/CC (Fin Serv) (BTEC 4M)
Hertfordshire - 16 pts (Acc/MIS) (BTEC 4D+Ms)
Humberside - 16 pts (Acc/Fin)
Kingston - CCD-CDD/BB (Acc/Fin) (BTEC Ds)
Leeds Met - CCD/CC (EFA)
Liverpool John Moores - 16 pts/CC (Acc/Fin) (6 AS) (BTEC M)
Manchester Met - 16 pts (Fin Services) (BTEC 4D+Ms)
Middlesex - CCD/BB approx (Acc/Fin)
Northumbria - 16-17 pts (Acc)
Oxford Brookes - CCD/BB (Acc; Modular)
Nottingham Trent - 16 pts (All courses) (4 AS)
Paisley - CCD/BB (Acc)
Plymouth - CCD/BB (Acc/Fin) (BTEC 3D+4M)
Portsmouth - CCD/CC (Fin/Serv; Acc)
Robert Gordon - CCC/BB (Acc/Fin)
Sunderland - 16 pts (Acc/Bus)
Teesside - CCD (Accy Fin)
14 pts. **Bristol UWE** - 14 pts (Fin Serv)
Dundee - CDD (Acc - BSc)
Glamorgan - CDD/BC (Acc/Fin) (BTEC D)
Huddersfield - 14 pts (Acc St) (4 AS)
Luton (CHE) - 14 pts (Acc/Fin) (4 AS)
Manchester Met - 14 pts minimum (Acc/Fin) (BTEC 4D+Ms)
Sheffield Hallam - 14 pts (Fin/Serv) (BTEC 3D+3M)
Thames Valley London - 14 pts (Acc/Law) (BTEC Ds+Ms)
12 pts. **Buckingham** - DDD/CC (Comp Sci/Acc)
Central Lancashire - 12 pts (Acc)
Dundee (IT) - (Acc)
East London - DDD/CD (Acc/Fin) (BTEC 3D)
Greenwich - DDD/BD (Acct) (4 AS) (BTEC M overall)
Guildhall London - (Acc)
Leeds Met - CC approx (Acc/Fin) (See **European Studies**)
South Bank - CC (Acc/Fin) (4 AS) (BTEC 4D+3M)
Southampton (IHE) - CC/12 pts (Acc; Acc/Law - subject to approval)
Sunderland - 12 pts (Acc/Maths; Acc Comp) (BTEC 4M)
Swansea (IHE) - 12 pts (Acc) (BTEC D+M)
Thames Valley London - 12-10 pts (Acc; Acc/Eur) (BTEC M overall)
10 pts. **and below**
Central Lancashire - CD-DD (Comb Hons)
Cheltenham & Glos (CHE) - 10 pts (Fin Ser) (BTEC 3D)
Guildhall London - CD (Modular)
Holborn (Coll) - (BSc Econ)
North London - (Acc) (Contact Admissions Tutor)
Thames Valley London - 10 pts (Acc St; Acc Fin)

Offers for Foundation, Certificate and Diploma courses (see Ch 5):

Foundation courses:
14 pts. Bristol UWE 14 pts.
12 pts. Brighton (or CC), Guildhall London, Hertfordshire, Kingston, Leeds Met, Oxford Brookes
(Dip Acc St), Sheffield Hallam, Westminster.
10 pts. Central England, De Montfort, South Bank.

8 pts. Bristol UWE (Fin Serv), Central Lancashire, Coventry, Derby, East London, Glamorgan, Gwent (CHE), Huddersfield, Liverpool John Moores, (Bus St) (Fin/Acc), Norwich City (CFHE), Northumbria, Nottingham Trent, Sheffield Hallam (Acc/Fin).

4 pts. Anglia (Poly Univ), East London, Farnborough (CT), Greenwich, Humberside, Manchester Met, Middlesex, Mid-Kent (CHFE), Nene (CHE), Northumbria, North London, Plymouth, Portsmouth, Sandwell (CHE), Southampton (IHE), Staffordshire, Thames Valley London.

Diploma and Certificate courses (England and Wales):

8 pts. Thames Valley London (ACCA course), Ulster DD.

6 pts. North London (HND).

4 pts. Bradford & Ilkley (CmC), Cheltenham & Glos (CHE), Leeds Met (HND) DE, Oxford Brookes (Int Dip).

2 pts. Coventry, De Montfort, Derby, East London, Gwent (CHE), Kilburn Polytechnic (not in the UCAS scheme), Leeds Met, Luton (CHE), Oxford Brookes, Sandwell (CHFE), South Bank, Southampton (IHE), Swansea (IHE), Worthing (CT).

Diploma and Certificate courses (Scotland):

10 pts. Scottish (CText).

6 pts. Dundee (IT).

2 pts. Aberdeen (Coll), Ayr (Coll), Bell (CT), Clackmannan (Coll), Moray (Coll), Glasgow Caledonian, Inverness (Coll), Kirkcaldy (Coll), Napier, Perth (Coll).

Alternative offers:

IB offers: **Aberdeen** 32 pts; **Aberystwyth** 30 pts; **Aston** 31 pts; **Bangor** 30-24 pts; **Belfast** H766 S555; **Brighton** 24 pts (4 pts in each of the 6 subjects); **Buckingham** 28-26 pts; **Cardiff** H665 + S level 15 pts; **Dundee** (Acc Subsid) H544; **Essex** 28 pts 11 pts at H; **Exeter** 32 pts; **Guildhall London** 28 pts 7 subjects, 24 pts 6 subjects; **Kent** 29 pts H 13 pts; **Lancaster** 32 pts; **Leeds** 30 pts - 5 in maths; **Manchester Met** 24 pts; **Newcastle** 30-28 pts, (Acct/ Law) 30 pts; **North London** H543 S65; **Plymouth** 28-26 pts; **Salford** H665; **Sheffield** H665; **Thames Valley London** 24 pts; **Warwick** 34 pts maths H6.

Irish offers: **Aberdeen** AAAB; **Brighton** BBB; **Bristol UWE** CCCC minimum; **Central England** BBBCC; **East Anglia** BBBBB; **Guildhall London** CCCCC; **Heriot-Watt** AAABC; **Leeds** AAB; **Sheffield** AABBB.

SCE offers: **Aberdeen** AAAB/ABBBB; **Aberystwyth** ABBB; **Brighton** BBB; **Bristol UWE** AAB; **Central Lancashire** CCC; **Dundee** BBBBC or BBBB in 2 sittings, (BAcc) ABB/BBBC (BSc); **East Anglia** AABB-ABBBB; **Edinburgh** AAABB (Law/Acc), AABB/BBBBB (Econ/Acc, Bus St/Acc); **Essex** BBBB; **Glasgow** AABBB at 1 sitting, AAABBB at 2 sittings; **Guildhall London** (Modular) BBC; **Heriot-Watt** AABB (Acc/Fin), ABBB (Acc/Comp Sci); **Huddersfield** BBBB; **Lancaster** ABBBB; **Leeds** AAB; **Liverpool** BBBBB; **Manchester Met** BBBCC; **Newcastle** AAAAB; **Paisley** BBBB; **Sheffield** AABBB; **Sheffield Hallam** BBC; **Stirling** ABBB (BAcc), BBBC (Fin St); **Strathclyde** AAAA.

Overseas applicants: Hull Living costs 30% lower than in London area.

CHOOSING YOUR COURSE (See also Ch 1)

> **Subject information:** All courses offer financial management and accountancy training. Students should note that a degree in Accounting is not the only method of qualifying as an accountant. On the UCAS form you should be able to demonstrate your knowledge of accountancy and to give details of any work experience or work shadowing undertaken. Other subjects for consideration include Actuarial Studies, Banking, Business Studies, Economics and even Quantity Surveying which requires the same attention to detail. In addition to degree courses applicants should note that many institutions offer Foundation Courses which provide opportunities to move directly into degree courses.

Course highlights: Aberystwyth Financial, management and business finance in yr 1; specialist options in years 2 & 3. Also offered with languages including Welsh. **Birmingham** (Comm Acc) Course includes law, economics, computer science and behavioural science. **Bournemouth** (Fin/Serv) Course based on four themes: accounting and financial management, marketing and financial sevices, applications of information technology and business strategy. **Brighton** Emphasis on European and international organisations. **Bristol UWE** Includes information technology; opportunity to study a foreign language and for placement study in Europe. **Buckingham** (Acc Fin Man) Options in accounting and financial management or business or economics or computer science. **Central England** (Acc) Options in years 2 & 3 in behavioural aspects and international accounting. **Central Lancashire** (Acc) Integrated approach to teaching of computing; an information technology course in year 2. **East Anglia** All students take computerised accountancy. **Essex** (A Fin M) First-year students also take courses in computer applications, or mathematics and politics, sociology, computer applications or philosophy. **Glamorgan** Year 1 common with Business Studies, transfers possible. **Greenwich** (Acc) Options in taxation, auditing and international finance. **Guildhall London** (Acc) Course includes study of law and economics and a considerable amount of mathematics, computing and statistics. **Heriot-Watt** (Acc/Fin) Students take one elective subject each year from a choice of 30 which include several modern languages. **Hertfordshire** (Acc/MIS) International accounting, financial and treasury management and company law are final year subjects. **Holborn (Coll)** (BSc Econ) External London University degree with accountancy option. **Huddersfield** (Acc St) Emphasis on use of financial information in business planning, control and decision-making. **Lancaster** (Fin/Acc) Students take Part I course in economics and third course which could include a language or science subject. **Leeds Met** (Acc/Fin) Second year options include French or German. **Liverpool John Moores** Common first year with Business courses. **Middlesex** International accountancy option. **Newcastle** Common first year for all related courses makes transfers possible. (Acct/Law) Choice between Accountancy and Law made in year 2. **North London** (Acc) French, German or Spanish may be taken as a minor subject. **Northumbria** (Acc) Options in human behaviour in business organisations, the accountant in management, the accountant in the public sector and international accounting and finance. **Nottingham Trent** (Acc/Fin) Languages offered as minor subjects. **Paisley** Options include finance, technology and engineering and international accountancy with a foreign language. **Portsmouth** (Acc) Course has computer option route in years 2 & 4 and a European studies route involving a year abroad. **Salford** (Fin/Acc) Degree course has leaning towards management accounting. **Sheffield Hallam** (Fin/Serv) Leads to careers in banking, insurance, building societies and pension funds. **Stirling** (Acc) Accountancy can be taken as major, minor or subsidiary course in Part I. **Strathclyde** (Acc) Students choose second principal subject usually from administration, economics, law, marketing or operational research. **Thames Valley London** (Acc/Law) Choice between Accountancy or Law in year 3. **Ulster** (Acc) First year options include French, German, European business studies and product design. **Warwick** Year 1 common with Management Science. NOW CHECK PROSPECTUSES FOR ALL COURSES.

Study opportunities abroad: Bangor (E); **Birmingham** (E); **Buckingham** (E); **Cardiff** (E); **Exeter** (E); **Glamorgan** (E); **Glasgow** (E); **Guildhall London** (E); **Lancaster** (E); **Liverpool John Moores** (E); **Loughborough** (E); **Oxford Brookes** (E); **Portsmouth**; **Sheffield Hallam** (E); **Thames Valley London** (E).

Work opportunities abroad: Glamorgan FR G NL; **Lancaster** FR G IT; **Leeds Met** EUR; **Nottingham Trent** EUR; **Portsmouth** FR G; **Sheffield Hallam** USA CAN AUS.

ADMISSIONS INFORMATION

Number of applicants per place (approx): Aberystwyth 18; **Bangor** 35; **Belfast** 5; **Birmingham** 11; **Bournemouth** 10; **Brighton** 22; **Bristol UWE** 17; **Buckingham** 15; **Cardiff** 12; **Central England** 20; **Central Lancashire** 17; **Cheltenham & Glos (CHE)** 5; **Dundee (IT)** 10; **East Anglia** 17; **East London** 11; **Essex** 7; **Exeter** 18; **Glamorgan** 15; **Glasgow** 10; **Glasgow Caledonian** 11; **Guildhall London** 20; **Hertfordshire** 4; **Holborn (Coll)** no limits; **Huddersfield** 18; **Hull** 18; **Kent** 16; **Kingston** (Acc/Fin) 33, (Acc/Law) 5; **Lancaster** 20; **Leeds** 25; **Liverpool** 25; **Liverpool John Moores** 12; **Loughborough** 12; **Manchester Met** 20; **Middlesex** 24; **Napier** 13; **Newcastle** 15, (Acc/Law) 10; **North London** 20; **Northumbria** 24; **Nottingham Trent** 17; **Oxford Brookes** 50; **Portsmouth** 25; **Salford** 30; **Sheffield** 40; **Sheffield Hallam** 30; **South Bank** 6; **Stirling** 11; **Thames Valley London** 7; **Ulster** 10; **Warwick** 11.

General Studies acceptable: Bangor (varies); Birmingham; Brighton (2); Bristol UWE; Bournemouth; Cardiff; Central England; Central Lancashire; Cheltenham & Glos (CHE) (2); Exeter (2); Guildhall London; Kent; Hull; Lancaster; Leeds; Leeds Met; Liverpool John Moores (2); Manchester Met (No); Newcastle (as 3rd A-level); North London; Oxford Brookes; Portsmouth (JMB only); Salford; Sheffield (JMB only); Sheffield Hallam; South Bank (No); Thames Valley London.

Selection interviews: Bangor; Belfast (some); Birmingham (40%); Brighton (T); Bristol UWE; Central Lancashire (some); East Anglia (some); East London (T); Glamorgan; Glasgow (about 10%); Guildhall London (some); Heriot-Watt; Huddersfield; Hull (some); Leeds Met (some); Liverpool John Moores (some); Northumbria (some); Portsmouth (some); Salford (some); South Bank (some); Stirling (some); Thames Valley London; Ulster (some); Warwick (some).

Offers to applicants repeating A-levels: No offer made Belfast, Lancaster (rare); **Higher** Bangor, Glasgow, Huddersfield, Hull, Liverpool (Acc/Comp), North London, Northumbria, Sheffield; **Possibly higher** Brighton, Bristol UWE, Central England, Central Lancashire, East Anglia, Liverpool, Manchester Met, Newcastle, Oxford Brookes, Sheffield Hallam; **Same** Holborn (Coll), Humberside, Liverpool John Moores, Loughborough, Newcastle, South Bank, Thames Valley London, Ulster.

Admissions Tutors' advice: Aberystwyth AS-level maths preferred. **Brighton** Grade B in GCSE maths required. **Hertfordshire** Art or art-related subjects not acceptable. **Holborn (Coll)** Entry grades CC-EE accepted by London University. **Leeds** GCSE maths grade A preferred. **Lancaster, Sheffield** and **Leeds Met** GCSE maths grades A or B preferred. **Liverpool John Moores** GCSE subjects should demonstrate numeracy and literacy. **Newcastle** AS-level maths if not taken at A-level. **Warwick** Essay-type subject should be taken at AS-level if not at A-level. **NB** It is likely that many institutions will expect applicants to have a GCSE Grade A or B in maths.

> **Examples of interview questions:** Why did you choose this course? What are the main branches of accountancy? Discuss your UCAS application. Which interests do you hope to pursue at university? Can you relate economic concepts to everyday life? What are your main problems at school? Discuss your A-level subjects (for example economics) Britain and the EC. What qualities are needed to be a successful accountant? Which of these qualities do you possess?

GAP YEAR ADVICE

Institutions accepting a Gap Year: Most institutions; **Brighton** (Int Acc/Fin) Not acceptable; **Cheltenham & Glos (CHE)** Work experience may give exemption from the placement year; **Dundee** Do something useful; **East London** Apply early; **Glasgow** It may interrupt the habit of study; **Heriot-Watt** Not recommended; **Newcastle** Make your plans clear on the UCAS application.

Institutions willing to defer entry after A-levels (see Ch 5): Aberystwyth; Bangor; Bournemouth; Buckingham; Cheltenham & Glos (CHE); Dundee; East Anglia (not for Acc/Eur); Glasgow; Heriot-Watt; Humberside; Kingston; Lancaster; Manchester Met; Newcastle; Northumbria; Paisley; Plymouth; Salford; Sheffield Hallam; South Bank (No); Sunderland; Thames Valley London.

AFTER A-LEVELS ADVICE

Institutions which may accept the same points score after A-levels: Bangor; Belfast; Bournemouth; Brighton; Bristol UWE; Central England; Central Lancashire; East Anglia; Exeter; Glasgow; Glamorgan; Guildhall London; Holborn (Coll); Kingston; Liverpool; Liverpool John Moores; Luton (CHE); Northumbria; Nottingham Trent; Oxford Brookes; Portsmouth; Sheffield (in some cases); Sheffield Hallam; Southampton (IHE); South Bank; Swansea (IHE); Thames Valley London.

Institutions demanding the actual grades offered after A-levels: Leeds; Leeds Met (EFA); Loughborough; Manchester Met; Newcastle; Sheffield.

Institutions which may accept under-achieving applicants after A-levels: Bangor; Bournemouth; Brighton; Central England; Dundee; East Anglia; Glamorgan; Guildhall London; Heriot-Watt; Holborn

(Coll); Hull (overseas students 16-14 pts); Leeds Met (EFA); Liverpool John Moores; Luton (CHE); Sheffield; Sheffield Hallam; Southampton (IHE); South Bank; Swansea (IHE).

Institutions with vacancies in Aug/Sept 1992 (see Ch 5): Aberystwyth; Bangor; Bournemouth 14-12 pts; Brighton; Buckingham; Central England; Cheltenham & Glos (CHE) 10 pts; Dundee; Heriot-Watt; Holborn (Coll); Glamorgan; Greenwich 8 pts; Kingston; Leeds; Manchester Met 12 pts; Newcastle 22-20 pts; North London DDD; Northumbria 14 pts; Oxford Brookes; Portsmouth; Sheffield Hallam; South Bank CD; Southampton; Sunderland; Thames Valley London 14 pts. Most other 'new' universities and colleges.

ADVICE FOR MATURE STUDENTS

On these courses approximately 5 per cent of students are 'mature'. Most applicants are interviewed. Formal qualifications are not necessarily sought for HND courses, similarly for courses at **Huddersfield** and **Central Lancashire**. Motivation and the ability to cope with the course are important. Banking, insurance and accountancy experience are helpful as are A-levels, OU credits and certain Access and Return to Study courses. **Aston** 4% mature students; **South Bank** 50% students on course are 'mature'; many local candidates.

GRADUATE EMPLOYMENT

New Graduates' destinations (percentages) 1991:
Permanent employment: U 87; P 69; C 69.
Unemployment: U 10; P 20; C 17.
Further studies (all types): U 14; P 13; C 16.
Main career destinations (approx): Business/Finance 94.

This subject had one of the best employment records during the recession in 1992.

ACTUARIAL SCIENCE/STUDIES

Special subject requirements: A-level mathematics and one other subject. Most institutions will require Grade A or B GCSE mathematics.

NB Institutions may raise or lower the level of published offers depending either on the quality or otherwise of individual applications or the numbers of applications received; grades/points offered may be adjusted downwards after A-level results. The level of an offer is not indicative of the quality of a course.

24 pts. **Kent** – ABC (Act Sci)
22 pts. **City** – BBC/BB (Act Sci)
 Heriot-Watt – BBC/AB (Act Maths)
 London (LSE) – BBC approx (Act Sci)

Alternative offers:

IB offers: **City** 36 pts H665; **Heriot-Watt** H665; **Kent** 31 pts H 14 pts.

Irish offers: **Heriot-Watt** BBBBC.

SCE offers: **City** AAAAA; **Heriot-Watt** ABBB.

CHOOSING YOUR COURSE (See also Ch.1)

Subject information: This is reputed to be one of the highest paid careers in finance, and so naturally attracts a number of applicants! Training as an actuary, however, is extremely demanding and must not be underestimated. A discussion of this career with an actuary is recommended to be included in the UCAS form. An alternative route for actuarial work would be a mathematics degree course. See also under **Accountancy** and **Banking**.

Course highlights: Heriot-Watt Courses lead to BSc Statistics and BSc Actuarial Mathematics and Statistics – transfer between courses possible at end of year 1. Substantial exemptions from professional examinations. NOW CHECK PROSPECTUSES FOR ALL COURSES.

ADMISSIONS INFORMATION

Number of applicants per place (approx): City 5; **Heriot-Watt** 5; **Kent** 10.

General Studies acceptable: Heriot-Watt.

Offers to applicants repeating A-levels: Possibly higher City.

Examples of interview questions: What is actuarial work? What qualifications are needed to become an actuary? Have you discussed this career with an actuary?

AFTER A-LEVELS ADVICE

Institutions with vacancies in Aug/Sept 1992 (see Ch 5): City; Heriot-Watt 22 pts; Kent.

AFRICAN STUDIES

Special subject requirements: usually GCSE (grades A-C) mathematics.

NB Institutions may raise or lower the level of published offers depending either on the quality or otherwise of individual applications or the numbers of applications received; grades/points offered may be adjusted downwards after A-level results. The level of an offer is not indicative of the quality of a course.

20 pts.   **Kent** – BCC (Af Car)
          Birmingham – BCC (African St Combined Honours)
16 pts.   **London (SOAS)** – BB (Af L & C; All Amharic, Hausa and Swahili courses) (Ref BC)

Alternative offers:

IB offers: **Kent** 27 pts, H 12 pts; **London (SOAS)** 32 pts.

CHOOSING YOUR COURSE (See also Ch.1)

Subject information: African Studies is often combined with Caribbean Studies and can involve geography, history, popular culture, political science and sociology (refer also to these particular tables).

Course highlights: Birmingham African Studies can also be taken as a main or subsidiary subject in the General Honours degree. Study of African history and culture focusing on West Africa in year 1. NOW CHECK PROSPECTUSES FOR ALL COURSES.

ADMISSIONS INFORMATION

Number of applicants per place (approx): Birmingham 4; **Kent** 4; **London (SOAS)** 3.

Admissions Tutors' advice: Birmingham Motivation very important.

Examples of interview questions: Why do you want to study this subject? What parts of Africa are of particular interest to you? What are your views on apartheid?

AFTER A-LEVELS ADVICE

Institutions which may accept the same points score after A-levels: London(SOAS).

Institutions demanding the actual grades offered after A-levels: Kent.

ADVICE FOR MATURE STUDENTS

Kent 13% of students are 'mature' and a range of formal qualifications are acceptable eg, A-levels, OU credits, Access courses, Return to Study courses.

AGRICULTURAL SCIENCES/AGRICULTURE (including Agricultural Economics)

Special subject requirements: 2-3 A-levels including chemistry and 1-2 other subjects from mathematics/science, except for Agric Econ/Agric/Food Marketing for which GCSE (grades A-C) mathematics is the only requirement. Practical experience for Agriculture courses required for entry to Aberystwyth, Bangor, Newcastle, Nottingham. Check entry requirements for other courses.

NB Institutions may raise or lower the level of published offers depending either on the quality or otherwise of individual applications or the numbers of applications received; grades/points offered may be adjusted downwards after A-level results. The level of an offer is not indicative of the quality of a course.

Agricultural Biochemistry
14pts.   **Newcastle** - CDD/CC (Agric Biochem/Nut) (BTEC Ms)
         Nottingham - CDD/CC (Agric Bioch)

Agricultural Biology
12pts.   **Hertfordshire** - 12-8 pts (App Biol)

Agricultural Biotechnology
18pts.   **Aberdeen** - CCC-CCD/BC (Agric/Bio T)

Agricultural Botany
18pts.   **Glasgow** - CCC-CCD/BC (Agric Bot)
14pts.   **Aberystwyth** - CDD/CC (Agric Sci)
         Bangor - CDD/CC (Agric Bot)
         London (Wye) - CDD (App Plant Sci)
         Newcastle - CDD/BC (Plant Sci; Agric Env; Crop Prot) (BTEC Ms)
         Nottingham - CDD/CC (Agric Bot; Plant Sci)
10pts.   **Harper Adams (CAg)** - (Agric/ICM)

Agricultural Business Management
20pts.   **Newcastle** - BCC/BB (Agri Bus Man)
18pts.   **Newcastle** - CCC/BB (Country Man) (4 AS) (BTEC Ms)
16pts.   **Cirencester (RAC)** - 16-14 pts (Int Ag Man)
         London (Wye) - CCD/BB-CC (Agric Bus Man)
14pts.   **Aberdeen** - CDD/BC (Country/Env Man) (6 AS)
         Aberystwyth - 14 pts (Agric/BS) (BTEC 5M)
         Newcastle - CDD/CC (Farm B/Man)
12pts.   **Cirencester (RAC)** - 12 pts (Int Ag Eq Man)

10 pts.   **Harper Adams (CAg)** – (Agric/LFM) (BTEC Ms)
6 pts.   **SAC (Ab)** – 6 pts (Agric Bus Man)

Agricultural Chemistry
18 pts.   **Glasgow** – CCC-CCD/BC (Agric Chem)
16 pts.   **Belfast** – CCD (Agric Chem)
          Brunel – CCD (MAE Chem)

Agricultural Economics
24 pts.   **Nottingham** – ABC-BCC/AB (Econ/Ag Econ)
22 pts.   **Aberdeen** – BBC (Econ/Ag Econ – MA)
          East Anglia – BBC (Dev Ag/Dev)
          Glasgow – (Agric Econ – MA)
20 pts.   **Aberystwyth** – BCC (BSc Econ)
          Exeter – BCC-CCC (Econ/Ag Ec)
          Manchester – 20 pts approx
18 pts.   **Belfast** – CCC (Agric)
          Glasgow – CCC (Agric Econ)
          Newcastle – CCC/AB-BB (Agric Econ) (4 AS)
16 pts.   **Aberystwyth** – CCD (Ag Econ; Econ/Ag Econ)
          Edinburgh – CCD/BB (Agric)
          London (Wye) – CCD (Agric Econ)
          Reading – CCD/BC (Agric Econ)
12 pts.   **Bangor** – DDD/CC (Agric Ag Ec) (4 AS)

Agricultural and Environmental Science
16 pts.   **Newcastle** – CCD/BC (Agric Env – all courses)
12 pts.   **Aberystwyth** – DDD/CC (Agric/Env) (BTEC 3M)

Agricultural and Food Marketing
16 pts.   **Newcastle** – CCD/BC (Agric/F Mar) (6 AS)
14 pts.   **Aberystwyth** – CDD (AFM)
          Cranfield (Silsoe) – CDD/CC (Food Mar/Dis)
10 pts.   **Harper Adams (CAg)** – DDD/CC (Agric Food Mar) (BTEC Ms)

Agricultural Microbiology
16 pts.   **Edinburgh** – CCD approx (Agric Micro)

Agricultural Zoology
16 pts.   **Belfast** – CCD (Agric Zoo)
14 pts.   **Leeds** – CDD/BC (AAZ)
          Newcastle – CDD/BC (Agric Zoo; Ag Env Sci/Ag Zool) (BTEC Ms)
10 pts.   **Harper Adams (CAg)** – 10 pts (Agric/An Sci)

Agroforestry
16 pts.   **Bangor** – CCD/BC-CD (Agrofor) (BTEC 3M)

Agriculture (See also **Engineering (Agricultural)**)
22 pts.   **East Anglia** – BBC (Dev/NR)
18 pts.   **Aberdeen** – CCC-CCD/BC (Crop Sci)
          London (Wye) – CCC (Country Man)
          Newcastle – CCC/BB (Country/Man) (4 AS) (BTEC Ms)
          Reading – CCC (Crop Prot)
16 pts.   **Edinburgh** – CCD (Agric; Ecol Sci) (4 AS)
          Leeds – CCD (Agric Sci An)
          Stirling – CCD approx (Cons Man)
14 pts.   **Aberdeen** – CDD (Agric)
          Aberystwyth – CDD/CC (Agric; Agric Sci; Agric/BS) (BTEC 3M)
          Cranfield (Silsoe) – CDD/CC (Rur Env Man; Ag Tech Man) (BTEC 75% overall)

Royal Agricultural College
Cirencester

Britain's First Agricultural College offers:

BSc Agriculture and Land Management

BSc Crop Production Ecology and Management

BSc International Agribusiness Management

BSc International Agricultural and Equine
     Business Management

BSc Rural Land Management

Professional Diploma Rural Estate Management

For further details contact: The Admissions Secretary,
Royal Agricultural College, Cirencester, Glos. GL7 6JS
Tel : 0285 652531/641404

Harper Adams (CAg) – CDD/BC (Rural Ent/Land Man)
London (Wye) – CDD/CD-DD (Agric; Agric/Env)
Newcastle – CDD/BC (All Agric courses)
Nottingham – CDD/CC (Agric; Plant Sci) (BTEC 3M)
Reading – CDD/CC (Agric; Rur Res Man; Crop Sci)

12 pts.   **Aberdeen** – DDD (Agric)
Askham Bryan (CAg) – CC (Land Res Man)
Bangor – DDD/CD (Agriculture; Rur Res Man) (4 AS)
Buckingham – DDD/CC (Agric/Land Man)
Cirencester (RAC) – 12 pts (Ag/Land Man; Crop Prod Ecol Man; Rural Land Man)
Hertfordshire – 12pts (Ag Bio)
Plymouth – CC (Rural Res Man; Agric CM)
Welsh (CAg) – 12 pts (Agric)

10 pts.   **and below approx**
Anglia (Poly Univ) – 8 pts (Rural Res Dev)
Central Lancashire – (Country Man) (4 AS)
Harper Adams (CAg) – 10 pts (Agric) (BTEC Ms)
Hertfordshire/Writtle (CAg) – (Agric)
Liverpool John Moores – DDE/DD (App Crop Sci)
Liverpool John Moores – (Country/Man)
Plymouth/Seale Hayne – DDD/CC (Agric) (1 yr farm experience before entry) (BTEC Ms)
Ripon & York St John (CHE) – (Modular/Rural Sci)
SAC (Ed) – (Rural Res)
Trinity Carmarthen (CHE) – (General)
Welsh (CAg) – (Agric)
Wolverhampton – DD (Agric Tech; Agric)
Writtle (CAg) – (Rural Resources)

Franchised degree and HND courses (see Ch 5):

> **Bristol UWE** - Sparshot (CAg)
> **Central Lancashire** - Cumberland (CAg), Lancashire (CAg)
> **Coventry** - Warwick (CAg)
> **Greenwich** - Hadlow (CAg)
> **Harper Adams (CAg)** - Staffordshire (CAg)
> **Humberside** - Bishop Burton (CAg)
> **Nottingham Trent** - Lincolnshire (CAg)
> **Southampton (IHE)** - Cannington (Coll)

Offers for Foundation, Certificate and Diploma courses (see Ch 5):

Higher National Diploma courses (England and Wales):
6 pts. Plymouth (SH) D-E in a science preferred (HND Ag/Rural Resources)
4 pts. and below
> Askham Bryan (CAg) (also Agribusiness), Bristol UWE (Golf Greenkeeping/Euro St), Harper Adams (CAg) (Ag; Agric Marketing/Bus Admin), Kingston (Golf St), Lancashire (CAg), Lincolnshire (CAg), Sheffield Hallam, Shuttleworth (CAg) Agric, Rural Env Man; Welsh (CAg), Writtle (CAg) D in a science subject.

Higher Diploma courses (Scotland):
4 pts. equivalent and below SAC (Ab) (Ag; Ag/Bus); SAC (Au) (Ag; Mech/Bus); SAC (Ed) (Agriculture; Rural Res).

Other Diploma courses:
4 pts. Cirencester (RAC) (Rural Est Man)

Alternative offers:

IB offers: **Aberystwyth** 27 pts maths H4; **Bangor** 28 pts H555; **Belfast** H555 S555; **Cirencester (RAC)** 26 pts; **Cranfield (Silsoe)** (Ag Tech) H554; **Edinburgh** 28 pts; **Exeter** 30 pts; **Harper Adams (CAg)** 24 pts; **Newcastle** H654, (Agric Biochem) H55 - 29 pts; **Nottingham** 24 pts 6 subjects 28 pts 7 subjects; **Plymouth** 3 merits; **Reading** 24 pts.

Irish Offers: **Aberdeen** BBCC; **Bangor** CCC; **Harper Adams (CAg)** CCCC.

SCE offers: **Aberdeen** BBC or BCCC (Ag Bus Man), AAB or BBB (Ag Econ), BBBC (other Ag courses); **Aberystwyth** (AFM) BBBB; **Bangor** BBCC; **Belfast** BBBB; **Edinburgh** BBBC; **Glasgow** BBB or BBBB or ABB; **Leeds** BBBBC; **Newcastle** (AFM) BBCC, (Agric; Agric Econ) AABB, (Agric Biochem) BBBC.

CHOOSING YOUR COURSE (See also Ch 1)

> **Subject information:** Farming, biochemical applications to plants and animals and agricultural surveying are just some of the specialisms within Agriculture courses; for some agricultural courses practical experience is required. There has also been a recent expansion in agri-business studies courses. Other courses for consideration include Animal Sciences, Estate Management, Food Science, Horticulture, Forestry, Soil Science (including Horse Studies).

Course highlights: Aberdeen (Crop Sci) Includes options in forestry, ecology and environmental science. (Agric) Common courses for all students in years 1 & 2, with the choice of options in year 3. **Aberystwyth** (Ag Econ) Includes a study of Britain in the EC, USA and Eastern Europe; an industrial year (possibly in the US) offered. (AFM) Covers processing and marketing from farm gate to supermarket. (Agric/BS) Course includes sandwich periods for practical experience (no previous practical experience needed). (Agric) In Part II students may choose agricultural botany, agricultural economics or applied nutrition. **Anglia (Poly Univ)** (Rural Res Dev) Options include wildlife and landscape conservation, farm business and countryside and leisure. **Bangor** (Rur Res/Man) Includes options in agriculture, agroforestry, forestry, arid zone and conservation. (Agroforestry) Social, ecological and economic aspects of food, fuel and timber production worldwide. **Bath** (Crop PE Man) Modular course covering plant biology, crop science and agricultural management. **Cirencester (RAC)** (Agric Bus) Very broad course covering farm gate to retail outlet in the food chain. Industrial sponsorships. Contacts with new developments in Eastern Europe. **Edinburgh** Flexible course system - transfers possible between Agriculture and Biological Sciences. **Harper Adams (CAg)** (Agric) Strong emphasis on application of science, economics and business techniques. **London (Wye)** (Agric) Emphasis on animal and crop production, management and marketing. **Newcastle** (Country Man) Covers natural and social sciences. Proximity of four National Parks and coastal countryside valuable for teaching and fieldwork. (Agric Econ) Options in marketing, rural planning. (Agric F/Man) Course covers marketing, research and design and consumer behaviour. **Nottingham** (Agric) Six streams chosen for third, fourth and fifth terms, giving flexibility of choice (agricultural, horticulture, plants science, animal science, food science, environmental biology). **Reading** (Agric) Part I (two terms) includes agriculture, crop production, animal production, plant and soil science and agricultural economics. Part II (three terms) includes crop physiology, crop protection, plant breeding and animal breeding. NOW CHECK PROSPECTUSES FOR ALL COURSES.

Study opportunities abroad: Aberdeen (E); **Aberystwyth** (Ag Econ; Ag FM) USA; **Bangor** (E); **Cirencester (RAC)** (E) Worldwide; **Edinburgh** (E); **Harper Adams (CAg)** (E); **Nottingham** (E); **Welsh (CAg)** (E).

Work opportunities abroad: Aberystwyth EUR; **Askham Bryan (CAg)** FR G NL IRE; **Bangor** CAN USA AUS; **Bath** EUR; **Cirencester (RAC)** EUR; **Cranfield** AUS EUR BZ COL K PA USA SWZ Z; **Hertfordshire** SZ B NL; **Newcastle** (Agric Bus Man) EUR; **Seale Hayne (CAg)** EUR; **Writtle (CAg)** N NL.

ADMISSIONS INFORMATION

Number of applicants per place (approx): Aberdeen (Agric) 10; **Aberdeen (SAC)** 1; **Aberystwyth** (Agric) 5; **Anglia (Poly Univ)** 3; **Bangor** (Agric) 12, (Agric Bot) 4; **Buckingham** (Agric) 3; **Cirencester (RAC)** (Ag) 4; **Cranfield (Silsoe)** (Ag Tech) 5; **Edinburgh** 9; **Harper Adams (CAg)** 4; **Hertfordshire** 10; **Leeds** (Agr) 3, (Agric Chem) 5; **London (Wye)** (Agric) 9; **Newcastle** (Agric Econ) 5, (Agric Bus Man) 10, (Agric Env) 4, (Country Man) 12, (Agric) 4, (Agric Zoo) 6, (Agric Bioch) 5, (Agric/F Mar) 6; **Nottingham** (Agric) 4; **Reading** (Agric) 9; **Welsh (CAg)** 20; **Wolverhampton** 4; **Writtle (CAg)** 4.

General Studies acceptable: Aberdeen; Anglia (Poly Univ); Askham Bryan (CAg); Bangor (Agriculture); Cirencester (RAC); Newcastle (Agric/F Mar).

Selection interviews: Anglia (Poly Univ); Bangor (Agriculture); Bath; Belfast (Agric); Cirencester (RAC); Edinburgh (Agric) (some); Newcastle; Plymouth/Seale Hayne (CAg).

Offers to applicants repeating A-levels: Higher Bangor (Agric Bot), Newcastle (Ag Econ); **Possibly higher** Edinburgh, Newcastle (Agric/F Mar; Agr), Plymouth/Seale Hayne (CAg) (Agr); **Same** Anglia (Poly Univ), Bangor (Agriculture), Harper Adams (CAg), Newcastle (Agric; Agric Bioch), Nottingham (Agric).

Admissions Tutors' advice: Newcastle (Country Man) GCSE grade C+ in biology preferred. **Nottingham** When offered, 2 AS-levels must be in sciences.

Examples of interview questions: Discuss your family background. What do you consider are the benefits of practical farming experience? Why do you want to study Agriculture? What special agricultural interests do you have? Why are you interested in Food Marketing? What types of farms have you worked on? What kind of future exists for farmers? Have you thought of doing anything else? What crops are grown on your own farm and what other enterprises are taking place? Are you struggling with any of your A-levels? If so, Why? Why did you choose your A-level subjects? Practical questions on dairy farming. What is Food Marketing? What sort of a career do you envisage on completing your degree course? How long has your father been a farmer? Is he successful? What system does he use? Can you see any problems with this system? Since you wish to be a farmer why are you not doing a diploma course at a college of agriculture? Do you read any farming publications? If so, which? How long will an egg last before going bad? Compare an egg with a potato. What is wrong with this tomato? (It had been frozen and defrosted.) What problems have the French created for British farmers?

GAP YEAR ADVICE

Institutions accepting a Gap Year: Most institutions; **Aberystwyth** Try to work in a related area; **Cirencester (RAC)** Strengthen language skills for the international courses and agriculture for the practical courses; **Harper Adams (CAg)** A pre-college year on a farm is recommended; **Newcastle** Keep a diary/photographs of anything done or seen relevant to the course; **Welsh (CAg)** Industrial placement year provides opportunity to travel.

Institutions willing to defer entry after A-levels (see Ch 5): Aberystwyth; Cirencester (RAC); Harper Adams (CAg); Newcastle; Plymouth/ Seale Hayne (CAg).

AFTER A-LEVELS ADVICE

Institutions which may accept the same points score after A-levels: Anglia (Poly Univ); Bangor (Agriculture; Agr Bot); Edinburgh; Harper Adams (CAg); Liverpool John Moores; Newcastle (Agr; Agr Econ; Agric Bioch; Country Man; Agric Zoo; Agr FM); Nottingham (Ag Bot); Plymouth/Seale Hayne (CAg); Writtle (CAg).

Institutions demanding the actual grades offered after A-levels: Belfast (Agr Bot).

Institutions which may accept under-achieving applicants after A-levels: Aberdeen; Bangor; Belfast; Edinburgh; Essex; Harper Adams (CAg); Liverpool John Moores; Newcastle (Agr, Agric Econ, Agric Bioch, Agric/F Mar); Nottingham; Plymouth/Seale Hayne (CAg); Writtle (CAg).

Institutions with vacancies in Aug/Sept 1992 (see Ch 5): Aberdeen; Aberystwyth 12 pts; Bangor; Cirencester (RAC); Harper Adams (CAg) 8 pts; Newcastle (Farm B/Man), (Agric Env Sci) 8 pts; Plymouth/Seale Hayne (CAg) 8 pts. Most new universities and agricultural colleges had vacancies; the more popular universities looked for a points score of 16-10 pts.

ADVICE FOR MATURE STUDENTS

Strong motivation and in some cases a good employer reference are required. Some institutions may require A-levels although at lower grades than for school leavers.

GRADUATE EMPLOYMENT

New Graduates' destinations (percentages) 1991:
Permanent employment: U 83; P 74; C 87.
Unemployment: U 12; P 16; C 2.
Further studies (all types): U 24; P 14; C 8.

Anglia (Poly Univ) (1991) (Rural Resource Development) Graduate employment from this course was extremely varied and included surveying, police, estate management, marketing and sales. Three students went on to further study in Land Economy, Environmental Assessment and Sociology and Anthropology.

AMERICAN STUDIES

Special subject requirements: A-level history and English are required for some courses; GCSE (grade A-C) in mathematics and a language for others.

NB Institutions may raise or lower the level of published offers depending either on the quality or otherwise of individual applications or the numbers of applications received; grades/points offered may be adjusted downwards after A-level results. The level of an offer is not indicative of the quality of a course.

24 pts.   **Birmingham** – BBB (Amer St)
         East Anglia – 24 pts (EAS/L; Am Eng Hist)
         Hull – BBB-BBC/AB (Amer Studs) (BTEC Ds+Ms)
         Lancaster – BBB-BBC (Amer St) (BTEC 4D+3M)
         Sheffield – BBB (Am St)
         Swansea – BBB (AMS (USA))
22 pts.   **East Anglia** – BBC-BCC/BC (EAS/AH; EAS/AHP; EAS/AS; EAS/AL) (GCSE English
         lit & history B)
         Essex – BBC-BCC/BB (US; LUS)
         Kent – BBC-BCC/BB (All courses except **20 pts**)
         Manchester – 22 pts approx (Amer St)
         Nottingham – BBC (Amer/Eng)
         Nottingham – BBC-BCC (Other courses)
         Ripon & York St John (CHE) – BBC (AM/Eng)
         Sussex – BBC (All courses)
         Warwick – BBC (Am Lit)
20 pts.   **Aberystwyth** – BCC/BB (Amer) (BTEC 3D+3M)
         Dundee – BCC (Am St)
         Exeter – BCC/BB (Am Arts; Engl/Am Arts) (4 AS)
         Keele – BCC-BCD/BB-BC (Joint Hons) (4 AS) (BTEC 3M)
         Kent – BCC-CCC/BB (Br Am Pol St)
         Leicester – BCC/BB (Amer St)
         Ripon & York St John (CHE) – BCC/BB (AM/Dr TV; AM/Hist)
         Reading – BCC (Am St)
         Swansea – BCC-BCD/BC (All Joint courses except AMS (USA))
         Warwick – BCC (CAS)
18 pts.   **Belfast** – CCC/BB (Amer St)
         Ripon & York St John (CHE) – CCC/BB (AM/Geog)
         Ulster · CCC-CCD (Hum Comb)
16 pts.   **Central Lancashire** – CCD (Amer St; Comb Hons) (4 AS)
         Middlesex – 16-12 pts approx (Modular)
14 pts.   **West London (IHE)** – 14 pts (Joint)
12 pts.   **and below approx**
         Derby – (Modular; Comb St) (4 AS)
         King Alfred's (CHE) – (Comb St)
         Liverpool (IHE) – CC (Comb St) (4 AS)
         North London – (Comb Hons; Caribbean St)
         Thames Valley London – (Comb St)

Alternative offers:

EB offers: **Keele** 60%.

IB offers: **Aberystwyth** 30 pts H6 in history or English; **Essex** 28 pts, H 11 pts; **Exeter** 30 pts; **Hull** 30 pts H66 in English and history; **Keele** 26 pts; **Kent** 29 pts, H 13 pts; **Lancaster** 32-30 pts; **Leicester** 20 pts; **Ripon & York St John (CHE)** 30 pts; **Swansea** 26 pts min.

Irish offers: **Keele** BBBCC.

SCE offers: **Dundee** BBBC; **Essex** BBBB; **Keele** BBCC; **Nottingham** BBCC; **Sheffield** AABB; **Sussex** ABBB.

CHOOSING YOUR COURSE (See also Ch 1)

> **Subject information:** American literature and history represent the core of most courses with a year in the USA (variations are given below). Alternative courses of possible interest include International Relations, Politics, Latin-American or Spanish-American Studies.

Course highlights: Aberystwyth Course covers US history, literature, politics, cinema. **Birmingham** (Amer St) Specialist studies include Latin American Studies and Canada. **Dundee** (Amer St) Courses on American and Canadian literature, US foreign policies, race and slavery in the South. **East Anglia** (EAS) Wide choice of Honours programmes covering English and American literature, history, drama, film studies, linguistics and philosophy. **Essex** (US) Also possible to take a degree in Government, History, Literature, or Sociology specialising in the United States, or optional courses on American topics in the School of Comparative Studies and in the School of Social Studies. **Exeter** (Am Arts) Emphasis not only on literature but on all the arts, including film, photography, painting and popular music. **Liverpool (IHE)** One year abroad. **Sussex** (Am St) Emphasis on history, literature or social aspects. **Warwick** (CAS) First year students do two courses on themes and problems in North America, Latin America and the Caribbean, and a beginner's course in Spanish. NOW CHECK PROSPECTUSES FOR ALL COURSES.

Study opportunities abroad: All institutions make some arrangements for period of study in USA or Canada (check with institution); **Nottingham** (E).

ADMISSIONS INFORMATION

Number of applicants per place (approx): Aberystwyth 19; **Belfast** 11; **Birmingham** 25; **East Anglia** 25; **Essex** 6; **Exeter** 20; **Hull** 8; **Keele** 7; **Kent** 15; **Lancaster** 25; **Liverpool (IHE)** 12; **Nottingham** 20; **Reading** 9; **Sheffield** 30; **Sussex** 12; **Swansea** 7; **Warwick** 11; **West London (IHE)** 8.

General Studies acceptable: Belfast; East Anglia; Exeter; Hull; Keele; Lancaster; Liverpool (IHE); Nottingham.

Selection interviews: East Anglia; Hull; Nottingham (BB offer without interview); Warwick.

Offers to applicants repeating A-levels: Higher Essex; **Possibly higher** Nottingham; **Same** East Anglia.

Admissions Tutors' advice: Admissions tutors expect some background reading in these fields. Details of any visits to the Americas should also be included on UCAS form.

> **Examples of interview questions:** What American literature have you read? Why do 'westerns' appeal more to men than women? What parts of America would you like to visit? Why? Why was it that Spain settled in America 100 years before the French, English and Dutch? What are your impressions of Americans? Which candidate would you have voted for in the presidential election? Why?

GAP YEAR ADVICE

Institutions accepting a Gap Year: Most institutions; **Swansea** Useful to spend part of the year in the USA.

Institutions willing to defer entry after A-levels (see Ch 5): Aberystwyth (prefer deferred entry application); Dundee; Hull; Lancaster; Ripon & York St John (CHE); Swansea.

AFTER A-LEVELS ADVICE

Institutions which may accept the same points score after A-levels: Aberystwyth; East Anglia; Essex; Hull; Keele; Kent; Liverpool (IHE); Swansea.

Institutions demanding the actual grades offered after A-levels: Birmingham; Dundee; Nottingham; Warwick.

Institutions which may accept under-achieving applicants after A-levels: Aberystwyth; Exeter; Hull; Keele.

Institutions with vacancies in Aug/Sept 1992 (see Ch 5): Hull 24 pts. Very few vacancies declared. The more popular universities asked for 20 pts.

ADVICE FOR MATURE STUDENTS

14% of students on American Studies courses are 'mature'. Some part-time courses are available.

GRADUATE EMPLOYMENT

New Graduates' destinations (percentages) 1991:
Permanent employment: U 64.
Unemployment: U 19.
Further studies (all types): U 25.

ANATOMICAL SCIENCE/ANATOMY

Special subject requirements: 2-3 A-levels in science/ mathematics subjects; chemistry sometimes 'required' or 'preferred'.

NB Institutions may raise or lower the level of published offers depending either on the quality or otherwise of individual applications or the numbers of applications received; grades/points offered may be adjusted downwards after A-level results. The level of an offer is not indicative of the quality of a course.

30 pts.	**Cambridge** - AAA potential recommended (Nat Sci/Anat)
20 pts.	**Birmingham** - BCC (Medical Sci - 2 from biol/chem/phys)
18 pts.	**Aberdeen** - CCC-CCD/BC (Anatomy)
	Bristol - CCC/BB (Anat Sci)
	Glasgow - CCC-CCD/BC (Anatomy)
	Liverpool - CCC/BB (Anat Comb; Anat/H Biol) (4 AS)
	London (King's) - 18 pts approx (Anat)
	London (UC) - CCC (Anat/Dev Biol)
	Manchester - 18 pts approx (Anat)
	Sheffield - CCC (Anatomy; Anat/Cell Biol) (6 AS) (BTEC Ms)
16 pts.	**Dundee** - (Anatomy; Anat/Physio)
14 pts.	**Dundee** - CDD/BC (Med Sci)

Alternative offers:

IB offers: **Aberdeen** 26 pts; **Bristol** H655.

SCE offers: **Aberdeen** BBBC; **Dundee** BBB or BBCC; **Glasgow** BBBB or BBB; **Sheffield** BBBB.

CHOOSING YOUR COURSE (See also Ch 1)

Subject information: Anatomical Science/Anatomy is a highly specialised scientific study covering the biological sciences and a variety of research techniques. The most appropriate alternative course would be Biological Sciences in which anatomy may be included as an option. The subject is an excellent basis for careers in neuroscience, molecular endocrinology, oral biology or skeletal tissue research. See also under **Physiology**.

Course highlights: Birmingham (Medical Sci) Year 3 options in anatomy, pharmacology, physiology. **Bristol** Unique in its emphasis on comparative mammalian anatomy but not based primarily on human material. High research rating for **Oxford**, **London (UC)** and **Bristol**. NOW CHECK PROSPECTUSES FOR ALL COURSES.

ADMISSIONS INFORMATION

Number of applicants per place (approx): Bristol 7; **Liverpool** 8; **Sheffield** 7.

Selection interviews: Bristol; Cambridge.

Offers to applicants repeating A-levels: Higher Bristol (BBC); **Possibly higher** Liverpool.

Examples of interview questions: What interests you about the study of anatomy? What career do you hope to follow when you graduate? (See also Interview questions under **Biology** and **Physiology**.)

AFTER A-LEVELS ADVICE

Institutions which may accept the same points score after A-levels: Liverpool.

Institutions demanding the actual grades offered after A-levels: Bristol.

Institutions with vacancies in Aug/Sept 1992 (see Ch 5): Aberdeen; Bristol 18 pts; Dundee; several other universities declared vacancies between 16 and 12 pts.

GRADUATE EMPLOYMENT

New Graduates' destinations (percentages) 1991:
Permanent employment: U 75.
Unemployment: U 19.
Further studies (all types): U 53.

ANIMAL SCIENCES

Special subject requirements: 2-3 A-levels from science/mathematics subjects; chemistry usually required.

NB Institutions may raise or lower the level of published offers depending either on the quality or otherwise of individual applications or the numbers of applications received; grades/points offered may be adjusted downwards after A-level results. The level of an offer is not indicative of the quality of a course.

30 pts.	**Cambridge** - AAA potential recommended (Nat Sci)
20 pts.	**St Andrews** - BCC (An Sci)
	York - BCC-CCC (Physiol; Animal Phys) (BTEC 4M)
18 pts.	**Aberdeen** - CCC-CCD/BC (Ani Sci PS)

        Glasgow - CCC-CCD/BC (Pl/An Sci)
        Leicester - BCD-CCC (An Phys)
        Sheffield - CCC-CCD (AP Biol)

16pts.   **Bangor** - CCD-CDD/BC-CC (Anim Man; Anim Biol) (4 AS)
        Edinburgh - CCD (Animal Sci)
        Glasgow - CCD (Dev/Biol)

14pts.   approx
        Coventry - CDD/BC (Equine St)
        Leeds - CDD (ANP; An Sci; ANP Biol)
        London (Wye) - CDD (Anim Sci)
        Newcastle - CDD/BC (Ag Env Sci/An Sci; An Prod/Sci)
        Nottingham - CDD/CC (Animal Sci) BTEC 3M)
        Reading - CDD/CC (Anim Sci A)
        SAC (Au) - CDD/CD (App Pl An Sci)

Higher National Diploma courses:
  4pts. **and below**
        Harper Adams (CAg) – (Animal Care)
        Horse Studies courses offered at Cheltenham & Glos (CHE), Coventry, Humberside, Welsh
          (CAg), West Oxfordshire (Coll).

Higher National Diploma courses (Scotland):
        SAC (Au)

Alternative offers:

IB offers: **Bangor** 30-28 pts inc H55 in biol/chem; **Nottingham** 28 pts in 7 subjects, 24 pts in 6 subjects.

SCE offers: **Aberdeen** BBBC; **Glasgow** BBBB or BBB; **Leeds** BBBCC; **St Andrews** BBBC; **Sheffield** BBBB.

CHOOSING YOUR COURSE (See also Ch 1)

Subject information: A popular course choice for those who fail to obtain a place in Veterinary Science. The course covers a biological study of animals, reproduction and nutrition. Horse Studies has also become popular in recent years, particularly at HND level. Check Agriculture courses for suitable alternative studies.

Course highlights: Bangor Course covers parasitology, immunology, farm animal welfare and behaviour. (Anim Biol) In year 3 options include Animal Biology, Applied Zoology or Marine Zoology. **Coventry** (Equine St) Modular core so Equine Studies can be combined with Business Studies or other courses; 70 horses in commercial stud. **Leeds** Good contacts and job prospects in animal nutrition and pharmaceuticals. NOW CHECK PROSPECTUSES FOR ALL COURSES.

Study opportunities abroad: Edinburgh (E).

Work opportunities abroad: Leeds D NL.

ADMISSIONS INFORMATION

Number of applicants per place (approx): Bangor 5; **Leeds** 3; **Liverpool** 6; **Reading** 10.

General Studies acceptable: Aberdeen; Leeds.

Selection interviews: Cambridge; Leeds (some).

Admissions Tutors' advice: Leeds Practical farming experience useful.

> **Examples of interview questions:** What interests you about a course in Animal Sciences? What do your parents think about your choice of course? (See also **Interview questions** under **Veterinary Science**).

GAP YEAR ADVICE

Institutions accepting a Gap Year: Most institutions; **Coventry** Experience of the equine industry useful. Gain riding experience during the gap year since this is not part of the course; **Newcastle** Keep a record or diary or photographs or anything seen relevant to the course.

Institutions willing to defer entry after A-levels (see Ch 5): Newcastle; York.

AFTER A-LEVELS ADVICE

Institutions which may accept the same points score after A-levels: Bangor; Leeds.

Institutions which may accept under-achieving applicants after A-levels: Aberdeen; Bangor; Leeds; Nottingham.

Offers to applicants repeating A-levels: Higher Nottingham; **Same** Bangor, Leeds.

Institutions with vacancies in Aug/Sept 1992 (see Ch 5): Aberdeen; Leeds 14 pts; Newcastle 8 pts; York 18 pts; most institutions likely to have vacancies in 1993.

ADVICE FOR MATURE STUDENTS

About 5% of students at **Leeds** and **Bangor** are 'mature'. A suitable background in biology and chemistry is helpful but formal qualifications may not be required.

ANTHROPOLOGY (See also Social Anthropology)

Special subject requirements: GCSE (grades A-C) mathematics may be required.

NB Institutions may raise or lower the level of published offers depending either on the quality or otherwise of individual applications or the numbers of applications received; grades/points offered may be adjusted downwards after A-level results. The level of an offer is not indicative of the quality of a course.

30 pts.	**Cambridge** – AAA potential recommended (Arch/Anth) (See also under **Archaeology**)
24 pts.	**St Andrews** – BBB (Soc Ant) (4 AS)
22 pts.	**Durham** – BBC (All courses) (4 AS)
	Edinburgh – BBC (Soc Anthr courses)
20 pts.	**Brunel** – BCC/BB (SA Soc; SA Psy) (4 AS) (BTEC Ms)
	Kent – BCC (All courses)
	London (Gold) – BCC (Anth Comm St; Anth/Soc)
	London (LSE) – BCC approx (Anth Arts)
	Sussex – BCC/BC (All courses)
	Swansea – BCC/BB (Soc Anth/Sociol) (BTEC 1-2D+Ms approx)
18 pts.	**Belfast** – CCC/BC (Anth Soc Sc)
	Hull – CCC/BC (Soc/S Ant)
	London (UC) – CCC (Anthrop Sci)
	Swansea – CCC-CCD/BB-BC (Dev St/S Anth; Soc Anth)
16 pts.	**London (SOAS)** – BB (All courses)
	Oxford Brookes – CCD/BC (Modular) (4 AS)

Alternative offers:

IB offers: **East Anglia** 30 pts; **Durham** H554; **St Andrews** 30 pts.

SCE offers: **Edinburgh** BBBBB; **St Andrews** BBBB.

CHOOSING YOUR COURSE (See also Ch 1)

> **Subject information:** The study will include some biology, some history and a study of the cultures, rituals and beliefs of mankind (ancient and modern) with extensions into art, kinship, family, religion, political and legal structures. Psychology, Sociology or Religious Studies courses might also be of interest as alternatives.

Course highlights: Belfast (Anth Soc Sc) Topics covered include modes of livelihood, perception and belief, marriage and organisation of public life. **Cambridge** (Arch/Anth) Areas of study cover archaeology, biological anthropology - involving evolution of the species and ecology - and social anthropology. **Durham** (Anth) Teaching offered in social and biological anthropology (no previous knowledge assumed). **Edinburgh** (Soc Anthr) Human perceptions of the supernatural and the systems of belief covered in this course. **Kent** (Soc Anth) Second year Foundation courses in political and economic anthropology, systems of ritual belief and research practices. **London (Gold)** First two years concentrate on basic anthropological concepts such as marriage and kinship, and religious and moral systems; wide range of course units are available in year 3. **London (LSE)** (Soc Anth) Course on the introduction to Social Anthropology should be taken by students embarking on Part I; special subject is chosen for study in years 2 & 3. **London (SOAS)** (Soc Anth) Year 1 students take courses in social anthropology and social theory, and study the ethnography of a selected area of Africa or Asia. **London (UC)** (Anthrop Sci) All three branches of anthropology - biological, social and material culture - covered. **St Andrews** (Soc An) Topics covered in years 3 and 4 include gender studies, communities in Britain, hunting and gathering societies, literacy and semiotics. **Sussex** Special emphasis given to study of Europe and UK. **Swansea** (Soc Anth/Sociol) In year 1 students take social anthropology, sociology and four other courses in Faculty of Economic and Social Studies. NOW CHECK PROSPECTUSES FOR ALL COURSES.

Study opportunities abroad: London (Gold) (E), **(UC)** (E); **Oxford Brookes** (E).

ADMISSIONS INFORMATION

Number of applicants per place (approx): Belfast 10; **Durham** 14; **Kent** 10; **London (SOAS)** 8; **Oxford Brookes** 17; **Sussex** 10; **Swansea** 10.

General Studies acceptable: Durham.

Selection interviews: Cambridge; Durham; Oxford Brookes (some).

Offers to applicants repeating A-levels: Possibly higher Durham, Oxford Brookes.

Admissions Tutors' advice: Durham (Nat Sci) A-levels exclusively in arts or science subjects not required. The average A-level points score for Combined courses with Archaeology, Geography and Psychology is 22-26 pts.

> **Examples of interview questions:** What stresses exist among the nomads of the North African desert? What is a society? What are the problems of relating to a foreign culture? What is speech? If you dug up a stone axe what could you learn from it? What are the values created by a capitalist society? Discuss the role of women since the beginning of this century. (Since anthropology is not an A-level subject, applicants should expect their knowledge of the subject to be tested.)

GAP YEAR ADVICE

Institutions willing to defer entry after A-levels (see Ch 5): Brunel; St Andrews; Swansea.

AFTER A-LEVELS ADVICE

Institutions which may accept the same points score after A-levels: Durham; Oxford Brookes.

Institutions with vacancies in Aug/Sept 1992 (see Ch 5): A small number of vacancies existed with offers in the 20 to 12 pts range, including **Swansea** 18 pts.

ADVICE FOR MATURE STUDENTS

Durham has several 'mature' students on its course and would consider applicants with qualifications other than A-levels.

GRADUATE EMPLOYMENT

New Graduates' destinations (percentages) 1991:
Permanent employment: U 62; P 44.
Unemployment: U 29; P 29.
Further studies (all types): U 29; P 20.

ARABIC

Special subject requirements: A-level in a language sometimes preferred.

NB Institutions may raise or lower the level of published offers depending either on the quality or otherwise of individual applications or the numbers of applications received; grades/points offered may be adjusted downwards after A-level results. The level of an offer is not indicative of the quality of a course.

30 pts.	**Cambridge/Oxford** - AAA potential recommended (Arab/Mod; Arab/Class)
24 pts.	**Durham** - BBB (Arab/Pol)
	St Andrews - BBB (Arab) (4 AS)
22 pts.	**Durham** - BBC (All courses except under **24 pts**)
	Edinburgh - BBC (Arabic courses)
	Glasgow - BBC (Arabic courses)
20 pts.	**Exeter** - BCC-CCC ((Arab/Islam; Arab St) (4 AS)
	Leeds - BCC (All joint courses; see also **18 pts**)
18 pts.	**Leeds** - 18 pts (Mod Arabic)
16 pts.	**London (SOAS)** - BB (All courses)
12 pts.	**Westminster** - CC-CD (All courses)

Alternative offers:

IB offers: **Exeter** 30 pts; **St Andrews** 30 pts.

SCE offers: **Edinburgh** BBBB; **Glasgow** BBBB; **St Andrews** BBBB.

CHOOSING YOUR COURSE (See also Ch 1)

Subject information: Linguists may wish to extend their interest into a different language form, although in this subject interests in the Middle Eastern cultures must also predominate. Such courses, however, should never be under-estimated as they involve considerable study. Alternative courses would depend on the student's preferences towards other unusual languages or courses in Middle Eastern or African Studies, Archaeology, History etc.

Course highlights: Durham Emphasis on written and spoken Arabic. **Exeter** Emphasis on Classical Arabic language and literature. **Leeds** Course concentrates on language as a tool for research, professional jobs and the media. **St Andrews** See under **Arts**. NOW CHECK PROSPECTUSES FOR ALL COURSES.

ADMISSIONS INFORMATION

Number of applicants per place (approx): Durham 4; **Leeds** 5.

General Studies acceptable: Exeter; Leeds.

Selection interviews: Cambridge; Durham; Leeds; Oxford.

Offers to applicants repeating A-levels: Same Durham, Exeter, Leeds.

Examples of interview questions: Why do you wish to study Arabic? What areas of interest have you concerning the Middle East?

GAP YEAR ADVICE

Institutions accepting a Gap Year: Leeds (background reading in history recommended).

Institutions willing to defer entry after A-levels (see Ch 5): Leeds; St Andrews.

AFTER A-LEVELS ADVICE

Institutions which may accept the same points score after A-levels: Leeds.

Institutions which may accept under-achieving applicants after A-levels: Leeds.

Institutions with vacancies in Aug/Sept 1992 (see Ch 5): Leeds 18 pts. Westminster had several vacancies on their combined courses with other languages.

ARCHAEOLOGY

Special subject requirements: Latin and Greek occasionally 'required' or 'preferred' at A-level. GCSE (grade A-C) language required.

NB Institutions may raise or lower the level of published offers depending either on the quality or otherwise of individual applications or the numbers of applications received; grades/points offered may be adjusted downwards after A-level results. The level of an offer is not indicative of the quality of a course.

30 pts. **Cambridge** - AAA potential recommended (Arch/Anth)
22 pts. **Bristol** - BBC-BCC/BB (All courses except under **20 pts**)
Durham - BBC (Arch/Anthrop; Arch/Hist)
Edinburgh - BBC (All courses)
Glasgow - BBC (Archaeol - MA)
London (SOAS) - BBC/BB (All courses)
Newcastle - BBC/BB (Anc Hist/Arch)
Nottingham - BBC-CCC (Archaeol; Arch Hist)
York - BBC/BB (Arch/Hist EQ) (BTEC Ds+Ms)

20 pts.	**York** - BBC-BCC/BB-BC (Archaeol; Archaeol/Ed) (6 AS) (BTEC Ds+Ms)
	Bradford - BCC/BB (Arch Sci; Arch) (BTEC 3M)
	Bristol - BCC/BB-BC (Arch/Geol)
	Cardiff - BCC-CCC/BB (Archaeol/AH; Archaeol/MH)
	Durham - BCC (Archaeol)
	Exeter - BCC/BB (A Hist/Arch) (4-6 AS) (BTEC Ms)
	Leicester - BCC-BCD (Arch Arts)
	London (UC) - BCC (approx) (All courses)
	Manchester - 20 pts approx (Combined courses)
	Newcastle - BCC-CCC/BB (Arch) (6 AS) (BTEC no standard offer)
	Reading - BCC (Arch)
	Sheffield - BCC-CCC-BCD/BB (Arch/Geog; Arch Pre/Med H; Arch Sci) (4 AS)
	Warwick - BCC (Anc Hist Arch)
18 pts.	**Belfast** - CCC/BC-CC (Arch Sci; Archaeol; Pal/Arch)
	Birmingham - BCD (Archaeol)
	Cardiff - CCC/BC (Archaeol Arts)
	Glasgow - CCC-CCD/BC (Archaeol - BSc)
	Leicester - CCC-BCD (Arch Sci)
	Liverpool - CCC/BB-BC (Archeol; Hominid St; Sci Arch) (4-5 AS)
	Southampton - BCD-CCC (All courses)
16 pts.	**and below**
	Cardiff - 16 pts (Archaeol Sci; Arch Cons)
	London (King's) - CCD approx (Class Arch)
	St David's - CCD/10 pts (AES; A Hist/Arch)
12 pts.	**Bournemouth** - (Arch BCT) (BTEC students assessed individually)

Higher National Diploma courses:
  2 pts.   Bournemouth

Alternative offers:

IB offers: **Bradford** 24 pts; **Bristol** (AAH/GK; AAH/Lat) H655, (Arch/Geol) H555; **Cardiff** 28 pts; **Edinburgh** H655; **Exeter** 30 pts; **Liverpool** 30 pts inc 5 and 6 in sciences; **York** 28 pts.

Irish offers: **Liverpool** BBCCC.

SCE offers: **Durham** BBB; **Edinburgh** AAB or BBBB; **Glasgow** AAB or BBBB (MA), ABB or BBB or BBBB (BSc); **Liverpool** BBBB; **Newcastle** BBBC; **Sheffield** BBBB; **York** BBBBB.

CHOOSING YOUR COURSE (See also Ch 1)

> **Subject information:** It would be unusual for an applicant to pursue this degree course without having been involved in some basic field work. Studies can cover European, Greek, Roman or African spheres etc. Details of any such experience should be given on the UCAS form. As alternatives, History, Classics or History of Art, and Design courses might also be considered.

Course highlights: Courses at **Oxford, Cambridge, London, Bradford, Liverpool, Sheffield, Durham** have a scientific emphasis. **Belfast** (Arch) Course covers prehistoric/Bronze Age, Great Britain and Europe. **Bradford** (Arch Sci) British and European history and scientific methods of investigation, attractive to A-level scientists. **Bristol** (Anc Med St) Emphasis on archaeology, ancient history and art. **Bournemouth** Course addresses present and foreseeable vocational needs in archaeology. Transfer possible to Heritage Conservation or vice-versa. New course in Building Conservation Technology also planned. **Cambridge** (Arch/Anth) Course focuses on three areas: Archaeology, Biological Anthropology, Social Anthropology. **Cardiff** (Arch) British and European archaeology. For students with appropriate science background, particularly chemistry, there is also a degree course in Archaeological Conservation. **Durham** (Arch) Prehistoric Roman and early medieval periods. **Edinburgh** (Arch) Emphasis on prehistoric periods, from origins of man to periods contemporary with Greek and Roman civilisation. Opportunities for practical training, the use of computers and processing of air-photographs. **Exeter** (Arch) Western Europe with special reference to British Isles from origins of man to Middle Ages. **Leicester** (Arch St) Study covers Europe, Western Asia, Africa, Australasia and the Americas. Archaeological methodology also studied. **London (SOAS)** (Art/Arch) Programme includes Africa, Islamic World, Iran, SE Asia and China. **London (UC)** (Arch) Six courses offered in arts, science, classical, western Asiatic and medieval archaeology. **Newcastle** (Arch) First year covers introduction to archaeology, prehistoric Britain, Britain in the first millenium AD, archaeological theory and practice, and the option to study a language. **Nottingham** (Arch) Study of development of civilisation in Britain and Europe over 11,000 years; Subsidiary language study possible. **Reading** (Arch) Techniques of excavation and theory, methodology and interpretation of archaeology. Subjects cover British and European archaeology and archaeology and science. **Sheffield** (Arch Sci) Students to bias studies towards prehistoric archaeology or Roman or medieval archaeology at beginning of second year. **Southampton** (Arch) Five themes in second year: subsistence and survival, emergence of complex societies, art and society, archaeology, and history and scientific methods. Options in third year range from Saxon England and Roman Spain to computers in archaeology. **York** (Arch) Course concerned with archaeological method and theory. Teaching concentrates on the archaeology of Britain and north-west Europe from Iron Age to high Middle Ages. NOW CHECK PROSPECTUSES FOR ALL COURSES.

Study opportunities abroad: Bradford (E); **Leicester** (E); **York** (E) IRE IT FR.

ADMISSIONS INFORMATION

Number of applicants per place (approx): Birmingham 9; **Bournemouth** 4; **Bradford** 5; **Cardiff** 6; **Durham** 6; **Liverpool** 9; **Newcastle** 12; **St David's** 2; **Sheffield** 5; **York** 12.

General Studies acceptable: Bournemouth (2); Bradford; Exeter (2); Liverpool; Newcastle; St David's (2).

Selection interviews: Bradford; Cambridge; Durham; Glasgow; Hull; Liverpool; Newcastle; St David's (some); Sheffield.

Offers to applicants repeating A-levels: Same Bradford, Durham, Liverpool; St David's.

Admissions Tutors' advice: Bournemouth Four weeks' archaeological experience required. **Bradford** Some archaeological experience preferred. **Newcastle** Prior experience desirable; offers depend on experience. **Nottingham** French or German useful.

> **Examples of interview questions:** How would you interpret archaeological evidence, for example a pile of flints, coins? How would you treat modern knowledge of tribal behaviour in connection with archaeology? What is stratification? How would you date archaeological remains? What books have you read on the subject? What career do you have in mind after completing the course? Is it archaeology's job to write world history? How did you become interested in archaeology? What do you hope to get from a university course in Archaeology? With what archaeological sites in the UK are you familiar? How do you see Man's position in the world?

GAP YEAR ADVICE

Institutions accepting a Gap Year: Most institutions; **Bournemouth** Obtain some practical experience or closely related work (museums or heritage). Only apply for gap year after exam results are known. **Bradford** Travel. Get some experience in field archaeology.

Institutions willing to defer entry after A-levels (see Ch 5): Newcastle; York (prefer not).

AFTER A-LEVELS ADVICE

Institutions which may accept the same points score after A-levels: Bradford; Bristol; Durham; Liverpool; St David's; York.

Institutions demanding the actual grades offered after A-levels: Newcastle.

Institutions which may accept under-achieving applicants after A-levels: Bradford; Edinburgh; Glasgow; Leicester; Liverpool; Newcastle; St David's; Sheffield; York.

Institutions with vacancies in Aug/Sept 1992 (see Ch 5): Bradford 20 pts; Bristol (Arch/Geol) 14 pts; St David's 10 pts. Popular universities with vacancies prepared to consider applicants with 20 to 12 pts.

ADVICE FOR MATURE STUDENTS

Some universities have up to 20% intake of mature students. Apart from motivation and academic potential, practical experience is essential.

GRADUATE EMPLOYMENT

New Graduates' destinations (percentages) 1991:
Permanent employment: U 60.
Unemployment: U 32.
Further studies (all types): U 25. *Main career destinations (approx):* Legal 41; Financial 12; Admin 11; Business 9; Medical/Social 9; Secretarial 8.

York (1987-91) Out of 40 graduates, 27 entered careers associated with the subject. The remainder entered library and museum work and other clerical occupations.

ARCHITECTURE

Special subject requirements: One A-level from mathematics or physics occasionally required. English language and mathematics GCSE (grades A-C) necessary.

NB Institutions may raise or lower the level of published offers depending either on the quality or otherwise of individual applications or the numbers of applications received; grades/points offered may be adjusted downwards after A-level results. The level of an offer is not indicative of the quality of a course.

30 pts.	**Cambridge** - AAA potential recommended
24 pts.	**Bath** - BBB/24 pts (Arch) (BTEC Ms)
	Edinburgh - BBB (Archit - MA)
	Newcastle - BBB (Archit) (4 AS) (BTEC 2M level IV + 1M level III)
	Sheffield - BBB/BB (Archit) (BTEC 2D+2M)
	Strathclyde - BBB (Archit; Arch/Env)
22 pts.	**Cardiff** - BBC (Arch) (BTEC 3D+2M)
	Dundee - BBC (Archit)
	Heriot-Watt - BBC (Archit)
	Liverpool - BBC/BB (Archit)
	Manchester - 22 pts approx (Arch)
	Nottingham - BBC (Archit; Arch/Env Des)
20 pts.	**Belfast** - BCC (Archit)
	Dundee - BCC (with a very good portfolio) (Archit)
	Edinburgh - BCC (Archit Hist)
	Glasgow - BCC (Archit)
	London (UC) - BCC (Architecture)
18 pts.	**Manchester Met** - CCC/CC (Arch) (4 AS) (BTEC 4M)
	Portsmouth - CCC (Arch)
	Westminster - CCC/CC (Arch)
16 pts.	**Brighton** - 16 pts (Arch)
	De Montfort - 16 pts (Arch) (BTEC 2D+4M)

Kingston - 16 pts (Arch) (4 AS) (BTEC 5M)
Liverpool John Moores - CCD/BC (Archit) (6 AS)
Robert Gordon - CCD/CD (Arch)
14 pts. Oxford Brookes - (Arch) (4 AS)
12 pts. Central England - CC (Arch) (BTEC 3+4M)
Greenwich - 12 pts (Arch) (4 AS) (BTEC 5M)
Leeds Met - CC (Arch) (BTEC 3+6M)
North London - 12 pts (Arch) (BTEC 3M)
Plymouth - 12 pts (Arch) (4 AS) (BTEC 5M)
South Bank - CC (Arch) (BTEC 3M)
Westminster - 12 pts (Arch Eng) (BTEC M in maths)
10 pts. and below
East London - 10 pts (Arch)
Huddersfield - (Arch St - overseas students only)
Humberside - EE (Architecture) (BTEC 4M)
Kent (IAD - Canterbury) - No standard offer
London (AA School) - (Arch)

Franchised degree and HND courses (see Ch 5):
South Bank - Guildford (Coll); Mid Kent (Coll); North East Surrey(CAT); South Bank (Coll); Vauxhall (Coll); Waltham Forest (Coll); Westminster (Coll).

Higher National Diploma courses (England and Wales):
Swansea (IHE) Arch Stained Glass

Higher National Diploma courses (Scotland):
Robert Gordon (Arch Tech)

Alternative offers:

IB offers: **Bath** 30 pts H655 inc 6 in maths; **Brighton** 24 pts inc 12 pts 3 Highers; **Cardiff** 20 pts; **Central England** 28 pts; **Glasgow** 24 pts; **Greenwich** 24 pts inc 12 pts 3 Highers; **Heriot-Watt** 30 pts; **Kingston** 24 pts; **Newcastle** 30 pts; **Nottingham** H555 in maths/physics/art; **Portsmouth** 26 pts.

SCE offers: **Cardiff** BBBB; **Dundee** BBBC; **Edinburgh** ABBBB or AAAB; **Glasgow** BBBC; **Greenwich** BBB; **Heriot-Watt** BBBC; **Liverpool** BBBB; **Newcastle** BBB; **Robert Gordon** BBC; **Sheffield** BBBB; **Strathclyde** ABBB/BBBBC.

CHOOSING YOUR COURSE (See also Ch 1)

Subject information: Institutions offering architecture have very similar courses (some variations are given below). An awareness of the relationship between people and the built environment is necessary, plus the ability to create and to express oneself in terms of drawings, paintings etc. Most architecture schools will expect to see a portfolio of art work, particularly drawings of buildings or parts of buildings. Some work experience or work shadowing is advisable prior to submitting the UCAS form. Landscape architecture, estate management, building, civil engineering or town and country planning courses might also be considered as alternatives.

Course highlights: Newcastle, Leeds Met, Brighton, Plymouth Emphasis on design. **Bath** Year 1 common with Civil Engineering and Building: some transfers possible. **Brighton** Parallel Interior Design course; language courses; European exchange. (Arch) Balance between environmental needs, technology and creative design **Cardiff** (Arch) Visual communication, interior design, town planning and landscape design are included throughout BSc course. School of Architecture works in close liaison with the Town Planning Department in urban design, housing and landscape. **Central England** (Arch) Reputed to be one of the largest Schools in country and draws strength from its association with the Departments of Planning, Landscape and Construction and Surveying. **De Montfort** (Arch) Some emphasis on information technology and computing. **Glasgow** Studio-orientated School of

Architecture. Emphasis on building design. **Greenwich** Studio-based course, multi-mode, with possibility of transfer between full-time and part-time study. **Heriot-Watt** School of Architecture housed in Edinburgh College of Art; students do joint courses with Planning and Housing. **Humberside** (Arch) Subject topics include interior design, computer-aided architectural design and architecture of developing countries. **Kent (IAD)** (Arch) Optional studies in graphic design, painting, sculpture and photography also available. **Liverpool** (Arch) Strong emphasis on design, having close links with building, civil engineering and civic design areas. **Manchester Met** Architecture, Landscape Design, Interior Design in same department. **Newcastle** (Arch) Course covers theory and history of architecture, building technology, studio design projects and environmental design. **North London** (Arch) Course includes environmental psychology and sociology, and architectural history and philosophy. **Nottingham** (Arch) Course stresses integration of technical work with projects but is without a strong scientific bias. **Portsmouth** (Arch) The second and third year studies focus on three themes: the house, urban residential and commercial buildings, and a public building. **Robert Gordon** Course includes computer aided design, architectural history and management studies. **Westminster** (Arch Eng) Gives exemption from RIBA Part I. Attention given to history and theory of architecture. NOW CHECK PROSPECTUSES FOR ALL COURSES.

Study opportunities abroad: Bath (E); **Brighton** (E) FR G IT SP; **Central England** (E) USA G D NL P SP; **De Montfort** (E); **Duncan of Jordanstone** (E); **Dundee** (E); **East London** (E); **Glasgow** (E); **Glasgow (SA)** (E); **Heriot-Watt** (E); **Humberside** (E); **Kent (Inst)** (E); **Kingston** (E); **Liverpool John Moores** (E); **Newcastle** (E) G IT, SI (British Council sponsored); **Oxford Brookes** (E); **South Bank** FR; **Strathclyde** (E).

Work opportunities abroad: De Montfort NL G; **Dundee** EUR; **Greenwich** FR IT G; **Heriot-Watt** USA SW D FE AUS; **Manchester Met** USA EUR HK G M.

ADMISSIONS INFORMATION

Number of applicants per place (approx): Bath 25; **Belfast** 9; **Brighton** 32; **Cambridge** 5; **Cardiff** 12; **Central England** 14; **De Montfort** 18; **Dundee** 10; **Edinburgh** 18; **Glasgow** 16; **Greenwich** 6; **Humberside** 5; **Heriot-Watt** 20; **Kent (IAD)** 4; **Leeds Met** 12; **Liverpool** 18; **Liverpool John Moores** 16; **Manchester Met** 25; **Newcastle** 20; **Nottingham** 30; **Oxford Brookes** 15; **Plymouth** 11; **Robert Gordon** 5; **Sheffield** 20; **Strathclyde** 10.

General Studies acceptable: Belfast; De Montfort; Glasgow; Greenwich; Huddersfield; Leeds Met (JMB only); Liverpool; Liverpool John Moores; Manchester Met as a third subject; Newcastle; Oxford Brookes; South Bank (discretionary).

Selection interviews: The majority of universities and colleges interview for Architecture and most require a portfolio of art work. **Oxford Brookes** set an aptitude test at interview.

Offers to applicants repeating A-levels: Higher Huddersfield (2 pts); **Possibly higher** Brighton, Central England, De Montfort, Glasgow, Liverpool, Manchester Met, Newcastle; **Same** Bath, Belfast, Greenwich, Heriot-Watt, Kingston, Liverpool John Moores, North London, Nottingham, Oxford Brookes, Robert Gordon, South Bank.

Admissions Tutors' advice: De Montfort All applicants must attend an open day and submit a portfolio or art/design work as evidence of creativity. **Dundee** Bring a portfolio of creative work (14 best pieces). **Newcastle** accepts design and technology at A-level. Some science/ technology study in 6th forms expected to promote broad educational experience. **Westminster** (Arch Eng) Portfolio of sketches, photographs, technical drawings preferred.

> **Examples of interview questions:** What is the role of the architect in society? If you were to design a building in Windermere what type of materials would you consider? Discuss one historic and one 20th century building you admire. Architects should be creative; how can you demonstrate that you are creative? Who is your favourite architect? What sort of buildings do you want to design? How are you suited to architecture? Talk about your A-level art work. Have you ever visited an architect's office? What do you do out of school? Do you like the university buildings? Do you read any architectural journals? What inspired you to take architecture? What do you understand

by the word 'design'? What books do you read for pleasure? What exhibitions have you visited recently? What are the Prince of Wales' views on architecture? Do you agree with them?

GAP YEAR ADVICE

Institutions accepting a Gap Year: Most institutions; **Bath** Get some architectural and drawing experience. **Brighton** Get involved in the subject area eg, exhibitions, lectures, visits, reading. **De Montfort** Work experience in an architect's office advantageous. **Dundee** Travel – with a sketchbook or camera or work in an architect's office. **Greenwich** Travel, sketch, but preferably work in an architect's office or surveying practice; **Heriot-Watt** Tell us what you plan to do in the gap year. **Newcastle** Do a one-year Foundation art course or work with an architect or travel. **Manchester Met, Cardiff, Glasgow** Travel and view modern architecture abroad.

Institutions willing to defer entry after A-levels (see Ch 5): Bath; De Montfort; Dundee; Glasgow (No); Greenwich; Heriot-Watt; Humberside; Kingston; Newcastle; South Bank (No); Westminster (Arch Eng).

AFTER A-LEVELS ADVICE

Institutions which may accept the same points score after A-levels: Brighton; Central England; De Montfort; Glasgow; Greenwich; Huddersfield; Kingston; Liverpool; Manchester Met; North London; Oxford Brookes; Plymouth; Portsmouth; Robert Gordon; South Bank; Strathclyde; Westminster (perhaps).

Institutions demanding the actual grades offered after A-levels: Bath; Belfast; Glasgow (in most cases); Leeds Met; Liverpool John Moores; Newcastle; Nottingham.

Institutions which may accept under-achieving applicants after A-levels: Bath; Brighton; Central England; Glasgow; Heriot-Watt; Liverpool; Liverpool John Moores; Newcastle; Nottingham; Portsmouth; South Bank; Strathclyde; Westminster (perhaps).

Institutions with vacancies in Aug/Sept 1992 (see Ch 5): Institutions included Dundee; Glasgow (offers depend on interview and portfolio); Kent (IAD) 10 pts; Kingston 12 pts from 2 A-levels; Robert Gordon (HND) 5 pts; Strathclyde; Westminster (Arch Eng) 12 pts. Offers from universities ranged from 24–16 pts and sometimes lower.

ADVICE FOR MATURE STUDENTS

Approximately 7% of students on Architecture courses are 'mature'. Formal qualifications may be waived but a portfolio of art/design work is important.

GRADUATE EMPLOYMENT

New Graduates' destinations (percentages) 1991:
Permanent employment: U 74; P 62; C 67.
Unemployment: U 19; P 31; C 17.
Further studies (all types): U 14; P 26; C 14.

ART (Fine/History/Design)

Art courses leading to degree qualifications can be divided into two main groups:

(1) Degree courses for which two A-level passes and five GCSE subjects at grade C or above are required as a minimum qualification in universities, colleges and institutes of higher education. (See table below.)

(2) Art and Design degree courses (specialist practical art courses) in universities, colleges and schools of art, for which applications are submitted through the Art and Design Admissions Registry (ADAR) (see Chapter 3). Entry to these courses is normally through a Foundation course in Art for which A-level passes may not be necessary if applicants have a minimum of five subjects at GCSE grade C or above. Details of these degree courses appear under the degree course titles as follows:- **Fine Art, Graphic Design, Textiles/Fashion, Three Dimensional Design, Furniture Design, Interior Design, Silversmithing, Industrial Design, Carpet Design** and **Theatre Design**.

(1) Courses for which two A-level passes are required.

Special subject requirements: modern language or art may be required at A-level for some courses. GCSE (grades A-C) in a modern language is usually required.

NB Institutions may raise or lower the level of published offers depending either on the quality or otherwise of individual applications or the numbers of applications received; grades/points offered may be adjusted downwards after A-level results. The level of an offer is not indicative of the quality of a course.

Universities below marked (P) require applicants to submit a portfolio of art work through a central scheme. Inspection of these portfolios takes place in London in January each year. Details of the scheme can be obtained from the Department of Fine Art, University of Reading (see Chapter 3 for address).

The following courses are outside the ADAR scheme:

30 pts.	**Cambridge** (Hist Art)/**Oxford** (Fine Art) - AAA potential recommended Foundation preferred.
24 pts.	**St Andrews** - BBB (Art; Art H/Class) (4 AS)
	Warwick - BBB-BBC (Hist Art)
22 pts.	**Bristol** - BBC (Hist of Art joint courses) (BTEC D+M)
	East Anglia - BBC/BB (Hist/Art; Art Hist/Lit; HAW) (BTEC 2/3M)
	Edinburgh - (P) BBC (Art; Art Hist; Fine Art; joint courses)
	Glasgow - BBC (Hist Art)
	Leeds - (P) BBC-BCC (All courses) (4 AS)
	Leicester - BBC/AB-BB (Art Hist)
	London (Court) - BBC (Art Hist)
	Manchester - BBC approx (Hist Art)
	Nottingham - BBC-BCC (Art Hist)
	Plymouth - BBC inc art (Fine Art/Lang)
	York - BBC (Hist/Art EQ)
21 pts.	**Lancaster** - (P) (Art/Mktg)
20 pts.	**Aberdeen** - BCC (Art Hist)
	Birmingham - BCC (Hist of Art)
	Edinburgh - BCC (Arch Hist)
	Essex - BCC/BB (Art courses)
	Exeter - 20 pts approx (Fine Art/Lang)
	Oxford Brookes - BCC (H of Art) (4 AS)
	Reading - BCC (Art/Hist Arch; Art/Art Hist; Typ/Graph; Art/Psy)
	Sussex - BCC (All courses)

18 pts.   **Aberystwyth** - (P) BCD-CCC/BB (All courses) (Lower offers may be made)
   Brighton - CCC/BC (Hist Des) (4-6 AS)
   Loughborough – CCC/CC (Des/Tech; Ind Des Tech; Prod Des; Hist Art)
   Northumbria - 18-14 pts (Hist of Art; Vis Arts) (4 AS)
   Sheffield Hallam - 18 pts (Hist Art/Des/Film) (BTEC 4M)
   Teesside - CCC/CC (Hist Des/Env)
16 pts.   **De Montfort** - CCD/BC (Hist of Art; Comb Arts; Joint Arts)
   London (SOAS) - 16 pts (Art/Arch)
   Middlesex - 16-12 pts (Art Hist; Vis Arts)
   Plymouth - CCD or Foundation + 1 A-level (Des Arts/Art Hist; Land/Des Heritage)
   Reading - (P) BB (Art)
   Warwick - CCD/BC (Art QTS)
14 pts.   **Brunel** - CDD/CC (Des Tech Ed - BSc QTS) (6 AS)
   Cambridge (Hom) - BC-CC (Art/Ed) (4 AS) (See also **Education**)
   London (QMW) - BC (Art Hist)
   Ripon & York St John (CHE) - CDD/BB (Des Tech/Dr TV) (BTEC Ms)
12 pts.   **Anglia (Poly Univ)** - CC (Modular)
   Bretton Hall (CHE) - CC-EE (Fine Arts; Fashion/Textiles) (Subsids: Dance/Drama/ English/Inter-Arts) (4 AS) (See also **Textile Courses**)
   Brunel - DDD/CD (Des/Tech/Ed - BA QTS; Prod Des; Ind Des Eng) (6 AS)
   Canterbury Christ Church (CHE) - CC-EE (Comb St)
   Glamorgan - CC (Creative Arts - new course) (BTEC 4/5M)
   Humberside - 12-10 pts (Comm Proc)
   Kent - 12 pts approx (Vis/Arts)
   Lancaster - CC (Vis Arts; Art/Media - check with Admissions Tutor)
   London (Gold) - (P) DDD/DD (Fine Art; Craft; Eng/Hist Art; Des)
   Northumbria - CC (Creative Arts - or via Foundation course) (4 AS)
   Nottingham Trent - CC (Creative Arts)
   Oxford Brookes - DDD/CC (Vis St)
   Ripon & York St John (CHE) - DDD/CC (Des Tech see also **14 pts**) (BTEC Ms)
   Staffordshire - CC (Hist Des)
   Thames Valley London - CC + portfolio (Des/Med Man) (BTEC Ms)
   Ulster - CC (Design) (For direct entry) (AS des tech/hist/econ/contrasting subjects)
10 pts.   **and below**
   Bath - DD (Creative Arts)
   Bolton (IHE) - (Comb St)
   Bournemouth - (Des/Vis; Prod Des; CVA; Med Prod)
   Brighton - (Des Tech)
   Bristol UWE - (Art/Soc)
   Buckingham - DDE/DD (Hist Art/Heritage) (BTEC 2D + Ms)
   Buckinghamshire (CHE) - (Furn Res; Furn Prod; Arts Med Cul St)
   Central Lancashire - (Hist Art; Vis St)
   Cheltenham & Glos (CHE) - (Modular)
   Chester (CHE) - (Comb St)
   Coventry - (Tech Comm; Art/Craft - part-time)
   Crewe & Alsager (CHE) - DD (Creative Arts; Crafts)
   Dartington (CA) - (Art)
   Derby - (Vis Cult) (4 AS)
   Dundee - (Design; Fine Art)
   East London - (Art Des; Prod Des)
   Edinburgh (CA) - (Design; Ptg; Sculp)
   Glasgow (SA) - (Art; Des) (Offers made on basis of academic quals/ portfolio)
   Guildhall London - CD (C in art or CDT) (Design St; Rest/Cons; Art/Des - part-time)
   Gwent (CHE) - (CDT)
   Heriot-Watt/Edinburgh (CA) - (Design/Crafts)
   Hertfordshire - (Fine Art)
   Humberside - (Euro Audio Prod; Vis St; Comb St)

King Alfred's (CHE) - (Des Tech)
Leeds Met - (Hist Art)
Liverpool (IHE) - 8 pts (Design; Comb St)
London (Inst - Camberwell) - (Hist Drg; Ptg; Cons)
London (Inst - St Martins) - (Fine Art)
London (UC) - (Art Hist; Fine Art) (Low offers for outstanding students)
Loughborough (CA) - (Fine Art - part-time)
Manchester Met - (Hist Des; Hum/Soc St)
Middlesex - (Modular)
Nene (CHE) - (Comb)
Newcastle - (Fine Art)
Norfolk (IAD) - 10 pts (Cult St)
Robert Gordon - (Des Craft; Fine Art; Des Ind - new course)
Roehampton (IHE) - (Art courses)
Salford (UC) - (Prod Des; Des St)
Southampton (IHE) - (Fine Art; Des Comm; Fine Art Val - subject to approval)
St Mark & St John (CHE) - (Rec St/Cr Des)
Sunderland - (Ex/Perf Arts)
Swansea (IHE) - C Minimum + foundation course + 1 A-level (not art) (Comb St; Vis Arts)
Teesside - Hist Des/Arch/Built Env)
West Herts (Coll) - (Gr Media St)
West London (IHE) - (Vis Perf Art)
West Sussex (IHE) - (Art; BEd) (6 AS)
Wolverhampton - (Modular)

Offers for Foundation, Certificate and Diploma courses (see Ch 5):

Diploma of Higher Education courses:
 4 pts. East London; Liverpool John Moores (Media/Cult St); Middlesex (Modular).

Higher National Diploma courses: See also under specialist Art headings.
 2 pts. West Herts (Coll) Typo Design.

Alternative offers:

IB offers: **Aberdeen** 30 pts; **Anglia (Poly Univ)** 28 pts; **Brighton** 24 pts inc H 12 pts; **Bristol** 33 pts; **Brunel** 26-24 pts; **Buckingham** 24 pts; **East Anglia** H444 (min); **Leeds** 30 pts; **London (Court)** 28 pts inc H 16 pts; **Ripon & York St John (CHE)** (Des Tech) 30-27 pts, (Art) 34 pts; **St Andrews** 30 pts; **Thames Valley London** 26 pts.

Irish offers: **Aberdeen** BBBB; **Guildhall London** CCCCC.

SCE offers: **Aberdeen** BBBB (Hist Art); **Dundee** CCC; **Edinburgh** AAB or BBBB (inc Hist Art); **Glasgow** BBBB (Hist Art); **Guildhall London** BBCCC; **Heriot-Watt** CCC; **St Andrews** BBBB.

CHOOSING YOUR COURSE (See also Ch 1)

Subject information: This is a wide field comprising many aspects of two and three dimensional work as well as art history. The well motivated art student with real ability will be a self-starter who never needs to be advised to choose this subject. See also under **Graphic Design**, **Industrial Design**, **Three Dimensional Design** and **Textile Fashion**.

Course highlights: Aberdeen Renaissance to the Modern tradition in the 19th and 20th centuries. Options in industrial design (18th - 20th century) and garden history. **Aberystwyth** Practical art and art history with year abroad possibly in USA. Department runs placement scheme - year out - between years 2 & 3. **Anglia (Poly Univ)** Studio work and history or art history on its own; course in Visual Studies covers drawing, printmaking, typography, photography and video work. **Brighton** (Hist Des)

Industrial revolution to the present day. **Bristol UWE** (Art/Soc) A practical art course. **Bournemouth** (CVA) Course includes computer programming graphics and animation. **Cambridge** (Hist of Art) The course covers art and architecture in Western Europe. **Crewe & Alsager (CHE)** Commitment to inter-relationship between theory and practice in the arts (performance, dance, TV and drama). **De Montfort** (Hist of Art/Des) The course covers art and design from mid-18th century to present day. **East Anglia** (Hist of Art) Programme built around two separate periods in history of art, selected from wide variety of subjects which range from antiquity to present day. **Edinburgh** (Fine Art) Course takes five years and combines the history of art and practical art with (in years 1 & 2) a second subject. **Essex** (Art Hist) Third year includes art theory, practical criticism, an extended essay and two options from European art, 20th century art, Latin American art and architecture, Russian art, art in USA or Spanish art and architecture. **Glasgow** (Hist Art) Course covers European, medieval, modern and Scottish art; reading knowledge of a European language an advantage. **Lancaster** (Vis Arts) In Part 1 Visual Arts taken with two other subjects and consists of practical studio work and theory. **Leeds** (Fine Art) Creative studio practice and research. (Hist of Dec Arts) Teaching in country house museums, art galleries etc involving 'hands on' and detailed examination of original works of art. **Leicester** (Hist Art) Two additional subjects studied, one in years 1 and 2 and one in year 1 only. Course covers the history of European art from the Renaissance to modern times – mainly painting, but with sections dealing with architecture and sculpture. **London (Court)** (Hist Art) General year 1 foundation leads to choice of specialist period of study (European art 1200-1350, 16th century, or 1848 to 1925). **London (Gold)** (Art/Hist Art) Studio work and art history studied equally. Specialist historical options include cinema, photography, Eastern art, and primitivism. **London (Inst - Camberwell)** (Hist Drg Prt) Combines art history with science-related studies - materials, processes, environmental effects. (Conservation) International reputation in paper conservation; course involves study of art, science, history, hand skills. Textile conservation also offered. **London (SOAS)** Hist Art) Course divided between European and non-European art. **London (UC)** (Fine Art) Practical study in Slade School of Fine Art; major part of course devoted to practical work with some course work in the history of art. **Manchester Met** Option of 25% of studio work. Placements in museums, galleries etc in year 2 (no previous graphical experience necessary). **Middlesex** History of art and design from Italian Renaissance to present as well as film and television studies. **Newcastle** (Fine Art) Four year course in the history of European art and architecture, with studio work in painting, sculpture or design. **Northumbria** (Hist Art) History of European and American art from 1770 to present day covering painting and sculpture, architecture, design, film, social history. **Nottingham** (Art Hist) Topics range from the Greek and Roman periods to modern art. Practical work available but not compulsory. **Oxford** (Fine Art) Full-time study of drawing, painting, printmaking, sculpture, history of art and anatomy. **Plymouth** (Des Arts) Major options in Stage 2 textile or environmental art or design; (Fine Art/Lang) Study of English, French or Italian fine art, 50% practical. **Reading** (Art) A four year practical course in painting with construction, painting with print, and sculpture with multi-media art and group projects. **Robert Gordon** (Des Tech) Technology and business feature prominently with practical and theoretical design. **St Andrews** (Art Hist) History of European painting, sculpture, architecture and graphic art forms from Middle Ages to 1800. **Sheffield Hallam** (Hist Art/Des/Film) Course draws mainly on 19th and 20th century material. **Staffordshire** (Hist Des) Students select six options: history of ceramics and glass, graphic design, architecture of the industrial society, history of painting and sculpture, film studies, history of fashion. **Sussex** (Hist Art) Course includes architecture, painting, sculpture and photography. **Teesside** Study covers popular design of 19th and 20th centuries, urban planning and architecture. **Warwick** (Hist Art) History of European art and architecture. **West Sussex (IHE)** Two and three dimensional art and textiles taught alongside dance, English and music. NOW CHECK PROSPECTUSES FOR ALL COURSES.

Study opportunities abroad: East Anglia IT H; **Lancaster** USA; **Leeds Met** SP; **Leicester** (E) I NL D; **Manchester Met** USA; **Newcastle** FR (yr 1); **Northumbria** CZ G SP IN; **Nottingham Trent** USA; **Robert Gordon** NL SP FR; **Roehampton (IHE)** FR; **West Sussex (IHE)** (E).

Work opportunities abroad: Bristol EUR; **Brunel** G; **Heriot-Watt** CIS FR IT; **Suffolk (CA)** USA.

ADMISSIONS INFORMATION

Number of applicants per place (approx): Anglia (Poly Univ) 17; **Bournemouth** (Des Vis) 3; **Brighton** (Hist of Des) 8; **Canterbury Christ Church (CHE)** 3; **Crewe & Alsager (CHE)** 8; **East**

Anglia 7; **Lancaster** (Vis Arts) 15; **Leeds** 29; **Leicester** 10; **London (Inst)** 2; **London (SOAS)** 4; **Loughborough** 7; **Manchester Met** 10; **Middlesex** (Vis Arts) 17, (Art Hist) 16; **Newcastle** 23; **Northumbria** 14, (Creative Arts) 37; **Nottingham Trent** 25; **Plymouth** (Fine Art/Lang) 25; **Robert Gordon** 5; **Roehampton (IHE)** 7; **Sheffield Hallam** 15; **Staffordshire** 5; **Suffolk (CA)** 3; **Teesside** 2; **Thames Valley London** 15; **West Herts (Coll)** 3; **West Sussex (IHE)** 3.

General Studies acceptable: Aberdeen; Aberystwyth; Bretton Hall (CHE) (2) (Not AEB); Brunel; Bristol; East Anglia; Essex (JMB); Lancaster; Liverpool (IHE); London (Court); Loughborough; Manchester Met (Hist of Des) plus an academic subject; Newcastle (2); Northumbria (Vis Arts); Nottingham Trent; Oxford Brookes; Robert Gordon (2); Roehampton (IHE) (2); Sheffield Hallam; Staffordshire; Swansea (IHE); West Herts (Coll); West Sussex (IHE) (2).

Selection interviews: Bradford (Coll); Brighton; Brunel; Cambridge; Cambridge (Hom); Canterbury Christ Church (CHE); Crewe & Alsager (CHE) (also audition); East Anglia; Edinburgh (also portfolio); Lancaster (also portfolio); Leicester (some); Leeds (also portfolio); Newcastle (also portfolio); Sheffield Hallam; Warwick. Details of the Fine Art portfolio inspection scheme are given in the UCAS handbook.

Offers to applicants repeating A-levels: Higher Brunel; **Possibly higher** Brighton, Essex, Loughborough, Northumbria, Oxford Brookes; **Same** Aberystwyth, Bretton Hall (CHE), Canterbury Christ Church (CHE), Leeds, Newcastle, Warwick.

Admissions Tutors' advice: Aberystwyth Portfolio with representational drawings required. **East Anglia** Good interview lowers offer. **Lancaster** GCSE maths A or B. Good practical skills and portfolio are most important criteria for selection. Many students benefit from Foundation course. **Leeds** (Art History) Good grounding required in history or language or English. **Liverpool John Moores** Preference given to Foundation course students. **London (Court)** Emphasis on visual memory; language important. **Loughborough** (Des/Tech) Good physics grade at GCSE. **Newcastle** Selection based on portfolio - emphasis on practical work. Portfolios required for all practical courses. **Northumbria** Essay-writing ability required. **Nottingham Trent** (Creative Arts) Music students need grade 6 in one instrument or ability in two instruments. **Oxford** Foundation coursework an advantage. **Oxford Brookes** Foundation art course often necessary.

Examples of interview questions:
History of Art courses: Discuss and compare two paintings (reproductions given). Tests may be given on slides covering both paintings and sculpture. (Some History of Art courses do not require an A-level pass in the subject but you are expected to know a lot about historical periods or paintings.) What art history books have you read? What did you think of them? They will test your knowledge of the history of art, possibly your favourite painter and work of art. Discuss any exhibitions you have attended.

Art and Design Foundation courses: How much art do you do inside and outside school? What do you want to do after your Foundation course? Discuss your thinking behind examples of your work in the portfolio. How often do you visit art galleries and exhibitions? Discuss the last exhibition you visited. What are the the reactions of your parents to your choice of course and career? What will you do if you don't get on the course? What are your interests outside school? How do they link up with art? Do you feel that modern art has anything to contribute to society compared with earlier art? In which medium do you prefer to work? Applicants are advised to take some trouble to mount their work carefully. Title and date each piece of work. A wide variety of work is important - include sketch books. Show signs of life - no apathy! Don't give the impression you're only doing art as a 'soft option'. Be eager and enthusiastic. Be prepared to answer questions about your work - why did you do it? How? What was your aim?

GAP YEAR ADVICE

Institutions accepting a Gap Year: Most institutions; **Leicester** If possible travel and visit art galleries and museums, also learn a foreign language. **Manchester Met** Increase knowledge of history of art and design by visits to museums, art galleries etc. **Newcastle** Acceptable. **Roehampton (IHE)**

Give reasons for gap year plus a summary of activities. **West Sussex (IHE)** Work experience abroad useful.

Institutions willing to defer entry after A-levels (see Ch 5): Aberystwyth; Buckingham; De Montfort; King Alfred's (CHE); Lancaster (No); Manchester Met; Newcastle (No); Roehampton (IHE); Sheffield Hallam (No); Thames Valley London; West Herts (Coll).

AFTER A-LEVELS ADVICE

Institutions which may accept the same points score after A-levels: Bretton Hall (CHE); Brighton; Brunel; Crewe & Alsager (CHE); East Anglia; Leeds; Liverpool John Moores; Loughborough (Des/Tech); Oxford Brookes; Sheffield Hallam; Teesside.

Institutions demanding the actual grades offered after A-levels: Anglia (Poly Univ); London (Court), (SOAS); Loughborough; Northumbria (Vis Arts); Nottingham Trent; Warwick (Hist of Art).

Institutions which may accept under-achieving applicants after A-levels: Brunel; Cambridge (Hom); Crewe & Alsager (Coll); East Anglia; Glasgow; Leeds; Loughborough; Most institutions.

Institutions with vacancies in Aug/Sept 1992 (see Ch 5): Anglia (Poly Univ); Bournemouth; Bradford & Ilkley (CmC); Brighton; Buckingham DDE; De Montfort 16-14 pts; Guildhall London; King Alfred's (CHE) 10-8 pts; Kingston; Plymouth (Art Hist) 16 pts; Ripon & York St John (CHE); Sheffield Hallam 16 pts; Southampton (IHE); Thames Valley London (Des/Med Man) 12 pts; West Herts (Coll).

ADVICE FOR MATURE STUDENTS

On these courses about 10% of students are mature. Some part-time courses are available. Applicants must show evidence of ability, and activities and experience appropriate to courses are also important. **Plymouth** Active policy of recruiting mature students.

GRADUATE EMPLOYMENT

New Graduates' destinations (percentages) 1991:
Permanent employment: (Creative Art) U 67; P 96; C 58. (Art History) U 63; P 59; C 60. (Design) U 69; P 61; C 66. (Fine Art) U 57; P 53; C 67.
Unemployment: (Creative Art) U 33; P5; C 26. (Art History) U 22; P 27; C 10. (Design) U 22; P 27; C 20. (Fine Art) U 38; P 32; C 13.
Further studies (all types): (Creative Art) U 25; P 16; C 25. (Art History) U 33; P 26; C 33. (Design) U 20; P 14; C 18. (Fine Art) U 28; P 20; C 26.
Main career destinations (approx): (Design) Creative 69; Teaching 7; Secretarial 6. (Fine Art) Creative 62; Secretarial 12; Teaching 5. (Art History) Creative 16; Administrative 16; Legal 14; Teaching 10.

ARTS (GENERAL/COMBINED/HUMANITIES/ MODULAR)

Special subject requirements: A-level subjects will relate to the course chosen.

NB Institutions may raise or lower the level of published offers depending either on the quality or otherwise of individual applications or the numbers of applications received; grades/points offered may be adjusted downwards after A-level results. The level of an offer is not indicative of the quality of a course. The grades shown below are approximate since offers made in Combined, General and Humanities courses may vary depending on the subjects chosen.

24 pts.   **Durham** - ABC (Comb St/Soc Sci)
        Manchester - BBB approx (Comb)
        Newcastle - BBB-BBC (Comb Studs inc Chin/Jap/Korean)
        St Andrews - BBB (Fac of Arts) (4 AS)

22 pts.   **Aberdeen** - BBC/BC (Arts Ord)
        Birmingham - BBC (Combined Hons)
        Durham - BBC (Comb St/Arts)
        Edinburgh - BBC (MA Gen)
        Glasgow - BBC/AA (MA Ord)
        Leeds - BBC-BCC/AA-BB (Joint courses Arts, Econ & Soc St)
        Liverpool - BBC-BCC (Arts Comb)
        Ripon & York St John (CHE) - BBC-DDD/BB-BC (BA/BSc depending on subject)

20 pts.   **Aston** - BCC/AA (Comb Hons) (BTEC 5D+5M)
        Birmingham - BCC-BCD (General)
        Bradford - BCC (I Hum St)
        Bristol UWE - 20-18 pts (Hum) (BTEC M overall)
        Dundee - BCC/BB (Arts/Soc Sci)
        Essex - BCC/BB (Joint/Comb Hons Def)
        Lancaster - BCC (Ind St)
        Leicester - BCC/CCC (Comb Arts)
        Swansea - BCC-CCC/BB (BSc Econ deferred choice joint hons)

18 pts.   **Belfast** - CCC/BB (Arts Comb)
        Heriot-Watt - CCC (Comb St)
        Portsmouth - CCC/BB (Cul St) (Ref 12pts)
        Strathclyde - CCC/BC (BBD 2nd year entry)

16 pts.   **Anglia (Poly Univ)** - 16 pts (Arts Comb)
        Bath (CHE) - (Comb St; Eng/Hist)
        Central Lancashire - CCD/CC (Varies by chosen subject) (4 AS)
        De Montfort - CCD/BC (Arts; Hum) (6 AS) (BTEC Ms)
        Exeter - CCD (Ed St/Hum)
        Manchester Met - CCD-CDD/CC (Hum/Soc St)
        Middlesex - 16-12 pts (Modular)
        Oxford Brookes - CCD-DDD/BC-CC (Modular)
        Plymouth - CCD/BC-CC (Comb Arts) (BTEC 5M)
        St Mark & St John (CHE) - 16-12 pts (BA Hons)
        Ulster - CCD/BC (Hum Comb)

14 pts.   **Bolton (IHE)** - CDD/CD (Comb St Mod)
        Canterbury Christ Church (CHE) - 14 pts (Comb St)
        Hertfordshire - (Hum)
        Nottingham Trent - CDD/CC (Hum)
        Teesside - CDD (Hum) (BTEC M overall)
        Worcester (CHE) - 14-8 pts (Comb St - depending on subject) (BTEC 3M)

12 pts.   **Bretton Hall (CHE)** - CC-EE (Eng; Inter Arts; Social St) (See under**English**) (4 AS)
        Chester (CHE) - 12 pts grade C in selected subject (Comb Arts) (BTEC 3M)
        Derby - 12-8 pts (Comb St)

East London - CC (Cul St)
Glamorgan - CC (Hum) (4 AS) (BTEC 4/5M)
Greenwich - CC (Hum)
King Alfred's (CHE) - (Comb St - BA) (BTEC 3M)
Kingston - CC (Hist of Ideas)
North London - 12 pts (Hum) (Contact Admissions Tutor)
Portsmouth - 12 pts (Cult St)
Sunderland - 12-8 pts varies depending on subjects (Arts)
Thames Valley London - 12-10 pts (Hum) (BTEC M overall)
West Sussex (IHE) - (Gen: Comb Hons)
Wolverhampton - 12 pts approx - varies depending on subjects chosen (Comb St; Hum)

10 pts. Bedford (CHE) - (Comb St) (4 AS)
Cheltenham & Glos (CHE) - 10 pts (Cult St)
Humberside - (Hum; Comb St) (BTEC 3M)
North East Wales (IHE) - (Comb St)

8 pts. and below
Brighton - (Hum) (6 AS)
Buckinghamshire (CHE) - (Arts/Soc - mature students part-time)
Cheltenham & Glos (CHE) - (Cult St)
Crewe & Alsager (CHE) - DEE/DD (Ind St; Hum)
Coventry - (Mod St)
East London - (Comb St)
Greenwich - (Cult/Belief - new course)
Guildhall London - (Mod)
Gwent (CHE) - (Cul St; Comb St)
La Sainte Union (CHE) - (Comb St)
Liverpool - (Comb St) (4 AS)
Manchester Met - 7-4 pts (Comb St) (4 AS)
Nene (CHE) - (Comb St) (4 AS) (BTEC 5M)
Norfolk (IAD) - (Cult St)
North Chesire (CHE) - (Comb Hons for mature students - flexible entry)
North Riding (Coll) - 8 pts (Hum Arts)
Paisley - 6 pts (Gen)
Roehampton (IHE) - DD-EE (Comb St)
Sheffield Hallam - DD approx (depends on combinations) (Comb St) (BTEC 5M)
St Mary's (CHE) - (Comb Hons)
Swansea (IHE) - (Comb St) (4 AS)
Trinity & All Saints (CHE) - (BA)
Trinity Carmarthen (CHE) - (Hum)
West London (IHE) - (Int Degree Scheme) (4 AS)
Wolverhampton - (Hum) (Part-time course for mature students)

Franchised degree and HND courses (see Ch 5):

De Montfort - Barnfield (Coll); Boston (Coll); Derby Tertiary (Coll); Henley (Coll); Loughborough (Coll); North Lincolnshire (Coll); Northampton (Coll); Peterborough (Coll); Trensham (Coll).
Humberside - North Lindsey (Coll).

Diploma of Higher Education courses:

10 pts. Crewe & Alsager (CHE) (4 AS)
4 pts. Bangor Normal (CHE); Bath (CHE); Bradford & Ilkley (CmC); Trinity Carmarthen (CHE); Central Lancashire; Doncaster (CFHE); East London; Edge Hill (CHE); Guildhall London; Humberside; King Alfred's (CHE); La Sainte Union (CHE); Leeds Met; Manchester Met (Modular); Nene (CHE); North Chesire (CHE); Oxford Brookes; Plymouth; Ripon & York St John (CHE); Westminster (CHE); Wolverhampton; Worcester (CHE).

Alternative offers:

IB offers: **Aberdeen** 30 pts; **Aston** 33-31 pts; **Bath (CHE)** 24 pts; **Belfast** H555 S555; **Brighton** 24 pts in 6 subjects inc 12 pts in 3 Highers; **Durham** 30 pts; **Glamorgan** 24 pts; **Glasgow** 30 pts; **Huddersfield** 30 pts; **King Alfred's (CHE)** 24 pts; **Leeds** 28-30 pts; **Liverpool** 30 pts; **Manchester Met** 28-30 pts.

SCE offers: **Aberdeen** BBBB; **Belfast** BBBB/BBBBC; **Birmingham** ABBC; **Bristol UWE** AAB; **De Montfort** BBB; **Dundee** BBBC; **Edinburgh** BBBC; **Glasgow** BBBB; **Huddersfield** BBB; **Leeds** AAABB; **Teesside** BBB; **Strathclyde** BBBB/BBBCC.

Overseas applicants: Oxford Brookes Special International Foundation Programme – details from institution.

CHOOSING YOUR COURSE (See also Ch 1)

> **Subject information:** Many different subjects are included in Arts courses which offer the student a wide choice and flexibility of study. At each institution the student normally chooses two or three subjects from a list of up to 30. Arts courses are thus ideal for students with a range of interests in non-scientific areas who do not wish to commit themselves to a single subject course.

Course highlights: Birmingham (Gen Hons) and **Newcastle** (Comb St) Three subjects chosen in year 1, further choices in years 2 & 3. **Bath (CHE)** Work placement during course. **Brighton** (Hum) Options in British society, world studies, self and society and Third World studies. **Bristol UWE** (Hum) Multi-disciplinary course with 4 main themes - Cultural/Social Studies; History, Literary, Geographical/Environmental - plus wide variety of other subsidiary subjects. American exchange in year 2 for one semester. **Chester (CHE)** Year 1 has termly assessment in modules; degree programme chosen in second term. One month work placement for all students. Good employer contacts. **De Montfort** Degree schemes cover 9 subjects including history of art, media studies, English, history, politics, drama and contemporary Asian studies. **Durham** Three-subject degree course. **Glasgow** Five subjects taken in year 1. **Humberside** Modular degree structure allowing students to build their own scheme within specific guidelines. **Leicester** (Comb St) 25 subjects offered, 3 subjects chosen. **Plymouth** Modular course. Options covering art (including history of art), drama, English, education, history and media studies. **Ripon & York St John (CHE)** Periods of work placement in the BA/BSc programme. **Sheffield Hallam** Combined Studies programme operates on credit accumulation and transfer basis. Students negotiate own programme of study by selecting units from full range of degree courses (credit may be awarded for prior certificated or experiential learning). **Thames Valley London** (Hum) Four subjects chosen in year 2. Psychology major accepted by the BPS. **Trinity Carmarthen (CHE)** Two subjects from 6 in year 1; two subjects equal in year 2; one major, one minor in year 3. **West London (IHE)** (Integrated Degree Scheme) Modular degree scheme for BA and BSc courses; students choose 2 subjects from 14 to be studied equally or as major/minor subjects; 3rd area of study can also be followed. **Worcester (CHE)** Flexible structure enables students to build personal programme choosing three courses, following 2 throughout 3 year programme, and 1 through years 1 and 2. NOW CHECK PROSPECTUSES FOR ALL COURSES.

Study opportunities abroad: De Montfort; Humberside FR G NL; **Norfolk (IAD)** (E) G NL P; **St Andrews** (E) USA FR G NL SP CAN; **St Mark & St John (CHE)** FR G NL B; **Thames Valley London** FR SP; **Wolverhampton** EUR.

Work opportunities abroad: Dundee C FR G SP USA; **Thames Valley London** USA; **Worcester (CHE)** USA.

ADMISSIONS INFORMATION

Number of applicants per place (approx): Bath (CHE) 10; **Bedford (CHE)** 6; **Bolton (IHE)** 5; **Bristol UWE** 16; **Central England** 14; **Central Lancashire** 9; **Chester (CHE)** 10; **Crewe & Alsager (CHE)** 5; **De Montfort** 8; **Derby** 5; **Dundee** 9; **Durham** (Arts) 5, (Soc Sci) 9; **East Anglia** 12; **East London** 4; **Glamorgan** 7; **Greenwich** 5; **Gwent (CHE)** 2; **Hertfordshire** 12; **La Sainte**

Union (CHE) 3; Leeds 15; Liverpool (IHE) 8; Manchester Met (Hum) 17; Nene (CHE) 8; North London 10; North East Wales (IHE) 2; 8; Nottingham Trent 23; Plymouth 11; Portsmouth 14; Ripon & York St John (CHE) 15; St Mark & St John (CHE) 5; Strathclyde 14; Swansea 8; Swansea (IHE) 3; Teesside 8; Thames Valley London 4; Trinity Carmarthen (CHE) 2; West London (IHE) 4; West Sussex (IHE) 6; Wolverhampton 13; Worcester (CHE) 10.

General Studies acceptable: Aberdeen; Anglia (Poly Univ); Bedford (CHE); Bolton (IHE) (2); Bristol UWE; Cheltenham & Glos (CHE); Chester (CHE); De Montfort; Derby; East London; Glamorgan; Greenwich; Liverpool; Liverpool John Moores; Liverpool (IHE); Manchester Met; Nene (CHE); Newcastle (Grade C); Norfolk (IAD); North Cheshire (CHE); Nottingham Trent; Oxford Brookes; Ripon & York St John (CHE) JMB only; St Mary's (CHE); Swansea (IHE); Teesside; Thames Valley London (2); Trinity Carmarthen (CHE); Worcester (CHE).

Selection interviews: Aberdeen (some); Anglia (Poly Univ); Bath (CHE) (some); Bedford (CHE); Bournemouth; Brighton; Bristol UWE; Central Lancashire (some); Chester (CHE); Cheltenham & Glos (CHE); Crewe & Alsager (CHE); De Montfort (some); Durham; Glamorgan (T); Greenwich (some); Humberside (T); La Sainte Union (CHE); Liverpool (some); Liverpool (IHE); Nene (CHE); North London; Nottingham Trent; Ripon & York St John (CHE); Roehampton (IHE); S Martin's (CHE); St Mark & St John (CHE); St Mary's (CHE); Teesside (some); Trinity Carmarthen (CHE); West London (IHE); Worcester (CHE) (some).

Offers to applicants repeating A-levels: Higher Chester (CHE), Glamorgan, Huddersfield, Ripon & York St John (CHE); Possibly higher Bristol UWE, De Montfort, Leeds, Liverpool, Liverpool (IHE), Newcastle, Roehampton (IHE), St Mary's (CHE), Teesside; Same Anglia (Poly Univ), Bath (CHE), Bedford (CHE), Birmingham, Bolton (IHE), Bournemouth, Cheltenham & Glos (CHE), Derby, De Montfort, Durham, Greenwich, Humberside, Kingston, La Sainte Union (CHE), Manchester Met, Nene (CHE), North London, Portsmouth, Swansea (IHE), Teesside, Wolverhampton, Worcester (CHE).

Admissions Tutors' advice: Liverpool A-level grade B in English for appropriate course. Glamorgan GCSE grade A-C in English required. Roehampton (IHE) A-level grade D for appropriate course.

Examples of interview questions: See under separate subject headings.

GAP YEAR ADVICE

Institutions accepting a Gap Year: Most institutions; Bath (CHE) Apply before gap year if travelling abroad. Crewe & Alsager (CHE) Book list provided. Dundee Voluntary Service Overseas encouraged. Ripon & York St John (CHE) Firm plans should be made before application. Teesside Encouraged. Thames Valley London Apply before gap year.

Institutions willing to defer entry after A-levels (see Ch 5): Aston; Heriot-Watt; Humberside; King Alfred's (CHE); Swansea (IHE).

AFTER A-LEVELS ADVICE

Institutions which may accept the same points score after A-levels: Anglia (Poly Univ); Bath (CHE); Bedford (CHE); Brighton; Bristol UWE; Central Lancashire; Cheltenham & Glos (CHE); Crewe & Alsager (CHE); De Montfort; Derby; Durham; Greenwich; Humberside; Kingston; La Sainte Union (CHE); Liverpool John Moores; Liverpool (IHE); Manchester Met; Nene (CHE); Nottingham Trent; Portsmouth; Ripon & York St John (CHE); Roehampton (IHE); St Andrews; St Mark & St John (CHE); St Mary's (CHE); Strathclyde; Swansea (IHE); Ulster; Worcester (CHE) (varies).

Institutions demanding the actual grades offered after A-levels: Aberdeen; Chester (CHE); Glamorgan; Huddersfield; Liverpool; Newcastle; North London.

Institutions which may accept under-achieving applicants after A-levels: Bedford (CHE); Bristol UWE; De Montfort; Durham; Glamorgan; Liverpool; Ripon & York St John (CHE); Roehampton (IHE); Strathclyde; Most institutions.

Institutions with vacancies in Aug/Sept 1992 (see Ch 5): Aston BBC-BCC; Glamorgan (CD); King Alfred's (CHE) 12 pts; Plymouth 16 pts; Sunderland; Swansea (IHE). Several institutions declared vacancies in Humanities courses.

ADVICE FOR MATURE STUDENTS

A large number of mature students follow these courses. Some institutions are actively recruiting mature students. In many cases preference is given to local students and part-time courses are often offered. Recent study is important in order that students can adapt to the academic demands of courses. **Cheltenham & Glos (CHE)** Flexible entry for BA Combined Studies.

GRADUATE EMPLOYMENT

New Graduates' destinations (percentages) 1991;
Permanent employment: P 48; C 57.
Unemployment: P 30; C 34.
Further studies (all types): P 29; C 39.
Main career destinations (approx): Universities: Finance 24; Marketing 21; Administration 17; Secretarial 9; Social Work 9; Legal 7 Polytechnics: Administration 24; Finance 24; Marketing 17; Secretarial 16; Social Work 16; Legal 8.

Teesside (Humanities) About 50% of graduates entered a wide range of careers. These included estate agency work, management, sales, marketing and child care.

ASTRONOMY/ASTROPHYSICS

Special subject requirements: 2-3 A-levels from science subjects; mathematics and physics important.

NB Institutions may raise or lower the level of published offers depending either on the quality or otherwise of individual applications or the numbers of applications received; grades/points offered may be adjusted downwards after A-level results. The level of an offer is not indicative of the quality of a course.

22 pts.	**Birmingham** - BBC-BCC (Phys/Astro)
	Manchester - 22 pts approx
20 pts.	**Newcastle** - BCC/BC (Astron)
	Sussex - BCC (P Astro/Maps)
18 pts.	**Cardiff** - CCC/CC (Phys/Astro)
	Edinburgh - CCC/BB (Astrophysics) (4 AS)
	Kent - BCD (Phys Ast)
	Leicester - CCC (Phys/Ast; Maths/Ast)
	London (QMW) - CCC/CC (Astron; Astrophys) (BTEC 3M)
	London (RH) - BCD (Phys Astro)
	London (UC) - CCC/CC (Astronomy)
16 pts.	**Glasgow** - CCD (Astron/Maths; Astron/Phys)
	Leeds - CCD-CDD/CC (Phys/Astrophys)
	St Andrews - CCD (Astronomy courses) (4 AS) (BTEC 65%)
	Sheffield - CCD (Astronomy courses)
12 pts.	and below
	Central Lancashire - DD (Comb Hons) (4 AS)
	Hertfordshire - (Comb St)
8 pts.	and below

Plymouth – (Comb Sci/Soc)

Alternative offers:

IB offers: **Cardiff** Individual offers; **Kent** 25 pts, H 11 pts; **London (QMW)** H777-H555; **Newcastle** 30 pts H5 phys; **St Andrews** 28 pts.

SCE offers: **Edinburgh** BBBB; **Newcastle** BBBB; **St Andrews** BBCC-BBB.

CHOOSING YOUR COURSE (See also Ch 1)

> **Subject information:** These courses have a mathematics and physics emphasis. Applicants, however, should must realise that subject-related careers on graduation are limited. Courses in Geophysics, Mathematics, Meteorology or Applied Physics could be suitable alternatives. Astrophysics courses involve both physics and astronomy and are more difficult than single honours; students weak in mathematics and physics should avoid them.

Course highlights: Birmingham (Phys/Astro) Astronomy and astrophysics combine with a training in basic physics. **Cardiff** European language can be studied, with placement in Europe. Transfers possible between courses. **Central Lancashire** Two observatories operate largest array of optical telescopes for undergraduate use in UK. **Edinburgh** (Astrophysics) In years 3 and 4 work divided between astronomy and physics. **Glasgow** (Astron/Phys) Courses cover the universe and methods used in assessing distances, motions and nature of celestial objects. **Leeds** (Phys/Astrophys) Transfers between Physics and Physics with Astrophysics courses possible up to end of year 1. **London (QMW)** (Astrophys) A physics programme accompanied by specialised topics such as stellar and galactic structure and cosmology. **London (UC)** (Astronomy) Year 1 provides introduction to the theory and practice of astronomy with maths and physics. Astrophysics, spectroscopy and astronomical methods follow in year 2. **Newcastle** (Astron) Maths, physics and another science subject studied in year 1. Years 2 and 3 introduce astronomy and astrophysics, computing, electronics and nuclear physics. **St Andrews** (Astronomy) Maths and physics predominate in year 2. NOW CHECK PROSPECTUSES FOR ALL COURSES.

Study opportunities abroad: Glasgow (E); **Kent** (E); **Leicester** (E); **London (QMW)** FR G IT; **St Andrews** (E).

ADMISSIONS INFORMATION

Number of applicants per place (approx): Cardiff 6; **Leicester** 12; **London (QMW)** 6, **(RH)** 6; **Newcastle** 8.

Selection interviews: Newcastle.

Offers to applicants repeating A-levels: Same Newcastle.

> **Examples of interview questions:** Can you name a recent development in physics which will be important in the future? Describe a physics experiment, indicating any errors and exactly what it was intended to prove! Why do you wish to study Astronomy/Astrophysics? Explain weightlessness. What is a black hole? (Expect some questions on rotational dynamics and thermo-dynamics.)

GAP YEAR ADVICE

Institutions accepting a Gap Year: Most institutions; **Newcastle** The experience of travel abroad is worthwhile, but your maths knowledge may fade.

Institutions willing to defer entry after A-levels (see Ch 5): Newcastle; St Andrews.

AFTER A-LEVELS ADVICE

Institutions demanding the actual grades offered after A-levels: Newcastle.

Institutions with vacancies in Aug/Sept 1992 (see Ch 5): London (QMW). There was a shortage of applicants in this subject with several universities offering places at 16, 14 and 12 pts.

GRADUATE EMPLOYMENT

New Graduates' destinations (percentages) 1991:
Permanent employment: U 53.
Unemployment: U 41.
Further studies (all types): U 61.

BANKING AND FINANCE

Special subject requirements: GCSE (grades A-C) in mathematics.

NB Institutions may raise or lower the level of published offers depending either on the quality or otherwise of individual applications or the numbers of applications received; grades/points offered may be adjusted downwards after A-level results. The level of an offer is not indicative of the quality of a course.

24 pts. **Birmingham** - BBB (Bank Fin; MBF/Lang) (BTEC D overall)
     City - BBB (Bank/Int Fin) (4 AS)
     Nottingham - BBB-BBC (Ind Ec/Ins)
22 pts. **Bangor** - BBC excluding gen studs/BB (Bank/Ins/Fin) (BTEC 3D+3M)
     Cardiff - BBC/22 pts (Bank/Fin) (BTEC 5D+2M)
     City - BBC (Ins/Invest) (BTEC Ds)
     Loughborough - BBC/AB (Bank/Fin 3 and 4) (BTEC 6D)
16 pts. **Guildhall London** - CCD-CDD/CC (Ins St - new course)
     Ulster - CCD (Bank/Fin) (AS (recommended) maths/econ/comp/eng)
14 pts. **Central England** - (Bank/Fin) (6 AS) (BTEC 3D+Ms)
12 pts. **and below Guildhall London** - DDD/CC (Banking - options in Bus St) (BTEC Ds+
     Ms)
     Holborn (Coll) - (BSc Econ)
     South Bank - DD (Fin/Maths - new course)

Higher National Diploma courses:
2 pts. De Montfort; Gwent (CHE); Stockport (CT).

Alternative offers:

IB offers: **Bangor** 30-32 pts inc H666; **Birmingham** H 16 pts S16 pts; **Cardiff** H665 + 15 pts Subsid; **City** (Ins/Invest) H655 S544, (Bank/Int Fin) H666 S65; **South Bank** 24 pts.

Irish offers: **Bangor** AAABB; **Holborn (Coll)** BBB.

CHOOSING YOUR COURSE (See also Ch 1)

> **Subject information:** These are specialised courses leading to a career in banking. Major banks offer sponsorships. Economics, Accountancy, Actuarial Studies and Business Studies courses could be appropriate alternatives.

Course highlights: Bangor Specialist topics - banking, insurance and finance - in year 3. **City** Insurance and Investment course only one in UK. **Loughborough** Course includes French or German option.

(Bank/Fin3) for sponsored students or those with 1 year banking employment. NOW CHECK PROSPECTUSES FOR ALL COURSES.

Study opportunities abroad: City (E).

Work opportunities abroad: Birmingham FR G SP; **Central England** EUR FE.

ADMISSIONS INFORMATION

Number of applicants per place (approx): Bangor 30; **Birmingham** 18; **Cardiff** 8; **Central England** 13; **City** 9; **Holborn (Coll)** No limits; **Loughborough** 35.

General Studies acceptable: Cardiff; Central England (2); South Bank.

Selection interviews: South Bank.

Offers to applicants repeating A-levels: Higher City (possibly ABB); **Possibly higher** Bangor; **Same** Holborn (Coll), Loughborough, South Bank, Ulster.

Admissions Tutors' advice: Bangor Motivation and commitment required. **Loughborough** Good GCSE maths grade required (A or B).

> **Examples of interview questions:** Where do you see yourself in ten years? What are your strengths and weaknesses? Why have you chosen a career in the banking profession? What do you like about our course? Describe the various activities in banking.

GAP YEAR ADVICE

Institutions accepting a Gap Year: Most institutions; **Birmingham** If we are willing to offer a place we would be willing to defer entry. **Cardiff** Try to gain some experience in the finance sector. **City** Deferred entry preferred.

Institutions willing to defer entry after A-levels (see Ch 5): Bangor; City; South Bank.

AFTER A-LEVELS ADVICE

Institutions which may accept the same points score after A-levels: Bangor; Holborn (Coll); Loughborough; South Bank; Ulster.

Institutions which may accept under-achieving applicants after A-levels: Bangor; Holborn (Coll); South Bank.

Institutions with vacancies in Aug/Sept 1992 (see Ch 5): Bangor 16 pts; City; South Bank DD/8 pts. Vacancies in this subject normally required 20 to 18 pts in the more popular universities.

ADVICE FOR MATURE STUDENTS

A small number of mature students apply for these courses. O-levels or equivalent and in some cases A-levels may be required.

BEHAVIOURAL SCIENCE (See also Psychology)

Special subject requirements: GCSE (grades A-C) English language and mathematics.

NB Institutions may raise or lower the level of published offers depending either on the quality or otherwise of individual applications or the numbers of applications received; grades/points offered may be adjusted downwards after A-level results. The level of an offer is not indicative of the quality of a course.

24 pts.	**Nottingham** - BBB-BBC (Bhv Sci) (BTEC 3M)
14 pts.	**Glamorgan** - 14-12 pts/12-8 pts (Bhv Sci) (4 AS) (BTEC 2D+M)
	Huddersfield - 14 pts (Bhv Sci) (4 AS)
8 pts.	**and below**
	Nene (CHE) - (Comb St) (See also **Psychology**)
	Westminster - (Sci/Life)

Alternative offers:

SCE offers: **Huddersfield** BB.

CHOOSING YOUR COURSE (See also Ch 1)

> **Subject information:** This is a study of animal as well as human behaviour, which offers an overlap between zoology, psychology and biological sciences. These courses could also be considered as alternative subject choices.

Course highlights: Glamorgan Community-based programmes form part of teaching scheme. Mixed programme of sociology, anthropology and psychology. Selection of certain options gives exemptions from elements of social work training and qualifies graduates for membership of the British Psychological Society. NOW CHECK PROSPECTUSES FOR ALL COURSES.

ADMISSIONS INFORMATION

Number of applicants per place (approx): Glamorgan 10.

Selection interviews: Glamorgan; Huddersfield; Nottingham.

> **Examples of interview questions:** See under **Psychology**.

GAP YEAR ADVICE

Institutions accepting a Gap Year: Most institutions.

AFTER A-LEVELS ADVICE

Institutions which may accept the same points score after A-levels: Glamorgan; Huddersfield.

Institutions demanding actual grades after A-levels: Nottingham.

ADVICE FOR MATURE STUDENTS

This is a popular course for mature students. Institutions often have links with local Access courses.

BIOCHEMISTRY

Special subject requirements: 2-3 A-levels from mathematics/science subjects. Chemistry often essential; physics sometimes preferred.

NB Institutions may raise or lower the level of published offers depending either on the quality or otherwise of individual applications or the numbers of applications received; grades/points offered may be adjusted downwards after A-level results. The level of an offer is not indicative of the quality of a course.

30 pts.   **Cambridge** - AAA potential recommended (Nat Sci/Biochem)
          Oxford - AAA potential recommended (Biochem)
24 pts.   **Bath** - BBB (Biochem) (BTEC D+2M)
22 pts.   **Bristol** - BBC/BC+CC at AS (All courses)
          Lancaster - BBC (Bioch/USA)
          Nottingham - BBC (Bio/Gen)
          Salford - BBC-CCD/AA-BB (Bioch Sci; Bioch USA) (4 AS) (BTEC 4M)
          Southampton - BBC/BCC (All courses)
20 pts.   **Birmingham** - BCC (Biochem; Bioch/Biot; Med Biochem; Bioch/Biol)
          Cardiff - BCC/BB (Bioch; Bioch Med) (BTEC M average)
          Lancaster - BCC (Biochem) (BTEC Ms)
          Leeds - BCC-CCC/BB (Biochem courses)
          Leicester - BCC (Med Bioch)
          Liverpool - BCC-CCC (Biochem; C Biol/Bioch) (4-5 AS)
          London (Imp) - BCC/BB (Biochem; Biotech; Bioch/Ind; Bioch Man/Ind)
          London (King's) - BCC/BB approx (Biochem; Biotech)
          London (RH) - BCC/BC (All courses) (6 AS) (BTEC 2M+2P)
          Manchester - BCC approx (Biochem)
          Nottingham - BCC (Bioch/Biol Ch)
          Sheffield - BCC-CCC/AC-BB (Biochem; Bio/Chem; Bio/Micro) (6 AS) (BTEC 3M)
          Sussex - BCC-BCD (BCB; BCH)
          UMIST - BCC/BB (All courses) (BTEC 3M)
          Warwick - BCC-CCC (Biochem)
          York - BCC (Biochem)
18 pts.   **Aberdeen** - CCC-CCD/BC (Biochem)
          Aberystwyth - CCC-CCD/BB-BC (C in biol & chem) (Bio/Micro) (BTEC 3M)
          Belfast - CCC/BB (Biochem)
          Brunel - BCD-CCC/BB (Biochem; Med Bioch; App Bioch) (4 AS) (A or AS to include
                 biol and phys **or** maths) (BTEC 3M)
          Cardiff - CCC/BB (Bioch Phys)
          Durham - CCC-CCD (M Biol/Bioch)
          East Anglia - BCD-CCC/BC (Biochem; Bioch/Biol) (4 AS) (BTEC 65% average)
          Edinburgh - CCC/BB (Biochem) (4 AS)
          Essex - CCC/BB (Biochem; Biol Med Chem) (BTEC Ms)
          Glasgow - CCC-CCD/BC (Biochem courses)
          Keele - BCD-CCC/BC-CC (Biochemistry - Single and Joint courses) (4 AS) (BTEC
                 3M)
          Leicester - BCD (Biol Chem)
          London (UC) - CCC (Biochem)
          Newcastle - CCC-BCD/BB (Biochem)
          Reading - BCD-CCC (Biochem; Biochem/Physio)
          Salford - CCC-CDD (Biochem/Chem; Biochem/Phys; Biochem/Econ) (BTEC 4M)
          Sheffield - CCC (Bio/Physio)
          Stirling - CCC-BCD/BB-BC (Biochem courses)
          Strathclyde - CCC-BCD (2nd yr entry) (Bioch; Bioch/Immun; Bioch/Pharm)
          Surrey - CCC/BC (All courses) (BTEC 3D+2M)
          Swansea - CCC/BB (Biochem) (BTEC 1D+Ms)
16 pts.   **Aberystwyth** - 16-14 pts (Biochem courses) (BTEC 3M)

Bradford - CCD/BB (Biochem) (BTEC 3M)
Kent - CCD (Biol Chem)
Leicester - BDD (Biol Chem)
London (QMW) - CCD/CC (Biochem)
Newcastle - CCD-CDD/BB-BC (Agric Biochem)
St Andrews - CCD (Biochem)
Ulster - CCD/BC (Ap Bio Sc)

14 pts. Bangor - CDD/BC (B in chem) (Biochem; Bioch 4) (BTEC 6M)
Dundee - CDD/BC (Biochem courses; Med Sci)
London (Wye) - 14 pts approx (Bioch)
Nottingham - CDD (Nut Bioch)

12 pts. and below approx
Aberystwyth - 4 pts (Bioch - Ord degree)
Bristol UWE - 8 pts (Bioch/Med Biol)
Buckingham - CDE (Phys Bioch)
Central Lancashire - CC-CD (Comb Hons; App Bioch) (4 AS)
Coventry - 10 pts inc E min in chem and pref biol (Bioch Sci) (BTEC 3M)
East London - (Bioch)
Greenwich - EEE/DE (Biochem) (BTEC 4M)
Heriot-Watt - DDD (CCC 2nd yr entry) (Biochem; Brewing/Dist) (BTEC 3M)
Hertfordshire - 12-8 pts (App Biol - Bioch)
Huddersfield - (App Chem)
Kingston - 8 pts (Bioch) (BTEC 6M)
Liverpool John Moores - DD (App Biochem) (4 AS)
North East Wales (IHE) - 6 pts (Bioch/Biol Sci)
Paisley - (App Bioch)
SAC (Ab) - (Aqua)
Westminster - DD (Bioch/Micro)
Wolverhampton - 10 pts (Biochem; Comb Studs; Ap Sci)

Diploma of Higher Education courses:
4 pts. Central Lancashire; Wolverhampton.

Alternative offers:

EB offers: **Aberystwyth** 70% in 2 named subjects; **Bangor** 65%; **Bath** 70%; **Bradford** 65%; **Keele** 60%; **Sheffield** 65%; **UMIST** 60%.

IB offers: **Aberdeen** 26 pts; **Aberystwyth** 28 pts + (minimum of 5 in each subject); **Bangor** 28 pts 5 in chem; **Bath** 24 pts or more inc 18 pts at Highers; **Bradford** 24 pts; **Bristol** 32 pts inc 6 in Chemistry; **Brunel** 28 pts min inc 15 pts Highers; **Cardiff** 28 pts + H555; **Dundee** H544; **Durham** H665; **East Anglia** 28 pts; **Heriot-Watt** 28 pts; **Keele** 26 pts; **Kent** 25 pts, H 11 pts; **Lancaster** 28-30 pts; **Leeds** 24 pts; **Liverpool** 30 pts inc H555; **London (RH)** 30 pts; **St Andrews** 28 pts; **Salford** H555; **Southampton** 6H55; **Surrey** 28 pts; **Swansea** 30 pts; **UMIST** 30 pts H555; **York** 28 pts H555.

Irish offers: **Aberdeen** BBCC/BCCC; **Aberystwyth** BBBCC; **Bangor** BBBDD; **Brunel** BBCCC; **Keele** BBCCC; **Liverpool** BBCCC; **Sheffield** BBBBB; **UMIST** ABBBBC.

SCE offers: **Aberdeen** BBBC; **Bangor** BBCC; **Bradford** BBBB inc chem/biol; **Dundee** BBB/BBCC; **East Anglia** BBBB; **Edinburgh** ABBC-BBBB; **Glasgow** ABB or BBBB or BBB; **Heriot-Watt** BBBB; **Keele** BBCC; **Lancaster** ABBB; **Leeds** AAAA; **Liverpool** ABBB; **London (RH)** BBB; **St Andrews** BBBC; **Salford** BBBB; **Sheffield** BBBB; **Stirling** BBCC; **Strathclyde** BBB; **Surrey** ABB/BBBB; **UMIST** AABB.

Overseas applicants: Bangor Courses in English available; also Foundation courses in chemistry. **Durham** No Foundation courses. **East Anglia** English courses for students.

CHOOSING YOUR COURSE (See also Ch I)

> **Subject information:** Many subjects can be covered in these courses eg. medical biochemistry, plant and animal physiology, microbiology, biophysics. Different courses will suit different students; check the prospectuses carefully. Other alternatives are equally varied eg, Agriculture, Brewing, Geochemistry, Medicine, Pharmacology and Pharmacy.

Course highlights: Dundee, London (Imp), Oxford, Leicester High research ratings. **Aberdeen** Options in immunology and parasitology. **Aberystwyth** New course offered in Genetics and Biochemistry and an ordinary degree in Biochemistry for applicants not wanting to commit themselves to Honours level study. Transfers to honours degree possible at the end of year I. **Bangor** Wide choice of modules covering botany, animal biology, applied and fisheries biology. **Bath** Biochemistry taken with chemistry and cell biology in year I; genetics and statistics taken in year 2, and a range of options in year 4 include biotechnology and medical biochemistry. **Belfast** Year I subjects include chemistry plus three from physics, mathematics, statistics, computer science, botany or zoology. **Birmingham** Choice of courses deferred until Easter of year 2. **Bradford** Options in year 3 – microbiology, biochemistry, cellular pathology, nutrition, pharmacology. **Bristol** Flexibility in years I and 2, transfer to other subjects possible in year I (eg, Chemistry, Psychology, Pharmacology, Microbiology (depending on 1st year course). Language option in year 2. **Brunel** Options in final year in field of medical biochemistry and genetic manipulation. **Cardiff** (Biochemistry Medical) In year 3 three special topics offered: biochemistry, biochemistry with an option in medical biochemistry, and biochemistry with option in biochemistry of drugs. **Durham** Year I students take courses in botany, zoology and chemistry going on to specialist areas. **East Anglia** Transfers to degree courses in Biological or Chemical Sciences possible. **East London** Compulsory subjects include biochemical techniques, metabolism, molecular biology and medical biochemistry. **Edinburgh** Common first year which includes biology, chemistry, introductory physics and maths; biochemistry specialism starts in year 3. **Heriot-Watt** In year 3 options with biochemistry include computer science, microbiology and chemical engineering. **Keele** Course emphasis on animal and human biochemistry. **Kent** Optional courses in medical biochemistry, cell and molecular biology or biotechnology. **Leeds** Biochemistry offered with chemistry and two other subjects from genetics, microbiology and physiology in year I. **Liverpool John Moores** Year 4 specialisms avilable in clinical, agrochemical, environmental and microbial biochemistry. **London (Imp)** Common life science course in year I includes chemistry and biochemistry with optional courses. **London (RH)** In year 3 specialist subject include parasite biochemistry, drug metabolism and plant and animal biochemistry. **Newcastle** Options in years 2 and 3 include nutrition, immuniology, gene cloning and protein engineering. **Nottingham** Nutritional Biochemistry allows for specialisation in either animal or human nutrition. **Sheffield** Year 2 studies divided between chemistry, physiology or microbiology. **Stirling** Department's main interests are developmental biochemistry, plant biochemistry and biochemistry of brain and nerve tissue. **Surrey** In year 4 Biochemistry students select three options from range including biotechnology, cancer biochemistry and pharmacological biochemistry. **UMIST** In year 3 some students take advanced biochemistry and either clinical biochemistry or applied molecular biology. **York** Biochemistry and Chemistry students taught together for first part of course. In remaining two parts, Biochemistry specialisms include microbiology and biophysical techniques and biology. NOW CHECK PROSPECTUSES FOR ALL COURSES.

Study opportunities abroad: Aberystwyth (E) G FR SZ; **Bangor** (E); **Birmingham** (E); **Brunel** G IT SZ FR USA; **Cardiff** (E); **Central Lancashire** FR SP G; **East Anglia** (E) FR G; **Kent** IT; **Lancaster** USA; **Newcastle** (E) SP NL; **Sussex** FR G SP; **Swansea** (E); **UMIST** GR.

Work opportunities abroad: Aberystwyth EUR; **Bath** EUR USA; **Brunel** G IT SZ FR; **Greenwich; Surrey** G SZ USA; **Warwick**.

ADMISSIONS INFORMATION

Number of applicants per place (approx): Aberystwyth 6; **Bangor** 6; **Bath** 7; **Birmingham** 9; **Bradford** 10; **Bristol** 7; **Brunel** 6; **Cardiff** 6, (Bioch/Phys) 2; **Dundee** 8; **Durham** 6; **East Anglia** 10; **East London** 2; **Edinburgh** 8; **Essex** 5; **Heriot-Watt** 7; **Keele** 7; **Kent** 11; **Lancaster** 10; **Leeds** 6; **Liverpool** 5; **Liverpool John Moores** 10; **London (Imp)** 6, **(RH)** 6; **Newcastle** 7;

Nottingham 10; **St Andrews** 10; **Salford** 6; **Sheffield** 11; **Strathclyde** 15; **Surrey** 6; **Swansea** 5; **UMIST** 6; **Warwick** 6; **York** 12.

General Studies acceptable: Aberdeen; Aberystwyth; Coventry (No); Dundee; East London; Keele; Westminster.

Selection interviews: Bangor (some); Bath (50%); Bradford (informal – after offer); Brunel (most); Cambridge; East Anglia; Keele (mature applicants only); Leeds (some); Liverpool; Liverpool John Moores; London (RH); Newcastle; Oxford; Salford; Sheffield; UMIST (some); Warwick; York.

Offers to applicants repeating A-levels: Higher Bangor, Durham (BCC), East Anglia, Nottingham (BBC or BCC), Strathclyde; **Possibly higher** Aberystwyth, Bath, Bristol, Brunel, Central Lancashire, Keele, Kent, Lancaster, Liverpool John Moores, Newcastle, York; **Same** Aston (Comb Hons), Birmingham, Bradford, Hull, Leeds, Liverpool, London (RH), Salford, Sheffield, Surrey, Swansea, UMIST (C in chemistry).

Admissions Tutors' advice: Aberystwyth GCSE maths grade A-C required. **Bath** A-level grades A-B in chemistry required. **Bradford** If not presented at A-level then biology, chemistry or maths must be passed at GCSE (grade C). **York** GCSE physics or science with physics very desirable. **Salford** Applicants are invited to visit in small groups and an informal solo interview is included.

> **Examples of interview questions:** What do you intend to do with a degree in Biochemistry? Discuss the process in which light energy is converted to energy in a form useful to plants. What does biochemistry consist of? What is microbiology? Problems about oxidation and reduction. What are catalysts? How do enzymes work? What developments are taking place in biochemistry? Questions on subjects covering Mendel, genetics, RNA and DNA. Which is more important – biochemistry, biology or chemistry? (Trick question, answer – None!) Question on the formation of the chemistry of proteins. (See also **Biological Sciences**.)

GAP YEAR ADVICE

Institutions accepting a Gap Year: Most institutions; **Aberystwyth** Apply before taking your year out so that you can visit the university of your choice. **Bristol** Adequate chemistry revision necessary before starting the course. **Brunel** Think beforehand since this course offers experience outside the academic world. **Cardiff** Have a positive plan. **Dundee** Do something useful. **London (RH)** Lab work beneficial. Overseas travel to develop independence and communication skills. **Surrey** Appropriate lab-based work can compensate for under-achievement at A-level. **Swansea** Try to obtain subject-related employment.

Institutions willing to defer entry after A-levels (see Ch 5): Aberystwyth (Contact the Admissions Tutor if you change your mind); Brunel; Heriot-Watt; Kingston; Lancaster; Salford; St Andrews; Surrey; Swansea (discouraged); UMIST.

AFTER A-LEVELS ADVICE

Institutions which may accept the same points score after A-levels: Aberystwyth; Bangor; Bath; Bradford; Bristol; Brunel; Cardiff; Central Lancashire; Durham; East Anglia; Hull; Keele; Kent; Lancaster; Leeds (grade C chem); Liverpool; Liverpool John Moores; London (RH); Newcastle; Nottingham; Salford; Sheffield; Southampton; Strathclyde; Surrey; Swansea; Warwick; UMIST; Wolverhampton; York.

Institutions demanding the actual grades offered after A-levels: Stirling.

Institutions which may accept under-achieving applicants after A-levels: Aberdeen; Aberystwyth; Bangor; Bath; Belfast; Bradford; Bristol; Brunel; Cardiff; City; East Anglia; Hull; Keele; Kent; Lancaster; Leeds (chem grade as in offer); Liverpool; Liverpool John Moores; London (RH); Newcastle; Salford; Sheffield; Surrey; Sussex; Swansea; UMIST; Wolverhampton; York.

Institutions with vacancies in Aug/Sept 1992 (see Ch 5): Aberdeen; Aberystwyth 12 pts; Bath; Bristol; Brunel 16 pts; Dundee; Essex; Greenwich 4 pts; Heriot-Watt 12 pts; Kent; Kingston 10-9 pts; Lancaster 12 pts; London (QMW); Newcastle 18 pts; Paisley; St Andrews; Sheffield; Strathclyde; St Andrews 16 pts; Surrey CDD; Swansea 16-14 pts; UMIST 16-14 pts; most institutions are likely to have vacancies in 1993. A very large number of universities declared vacancies in 1992 and places could be obtained on 12 pts or lower.

ADVICE FOR MATURE STUDENTS

About 4% of students on these courses are 'mature'. Science qualifications are important.

GRADUATE EMPLOYMENT

New Graduates' destinations (percentages) 1991:
Permanent employment: U 73; P 67.
Unemployment: U 18; P 24.
Further studies (all types): U 58; P 49
Main career destinations (approx): Scientific 36; Business/Finance 27.

Surrey (1991) Five graduates went into subject-related full-time employment, the remainder following post-graduate courses. Many of those following the Biochemistry (Medical) course also entered scientific occupations in hospitals or laboratories. Nine students went on to study for PhDs in such areas as biochemistry, equine embryology, genetics and cancer, nutrition and drug metabolism. One student went on to a Master's course in Business Administration. A similar pattern of employment is reflected in the destinations of those following the Biochemistry (Toxicology) course. See also under **Science**.

York (1988-91) Work in hospitals, animal research industry including phamaceuticals, and agriculture and conservation attracted a number of students; 52% went on to higher degrees in research, business studies, law and teacher training.

BIOLOGICAL SCIENCES (including Ecology)

Special subject requirements: 2-3 A-levels from mathematics/science subjects. Chemistry usually essential; GCSE (grades A-C) in mathematics/science subjects. The general requirement for a foreign language at York may be waived.

NB Institutions may raise or lower the level of published offers depending either on the quality or otherwise of individual applications or the numbers of applications received; grades/points offered may be adjusted downwards after A-level results. The level of an offer is not indicative of the quality of a course.

30 pts.	**Cambridge** - AAA potential recommended (Nat Sci)
28 pts.	**East Anglia** - AAB-ABB (Bio/USA)
	Oxford - AAB-ABB (Science - Biology)
24 pts.	**Lancaster** - BBB (Ecol/USA)
22 pts.	**Cardiff** - BBC-BCC (Neurosc) (BTEC 2D+4M)
	Lancaster - BBC (Biol/USA)
	Leeds - BBC-BCC/AB (Ecol)
	Salford - BBC-CCD/AA-AB (Biol USA) (4 AS) (BTEC 4M)
20 pts.	**Birmingham** - BCC (Biol Sci; Bio/Geog)
	Bristol - BCC/BB (Path) (AS from phys/maths/bot)
	East Anglia - BCC/AA-BB (Cell Biol; Bio/Eur) (BTEC 65%)
	Exeter - BCC/BB (Biol Sci; Bio/Med Chem) (4-6 AS) (BTEC M overall)
	Lancaster - BCC/BB (Ecology)
	Leeds - BCC (Ecol) (BTEC 5M)
	London (Imp) - BCC (Neuro)

London (RH) – BCC (Ecol; Env Biol) (4 AS)
St Andrews – BCC-CCC (Neuro) (4 AS)
Sheffield – BCC-CCC (Ecol courses) (BTEC Ms)
Swansea – BCC/BB (Biol Sci/Lang) (BTEC 2-3M)
Warwick – BCC-CCC (Bio Sci)
York – BCC-CCC (Ecology)

18pts. **Aberdeen** – CCC-CCD/BC (Biomed Sci; Biol Sci)
Belfast – CCC/BB (Biol Sc)
Cardiff – BCD (Ecol)
Durham – CCC (Biol Sci; M Biol/Bioch) (4 AS)
East Anglia – BCD/BC (Biol Sci – C100)
Edinburgh – CCC-CCD/BB (Ecol Sci; Biol; Immun) (4 AS)
Essex – BCD (Biol)
Heriot-Watt – CCC (Biol Sci; Brewing)
Lancaster – CCC/BC (Biol Sci)
Leicester – BCD (Biol Sci; An Phys; Ecol)
Liverpool – CCC (All courses)
London (QMW) – CCC (Biology)
London (UC) – CCC-CCD/BC (Ecology; Immun)
Newcastle – BCD/BB (Biol Sci)
Reading – CCC-BCD (Biol Sci; Molec Biol; Animal Sci S)
Salford – CCC (Biol Sci)
Sheffield – CCC (Biomed Sci; Neurosci) (6 AS) (BTEC Ms)
Stirling – CCC (Ecol)
Strathclyde – CCC-BCD (2nd yr entry) (Biol Sci; Immun)
Sussex – 18 pts approx (Ecol/Cons; Biol Sci)
Ulster – BCD/BB (Biomed Sci) (6 AS)
Ulster – CCC/BB (Biol Sci) (6 AS)
York – CCC (Ecol/Cons Env)

16pts. **Bradford** – CCD/BB (Biomed Sci) (BTEC 3M)
Glasgow – CCD (Biol courses)
Leicester – CCD (Sci Comb)
London (King's) – CCD approx (Biol Sci)
London (QMW) – CCD (Ecol)

14pts. **Cambridge (Hom)** – BC-CC (Bio Ed) (4 AS) (See also **Education**)
Dundee – CDD/BC (Biol Sci)
Huddersfield – CDD-DDD/CC (Human Ec)
Newcastle – CDD/BC (Ag Eur Sci/Ecol)
Warwick – CCE-CDE (C in Biol) (BA (QTS) Biol)

12pts. **Brighton** – 12-10 pts (Biomed Sci) (BTEC 3M)
Kingston – 12 pts (Biomed Sci)
Plymouth – CDE/CD-DD (Biol Sci) (BTEC 4M)
Portsmouth – 12 pts (Biomed Sci) (4 AS)
Wolverhampton – DDD/CC (Biomed Sci) (BTEC 3M)

10pts. **Bedford (CHE)** – 10 pts (Comb St)
Buckingham – 10-8 pts (Ag Fish Bio; Biol Sci) (BTEC 2-3M)
Cardiff (IHE) – CD (Biomed Sci)
Glasgow Caledonian – DDE/CD (App Bio Sci)
Heriot-Watt – DDD (CCC for 2nd yr entry) (Biol Sci)
Kingston – DDE-DEE/CD-DD (Bio Sci; Cell/Mol Biol)
Liverpool John Moores – DDE/DD (App Ecol)
Manchester Met – 10 pts (App Biol Sci – 3 yr course) (BTEC 5M)
Napier – 10 pts (Biol Sci)
Sheffield Hallam – CD (Biol Man)
Worcester (CHE) – 10 pts (Biol Sci) (4 AS)

8pts. and below
Bell (CT) – (App Bio Sci)
Bristol UWE – 8 pts (Ap Biol; Biomed Sci) (BTEC 5M)
Central Lancashire – DD (Neuro) (4 AS)

Derby - (Earth/Life St)
East London - (App Ecol; Immun; Inf Diseases)
Glamorgan - EEE/DD (App Sci/Biol Sci)
Guildhall London - DEE/DD-CE (Ecol - modular; Neuroscience - modular) (BTEC 4M)
Manchester Met - 6 pts (App Biol Sci - 4 yr course) (BTEC 5M)
Robert Gordon - (App Biosci/Chem)
Roehampton (IHE) -
Westminster - DD (Biomed Sci) (BTEC 3M)
Wolverhampton - DD (Biol Sci; Comb St)
Wolverhampton - (Part-time course for mature students)

Diploma of Higher Education courses:
2pts.   Edge Hill (CHE).

Higher National Diploma courses (England and Wales):
2pts.   Bristol UWE; Westminster (App Biol).

Higher Diploma courses (Scotland):
2pts.   and below. Bell (CT); Dundee (IT); Napier EE; Paisley.

Alternative offers:

EB offers: **Newcastle** 65%.

IB offers: **Aberdeen** 24 pts; **Birmingham** H655; **Bradford** 24 pts; **Brighton** 27 pts; **Buckingham** 24 pts; **Durham** H665; **East Anglia** (Biol Eur) 30 pts, (Ecol) 444, (Biol Sci) 28 pts inc 15 pts Highers, (Biol/USA) 32 pts inc 6 in relevant sciences; **Essex** 28 pts; **Exeter** 30 pts; **Kent** 25 pts, H 11 pts; **Lancaster** 28 pts; **Newcastle** 30-28 pts; **Plymouth** 28-26 pts inc 15 pts from 3 science subjects; **Salford** H555; **St Andrews** 28 pts; **Swansea** 28 pts, (Biol Sci/Lang) 32 pts; **York** H555.

Irish offers: **Aberdeen** BBCC/BCCCC; **Guildhall London** CCCCC; **Newcastle** AABB.

SCE offers: **Aberdeen** BBBC; **Bristol** ABBB; **Bristol UWE** BBC; **East Anglia** BBBB-BBBCC; **Edinburgh** BBBB; **Guildhall London** BBCCC; **Heriot-Watt** BBBB; **Lancaster** BBCCC; **Leeds** ABB; **Loughborough** ABBB; **Manchester Met** BBB; **Napier** BCC; **Newcastle** AABB; **Salford** ABBB; **Sheffield** BBBB; **Strathclyde** ABBC/BBBB; **Warwick** AAABB; **York** BBBB.

CHOOSING YOUR COURSE (See also Ch 1)

Subject information: Biological Sciences crosses many boundaries eg, biochemistry, botany, zoology, microbiology, biotechnology, genetics, physiology. Biology and Applied Biology courses should also be considered.

Course highlights: Cambridge, London (Imp), Manchester Met Emphasis on mammalian physiology, biochemistry, ecology and behaviour. Course work 30% assessment. **Bangor** Main areas of interest - animal physiology, ecology, genetics, microbiology, biology and biochemistry. **Birmingham** Options to specialise in animal biology, environmental biology, genetics, microbiology or plant biology. **Bradford** Year 3 options offered in cellular pathology, metabolic biochemistry, microbiology and pharmacology. **Bristol UWE** Two named routes - Biotechnology and Biomedical Science. **Brunel** Option to transfer to Applied Biochemistry in year 2. **Buckingham** (Biol Sci) Options in physiological biochemistry, aquatic and fisheries. Biology or Environmental Physiology courses commence in January. **Durham** Year 1 programme includes botany and zoology. **East Anglia** Year 3 specialist programmes include biochemistry, genetics, plant biology and ecology. **Edinburgh** Transfer possible from Biological Science to Agriculture up to the end of year 2. **Exeter** Ancilliary subject taken in year 1 from chemistry, geography, geology or psychology. **Heriot-Watt** Combined course across biochemical, microbiological and marine biological subjects. **Lancaster** Year 1 covers biological sciences and one subject from chemistry, environmental sciences, physics, psychology, statistics, maths computer studies. **Leicester** Year I includes Biological Sciences and supplementary subject from chemistry, geography, geology, psychology, pure maths, statistics or economics. **Liverpool John Moores** (App Ecol) Course covers population biology, resource management and conservation. **Newcastle** Biological Sciences covers degree courses in cell biology, biology of plants and animals, marine biology and plant biology. **Plymouth** Two options chosen in the final four terms including marine and fish biology, medical biology, agricultural physiology, crop protection and pollution. **Reading** Specialist studies in three main areas: animal sciences, molecular biology, biology and statistics. **Salford** Year 2 options in psychology, applied biology or biochemistry. **Ulster** Optional courses in animal behaviour, biochemistry, statistics, psychology, chemistry. **Warwick** Flexible course with opportunity to transfer to degree courses in Biochemistry, Microbiolgy and Virology and Microbiology and Microbial Technology. **Wolverhampton** Opportunities to specialise in specific areas of biotechnology, biomedical sciences, applied human biology, microbiology, biochemistry and ecology. NOW CHECK PROSPECTUSES FOR ALL COURSES.

Study opportunities abroad: Birmingham; Buckingham (E) SP; **East Anglia** USA FR G; **Lancaster** USA; **Sussex** FR G SP; **Swansea** (E); **Ulster** (E) GR; **York** USA CAN.

Work opportunities abroad: Worcester (CHE) USA.

ADMISSIONS INFORMATION

Number of applicants per place (approx): Birmingham 10; **Bristol UWE** 11; **Cambridge (Hom)** 4; **Cardiff (IHE)** 2; **Durham** 4 inc biol; **East Anglia** (Biol/USA) 15, (Biol/Eur) 5, (Biol Sci) 15; **Edinburgh** 8; **Essex** 10; **Lancaster** (Biol Sci) 12; **Leeds** (Ecol) 5; **Leicester** 7; **Manchester Met** 23; **Napier** 8; **Newcastle** 9; **Plymouth** 10; **Reading** 8; **Salford** 6; **Strathclyde** 30; **Swansea** 5; **Wolverhampton** 17; **Worcester (CHE)** 18.

General Studies acceptable: Aberdeen; Bedford (CHE); Birmingham; Bristol UWE; Essex (JMB only); Exeter (2); Manchester Met (2); Salford; Wolverhampton (2); Worcester (CHE) (2).

Selection interviews: Cambridge (Hom); East Anglia; Essex (some); Huddersfield; Kent; Leeds (Ecol); Liverpool; London (RH); Manchester Met (some); Nottingham; Oxford; Plymouth (some); Salford; Stirling; Southampton; Sussex; Warwick; York.

Offers to applicants repeating A-levels: Higher Bristol, Durham, East Anglia (BCC), Bristol UWE, Leeds (BBC), Newcastle, Swansea; **Possibly higher** Cambridge (Hom), Essex, Lancaster, Leeds (Ecol), Manchester Met; **Same** Exeter, London (RH), York (or 2 pts higher).

Admissions Tutors' advice: Leeds (Ecology) Ability in science subjects important. See also under **Biology. London (RH)** (Ecology) Some experience preferred. **Salford** Candidates are invited to visit in small groups and an informal solo interview is included.

> **Examples of interview questions:** What do you know about microbiology and genetics? What research interests do you have? What could be the role of the microbiologist in industry? What are your main interests in biology? How would you teach children biology? (BEd course) What do you understand by biotechnology and genetic engineering? How is insulin produced? Give examples of where microbes might be used in industry. What field work courses have you attended? *(If you have a field course work book take it with you.)* Why is photosynthesis necessary? Describe it. Describe the dentition of a herbivor. Argue for and against investing money in industry rather than education. (BEd course).

GAP YEAR ADVICE

Institutions accepting a Gap Year: Bradford (Prefer gap year); Lancaster; Plymouth (Stay tuned to biology, chemistry, maths); Robert Gordon; Swansea (Try to obtain relevant experience, but enjoy yourself!); most institutions.

Institutions willing to defer entry after A-levels (see Ch 5): Bell (CT) (No); Bradford; Buckingham; Heriot-Watt; Kingston; Leeds; Manchester Met; Plymouth (decide quickly!); Roehampton (IHE); Salford; Swansea (discouraged); Westminster.

AFTER A-LEVELS ADVICE

Institutions which may accept the same points score after A-levels: Birmingham; Bristol UWE; Brunel; Cardiff (Neuro); Durham; East Anglia; Essex; Exeter; Lancaster; London (RH); Loughborough; Manchester Met; Salford; Strathclyde; Warwick; Wolverhampton; Worcester (CHE).

Institutions demanding the actual grades after A-levels: Plymouth.

Institutions which may accept under-achieving applicants after A-levels: Bristol UWE; Cambridge (Hom); Cardiff; East Anglia (not Biol/USA); Essex; Exeter; Leeds (Ecol); Leicester; Liverpool John Moores; London (RH); Newcastle; Reading; Salford; Swansea; most other new universities and colleges.

Institutions with vacancies in Aug/Sept 1992 (see Ch 5): Aberdeen; Bangor; Bell (CT); Bradford above 12 pts; Buckingham 8 pts; East London; Glamorgan; Heriot-Watt 12 pts; Kingston 10 pts; Lancaster 16 pts; Leeds (Ecol) 18 pts; London (QMW), (RH); Manchester Met; Plymouth 10 pts; Robert Gordon 4 pts; Roehampton (IHE); Swansea 16 pts; Westminster; most institutions are likely to have vacancies in 1993 in Biological and Biomedical Sciences and Biology. 12 pts and lower are likely to secure places. Vacancies for Ecology courses normally required 14-18 pts.

ADVICE FOR MATURE STUDENTS

A small number of students embark on these courses. Science qualifications are usually required.

GRADUATE EMPLOYMENT

New Graduates' destinations (percentages) 1991:
Permanent employment: U 64; P 76; C 100.
Unemployment: U 24; P 18; C 0.
Further studies (all types): U 44; P 33; C 18.

For other Biological Science subjects see also under **Biology, Botany, Genetics, Microbiology, Science, Zoology.**

BIOLOGY (including Applied, Human, Marine and Plant Biology and Biomedical Science) (For Environmental Biology see also Environmental Science)

Special subject requirements: see **Biological Sciences.**

NB Institutions may raise or lower the level of published offers depending either on the quality or otherwise of individual applications or the numbers of applications received; grades/points offered may be adjusted downwards after A-level results. The level of an offer is not indicative of the quality of a course.

30 pts.	**Cambridge** (Nat Sci)/**Oxford** (Biology) – AAA potential recommended
22 pts.	**Aberdeen** - BBC (Marine Res Man)
	London (Imp) - BBC (App Biol)
	Newcastle - BBC-BCC/BB (Marine Bio)
	St Andrews - BBB (Env Biol courses) (BTEC 65% overall)
20 pts.	**Aston** - BCC/AB (Ap Hum Biol)
	Bath - BCC-BCD (Biol) (BTEC 75% average)

Cardiff - BCC-BCD/BB (Biol courses) (BTEC 70% average)

Leeds - BCC/BB (Biol; App Biol; App Biol/Man St; App Biol/Chem; Ecol) (BTEC 5M)

London (Imp) - BCC (Biology; Biol/Eur)

London (RH) - BCC-BCD/BC (Biology; Biol/Geog; Bot) (4 AS)(BTEC 3M)

Manchester - BCC-CCC approx (Biol courses)

Newcastle - BCC-BCD/BB (Biol/PA; Env Biol/Lang) (4 AS)

Nottingham - BCC (Biol)

Nottingham - BCC-CCC (Mol Cell Biol)

Southampton - BCC-BCD (All courses)

Swansea - BCC-CCC/BB (Env Biol; Mar Biol) (BTEC 3M, (HND) 1D+Ms for yr 2 entry)

York - BCC-CCC (All courses) (BTEC 4M)

18 pts. **Aberdeen** - CCC-CCD/BC (Biol; Biomed Sci)

Aberystwyth - CCC-CCD/BB-BC(Biology courses; Biometry) (BTEC 3M)

Aston - CCC/AA (Biol Comb)

Bangor - CCC-CCD/BB (Mar Biol courses) (BTEC 3M)

Belfast - CCC/BB (Biol Sci; Mol Biol)

Bristol - CCC (Biol)

Brunel - BCD/14 pts (Biol) (BTEC 65% average)

Cambridge (Hom) - BCD/CC (Bio/Ed) (See also under **Education**)

Durham - CCC (Nat Sci; M Biol/Bioch)

East Anglia - BCD/BB (Plant Biol)

East Anglia - CCC-CCD/CC (Bio/Chem; Molec Biol)

Edinburgh - CCC (Biol)

Essex - BCD-CCC/BC (Env Biol; Cell Biol)

Glasgow - CCC-CCD/BC (Aquat; Cell Biol; Mol Biol)

Keele - CCC (All courses) (4 AS) (BTEC 3M)

Leicester - BCD (Biol Sci)

Liverpool - CCC/BB (Biol; App Biol; Mar Biol; App Cell Sci; Biol/Med Sci; M Cell Biol) (4 AS)

London (King's) - CCC-CCD approx (Biol courses)

London (QMW) - CCC-CDD (Biology)

London (UC) - CCC-CCD (Biol)

Loughborough - CCC (H Biol 3 & 4) (BTEC 2D+5M)

Manchester - 18 pts approx (Plant Biol/Science courses)

Newcastle - CCC-BCD/BB-BC (Plant Biol; Mol Biol)

Reading - CCC-BCD (All courses)

Salford - CCC-CDD approx (Ap Biol/Geog; Ap Biol/Chem)

Sheffield - CCC (Ap Biol) (6 AS) (BTEC 3M)

Stirling - BCD-CCC/BC (All courses)

Surrey - CCC/BC (Mol Biol) (BTEC 5M)

Sussex - BCD-CCC (B/Biols)

Swansea - CCC-CCD/BB (Biol) (BTEC 3M, (HND) 1D+Ms for yr 2 entry)

Warwick - CCC (Bio Sci)

16 pts. **Bangor** - CCD/BC (Biology; Biol/Bioch; App An Biol; Biol 4; Bio Bioch 4) (BTEC 3M)

Bradford - CCD/BB (Biomed Sci - all options)

Central Lancashire - CCD/CC (App Biol)

Hull - CCD-CDD/BC (Biol; Biol Educ) (1 complementary AS)

London (QMW) - CCD/CC (Biol/Chem)

London (QMW) - CCD (Biomed Sci)

London (Wye) - CCD (Biol)

Salford - (Biomedical Engineering) (See under **Engineering (Electronic)**)

14 pts. **Aberystwyth** - CDD/BC (AP Biol)

Bangor - CDD/CC (Ap Biol) (BTEC 3M)

Dundee - CDD/BC (Biol Sci)

Kingston - 14 pts (Biomedical Sci; Biol/Geog) (4 AS)

Nottingham - CDD/CC (Env Biol)

	Ulster – CDD/CC (Bio Sc; Biol Sc) (Bio Sc – AS des tech/maths/ biol/phys/eng)
12pts.	**Brighton** – 12-8 pts (Biol courses) (4 AS) (BTEC 3M)
	Bristol UWE – DDD/CC (Ap Biol)
	Buckingham – CDE/DD (Biol)
	Derby – 12 pts (Biol Image)
	Hertfordshire – 12-8 pts (Ap Biol) (BTEC 2M)
	Heriot-Watt – DDD (1st yr entry) CCC (2nd yr entry) (App Mar Biol)
	Portsmouth – 12-10 pts (D in chemistry) (Biol)
	Ripon & York St John (CHE) – DDD/CC (Biol/Geog; Biol/App Soc Sci)
	Warwick – CDE/CC (Biol BA(QTS))
10pts.	**Aberdeen** – CD (Aquaculture)
	Brighton – 10 pts (Bio/Med Sci)
	Central Lancashire – DDE/DD (Biomed Sci) (6 AS)
	Coventry – 10 pts (All courses) (BTEC 3M)
	Glasgow Caledonian – DDE (App Biol)
	Kingston – 10 pts (Biol/Fr; Cell Biol) (4 AS)
	Liverpool John Moores – DDE/DD (App Biol) (NMI)
	Manchester Met – 10 pts (Comb St)
	Nottingham Trent – 10 pts (Ap Biol)
	Oxford Brookes – CD (Hum Biol) (4 AS)
	Ripon & York St John (CHE) – DDE/CD (Biol/App Env Sci)
8pts.	**and below**
	Anglia (Poly Univ) – (Cell and Mol Sci)
	Bath (CHE) – (Comb St)
	Bournemouth – (Clin Sci)
	Cardiff (IHE) – (Biomed Sci)
	Chester (CHE) – (Comb Sci)
	De Montfort – (Comb St; Biol/Med Lab Tech)
	Derby – (Earth/Life St)
	East London – (Sci; App Biol)
	Glamorgan – (All Biology courses)
	Greenwich – (Env Biol; Ap Biol) (BTEC 4M)
	Guildhall London – DD (Biology – Modular)
	Hertfordshire – (Comb St)
	Humberside – EE (Comb St; Contemp St)
	Kingston - DEE-EEE/DD (Biol/Chem; Biol/App Phys; App Biol courses) (4 AS)
	Liverpool (IHE) – (Comb St)
	Liverpool John Moores – DEE/DD (Bio Med Sci; Nat Sci)
	Luton (CHE) – DEE/DD (Biol) (4 AS)
	Nene (CHE) – (Env Biol)
	North London – (Biol/Chem; Biol/Nutr)
	Nottingham Trent – (All Biology courses except under **10 pts**)
	Paisley – (Biol)
	Plymouth – (Biology courses)
	Portsmouth – 8 pts in 2 sci subjects (Biomed Sci; M Biol) (BTEC 65% average)
	Roehampton (IHE) – (All courses)
	SAC (Ab) – (Aquaculture)
	Sheffield Hallam – (Biomed Tech)
	South Bank – 4 pts (Env Biol; App/Ind Biol)
	St Mary's (CHE) – (Biol)
	Staffordshire – (Applied Sci)
	Sunderland – (All courses)
	Trinity Carmarthen (CHE) – (Rural Env; Biol)
	Westminster – (Sci/Life; Modular – Ecology; Biomed Sci)
	Wolverhampton – (All Biology courses; Biomedical Sci) (4 AS)
	Worcester (CHE) – (All Biology courses)

Franchised degree and HND courses (see Ch 5):

South Bank – South London (Coll); Waltham Forest (Coll).

Offers for Foundation, Certificate and Diploma courses (see Ch 5):

Diploma of Higher Education courses:
4 pts.   Hertfordshire; Luton (CHE); Oxford Brookes; Plymouth; Wolverhampton.

Higher National Diploma courses: (Applied Biology)
6 pts.   Bristol UWE EEE/DE; Plymouth EEE/DE/C; Sheffield Hallam.
4 pts.   East London EE/D; Luton (CHE) D; Nottingham Trent; Sunderland EE; Wolverhampton.
2 pts.   Brighton; Cardiff (IHE); Central Lancashire; De Montfort; Manchester Met; North East Surrey (CT); Nottingham Trent; Portsmouth; South Bank; Westminster.

Higher National Diploma courses:
        Bristol UWE (Med Lab Sci); Cardiff (IHE) (Science - Med Lab).

Alternative offers:

EB offers: **Bradford** 65%; **Keele** 65%; **Liverpool John Moores** 60%; **Newcastle** 65%; **Sheffield** 65%.

IB offers: **Aberdeen** 26 pts, (Marine Res Man) 32 pts; **Aberystwyth** 28 pts; **Bangor** 30-28 pts H665; **Bradford** 24 pts H6/7 chem, biol, maths or physics; **Bristol** 30 pts inc H655; **Cardiff** 27 pts, H 15 pts; **Coventry** (App Biol) 6 certificates at grade 4 or 3 at Higher level; **Guildhall London** 28 pts 7 subjects 24 pts 6 subjects; **Keele** 26 pts; **Lancaster** 33 pts; **Leeds** 30-28 pts; **Liverpool** 30 pts inc H655-555; **Liverpool John Moores** 24 pts; **London (RH)** 27 pts; **Newcastle** 28 pts; **Portsmouth** 24 pts; **Reading** 30 pts; **St Andrews** 30-28 pts; **Sheffield** 30 pts; **Southampton** H655; **Swansea** 32-30 pts; **York** 28 pts H55 S55.

Irish offers: **Aberdeen** BBCC/BCCCC; **Aberystwyth** BBBCC; **Bangor** BBCCC; **Bradford** BBBB; **Bristol** Overall 32 pts: H655 inc Biol; **Guildhall London** CCCCC; **Keele** BBBCC; **Liverpool** BBCCC; **Liverpool John Moores** CCC; **Newcastle** BBCC; **Sheffield** BBBCC; **South Bank** DDD.

SCE offers: **Aberdeen** BBBC; **Aston** ABBB; **Bangor** BBBC; **Bradford** BBBB inc chem/biol; **Bristol** BBBCC; **Bristol UWE** BBB; **East Anglia** BBBB; **Glasgow (CT)** BCC; **Guildhall London** BBCCC; **Heriot-Watt** BBBB; **Hull** BBBB; **Keele** BBCC; **Leeds** BBBC; **Liverpool** AABB; **Liverpool John Moores** DDD; **Newcastle** BBC; **St Andrews** BBBC; **Sheffield** BBBC; **Stirling** BBCC; **York** BBBB.

Overseas applicants: East Anglia English courses available for overseas students. **Heriot-Watt** No remedial courses available. **South Bank** Foundation courses in year 1.

CHOOSING YOUR COURSE (See also Ch 1)

> **Subject information:** These courses usually are more specialised than Biological Sciences with such options as aquatic biology, human biology, animal and plant biology. Many of these options are also offered on Applied Biology courses.

Course highlights: Aberystwyth Year 3 options cover immunology, animal sciences, biotechnology and physiology. **Anglia (Poly Univ)** Course covers biomedical studies, microbiology, environmental biology and environmental toxicology. **Bangor** Topics covered include freshwater, terrestrial and aquatic biology, evolution and marine and animal behaviour. **Bath** Language options in French and German in years 1 & 2. **Belfast** (Mol Biol) Students need to have a strong interest in genetics and microbiology. **Bournemouth** (Clin Sci) New course combines classical science and technology, and options range from health care to medical ultrasonics. **Bristol** Changes possible between Biology, Botany and Zoology. **Cardiff** Specialisms in final year include medical and public health, fishery biology, biochemistry, toxicology and land use ecology. **East London** (Applied Biology) Options include biochemistry, microbiology (industrial or medical), pharmacology, medical sciences, plant physiology and pathology. **Greenwich** Course biased towards biotechnology, biochemistry, biomedical analysis and horticulture. **Hertfordshire** Seven parallel schemes offered - agricultural, biology, biochemistry, biotechnology, microbiology, molecular biology, physiology, pharmacology. **Hull** Five different areas of specialisation: biotechnology, molecular biology, plant biotechnology and microbiology, coastal, estaurine and wetland biology, and fisheries science. **Keele** Studies cover genetics, population and ecology of marine, freshwater and terrestrial environments and animal behaviour. **Leeds** Applied Biology covers pharmacology of parasites, pesticide biochemistry and environmental conservation. **Liverpool** Students select units to include environmental and marine biology. **London (QMW)** Biological Sciences organised into 7 academic groups: animal physiology, biochemistry, environmental biology, genetics, microbiology, plant biology and zoology. **London (UC)** In year 2 students choose broad-based study of biology with other courses from anatomy, anthropology, computer science and psychology, biochemistry, genetics, microbiology. **Loughborough** (Hum Biol) No animal work. Options to study other aspects of biology, eg psychology, ergonomics. **Portsmouth** After common first year students choose one of two elective streams in either cellular and molecular biology or environmental systems and population biology. **St Andrews** Includes animal biology, experimental pathology, marine and environmental biology, plant and environmental biology and neuroscience physiology. **Southampton** Students can specialise in eg, cell biology, developmental biology, ecology or genetics. **Stirling** Students choose one of four specialist areas: animal physiology, plant biology, ecology, marine and freshwater biology. **Sunderland** Subjects focus on a choice from biochemistry, biotechnology, microbiology and applied ecology. **York** Part I (5 terms) common to degree programmes in Biology, Applied and Environmental Biology, Cell Biology, Ecology, Genetics and Animal Physiology. NOW CHECK PROSPECTUSES FOR ALL COURSES.

Study opportunities abroad: Bangor (E); **Coventry** (E); **Greenwich** (E); **Portsmouth** USA; **Salford** USA; **Swansea** (E); **Wolverhampton** (E); **York** (E) G.

Work opportunities abroad: Greenwich FR G GR NL IT P SZ; **Ulster** USA FR CAN IRE; **Wolverhampton** USA FR.

ADMISSIONS INFORMATION

Number of applicants per place (approx): Aberdeen 8; **Aberystwyth** 8; **Aston** 5; **Bangor** (Marine Biol) 5; **Bath** 10; **Bradford** 10, (Biomed Sci) 9; **Bristol** 12; **Brunel** 5; **Cardiff** 7; **Cardiff (IHE)** 2; **Coventry** 11; **Dundee** 4 inc biol sci; **Durham** 15; **Glasgow Caledonian** 9; **Greenwich** 5; **Hertfordshire** 10; **Hull** 6; **Leeds** 5; **Liverpool** 10; **Liverpool John Moores** 11; **London (Imp)** 4; **London (RH)** 5; **Loughborough** 6; **Luton (CHE)** 3; **Newcastle** (Plant Biol) 4, (Marine Biol) 15; **Nottingham** 14; **Nottingham Trent** 17; **Oxford Brookes** 13; **Portsmouth** 15; **Roehampton (IHE)** 7; **South Bank** 8; **Stirling** 6; **Sunderland** 9; **Sussex** 4; **Swansea** 12; **York** 11.

General Studies acceptable: Aberdeen (Aqua); Aberystwyth; Aston; Bristol UWE; Cardiff (IHE); Coventry (2); Greenwich (2); Liverpool (Biol) (JMB/Camb/Oxford only); Liverpool (IHE); Nottingham Trent; Oxford Brookes.

Selection interviews: Aston; Bangor (some); Bath; Birmingham; Bradford (informal, after offer); Brunel; Buckingham (UC) (very important); Cambridge; Coventry; Durham; East Anglia; East London (T); Leeds; Leicester; Liverpool; London (RH); Manchester Met (some); Newcastle (some); Oxford Brookes; Salford (some); Southampton; South Bank (some); Warwick (BA(QTS)); York.

Offers to applicants repeating A-levels: Higher Brunel, Cardiff, East London, Nottingham, Strathclyde; **Possibly higher** Bath, Bradford, Durham, Leeds, Liverpool John Moores, London (RH), Portsmouth; **Same** Aston, Bangor, Coventry, Bradford, Hull, Liverpool, Liverpool John Moores, Liverpool (IHE), Luton (CHE), Manchester Met, Newcastle (Plant Biol, Biol/PA), South Bank, Ulster.

Admissions Tutors' advice: Brunel (App Biol) For interview, be prompt, smart and talkative. **Buckingham** Competence in maths required. **De Montfort** GCSE grades A-C in maths and chemistry required. **East Anglia** Broad range of interests on UCAS application required.

Examples of interview questions: Why have you chosen this course when there are few jobs in biology? Discuss developing countries. Is the computer like a brain and, if so, could it ever be taught to think? Be prepared for searching questions on various micro-organisms. Questions on food chains and food webs. Why do animals fight? What do you think the role of the environmental biologist will be in the next 40 to 50 years? Have you any strong views on vivisection? Do you read the *New Scientist*? Questions about ova transplants in cows and artificial insemination - reasons for these and problems arising. You have a micro-organism in the blood - you want to make a culture - what conditions should be borne in mind? What is a pacemaker? What problems will a giraffe experience? When did you first become interested in biology? What exactly is molecular biology? Why did you choose Molecular Biology rather than Biochemistry? What aspects of biology interests you the most? Discuss your personality. How does water enter a flowering plant? What do you know about marine biology? Compare an egg and a potato. Discuss a family tree of human genotypes. If you were in control of a hospital what changes would you make? (The applicant had done some hospital voluntary work.) Do you see this degree as the key to a good job in industry? If so, why?

GAP YEAR ADVICE

Institutions accepting a Gap Year: Most institutions; **Aberystwyth** Apply before taking a year out so that you can visit the universities of your choice; **London (RH)** Do something constructive, don't just take a holiday! **Loughborough** Do something related to Human Biology; **Newcastle** Do something relevant or useful; **Westminster** Apply year before but mark form for year of entry.

Institutions willing to defer entry after A-levels (see Ch 5): Aston; Bristol; Brunel; Heriot-Watt; Leeds; Newcastle (Mar Biol); Plymouth; Ripon & York St John (CHE) (No); Roehampton (IHE); St Andrews; Swansea (discouraged); York.

AFTER A-LEVELS ADVICE

Institutions which may accept the same points score after A-levels: Aberystwyth; Aston; Bangor; Bath; Bradford; Bristol UWE; Brunel; Coventry; Essex; Greenwich; Hull; Humberside; Leeds; Liverpool; Liverpool John Moores; Loughborough; London (RH); Luton (CHE); Newcastle; Nottingham Trent; Portsmouth; Southampton; Sunderland; Swansea; York; most new universities and colleges.

Institutions demanding the actual grades offered after A-levels: Guildhall London; Nottingham; Stirling.

Institutions which may accept under-achieving applicants after A-levels: Aberdeen; Bangor; Bath; Belfast; Bradford (Biomed Sci); Brunel; Coventry; Durham; Hull; Humberside; Keele; Leeds; Liverpool; Liverpool John Moores; London (RH); Newcastle; Nottingham; Portsmouth; St Andrews; York; most new universities and colleges.

Institutions with vacancies in Aug/Sept 1992 (see Ch 5): Aberdeen; Aberystwyth 14 pts $+$; Anglia (Poly Univ); Aston CCC; Bath; Brunel 14 pts; Coventry 8 pts; Derby; Dundee; East London; Essex; Greenwich 4 pts; Heriot-Watt 12 pts; Kingston; Leeds 18 pts; Liverpool; London (QMW), (RH); Manchester Met; Oxford Brookes; Plymouth 6 pts; Portsmouth 6 pts; Ripon & York St John (CHE) some; Roehampton (IHE); St Andrews 16 pts; Sunderland; Surrey CDD; Swansea 16-14 pts; York 18 pts; most institutions are likely to have vacancies in 1993.

ADVICE FOR MATURE STUDENTS

Science qualifications are usually required for these courses. Approximately 4% of students are mature; **Aston** 10%.

GRADUATE EMPLOYMENT

New Graduates' destinations (percentages) 1991:
Permanent employment: U 63; P 58.

Unemployment: U 25; P 29.
Further studies (all types): U 44; P 31.
Main career destinations (approx): Scientific 40; Business 42; Social 8; Teaching 1.

Newcastle 33% of graduates enter non-biological employment areas.

York (1987-91) 15 % of graduates enter subject-related careers in hospitals, agriculture and food science; 7% went into careers in finance and 4% into management. The remainder went into various careers including pollution, computer work, social work, physiotherapy, conservation and professional horse riding!

See also under **Science**.

BIOPHYSICS

Special subject requirements: 2-3 A-levels in mathematics/science subjects.

NB Institutions may raise or lower the level of published offers depending either on the quality or otherwise of individual applications or the numbers of applications received; grades/points offered may be adjusted downwards after A-level results. The level of an offer is not indicative of the quality of a course.

18 pts.	**East Anglia** - BCD/BC (Biophys; Biophys/Phys) (BTEC 65% average)
	Leeds - CCC/CC (All courses)
	London (King's) - CCC (Biophys)
8 pts.	**and below approx**
	East London - EE (Biophys Sci)
	Kingston - 8 pts (Biophys)
	Liverpool John Moores - DD (Biophys) (4 AS)

Alternative offers:

IB offers: **East Anglia** 28 pts at least 5 in maths and physics/physical science.

SCE offers: **East Anglia** BBBB.

CHOOSING YOUR COURSE (See also Ch 1)

> **Subject information:** Biophysics is a study of the physical techniques related to fundamental biological processes including computer methods employed in the natural science. Also check Physics, Biology and Biotechnology courses.

Course highlights: Liverpool John Moores Small group teaching; more than £300,000 in external funding for research. NOW CHECK PROSPECTUSES FOR ALL COURSES.

Work opportunities abroad: Liverpool John Moores G.

ADMISSIONS INFORMATION

Number of applicants per place (approx): East Anglia 6; **East London** 3; **Leeds** 2.

Selection interviews: East Anglia; East London.

Offers to applicants repeating A-levels: Higher East Anglia (BCC); **Same** Leeds.

Admissions Tutors' advice: East Anglia Standard (not variable) offers are made to appropriate candidates. Courses in Biophysics demand good abilities in mathematics, physics and biology. We are looking for enthusiasts, not simply those who are academically and technically competent.

> **Examples of interview questions:** Questions were asked on the structure of amino-acids and proteins, integration and differentiation. Why have you chosen Biophysics? What career do you hope to follow when you graduate?

GAP YEAR ADVICE

Institutions willing to defer entry after A-levels (see Ch 5): Leeds.

AFTER A-LEVELS ADVICE

Institutions which may accept the same points score after A-levels: East Anglia; Leeds (or slightly less); Liverpool John Moores.

Institutions which may accept under-achieving applicants after A-levels: East Anglia; Leeds; Liverpool John Moores.

Institutions with vacancies in Aug/Sept 1992 (see Ch 5): Leeds 12-10 pts; most institutions are likely to have vacancies in 1993.

BIOTECHNOLOGY

Special subject requirements: 2-3 A-levels in mathematics/science subjects; GCSE mathematics at grades A-C.

NB Institutions may raise or lower the level of published offers depending either on the quality or otherwise of individual applications or the numbers of applications received; grades/points offered may be adjusted downwards after A-level results. The level of an offer is not indicative of the quality of a course.

20 pts.	**Leeds** - BCC (Biotech) (AS-levels not accepted)
	London (Imp) - BCC/BB (Biotech; Biol/Eur; Biol/Ind)
	Surrey - BCC (Proc Biotech) (BTEC 3M)
18 pts.	**Aberdeen** - CCC-CCD/BC (Biotech)
	Birmingham - BCD (Bio Sc/Biol)
	Cardiff - BCD/AB (Biotech)
	Liverpool - CCC/BB (Mic Biotech)
	London (King's) - 18 pts approx (Biotech)
	London (UC) - CCC (Biotech)
	St Andrews - BCC-CCC (Bioch/Biotech) (4 AS)
	Strathclyde - BCD-CCC (Biotech) (2nd yr entry)
	Swansea - CCC/BB (Proc Bio) (BTEC 3M)
	Warwick - CCC (Microtech Biotech)
14 pts.	**Cranfield (Silsoe)** - CDD/CC (App Biotech)
	Nottingham - CDD/CC (Agric Bioch)
	Reading - CDD/CC (Biotech)
8 pts.	**De Montfort** - (Biotech) (4 AS)
	Glamorgan - DD (Biotech) (4 AS) (BTEC 3M)
	Sheffield Hallam - DD-EE (Biomed Tech)
	South Bank - 8 pts (Sci Comp; Biotech courses) (BTEC 3M)
	Sunderland - 8 pts (Biotech)
	Teesside - 8 pts inc 1 science at A-level (Pro Bio) (4 AS)
	Westminster - DD (Sci Biotech; Biotech) (BTEC 3M)

4pts. **Central Lancashire** – EE (Biotech)
Dundee (IT) – (Biotech)
East London – (Biotech; Med Biotech)

Offers for Foundation, Certificate and Diploma courses (see Ch 5):

Higher National Diploma courses (England and Wales):
2pts. Bristol UWE (Food Tech).

Higher National Diploma courses (Scotland):
SAC (Au).

Alternative offers:

IB offers: **Aberdeen** 26 pts; **Glamorgan** 26 pts; **Leeds** 28 pts H biol 6, chem 5 maths 4; **St Andrews** 28 pts; **Liverpool** H555; **South Bank** 24 pts; **Surrey** H5555 (maths/chem/phys/biol) 28 pts; **Swansea** 28 pts.

Irish offers: **Aberdeen** BBCC/BCCCC; **Leeds** BCC; **South Bank** CCCC.

SCE offers: **Aberdeen** BBBC; **Leeds** AAB; **Surrey** AAAA.

CHOOSING YOUR COURSE (See also Ch 1)

Subject information: This is an interdisciplinary subject which covers biochemistry, microbiology, genetics, chemical engineering, biophysics etc (courses in these subjects also should be explored).

Course highlights: Cranfield (Silsoe) Emphasis on food production, agricultural and environmental protection. **Glamorgan** Cross-disciplinary course covering chemical engineering, biological science and chemistry. **Leeds** Inter-departmental teaching from science and engineering departments; research project in final year. Overseas students often enter the course after one year on a BTEC HND course. **South Bank** Course includes fermentation and DNA enzyme technology, environmental biotechnology. **Swansea** Optional sandwich year. **Teesside** Interdisciplinary course taught by chemists, biotechnologists and process engineers. Strong European element with language studies eg French. **Westminster** Course decisions can be delayed until end of year 1. NOW CHECK PROSPECTUSES FOR ALL COURSES.

Study opportunities abroad: Glamorgan (E); **Teesside**.

Work opportunities abroad: South Bank EUR; **Surrey** G FR USA CAN AUS N SZ NZ; **Teesside**.

ADMISSIONS INFORMATION

Number of applicants per place (approx): Dundee (IT) 3; **Glamorgan** 3; **Leeds** 7; **London (Imp)** 4; **Reading** 10; **South Bank** 5; **Strathclyde** 10; **Surrey** 2; **Swansea** 4; **Teesside** 3; **Westminster** 3.

General Studies acceptable: South Bank (No); Teesside (2); Westminster.

Selection interviews: South Bank.

Offers to applicants repeating A-levels: Possibly higher Leeds; **Same** South Bank.

Examples of interview questions: See under **Biology** and **Biological Sciences**.

GAP YEAR ADVICE

Institutions accepting a Gap Year: Most institutions; **Teesside** Apply as for direct entry but explain your plans at interview for deferred entry. **Westminster** Apply as normal but mark your application form one year later.

Institutions willing to defer entry after A-levels (see Ch 5): Cranfield (Silsoe); Glamorgan; South Bank; Westminster.

AFTER A-LEVELS ADVICE

Institutions which may accept the same points score after A-levels: Leeds; South Bank; Surrey; most new universities and colleges.

Institutions which may accept under-achieving applicants after A-levels: Leeds; South Bank; Surrey; most new universities and colleges.

Institutions with vacancies in Aug/Sept 1992 (see Ch 5): Aberdeen; De Montfort; Glamorgan DE; Leeds; South Bank 6 pts; Strathclyde; Sunderland; Westminster; most institutions are likely to have vacancies in 1993. Vacancies were advertised for applicants with a wide range of results from 20 to 8 pts.

ADVICE FOR MATURE STUDENTS

Science qualifications are offered by the small number of mature students applying. At **Leeds** 5% of students are 'mature'.

GRADUATE EMPLOYMENT

New Graduates' destinations (percentages) 1991:
Permanent employment: U 63; P 54.
Unemployment: U 33; P 46.
Further studies (all types): U 38; P 38.

BOTANY (See also Biology)

Special subject requirements: 2-3 A-levels in mathematics/science subjects.

NB Institutions may raise or lower the level of published offers depending either on the quality or otherwise of individual applications or the numbers of applications received; grades/points offered may be adjusted downwards after A-level results. The level of an offer is not indicative of the quality of a course.

30 pts.	**Cambridge** (Nat Sci)/**Oxford** - AAA potential recommended
20 pts.	**London (Imp)** - BCC (Plant Sci)
	St Andrews - BCC approx (Plant/Env Biol)
	Southampton - BCC-BCD (Bot)
18 pts.	**Aberystwyth** - CCC-CCD/BB-BC (Botany; Plant Phys; AP Biol)(BTEC 3M)
	Birmingham - BCD (Bio Sc/Plant)
	Bristol - CCC (Botany)
	East Anglia - BCD/BB (Plant Biol)
	Edinburgh - CCC/BB (Ecol Sci) (4 AS)
	Glasgow - CCC-CCD/BC (Bot)
	Leeds - BCD (B Plant) (BTEC 5M)
	Leicester - BCD (Biol Sci)
	Liverpool - 18 pts approx (Plant Sci)
	London (RH) - 18-14 pts (All courses) (4 AS)

Manchester – 18 pts approx (All courses)
Newcastle – CCC/BC (Plant Biol; Biol/PA)
Sheffield – CCC (LD/P Sci; Plant Sci) (6 AS) (BTEC 3M)
Swansea – CCC/BB (Botany) (BTEC 3M, (HND) ID+Ms for yr 2 entry)

16 pts.   Belfast – CCD/BB (Plant Sci)
London (QMW) – CCD (Plant Biol)
Nottingham – CCD-CDD-CCE (Bot Micro)
Reading – CCD/BC (Botany; Bot/Zoo)

14 pts.   Aberdeen – CDD/BC (Bot)
Bangor – CDD/CC (Botany; Bot M Bot)
Dundee – CDD/BC (Biol Sci)
London (Wye) – (Plant Biotech)
Newcastle – CDD/BC (Ag Sci/Plant Sci)
Nottingham – CDD/CC (All Plant Sci courses)
SAC (Au) – CDD (App Plant/An Sci)

8 pts.   and below approx
Plymouth – (BIOA)
Westminster – (Sci/Life)
Wolverhampton – (Biol Sci)

Alternative offers:

EB offers: **Aberystwyth** 70%; **Newcastle** 60%; **Sheffield** 65%.

IB offers: **Aberdeen** 28 pts; **Aberystwyth** 28 pts and above (26 pts for Ag Bot); **Bangor** 28 pts; **Belfast** H555 S555; **Bristol** 30 pts inc H655, 6 in biology; **Dundee** H544; **Leeds** 30-28 pts; **London (RH)** 25 pts; **Sheffield** 30 pts; **Swansea** 28 pts.

Irish offers: **Aberdeen** BBCC/BCCCC; **Aberystwyth** BBBCC, (Ag Bot) BBCCC; **London (RH)** BBCCC; **Newcastle** BBCCC; **Sheffield** BBBCC.

SCE offers: **Aberdeen** BBBC; **Bangor** BBBC; **Belfast** BBBB/BBBC; **Bristol** BBBBC; **Edinburgh** ABBC or BBBB; **Glasgow** BBBB; **Leeds** BBBBC; **Sheffield** BBBB.

CHOOSING YOUR COURSE (See also Ch 1)

Subject information: Botany is also sometimes referred to as Plant Science in which final year studies lead to specialised studies of plant physiology or broader areas of ecology or environmental aspects. Biological Science courses should also be checked since botany could be an optional study.

Course highlights: Aberdeen Subjects covered include zoology, genetics and microbiology. **Aberystwyth** Years 2 and 3 courses include ecology, plant-soil relations, genetics and evolution of land flora, plant physiology and floral biology. Final course decisions can be delayed until start of year 2. Optional year in employment. **Bangor** Botany studied in year 2 with one subject from biochemistry, marine biology, mathematics, soil science, zoology. **Belfast** In year 3 students select five unit courses from ten from Departments of Botany, Zoology, Genetics and Marine Biology. **Bristol** Course transfers possible in year 2 between Biology, Botany, Zoology and joint courses. Students control course choice in final 2 years, selecting from many options. Course covers environmental studies, ecology, plant physiology, pollution studies. **Dundee** Final course decisions can be delayed. **East Anglia** Plant Biology programme includes courses in molecular biology, biochemistry, physiology, pathology, genetic manipulation of plants and ecology. **Glasgow** Honours course focuses on plant physiology and biochemistry, the study of fungi (mycology) and ecology. **London (Imp)** Common first year offered, leading to degrees in Biology, Microbilogy, Plant Science and Zoology. **London (QMW)** Plant Biology involves study of the principles of genetics, cytology, morphology, physiology, biochemistry and ecology. **London (RH)** Broad courses available with chance to specialise in applied plant biology (plant pathology, breeding and genetics) or botany and microbiology. **London (UC)** In years 2 and 3 as well as specialised botany topics, courses also available in chemistry, maths, zoology, geology, biochemistry and biology. **Reading** Botany plus 2 other subjects in terms 1 & 2. **St Andrews** Third year focuses on environments, population biology and adaptive physiology. **Sheffield** In year 2 botany combined with biochemistry, genetics, geography, geology, microbiology or zoology. **Southampton** The course is unitised. Biology, Botany and Zoology courses have common first year. **Swansea** Botany, zoology and biology are taught in Part I (year I); wide range of units specialising in plant biology. NOW CHECK PROSPECTUSES FOR ALL COURSES.

Study opportunities abroad: Swansea (E) IT FR G SP.

ADMISSIONS INFORMATION

Number of applicants per place (approx): Aberystwyth 8; **Bangor** 4; **Bristol** 5; **Dundee** 10; **Edinburgh** 6; **Glasgow** 4; **Leeds** (B Plant) 3; **London (RH)** 3; **Newcastle** 6; **Nottingham** 5; **Reading** 3; **Sheffield** 5; **Swansea** 6.

General Studies acceptable: Aberdeen; Aberystwyth; Dundee.

Selection interviews: Cambridge; Hull; London (RH); Newcastle; Nottingham; Oxford.

Offers to applicants repeating A-levels: Higher Nottingham; **Same** Bangor, London (RH), Newcastle, Sheffield.

> **Examples of interview questions:** What do you consider are important reasons for studying botany? What future career do you have in mind? Questions about photosynthesis. Discuss Darwin's Theory of Evolution. What is the function of DNA?

GAP YEAR ADVICE

Institutions accepting a Gap Year: Aberystwyth (Apply before taking a year out so that you can visit your university choice); most institutions.

Institutions willing to defer entry after A-levels (see Ch 5): Bristol; Leeds; Plymouth; Swansea (discouraged).

AFTER A-LEVELS ADVICE

Institutions which may accept the same points score after A-levels: Bangor; Leeds; London (RH); Newcastle (Plant Biol); Nottingham (not for joint courses); Sheffield.

Institutions which may accept under-achieving applicants after A-levels: Aberdeen; Bangor; Leeds; London (RH); Newcastle.

Institutions with vacancies in Aug/Sept 1992 (see Ch 5): Aberdeen; Aberystwyth 14 pts; Leeds 16 pts; London (RH) 14 pts; Plymouth 6 pts; Swansea 16-14 pts; most institutions are likely to have vacancies in 1993.

ADVICE FOR MATURE STUDENTS

Approximately 8% of students admitted to these courses are mature. Familiarity with A-level work or equivalent is advisable.

GRADUATE EMPLOYMENT

New Graduates' destinations (percentages) 1991:
Permanent employment: U 53.
Unemployment: U 29.
Further studies (all types): U 47.
Main career destinations (approx): Scientific 31; Business/Finance 57; Computing 10.

BUILDING (including Building Services Engineering, Building Design Engineering and Building Surveying)

Special subject requirements: 2-3 A-levels from mathematics/physics/ chemistry.

NB Institutions may raise or lower the level of published offers depending either on the quality or otherwise of individual applications or the numbers of applications received; grades/points offered may be adjusted downwards after A-level results. The level of an offer is not indicative of the quality of a course.

22 pts.	**Reading** - BBC/AB (Buil Con; Build Surv)
	Salford - BBC (Cons Man) (4 AS) (BTEC 2D+4M)
20 pts.	**London (UC)** - BCC (Building)
	Loughborough - 20 pts (Con Eng 4) (BTEC 2D+Ms)
	Reading - BCC (Build Serv)
	Salford - BCC/BB (Build Surv) (4 AS) (BTEC 1D+4M)
	Strathclyde - BCC (BBB - 2nd yr entry) (Bldg Des Eng)
18 pts.	**Bath** - CCC (Build Env) (BTEC 2D+3M)
	Brighton - CCC/BC (Con Man; Build St; Build Surv)
	Cardiff - CCC (Arch Eng)
	Heriot-Watt - CCC/CC (All courses)
	Loughborough - 18 pts (Build Serv 3 & 4) (BTEC 1D maths+3M)
	UMIST - CCC/BB (Building; Build Serv; Constr Man) (BTEC 2D+2M)
16 pts.	**Central Lancashire** - CCD (All courses inc Cons Econ except **12 pts**)
	Glasgow Caledonian - CCD (Building)
	Liverpool - 16-12 pts (Build Man; Build Env; Bldg/Env Eng) (4 AS) (BTEC 80% average maths +75% overall)
14 pts.	**Brighton** - CDD/CC (Build Eng Man) (BTEC 3M)
	Central England - 14-12 pts (Build Surv) (BTEC 5M)
	Northumbria - 14-12 pts (Build Man) (BTEC 6/5M)
	Robert Gordon - CDD/CC (Build Surv) (BTEC 5M, (HND) 5M yr 2 entry)
	Ulster - CDD/CC (Bldg Serv; Bldg) (Bldg Serv - AS des tech/ contrasting subjects; Bldg - AS des tech/biol/chem/geol)
12 pts.	**Bristol UWE** - 12-10 pts (Build Surv) (4 AS) (BTEC 3M)
	Central Lancashire - 12-9 pts (Build Man)
	De Montfort - 12 pts (Building Surv) (BTEC 1D+4M)
	Greenwich - 12 pts minimum (Building Surv) (BTEC 3M)
	Heriot-Watt - CC (BBC 2nd yr entry) (Build Serv)
	Liverpool John Moores - CC (Build Surv) (BTEC 75% average)
	Liverpool John Moores - DDD/CD (Build) (BTEC 3-5M)
	South Bank - 12 pts (Building Surv; Build Eng; Con Man) (4 AS) (BTEC 3-5M))
	Westminster - 12 pts (Con Man) (4 AS)
10 pts.	**Glamorgan** - 10 pts (Building) (4 AS)
	Nottingham Trent - 10-8 pts (Building; Con Man)
	Robert Gordon - 10 pts (Con Man)
	Sheffield Hallam - 10 pts (approx) (Constr) (BTEC 4M)
	Wolverhampton - (Build Man)
8 pts.	**and below**
	Anglia (Poly Univ) - (Building)
	Bell (CT) - DE (Con Man)
	Brighton - 6-4 pts (Foundation) (4 AS) (BTEC 3M)
	Bristol UWE - DEE/DD (Con Man; Build Eng Man)
	Coventry - (All courses)
	Leeds Met - DD approx (Building)
	Middlesex - 8 pts (Con Eng Man) (4 AS)
	Napier - 8 pts (Build)
	North East Wales (IHE) - 8 pts (Build Tech Man)

Northumbria - (Building Eng) (4 AS)
Paisley - 8 pts (Cons Man)
Westminster - DD (Building) (4 AS)

Franchised degree and HND courses (see Ch 5):
Cheltenham & Glos (CHE) – Gloucester (CAT)
Greenwich - West Kent (Coll)
Hertfordshire - Oaklands (Coll)
Plymouth - Somerset (CAT)
South Bank - Guildford (Coll); Mid Kent (Coll); North East Surrey (CT); South Bank (Coll); Vauxhall (Coll); Waltham Forest (Coll); Westminster (Coll).

Offers for Foundation, Certificate and Diploma courses (see Ch 5):

Higher National Certificate courses:
Southampton (IHE) Part-time course leading to a degree.

Higher National Diploma courses (England and Wales):
6 pts. Central Lancashire EEE/DD.
4 pts. Anglia (Poly Univ); Brighton; Mid-Kent (CHFE); South Bank EE/E; Wolverhampton.
2 pts. Blackpool (Coll); Bolton (IHE); Bristol UWE; Buckinghamshire (CHE); Cardiff (IHE) (Eng Build Services); Central Lancashire; Cheltenham & Glos (CHE); De Montfort; Doncaster (Coll) (Asphalt Technology); Glamorgan; Guildford (CT); Hammersmith and West London (Coll); Hertfordshire (Build Surv); Huddersfield; Leeds Met; Mid-Kent (CHFE) inc grade C in maths or physics; Liverpool John Moores; Nene (CHE); North East Surrey (CT); North East Wales (IHE); Northumbria; Nottingham Trent; Oxford Brookes; Plymouth; Robert Gordon (Build Surv; Con Man); Sheffield Hallam; Southampton (IHE); Stoke on Trent (Coll); Willesden (CT) (Build Serv), (Eng Refrig).

Higher National Diploma courses (Scotland):
2 pts.   or equivalent:
Bell (CT); Dundee (IT); Glasgow (CB); Kirkcaldy (CT); Napier EE; Robert Gordon.

Polytechnic and College Diploma courses:

2 pts.   or equivalent:
Glasgow (CB) (Building Surv); Northumbria.

Alternative offers:

IB offers: **Bath** 28 pts H5 maths; **Brighton** 24 pts inc 12 pts Highers 3 subjects; **Bristol UWE** 26 pts (Build Surv); **UMIST** 28 pts inc H55.

Irish offers: **Bristol UWE** CCCC; **Liverpool** BBCCC.

SCE offers: **Bell (CT)** CCC; **Bristol UWE** BBC; **Glasgow (CB)** BBB; **Heriot-Watt** BBBC; **Robert Gordon** BBCC; **Strathclyde** BBBB; **UMIST** AAAB.

Overseas applicants: Sheffield Hallam Courses available in language and study skills.

CHOOSING YOUR COURSE (See also Ch I)

> **Subject information:** These courses involve the techniques and management methods employed in the building industry. Similar subject areas are covered in Civil and Structural Engineering courses and Architecture.

Course highlights: Bath Course shares common first year with Civil/ Structural Engineering. Option to change to Building Services Engineering at the end of year 2. **Brighton** Course covers materials science, environmental science, building services, structural design and economics. **Coventry** All students take common first year and then opt for the BSc degrees in Building, Building Management or Building Services Engineering. **De Montfort** (Build Surv) Bias towards continuous assessment. **Heriot-Watt** Course also includes valuation and quantity surveying. **Leeds Met** Special studies include environmental science and services engineering, systems management, construction engineering and financial management. **Liverpool** Year 1 course covers building construction engineering or building services engineering. **Loughborough** Common first year with Civil Engineering; option to choose between Building Services Engineering or Civil Engineering (shortage of applicants for Building Services Engineering) at end of year 1. **Nottingham Trent** Course emphasises both building technology and management. **Reading** First year common with courses in Quantity Surveying and Building Services. **Robert Gordon** Most of year 1 is common with Building Surveying and Quantity Surveying. **Salford** All students sponsored by major construction companies guaranteeing industrial placement and employment on graduation. Bursaries of £300 are available each term while students are at university. **Sheffield Hallam** Four options offered: quantity surveying, production organisation, construction engineering and building surveying. **Strathclyde** Course includes architecture, civil engineering, building science, environmental engineering, computer-aided design and energy structures. **UMIST** Emphasis on planning, legal, cost and administrative aspects of the production of construction projects particularly at site level. **Westminster** All students take French, German or Spanish. NOW CHECK PROSPECTUSES FOR ALL COURSES.

Study opportunities abroad: Central Lancashire EUR; **Coventry** F G; **Liverpool John Moores** (Build Surv) (E); **Northumbria** (Building Eng) (E); **South Bank** (E) AUS HK.

Work opportunities abroad: Central Lancashire FR G D SP; **Coventry** FR G; **Liverpool John Moores** NL FR; **Northumbria** EUR USA CAN AUS NZ IN HK; **South Bank** HK AUS ME EUR; **Westminster** USA FR G SP IT PL TY GR.

ADMISSIONS INFORMATION

Number of applicants per place (approx): Anglia (Poly Univ) 6; **Bath** 8; **Brighton** 7; **Bristol UWE** 3, (Build Surv) 8; **Coventry** 5, (Build Eng) 1; **De Montfort** (Build Surv) 17; **Glamorgan** 3; **Glasgow Caledonian** 10; **Greenwich** 13; **Leeds Met** 7; **Liverpool** (Building; Buil Serv) 8; **Liverpool John Moores** 15; **Loughborough** (Con Eng 4) 5; **Napier** 8; **Northumbria** (Build Eng) 4; **Nottingham Trent** (Con Man) 9; **Sheffield Hallam** 9; **South Bank** 4; **Strathclyde** 5; **UMIST** 5; **Wolverhampton** 6.

General Studies acceptable: Anglia (Poly Univ); Brighton; Bristol UWE; Coventry; Glamorgan; Liverpool; Liverpool John Moores (Building); Robert Gordon; South Bank.

Selection interviews: Bath; Brighton (some); Bristol UWE; De Montfort; Glamorgan; Glasgow Caledonian; Greenwich; Leeds Met; Liverpool John Moores; Northumbria; South Bank (some); Westminster.

Offers to applicants repeating A-levels: Higher Bath, Liverpool John Moores, Strathclyde; **Possibly higher** Bristol UWE, Liverpool; **Same** Brighton, Coventry, De Montfort, Leeds Met, Northumbria, South Bank.

Admissions Tutors' advice: Bath A-level physics preferred. **Salford** Sponsorship mandatory.

Examples of interview questions: Have you visited a building site? What is the difference between a builder, a civil engineer and an architect? Discuss any building project with which you are familiar. What problems do you envisage in organising workers on a building site?

GAP YEAR ADVICE

Institutions accepting a Gap Year: Most institutions; **Anglia (Poly Univ)** Work experience useful. **Bath** Use it wisely. **Glamorgan** (No). **Loughborough** (Con Eng 4) Fully sponsored course - see sponsor.

Institutions willing to defer entry after A-levels (see Ch 5): Bath; Brighton; De Montfort (Build Surv); Glamorgan; Heriot-Watt; Northumbria; Robert Gordon (Build Surv); Salford (No); South Bank (No); UMIST.

AFTER A-LEVELS ADVICE

Institutions which may accept the same points score after A-levels: Bath; Brighton; Bristol UWE; Coventry; De Montfort; Glamorgan; Leeds Met; Liverpool; Liverpool John Moores; Northumbria; Nottingham Trent; Salford; South Bank (Build Surv); Strathclyde; UMIST; Westminster.

Institutions which may accept under-achieving applicants after A-levels: Bath; Coventry; Liverpool; Reading; Salford; South Bank; Westminster.

Institutions with vacancies in Aug/Sept 1992 (see Ch 5): Most institutions; Anglia (Poly Univ); Bath 16 pts; Brighton 14-8 pts; Glamorgan (apply early); Greenwich 10 pts; Heriot-Watt 18 pts, (Build Serv) 16 pts; Northumbria 12 pts or BTEC 5M; Robert Gordon 10 pts or SCE CCCC; Salford 18 pts; South Bank EE. This was a very undersubscribed subject at all institutions and university places could be gained on 16 pts and below.

ADVICE FOR MATURE STUDENTS

A large number of mature students with background qualifications and work experience apply for this course. At **Robert Gordon** advanced entry to year 3 is permitted for those with HNC qualifications.

GRADUATE EMPLOYMENT

New Graduate destinations (percentages) 1991:
Permanent employment: U 81; P 73.
Unemployment: U 17; P 19.
Further studies (all types): U 8; P 4.

Anglia (Poly Univ) (1991) (HND) Four students entered full-time employment in building careers. The appointments were those of an assistant planning engineer, an assistant quantity surveyor and as management trainees.

The following institutions are perceived as being above average in producing graduates for employment: Coventry, Loughborough, Nottingham Trent, Reading, Salford, UMIST. See PIP reference in Chapter 5.

BUSINESS COURSES (including Advertising, Administrative Science, Applied Consumer Sciences, Bilingual Administration, Company Administration, European Business Studies, Finance, Industrial Relations, Industrial Studies, Journalism, Language for Business, Management Sciences, Organisation Studies, Retail Management, Travel and Tourism)

Special subject requirements: GCSE (grades A-C) English and mathematics. Some university courses require mathematics at A-level.

Choosing your degree course?

Would you like advice on...

...choosing 'A' Level subjects for Degree Courses
...choosing your degree subjects or courses?
...choosing your university or college?
...completing your UCAS form?
...preparing for interview?
...deciding what to do if you haven't got the right 'A' level grades?

Then why not contact Brian Heap and arrange for a personal or telephone consultation.

Full details of all advisory services for students together with fees and details of special HEAPS publications are available from the Service.

Brian Heap also offers lectures on entry to higher education, to schools and colleges, parents, teachers and careers advisers groups

For further information contact: The Director
Higher Education Advice Planning Service,
200 Greyhound Road, London W14 9RY. Tel: 071-385 3377

NB Institutions may raise or lower the level of published offers depending either on the quality or otherwise of individual applications or the numbers of applications received; grades/points offered may be adjusted downwards after A-level results. The level of an offer is not indicative of the quality of a course.

26 pts. **Bath** - ABB (Man/French - B in French; Int Man/Modern Lang) (BTEC 6D, 3D minimum)
Edinburgh - ABB (MA)
Glasgow - ABB (Arts - MA)
Nottingham - ABB-ABC (Maths/Man)
St Andrews - ABB (Man Sci - MA)
Salford - ABB-BBC (BOAC N Am) (4 AS)
UMIST - ABB (Int Man/ABS; Int Man/Fr)

24 pts. **Aston** - BBB-BBC (Man/Admin; Int Bus/Fr; Int Bus/Ger; Man/Comp) (BTEC D+M)
Bath - BBB/AB (Bus Admin) (BTEC 6D; 3M minimum)
Birmingham - BBB (B Comm) (BTEC D overall)
Bournemouth - 24 pts (Advert) (BTEC Ds)
Bradford - BBB (B in lang) (Man St/Fr/G/Sp)
Brunel - BBB/24 pts (Man St) (BTEC 5D)
City - BBB-BBC (Bus Stud)
Durham - BBB (Eng/Man)
East Anglia - BBB-BBC (Bus Fin/Ec)
Glasgow - BBB (Man Sci; BA Soc Sci)
Hull - BBB-BBC (Bus St) (BTEC mainly D)
Kent - BBB-BBC (Eur Man Sci)
Lancaster - BBB approx (BBA)
Leeds - BBB (Man St)
London (King's) - 24 pts approx (Bus)
London (LSE) - 24 pts approx (Man Sci)
London (RH) - BBB/AB (Man/Lang; Man St) (BTEC mainly D)
Newcastle - BBB/AA (Bus Man; Int Bus Man; Eur Bus man) (BTEC 5D+2M)
Nottingham - BBB-BBC (All Man St courses)
Reading - BBB (Man Bus Admin)
St Andrews - BBB (Man Sci Bsc)
Sheffield - BBB (Bus Stud/Jap; Bus Stud/Econ; Bus Stud) (BTEC 2D+Ms)
Stirling - BBB (Bus Man; Bus St)
Swansea - BBB/AB (Bus Stud; AMS (USA); EBS; EMS; Man Sci; Op Res; Bus St/Abroad) (BTEC 5D+M)
UMIST - BBB (Man Sci) (BTEC 4D+Ms)
Warwick - BBB (Man Sci; Int Bus) or (BBBB in 2 As + 2 AS or BB in 2 As + CC in 1A + 1 AS)
York - BBB (Bus Man/Lang - course awaiting approval) (6 AS)

22 pts. **Aberystwyth** - BBC-BCC/AB-BB (Bus Admin) (BTEC 3D+3M)
Birmingham - BBC (Commerce)
Bradford - BBC (Int Man/Fr/Ger/Sp) (BTEC 5D+Ms)
Bradford - 22 pts (Bus Man St) (BTEC 5D+Ms)
Brunel - BBC-BCC/BB (Mats/Man; Man/Tech) (BTEC Bus course not suitable)
Cardiff - BBC (Bus Admin; Bus/Jap) (BTEC 4D)
City - BBC/BB + 2 AS (Mgt/Sys) (BTEC Ds+Ms)
Durham - BBC (Arab/Is; Chin/Man; Jap/Man)
East Anglia - BBC/BB (Lang Bus - Fr/Ger/Danish)
Edinburgh - BBC (B Com courses)
Heriot-Watt - BBC/AB (Int Bus; Bus Org; I Bus Lang - B in French) (BTEC 2D+3M)
Hull - BBC-BCC/BB (Bus St/Germ; Man Sys) (4 AS) (BTEC mainly D)
Kent - BBC/AB (Man Sci)
Lancaster - BBC-BCC (MS/Econ; MS/OR; Org/Psy; also Marketing courses) (BTEC D+M)
Loughborough - BBC/AB (Bus/Lang; Man Sci)
Oxford Brookes - BBC (Retail Man) (BTEC 3D+M)

Salford - BBC-CCC/AB-BB (BOAC; Bus/Mang) (4 AS)
Southampton - BBC (Bus Econ courses)
Surrey - BBC (Bus Econ/Comp) (BTEC 3D+M)
Swansea - BBC/BB (Man Sci/Maths)
UMIST - BBC (Int Man/Ger)

20 pts.   **Aberdeen** - BCC (Bus)
Aberystwyth - BCC (BSc Econ; Bus Wels) (BTEC 3D+3M)
Aston - BCC/AA (Bus Ad - comb hons)
Hull - BCC/BB (Maths MS; Bus St/Scand) (6 AS) (BTEC mainly D)
Keele - BCC-BCD/BB-BC (Man Sci joint courses) (4 AS) (BTEC 3M)
Lancaster - BCC (Org St; Op Man)
Liverpool - BCC-BCD-CCC/BB (Bus/Comp)
Manchester Met - BCC/AA (Retail Mark; Bus St) (4 AS) (BTEC mainly D)
Paisley - BCC/AA (Bus/Man) (BTEC 3D+5M)
Robert Gordon - BCC/BB (EBS - Fr/Ger)
Stirling - BCC/BB (HRM courses; Soc Pol/Tech Man; Man Sci courses)
Strathclyde - BCC (BBB 2nd yr entry) (BA Bus School)
Swansea - BCC/BB (Man Sci/Maths)
UMIST - BCC (MACS; MMT)

18 pts.   **Bournemouth** - CCC-BCD/BB (Public Rel)
Bradford - CCC/BB (Tech/Man)
Brighton - 18-16 pts (Bus St; Int Tour Man; Int Bus) (4 AS) (BTEC M overall - Int Bus 5D)
Bristol UWE - CCC/BB (Bus St; Int Bus) (BTEC 2D+3M)
Brunel - CCC/AB (Mats/Man; Manmt)
Buckingham - 18-14 pts (Bus St) (BTEC 3D)
Canterbury Christ Church (CHE) - CCC-EEE/BB-EE (Comb St)
Cardiff - CCC/BB (Mar Comm)
Central Lancashire - 18 pts (Bus) (BTEC 3D+3M)
De Montfort - 18 pts (Bus St) (4 AS) (BTEC 3D+Ms - M overall)
Edinburgh - CCC (BSc; BEng)
Essex - CCC/BC (PMA)
Essex - BCD (IMA)
Glamorgan - 18-14 pts (Eur Bus Ad) (BTEC 3D+Ms)
Glasgow Caledonian - CCC/BC (Bus)
Greenwich - CCC/BC (Int Bus; Bus Admin) (BTEC Ms)
Guildhall London - CCC/BC (Bus Law)
Hull - (Bus/Dutch - Contact Admissions Tutor)
Kent - CCC/BC (E Man Comp; Ind Rel courses)
Kingston - CCC-BCD/AB (Bus St; Bus St Eur - Fr/Ger/Sp)
Leeds Met - CCC/BB approx (Bus St)
Manchester Met - CCC (Bus/Eur - Fr/Ger) (BTEC mainly D)
Middlesex - CCC/BB (Bus St)
Northumbria - 18-14 pts (Trav/Tour; Bus St; Int Bus St - Fr/Ger/Sp)
Oxford Brookes - BCD/CCC (Bus St) (BTEC 3D+Ms)
Portsmouth - CCC (Eur Bus St; Bus St/Lang) (A-level Grade C or equivalent in language required)
Robert Gordon - CCC/BB (Bus St; Comm)
Sheffield Hallam - CCC (Int Bus) (BTEC 5D)
Stirling - CCC/BB (Bus St; Man Sci - all courses)
Strathclyde - CCC/BB (BBD - 2nd yr entry) (BA Arts/Soc Sci; BSc)
Surrey - CCC/BB (Retail Man - N110) (BTEC 3D+Ms)
Thames Valley London - 18-14 pts (Bus St)
Ulster - CCC (Ent Dev)
Westminster - (Int Bus - Fr/Ger/Ital/Russ/Sp) (Contact Admissions Tutor)

16 pts.   **Anglia (Poly Univ)** - 16 pts (Euro Bus Ad)
Bournemouth - 16-14 pts (Bus St) (BTEC (Int Market) 1D+Ms, other courses 4D+3M)
Central England - CCD/CC (Bus) (BTEC 3D)

Central Lancashire - CCD/BC (Comb Hons)
Cirencester (RAC) - 16-14 pts (Int Agri Man)
Coventry - 16 pts (Bus/Fin; Bus; Eur Bus St) (BTEC 2D+3M - 3M)
De Montfort - 16 pts (Bus St) (For students able to take Eur Bus stream) (BTEC 4D - D+M)
East London - CCD (Bus St; Man Syst; Mangt)
Glamorgan - 16-12 pts (Bus St; HRM; Bus Inf Man) (BTEC 3D+2M)
Glasgow Caledonian - (Risk Man; Commerce; Bus St)
Greenwich - CCD/BC (Bus St; Bus Media Comm; IM courses) (BTEC Ds+Ms)
Guildhall London - CCD-DDD/CC (Fin Econ; Fin Serv) (BTEC 3D+3M)
Hertfordshire - 16-14 pts (Bus St; Euro Bus St; Trav/Tour) (BTEC D+M)
Huddersfield - CCD-CDD/BC (Bus St) (4 AS) (BTEC mainly D)
Liverpool John Moores - 16 pts (Bus St; Bus/Fr/Ger/Sp/Jap; Int Bus St; Bus Inf Man) (6 AS) (BTEC 4D+3M)
London (Wye) - CCD/BC (Agric Bus Man)
Middlesex - 16 pts (EBA - Fr/Ger/Sp)
Napier - CCD/BB (Bus St)
North London - 16-14 pts (Bus St; Eur Bus St; Bus Ad) (BTEC Ds+Ms)
Nottingham Trent - CCD (Bus St; Eur Bus/Fr/Ger/Sp) (BTEC 3D+Ms)
Oxford Brookes - CCD/BB (Lang Bus - Fr/Ger; Tourism; Modular) (4 AS) (BTEC 3D+Ms)
Plymouth - CCD/AB-BB (Int Bus - Fr/Ger/Sp) (BTEC 3D+4M)
Portsmouth - 16 pts (Bus St) (BTEC 2D+Ms)
Sheffield Hallam - 16-14 pts (Eur Bus)
Staffordshire - 16-14 pts (Bus) (BTEC 3D+Ms)
Sunderland - 16 pts (Bus courses) (BTEC 5D+2M)
Swansea - CCD/BC-CC (Welsh BS)
Teesside - CCD (Bus St; Mark; Int Bus Stds; Bus Comm) (BTEC mainly Ds)
Ulster - CCD/BC (Bus St; EBS courses; Int Bus Com) (AS (recommended) maths/mod lang/comp/econ/eng)
Wolverhampton - 16 pts (Eur Bus Ad; Bus; Bus/Fr/Ger/Russ/Sp)(4 AS) (BTEC mainly D)

14 pts.
Bournemouth - 14-12 pts (Tourism; Retail Man) (BTEC 3D+Ms)
Brighton - 14 pts (Eur Bus/Tech) (4 AS) (BTEC 2D)
Bristol UWE - 14-10 pts (Bus Sci) (BTEC 4D+3M)
Buckinghamshire (CHE) - 14-12 pts (Int Bus Ad - Fr/Ger/Ital/Sp; IOM; Bus St; EBS) (BTEC 2D+3M)
Cardiff (IHE) - 14 pts (Euro Admin; Tourism)
Central Lancashire - CCE/CC (Bus Inf Tech) (NMI) (4 AS - mod lang considered)
Derby - 14 pts (Bus St) (4 AS) (BTEC 2D)
Dundee (IT) - CDD/BC (Bus St; Comm)
Guildhall London - CCE/BC (Bus St) (BTEC 3D+3M)
Humberside - 14 pts (Euro Bus St/Lang)
Nene (CHE) - 14-12 pts (Bus St)
North London - CCE/BC (Bus St Comb - varies depending on subjects)
Northumbria - CDD/CC (Bus Inf Tech; Int Bus Tech)
Robert Gordon - 14 pts (Bus; Euro Bus Admin)
Sheffield Hallam - 14 pts (Bus St - sandwich) (BTEC 3D+3M)
Sheffield Hallam - BC-CC (Indust St) (4 AS) (BTEC 4D+3M)
Southampton (IHE) - CDD (Bus; Bus/Law; Bus Ad - subject to approval) (4 AS)
Westminster - CDD/CC (Bus St (Serv)) (BTEC Ms)
Wolverhampton - 14 pts (Bus Inf Sys) (BTEC M)

12 pts.
Bournemouth - 12 minimum (Retail Man)
Brighton - 12 pts (Service Sector/Modular; ITM) (BTEC Ds+Ms)
Bristol UWE - 12 pts (BDA) (6 AS)
Buckingham - DDD/CC (EBS) (BTEC Ms)
Cheltenham & Glos (CHE) - 12 pts (Bus St; Tourism) (BTEC 3D+Ms)
Cirencester (RAC) - DDD/CC (Int Agri Man)
Coventry - 12 pts (Bus Ad; Eur Bus Tech - Fr/Ger) (BTEC 3D)

De Montfort – 12 pts (Man Sci)
Dundee – CDE/BB-CC (Retail Man; Con Prod Man)
Humberside – 12 pts (Euro Ad; Ad Man; Euro Tourism) (BTEC Ms)
Luton (CHE) – 12-10 pts (Bus) (4 AS) (BTEC 3D)
Plymouth – 12 pts (Tourism)
Robert Gordon – DDD/CC (Comm; Cons Prod Man)
Salford (UC) – CC (Bus St)
South Bank – CC-CD (All courses; Int Bus – Fr/Ger/Sp)
Swansea (IHE) – CC (Bus St) (6 AS)
Teesside – 12 pts (QDB)
West London (IHE) – 12 pts (Bus St)
Westminster – CDE/CC (Inf Man/Fin; Int Bus) (4 AS)
Wolverhampton – CC (Languages for Business Dip HE)

10 pts. **Anglia (Poly Univ)** – 10 pts (Bus St) (BTEC 2D)
Bolton (IHE) – (Bus St; Tourism)
De Montfort – 10 pts (Ind Bus Syst) (4 AS)
Glamorgan – 10 pts approx (Tech/Bus)
Guildhall London – CD (Bus St modular; Org Behav modular)
Humberside – 10 pts (Int Euro Bus/Tech – Fr/Ger/Sp) (BTEC Ms)
Northumbria – (App Cons Sci)
Trinity & All Saints (CHE) – CD-DD (Bus Man/Admin)
Wolverhampton – 9 pts (Maths Bus An)

8 pts. **and below**
Bangor Normal (CHE) – (Admin)
Bedford (CHE) – (Comb St)
Bournemouth – (Eng Bus Dev; Inf Syst Mgt)
Bradford & Ilkley (CmC) – EE (Org St)
Brighton – (Bus Comp; Sec BEd) (4 AS)
Bristol UWE – (Bus in Sci)
Buckinghamshire (CHE) – 8 pts (Bus/Env Man)
Central Lancashire – (Comb St)
Cheltenham & Glos (CHE) – 8 pts (BCS; Tour Mgt)
Derby – (Modular; Comb St) (4 AS)
Edge Hill (CHE) – (Org/Man St)
Glasgow Caledonian – (Con Man St)
Guildhall London – 8 pts (Euro Bus Syst – Fr/Ger)
Hertfordshire – (Comb St; Dec Sci)
Holborn (Coll) – (BSc Econ)
Humberside – (Bus St; Bus Inf Syst)
Inverness (Coll) – (Bus Ad)
Napier – (Export St/Lang)
Nene (CHE) – DD (Euro Bus – Fr/Ger/Ital/Sp)
North Cheshire (CHE) – (Bus Inf Man/Media)
North East Wales (IHE) – (Bus Man)
Queen Margaret (Coll) – (Commer St; Retail Bus; Retail Man) (See **Home Economics**)
Roehampton (IHE) – (All courses) (BTEC Ms)
Salford (UC) – DD (Qual Man)
South Bank – DD (Con Prod Mgt; Bus St) (NMI)
Suffolk (CFHE) –
Teesside – 4 pts (Bus Comm)
Thames Valley London – DD (Bus Fin; Inf Man)
Wolverhampton – (Bus Man Sys) (Also part-time course for mature students)

Franchised degree and HND courses (see Ch 5):
Bournemouth – Isle of Wight (CAT); Salisbury (CT); Yeovil (CFE)
Greenwich – West Kent (CFE)
Hertfordshire – North Herts (CFE); Hertford Regional (CFE); Oaklands (CFE)

Humberside - Beverley (CFE); Grimsby (CT); North Lindsey (CFE); Scarborough (CT); York (CAT)
Kingston - South Thames (CFE)
Leeds Met - Barnsley (CAT); Harrogate (CAT)
Liverpool John Moores - City of Liverpool (CmC); Wirral Met (CFE)
Northumbria - Carlisle Campus
Plymouth - Cornwall (CFE); Somerset (CAT)
South Bank - South London (CFE); Waltham Forest (CFE)

Offers for Foundation, Certificate and Diploma courses (see Ch 5):

Diploma of Higher Education courses:
4 pts.   Anglia (Poly Univ) (Corp Admin), East London, Leeds Met (Eur Bus Comm), South West London (CFE), Wolverhampton (Lang for Business).

Higher National Diploma courses (England and Wales):
12 pts.   Anglia (Poly Univ) (Dip Corp Admin).
10 pts.   Buckinghamshire (CHE) (Bus/Fin), Hertfordshire (Bus St), Manchester Met 10 pts.
8 pts.   Brighton (Bus Fin), Bristol UWE, Central England 8-6 pts, Central Lancashire DD-DEE (Bus Inf Tech; Bus Fin), Coventry, Guildhall London DD/EEE; Kingston varies, Northumbria (Bus St; Bus Inf Tech), Nottingham Trent 8-6 pts, Oxford Brookes DD, Portsmouth, South Bank DD, Swansea (IHE) (Tourism, Euro Bus); Teesside (Bus Inf Tech; Fin St), West Herts (CFE) (Advt Dip).
6 pts.   Buckinghamshire (CHE) CE-EE (IOM Bus Fin; Travel/Tourism), Glamorgan, Greenwich, Hertfordshire (Quant Methods), Huddersfield (Bus/Fin), Humberside, Leeds Met, Plymouth EEE/EE (Bus Fin), Richmond-on-Thames (Coll) DE-E, Sheffield Hallam also HNC, Suffolk (CFHE) DE-EE, Sunderland DE, Thames Valley London, West London (IHE), Wolverhampton DE (HND - Bus Fin; Public Admin).
4 pts.   Blackburn (CT), Bolton (IHE), Bournemouth, Cheltenham & Glos (CHE), Crawley (CT), Crewe & Alsager (CHE), Croydon (CFE), Derby, Durham (New Coll), East London, Farnborough (CT), Guildford (CT), Gwent (CHE), Hammersmith and West London (Coll), Liverpool John Moores DD, London (Coll/Dist Tr), London (CP), Loughborough (CT), Luton (CHE), Nene (CHE), North London, North Worcs (Coll), Northumbria (Mus; Retail), Norwich City (CFE), Salford (UC), Sandwell (CFE), Staffordshire, Stockport (CT), Thames Valley London (Bus Inf Tech).
2 pts.   Blackpool (Coll), Bradford & Ilkley (CmM), Buckinghamshire (CHE) (Bus Inf Tech), Cardiff (IHE), De Montfort, Glasgow Caledonian, Llandrillo (CFE), North East Wales (IHE), North Herts (CFE), Northumbria (Bus St Lang), Salford (UC) (Bus/Finance for Linguists), Shuttleworth (CAg), Southampton (IHE), Stoke on Trent (Coll) (Motor Vehicle Management), West Herts (Coll) (Bus/Fin St); Suffolk (CFHE), Thames Valley London.

Higher Diploma courses (Scotland):
4 pts.   **and below or equivalent** Aberdeen (CC), Ayr (Coll), Bell (CT), Clydebank (Coll) Dumfries & Galloway (CT), Dundee (IT), Glasgow Caledonian, Inverness (Coll), Moray (Coll), Napier EE (Bus St/Lang, Office Studies, Bus St; Journalism), Perth (Coll), Scottish (CText), Lews Castle (Coll).

College Diploma courses:
8 pts.   West Herts (CFE) (Advertising).
2 pts.   Kingston (Personnel Man), Robert Gordon (Commerce).

Alternative offers:

EB offers: **Lancaster** 70%; **Manchester Met** 70%; **Salford** (BOAC) 70%; **UMIST** 70%.

IB offers: **Aberdeen** 30 pts; **Aberystwyth** 30 pts; **Aston** (Man/Admin; Int Bus/Lang) 31 pts; **Bath** 30 pts inc or H66; **Bournemouth** 24 pts; **Bradford** (Bus Man St) 31 pts, H 16 pts H5 Eng S5 maths, (Man St/Lang) 33-31 pts, H6 Fr/German H5 Span; **Brighton** 24 pts inc 12 pts Highers; **Bristol UWE**

24 pts with 12 pts 3 Highers; **Brunel** 28 pts; **Buckingham** 26 pts; **Buckinghamshire (CHE)** 27 pts; **Cardiff** 28 pts, H655 + 14 pts; **Central England** H555; **City** H666 - 34 pts overall, (Mgt/Syst) 26 pts min; **Coventry** 24 pts; **De Montfort** 28 pts inc 14 pts Highers; **Essex** 28 pts inc 10 pts 2 Highers; **Greenwich** 27 pts; **Guildhall London** 24 pts; **Heriot-Watt** 30 pts; **Hull** (MS) 30 pts; **Keele** 28-27 pts; **Kent** 29 pts, H 13 pts; **Kingston** 29 pts; **Lancaster** 32-30 pts; **Liverpool John Moores** 25 pts; **London (RH)** 30 pts; **Manchester Met** 30 pts; **Plymouth** 26 pts; **Portsmouth** 24 pts plus mathematical ability, Lang at H level for Bus/Lang; **Salford** 30 pts; **South Bank** 24 pts; **St Andrews** 28 pts; **Surrey** (Retail Man) 28 pts; **Swansea** 32 pts, H 16 pts; **UMIST** 30 pts inc 15 pts Highers, (Int Man) 35 pts; **Warwick** 32-30 pts; **Westminster** 30 pts inc 15 pts Highers.

Irish offers: **Aberdeen** BBBB; **Bristol UWE** CCCC; **Guildhall London** CCCCC; **Holborn (Coll)** BBB; **Salford** (BOAC) BBBCCC; **South Bank** CCCC; **UMIST** AABBBC.

SCE offers: **Aberdeen** BBBB; **Aberystwyth** ABBB; **Aston** (Man/Admin) AABB, (Comb Hons) AAAAB; **Bournemouth** BBB; **Bradford** AAABB; **Bristol UWE** ABB; **City** (Bus Stud) BBCCC, (Mgt/Sys) AABB; **Edinburgh** BBBBB; **Essex** BBBB; **Glasgow** AAAB or AABB; **Heriot-Watt** ABBB; **Hull** AABB; **Lancaster** ABBBB; **Liverpool** BBBB/BBBBB; **Napier** BBCC; **Nottingham** BBBB; **Robert Gordon** BBBB; **Sheffield** AABB; **St Andrews** BBBB; **Stirling** ABBB; **Strathclyde** BBBB or AABB (Ind Rel).

Overseas applicants: Competence in written and spoken English essential at **Northumbria, Nottingham Trent, Manchester Met, Staffordshire** and **South Bank. Coventry** 8 pts offer. **Buckinghamshire (CHE)** Interview essential. **Holborn (Coll)** Language classes and help with essay writing given. **North London** Induction course available. **Hull** Living expenses 30% lower than in London. **Sheffield Hallam** Orientation programme and English tuition available. **Tile Hill (CFE)** and **Warwick** Offer 1 year preparatory course for international students who have failed to obtain the right entry grades. Details from the International Office, Warwick University.

CHOOSING YOUR COURSE (See Also Ch 1)

Subject information: These are very popular courses with GCSE mathematics at Grades A or B often being preferred. Many other courses also lead to management careers. Other appropriate but less competitive courses include Hotel Management, Tourism, Transport Management, Estate Management, Teaching, Textile Management etc. Exemptions from the various professional bodies examinations apply to most courses.

At HND level many institutions offer Business Studies courses with specialist streams as follows: accountancy, advertising, broadcasting/ media, business administration, company secretaryship, computer studies, distribution, European business and marketing, fashion, food, health, horticulture, journalism, languages, law, leisure, marketing, media, personnel, printing, publicity, purchasing and tourism. Full details in the *Compendium of Higher Education,* available from the London Advisory Council, 232 Vauxhall Bridge Road, London SW1V 1AV.

Course highlights: Aston Options in marketing, accountancy, personnel, information management, legal studies, public sector management; year 3 in industry. **Anglia (Poly Univ)** (Bus St) Modules in accountancy, company admin, banking, financial services, marketing, personnel or information systems. **Bath** (Int Man) Options in languages, European business, political and social studies. **Birmingham** (Comm) Language options in French, German, Italian, Spanish. **Bournemouth** (Pub Rel) Options in consumer advertising, public affairs, crisis management, European public relations. **Brighton** (Euro Bus/Tech) Joint course with Polytechnic of Turin leads to joint qualifications. (Int Bus St) Contacts with business schools in Italy, Netherlands, Germany, Sweden and Greece. (Int Tour Man) Six month placements in Europe, USA, Far East and Australia. (Bus St) Choice of specialist options in final year from marketing, finance, employment studies and materials management. **Bristol UWE** (Bus St) Special 4-year options in business policy finance, marketing, employee relations and production. **Buckingham** (EBS) Specialist language tuition. (Bus St) Course starts in February. **Buckinghamshire (CHE)** Specialisations in finance, marketing, human resources, languages. (EBS) is the only Business Studies course operating in six countries. **Central England** (Bus) Core subjects in accounting, economics and behavioural studies. **Cheltenham & Glos (CHE)** Modular scheme includes languages. **City** (Man/Sys) Mature students via Access courses welcome. (Bus Stud) First 2 years cover business economics, law and accounting, business management and industrial relations; final year leads to 1 of 2 main areas - finance or marketing. **Coventry** (Bus Ad) Final year optional subjects include marketing communications, market research accounting, information systems, financial management, capital investment, law, industrial relations, personnel studies and purchasing. **Edinburgh** Course includes economics and accounting. Honours students study at least one other subject for 2 years eg, sociology, economic history and computer science; specialisation possible in marketing, personnel management and business finance. **Glamorgan** Specialisation in European Studies, marketing, human resource management or small businesses. **Guildhall London** Banking, business finance, marketing and transport are the 4 main options. **Heriot-Watt** (Bus Org) Broad-based course includes accounting, marketing, organisational behaviour and personnel studies. **Holborn (Coll)** Full- or part-time course with pathways in accounting, management studies or economics and management lead to a BSc Econ London University degree and exemptions from professional examinations. **Huddersfield** (Bus St) Common course for 2 years followed by specialist study from finance, building society studies, marketing or organisational studies. **Hull** (Man Sci) BA course covers analysis and management of organisations; BSc courses offer emphasis in mathematical methods or operations analysis and include computing and statistics. **Humberside** (Euro Ad) Language options in French, German, Spanish and Dutch. **Kingston** (Bus St) Students with A-level European language may join the European Programme, spending term at French or German Business School. **Leeds** (Man St) First 2 years focus on major disciplines of management, economics, psychology, sociology, information science and quantitive methods. In year 3 students select optional courses covering the major areas of business eg, marketing, personnel management, international management. **Leeds Met** (Bus St) Students taking the language options spend their first placement abroad and third in a Business School in France or Germany. **Liverpool John Moores** 5 modern languages offered including Japanese; specialisation in marketing, purchasing, finance, human resources. **London (LSE)** (Man Sci) Year 1 covers economics, quantitive methods and data management systems; years 2 and 3 provide considerable course choice. **London (Wye)** Main focus on managerial problems of agricultural, food and related industries. **Loughborough** (Man Sci) Courses are offered in Management Sciences, Accounting and Financial Management, Banking and Finance, Business Administration with a Foreign Language and also Transport Management. **Manchester Met** (App Cons Sci) Electives from year 2 with specialisation in one area from food, clothing or housing sandwich course options. **Middlesex** (Bus St) Broad course with language option - French, German or Spanish. **Northumbria** (Secretarial Administration) Secretarial studies, business information and organisation with one optional subject from international business or a modern language (French, German or Spanish). **Nottingham Trent** (Bus St) Final year students select 2 optional subjects from finance, marketing, personnel, computing or operations management. **Oxford Brookes** (Bus St) Final year options cover finance and accounting, manpower studies or marketing. **Plymouth** (Bus St) Business Studies may be combined with French, German or Spanish. **Portsmouth** (Bus St) In final year business analysis and planning taken, plus four from twelve options covering accounting, personnel, marketing and information systems and technology, travel and tourism. **Robert Gordon** (Cons Prod Man) Food, textiles and finance. Retail marketing and language options. (Euro Bus Admin) French or German languages with year 3 abroad. **Salford** (Bus Mang) Options are offered in quantitive business analysis, industrial administration or personnel management. **Sheffield** (Bus St) First year covers economics, maths and statistics. **Sheffield Hallam** (Bus St) Business coupled with a study of language (choice of four). Options include marketing, tourism and industrial relations. **Stirling** (Bus St) Part II includes accountancy, management science, marketing, retail studies, venture management, taxation and personnel management. **Strathclyde** (Bus) BA Single Honours courses in Accounting, Administration, Economics, Industrial Relations, Marketing and Operational Research. **Sunderland** (Bus St) Course also offered with a language pathway involving French or German language studies and a year abroad, or an accounting pathway. **Swansea** Emphasis on quantitative applications in business and management; excellent computer facilities. **Thames Valley London** (Bus St) With Business Studies subjects in years 1 and 2 one elective subject taken from: politics, psychology, or modern languages (French, German, Spanish). **Ulster** (Bus St) Elective choices in year 4 from personnel, marketing, finance, production, agribusiness and small businesses. **UMIST** (MACS) Students can major in management or chemistry in final year. **Westminster** (Bus St) Options include European languages, law and computation. NOW CHECK PROSPECTUSES FOR ALL COURSES.

Study opportunities abroad: Aston; Bath (E) FR NL G D; **Birmingham** FR G SP; **Bournemouth** (Public Rel) (E); **Bradford** (E) USA AUS CAN; **Brighton** IT; **Bristol UWE** FR; **Buckinghamshire (CHE)** (E) USA; **Cardiff** (E); **Central Lancashire** (E); **Coventry** G; **De Montfort** (E); **Glamorgan** (E); **Glasgow Caledonian** (E); **Guildhall London** (E) G; **Kingston** FR G; **Lancaster** FR G IT EUR;

Leeds Met FR G; **Liverpool John Moores** (E); **London (RH)** (E) FR G IT SP IRE SW; **Manchester Met** (E) EUR G FR; **Middlesex** EUR USA; **Portsmouth** FR G; **Robert Gordon** (E) FR G; **Salford** (BOAC N Am) USA; **Sheffield Hallam** EUR USA; **South Bank** EUR; **Swansea** (E) FR G IT SP GR P D NL; **Teesside** (E) G NL FR SP D; **Wolverhampton** FR G.

Work opportunities abroad: Aston FR G JAP USA; **Bath** FR G B; **Bournemouth** FR SP P NL AU AUS EG ML, (Public Rel) EUR; **Brighton** IT; **Buckinghamshire (CHE)** F G SP; **Cardiff (IHE)** (Tourism) USA EUR AUS; **Central England** FR G SP; **Coventry**; **De Montfort** FR G SP; **Edinburgh (QM)** (Retail Bus) USA CAN; **Glamorgan** FR G; **Glasgow Caledonian** FR SP G; **Greenwich** (Int Mkt) EUR MEX; **Hertfordshire** FR SP G; **Humberside** FR SP G; **Kingston** EUR; **Lancaster** FR G IT; **Leeds Met** FR G SP IT; **Liverpool John Moores** F G JAP SP; **Liverpool (IHE)**; **Manchester Met** USA G FR B; **Middlesex** EUR; **Northumbria** FR G SP; **Nottingham Trent**; **Oxford Brookes**; **Plymouth** CAN BUL G FR USA NL SP; **Robert Gordon** HK SA AUS; **Salford** (BOAC) EUR USA; **Sheffield** EUR AUS USA; **Sheffield Hallam**; **South Bank** EUR; **Sunderland** FR G; **Swansea** AU CIS; **Teesside** G; **Wolverhampton** EUR; **Ulster** EUR USA.

ADMISSIONS INFORMATION

Number of applicants per place (approx): Aston 6; **Bath** (Bus Admin) 12, (Int Man Lang) 21; **Birmingham** 13; **Bradford** 15; **Brighton** 20, (Euro Bus St) 20, (Euro Bus Tech) 11; **Bristol UWE** 12; **Bolton (IHE)** 3; **Bournemouth** (Tourism) 11, (Bus St) 22, (Adv) 33, (Retail M) 6; **Buckingham** 10; **Buckinghamshire (CHE)** (EBS) 11; **Canterbury Christ Church (CHE)** 20; **Cardiff** 12; **Cardiff (IHE)** (Tourism) 10; **Central England** 25; **Central Lancashire** 29; **Cheltenham & Glos (CHE)** (Tour Man) 8; **City** 40, (Mgt/Syst) 6; **Coventry** 30; **De Montfort** 14; **Dundee (IT)** (Bus St) 11; **East Anglia** (Bus/Fin) 18; **Glamorgan** 5; **Glasgow Caledonian** 18; **Greenwich** 24; **Guildhall London** 20; **Hertfordshire** 20; **Heriot-Watt** 15, (Eur Bus) 8; **Holborn (Coll)** no limit; **Huddersfield** 21; **Hull** (Bus St) 33; **Humberside** 50; **Kent** 30; **Kingston** 50; **Liverpool John Moores** 21; **Manchester Met** (Bus St) 26, (Retail M) 10; **Middlesex** 20, (EBA) 17; **Newcastle** 50; **North London** 15; **Northumbria** 27; **Nottingham Trent** 40, (Eur Bus) 30; **Oxford Brookes** 40; **Portsmouth** 44; **Paisley** 5; **Robert Gordon** 5; **Roehampton (IHE)** 12; **Salford** (BOAC) 50, (Bus Op) 4; **Sheffield Hallam** 35; **South Bank** 5; **Strathclyde** 12; **Sunderland** 20; **Surrey** 8 (Retail M); **Swansea** (All courses average) 10; **Swansea (IHE)** 7; **Teesside** 9; **Thames Valley London** 4; **Trinity & All Saints (CHE)** 3; **UMIST** 10; **West London (IHE)** 7; **Westminster** 12; **Wolverhampton** 20, (Maths Bus An) 2.

General Studies acceptable: Aberdeen; Aston; Birmingham; Bournemouth (not Int Market); Bradford; Bristol UWE; Cardiff; Cardiff (IHE); Central England; Central Lancashire; Cheltenham & Glos (CHE) (2); De Montfort (2); Dundee (IT); Glasgow Caledonian; Greenwich (2); Guildhall London (2); Heriot-Watt (2); Huddersfield; Hull; Humberside; Keele; Lancaster; Leeds (Tr/All Sts); Liverpool; Manchester Met (2); Oxford Brookes (No); Paisley; Portsmouth; Salford (BOAC); South Bank (No); Sunderland; Surrey (Retail Man) (2); Teesside; Thames Valley London; UMIST (as 1 of 3 subjects); Westminster; Wolverhampton.

Selection interviews: Bournemouth; Bradford; Brighton (T); (some); Cardiff (IHE); De Montfort; Dundee (IT); East Anglia; Glamorgan (T); Greenwich; Huddersfield (T); Humberside; Kingston (some); Leeds Met (some); Loughborough; Manchester Met; Northumbria; Oxford Brookes (T); Portsmouth (some); Robert Gordon (T); Salford (BOAC); Sheffield Hallam; South Bank; Stirling (some); Sunderland (T); Swansea; Teesside; Thames Valley London; Warwick (some).

Offers to applicants repeating A-levels: Higher Bristol UWE, Cardiff, Central England, East Anglia (2 pts), Greenwich, Hertfordshire, Huddersfield, Kingston, Lancaster, Leeds Met, Liverpool, Manchester Met, Oxford Brookes, South Bank, Staffordshire, Strathclyde, Swansea, Teesside, West Glamorgan (IHE); **Same** Aston, Bath, Bournemouth, Brunel, Cardiff (IHE), De Montfort, Greenwich (Int Mktg), Hull, Humberside, Loughborough, Northumbria, Salford (BOAC), Sheffield Hallam, South Bank, Ulster, UMIST; **Rare** Lancaster (Mktg).

Admissions Tutors' advice: Bath Ability in arts, science and maths important. **Bournemouth** (Adv/Med/Mar) Motivation and knowledge of subject important. **Hertfordshire** Look for leadership and initiative. **Northumbria** Some lower offers for gap year applicants. **Portsmouth** Grade B in GCSE

English and maths required. **Robert Gordon** Candidate's appearance at interview is important. Interview the interviewer! Ask questions - be positive. Art or art-related subjects not accepted. **Salford** (BOAC) Good A-level grades (C or higher) in maths; be prepared to come for interview. Course leaflet available. **UMIST** Applicants welcomed from both arts and science A-levels.

Examples of interview questions: Tell me about yourself. What is the largest trade union? How large? What do you think about the Government's policy of de-nationalisation? What aspects of the Business Studies course will interest you? What career in the field of management would you like to pursue? What newspapers do you read? What are invisible exports? Describe your strengths and weaknesses. What qualities do you have which are suitable and important for this course? What do you think are the differences between being a personnel manager for Marks and Spencer and British Rail? Why should we give you a place on this course? What is marketing? Is advertising fair? What qualities does a person in business require to be successful? What is the difference between marketing and selling? What makes a good manager? What is a cash-flow system? What problems can it cause? How could supermarkets improve customer relations? What special qualities do you think you have to be of use in the tourist industry? Applicants are always advised to be able to convince the admissions tutor on why they chose that institution and its Business Studies course.

GAP YEAR ADVICE

Institutions accepting a Gap Year: Most institutions; **Bath** Applicants should show willingness to do something complementary to their studies. **Bournemouth** Set yourself personal development goals. **Buckinghamshire (CHE)** Applicants taking a gap year get a lower offer! **City** Do something useful. **De Montfort** Don't drift! **Glamorgan** Obtain work and travel. **Guildhall London** Prefers gap year to be spent gaining work experience. **Heriot-Watt** Relevant work experience useful. **Liverpool John Moores** Go abroad and study your chosen language. **London (Wye)** Probably not. **Manchester Met** (Bus St) Spend a year working in Germany or France. (App Cons Sci) Try to find work in food, housing or work with the elderly or homeless. **Oxford Brookes** Explain your reasons. **Plymouth** Exact conditions of offer must be met. **Salford** (BOAC) Prefer not.

Institutions willing to defer entry after A-levels (see Ch 5): Bath; Bournemouth (possibly); Bradford; Brighton; Bristol UWE (No); Brunel (Prefer not); Buckingham; Cheltenham & Glos (CHE); City; De Montfort; East Anglia; Glamorgan (HRM) (No); Heriot-Watt; Hull; Humberside; Lancaster; London (RH); Manchester Met (No); Northumbria (No); Oxford Brookes; Paisley; Plymouth; Portsmouth (Deferred entry application preferred); Queen Margaret (Coll); Robert Gordon; Roehampton (IHE) (No); Salford; St Andrews; South Bank (No); Staffordshire; Surrey; UMIST; Westminster (Defer entry only rarely).

AFTER A-LEVELS ADVICE

Institutions which may accept the same points score after A-levels: Bath; Belfast; Bournemouth; Brighton; Bristol UWE; Brunel; Cardiff (IHE); Central England; Central Lancashire; Coventry; De Montfort; East Anglia; East London; Glamorgan; Greenwich; Guildhall London; Hull; Holborn (Coll); Huddersfield; Kingston; Liverpool John Moores; Loughborough (varies); Luton (CHE); Manchester Met; Middlesex; Nene (CHE); North London; Northumbria; Nottingham Trent; Oxford Brookes; Plymouth; Portsmouth; Robert Gordon; Salford; Sheffield Hallam; South Bank; Southampton (IHE); Staffordshire; Strathclyde; Sunderland; Surrey (Retail Man); Swansea; Swansea (IHE); Teesside; Ulster; UMIST; Wolverhampton.

Institutions demanding the actual grades offered after A-levels: Bradford (Man Stud/Fr); Dundee (IT); Greenwich (Int Mark); Hull; Lancaster (Marketing); Liverpool; Loughborough (varies); Stirling; Warwick (Man Sci).

Institutions which may accept under-achieving applicants after A-levels: Bath; Bournemouth; Bradford; Brighton; East Anglia; Edinburgh; Hertfordshire; Heriot-Watt; Holborn (Coll); Hull (Overseas students 18-16 pts); Luton (CHE); Manchester Met; Oxford Brookes; Plymouth;

Portsmouth; St Andrews; Salford (BOAC); South Bank; Staffordshire; Thames Valley London; Trinity & All Saints (CHE); Westminster; Check with other institutions.

Institutions with vacancies in Aug/Sept 1992 (see Ch 5): Anglia (Poly Univ); Aston BBC; Bournemouth (Int Market) 14 pts + A-level German, French or Spanish preferred; Bradford (Bus Man St) 22 pts; Bradford & Ilkley (CmC); Bristol UWE (Bus Sci); Brunel (Man/Tech) 18 pts, (Man St) 20 pts; Buckingham 10 pts; Buckinghamshire (CHE) 8 pts; Cheltenham & Glos (CHE) (Bus St) 10 pts, (Tourism) 14 pts; City (Man/Sys); De Montfort 6 pts; Glamorgan 12 pts; Greenwich 12 pts; ; Heriot-Watt (Bus Org) 22 pts; Holborn (Coll); Hull; Humberside; Kingston 16-14 pts + maths A-level; Lancaster; Leeds; Newcastle 22 pts; North London; Northumbria 14 pts, 10 pts at Carlisle campus; Oxford Brookes CCE-BDE; Paisley; Portsmouth 16 pts min, (Bus Lang) CCC; Queen Margaret (Coll) (Retail Man) 4 pts; Salford (BOAC) 18-16 pts; Sheffield Hallam (Portuguese) 6 pts; South Bank; Staffordshire 14 pts; Strathclyde; Sunderland 14 pts; Swansea 10 pts; UMIST (MACS) 16 pts, (Int Man/Ger) 20-18 pts; Westminster 10 pts. Personnel courses also declared several vacancies as did institutions offering Tourism and Travel.

ADVICE FOR MATURE STUDENTS

About 10% of students on these courses are 'mature'. Part-time courses are available at several institutions. Whilst A-levels or equivalent may be required for some courses relevant work experience is often considered equally important. **City** (Man/Sys) Mature students via Access courses welcome.

GRADUATE EMPLOYMENT

New Graduates' destinations (percentages) 1991:
Permanent employment: U 80; P 68; C 69.
Unemployment: U 14; P 19; C 17.
Further studies (all types): U 14; P 7; C 16.
Main career destinations (approx): Business/Finance 77; Computing 10; Social/Medical 6.

Teesside Over 50 graduates entered a wide range of business and administrative occupations. These included accountancy, sales work, personnel work, purchasing, quantity surveying, marketing and hospital administration; 25 HND students transferred to degree courses in business, law and recreation management.

Anglia (Poly Univ) (1991) (Business Studies HND) 24 students went into full-time employment and 13 transferred to degree courses. Of those in employment there was a wide range of destinations including trainee management in hotels and restaurants, and administration posts in the Victoria and Albert Museum, British Standards Institute, Federal Express and Aviation Security. Four students went on to train in accountancy and three went into insurance.

The following institutions are perceived as being above average in producing graduates for employment: Aston, Bath, Bradford, Bristol, Edinburgh, Lancaster, Leeds, London Business School, Manchester Business School, Manchester Met, Nottingham Trent, UMIST, Warwick. See PIP reference in Chapter 5.

This was one of the subjects with the best employment records in 1991-92 during the period of recession.

CELTIC STUDIES

Special subject requirements: For courses in Celtic, A-level in Gaelic is required. For Welsh, A-level Welsh 'required' or 'preferred'.

NB Institutions may raise or lower the level of published offers depending either on the quality or otherwise of individual applications or the numbers of applications received; grades/points offered may be adjusted downwards after A-level results. The level of an offer is not indicative of the quality of a course.

30 pts.	**Cambridge** - AAA potential recommended (Ang-Saxon)
22 pts.	**Aberdeen** - BBC (Celtic; Gaelic)
	Edinburgh - BBC (All Celtic courses)
	Glasgow - BBC (All Celtic courses)
20 pts.	**Cardiff** - BCC (B in history) (Hist/Welsh Hist)
18 pts.	**Belfast** - CCC/BB (Celtic; Irish)
	Cardiff - CCC/BB (Welsh joint degrees; Welsh Studs joint degrees)
16 pts.	**Aberystwyth** - CCD/BC (Celtic; Welsh) (4 AS)
	Bangor - CCD/BC (Welsh Lang Lit; Welsh History; Welsh Lit/LM)
	Swansea - CCD/BC-CC (Welsh; Welsh BS)
	Ulster - CCD-DDD/BC-CD (Irish; Ir Pol Soc)
12 pts.	**St David's** - CC (Welsh; Welsh Stds)
10 pts.	**and below approx**
	St Mary's (CHE) - (Irish St)
	Trinity Carmarthen (CHE) - (Hum)

Alternative offers:

IB offers: **Aberdeen** 30 pts.

Irish offers: **Aberdeen** BBBB; **Aberystwyth** BBBCC.

SCE offers: **Aberdeen** BBBB; **Belfast** BBBB/BBBC; **Glasgow** BBBB.

CHOOSING YOUR COURSE (See also Ch 1)

Subject information: There are five living Celtic languages – Irish, Scottish, Gaelic, Welsh and Breton. But this subject area also covers the extinct languages – Manx, Cornish, Gaulish and Celtiberian – and also the history and civilisation of the Celtic peoples.

Course highlights: Aberystwyth Course option in creative writing. **Bangor** Option in writing for the media. **Cardiff** Mediaeval Welsh literature and linguistics of modern Welsh; course in Welsh and the Media. NOW CHECK PROSPECTUSES FOR ALL COURSES.

Study opportunities abroad: Aberdeen (E); **Belfast** (E); **Glasgow** (E); **Swansea** (E) B SP P D.

ADMISSIONS INFORMATION

Number of applicants per place (approx): Aberystwyth 5; **Bangor** 5; **Cardiff** 5; **St David's** 3; **Swansea** 7.

General Studies acceptable: Aberdeen; Bangor; Cardiff; St David's.

Selection interviews: Aberystwyth; St David's.

Examples of interview questions: Why do you want to study this subject? What specific areas of Celtic culture interest you?

GAP YEAR ADVICE

Institutions accepting a Gap Year: Most institutions.

Institutions willing to defer entry after A-levels (see Ch 5): Aberystwyth; Bangor.

AFTER A-LEVELS ADVICE

Institutions which may accept the same points score after A-levels: Bangor; Cardiff; St David's.

Institutions with vacancies in Aug/Sept 1992 (see Ch 5): Aberystwyth; Bangor 14 pts.

ADVICE FOR MATURE STUDENTS

5% of students on these courses in the Welsh universities come into the 'mature' category

---

CHEMISTRY

Special subject requirements: 2-3 A-levels from mathematics/science subjects. Chemistry 'required' or 'preferred' in most cases.

NB Institutions may raise or lower the level of published offers depending either on the quality or otherwise of individual applications or the numbers of applications received; grades/points offered may be adjusted downwards after A-level results. The level of an offer is not indicative of the quality of a course.

30 pts.	**Cambridge** (Nat Sci)/**Oxford** - AAA potential recommended in most cases
26 pts.	**East Anglia** - ABB (Chem/USA)
24 pts.	**Lancaster** - BBB/AB (Chem/USA; Chem/P USA)
	Leicester - BBB (Chem USA; Chem Eur)
	Nottingham - BBC (Chem Man)
	Salford - BBB/AB (Chem/USA)
	Southampton - BBB (Chem 4-yr courses)
	Strathclyde - BBB (Forensic Chem)
22 pts.	**Aston** - BBC-BCC/AA-AB (Comb Hons) (BTEC D+M overall)
	Surrey - BBC/AB (Comp Aid Chem) (4 AS) (BTEC Ms)
	Swansea - BBC/AB (CCC/BC yr in industry) (Chem courses with a year in USA/Europe)
	UMIST - BBC/AB (Chem/Fr; Chem/Ger)
20 pts.	**Bradford** - BCC/BB (Chem/Pharm for Sci) (BTEC 5D)
	Bristol - BCC (Chemistry; Chem Phys; Chem/Ind St) (BTEC D+M overall)
	East Anglia - BCC (Euchem) (4 AS)
	Essex - BCC (CEBS)
	Heriot-Watt - BCC (2nd yr entry) (Chemistry courses also Chem/Lang)
	Leeds - BCC/BB (All Comb St courses) (BTEC 3M)
	London (Imp) - BCC (BB offers rare) (All Chem courses)
	London (QMW) - BCC/BC (Chem/Comp Sci)
	Nottingham - BCC-CCD (Chemistry)
	Salford - BCC/BB (Chem/Fr/Ger/Jap)
	Sheffield - BCC-CCC/BC-CC (Chemistry courses) (6 AS) (BTEC M overall 70% average)
	Southampton - BCC (Chem 3-yr courses)

Strathclyde - BCC (Chem; Ap Chem)
Surrey - BCC/AB (Chem France; Chem Germ; Chem Man) (4 AS)(BTEC Ms)
Warwick - BCC-CCD (Chem; Chem Bus; Chem/Med Chem)

18 pts.   **Aberdeen** - CCC-CCD/BC (All courses)
Aston - CCC/AB (Chem Comb Hons) (BTEC Ds+Ms)
Bangor - 18 pts (Chem/PE) (BTEC 3M)
Bath - CCC/BB (Chem) (BTEC 3M)
Belfast - CCC/BB (Chem; Chem Comp)
Birmingham - CCC-DDD (Chemistry)
Durham - CCC (Phys/Chem) (BTEC 3M)
East Anglia - CCC-CCD (Env/Chem; Chem/Maths; Chem/An Sci; Chem; Chem/Bus)
   (4 AS) (BTEC 3M)
Essex - CCC-CCD (Chem courses)
Glasgow - CCC-CCD/BC (All courses)
Hull - CCC-CDD/BC-CC (Chem Sur Mol) (BTEC M overall)
Hull - BCD (Chem/Maths) (BTEC M overall)
Keele - BCD-CCC/BC-CC (All courses) (4 AS) (BTEC 3M)
Lancaster - CCC-CCD/BB (Env Chem) (BTEC Ms)
Leeds - CCC/BB (Chem; Chem Sci; Fuel) (4 AS) (BTEC 3M)
Liverpool - CCC/BB (Chem; Chem/Mat Sci; Chem Pharm) (4 AS)
London (King's) - CCC approx (Chem courses)
London (RH) - CCC (Geochem) (6 AS)
London (UC) - CCC (Chem courses)
Loughborough - CCC-CCD/BB-BC (Chemistry courses)
Manchester - CCC approx (Chemistry courses)
Nottingham - CCC (Chem/Mol Phys; Mat Chem)
Reading - CCC-CCD (All courses)
St Andrews - CCC (Chem) (4 AS)
Salford - CCC/BC (Chem) (BTEC 3M)
Sheffield - BCD (Chem/PM) (BTEC M overall 70% average)
Sheffield - CCC (Chem/Mat) (BTEC M overall 70% average)
Sheffield - CCC/BB (Chem/Ast) (BTEC M overall 70% average)
Strathclyde - CCC (2nd yr entry) (Chem)
Surrey - CCC/BC (Chem) (4 AS) (BTEC 4M)
Sussex - CCC (Chemistry courses)
Swansea - CCC/BC (Chem; Chem Bus; Chem/Man Sci; Chem/Comp Sci; Chem/Env
   Sci; Bio/Biomed Chem; Chem/An Sci)
UMIST - BCD/BC (All courses except under **20/14 pts**)
York - CCC (Average - all courses) (4 AS inc phys and maths) (BTEC 3D or 3M)

16 pts.   **Brunel** - CCD/BD (C/B in chem) (Chemistry courses)
Cardiff - CCD/BC (Chemistry courses)
Dundee - CCD/BC (Med Chem)
Durham - CCD (Chemistry) (4 AS) (BTEC 3M)
East Anglia - CCD (Chem Phys)
Edinburgh - CCD/BB (Chemistry; Env Chem) (4 AS)
Exeter - CCD/BC (Chem) (BTEC M overall)
Hull - CCD/BC-CC (Chem Bio/Tox; Chem; Chem/Educ) (BTEC M overall)
Kent - CCD/BB (Chemistry)
Lancaster - CCD (Chemistry/Polymer; Chem Sci) (BTEC Ms)
Leicester - CCD (Chem)
London (QMW) - CCD/CC (All Chemistry courses except under **20 pts**)
Manchester Met - 16-10 pts (Comb St)
Newcastle - CCD/BC (B or C in Chem) (Chem courses)
St Andrews - CCD (Geochem)

14 pts.   **Bradford** - CDD/CC (Chem/Chem Tech) (BTEC 3M)
Dundee - CDD/BC (All courses except **16 pts**)
Heriot-Watt - CDD (All courses except **20/12 pts**)
Leeds - CDD/CC (Col Chem) (BTEC 3M)
Paisley - 14 pts (Chem; Ind Chem)

Stirling – CDD (1st yr entry) BCC (2nd yr entry) (Chem)
UMIST – CDD/CC (Polymer Chem)
12 pts. Bangor – 12 pts (D in chem from 3 subjects; C in chem from 2 subjects) (All Chemistry courses except under 18 & 8 pts) (4 AS)
Brighton – 12-8 pts (Chem courses) (4 AS) (BTEC 3M)
Central Lancashire – CC (Comb Hons)
Dundee (IT) – CC (Chem/Bus)
Greenwich – 12 pts (Ap Geochem)
Heriot-Watt – DDD (CCC 2nd yr entry) (Brewing/Dist; Col Chem)
10 pts. Central Lancashire – CD (Bio Chem; Chem) (3 AS)
De Montfort – 10 pts (Chem/Bus St – for all non-science students, flexible entry) (4 AS)
Nottingham Trent – CEE/CD (All courses)
8 pts. and below
Anglia (Poly Univ) – (Cell Mol Sci)
Bangor – 1 A-level (Wide Access course)
Bell (CT) – (Chem/Inst Anal)
Coventry – (Modular; Comb Sci)
De Montfort – (Comb St)
Derby – (Modular) (4 AS)
Glamorgan – (All courses)
Glasgow Caledonian – (Chem/Inf)
Hertfordshire – CD-DD (Chem/Nat Sci; Env Chem)
Huddersfield – DE (Ap Chem)
Humberside – (Chem; Chem/Chem Eng) (4 AS)
Kingston – 8 pts (All courses) (4 AS) (BTEC)
Liverpool John Moores – DD (Nat Sci)
North East Wales (IHE) – 4 pts (Chem Sci)
North East Wales (IHE) – EE (Chem Sci Inf Tech) (4 AS)
North London – (Chem; Comb)
Oxford Brookes – DD (Modular) (NMI) (4 AS)
Plymouth – (Comb Sci/Soc)
Ripon & York St John (CHE) – (Modular)
Robert Gordon – (Chem)
Salford – 6 pts (Chem Sci)
Salford/North East Wales (IHE) – DE (2x2 courses)
Sheffield Hallam – 8 pts (Chem/Man)
South Bank – DD (Sci Comp) (BTEC 5M)
Staffordshire – (Comb Sci)
St Mary's (CHE) – (Comb St)
Sunderland – (Chem Pharm Sci; joint courses)
Teesside – (Chem)
Wolverhampton – (All Chemistry courses)

Offers for Foundation, Certificate and Diploma courses (see Ch 5):

Diploma of Higher Education courses:
4 pts. Wolverhampton.

Higher National Diploma courses (England and Wales):
2 pts. Central Lancashire; De Montfort (Chem; Cosmetic); Glamorgan; Greenwich; Hertfordshire; Huddersfield; Kingston; Manchester Met; North East Wales (IHE); Nottingham Trent; Portsmouth; Salford (UC); Sheffield Hallam; Staffordshire; Teesside.

Eligible students on BTEC HND courses in Science (Chemistry) may elect to take an additional paper for Graduate Membership Part 1 of the Royal Society of Chemistry.

Higher National Diploma courses (Scotland):
  2 pts.   **or equivalent** Bell (CT); Dundee (IT); Falkirk (CT); Glasgow Caledonian; Kirkcaldy (CT); Napier; Robert Gordon.

Alternative offers:

EB offers: **Aston** 70%; **East Anglia** (Chem) 60%; **Edinburgh** Grades 7 or 8 in 3 relevant subjects; **London (RH)** 60%.

IB offers: **Aberdeen** 26 pts; **Aston** 30 pts; **Belfast** H555 S555; **Brunel** varies; **Bangor** 28 pts; **Bath** 28 pts, H5 chem; **Bradford** 26 pts; **Bristol** 30 pts; **Cardiff** 25 pts H6 chem; **City (Poly)** 28 pts 7 subjects, 24 pts 6 subjects; **Durham** H555; **East Anglia** (Chem) 28 pts inc 15 pts Highers, (Chem/USA) 32 pts, (Euchem) 30 pts; **Edinburgh** 28 pts inc 5 or 6 in relevant subjects; **Exeter** 30 pts; **Heriot-Watt** 28 pts; **Hull** 27 pts; **Keele** 26 pts; **Kent** 25 pts, H 11 pts; **Lancaster** 28 pts; **Leeds** 30-28 pts Chem H5 pts, (Col Chem) 30-25 pts; **Liverpool** 30 pts inc H555; **London (RH)** 30 pts; **Newcastle** H6 chem + H55; **North London** 24 pts inc H444; **Nottingham** 30-28 pts H555; **St Andrews** 28 pts; **Salford** 30 pts; **Sheffield** 26 pts inc H655; **South Bank** 24 pts; **Surrey** 36-30 pts; **UMIST** 30 pts inc 16 pts Highers; **York** 27 pts H555.

Irish offers: **Aberdeen** BBCC/BCCCC; **Aston** BBBBBB; **Bangor** BBCCC; **Brunel** BBBCC; **East Anglia** (Chem) BBBC; **Edinburgh** BBBB; **Keele** BBBCC; **Liverpool** BBCCC; **London (RH)** BBBBC; **Newcastle** BBBCCC; **Sheffield** AABBB; **South Bank** CCCC; **UMIST** ABBBBC.

SCE offers: **Aberdeen** BBBC; **Aston** BBBBB; **Belfast** BBBB/BBBC; **Brunel** 5 satis passes; **Dundee** BBB; **East Anglia** AAAB; **Edinburgh** BBBC; **Glasgow** BBB; **Heriot-Watt** BBB; **Keele** BBCC; **Lancaster** BBBB; **Leeds** AAAA; **Liverpool** AABB; **London (RH)** BBBB; **Newcastle** BBB; **North London** CCCC; **Sheffield** AABB; **St Andrews** BBB; **Strathclyde** (Forensic) AABB, (Chem) BBBB/ABB; **UMIST** BBBB; **York** BBBBB.

Overseas applicants: East Anglia, London (RH) Offer language courses. **Surrey** English proficiency required. **UMIST** 25% overseas students. **York** Some scholarships available.

CHOOSING YOUR COURSE (See also Ch 1)

> **Subject information:** There is a considerable shortage of applicants for this subject which has very many career applications. These include oceanography (marine chemistry), agricultural and environmental work, colour chemistry, medical chemistry, pharmacy, pharmacology and polymer science. Refer to tables covering these subjects.

Course highlights: Aston Choice between full-time or sandwich courses made in year 2. Transfer to Chemical Process Engineering possible. **Bath** Choice between full-time and sandwich course on UCAS applications not binding. Optional courses in biochemistry, physics, chemical engineering, languages in year 1. **Bangor** Aspects of chemistry with particular relevance to the ocean as a chemical system. This involves the natural organic and inorganic componenets of the sea and the assessment of pollution problems in estuaries and coastal waters. **Bell (CT)** (Chem/Inst Anal) A pass degree course with option to transfer to **Strathclyde** in year 3. **Birmingham** Year 1 students also take course chosen from physics, biological sciences, geological sciences or computer science. **Bradford** Course has 4 equal components – inorganic, physical and organic chemistry and chemical technology. **Bristol** Chemistry taken in yr 1 plus 2 subjects from: biochemistry, physics, geology, maths or computer methods. **Brunel** Common first two years for all courses, specialisation in medical, environmental and agricultural chemistry in years 3 and 4, German and French available as options. **Durham** Year 1 includes wide range subsidiary courses: computing, electronics, biology, business studies, history and philosophy of science. **Hertfordshire** 4 named routes – analytical chemistry, chemical computing, chemical technology, medicinal chemistry. **Heriot-Watt** Optional subjects include computer science, physics and accountancy and finance. Five courses offered, four common in year 1. (Brewing) Scholarships available. **Leeds** (Col Chem) General degree in applied chemistry and specialised training in all aspects of dye chemistry, textile, paint and ink technology, photochemistry and spectroscopy; 7 scholarships available. **Liverpool** Year 2 options include materials science, oceanography, computer science, biochemistry or pharmacology. **London (Imp)** In year 1 students take maths and second ancilliary subject from cell biology, physics or a modern language. Special feature of course is training in computing – and absence of comprehensive exams in final year. **London (QMW)** Year 1 supporting subject taken with chemistry such as computer science, maths or physics, or a subject involving the applications of chemistry such as biochemistry or geology. **London (UC)** (Medicinal Chemistry) This includes biology, pharmacology, physiology and biochemistry. **Newcastle** Transferability possible between Chemistry, Chemistry with Applied Chemistry and Medicinal Chemistry until start of year 2. Optional year out. **South Bank** (Sci Comp) Major options – physical science or biotechnology. **Surrey** Optional language; management studies taken in all years. **Southampton** In year 2 chemistry combined with oceanography and biology. **Strathclyde** All students take same course in first three years. A subsidiary subject taken in year 3 from physics, materials science biochemistry or biology. Options for Applied Chemistry students include polymer or chemixcal technology and fuel science. **Swansea** Covers all 3 branches of Chemistry (organic, inorganic and physical); scholarship scheme. **UMIST** Years 1 and 2 cover chemistry, industrial chemistry, chemical physics, polymer chemistry and analytical chemistry; final choice made in year 3. NOW CHECK PROSPECTUSES FOR ALL COURSES.

Study opportunities abroad: Bangor (E); **Belfast** (E); **Birmingham** (E); **Bristol** (E); **Brunel** (E); **Central Lancashire** (E); **Cardiff** (E); **City** USA EUR; **Coventry** FR G IRE; **East Anglia** (E) D FR G IT NL SP; **Edinburgh** (E); **Exeter** (E); **Heriot-Watt** (E); **Hertfordshire** (E); **Hull** (E) G; **Humberside**; **Kent** (E) EUR; **Kingston** (E); **Lancaster** USA; **Leeds** (E); **Leicester** (E); **Liverpool** (E); **London (Imp)** (E) EUR, **(QMW)** (E), **(RH)** (E); **Newcastle** (E) G B IT SP; **Reading** (E); **Salford** (E) USA EUR; **Sheffield** (E); **Southampton** (E); **St Andrews** (E); **Stirling** FR; **Strathclyde** (E); **Surrey** (E) USA (some) FR; **Sussex** FR G SP; **Swansea** (E); **Teesside** (E) FR G; **UMIST** FR G; **York** FR G.

Work opportunities abroad: Brunel NL SZ FR; **Cardiff** FR G IRE; **City**; **Coventry** EUR; **Heriot-Watt** FR G SP; **Hull** G; **Kingston** G USA; **London (Imp)** EUR; **Loughborough**; **Northumbria** FR; **Nottingham Trent** FR G USA; **Portsmouth** EUR; **Salford** EUR; **South Bank** EUR; **Southampton**; **Strathclyde**; **Surrey** FR G SZ AUS NZ; **York** FR NL G.

ADMISSIONS INFORMATION

Number of applicants per place (approx): Aston 6; **Bangor** 3, (Mar/Chem) 2, (Chem) 2; **Bath** 8; **Bradford** 3; **Bristol** 4; **Brunel** 4; **Cardiff** 3; **Coventry** 10; **Dundee** 9; **Dundee (IT)** 25; **Durham** 4; **East Anglia** (Euchem) 4, (Chem/USA) 7; (Chem) 10; **Edinburgh** 5; **Essex** 9; **Exeter** 8; **Glamorgan** 1; **Glasgow Caledonian** 4; **Hertfordshire** 10; **Heriot-Watt** 6, (Brewing) 5; **Huddersfield** 22; **Hull** 5; **Keele** 9; **Kent** 5; **Kingston** 4; **Lancaster** 14; **Leeds** 7; **Liverpool** 6; **London (Imp)** 3, **(QMW)** 4; **Loughborough** 9; **Newcastle** 5, (Med Chem) 1; **North East Wales (IHE)** 2; **North London** 4; **Nottingham Trent** 20; **Oxford Brookes** 8; **Reading** 5; **Salford** (Chem/USA) 5, (2-2 course) 4, (Chem/Fr) 4; **Sheffield** 6; **South Bank** 5; **Surrey** 7, (Comp Aid Chem) 5, (Chem) 8; **Strathclyde** 6; **Swansea** 5; **Teesside** 2; **UMIST** 7; **York** 7.

General Studies acceptable: Aberdeen; Aberystwyth; Bradford; Brunel; Central Lancashire; Exeter; Lancaster (JMB); London (QMW); North East Wales (IHE); North London; Salford; South Bank; Strathclyde; Surrey; UMIST.

Selection interviews: (some); Bangor; Bath; Brunel; Cambridge; Durham (Approximately 75-60% offered places); East Anglia; Greenwich; Guilhall London (some); Hull; Keele (mature students only); Kingston (some); Lancaster; Liverpool; London (RH); Loughborough; Newcastle (usually); Nottingham; Oxford; Portsmouth; Salford; Sheffield; South Bank; Staffordshire; Surrey; Warwick.

Offers to applicants repeating A-levels: Higher Bangor, Brunel (Ind Chem), Hull, Kingston, Loughborough (2-4 pts), Nottingham; **Possibly higher** Brunel, East Anglia, Edinburgh, London (RH), Newcastle; **Same** Bath, Bristol (no offer if first time grades are low), Exeter, Huddersfield, Keele, Lancaster, North London, Salford, Sheffield, South Bank, Surrey.

Admissions Tutors' advice: Bath Students not attending interview may not receive an offer. **Bangor** Great weight placed on students' ability to pass 1st year exams; character as important as A-level grades. **Brunel** Transfers possible at appropriate level from other universities or colleges. **East**

Anglia Lower offers possible for applicants with A- and AS-levels depending on subjects breadth. GCSE grades A-C in maths at least required. **Greenwich** Looks for all-round achievement. **Kingston** Looks for motivation. **Leeds** GCSE maths grades A-C required. **Newcastle** Applicants normally asked to attend for interview before an offer is made (except in cases of financial hardship). **Northumbria** Offer depends on academic ability and school report. **Swansea** Apply for scholarship scheme. **Wolverhampton** Looks for desire to develop computing expertise with reference to chemical applications.

Examples of interview questions: Why is carbon a special element? Why do you find chemistry interesting? What use is chemistry? Discuss the nature of forces between atoms with varying intermolecular distances. Describe recent practicals. What is acid rain? What other types of pollution are caused by Man? With what could you react oxides of nitrogen? What evidence is there for the 'lock and key' hypothesis? Is it in fact an hypothesis or has it been proven? What is an enzyme? What are the general properties of benzene? Why should sciences be less popular among girls at school? What can a mass spectrometer be used for? What would you do if a river turned bright blue and you were asked to test a sample? What would be the difference between metal and non-metal pollution? Identification of crystals. Questions on resources for example, oil, gas, coal.

GAP YEAR ADVICE

Institutions accepting a Gap Year: Most institutions; **Brunel** Industrial training lasts 15 months. Students may prefer not to take a gap year. **Heriot-Watt** Some revision desirable during the year. Intensive courses available in some subjects a month before starting course. **London (QMW)** Take up some worthwhile employment; learn a language, VSO etc. **UMIST** Try to keep in touch with chemistry if year not spent on scientific pursuits. **York** Have a definite plan. Apply for deferred entry.

Institutions willing to defer entry after A-levels (see Ch 5): Aston; Bangor; Bath (providing decision is made early on); Bradford; Brunel; Glamorgan; Heriot-Watt; Kingston; Lancaster; Leeds; Newcastle; Robert Gordon; Salford; St Andrews; South Bank; Swansea; York; most institutions.

AFTER A-LEVELS ADVICE

Institutions which may accept the same points score after A-levels: Aston; Bangor; Bath; Bristol (actual grades); Brunel; Cardiff; Central Lancashire; Durham; East Anglia; Edinburgh; Heriot-Watt; Hull; Humberside; Keele; Lancaster; Leeds; Liverpool; London (RH); Loughborough; Manchester Met; Newcastle (provided offer was firmly accepted and at least D in chemistry); North London; Northumbria; Oxford Brookes; Portsmouth; Salford; Sheffield; South Bank; Strathclyde; Sunderland; Surrey; most other institutions.

Institutions demanding the actual grades offered after A-levels: Kingston, Nottingham.

Institutions which may accept under-achieving applicants after A-levels: Cardiff; Heriot-Watt; Leeds; South Bank; most other institutions.

Institutions with vacancies in Aug/Sept 1992 (see Ch 5): Aberdeen; Anglia (Poly Univ); Aston CCC; Bangor 10 pts; Bath 14 pts; Brighton; Bristol; Brunel 10 pts; Dundee; Essex; Glamorgan; Greenwich 4 pts; Heriot-Watt 12 pts, (Col Chem) 10 pts; Kingston 6-4 pts; Lancaster (Chem/USA) 22 pts; Leeds (Col Chem) 10 pts; Leicester; London (QMW); Manchester Met; Newcastle 14 pts; Oxford Brookes; Paisley; Portsmouth; Robert Gordon; Salford (Chem/USA) 18 pts, (Chem/Lang) 16 pts, (Chem) 10 pts; St Andrews 16 pts; St Mary's (CHE); Scottish (CText); Sheffield; Sheffield Hallam; South Bank 6 pts; Strathclyde; Surrey; Swansea 14 pts.

ADVICE FOR MATURE STUDENTS

These courses attract about 4% of mature students who invariably must have a science background. **Sheffield** Non A-level applicants should send details before making application.

GRADUATE EMPLOYMENT

New Graduates' destinations (percentages) 1991:
Permanent UK employment: U 69; P 59.
Unemployment: U 24; P 31.
Further studies (all types): U 51; P 40.
Main career destinations (approx): Scientific 43; Business/Finance 40; Computing 7; Teaching 1.

Surrey (1991) Chemists entering full-time employment went into development work, paint technology, technical sales and quality control. Almost all graduates entered subject-related employment.

York (1986-91) 48% of graduates entered employment, almost half moving into subject-related careers. These included scientific research in industry analytical chemistry, product development, technical management, quality control, laboratory and environmental work. 8% chose management training, sales, marketing and production management sometimes in industries associated with chemicals. 7% went into accountancy and banking and the remainder went into management, publishing, law, information work and voluntary work in India and Brazil.

See Also under **Science**.

CHEMISTRY (APPLIED)

Special subject requirements: see Chemistry.

NB Institutions may raise or lower the level of published offers depending either on the quality or otherwise of individual applications or the numbers of applications received; grades/points offered may be adjusted downwards after A-level results. NB The level of an offer is not indicative of the quality of a course.

20 pts.	**Aston** - 20-18 pts (Ap Chem)
18 pts.	**Salford** - CCC/BC (App Chem)
	Strathclyde - CCC (2nd yr entry) (App Chem)
16 pts.	**Brunel** - CCD/CC (Chem) (5 AS) (BTEC 3M)
	Cardiff - CCD/BB (App Chem)
14 pts.	**Strathclyde** - CDD (1st yr entry) (App Chem)
12 pts.	**Heriot-Watt** - CC (App Chem)
	Scottish (CText) - CC minimum (App Chem)
10 pts.	**Central Lancashire** - CD (Ap Chem) (3 AS)
	Huddersfield - 10-8 pts (Ap Chem)
	Kingston - CEE/CD (Ap Chem)
	Sheffield Hallam - DDE/CD (Ap Chem)
8 pts.	**and below**
	Bristol UWE - 6 pts (Ap Chem Sci)
	Coventry - 8 pts (Ap Chem) (4 AS) (BTEC 2M)
	De Montfort - DD (Ap Chem) (BTEC 3M)
	Greenwich - (App Chem Bus) (BTEC 3M)
	Hertfordshire - DD (App Chem) (BTEC 2M)
	Liverpool John Moores - DD (Ap Chem) (BTEC 3M)
	Napier - DD-EE (App Chem) (4 AS)
	North London - (Chem/Polymers)
	Northumbria - DEE (Ap Chem)
	Nottingham Trent - 6 pts (Ap Chem)
	Plymouth - (App Chem)
	Portsmouth - 6 pts (Ap Chem) (4 AS)
	Staffordshire - DD (Ap Chem)
	Wolverhampton - DE (Ap Chem)

Offers for Foundation, Certificate and Diploma courses (see Ch 5):

Higher National Diploma courses:
2 pts.   and below
         Cardiff (IHE) (Medical Lab Tech), Coventry (Phys Sci), Nene (CHE) (Leather Technology),
         Portsmouth, Westminster (Medical Lab Tech).

Higher National Diploma courses (Scotland):
2 pts.   Dundee (IT)

Alternative offers:

EB offers: **Hertfordshire** 60%.

IB offers: **Brunel** 26 pts - each case considered on merit; **Cardiff** H554 + 13 pts; **Hertfordshire**
24 pts; **Northumbria** 24 pts inc H444.

Irish offers: **Brunel** BBBCC; **Coventry** CCCC; **Hertfordshire** DDD; **Liverpool John Moores**
CCC.

SCE offers: **Brunel** 5 satisfactory passes; **Scottish (CText)** DD; **Strathclyde** BBBB/ABB.

Overseas applicants: Brunel Overseas applicants must be fluent in spoken English. **Hertfordshire**
Foundation courses offered in science subjects. **Huddersfield** Two week induction course -
information pack available.

CHOOSING YOUR COURSE (See also Ch 1)

> **Subject information:** These courses often cover the same range of diverse topics as those listed
> under **Chemistry**. Many courses include a year spent in industry.

Course highlights: Central Lancashire Language options in French, German and Spanish. **Coventry**
Modular course allows choice between single or joint honours. Language study possible. **De Montfort**
Two specialist areas chosen in final year from electrochemistry, polymer science, pharmaceutical
chemistry and computer methodology in chemistry. **Huddersfield** Course covers basic chemistry,
chemical engineering and biochemistry. **Kingston** Major options in medicinal chemistry or polymer
chemistry. **Liverpool John Moores** Industrial chemistry, radio-chemistry and natural products
chemistry offered in final year. **Northumbria** Major options in analytical chemistry, applied
biochemistry and chemical process technology. **Plymouth** Bias towards environmental, marine and
analytical chemistry. **Portsmouth** Options include analytical chemistry, corrosion and protection and
fuels and energy. **Sheffield Hallam** In final year up to one third of chemistry studies can be replaced
by industrial studies (operational planning and marketing). **Staffordshire** Options in years 2 and 3
include computing, geology, mathematics, polymers, pharmaceutical and toxicological chemistry.
NOW CHECK PROSPECTUSES FOR ALL COURSES.

Study opportunities abroad: Brunel (E); **Coventry** (E); **Greenwich** (E); **Huddersfield** (E);
Nottingham Trent (E).

ADMISSIONS INFORMATION

Number of applicants per place (approx): Aston 8; **Bristol UWE** 14; **Brunel** 7; **Coventry** 13;
De Montfort 12; **Greenwich** 10; **Hertfordshire** 8; **Huddersfield** 18; **Liverpool John Moores** 7;
Napier 4; **Northumbria** 10; **Nottingham Trent** 12; **Portsmouth** 11; **Scottish (CText)** 3;
Sheffield Hallam 16; **Staffordshire** 5; **Wolverhampton** 3.

General Studies acceptable: Aston; Brunel; De Montfort; Greenwich; Staffordshire;
Wolverhampton.

Selection interviews: Aston; Brunel (some); De Montfort (some); Greenwich; Huddersfield; Kingston; Liverpool John Moores (some); Northumbria; Portsmouth; Scottish (CText),

Offers to applicants repeating A-levels: Higher Liverpool John Moores, Northumbria, Sheffield Hallam; **Possibly higher** Brunel, Coventry, De Montfort, Huddersfield, Portsmouth; **Same** Aston, Greenwich.

Admissions Tutors' advice: See under **Chemistry.**

Examples of interview questions: See under **Chemistry**.

GAP YEAR ADVICE

Institutions accepting a Gap Year: Most institutions; **Brunel** Since industrial training lasts 15 months, students may prefer not to take a gap year. **Staffordshire** Increase your communication skills; **Wolverhampton** You should aim to spend it in the chemical industry.

Institutions willing to defer entry after A-levels (see Ch 5): Coventry; Plymouth; Salford.

AFTER A-LEVELS ADVICE

Institutions which may accept the same points score after A-levels: Aston; Brunel; Coventry; De Montfort; Hertfordshire; Liverpool John Moores; Napier; Northumbria; Nottingham Trent; Portsmouth; Strathclyde; Wolverhampton; most other new universities.

Institutions demanding the actual grades after A-levels: Northumbria; Scottish (CText).

Institutions with vacancies in Aug/Sept 1992 (see Ch 5): Coventry; Greenwich (open access admission) 4 pts; Plymouth 8 pts; Salford 10 pts.

ADVICE FOR MATURE STUDENTS

See under **Chemistry.**

CHINESE

Special subject requirements: 2 A-levels. Modern language at A-level.

NB Institutions may raise or lower the level of published offers depending either on the quality or otherwise of individual applications or the numbers of applications received; grades/points offered may be adjusted downwards after A-level results. The level of an offer is not indicative of the quality of a course.

30 pts.	**Cambridge/Oxford** – AAA potential recommended (Oriental)
24 pts.	**London (SOAS)** – BBB/AB (Chinese and all courses)
	Sheffield – BBB (Korean)
22 pts.	**Durham** – BBC (All Chinese courses)
	Edinburgh – BBC (Chin)
	Leeds – BBC (Mod Chinese and all joint Hons courses)
	Newcastle – 22-20 pts (Pol/EA St – Chinese/Korean; Comb St/ Asian St)
20 pts.	**York** – BCC/BB (Language)
12 pts.	**Westminster** – CC-CD (All courses)

Alternative offers:

EB offers: **Durham** 65-60%; **Leeds** 70%.

IB offers: **Leeds** 17 pts in 3 Highers.

SCE offers: **Durham** ABBBB; **Edinburgh** BBBB; **Sheffield** AABB.

Overseas applicants: Leeds English tuition, some scholarships.

CHOOSING YOUR COURSE (See also Ch 1)

Subject information: This is not a language to be studied for its novelty! An interest and appreciation of the Chinese, their lives and culture are important considerations in selection.

Course highlights: Durham Mainly Classical Chinese but Modern Chinese and history covered. **Leeds** Intensive language study and year 2 placement in China or Japan for joint courses. NOW CHECK PROSPECTUSES FOR ALL COURSES.

ADMISSIONS INFORMATION

Number of applicants per place (approx): Durham 5; **Leeds** 3; **London (SOAS)** 8; **Westminster** 18.

General Studies acceptable: Durham; Leeds (JMB only).

Selection interviews: Cambridge; Durham; Leeds; London (SOAS); Oxford.

Admissions Tutors' advice: Leeds Applicants must be able to cope well with language training. B grade required in a foreign language. Read up on China. **London (SOAS)** Experience in learning a language a plus point. **Durham** 'Actual' A-level grade required. BBB for repeaters.

Examples of interview questions: What interests you about China and the Chinese? Would you object to studying in China? How do you see your future career developing once you have graduated?

GAP YEAR ADVICE

Institutions accepting a Gap Year: Leeds.

Institutions willing to defer entry after A-levels (see Ch 5): Leeds (Prefer not).

ADMISSIONS INFORMATION

Institutions which may accept under-achieving applicants after A-levels: Leeds.

Institutions with vacancies in Aug/Sept 1992 (see Ch 5): Some vacancies were declared for students with 18-22 pts. Leeds 20 pts.

ADVICE FOR MATURE STUDENTS

5% of students at **London (SOAS)** are 'mature'. Ability required to A-level standard in a language.

GRADUATE EMPLOYMENT

New Graduates' destinations (percentages) 1991:
Permanent employment: U 81.
Unemployment: U 14.
Further studies (all types): U 34.

Anglo-European College of Chiropractic

THINKING OF A CAREER IN CHIROPRACTIC?

* Four year Honours degree course followed by fifth year Post Graduate Diploma in Chiropractic, for entry to the third largest health-care profession in the world

* AECC is the foremost Chiropractic college in Europe with one of the finest reputations in the world

* A young and rapidly expanding career with exciting opportunities for graduates wishing to practise or undertake research in a primary health care profession

For further details, write to:

Academic Registrar (Dept DCO/93), AECC, 13 Parkwood Road, Bournemouth, BH5 2DF,

Telephone (0202) 431021 Fax (0202) 417352

CHIROPRACTIC

Special subject requirements: Three A-levels, including chemistry and one other science.

14pts.   **Bournemouth (Anglo Euro Coll)** – BC/CDD (Chiropractic)

CHOOSING YOUR COURSE (See also Ch 1)

Subject information: A specialism of alternative medicine which aims at healing by manipulation, mainly in the spinal region.

Details from Anglo European College of Chiropractic, Parkwood Road, Bournemouth, Dorset BH 5 2DF. Tel 0202 431021.

CLASSICAL STUDIES/CLASSICAL CIVILISATION

Special subject requirements: A GCSE (grade A-C) language occasionally specified. For Classical Studies the following universities 'require' or 'prefer' a foreign language at A-level or GCSE (grade A-C) as a subject requirement: Aberdeen, Bristol, Durham, London (QMW), (RH). For AS-level subject requirements check with prospectus and admissions tutors.

NB Institutions may raise or lower the level of published offers depending either on the quality or otherwise of individual applications or the numbers of applications received; grades/points offered may be adjusted downwards after A-level results. NB The level of an offer is not indicative of the quality of a course.

24 pts. **Newcastle** – 24-16 pts (Class Studs; Classics; Anc Hist; Latin; Greek)
22 pts. **Bristol** – BBC-BCC/BB-BC (Class Studs)
          Edinburgh – BBC approx (Cl Stud) (BTEC N/A)
          Glasgow – (Class Civ courses)
          Manchester – 22 pts approx (Cl St)
          St Andrews – BBC (Class St) (4 AS)
20 pts. **Durham** – BCC (Class Studies)
          Leeds – BCC/BB (All courses) (6 AS)
          London (King's) – 20 pts approx (Cl St)
          London (RH) – BCC/BC (Cl Studs)
          London (UC) – BCC (Anc World)
          Reading - BCC (Class/Med; Class St)
          Nottingham – BCC-CCD (Class Civ)
          Warwick – BCC (Class Civ; Class Civ Phil)
18 pts. **Belfast** – CCC (All courses)
          Keele – CCC/CC (Joint courses) (4 AS) (BTEC 3M)
          Kent – CCC/BB-BC (Class Civ courses)
          Liverpool - CCC/BC (Class Studs) (Ref CDD)
          Swansea – CCC-BCD (Gk/Roman St)
16 pts. **Aberystwyth** – CCD (Class St)
          Exeter – BCE (Gr/Rom St)
14 pts. **London (QMW)** – CCE/BE (Class St)
          St David's – CDD/BC (Class St and approx offer for joint courses)
12 pts. **North London** – (Hum)
 8 pts. **and below**
          St Mary's (CHE) – (Comb St)

Alternative offers:

EB offers: **Keele** 60%; **Leeds** 67%.

IB offers: **Bristol** 30-28 pts H555; **Edinburgh** H665; **Keele** 26 pts; **Kent** 25 pts, H 11 pts; **Leeds** 26 pts; **St Andrews** 30 pts.

Irish offers: **Keele** BBBCC; **Leeds** BBBCC.

SCE offers: **Edinburgh** BBBB; **Glasgow** BBBB; **Keele** BBCC; **Liverpool** BBBB; **St Andrews** BBBB.

CHOOSING YOUR COURSE (See also Ch 1)

Subject information: The literature, history, philosophy and archaeology of Ancient Greece and Rome are covered by these subjects. A knowledge of classical languages is not necessary for many courses. Ancient History and Archaeology may also be of interest as alternative courses.

Course highlights: Belfast Courses are offered in Byzantine Studies covering history, literature, art and theology from 300 AD to 1500 AD; Greek and Roman Civilisation. **Bristol** Emphasis on literature and philosophy, not archaeology or history. Gives access to study of classical literature and culture without previous knowledge of ancient languages. **Leeds** Wide range of teaching and research skills supported by computer applications. **Liverpool** Greek and Latin not required for Greek and Roman history and/or Archaeology. **London (RH)** Wide range of options covering classical literature, history, philosophy, art and archaeology. **Newcastle** Wide choice of courses covering literature, history, philosophy, science, art and archaeology. **St David's** Options in art, archaeology and philosophy. **Warwick** Course covers languages, literature, history, philosophy and archaeology of Ancient Greece and Rome. NOW CHECK PROSPECTUSES FOR ALL COURSES.

Study opportunities abroad: Leeds (E); **London (QMW)** (E).

ADMISSIONS INFORMATION

Number of applicants per place (approx): Bristol 8; **Durham** 12; **Exeter** 12; **Leeds** 4; **Liverpool** 8; **London (RH)** 4; **Newcastle** 8; **Nottingham** 9; **Reading** 10; **St David's** 8; **Warwick** 10.

General Studies acceptable: Leeds; Liverpool.

Selecton interviews: Durham; Leeds, London (RH); Newcastle; Warwick.

Offers to applicants repeating A-levels: Higher Nottingham (BCC); **Possibly higher** Leeds; **Same** Aberystwyth, Bristol, Durham, London (RH), Newcastle.

> **Examples of interview questions:** What special interests have you in classical civilisation? Have you visited Greece or Rome? What were your impressions?

GAP YEAR ADVICE

Institutions accepting a Gap Year: Most institutions; **London (RH)** We send a reading list and also advise attendance at a summer school in Latin or Greek.

Institutions willing to defer entry after A-levels (see Ch 5): Leeds; London (RH) (Applications post A-level ie, in 1994 for 1995 also acceptable); Newcastle; St Andrews.

AFTER A-LEVELS ADVICE

Institutions which may accept the same points score after A-levels: Brunel; Durham; Hull; Keele; Leeds; Liverpool; London (RH); Warwick.

Institutions demanding the actual grades offered after A-levels: Newcastle; Nottingham.

Institutions which may accept under-achieving applicants after A-levels: Durham; Keele; Lancaster; Leeds; Liverpool; London (RH); Warwick.

Institutions with vacancies in Aug/Sept 1992 (see Ch 5): London (RH) 18 pts.

ADVICE FOR MATURE STUDENTS

Linguistic ability is required for most courses. About 6% of students on courses are 'mature'.

CLASSICS

Special subject requirements: Latin and/or Greek at A-level usually required. (1) = one A-level language required (2) = two A-level languages required. For AS-level subject requirements check with prospectus and admissions tutors.

NB Institutions may raise or lower the level of published offers depending either on the quality or otherwise of individual applications or the numbers of applications received; grades/points offered may be adjusted downwards after A-level results. NB The level of an offer is not indicative of the quality of a course.

30 pts.	**Cambridge/Oxford** (Class; Class/ML) - AAA potential recommended)
26 pts.	**Newcastle** - 26-16 pts(Classics)
22 pts.	**Bristol** - BBC-BCC/BC (1) (Classics)
	Edinburgh - 22 pts (2) (Classics courses)
	Newcastle - BBC/AB (1) (Class Stud; Anc Hist; Latin; Greek)
	Nottingham - BBC-CCC (1) (Classics)
	St Andrews - BBC (Classics)
20 pts.	**Birmingham** - BCC-CCC (2) (Classics; Cl/Cl Arch)
	Durham - BCC (1 or 2) (Classics; Class Studies; Latin; Anc H-Gk; Anc H-Lat)
	Exeter - BCC/BB (2) (Classics)
	Leeds - BCC (1) (Classics) (4 AS)
	London (RH) - BCC/BC (1) (Classics; Cl/Anc Hist)
	Manchester - 20 pts approx (Classics)
	Reading - BCC (Classics)
	Warwick - BCC (Classics)
18 pts.	**Kent** - CCC/BC (1) (Classics)
	Liverpool - CCC/BC (2) (Classics) (4 AS)
	London (King's) - 18 pts approx (Classics)
	Swansea - BCD-CCC/BC (2) (Classics)
16 pts.	**St David's** - CCD/BC (2) (Classics)
12 pts.	**Belfast** - CC (1) (Classics)
	London (UC) - CC (1) (Classics)

Alternative offers:

IB offers: **Bristol** 30 pts H655; **Exeter** 30 pts; **Kent** 25 pts, H 11 pts; **St Andrews** 30 pts.

SCE offers: **Edinburgh** BBBB; **Liverpool** BBBB; **St Andrews** BBBB.

CHOOSING YOUR COURSE (See also Ch 1)

> **Subject information:** This subject covers the study of the classical languages Greek and Latin but also may include topics related to drama, philosophy and art and architecture. See also under **Classical Studies.**

Course highlights: Exeter, Bristol Courses for those without Latin or Greek. **Cambridge** Classics is an appropriate subject for anyone aiming to read another Tripos in their third year, for students reading Archaeology and Anthropology, English, History, Law, Philosophy or Theology and Religious Studies. **Durham** Courses available for students whose main interest lies in literature but also courses for ancient historians and philosophers. **Edinburgh** Study is made of Greek and Roman civilisations with equal amounts of Greek and Latin. **Kent** Course explores literary, political and intellectual aspects of Athenian and Roman Empires. **London (RH)** See **Classical Studies. London (UC)** Topics for detailed study include Greek philosophy, sculpture, drama and history, Roman Britain, law and history and Latin satire, elegy and late and medieval Latin, art and architecture. **Newcastle** High research rating. **Oxford** The Honours School of Literae Humaniores provides a unique combination of classics, philosophy and ancient history. **Swansea** Emphasis on language and literature. NOW CHECK PROSPECTUSES FOR ALL COURSES.

Study opportunities abroad: Birmingham (E); **Edinburgh** (E); **Leeds** (E) IT G B; **Newcastle** (E); **St Andrews** (E).

ADMISSIONS INFORMATION

Number of applicants per place (approx): Birmingham 10; **Bristol** 10; **Durham** 9; **Kent** 5; **Liverpool** 10; **London (RH)** 6; **Newcastle** 14; **St David's** 5; **Swansea** 3.

General Studies acceptable: Exeter; Liverpool.

Selection interviews: Birmingham; Cambridge; Durham; Exeter; Liverpool; Leeds; London (RH); Newcastle.

Offers to applicants repeating A-levels: Higher Nottingham (BCC); **Same** Birmingham, Durham, Newcastle.

Examples of interview questions: What aspects of your Latin (or Greek) A-level course do you enjoy? Have you visited Greece or Italy? (If so, be prepared to discuss any sites of classical architecture you have visited.) Knowledge of culture, art and architecture of Ancient Greece or Rome important. See also under **Classical Studies**.

GAP YEAR ADVICE

Institutions accepting a Gap Year: Leeds (Do not apply two years in advance); Most institutions.

Institutions willing to defer entry after A-levels (see Ch 5): Leeds; Newcastle; St Andrews; Swansea.

AFTER A-LEVELS ADVICE

Institutions which may accept the same points score after A-levels: Durham; Leeds; Liverpool; London (RH).

Institutions demanding the actual grades offered after A-levels: Durham (2 A-levels); Newcastle (some flexibility); Nottingham.

Institutions which may accept under-achieving applicants after A-levels: Durham; Leeds; London (RH); Liverpool; St David's.

Institutions with vacancies in Aug/Sept 1992 (see Ch 5): Bristol; Leeds 18 pts. University vacancies normally required 14 to 18 pts.

ADVICE FOR MATURE STUDENTS

Evidence of ability to cope with the course is a condition of entry to all courses.

GRADUATE EMPLOYMENT

New Graduates' destinations (percentages) 1991:
Permanent employment: U 66.
Unemployment: U 18.
Further studies (all types): U 35.

COMMUNICATIONS STUDIES (See also under Film & Video Studies and Media Studies)

Special subject requirements: none.

NB Institutions may raise or lower the level of published offers depending either on the quality or otherwise of individual applications or the numbers of applications received; grades/points offered may be adjusted downwards after A-level results. The level of an offer is not indicative of the quality of a course.

24 pts.	**Kent** - BBB approx (Com/Im)
	Leeds - BBB (Comm St)
22 pts.	**Glasgow Caledonian** - 22 pts (Comm St) (6 AS)
	Lancaster - BBC (C Comm) (BTEC Ds+Ms)
	Leicester - BBC/BB (Comm/Soc) (BTEC 3M)
20 pts.	**Birmingham** - BCC-BCD/AB-BB (Media Cult Soc)
	Bradford - BCC/BB (Com) (BTEC 2D+3M)
	Brunel - BCC/AB (Comm Stud) (4 AS) (BTEC 5Ms)
	Coventry - 20-16 pts (Comm St) (BTEC 3D+M)
	Lancaster - BCC (Hum Comm) (BTEC Ms)
	Sheffield Hallam - 20-16 pts (Comm St) (6 AS) (BTEC 4M)
18 pts.	**Bournemouth** - 18 pts (Comm) (6 AS) (BTEC D+M overall)
	Central England - 18 pts (Comm St) (4 AS)
	Glamorgan - CCC/BC (Comm St) (6 AS)
16 pts.	**London (Gold)** - BB (Comm St/Soc)
	Middlesex - 16 pts (Comm St - Modular)
	Nottingham Trent - BB-CC (Comm St)
	Queen Margaret (Coll) - 16 pts (Comm St)
	Sunderland - 16 pts (Comm St)
14 pts.	**Huddersfield** - 14 pts (Comm Arts)
	Humberside - (Doc Comm - contact Admissions Tutor)
	Oxford Brookes - CDD/CD (Vis Studs - Modular)
12 pts.	**North London** - 12 pts (Comm/Cult St) (BTEC Ds+Ms)
10 pts.	**Guildhall London** - CD (Comm St) (BTEC 4M)
8 pts.	**and below**
	Bangor Normal (CHE) - (Comm)
	Heriot-Watt (Moray House) - (Comm Ed)
	Kent (Inst - Maidstone) - (Comm Media)
	North Cheshire (CHE) - (MSBM)

Offers for Foundation, Certificate and Diploma courses (see Ch 5):

Higher National Diploma courses (England and Wales):
  4 pts.   and below
        Cheltenham & Glos (CHE) (Des Comm - Electronics); Northumberland (CA) (Communications); Ravensbourne (CDC) - Design (Communications); Wolverhampton; Worthing (CT).

Higher National Diploma courses (Scotland):
  2 pts.   or equivalent
        Aberdeen (CC); Bell (CT); Dundee (IT); Falkirk (CT); Kirkcaldy (CT); Napier EE (also HND Journalism); Queen Margaret (Coll); Robert Gordon.

Alternative offers:

EB offers: **Coventry** 60%.

IB offers: **Coventry** 24 pts; **Lancaster** 30 pts; **Leicester** 28 pts; **Sunderland** 26 pts 6 subjects inc 3 Highers.

Irish offers: **Guildhall London** CCCCC.

SCE offers: **Coventry** BBBB; **Guildhall London** BBCCC; **Lancaster** ABBBB.

Overseas applicants: Glamorgan Proficiency in English required.

CHOOSING YOUR COURSE (See also Ch 1)

> **Subject information:** Communications Studies courses are not necessarily a training for the media (see **Media Studies**) but extends to management, international communications and psychology. HND Communications courses relate to TV operations. See also under **Media Studies** and **Film & Video Studies.**

Course highlights: Birmingham Cultural analysis (literary, historical and sociological) with historical debate about culture. **Bournemouth** (App Com) Course choices in management or media marketing. **Brunel** Options include television and the media, medical sociology, mental illness and psychiatry and soap opera symbolism. **Central England** Course 50% academic, 50% vocational. **Coventry** Specialisation possible in European communications, international communications and analysis of communication. **Glamorgan** Hugely popular course covering media, cultural and language studies. **Heriot-Watt** (Comm Ed) Option to specialise in youthwork, adult education or Community work. **Kent** In year 1 students take three humanities courses and the 'Pop, Porn, Pulp and Politics' course. Years 2 and 3 include courses in critical issues and communications, images and culture, and the history and theory of imaging. **London (Gold)** Course 50% practical in fields of TV, film, radio, journalism and photography. **Nottingham Trent** Course covers literature, linguistics, psychology, sociology and practical work. **Sheffield Hallam** Human communication with particular reference to role of language in British society; not a course in media training. **Sunderland** Largely academic course covering sociology, linguistics, psychology and cultural studies. All students study documentary film, television and media audience research. **Trinity & All Saints (CHE)** Emphasis on analysis and communication and cultural policy. NOW CHECK PROSPECTUSES FOR ALL COURSES.

Study opportunities abroad: Coventry (E) B FR SP SW IT; **Nottingham Trent.**

Work opportunities abroad: Glamorgan; Queen Margaret (Coll) USA.

ADMISSIONS INFORMATION

Number of applicants per place (approx): Birmingham 37; **Bournemouth** 22; **Brunel** 15; **Central England** 50; **Coventry** 28; **Glamorgan** 20; **Glasgow Caledonian** 30; **Middlesex** 21; **Nottingham Trent** 37; **Sheffield Hallam** 47; **Sunderland** 20; **Trinity & All Saints (CHE)** 46.

General Studies acceptable: Brunel; Central England; Coventry (2); Lancaster; Nottingham Trent; Trinity & All Saints (CHE) (2).

Selection interviews: Brunel; Bournemouth; Central England; Glamorgan (T); Glasgow Caledonian; Nottingham Trent; Sheffield Hallam; Sunderland.

Offers to applicants repeating A-levels: Possibly higher Coventry; **Same** Brunel; Nottingham Trent, Sheffield Hallam.

Admissions Tutors' advice: Central England Applicants must demonstrate clear interest in working in the media and preferably have some experience. **Sheffield Hallam** Both science and arts subjects acceptable.

Examples of interview questions: What does 'public media' mean? Discuss some of this week's main issues in current affairs. What is the difference between *The Daily Telegraph* and *The Guardian* ? Which are the most popular newspapers? Why? What do you feel about the ethics of public relations? Would you represent your firm on an issue in which you disagreed with management policy? What are the effects of the mass media? What do you think of the national press? Why do you want to be a journalist? What are the criteria for a good film or TV programme? How can TV be used in education? What do you think about censorship in the cinema? What are the roles of national and local radio?

GAP YEAR ADVICE

Institutions accepting a Gap Year: Most institutions; **Bournemouth** Secure a place before your gap year; working in the media very beneficial. **Coventry** Deferred applicants not normally considered; applicants should apply during the gap year. No interviews so students abroad are not at a disadvantage. **Trinity & All Saints (CHE)** Try not to get into debt!

Institutions willing to defer entry after A-levels (see Ch 5): Bournemouth; Bradford; Brunel; Heriot-Watt/Moray House (No); Lancaster (Not Hum Comm); Leeds; Queen Margaret (Coll).

AFTER A-LEVELS ADVICE

Institutions which may accept the same points score after A-levels: Birmingham; Bournemouth; Brunel; Central England; Glamorgan; Sheffield Hallam; Trinity & All Saints (CHE).

Institutions which may accept under-achieving applicants after A-levels: Bournemouth; Brunel; Central England; Trinity & all Saints (CHE).

Summary of vacancies in Aug/Sept 1992: A number of vacancies were advertised with various points scores being acceptable.

ADVICE FOR MATURE STUDENTS

About 15% of students come into the 'mature' category.

GRADUATE EMPLOYMENT

New Graduates' destinations (percentages) 1991:
Permanent employment: P 60.
Unemployment: P 23.
Further studies (all types): P 17.

COMMUNITY STUDIES (including **Health Studies**) (See also NURSING)

Special subject requirements: Mathematics GCSE (grades A-C) in some cases.

NB Institutions may raise or lower the level of published offers depending either on the quality or otherwise of individual applications or the numbers of applications received; grades/points offered may be adjusted downwards after A-level results. The level of an offer is not indicative of the quality of a course.

20 pts.	**Bangor** - 20-18 pts (Health/Educ/Dev)
	Reading - 20-18 pts approx (Comm St courses - Contact Admissions Tutor)
18 pts.	**Durham** - CCC (Com St)
	Strathclyde - CCC-BCD (Health) (2 AS)
16 pts.	**Ulster** - CCD/BC (Comb Soc Bhv)

12 pts. **Bournemouth** – 12 pts (Health Comm St; App Com; Clin Sci) (6 AS) (BTEC Ms)
  Central Lancashire – CC (Comb Hons)
  Luton (CHE) – CC (Comm Man)
  North London – 12 pts approx (App Soc St/Health; Health St)
10 pts. **De Montfort** – 10 pts approx (Health Studies)
  Sunderland – 10 pts (Health St)
 8 pts. **and below**
  Bradford & Ilkley (CmC) – 8 pts (Comm St; Ho/Comm St) (BTEC 60% average)
  Canterbury Christ Church (CHE) – (Comm Ed)
  Chester (CHE) – 4 pts (Health/Comm Studs) (BTEC 3M)
  Edge Hill (CHE) – 8 pts (UPRR)
  Heriot-Watt/Moray House - (Comm Ed)
  Liverpool John Moores – DD (App Comm St; Health and Comm St)(4 AS)
  Manchester Met – (Ap Com St; Youth Comm; Health St; App Hum Comm)
  Northern (Coll Ab) – (Comm Ed)
  Ripon & York St John (CHE) – (Modular)
  Roehampton (IHE) – (Health St)
  S Martin's (CHE) – (Youth St; Health Promotion)(4 AS) (BTEC 1D+3M)
  St Mark & St John (CHE) – (Rec/Comm St) (2 AS)
  West Sussex (IHE) – (Health St)

Franchised degree and HND courses (see Ch 5):
  Canterbury Christ Church (CHE) - YMCA College Walthamstow.

Offers for Foundation, Certificate and Diploma courses (see Ch 5):

Diploma of Higher Education courses:
  Bristol UWE; Crewe & Alsager (CHE); Manchester Met; Newman & Westhill (CHE).

Certificate courses (England and Wales):
  5 GCSE (grades A-C) Manchester Met; Newman & Westhill (CHE).

College Diploma courses (Scotland):
  3 pts. or equivalent Heriot-Watt/Moray House; Strathclyde/Jordanhill.

Alternative offers:

IB offers: **Bangor** 28-24 pts.

Overseas applicants: St Mark & St John (CHE) Strong multi-cultural policy. EFL offered.

CHOOSING YOUR COURSE (See also Ch 1)

Subject information: These courses also cover aspects of health and may include human biology, stress, prevention in health care, social problems, welfare and counselling. Refer also to tables under **Social Administration, Social Policy, Social Work, Social Studies, Sociology.**

Course highlights: Bangor Innovative teaching methods. Emphasis placed on personal skill acquisition in year 1. Research in psychological aspects of learning, behaviour, health promotion and development. Close ties with health authority and schools. **Bournemouth** A general degree for those wishing to enter health and social care careers but who do not have a defined vocational focus. (Health Comm St) Covers biological and social aspects of human life including health care and counselling. **Chester (CHE)** Integrated course combining natural and social sciences. One month's work placement as part of course. **De Montfort** Topics covered include sociology. psychology, politics, management and biological science. **Luton (CHE)** Option to study Urdu. **S Martin's (CHE)** Practical work emphasis. **West Sussex (IHE)** Modular degree offers students choice in year 3; module choice based on career pathways. NOW CHECK PROSPECTUSES FOR ALL COURSES.

ADMISSIONS INFORMATION

Number of applicants per place (approx): Bradford & Ilkley (CmC) 5; **Chester (CHE)** 3; **Edge Hill (CHE)** 5; **Heriot-Watt/Moray House** 3; **Manchester Met** 5; **S Martin's (CHE)** 4; **St Mark & St John (CHE)** 7.

General Studies acceptable: Bradford & Ilkley (CmC); Chester (CHE) (2); Manchester Met; St Mark & St John (CHE).

Selection interviews: Bradford & Ilkley (CmC); Manchester Met.

Offers to applicants repeating A-levels: Higher Chester (CHE); **Same** Bradford & Ilkley (CmC), St Mark & St John (CHE).

Admissions Tutors' advice: Lancaster (SM) Applicants should be 19 on entry with experience (voluntary or paid) in a youth work setting. **Manchester Met** GCSE English and maths grades A-C required. Substantial experience working with young people needed. **S Martin's (CHE)** A prerequisite for course entry is relevant work experience.

Examples of interview questions: What problems exist in the community in which you live? The Swiss are very strict when granting work permits to foreigners - their stated aim is to maintain a social and economic balance in their country. Have we achieved this in Britain? Discuss. What are the major community or youth problems at present? How would you solve them?

GAP YEAR ADVICE

Institutions accepting a Gap Year: Most institutions; **Bournemouth** Aim to get paid or voluntary experience in health or community care work. **Heriot-Watt/Moray House** Work experience related to community education useful.

Institutions willing to defer entry after A-levels (see Ch 5): Bournemouth (Preferred); Sunderland.

AFTER A-LEVELS ADVICE

Institutions which may accept the same points score after A-levels: Bournemouth; Luton (CHE); Manchester Met.

Institutions with vacancies in Aug/Sept 1992 (see Ch 5): Bournemouth 14-12 pts; Bradford & Ilkley (CmC); Manchester Met; Sunderland; West Sussex (IHE); most institutions are likely to have vacancies in 1993.

ADVICE FOR MATURE STUDENTS

These courses are very popular with and very appropriate for mature students who make up some 75% of the student cohort in some colleges.

COMPUTER COURSES (including Information Technology)

Special subject requirements: For some courses mathematics A-level is specified. Mathematics at GCSE (grade A-C) usually essential.

NB Institutions may raise or lower the level of published offers depending either on the quality or otherwise of individual applications or the numbers of applications received; grades/points offered may be adjusted downwards after A-level results. The level of an offer is not indicative of the quality of a course.

30 pts. **Cambridge** - AAA potential recommended (Maths)

24 pts. **Bath** - ABC (Comp)

Durham - ABC (Comp/Maths)

London (Imp) - BBB (Soft Eng)

London (UC)) - BBB-BBC (AAB-CC) (Comp/Elec)

Nottingham - BBB-BCC (Comp Sci; Comp/Cog; Comp/Man; Art Int/Psy)

St Andrews - BBB (Inf Proc)

Warwick - BBB (Comp Sci; Comp Man)

Warwick - BBB-BCC (Comp Sys Eng)

York - BBB (Comp SS Eng; Comp Sci/Human Factors; Comp Sci conversion; Inf Tech/Bus/Man) (4 AS)

22 pts. **Aberdeen** - BBC (MA course)

Aston - BBC-BCC/AA (Comb Hons; Comp Sci/Eur St)

Bath - ACC (CST)

Brunel - BBC-BCC/BB (Comp/Maths; Data Proc; Comp/Econ; Comp/Psy)

East Anglia - BBC-BCC (Comp (USA))

Edinburgh - BBC (Ling/AI)

Glasgow - BBC (MA joint courses)

Leeds - BBC (Comp/Mus)

London (QMW) - BBC/BB (Comp Sci; Comp/Maths; Comp/Stats; Comp/Bus)

London (RH) - BBC/BC (All courses except **20 pts**) (6 AS) (BTEC Ms)

London (UC) - BBC (Comp Sci)

Manchester - BBC approx (Comp Sci)

Southampton - 22 pts C in maths (Computer courses)

Surrey - BBC/AB-BB (Comp/Inf T) (BTEC Ds+Ms)

York - 22 pts (Comp Sci; Comp/Maths EQ; Comp SS Eng; Inf Tech) (4 AS) (BTEC Ds+Ms)

20 pts. **Aberystwyth** - BCC/BB (Comp Sci; Comp S/Mod L) (4 AS) (BTEC 2D+2M)

Aston - 20 pts (Comp Sci) (BTEC 3D+2M)

Birmingham - BCC-CCC (Comp/Software; Comp Elec Eng) (BTEC M overall)

Bristol - BCC (Comp Sci; Comp/Maths)

Bristol - BCC/BC (Comp Sci/Mod Lang)

Brunel - BCC (Soc Comp Sci) (BTEC 5M)

Cardiff - BCC (Comp Syst)

City - BCC-CCC/BB-BC (Comp Sci; Bus Comp Sys)

Durham - BCC (Comp Sci)

East Anglia - BCC-BCD (Comp; Bus Info Sys; Comp/Maths) (BTEC 6D)

East London - 20-12 pts (New Tech Euro)

Essex - BCC/BB-BC (All courses) (BTEC Ds+Ms)

Exeter - BCC/BB (Comp Sci) (6-4 AS) (BTEC 3M)

Hull - BCC/BB (Comp/MS) (BTEC 1D+Ms)

Kent - BCC (Comp Sci)

Lancaster - BCC (Comp Sci) (BTEC Ds+Ms)

Leeds - BCC/BB (Computer/Inf Sci courses) (BTEC Ds+Ms)

London (Imp) - BCC (B in maths) (Computing) (4 AS)

London (LSE) - 20 pts approx (Comp)

London (QMW) - BCC/BB-BC (Comp Sys/Dig Elect)

London (RH) - BCC/BB (Comp Sci/Maths) (4 AS)

Loughborough - BCC/AA (Comp 3/4)
Reading - BCC (Comp/Stats)
Salford - BCC-CCC (Inf Tech all courses)
Salford - BCC-CCD/BB-BC (Comp/Econ; Bus Inf Sys; Comp/Maths)
Sheffield - BCC/BB (Comp Sci; Comp/Maths; Comp/Stats; Software Eng; Cog Sci) (4 AS)
Sheffield - BCC/AB-BB (Accg/Comp)
Sussex - BCC-BBD (CS Eng/Eaps; Comp Al/Cog)
Ulster - BCC-CCD (Computing courses)
UMIST - BCC/20 pts (Comp; Comp Ger; Comp/Fr) (BTEC Ds+Ms)

18 pts. **Aberdeen** - CCC-CCD/BC (All courses except under **22 pts**)
Aston - CCC (Comp Sci Comb Hons) (BTEC 3D+2M)
Bangor - CCC/BB (Cog Sci) (BTEC 3M)
Belfast - CCC/BB (Comp Arts; Comp Sc; Inf Tech)
Bradford - CCC/AB (All courses) (BTEC 1D+3M)
Cardiff - CCC (Comp Sci Comp Stats)
Cranfield (Shrivenham) - CCC (Comp Sci; Inf Tech) (4 AS)
East Anglia - CCC-BCD/BC (Comp Syst Eng; App Comp)
Edinburgh - CCC/BB (All courses except under **22 pts**) (4 AS)
Glasgow - CCC-CCD/BC (All courses except under **22 pts**)
Hull - BCD/BB (All courses except under **20 pts**) (BTEC 1D+3M)
Keele - CCC/BC-CC (Comp Sci combinations; Comp Chem) (4 AS) (Inf Tech) (BTEC 3M)
Kingston - CCC/AB (Bus IT) (BTEC 1D+3M)
Lancaster - BCD (Computer courses except 20 pts)
Leicester - BCD (Maths/Comp)
Liverpool - CCC-BCD (All courses) (5 AS)
Loughborough - CCC/BC (Inf Comp 3 & 4)
Newcastle - BCD-CCC (Computing; Comp/Soft Eng; Mapping Inf Sci) (BTEC 2D+3M)
Newcastle - BBE/BB (Math Sci)
Reading - 18 pts (Comp Sci)
Reading - (Comp Sci/Cyb)
St Andrews - CCC (Comp Sci) (4 AS)
Salford - CCC-BCD (Comp/Biol; Comp/Chem; Comp/Phys; CS Inf; Comp/Mgt/El; Elect Comp Sys) (6 AS)
Stirling - CCC/BB (All courses)
Strathclyde - CCC (All courses)
Swansea - BCD/BB (Comp Sci; Comp/Maths; Elec/Comp Sci)(BTEC 4D+2M)
UMIST - CCC/BB (Comp Ling/GF; Comp Ling/GS)

16 pts. **Bangor** - CCD (Comp Sys Eng)
Central Lancashire - CCD (Comp/Eur Lang)
City - CCD/BC (Comp Sys Eng) (BTEC 2D+Ms)
Dundee - CCD/BC (All courses)
Glasgow Caledonian - CCD (Comp Inf Syst)
Liverpool John Moores - 16 pts (Bus Inf Tech; Bus Inf Sys)
Middlesex - 16 pts (Inf Tech)
Plymouth - CCD/BB (Bus Inf Man Sys) (BTEC 3D+4M)
Portsmouth - CCD/CC (Comp Sci; Bus Inf Tech; Inf Tech/Soc Inf Sys) (4 AS) (BTEC Ms)
St David's - CCD/BC (Informatics)
Southampton - BB (Comp/Mod Lang)
Teesside - 16 pts (IBIT) (4 AS)

14 pts. **Bournemouth** - 14 pts (Inf Syst Man; Strat Syst Man)
Bristol UWE - CDD-CDE/BC-CD (BDA) (BTEC 3M)
De Montfort - 14-12 pts (Bus Inf Syst)
Heriot-Watt - CDD/BC (All courses)
Hertfordshire - 14 pts (Cog Sci; Comp Sci) (6 AS) (BTEC All Ms)
Leeds Met - 14 pts (Inf Syst Bus)

Loughborough - CDD/BC (Inf Tech 3 and 4)
Northumbria - 14 pts (Bus Inf Tech)
St David's - 14 pts (Inf)
Sheffield Hallam - CDD/BC (Comp St) (4 AS)

12 pts. **Bolton (IHE)** - DDD/CD (Comb St)
Brighton - 12 pts (Comp Inf Syst; Comp Sci) (6 AS)
Brighton - 12-8 pts (Joint/modular)
Bristol UWE - 12-10 pts (Syst An; CRTS) (BTEC 3M)
Buckingham - DDD/CC (All courses) (BTEC 3M)
Canterbury Christ Church (CHE) - CC-EE (Inf Tech; Comb St)
Central England - 12 pts (All courses)
Central Lancashire - CC (Comb Hons Computing; Bus Inf Tech) (BTEC 3M)
Cranfield (Shrivenham) - CC (Inf Sys Man) (BTEC 4M inc maths)
De Montfort - 12 pts (Comp Sys Bus; Bus Inf Sys) (BTEC 2D+2M)
East London - 12 pts (New Tech; Computer courses except **20 pts**)
Glamorgan - DDD/DD (Inf Tech - part-time)
Huddersfield - 12 pts (Comp in Bus; Info Tech)
Humberside - 12 pts (BIS) (BTEC 3M)
Kingston - DDD/CC-CD (Comp Inf Sci; Comp Sci) (BTEC 1D+3M)
Leeds Met - CC approx (Comp St; Infor St) (BTEC 2D+3M)
Manchester Met - 12 pts (Computer courses; Bus Infor Tech) (BTEC Ms)
North London - CC (Inf/Comm) (4 AS)
Oxford Brookes - DDD/CC (Modular) (4 AS)
Paisley - 12 pts (Comp Sci)
Plymouth - 12 pts (Comb Sci/Soc; Sci/Marine; Comp/Infor)
Sheffield Hallam - DDD/CC (Bus Infor Tech; Eur Bus Infor Tech) (4 AS) (BTEC 1D+5M)
Sheffield Hallam - 12 pts (Comp St) (BTEC 2D+4M)
Sunderland - 12 pts (Bus Comp/Fr/Ger) (BTEC Ms)
Teesside - 12 pts (Comp Sci; Inf Tech)
Westminster - DDD (Bus Inf Tech)

10 pts. **Bedford (CHE)** - 10 pts (Comb St)
Cheltenham & Glos (CHE) - 10 pts (Comp; RTCS)
Cheltenham & Glos (CHE)- 10-8 pts (Inf Tech)
De Montfort - 10 pts (Comp Sci; Comb St)
Glamorgan - 10 pts (All courses except under **12 pts**) (4 AS) (BTEC 4-5M)
Guildhall London - DDE (Comp Inf) (BTEC 1D+3M)
Guildhall London - CEE/CD (Comp Hum Factors) (BTEC 1D+3M)
Middlesex - 10 pts (Comp/Bus)
Northumbria - 10 pts (Comp; Comp Ind)
Nottingham Trent - 10 pts (Comp Sys) (BTEC 6M)
Paisley - (Bus Inf Tech)
Plymouth - (Comp/Inf) (BTEC Ds)
Sheffield Hallam - 10 pts (Sys Mod; Infor Tech) (4 AS)(BTEC 1D+5M)
Sunderland - 10-4 pts (Inf Tech)
Thames Valley London - 10 pts (IM/BT)
Westminster - DDE (Comp)

8 pts. and below
Anglia (Poly Univ) - (Syst Mod; Comm Syst Man)
Bangor - DD (Comp/Bus St) (BTEC 3M)
Bell (CT) - (Comp)
Bristol UWE - 6 pts (Inf Tech Sci)
Buckinghamshire (CHE) - 6 pts (Euro Infor; Inf Sys Eur) (4 AS)
Cardiff (IHE) - (Bus Inf Syst)
Central Lancashire - 8 pts (Ind Inf Tech)
Cheltenham & Glos (CHE) - 8 pts (BCS)
Chester (CHE) - (Comb St)
Coventry - 8 pts (All courses) (BTEC 4M)
De Montfort - 8 pts (Infor Tech) (BTEC 5M, 4M, 3D)

Derby - (Modular) (4 AS)

Greenwich - (Comp/Com Sy) (BTEC 3M)

Guildhall London - DD (Computer courses - Modular)

Heriot-Watt - (Man/Comp St)

Hertfordshire - (Comb St) (BTEC 3M)

Inverness (Coll) - (App Comp)

Liverpool (IHE) - (Comb)

Liverpool John Moores - (Comp St) (4 AS)

Napier - (Comp Dat Proc; Comp; Inf Tech/Elec)

Nene (CHE) - (Comb St)

North East Wales (IHE) - (Comp St) (4 AS) (BTEC 4M)

North London - Offers not released (Comb Sci; Comb Hum)

Nottingham Trent - (Comp/Phys; Bus Inf Sys)

Queen Margaret (Coll) - (Inf Man)

Robert Gordon - (Comp Sci; Bus Comp) (BTEC Ds+Ms)

Roehampton (IHE) - (Comb St)

Sheffield Hallam - DE/C + HND (Comp St) (BTEC 2D+4M)

Sheffield Hallam - DDE (Comp Maths) (4 AS)

South Bank - DD (All courses) (4 AS) (BTEC 3M)

Southampton (IHE) - (Bus Inf Tech; Comp Stud) (4 AS)

Staffordshire - (All courses) (4 AS)

Sunderland - (Dig Sys)

Teesside - 8 pts (Bus Comp; Inf Tech) (4 AS) (BTEC 5-3M)

Thames Valley London - 6 pts (Inf Sys)

West London (IHE) - (Comp St)

Wolverhampton - (Comp Sci; Bus Inf Sys)

Worcester (CHE) - (Comb St)

Franchised degree and HND courses (see Ch 5):

Bournemouth - Isle of Wight (CFE); Salisbury (CT); Yeovil (CFE).

Canterbury Christ Church (CHE) - Canterbury (CFE)

Central England - Dudley (CFE); Sutton Coldfield (CFE).

De Montfort - Bedford (CFE); Broxtowe (CFE); Charles Keene (CFE); Milton Keynes (CFE).

Humberside - Scarborough (CFE).

Leeds - Wakefield District (CFE).

Liverpool John Moores - Southport (CFE); Wirral (CFE).

South Bank - South Bank (CFE).

Surrey - Roehampton (IHE).

Offers for Foundation, Certificate and Diploma courses (see Ch 5):

Diploma of Higher Education courses:

4 pts. Glamorgan; Guildhall London; Northumbria; Staffordshire; Wolverhampton.

Higher National Diploma courses (England and Wales) (including **Computer Science Studies** combined with **Business Studies** and other subjects):

8-6 pts. Central Lancashire DD (Bus Inf Tech); Greenwich; Hertfordshire; Northumbria 8 pts; Nottingham Trent; Plymouth 6 pts; Sheffield Hallam (Comp St); Teesside DE; Thames Valley London (Bus Inf Tech).

4pts.   **and below** Anglia (Poly Univ); Bolton (IHE); Bournemouth; Brighton (Comp); Bristol UWE (Foundation course); Buckinghamshire (CHE); Cardiff (IHE); Central England; Central Lancashire (Comp St); Cheltenham & Glos (CHE); Coventry; De Montfort; Derby; East London; Farnborough (CT); Glamorgan; Greenwich; Hastings (CT); Hertfordshire; Huddersfield; Leeds Met; Liverpool John Moores; Manchester Met; Middlesex; Nene (CHE); North East Surrey (CT); North East Wales (IHE); North London (Inf Tech); Northumbria; Nottingham Trent; Oxford Brookes; Portsmouth (HND Comp; Soft Eng); Salford (UC); Sheffield Hallam; South Bank; Southampton (IHE); Staffordshire; Stoke on Trent (Coll) Mature students only; Sunderland; Teesside; Thames Valley London; West London (IHE); Westminster; Wolverhampton (Comp St; Inf Tech).

Higher National Diploma (Computer Data Processing) and Higher Diploma (Computer Studies) courses (Scotland):
12pts.   Scottish (CText).
8pts.   **and below** Aberdeen (CC); Ayr (Coll); Bell (CT); Dundee (IT); Falkirk (CT); Kirkcaldy (CT); Moray (Coll); Napier EE; Perth (Coll); Robert Gordon.

Alternative offers:

IB offers: **Aberdeen** 30 pts (Arts), 26 pts (Sci); **Aberystwyth** 30 pts; **Birmingham** 30 pts inc H5 maths H5 (Phys Sci); **Bradford** 30 pts inc H5 maths; **Brighton** 25 pts over 6 subjects 16 at Highers; **Bristol** H665 inc 15 pts overall; **Brunel** H666; **Buckingham** 26 pts; **City** 31 pts inc 16 pts Highers; **Cranfield** 28 pts inc H5 maths; **De Montfort** H 13 pts; **Essex** H765; **Exeter** 30 pts; **Greenwich** 24 pts; **Guildhall London** 28 pts 7 subjects 24 pts 6 subjects; **Hertfordshire** 20 pts; **Heriot-Watt** 24 pts; **Hull** 28 pts inc 16 pts Highers; **Keele** 26 pts; **Kent** 27 pts, H 12 pts; **Lancaster** 30 pts; **Leeds Met** 26 pts; **Liverpool** 30 pts inc H555; **London (QMW)** 24 pts, **(RH)** 30 pts; **Newcastle** 30 pts; **St Andrews** 28 pts; **Salford** 30 pts; **Staffordshire** 24 pts; **Surrey** 32 pts; **UMIST** H655; **Westminster** 26 pts; **York** 30-28 pts in 6 subjects inc H5 maths + physics.

Irish offers: **Aberdeen** BBBB (Arts) BBCC/BCCCC (Sci); **Central Lancashire** CCCD; **Glamorgan** CCCC; **Liverpool** BBCCC; **Robert Gordon** BBBB; **Surrey** BBBB; **Teesside** (Comp Sci) BBB, (Infor Tech) CCC.

SCE offers: **Aberdeen** BBBB (Arts) BBBC (Sci); **Bristol** ABBBB; **Bristol UWE** BBC; **City** AABB; **Dundee** BBBC; **East Anglia** AAABC; **Edinburgh** BBBB; **Essex** BBBB; **Glasgow** BBBB; **Heriot-Watt** BBBC; **Keele** BBCC; **Lancaster** ABBB; **Liverpool** BBBB; **Loughborough** ABBB; **Napier** BBB; **Newcastle** AAAB; **Sheffield** BBBB; **Southampton** BBBB; **St Andrews** BBCC; **Stirling** BBCC; **Strathclyde** BBBB; **Surrey** BBBB; **Sussex** AABB; **UMIST** BBCC.

Overseas applicants: Coventry Good English required. **Glamorgan** Induction course and EFL offered. **Hull** Living costs 30% lower than in London. **Nottingham Trent** A-level course advised + GCSE maths and English. **Sheffield Hallam** Introductory and English programme - 1300 overseas students. **Teesside** English O-level/GCSE grades A-C required.

CHOOSING YOUR COURSE (See also Ch 1)

> **Subject information:** Programming languages, data processing, systems analysis, artificial intelligence, graphics, software and hardware are all aspects of these courses. Several institutions offer courses with European languages and placements.

Course highlights: Aberystwyth Practical course emphasising software engineering aspects of computing. **Bradford** Common 1st year with Computing in Information Systems - transfers possible. **Brighton** Course has 3 main themes: software engineering, computer structure and information processing systems. **Bristol** In year 2 course involves programming, file structure, design operating systems and comparisons of programming languages. **Bristol UWE** (BDA) Cross between business studies and applied statistics with language option. (CRTS) Advanced IT facilities; option to study French, German, Spanish or Business Studies. **Brunel** Emphasis on software engineering, knowledge-based systems and artificial intelligence; language options possible. **Cambridge** 2 courses offered: 2-year course for students who have spent a year studying another subject, eg, Mathematics, Natural Sciences, Engineering; 1-year course, Computer Science Tripos for those who have spent two years reading another subject. **City** Course concerned with design of information systems and its links with hardware and software applications. **Cranfield** (Inf Sys Man) Combination of computing and management. A-level maths not required. **De Montfort** (Bus Inf Syst) Strongly biased towards business studies and ideal for non-scientists. **Durham** Course covers all aspects of computer science and underlying principles as applied to software engineering, artificial intelligence and computer systems architecture; large practical element. **Edinburgh** 4 other courses taken in years 1 and 2 include choice from maths, engineering, physics, artificial intelligence, economics and business studies. **Essex** First year scheme taken with another subject from a range including sciences, electronics, modern languages and economics. **Heriot-Watt** (Man/Comp St) Bias towards science or maths. **Hertfordshire** (Cog Sci) Interdisciplinary course involving psychologists, linguistics, computer scientists and philosophers. A European language may be studied. **Liverpool** In year 3 optional subjects available in software engineering, data management, microprocessors and networks, artificial intelligence and graphics. **London (Imp)** In year 3 students select optional courses for specialisation drawn from the areas of applications, languages, systems and management. **Loughborough** Course includes exposure to industry and commercial applications. **Manchester Met** Common year 1 for Computing and Software Eng. **Newcastle** (Comp Sci) Year 1 covers 3 subjects - computing science, mathematics and one other from chemistry, economics, maths, physics, psychology, statistics, surveying (depending on the timetable). (Mapping Inf Sci) Unique course in UK, modules in geography, computing. **Northumbria** Course offers 3 routes - business, industrial or European, the latter involving a year in Europe. Language options. (Comp Ind) Study covers computer-based applications within manufacturing industry. Main subjects in the final tear include software engineering, systems analysis and project management. **Paisley** Options in Finance Marketing and Management. **Salford** Software-based degree with industrial involvement. (Elect Comp Sys) Optional 4 year thick sandwich course. Opportunities in hardware and software. (Comp Sci) Course has bias towards software. **St David's** (Informatics) Specially tailored for Arts and Humanities students who all complete 8 or 12 week placements. **Sheffield Hallam** Course includes computing, statistics operational research. **South Bank** Includes study of physics and chemistry. **Southampton (IHE)** Course covers systems analysis, accountancy, business operations. **Staffordshire** Year 1 common with Computing Science and Software Engineering and transfers possible up to end of year. All 3 degrees may be combined with French or German, including year abroad. **Sunderland** Degree courses in Business Computing with a foreign language (French, German or Spanish) for those who already possess some language skills. **Teesside** All students complete a supervised work experience year. Currently students placed with over 120 companies throughout the UK. Assessment by course work and end of year exams. **UMIST** A vocationally-oriented course with roughly equal emphasis on 3 major sub-divisions: information systems (data processing, databases, systems analysis); software engineering; systems software and hardware. **Warwick** Year 3 options include artificial intelligence and psychology, robot technology and computers in business. **Westminster** Option to specialise in Information Systems or Software Engineering after a common first year. High research ratings at **Cambridge, Edinburgh, London (Imp), (UC), Manchester, Newcastle, Oxford, Sussex, Warwick**. NOW CHECK PROSPECTUSES FOR ALL COURSES.

Study opportunities abroad: Belfast (E); **Brighton** (E); **Brunel** (E); **Buckingham** (E); **Coventry** (E); **De Montfort** (E); **Edinburgh** (E); **Glamorgan** (E); **Hertfordshire** (E); **Kent** (E); **Lancaster** not USA; **Leeds Met** FR G; **Liverpool** (E); **London (QMW)** (E); **Newcastle** (E); **Nottingham** (E); **Paisley** (E); **Sheffield** (E); **York** (E).

Work opportunities abroad: Aberystwyth EUR USA; **Brighton** FR G IT P; **Bristol** EUR; **Bristol UWE**; **Brunel** FR SZ SP NL; **Central Lancashire** FR G NL USA; **Coventry**; **Cranfield** USA WI; **De Montfort** G NL FR USA SZ; **Edinburgh (QM)** USA; **Glamorgan** G FR SZ P; **Kingston** EUR; **Leeds Met**; **Liverpool John Moores** FR; **Portsmouth** EUR; **Robert Gordon**; **Sheffield Hallam** EUR USA AUS D CAN; **South Bank** EUR; **Staffordshire** FR G SZ; **Sunderland**; **Teesside**; **York** SW IT G GR.

ADMISSIONS INFORMATION

Number of applicants per place (approx): Aberystwyth 6; **Aston** 10; **Bath** (CST) 8; **Birmingham** 10; **Bradford** 13; **Brighton** 26, (Comp Sci) 13; **Bristol** 11; **Bristol UWE** 5; **Brunel**

10; **Buckingham** 10; **Buckinghamshire (CHE)** 2; **Canterbury Christ Church (CHE)** 15; **Central Lancashire** 8; **Cheltenham & Glos (CHE)** 4; **City** 7; **Coventry** 10; **De Montfort** (Inf Tech) 3, (Comp Sci) 15, (inf Syst) 6; **Durham** 5; **East Anglia** (Comp/Maths) 3; **East London** 7; **Edinburgh** 4; **Essex** 2; **Exeter** 14; **Glamorgan** 3; **Glasgow Caledonian** 6; **Greenwich** 15; **Guildhall London** 7; **Hertfordshire** 8; **Heriot-Watt** 15; **Hull** (Comp Sci) 6, (Comp/Elect Eng) 12, (Comp/Maths) 12; **Kent** 14; **Kingston** (BIT) 6; **Lancaster** 12; **Leeds** 10; **Liverpool** 10; **Liverpool John Moores** 18; **London (Imp)** 6, **(RH)** 5; **Newcastle** 7; **North East Wales (IHE)** 2; **Northumbria** (Comp Inf) 8; **Nottingham Trent** 4; **Oxford Brookes** 18; **Paisley** 2; **Plymouth** 12; **Portsmouth** 17; **Robert Gordon** 3; **Salford** (Inf Tech) 5, (Comp Sci) 14; **Sheffield Hallam** (Comp St) 10; **South Bank** (Comp St) 7; **Southampton** 8; **Staffordshire** 5; **Strathclyde** 16; **Sunderland** 10; **Surrey** (Comp Inf Tech) 15; **Swansea** 10; **Teesside** 8, (Comp St) 5; **UMIST** 7; **West London (IHE)** 5; **Westminster** 5; **Wolverhampton** 6; **York** (Comp Sci) 6, (Comp SS Eng) 10.

General Studies acceptable: Aberdeen; Aberystwyth (2); Aston; Bedford (CHE); Bradford; Brighton; Bristol UWE; Cardiff (IHE); Central England; Cheltenham & Glos (CHE) (2); De Montfort; Exeter (2); Guildhall London (2); Hertfordshire (2); Huddersfield; Hull; Kingston; Lancaster; Liverpool (Cambs, JMB, Oxford); Liverpool (IHE); Liverpool John Moores; Oxford Brookes; Paisley (2); Salford; Sheffield (Cambs, JMB, Oxford); Sheffield Hallam; South Bank (No); Staffordshire (2); Sunderland (Data Pro); Surrey; Teesside; Thames Valley London; York.

Selection interviews: Aston (some); Bath; Bradford (some); Bristol (UWE); Brunel; Cambridge; City; Coventry (some) (T); De Montfort (some); Durham, East Anglia, Edinburgh (some); Exeter; Greenwich; Kingston (some); Liverpool; London (RH); Loughborough; Newcastle; Nottingham; Plymouth (some); Portsmouth (some); Salford; South Bank (some); Sunderland; Warwick.

Offers to applicants repeating A-levels: Higher Brighton, City (Bus Comp Syst), De Montfort, Greenwich, Kingston, Leeds (BBC or equivalent), Salford, Sussex, Teesside, Wolverhampton; **Possibly higher** Bath, Bristol UWE, City (Comp Sys Eng), Durham, East Anglia, Edinburgh, Lancaster, Leeds, Newcastle, Oxford Brookes, Portsmouth, Sheffield, Teesside; **Same** Aston, Brunel, Hull, Liverpool, Loughborough, London (RH), Manchester Met, Sheffield Hallam, South Bank, Ulster.

Admissions Tutors' advice: Aston A-level maths or computing experience not required. **Bath** Double maths an advantage. **Bradford** GCSE grade B maths required. **Brunel** At present we are trying to cater for good arts-based candidates for a degree course in Computer Science. We look for applicants who can present themselves well at interview since our courses require students to obtain employment. A-level maths grade B advised for course G500. Computer Science acceptable as a 3rd A-level – not a substitute for maths. **Cranfield** (Inf Tech) Maths plus two subjects required. **Newcastle** Interview important to offers made. **Portsmouth** Do not apply for more than one degree scheme. Option to change at the end of year 1. **York** Applicants taking 4 AS-levels receive slightly lower offer.

> **Examples of interview questions:** Why are you interested in specialising in software/hardware? What experience have you had with computers? Discuss the differences between hard and floppy discs. Can you name two restrictions on the speed of a computer? What kind of software have you written? How would you 'debug' a computer listing? A test was given on a computerised flight booking system. Which computer journals do you read?

GAP YEAR ADVICE

Institutions accepting a Gap Year: Most institutions; **Cheltenham & Glos (CHE)** Relevant experience can count instead of a year's industrial placement; **Salford** Try to do something relevant; **Surrey** Broaden experience by travel or work; **Thames Valley London** Try to work in a business environment; **York** Apply early.

Institutions willing to defer entry after A-levels (see Ch 5): Aberystwyth; Aston; Bell (CT); Buckingham; Coventry; Cranwell; Glamorgan; Heriot-Watt; Hull; Kingston; Leeds; London (RH); Manchester Met; Plymouth; Portsmouth; Robert Gordon; Roehampton (IHE); South Bank; Staffordshire; Sunderland (Inf Tech) (No); Surrey, Swansea; Thames Valley London; UMIST.

AFTER A-LEVELS ADVICE

Institutions which may accept the same points score after A-levels: Aberystwyth; Aston; Bournemouth; Bradford; Brighton; Bristol UWE; Brunel; Buckinghamshire (CHE); Central Lancashire; Coventry (reduced points in some cases); Durham; East Anglia; East London; De Montfort; Edinburgh; Glamorgan; Huddersfield; Hull; Kingston; Leeds (depending on A-levels); Liverpool; Liverpool John Moores; London (RH); Newcastle; North East Wales (IHE); Oxford Brookes; Plymouth; Portsmouth; St David's (perhaps); Sheffield (usually); Sheffield Hallam; South Bank; Staffordshire; Strathclyde; Sunderland; Teesside; Westminster; Wolverhampton; York.

Institutions demanding the actual grades after A-levels: Bath (CST); Hertfordshire; Loughborough; Stirling; Warwick.

Institutions which may accept under-achieving applicants after A-levels: Aberystwyth; Bournemouth; Brighton; Buckinghamshire (CHE); Hertfordshire; Hull (overseas students 18-16 pts); Leeds; Liverpool; Liverpool John Moores; London (RH); Newcastle; St David's; Sheffield; South Bank; York; most institutions and colleges consider applicants who have missed their offer by one or two points.

Institutions with vacancies in Aug/Sept 1992 (see Ch 5): Aberystwyth 14 pts; Anglia (Poly Univ); Aston BCC; Bangor 4 pts; Bournemouth; Brighton; Bristol 18-16 pts; Buckingham 6 pts; Cheltenham & Glos (CHE); Coventry 8 pts; Cranfield 12 pts; Derby; Dundee; East Anglia 17 pts; Essex 16 pts, (Comp Ling) 20 pts; Heriot-Watt 14 pts; Glamorgan 10 pts; Greenwich; Kent; King Alfred's (CHE); Kingston; Leeds; London (QMW), (RH); Manchester Met; Newcastle; Oxford Brookes; Paisley; Plymouth 12 pts; Portsmouth 12 pts; Roehampton (IHE) 8 pts; Robert Gordon; Salford 16 pts, (Inf Tech) 14-12 pts; St David's 12 pts; Sheffield; Sheffield Hallam; South Bank; Southampton (IHE); Staffordshire 8 pts; Strathclyde; Sunderland 4 pts; Surrey 18 pts; Thames Valley London; UMIST (Comp/Fr/Ger) 18 pts; York (Inf Tech) 18 pts; most institutions are likely to have vacancies in 1993.

ADVICE FOR MATURE STUDENTS

Mathematics at A-level or BTEC are required by several universities although a similar number of institutions will look for less formal qualifications. **Brighton** Attracts significant numbers of mature students.

GRADUATE EMPLOYMENT

New Graduates' destinations (percentages) 1991:
Permanent employment: U 74; P 73; C 100.
Unemployment: U 22; P 21; C 0.
Further studies (all types): U 17; P 7; C 50.
Main career destinations (approx): Computing 77; Business/Finance 8.

Anglia (Poly Univ) (1991) (Computer Studies HND) All graduates entered full-time employment as analysts and programmers. Three students proceeded to degree courses.

Teesside (1991) (Information Technology) All students entering full-time employment obtained work as programmers. (Computer Science) 50 graduates secured appointments in subject-related work areas as software engineers, systems analysts or programmers, many with well-known leading UK employers.

York (1987-91) 80% of graduates entered employment, 60% in computer-related occupations. The remainder went into finance, sales, marketing, social and information work.

The following institutions are perceived as being above average in producing graduates for employment: Aston, Bradford, Brighton, Cambridge, Heriot-Watt, Hertfordshire, Leeds, Loughborough, Manchester, Newcastle, Portsmouth, Sheffield Hallam, Staffordshire, Southampton, UMIST, Warwick. See PIP reference in Chapter 5.

UNIVERSITY OF SURREY

DANCE STUDIES

BA (HONS) DANCE IN SOCIETY

First undergraduate degree in dance at a British University; four year course
with a substantial period spent gaining professional qualifications or experience.

CORE STUDIES
Choreography, Performance and Appreciation of Western and non-Western theatre and
social dance forms.

CONTEXTUAL STUDIES
Social and Historical aspects of dance.

PROFESSIONAL STUDIES
Training for a career within the dance profession:
Community Dance; Education: private and public sector, companies and special needs;
Management; Notation and Reconstruction.

For further details please contact: Dance Studies, University of Surrey, Guildford, Surrey GU2 5XH
Telephone: 0483 509326 (direct line and ansaphone) Fax: 0483 509392

DANCE

Special subject requirements: None.

*NB Institutions may raise or lower the level of published offers depending either on the quality or otherwise
of individual applications or the numbers of applications received; grades/points offered may be adjusted
downwards after A-level results. The level of an offer is not indicative of the quality of a course.*

22 pts.	**Surrey** - BBC-BCC/BB (Dance) (6 AS) (BTEC 6D)
16 pts.	**Bedford (CHE)** - (Modular)
	Middlesex - 16-12 pts (Dance)
14 pts.	**North Cheshire (CHE)** - 14-12 pts (PABM) (BTEC 2D+3M)
12 pts.	**Bretton Hall (CHE)** - CC-EE (Dance courses) (4 AS)
10 pts.	**Bedford (CHE)** - 10 pts (B Ed) (4 AS) (BTEC 3P)
	Roehampton (IHE) - CD (Comb St) (BTEC 3M)
8 pts.	**De Montfort** - (Per Arts)
4 pts.	**Laban Centre** - (Dance Theatre) (Apply early)
	Middlesex - EE (Dance/PA)
	West Sussex (IHE) - (BEd Dance; Rel Arts/Dance) (4 AS)

Franchised degree and HND courses (see Ch 5):
Coventry - Coventry Centre for the Performance Arts.

Offers for Foundation, Certificate and Diploma courses (see Ch 5):

Higher National Diploma courses:
Coventry - (Dance)

Alternative offers:

IB offers: **North Cheshire (CHE)** 24 pts; **Surrey** H555 30-28 pts.

SCE offers: **Surrey** BBB/BBCC.

Irish offers: **Bedford (CHE)** BCCC.

CHOOSING YOUR COURSE (See also Ch 1)

> **Subject information:** Be prepared for theory, educational, historical and social aspects of dance as well as practical studies. Performance arts and human movement courses should also be considered.

Course highlights: Bretton Hall (CHE) Performance-based course covering dance, theatre, performance and dance in the community. **North Cheshire (CHE)** 40% media, 40% business, 20% subsidiary modules. **Surrey** Training for a career in the dance profession (community dance, dance company education, dance for people with special needs, education management, journalism and media, notation/reconstruction, therapy, resources/ archives). National Resource Centre for Dance and Labanotation Institute on site for teaching. **West Sussex (IHE)** Dance criticism and analysis. Dance and the national curriculum. Contacts with dance profession, companies, administrators, promoters, agents, associations, Arts Council. NOW CHECK PROSPECTUSES FOR ALL COURSES.

Study opportunities abroad: Roehampton (IHE) USA.

ADMISSIONS INFORMATION

Number of applicants per place (approx): Bedford (CHE) 2; **Laban Centre** 5; **Middlesex** 12, (Perf Arts) 23; **Roehampton (IHE)** 5; **Surrey** 3; **West Sussex (IHE)** 6.

Admissions Tutors' advice: Bretton Hall (CHE) Adequate practical background in contemporary dance or ballet required, preferably with recognised dance qualification. Students auditioned and asked to choreograph a short solo. **Laban Centre** Candidates should apply early. Applicants selected for the BA(Hons) Dance course by interview and audition. Vitality, stamina, good appearance, intelligence and good powers of self-expression are sought. **Middlesex** (Performance Arts) Performance experience in more than one discipline required. Audition important. **Surrey** Interested in applicants with above-average A-level scores and considerable dance experience in one or more styles and motivation to pursue career in wider dance profession. Any combination of A-levels, new A-level in dance. General Studies, and AS-level dance, acceptable. Course self-financing. Applicants are advised on potential sources of funding. Interview day includes practical work.

> **Examples of interview questions:** How long have you been interested in a degree course in Dance? What particular aspects of dance interest you? (Questions will then follow from this.) What career do you hope to enter at the end of the course?

GAP YEAR ADVICE

Institutions accepting a Gap Year: Roehampton (IHE) Advisable to give reasons and information on intended activities; **West Sussex (IHE)** Continue with some practical dance work and study performances.

AFTER A-LEVELS ADVICE

Institutions with vacancies in Aug/Sept 1992 (see Ch 5): North Cheshire (CHE); Roehampton (IHE) CD; Surrey.

Institutions willing to defer entry after A-levels (see Ch 5): North Cheshire (CHE); Roehampton (IHE) (No); Surrey.

ADVICE FOR MATURE STUDENTS

Surrey in particular welcomes mature students.

GRADUATE EMPLOYMENT

Surrey There were eight graduates in 1990. Three went into teaching (one self-employed), one has specialised as a self-employed dance therapist, one has joined an American ballet theatre and one has gone into secretarial work. The destinations of the remaining two are unknown.

DENTISTRY

Special subject requirements: 2-3 A-levels from science/mathematics subjects. Chemistry often 'required' or 'preferred'.

NB Institutions may raise or lower the level of published offers depending either on the quality or otherwise of individual applications or the numbers of applications received; grades/points offered may be adjusted downwards after A-level results. The level of an offer is not indicative of the quality of a course.

24 pts. **Belfast** - BBB (Second attempt ABB) (Dentistry)
22 pts. **London (HMC)** - BBC (Dentistry)
    Manchester - BBC-BCC (Dentistry)
20 pts. **Birmingham** - BCC (Dentistry) (2 approved AS) (BTEC 3M)
    Bristol - BCC (Dentistry) (Pre-dental any 2 AS; pre-clinical 1 science AS)
    Cardiff (UWCM) - BCC; AB for A204 only (Dentistry) (BTEC mainly M)
    Dundee - BCC (Dentistry)
    Glasgow - BCC (Dentistry)
    Leeds - BCC or BC + AS-levels CC (Dentistry)
    Liverpool - BCC (Dentistry)
    London (King's) - BCC (1st attempt) (Dentistry)
    London (UMDS) - BCC (Dentistry)
    Newcastle - BCC/BB (Dentistry)
    Sheffield - BCC (Dentistry) (2 AS - 1 science AS) (BTEC 3M)

Higher National Diploma courses:
    Cardiff (IHE) - (Dental Tech)
    Manchester Met - (Dental Tech)

Alternative offers:

IB offers: **Belfast** H666 S555; **Birmingham** 28 pts inc H55 inc chem; **Bristol** 30 pts inc H665; **Cardiff** 30 pts, H666 S444; **Leeds** 30 pts inc H666 in science subjs; **London (HMC)** 34-32 pts inc H555; **London (King's)** H666; **London (UMDS)** H655 - first attempt.

Irish offers: **Liverpool** AABBB.

SCE offers: **Belfast** ABBBB; **Bristol** AAAAB; **Dundee** AAABB; **Glasgow** BBBBB; **Manchester** BBBB; **Newcastle** BBBBB; **Sheffield** BBBBB.

Overseas applicants: Liverpool Preference for those taking A-levels with English and able to attend for interview. **London (King's)** Three students per year admitted from UK schools (if available for interview). **London (UMDS)** Maximum four places available for overseas (non-EC) students. Must meet normal entry requirements and be available for interview in UK. **Sheffield** Three students taken per year - interviews not held (intake 45).

CHOOSING YOUR COURSE (See also Ch 1)

> **Subject information:** Work shadowing or experience of this career beyond that of the ordinary patient is important. Possible alternative courses are Medicine, Pharmacy, Speech Therapy, Biochemistry, Biological Sciences, Anatomy and Physiology.

Course highlights: Birmingham Recently revised curriculum; emphasis on preparation for present-day dental practice and future changes. **Bristol** Emphasis on concept of whole-patient care through clinical teaching and early experience of clinical procedures. **Cardiff (UWCM)** Teaching based on whole-patient care; newly equipped areas for children and adult dentistry. Top research rating. **Dundee** Practical experience in hospital commences in the 2nd professional year. **Glasgow** In April year 3 students embark on the practical aspects of clinical dentistry with patients. **Liverpool** Opportunity to take 1 year BSc open to most students. **Newcastle** New integrated 5-term course in basic sciences. Opportunity for intercalated degree. New 6-term course in human disease. **Sheffield** Students treat patients, under supervision, from year 3 onwards. High research ratings also at **Manchester, Wales, London (UMDS), Nottingham, Glasgow, London (Imp).** NOW CHECK PROSPECTUSES FOR ALL COURSES.

Study opportunities abroad: Cardiff; Glasgow (E); **London (HMC)** (E).

ADMISSIONS INFORMATION

Number of applicants per place (approx): Belfast 5; **Birmingham** 11; **Bristol** 7; **Cardiff (UWCM)** (2nd BDS) 10, 1st BDS) 8; **Dundee** 8; **Glasgow** 5; **Leeds** 12; **Liverpool** 12; **London (HMC)** 7, **(King's)** 10, **(UMDS)** 7; **Newcastle** 6; **Sheffield** 16.

Selection interviews: Birmingham; Cardiff (UWCM); Dundee; Glasgow; Leeds; Liverpool; London (Hospital MC), (King's - for candidates likely to receive an offer), (UMDS) 50%; Newcastle; Sheffield.

Offers to applicants repeating A-levels: Higher Birmingham (BBB), Cardiff (UWCM), Glasgow (BBC required), Leeds (Preference given to those re-sitting who previously received an offer but did not achieve first-time grades of BCC - BBB required), Liverpool (BBC), London (UMDS) Resit applicants considered, London (King's) (BBC), Newcastle (BBB), Sheffield; **Same** Belfast.

Admissions Tutors' advice: Leeds, London (HMC) Knowledge of dentistry as a career important. Visit to a dental practice important for all applicants; **London (King's)** The average A-level points score is 22.4; **(UMDS)** Operates an equal opportunities policy for student admissions and welcomes applications from enterprising and well-motivated candidates from wide variety of backgrounds. Academic ability, personal qualities, interests and accomplishments all taken into account when selecting candidates for interview. Prospective students very welcome to attend annual UMDS Open Days in May.

> **Examples of interview questions:** Why do you want to do dentistry? What annoys you? Have you ever thought of doing medicine? What is your opinion of nuclear disarmament? What is your study pattern? What is conservative dentistry? What does integrity mean? Do you think the first year syllabus is a good one? What qualities are required by a dentist? Are there any dentists in the family? How are dentists paid? Is it important for dentists to keep up to date with current affairs? If you were given one million pounds what would you do with the National Health Service? How do you use your hands (eg knitting)? What are prosthetics, periodontics, orthodontics? What causes tooth decay?

GAP YEAR ADVICE

Institutions accepting a Gap Year: Most institutions; **Birmingham** Applicants should have specific aims; **Cardiff (UWCM)** Explain your reasons on UCAS application.

AFTER A-LEVELS ADVICE

Institutions which may accept the same points score after A-levels: Birmingham, Cardiff (UWCM); Leeds; London (King's) perhaps, (UMDS) usually; Newcastle; Sheffield.

Institutions demanding the actual grades offered after A-levels: Glasgow, Leeds; Liverpool (varies); London (King's); Newcastle (in most cases).

Institutions which may accept under-achieving applicants after A-levels: Birmingham; Cardiff (UWCM); Dundee; Leeds; Liverpool; London (King's) perhaps, (HMC), (UMDS); Newcastle; Sheffield.

Institutions with vacancies in Aug/Sept 1992 (see Ch 5): Leeds 20 pts; London (HMC) 20 pts.

Institutions willing to defer entry after A-levels (see Ch 5): Cardiff (UWCM) (No).

ADVICE FOR MATURE STUDENTS

Two or three mature students each year are accepted by dental schools. Entry requirements are the same as those for schools and college leavers. Some dental schools ask for honours degrees in other subjects.

GRADUATE EMPLOYMENT

This was one of the subjects with a good employment record during the period of recession in 1991-92.

DEVELOPMENT STUDIES

Special subject requirements: GCSE (grade A-C) mathematics.

NB Institutions may raise or lower the level of published offers depending either on the quality or otherwise of individual applications or the numbers of applications received; grades/points offered may be adjusted downwards after A-level results. The level of an offer is not indicative of the quality of a course.

24 pts.	**Sussex** - BBB-BCC (Dev St)
22 pts.	**East Anglia** - BBC (All Development Studies courses) (See also under **Agricultural Sciences**) (6 AS) (BTEC 5M)
	Leeds - BBC (Dev St - Comb St)
20 pts.	**Bradford** - BCC/BB (Dev St) (BTEC 2D+M)
	Leeds - BCC (Dev St - contact Admissions Tutor)
	Swansea - BCC-BCD/BC (All Development Studies courses)
18 pts.	**Belfast** - CCC/BC (Soc Sc Comb)
	Kent - CCC/BC (Dev St/EcH; Dev St/Ec; Dev St/Soc)
16 pts.	**Central Lancashire** - CCD (Comb Hons)

Alternative offers:

IB offers: **Bradford** 28 pts; **East Anglia** 31 pts; **Kent** 25 pts, H 11 pts; **Swansea** 26 pts.

Overseas applicants: East Anglia Competence in English required.

CHOOSING YOUR COURSE (See also Ch 1)

> **Subject information:** This is a multi-disciplinary course covering economics, sociology, social anthropology, politics and natural resources.

Course highlights: Belfast Multi-disciplinary course covering African politics, child care, economics, regional geography and sociology. **Bradford** Focus on issues of peace and conflict and conflict resolution. **East Anglia** Interdisciplinary programme covering social anthropology, natural resources, economics, sociology and politics. **Leeds** (New course) Joint course in combination with Economics, Geography, Politics and Sociology concentrating on past and present relationships between industrialised nations and poorer developing countries. NOW CHECK PROSPECTUSES FOR ALL COURSES.

ADMISSIONS INFORMATION

Number of applicants per place (approx): Bradford 6; **East Anglia** 8; **Swansea** 6.

General Studies acceptable: Bradford; East Anglia.

Admissions Tutors' advice: East Anglia Applicants considered on individual circumstances. Higher offers for re-sits. Some candidates interviewed but all encouraged to visit the school on an open day. Vacancies after A-levels last summer. **Swansea** Interviews often held; higher grades are required for re-sits. Primarily interested in applicants with background in history, geography and economics, but applicants with any experience of developing countries (even a year's travel or voluntary work) receive sympathetic consideration.

> **Examples of interview questions:** See under separate subjects (for example, **History, Geography, Economics**).

AFTER A-LEVELS ADVICE

Institutions with vacancies in Aug/Sept 1992 (see Ch 5): Swansea.

Institutions willing to defer entry after A-levels (see Ch 5): Swansea.

ADVICE FOR MATURE STUDENTS

These courses attract a number of mature applicants.

DIETETICS

Special subject requirements: Chemistry and one other science subject preferred, with GCSE (grades A-C) in English and mathematics.

NB Institutions may raise or lower the level of published offers depending either on the quality or otherwise of individual applications or the numbers of applications received; grades/points offered may be adjusted downwards after A-level results. The level of an offer is not indicative of the quality of a course.

16 pts.	**Leeds Met** - CCD/CC (Dietetics) (4 AS) (BTEC 3M inc chem)
14 pts.	**Cardiff (IHE)** - CDD (Human Nutn/Diet)
12 pts.	**Glasgow Caledonian** - CC (Dietetics)
10 pts.	**North London** - CD/EEE approx (Nutr/Biol)

8 pts. **Paisley** - (Dietetics)
Queen Margaret (Coll) - DEE/CE-EE (Dietetics)
Robert Gordon - (Dietetics)

Alternative offers:

IB offers: **Leeds Met** 30-28 pts inc Chem H5.

Irish offers: **Leeds Met** BBCCC inc Chem + 2 at Higher level.

SCE offers: **Glasgow Caledonian** BBC; **Queen Margaret (Coll)** BCC-CCC.

Overseas applicants: Leeds Met English language required.

CHOOSING YOUR COURSE (See also Ch 1)

Subject information: This subject includes scientific and medical topics. Work experience (usually in hospitals) is very important prior to submitting your application. Alternative course choices will depend on whether your interest lies in food or medical aspects eg, Food Science or paramedical careers such as Speech Therapy, Occupational Therapy. NOW CHECK PROSPECTUSES FOR ALL COURSES.

ADMISSIONS INFORMATION

Number of applicants per place (approx): Cardiff (IHE) 10; **Glasgow Caledonian** 11; **Leeds Met** 18; **Queen Margaret (Coll)** 5.

Selection interviews: All institutions.

Offers to applicants repeating A-levels: Higher Cardiff (IHE), Leeds Met;

Possibly higher Glasgow Caledonian.

Admissions Tutors' advice: Leeds Met Normally expects students to have discussed their courses with a hospital dietitian. Predicted grades important. GCSE grades A-C required, physics or biology preferred.

Examples of interview questions: What is your present state of health? What experience have you had in visiting hospitals and talking to dietitians? What experience have you had in dealing with people in different situations? Have you done any social or voluntary work? What does a dietitian do? What other careers have you considered in addition to dietetics?

AFTER A-LEVELS ADVICE

Summary of vacancies in Aug/Sept 1992: Several courses advertised vacancies.

Institutions willing to defer entry after A-levels (see Ch 5): Queen Margaret (Coll).

DRAMA (including Theatre Arts and Theatre Studies)

Special subject requirements: Vary, but A-level English, a language and history are relevant for some courses with mathematics and a language at GCSE (grade A-C).

NB Institutions may raise or lower the level of published offers depending either on the quality or otherwise of individual applications or the numbers of applications received; grades/points offered may be adjusted downwards after A-level results. The level of an offer is not indicative of the quality of a course.

24 pts.	**East Anglia** - BBB-BBC/BB-BC (Drama)
	London (RH) - ABC/AB (Drama/TS; Drama/Mus) (6 AS)
22 pts.	**Birmingham** - BBC-BCC (Arts Group - offers tailored to applicant)
	Glasgow - BBC (All Theatre courses)
	Hull - BBC-BCC/BB (Drama and joint courses) (BTEC D+M)
	Kent - BBC (Drama)
	Lancaster - BBC (All Theatre St courses)
	London (Gold) - BBC (Drama)
	Loughborough - 22-20 pts (Drama; Engl/Drama)
	Warwick - BBC (Thea/Dram Art)
20 pts.	**Aberystwyth** - BCC/BB (Drama (4 AS) (BTEC D+M)
	Bristol - BCC (Drama)
	Exeter - BCC/BB (Drama)
	Manchester - 20 pts approx (Drama)
18 pts.	**Dartington (CA)** - 18 pts (Perf Writings)
16 pts.	**Bristol** - BB (Joint courses except under 14 pts)
	London (Central Sch) - CCD/CC (Drama/Comm)
	Plymouth - CCD/16 pts (Theatre Arts/Dr) (BTEC 5M)
	St Mary's (CHE) - CCD/CC (Comb)
	Warwick - CCD/BC (Drama QTS)
14 pts.	**Bristol** - BC (Drama/Lang)
	Cambridge (Hom) - BC/CC (Drama/Ed) (See also **Education**)
	Dartington (CA) - BC (Theatre; Perf Arts)
12 pts.	**Bretton Hall (CHE)** - CC-EE (Drama Theatre Arts/Dramatic Arts; Hist/Drama; Theatre Crafts/Tech) (4 AS)
	Kent - 12 pts approx (Vis/Perf Arts)
	King Alfred's (CHE) - CC (DT/TVS; Eng/Drama) (4 AS)
	North Cheshire (CHE) - (Perf Arts/Bus)
	North London - (Hum)
	Northumbria - (Perf Arts)
	Roehampton (IHE) - CC (Comb St)
	West London (IHE) - (Joint)
10 pts.	**Bedford (CHE)** - (Comb St)
	Dartington (CA) - B (Arts) E (Vis Perf)
8 pts.	and below
	Cheltenham & Glos (CHE) - (Modular; Perf Arts)
	Chester (CHE) - (Comb St)
	Crewe & Alsager (CHE) - (Comb St; Creative Arts)
	De Montfort - (Perf Arts)
	Derby - (Modular) (4 AS)
	Glamorgan - (Hum; Theatre/Media Drama)
	Glasgow/Royal Scot Ac - (Drama St)
	Greenwich (Central School) - EE (Speech and Drama BEd)
	Huddersfield - (Comm Arts)
	Liverpool (IHE) - (Comb St)
	London (Cent Sch Sp/Dr) - (Drama)
	London (Laban) - (Dance; Theatre)

London (Rose Bruford Coll) – (Theatre Arts – Directors/Writers/ Actors) (See **Admissions Tutors' advice**)
London (Rose Bruford Coll) – (Technical Theatre – Stage Manager/ Technican/ Designer)
Manchester Met – (Theatre Arts)
Middlesex – (Drama/PA)
Nene (CHE) – (Comb St)
Nottingham Trent – (Creative Arts)
Paisley/Craigie – (BEd)
Queen Margaret (Coll) – (Drama Diploma)
Ripon & York St John (CHE) – (Modular)
Roehampton (IHE) – (Drama – QTS)
Royal Scottish Academy – (Drama St)
St Mary's (CHE) – DD-EE (Comb St – QTS)
Sunderland – (Ex/Perf Arts)
Welsh (CMus) – (Theatre St; BEd) (BTEC acceptable) Apply direct
Worcester (CHE) – (Comb St)

Franchised degree and HND courses (see Ch 5):

Cheltenham & Glos (CHE) – Coventry Centre for Performance Arts; South Warwickshire (CFE).
Plymouth – South Devon (CAT).
Westminster – Central School of Speech & Drama.

Offers for Foundation, Certificate and Diploma courses (see Ch 5):

Diploma of Higher Education courses:
4pts.   Crewe & Alsager (CHE).

Higher National Diploma courses (one A-level required):
2pts.   London (Central Sch/Sp and Drama) (Stage Management); Salford (Univ Coll) (Media Performance).

Polytechnic Diploma courses:
4pts.   Manchester Met; Middlesex; Welsh (CMus).

College Diploma courses: Birmingham (Sch Sp/Drama) Entry by audition; Bretton Hall (CHE) (for overseas students); London (Rose Bruford) Tech Theatre Arts; Mountview Theatre School (Acting and Musical Theatre; Stage Management Technical and Design course); Royal Scottish Academy (Dramatic Art; Stage Management).

Alternative offers:

IB offers: **Aberystwyth** 30 pts; **Bristol** 28 pts inc 5 in Eng/history or other appropriate subject; **Exeter** 30 pts; **Hull** Average of 5; **Kent** 29 pts, H 13 pts; **Lancaster** 32-30 pts; **London (RH)** 30 pts; **Plymouth** 26 pts.

SCE offers: **Bangor** BBBC; **East Anglia** AAB; **Glasgow** BBB (Drama), BBBB (Theatre St); **Kent** ABBB; **Lancaster** ABBBB.

Overseas applicants: Bretton Hall (CHE) Offers one, two or three year diploma which provides an individually designed programme of study and does not require standard entry requirements; gives an opportunity for overseas students to work alongside Honours Degree students in very rich Arts context.

CHOOSING YOUR COURSE (See also Ch 1)

Subject information: Your choice of course will vary depending on your preferences. For example, how much theory or practice do you want? It is worth remembering that by choosing a different degree course your interest in drama can be maintained by joining amateur drama groups. Performance arts courses should also be considered as well as courses offered by the stage schools.

Course highlights: Aberystwyth Emphasis on performing. Final decisions on Honours course can be delayed until start of year 2. Department characteristically a performing unit but also offers a historical perspective and study of selected periods and playwrights. **Birmingham** Strong practical element. **Birmingham (Sch Sp/Drama)** Totally practical course. **Bretton Hall (CHE)** Wide-ranging course for those aiming to be actors or technical staff. **Bristol** Integration of theory and practice. Teaching in a wide field of theatre, film and TV studies. **De Montfort** (Perf Arts) Options in arts administration, dance, drama or music. **East Anglia** Film Studies can be taken with Drama. Indivisibility of theory and practice in theatre; a vocational course. **Exeter** Course based on study of medium of theatre from inside as dramatic participant, rather than as critic. Emphasis on practical work. **Glasgow** Course covers various aspects of the arts of theatre including production, play construction and playing spaces. **Hull** Strong practical element plus technical opportunities offered by the Gulbenkian Centre. **Kent** Broad year 1, theoretical and practical years 2 & 3, practical year 4. **London (Gold)** Broad study of theatre, radio, film and TV as well as drama in the community. **London (RH)** Theory and practice combined with television and radio drama. **London (Rose Bruford Coll)** (Tech Th Arts) Final year options in stage management, properties and scenic techniques, scenic construction, lighting and sound, costume and wardrobe. Mandatory grants available; (Theatre) Options in classic and modern stage, educative theatre, acting, popular theatre forms, actor/musician, writing, directing. **Loughborough** Theory and practical work in equal parts; sound and TV drama. **Manchester Met** BA a training course for professional actors. (All applicants considered by audition.) **Middlesex** Each student chooses a First Study in dance or drama or music which occupies minimum of one-third of study time throughout course. **Plymouth** Course covers dance, African theatre, drama. **Queen Margaret (Coll)** Very practical course with options in acting and stage management. **Royal Scottish Academy** Mainly practical course. **St Mary's (CHE)** Options in set design, lighting, make-up, costume design and stage management. Techniques of theatre and TV in years 2 and 3. **Warwick** Emphasis on modern theatre. Years 2 and 3 allow students to specialise in either practical work or historical and analytical studies. **Welsh (CMus)** Theatre Studies course has options in acting, stage design and stage management. NOW CHECK PROSPECTUSES FOR ALL COURSES.

Study opportunities abroad: Hull IT G FR; **Kent** (E); **Lancaster** USA; **London (Central Sch)** (E).

ADMISSIONS INFORMATION

Number of applicants per place (approx): Aberystwyth 10; **Birmingham** 55; **Bretton Hall (CHE)** 10; **Bristol** 35; **Cambridge (Hom)** 4; **East Anglia** 20; **Exeter** 30; **Hull** 25; **Kent** 24; **King Alfred's (CHE)** 15; **Lancaster** 18; **London (Central Sch)** 4, **(RH)** 14, **Rose Bruford** (Tech Th) 10, (Theatre) 14 ; **Loughborough** 22; **Manchester Met** 48; **Middlesex** 26; **Northumbria** 40; **Reading** 17; **Roehampton (IHE)** 8; **Royal Scottish Academy** 3; **Warwick** 18; **West London (IHE)** 21.

General Studies acceptable: Bedford (CHE); Bretton Hall (CHE) (Not AEB); Bristol; Cheltenham & Glos (CHE) (2); East Anglia; Exeter (2); Hull; Lancaster; Liverpool (IHE); London (Central Sch), (Rose Bruford) (2); Loughborough (2); Manchester Met (2); Northumbria (2); North Cheshire (CHE);

Selection interviews: All institutions, usually with auditions.

Offers to applicants repeating A-levels: Higher Hull; **Possibly higher** Cambridge (Hom), London (RH); **Same** Bretton Hall (CHE) (Further audition required), East Anglia, Loughborough.

Admissions Tutors' advice: Aberystwyth Drama is a rigorous academic and practical discipline and not a soft option. It is thought, wrongly, to be unsuitable for men. Best preparation is A-level English, acquaintance with a wide variety of dramatic texts, theatre-going and practical experience. **Bristol** Assesses each case on its merits, paying attention to candidate's educational and cultural opportunities. Particularly interested in applicants who have already shown some evidence of commitment in their approach to drama - in practical work, theatre-going, film viewing or reading. One fifth of applicants are called for interview and take part in practical sessions. They may present any art work, photography or similar material. (London Board Practical Music not acceptable for Drama/Music unless offered with theoretical music + one other A-level.) **East Anglia** Looks for candidates with a sound balance of academic and practical skills. **Hull** Interviews two groups of 18 for whole day which presents a mini-version of the course, with entire staff and number of current students present. Offers then made to about half. Selection process is all-important. More applicants for the Joint Honours courses with English, Theology, Classical Studies, American Studies or Modern Language who have a conventional half-hour interview. Drama/English is the most popular combination and the offer includes a B in English. **King Alfred's (CHE)** Attaches importance to experience outside school. **Lancaster** (Theatre Studies) Candidates invited for interview and should be prepared to take part in a workshop with other candidates. Use the interests section on your UCAS application to the full. We are just as interested in backstage people as actors and now have an arts administration option. **London (RH)** At interview we look for students who are mentally agile and versatile, who enjoy reading as well as taking part in productions. **London (Rose Bruford College)** Entry by competitive audition and interview. College does not use any central clearing agency. Sees all applicants, including those with less than two A-levels. **Loughborough** Offers in terms of A-levels not set. Candidates judged as individuals. Applicants with unconventional subject combinations and mature students considered. Final selection based on interview and audition. Applicants ought to show experience of practical drama, preferably beyond school plays. **Middlesex** (Performing Arts) Audition important; ability to perform in more than one discipline essential. A-levels not required but the following add weight to an application: for Dance, A-level dance; for Drama, A-levels in theatre studies, drama or English literature; for Music, A-level music. **Northumbria** Work with people important. **Warwick** Interview is important to assess academic potential and particularly commitment to, and suitability for, teaching; offers therefore variable. **Welsh (CMus)** Applicants should acquire additional relevant experience before commencing studies.

Examples of interview questions: What dramatic productions have you been involved in? (Questions will then follow on aspects of these productions.) What recent theatre performances have you attended? What West End productions? Who was the producer? What were your views on the production? What do you watch on TV? What outstanding plays have you seen on TV? Discuss.

GAP YEAR ADVICE

Institutions accepting a Gap Year: Most institutions; **Bristol** We prefer applications in the year of entry but candidates must be available for interview between December and March. **Loughborough** Cannot consider deferred options. **Manchester Met** Prefer a gap year. **Plymouth** Go to as many performances as possible. **Royal Scottish Academy** No.

AFTER A-LEVELS ADVICE

Institutions which may accept the same points score after A-levels: Birmingham; Bretton Hall (CHE); Bristol; East Anglia; Hull; London (RH), (Sch Sp/Dr); London (Rose Bruford Coll); Loughborough; Manchester Met; Middlesex; Roehampton (IHE).

Institutions demanding the actual grades offered after A-levels: Lancaster; London (RH).

Institutions which may accept under-achieving applicants after A-levels: Bristol; Cambridge (Hom); East Anglia; Exeter; Glasgow; London (RH); London (Rose Bruford Coll); Loughborough; Manchester Met; Roehampton (IHE); most institutions.

Institutions with vacancies in Aug/Sept 1992 (see Ch 5): Cheltenham & Glos (CHE); Dartington (CA) All courses; Glamorgan CC; King Alfred's (CHE); North Cheshire (CHE); Northumbria; Plymouth (very few) 16 pts. Some vacancies existed for applicants with quite low points scores. There were also vacancies on Performance and Movement Studies courses and on Theatre Studies courses.

Institutions willing to defer entry after A-levels (see Ch 5): Glamorgan; Hull; Lancaster; London (RH); London Rose Bruford (No - they prefer to interview candidates during the year immediately prior to entry); Plymouth; Roehampton (IHE); Royal Scottish Academy (No); Welsh (CMus).

ADVICE FOR MATURE STUDENTS

A large number of mature students apply for and are accepted on these courses. Recent A-level or similar studies are required by a number of drama schools.

GRADUATE EMPLOYMENT

New Graduates' destinations (percentages) 1991:
Permanent employment: U 71; P 56; C 66.
Unemployment: U 18; P 19; C 23.
Further studies (all types): U 25; P 23; C 41.
Main career destinations (approx): Creative 42; Business/Admin 20; Secretarial 15; Teaching 9.

DUTCH

Special subject requirements: GCSE passes grades A-C in Dutch or German required.

NB Institutions may raise or lower the level of published offers depending either on the quality or otherwise of individual applications or the numbers of applications received; grades/points offered may be adjusted downwards after A-level results. The level of an offer is not indicative of the quality of a course.

30 pts.	**Cambridge** - AAA potential recommended (Mod/M Lang)
18 pts.	**Hull** - 18 pts approx (Bus/Dutch) (Contact Admissions Tutor)
	London (UC) - CCC/CC (All Dutch courses)
16 pts.	**Hull** - CCD (Dutch; Dut/SE Asian) (BTEC Ms)

CHOOSING YOUR COURSE (See also Ch 1)

Subject information: Students wishing to study unusual languages *must* have very good reasons for doing so.

ADMISSIONS INFORMATION

Number of applicants per place (approx): Hull 2.

Examples of interview questions: Why Dutch? The Dutch are said to speak English better than the English - why should you want to study their language?

GAP YEAR ADVICE

Institutions accepting a Gap Year: All institutions.

AFTER A-LEVELS ADVICE

Institutions with vacancies in Aug/Sept 1992 (see Ch 5): Hull CDD.

Institutions willing to defer entry after A-levels (see Ch 5): Hull.

EARTH SCIENCES (See also Geology and Biology)

Special subject requirements: A-levels in science and/or mathematics subjects. Geology, geography, environmental studies also accepted at Derby.

NB Institutions may raise or lower the level of published offers depending either on the quality or otherwise of individual applications or the numbers of applications received; grades/points offered may be adjusted downwards after A-level results. The level of an offer is not indicative of the quality of a course.

14 pts.	**Plymouth** - CDD/BC-CC (Earth Sci)
12 pts.	**Greenwich** - 12 pts (Env Earth Sci; Geol)
10 pts.	**Kingston** - DDE/CD (Earth Sci)
8 pts.	**and below**
	Anglia (Poly Univ) - (Earth Sci)
	Cheltenham & Glos (CHE) - EE (Earth Res)
	Derby - (Earth/Life St) (4 AS)
	Liverpool John Moores - (Earth Sci - Int Credit Scheme)
	Nene (CHE) - DD-EE (Comb St)
	West London (IHE) - (Eth Sci)
	Worcester (CHE) - (Comb St)

Alternative offers:

IB offers: **Kingston** H555 13 pts in Subsid inc Maths 5; **Nene (CHE)** 24 pts inc 12 pts Highers.

CHOOSING YOUR COURSE (See Ch 1)

> **Subject information:** Earth Sciences cover geology, environmental science and physical geography (check these courses also) and can also include modules in business studies and languages.

Course highlights: Cheltenham & Glos (CHE) Combination of applied geography and geology. **Greenwich** Option in remote sensing environmental change, waste disposal, resource management, natural hazards. **Plymouth** Integrates physical geography and geology. NOW CHECK PROSPECTUSES FOR ALL COURSES.

ADMISSIONS INFORMATION

Number of applicants per place (approx): Derby 2; **Greenwich** 2; **Kingston** 8.

Selection interviews: Derby.

Offers to applicants repeating A-levels: Possibly higher Derby.

> **Examples of interview questions:** See under **Geology**.

GAP YEAR ADVICE

Institutions accepting a Gap Year: Most institutions; **Greenwich** Obtain advice from admissions tutor.

Institutions willing to defer entry after A-levels (see Ch 5): Cheltenham & Glos (CHE); Kingston; Plymouth (No).

AFTER A-LEVELS ADVICE

Institutions which may accept the same points score after A-levels: Derby.

Institutions with vacancies in Aug/Sept 1992 (see Ch 5): Cheltenham & Glos (CHE) 8 pts; Greenwich 4 pts; Kingston 10 pts; Plymouth 12 pts.

EAST EUROPEAN STUDIES (See also **Russian**)

Special subject requirements: None.

NB Institutions may raise or lower the level of published offers depending either on the quality or otherwise of individual applications or the numbers of applications received; grades/points offered may be adjusted downwards after A-level results. The level of an offer is not indicative of the quality of a course.

30 pts.	**Cambridge/Oxford** - AAA potential recommended (Mod/M Lang)
22 pts.	**Glasgow** - BBC (Slav/EES)
18 pts.	**London (SSEES)** - CCC (Bulgarian; Czech; Finnish; Hungarian; Polish; Pol/Russ; Romanian; Serbo/Croat; Cont EE St) (4 AS)
	Sheffield - CCC/CC (E Eur St)

Alternative offers:

IB offers: **London (SSEES)** 30-28 pts.

SCE offers: **Glasgow** BBBB.

CHOOSING YOUR COURSE (See also Ch 1)

> **Subject information:** East European languages cover Bulgarian, Czech, Hungarian, Polish and Romanian. Their applications in the world of commerce in the future could be on the increase.

ADMISSIONS INFORMATION

Number of applicants per place (approx): London (SSESS) (Bulgarian) 1.

> **Examples of interview questions:** In which particular country in Eastern Europe are you interested? (Questions will then follow from this answer.) Justify the taxpayers' money in being allowed to study this subject.

AFTER A-LEVELS ADVICE

Institutions with vacancies in Aug/Sept 1992 (see Ch 5): London (SSEES) 18 pts.

ECONOMICS (See also Agricultural Economics under Agriculture)

Special subject requirements: Mathematics required in GCSE (grades A-C) and occasionally at A-level.

NB Institutions may raise or lower the level of published offers depending either on the quality or otherwise of individual applications or the numbers of applications received; grades/points offered may be adjusted downwards after A-level results. The level of an offer is not indicative of the quality of a course.

30 pts.	**Cambridge** (Econ)/**Oxford** (PPE) – AAA potential recommended
28 pts.	**Bristol** – AAB-ABB (Economics; Econ/Stats; Econ/Pol)
26 pts.	**Bristol** – ABB (Econ/Maths)
	Durham - ABB (Econ/Law)
	Nottingham – ABB-BBC (All courses except under **24 pts**)
24 pts.	**Aberystwyth** – BBB/AB (Econ/Law)
	Bath – BBB (Ec/Comp Stat)
	Birmingham – BBB (Econ Stats)
	Durham – ABC (All courses except under **26 pts**)
	Exeter – BBB (Econ) (4 AS) (BTEC D+M)
	Kent – BBB (Econ/Law)
	Leicester – BBB (Econ/Law)
	London (LSE) – ABC-BBB (BSc Econ)
	London (RH) – ABC/AB (Econ/Man) (BTEC Ds)
	Newcastle – BBB (Econ/Bus Man; Econ Bus Econ; Econ) (4 AS) (BTEC Ds+Ms)
	Nottingham – BBB (Ind Econ)
	Reading – BBB (Acc/Econ)
	Sheffield – BBB (Economics)
	Surrey – BBB-BBC (Bus Econ/Comp)
	Warwick – ABC-BBB (All courses)
	York – BBB/BB-BC (Econ/Stats; Ec/Ecmt EQ)
	York – BBB (Econ/Pol; Econ/Phil; PPE) (BTEC Ds)
22 pts.	**Aberdeen** – BBC (Econ) (BTEC 3D+3M)
	Aberystwyth – BBC-BCC/AB-BB (Econ/Acctg; Econ/Geog; Econ/Mktg) (2 AS inc maths if not at A-level)
	Bath – BBC/possibly AA (Econ/Pol; Economics)
	Belfast – BBC (Econ)
	Birmingham – BBC-BCC (Econ/Mod EH; Soc ES; Econ/Pol; Maths Econ)
	Bristol – BBC/AB (Econ/Ec Hist) (6 AS)
	Bristol – BBC (Econ/Accy) (6 AS)
	Brunel – BBC (Econ; Econ Bus/Fin) (6 AS)
	Cardiff – BBC (B in hist; BSc Econ courses; Econ/Hist)
	Durham – BBC (Econ courses except under **26 pts**)
	East Anglia – BBC (Econ; Bus Fin Econ)
	Edinburgh – BBC-BCC (All courses)
	Heriot-Watt – BBC (B in lang) (Econ/Lang)
	Hull – BBC/AB-BB (All courses) (BTEC Ds+Ms)
	Keele – BBC-BCD-CCC/BB-BC (All courses) (4 AS)
	Kent – BBC-BCC/BB (Econ courses) (See also **24 pts**)
	Lancaster – BBC (Econ; Acc/Econ) (BTEC D+M)
	Leeds – BBC (Econ/Hist; EHA; Econ/Pol; EPA) (4 AS)
	Liverpool – BBC/BB (Econ M Stat; Man Econ Acc; Econ M Econ)
	London (RH) – BBC/BB (Econ/Pub Ad)
	Loughborough – BBC-BCC/BB (Econ/Account; Econ)
	Newcastle – BBC/AB; (Econ/Geog; Econ Acct) (BTEC mainly Ds)
	St Andrews – BBC (Econ – MA/BSc) (4 AS)

Southampton - BBC (All courses)
Surrey - BBC-BCC (Econ) (BTEC D+M)
York - BBC/BB (Econ) (4 AS) (BTEC Ds)

20 pts.	**Aberystwyth** - BCC (BSc Econ)
Bristol - BCC/AB (Econ/Social)
City - BCC/BB (Econ/Acy)
City - BCC-CCC/BB (Econ)
Dundee - BCC (Econ MA)
East Anglia - BCC (Econ/Acc)
Essex - BCC (Econ courses)
Exeter - BCC/BB (Econ/Ag Econ; Econ/Stats; Food Econ) (4 AS) (BTEC Ms) (See Agriculture)
Glasgow - BCC (Ec Stud)
Leeds - BCC-CCC/BB (Economics) (See **22 pts**)
Leicester - BCC (Econ BA BSc; Ec/Ec Hist) (BTEC 3M)
Liverpool - BCC/BB (Bus/Comp) (4 AS)
Liverpool - BCC-CCC/AB-BB (Economics)
Liverpool - BCC/BB (Econ/Maths)
London (QMW) - BCC (Economics)
London (RH) - BCC/BC (Econ Soc/P; Econ Pub Ad)
London (UC) - BCC (Economics)
Loughborough - 20 pts (Econ/Minor)
Manchester - 20 pts approx (Econ)
Reading - BCC (Economics; Bus Org; Econ/Economet; Bus Econ; Econ/Soc)
Salford - BCC (Econ; Bus Econ) (BTEC 5D+1M)
Sheffield - BCC/AB (Econ/Maths; Econ/Stats)
Strathclyde - BCC/BB (BA Bus School)
Surrey - BCC/BB (Ec/Soc) (BTEC 3D+Ms)
Sussex - BCC (All Economics courses)
Swansea - BCC/AB (Econ Arts; Econ; Econ Soc St and joint courses) (BTEC 5M)

18 pts.	**Aberystwyth** - CCC/BB (Econ) (AS maths preferred if not at A-level)
Bangor - 18-16 pts (Econ) (4 AS)
Belfast - CCC/BB (Econ Comb Hons) (GCSE or AS in maths required)
Bradford - CCC/BB (BSc Econ)
Buckingham - 18-16 pts (Econ; Bus Econ) (BTEC 2D+Ms)
Central England - CCC/BC (Econ)
Heriot-Watt - CCC-BCD/AB (Econ) (6 AS)
Manchester Met - CCC inc gen stds or CCD exc gen stds/BB (Econ) (BTEC 4D+Ms)
Newcastle - CCC/BC (Ec/Soc Pol)
Nottingham Trent - CCC/BB (Econ)
Salford - CCC (Econ Pol; Econ Soc)
Stirling - CCC/BC (All courses)
Strathclyde - CCC (BBD 2nd yr entry) (Economics; BA Arts/Soc Sci)

16 pts.	**Central Lancashire** - 16 pts (Comb Hons)
Edinburgh - CCD (Agric Ec)
Hertfordshire - 16 pts (Ap Econ) (4 AS)
Kingston - CCD/BB (Econ) (BTEC 3D+Ms)
Leicester - CCD (Sci Comb)
Liverpool - CCD/BC (Econ Hist)
London (SOAS) - BB (Econ with another subject)
Manchester Met - CCD (Int Ec St)
Middlesex - 16-12 pts (Modular)
Northumbria - 16-14 pts/12 pts (Econ) (4 AS)
Oxford Brookes - CCD/BB (Modular) (4 AS)
Reading - CCD/BB (Agric Econ)
Ulster - CCD (App Econ)

14 pts.	**Aberystwyth** - CDD-CDD/BC-BD (Ag Econ)
Bristol UWE - 14 pts (Soc Sci/Econ; Econ) (BTEC 2D+2M)

Coventry – 14-12 pts (Econ; Fin Ec; Ind Ec) (6 AS) (BTEC 3D)
De Montfort – 14-12 pts (Econ)
Dundee – CDD/BC (BSc)
Harper Adams (CAg) – CDD/BC (Ecol Econ)
North London – CDD/BC (Bus Econ Fin) (BTEC 4D+Ms)
Plymouth – 14 pts (App Econ)
Portsmouth – CDD/CC (Econ; Econ/Geog) (2 AS Econ; 4 AS Econ/Geog)
Staffordshire – 14 pts (Econ; Euro Econ; Bus Fin Econ)
Trinity & All Saints (CHE) – CCE (Econ Comb St)
Wolverhampton – 14 pts (Econ; Bus Econ) (BTEC 4M)

12 pts.   **Anglia (Poly Univ)** – 12 pts (All Economics courses) (BTEC 2D+4M)
Buckingham – DDD/CC (Econ/Lang)
Dundee (IT) – DDD/CC (App Econ)
Greenwich – 12 pts (Econ) (6 AS)
Guildhall London – CC (Econ; Fin Econ) (BTEC 4M)
Leeds Met – CC approx (Econ P Pol) (2 AS)
Liverpool John Moores – 12 pts (Econ)
Portsmouth – DDD/CC (Econ/Geog)
Sunderland – 12 pts (Econ courses) (BTEC 2D+3M)
Westminster – CC (Soc Sci; Econ for Business)

10 pts.   **Manchester Met** – (Int Bus Econ)
Thames Valley London – 10 pts (Econ) (BTEC D+Ms)

8 pts.   and below
Coventry – (Econ Dev Plan)
Derby – (Modular) (4 AS)
East London – (Ap Econ) (BTEC 5M)
Guildhall London – DD (Economics – Modular)
Holborn (Coll) – (BSc Econ)
Huddersfield – (Hum)
Kingston – (Lang/Econ/Pol)
Liverpool John Moores – (Econ – Int Credit Scheme)
Nene (CHE) – (Comb St)
Paisley – (Bus Econ; Land Econ)
Plymouth – (Sci/Soc)
Swansea (IHE) – (Comb St)
Thames Valley London – 8 pts (Econ/Ger)
Worcester (IHE) – (Comb St)

Franchised degree and HND courses (see Ch 5):
Bristol UWE – Bridgewater (CFE); Chippenham (CT).

Diploma of Higher Education courses:
4 pts.   Central Lancashire; Oxford Brookes.

Open Access course: Holborn (Coll) Dip in Economics.

Alternative offers:

EB offers: **Aberystwyth** 70%; **Bath** 70%; **De Montfort** 60%; **Keele** 65%; **Lancaster** 70%.

IB offers: **Aberdeen** 30 pts; **Aberystwyth** 30 pts; **Anglia (Poly Univ)** 28 pts; **Bangor** 32 pts; **Bath** 28 pts inc H666-665-66; **Bristol** 32-30 pts inc H766, (Econ/Ec Hist) 34 pts, (Econ/Soc) 28 pts, (Econ/Acc – syll 2) 35 pts; **Brunel** 30 pts; **Buckingham** 27 pts; **Cambridge** H777; **Cardiff** H655 + 14 pts; **City** H655 S655; **Dundee** 29 pts H 15 pts; **East Anglia** 30 pts; **Exeter** 33-30 pts; **Greenwich** 24 pts; **Guildhall London** 28 pts 7 subjects 24 pts 6 subjects; **Harper Adams (CAg)** 28 pts; **Heriot-Watt** 27 pts; **Hull** 30 pts; **Keele** 27 pts; **Kent** 29 pts, H 13 pts; **Kingston** 26 pts; **Lancaster** 32-30 pts; **Leeds** 30 pts inc 15 pts Highers; **Leicester** (Econ/Law) 30 pts, (Econ) 28 pts; **Liverpool** 28 pts H5 maths; **London (RH)** 30 pts; **Loughborough** 30-28 pts inc H555; **Manchester Met** 24 pts; **Newcastle** H666; **Nottingham** H655, (Econ/Bus) H766; **Oxford** H777;

St Andrews 30 pts (BA), 28 pts (BSc); **Surrey** 30 pts; **Sussex** 15 pts Highers; **Swansea** 30 pts; **York** 30-28 pts inc H555.

Irish offers: **Aberdeen** BBBB; **Aberystwyth** BBBCC; **Bangor** BBBCC; **Brunel** AAAABB; **East Anglia BBBCC; Greenwich** CCCCC; **Guildhall London** CCCCC; **Holborn (Coll)** BBBCC; **Keele** BBBCC; **Leeds** ABB; **Surrey** BBBBC.

SCE offers: **Aberdeen** BBBB; **Aberystwyth** BBBB; **Birmingham** BBCC; **City** AABB; **Dundee** BBBC; **Edinburgh** BBBBB; **Glasgow** BBBB; **Guildhall London** BBCCC; **Heriot-Watt** BBBB; **Lancaster** ABBBB; **Liverpool** BBBBB; **Newcastle** BBBB; **St Andrews** BBBB; **Stirling** BBCC; **Strathclyde** BBBB; **Surrey** BBBB.

Overseas applicants: Leeds, **East Anglia**, and **Newcastle** English courses available. **Holborn (Coll)** Students from Kenya and Far East. **East Anglia** Far Eastern, Nigerian and Cypriot students. **De Montfort** Induction courses available. **Hull** Living costs 30% lower than in London.

CHOOSING YOUR COURSE (See also Ch 1)

Subject information: If you haven't taken economics at A-level be prepared for a study involving some mathematics, statistics and, depending on which course you choose, economic and social history, industrial policies, the British economy and labour history, money, banking and regional economics. Business Studies, Accountancy, Estate Management and Quantity Surveying degree courses might also be considered. Since suitability for employment is an important factor, interviews for sandwich courses are designed, in part, to assess this.

Course highlights: Anglia (Poly Univ) Part of the modular system, bias to maths and statistics, history of economics and sociology. **Bangor** Specialisms in regional economics, international economics in year 3. Institute of Economic Research at Bangor financed by World Bank and United Nations. **Bath** (Econ/Pol) Transfer to Economics possible at end of year 1. **Bristol** Rigorous mathematical analysis of economic theory. Students well equipped for further practical training. High research rating. Strong mathematical emphasis, wide range of subject options in Syllabus 2 (no maths required). **Brunel** Students also read two other courses each year from law, government and politics, sociology and psychology; language options. **Cambridge** Wide range of options offered in Part II including public economics, banking and credit, industry, labour, world depression in the inter-war years and aspects of sociology. **City** Wide range of economic subjects, including domestic and international finance, Marxist political economy and Russian and Chinese economic and social development. **Coventry** Emphasis on financial and industrial economics. **Durham** Single and joint Honours course students follow the same first year course in economics plus three from 11 other subjects leading to flexibility in choice of degree at end of year 1. **East Anglia** Common programme of courses in the first two terms introducing economics, economic and social history, sociology, philosophy and politics. **Exeter** Options include business techniques, management accountancy, investment and the economics of banking and financial institutions. **Leeds Met** (Econ P Pol) Degree focuses on economic, political and social issues. **Liverpool** Optional subjects include mathematics, business organisation, labour economics, English law, transport economics, commercial law and international economics. **Northumbria** Options include financial studies, urban and regional studies, industrial organisation and public policy studies. **Nottingham** In the third year specialist topics include money, banking, marketing and agricultural economics. **Portsmouth** In year 2 students choose pathways leading to one of four degrees in Economics. **Reading** Optional subjects in years 2 and 3 include money and banking, business economics and urban and regional economics. **Strathclyde** Course presented in two major parts: consumers, enterprises and industries; markets and governments. **Surrey** Courses are highly applied and vocational. Years 1 and 2 focus on economics and related subjects, including computing, maths, statistics, sociology, politics and history. **Swansea** Course decisions can be delayed until beginning of year 2. **Wolverhampton** A broad course with options including accounting, business law, public finance and French or German.

Study opportunities abroad: Bangor (E); **Bristol** (E); **De Montfort** (E); **Dundee** (E) FR; **East Anglia** (E); **East London; Exeter** (E); **Greenwich** (E); **Guildhall London** (E); **Lancaster** (E) USA FR G; **Keele** (E); **Kingston; Liverpool John Moores** (E); **London (QM)** (E); **Loughborough** (E)

G; **Manchester Met** FR; **Middlesex** FR; **Nottingham Trent** (E); **Portsmouth** (E); **Reading** (E); **Staffordshire** B LUX; **Surrey** USA; **Warwick** (E); **Westminster** (E); **Wolverhampton** (E).

Work opportunities abroad: Bangor; Bath EUR AF; **Bristol** B NL; **Brunel** FR G SZ AUS; **Greenwich** FR IT SP G B GR; **Manchester Met** FR; **Newcastle; York** USA CAN.

ADMISSIONS INFORMATION

Number of applicants per place (approx): Aberystwyth 10; **Anglia (Poly Univ)** 10; **Bangor** 15; **Bath** 10; **Belfast** 10; **Birmingham** (Econ/Stats) 6; **Bradford** 15; **Bristol** 7; **Brunel** 11; **Buckingham** 10; **Cambridge** 4; **Cardiff** 8; **Central England** 16; **City** 18; **Coventry** 10; **De Montfort** 15; **Dundee (IT)** 8; **Durham** 7; **East Anglia** 15; **Exeter** 12; **Greenwich** 8; **Guildhall London** 9; **Heriot-Watt** 11; **Holborn (Coll)** no limits; **Hull** 22; **Kent** 14; **Kingston** 9; **Lancaster** 14; **Leeds** 16; **Leeds Met** 10; **London (RH)** (Econ Soc Pol) 10, (Econ Pub Ad) 10; **Loughborough** 15; **Manchester Met** 16; **Middlesex** 6; **Newcastle** 20, (Econ/Bus Man) 8, (Econ/Acct) 10; **Northumbria** 11; **Nottingham** (Econ) 15; **Nottingham Trent** 19; **Oxford Brookes** 51; **Paisley** 7; **Portsmouth** 17; **Salford** 13; **Sheffield** 10; **Staffordshire** 5; **Stirling** 6; **Sunderland** 8; **Surrey** 10; **Swansea** 9; **Thames Valley London** 3; **Trinity & All Saints (CHE)** 16; **Warwick** 10; **Wolverhampton** 5; **York** 16.

General Studies acceptable: Aberdeen; Aberystwyth (as one of 4 A-levels); Bangor; Birmingham; Bradford; Brunel (JMB); Buckingham; Cardiff; Central England; Coventry; De Montfort; Dundee (IT); Essex (JMB); Exeter; Guildhall London; Heriot-Watt; Kent; Lancaster; Leeds; Leicester; Loughborough; Manchester Met; Newcastle; Northumbria; Nottingham Trent; Oxford Brookes; Surrey (Ec/Soc); Sheffield (Not AEB); Sunderland; Thames Valley London; Trinity & All Saints (CHE); Wolverhampton; York.

Selection interviews: Bangor (some); Bath (35%) (Maths aptitude test for those with GCSE grades A-C); Brunel (some); Cambridge; City (some); Durham; East Anglia (some); East London (some); Edinburgh; Essex (some); Guildhall London (some); Hull (some); Keele; Leeds (some); Leeds Met (some); Liverpool (some); London (RH); Loughborough; Manchester Met; Newcastle (some); Portsmouth (some); Staffordshire; Surrey (some); Swansea (some); Trinity & All Saints (CHE); UMIST (some); Warwick (some); York (some).

Offers to applicants repeating A-levels: Higher Aberystwyth, Bangor, Belfast, Central England, City, De Montfort, Essex, Hull, Leeds (2 pts), Leeds Met, Liverpool, Newcastle, Northumbria, Nottingham, Sheffield, Staffordshire, Swansea, York (BBC); **Possibly higher** Bath, Bradford, Brunel, Durham, Lancaster, Nottingham Trent, Oxford Brookes, Surrey; **Same** Brunel, Coventry, Durham, East London, Kingston, Leeds Met (Econ/Pub Pol), London (RH), Loughborough, Ulster.

Admissions Tutors' advice: Brunel Interviews important in order to assess applicants' employment prospects for sandwich placements. **Holborn College** (BSc Econ) London University (external) degree, a full-time course with low offers (EE) since no quota system applies. **Wolverhampton** Mathematical skills required.

Examples of interview questions: Why do you like economics? What is the ERM? How does it work? What aspects interest you? What is happening to sterling at present? What is happening to the dollar? How relevant is economics today? What are your views on government economic policy? What career have you in mind when you graduate? Do you think that the family is declining as an institution? What perspectives do you hold in sociology, functionalism or Marxism? How do you view the Hong Kong/China problem? Discuss Keynesian economics. If you were given £200 in addition to your grant at the beginning of the first year, what would you spend it on? What is your opinion of capital punishment? Discuss the Common Agricultural Policy (Agricultural Economics). Is the power of the Prime Minister increasing? What is a recession? How would you get the world out of recession? What caused it? What newspapers do you read? Is the study of economics an art or a science? What do you argue with your father about? How would you solve the unemployment problem? Is the cyclic economy true? Does the Government's policy care for the poor? Social conscience versus profitability - does a paradox exist between payment for education and payment for technical training? How would you solve the problems of the NHS?

GAP YEAR ADVICE

Institutions accepting a Gap Year: Most institutions; **Brunel** Tell us when you apply; **Guildhall London** Travel and read widely; **Manchester Met** (Int Ec St) A year in a French-speaking country invaluable. **Newcastle** (Econ/Acct) Summarise your plan on your UCAS form. **York** Use it constructively; paid or voluntary work and travel recommended.

Institutions willing to defer entry after A-levels (see Ch 5): Bradford; Brunel (No); Buckingham; Coventry; Dundee; East Anglia; Heriot-Watt; Hull; Lancaster; London (RH); Manchester Met; Newcastle (Econ/Acct) only; Northumbria (No); Plymouth; St Andrews; Surrey (Preferred); Swansea; Thames Valley London; Trinity & All Saints (CHE); Westminster (No); Wolverhampton; York.

AFTER A-LEVELS ADVICE

Institutions which may accept the same points score after A-levels: Aberystwyth; Bangor; Bath; Belfast; Brunel; Coventry; De Montfort; Essex; Exeter; Guildhall London; Holborn (Coll); Hull; Kent; Kingston; Leeds Met; London (RH); Loughborough (higher points score required); Manchester Met; Middlesex; Nottingham Trent; Oxford Brookes; Portsmouth; Staffordshire; Surrey (perhaps); Swansea; UMIST; Wolverhampton; York.

Institutions demanding the actual grades offered after A-levels: Dundee; Durham; Leeds; Lancaster; Loughborough (Econ/Minor); Newcastle (Econ/ Geog); Nottingham; Sheffield; Stirling.

Institutions which may accept under-achieving applicants after A-levels: Aberystwyth; Bangor; Brunel; Buckingham; Coventry; East Anglia; Glasgow; Holborn (Coll); Hull (Overseas students 18-14 pts); London (RH); Loughborough; Manchester Met; St Andrews; Surrey; Swansea; most new universities and colleges.

Institutions with vacancies in Aug/Sept 1992 (see Ch 5): Anglia (Poly Univ); Bangor; Brunel 22 pts; Buckingham 12 pts; Central England; City; Coventry; East Anglia (Bus Fin Econ) 22 pts; Greenwich 10 pts; Heriot-Watt 18 pts; Holborn (Coll); Kingston; Lancaster 20 pts; Leeds; London (QMW), (RH) 20-18 pts; Manchester Met (Int Ec St) but exceptional; Newcastle (Econ/Acct) 20 pts; North London 12 pts; Northumbria 14 pts; Oxford Brookes; Plymouth 12 pts; Portsmouth; Sunderland 10 pts; Surrey 18 pts; Thames Valley London; Trinity & All Saints (CHE) 12-10 pts; York (Econ/Stats; Ec/Ecmt) 20 pts.

ADVICE FOR MATURE STUDENTS

An average of 5% of mature students are accepted each year on these courses. Evidence of study to GCSE or equivalent and in many cases A-level is required by most universities.

GRADUATE EMPLOYMENT

New Graduates' destinations (percentages) 1991:
Permanent employment: U 76; P 55.
Unemployment: U 16; P 28.
Further studies (all types): U 24; P 21.
Main career destinations (approx): Finance 66; Business Management 20; Computing 7.

Surrey This degree course is often used as a preparation for careers in the accountancy profession with graduates entering as trainees; 15 students chose this career. Others went into programming and systems engineering, banking, taxation, the police and market research.

York (1988-91) Half those graduates obtaining employment went into a wide range of finance careers (merchant banks, actuarial work, stock broking, tax consultancy, investment analysis etc); personnel work, advertising, marketing and public administration accounted for a further 12%.

EDUCATION

Special subject requirements: A-levels in chosen subjects in most cases. GCSE (grade A-C) in English and mathematics.

NB Institutions may raise or lower the level of published offers depending either on the quality or otherwise of individual applications or the numbers of applications received; grades/points offered may be adjusted downwards after A-level results. The level of an offer is not indicative of the quality of a course.

Subjects attracting the most applicants include Drama, History, PE, Social Science, English and Art. Subjects attracting the least applicants include Modern Languages, Sciences, CDT, Music, Religious Education, Maths and Home Economics. The choice of subject will affect the level of the offer made.

Abbreviations: P – Primary Teaching; S – Secondary Teaching; N – Nursery; QTS – Qualified Teacher Status.

It should be noted that some university courses do not confer a teacher training qualification.

24 pts.	**Cardiff** – BBB (Educ/Eng)
22 pts.	**Cardiff** – BBC (Educ/Psy; Educ/Phil; Educ/Hist Ideas)
	Lancaster – BBC (Theatre/Educ; Educ/Psy)
	Warwick – BBC-BCC (Ed/Psy)
	York – BBC-CCD/BB-CC (Joint courses) (BTEC 5M)
20 pts.	**Bangor** – BCC/BB (Health Education and Development)
	Cardiff – BCC-CCC (Educ/Soc; Educ/Lang)
	Lancaster – BCC-CCC (Educ/Lang; Educ/Maths; Educ/Hist; Educ/SA; Ed/Soc; Educ/E Lang) (4 AS) (BTEC mainly M)
	Warwick – BCC-CCC/BC (P – BA (QTS), English; Soc/Ed; Phil/Ed) (S – PE)
18 pts.	**Aberystwyth** – CCC-CCD/BC (Joint courses Eng/Hist/Dr/Geog/Irish/ Maths/Arts/ Welsh/Libr) (BTEC Ds+Ms)
	Bangor – CCC-EEE/BB-EE (Educational Studs joint courses)
	Cambridge (Hom) – BCD-CCC/BC-CC (BEd) (BTEC 3M inc one in area of chosen subject)
	Lancaster – CCC (Educ; Educ/Rel; WS/Educ) (4 AS)
	Ripon & York St John (CHE) – CCC (N; P; Eng Lit)
	Stirling – CCC/BB (P/S – All Education courses)
	Warwick – CCC-CCD (P – BA (QTS) Hist)
16 pts.	**Central Lancashire** – CCD (Comb Hons)
	Dundee – CDD/BC (Maths/Ed)
	Exeter – CCD/CC (P/S – All Education courses) (6-4 AS)
	Loughborough – BDD-CDD (S – Des/Tech/Educ)
	Middlesex – 16-12 pts (Modular)
	Strathclyde/Jordanhill – CCD-CDD (S – B Tech Ed)
	Ulster – CCD/BC (Educ)
	Warwick – CCD/BC (P – QTS Art; RS; Drama)
14 pts.	**Brunel** – CDD/CC (S – Des/Tech/Ed – BSc/QTS) (6 AS)
	Cheltenham & Glos (CHE) – 14-10 pts (P BEd)
	Oxford Brookes – CDD/BC (Ed St Field)
12 pts.	**Brunel** – CDE/CC (S – Des Tech Ed – BA/QTS) (6 AS) (BTEC 4M)
	Cambridge (Hom) – CC (P – Music)

Canterbury Christ Church (CHE) - CC-EE (P)
Cheltenham & Glos (CHE) - 12-10 pts (BEd PE)
Cheltenham & Glos (CHE) - 12 pts (Ed St Mod/Hist/Eng/Geog) (BTEC 3M)
Durham - CC (BA) (P/S - Educ) (BTEC 3M)
Glasgow - CC (Tech Ed)
Heriot-Watt - CC (Phys/Ed)
Liverpool John Moores - CC (P - Des Tech/Pe/Outdoor)
Loughborough - CDE/CC (S - Maths/Educ)
Ripon & York St John (CHE) - CC (N; P; Geog)
Warwick - CDE/CC (P - BA(QTS) Biol; Geog; Music)
West Sussex (IHE) - DDD/CC (S - BEd)

10 pts. **Bath (CHE)** - 10 pts (P;S) (BTEC Ds+Ms)
Bedford (CHE) - 10pts (Comb St; Dance)
Bretton Hall (CHE) - CD-EE (P)
Cardiff - CD (S - Ed (Home Ec))
Cheltenham & Glos (CHE) - 10 pts (BEd RS)
King Alfred's (CHE) - 10-8 pts (P) (BTEC 3M)
Oxford Brookes - DDE (P/S)
Ripon & York St John (CHE) - DDE/CD (N; P; All courses except under 18, 12, 8 pts)
Warwick - CD (BA (QTS); S - Maths)

8 pts. **and below** (Most courses will accept 4 AS instead of 2 A-levels)
Anglia (Poly Univ) - (P) (BTEC 4M)
Bedford (CHE) - EE (P)
Bishop Grosseteste (CHE) - DD (P) (BTEC and Access courses by prior arrangement)
Bradford & Ilkley (CmC) - 8 pts (P)
Brighton - (P; S - PE with Eng/Bus St/Geog/Maths; Bus Ed; Bus Inf Tech)
Bristol UWE - (P; S - Bus St/Des Tech/Maths/Eng)
Cardiff (IHE) - (P/S - Music; Drama)
Charlotte Mason (CEd) - DD-CE (P)
Chester (CHE) - 8 pts minimum D for main subject (P) (BTEC 3M)
Crewe & Alsager (CHE) - 9P; S - Bus/Des Tech/Biol/Env Sci/Fr/ Maths/PE/Sci)
Derby - (P) (BTEC 3M)
Edge Hill (CHE) - (P) (BTEC 1D+3M)
Gwent (CHE) - (P; S - Des Tech/Maths/Sci)
Heriot-Watt/Moray House - (P/S)
Hertfordshire - (P/S)
King Alfred's (CHE) - (S - Des Tech; Soc/Prof St)
Kingston - (BEd Hons)
La Sainte Union (CHE) - (P)
Leeds Met - (P; S - Des Tech/Maths)
Liverpool (IHE) - 8 pts (P) (BTEC 3M)
Liverpool John Moores - (P; S - Des Tech/PE/Outdoor) (BTEC 4M CDT)
London (Central Sch Sp/Dr) - (S)
London (Gold) - (P; S - Des Tech)
Manchester Met - EE (P; S - Maths/Chem/Phys)
Middlesex - (P; S - Tech/Music)
Nene (CHE) - (P) (BTEC P overall)
Newman & Westhill (CHE) - 4 pts (P Maths, D in maths or C at AS-level; S - Music) (BTEC 3M)
North East Wales (IHE) - (P; S - Bus St)
North London - EE (P)
North Riding (Coll) - (P)
Northern Aberdeen - (P)
Northumbria - (P)
Nottingham Trent - (P) (BTEC P overall)
Oxford Brookes - (App Ed) (4 AS) (BTEC 3M)
Paisley/Craigie - (P)

Plymouth - (P) (BTEC 5M)
Reading - (P)
Ripon & York St John (CHE) - DD (N; P; Maths, Music, Theol)
Roehampton (IHE) - (P - Comb St)
S Martin's (CHE) - D (P; S - Maths)
St Mark & St John (CHE) - (P; S - Des Tech/PE)
St Mary's (CHE) - (P/S)
Sheffield Hallam - (P; S - PE/Des Tech/ Sci/Maths/HE; BEd 2yr Chem, Physics) (BTEC 3-6M)
South Bank - (P)
Strathclyde - EE (P)
Strathclyde/Jordanhill - EE (P/S)
Strathclyde/St Andrews - (P; S - Music)
Sunderland - (P; S - Des Tech/Bus St)
Swansea (IHE) - (P; S - Bus St)
Trinity & All Saints (CHE) - (QTS; P/S)
Trinity Carmarthen (CHE) - (P)
Welsh (CMus) - (S)
West London (IHE) - (P; S; BEd QTS)
West Sussex (IHE) - (P - All courses)
Westminster (CHE) - (P/S)
Wolverhampton - (P; S - Maths/Tech) (BTEC P overall)
Worcester (CHE) - (P; S - Biol/HE)

Alternative offers:

IB offers: **Aberystwyth** 30-28 pts; **Bangor** 30-28 pts; **Bath (CHE)** 24 pts; **Brighton** 28-24 pts; **Brunel** 28-25 pts; **Cambridge (Hom)** 28 pts inc H6 in chosen subject S5 maths and English; **Durham** 25 pts; **Exeter** 30 pts; **Lancaster** 30 pts; **Oxford Brookes** H444.

Irish offers: **Aberystwyth** BBBBC; **Bangor** BBCCC; **Bedford (CHE)** CCCC; **Durham** BBCCC; **Newman & Westhill (CHE)** CCC + maths and English at pass (ordinary level).

SCE offers: **Aberystwyth** BBBB; **Cambridge (Hom)** BBCC; **Dundee** BBBC (Maths/Ed); **Durham** BBB; **Glasgow** BBCC/BBB, BBC (Tech Ed); **Heriot-Watt** BBCC (Maths/Educ), ABBB (Phys/Ed); **Lancaster** ABBB; **Newman & Westhill (CHE)** CCCC; **Northern Aberdeen** BBC; **Stirling** BBCC; **Worcester (CHE)** CCC.

Overseas applicants: English language ability crucial in all cases. **Bath (CHE)** Special course for Japanese students. **Roehampton (IHE)** No foundation course. **West London (IHE)** GCSE maths and English grades A-C or British Council test of 6-5.

Applications to Colleges in Scotland: Applications for teacher training in Scotland are submitted through TEACH. Details are obtainable from Teacher Admissions Clearing House, PO Box 165, Edinburgh EH8 8AT.

CHOOSING YOUR COURSE (See Ch 1)

> **Subject information:** These studies cover the history, philosophy and theory of education; however they are not necessarily teacher training courses. Read prospectuses carefully. Candidates should be well motivated towards teaching and education - interview important. Interview panels look for candidates with confidence in their own ability, a lively personality, patience and optimism. Experience of working with children important. Teacher training courses are offered in the following subject areas: Art/Design (P); Biology (P/S); Business Studies (S); Chemistry (P/S); Childhood (P); Computer Education (P); Creative/Performing Arts (P); Dance (P/S); Design/Technology (P/S); Drama (P/S); English (P/S); Environmental Science (P/S); Environmental Studies (P); French (P/S); General Primary; Geography (P/S); History (P/S); Home Economics (P/S); Maths (P/S); Music (P/S); Physical Ed/Movement St (P/S); Religious St (P); Science (P/S); Sociology (P); Textile Design (P); Welsh (P).

Two-year BEd courses are also offered for holders of HND or equivalent qualifications (minimum age in some cases 23-25) in the following subject areas. Business Studies (S); Chemistry (S); Design and Technology (S); English (P); French (S); General Primary; German (S); Home Economics (S); Language Studies (P); Mathematics (S); Music (S); Physics (S); Science (S); Spanish (S); Welsh (S). Full details of the colleges offering these courses are published in the *Compendium of Higher Education* (London Advisory Council for Education), 232 Vauxhall Bridge Road, London SW1V 1AU (price £6.00).

Course highlights: Bishop Grosseteste (CHE) Choral and organ scholarships available. **Brunel** 70% of course covers design. Degree confers design and teaching qualifications. **Cambridge (Hom)** Course firmly rooted in practical, school-based experience. Coursework a major element of assessment. **Cardiff** Course covers psychological and social development of children from birth to adult and educational influences. Also focuses on inter-relationships between the child and the educational system, child and parent, and study of the deprived and disturbed child. **Chester (CHE)** Enterprise programme for additional work experience. **Heriot-Watt/Moray House** (BEd Tech) Course includes computing, CAD CAM/Electronics and teaching. **Lancaster** A general training in social sciences involving application of psychology, economics, sociology, history, philosophy and educational issues. **Loughborough** Years 1 and 2 Joint BEd common with single Honours specialist subject courses; years 3 and 4 have substantial education component, with teaching practice leading to degree and teaching qualification. **Ripon & York St John (CHE)** Students can opt out of QTS course and qualify for a BA or BSc degree. **S Martins (CHE)** Students able to choose between upper and lower primary after year 1. **Sheffield Hallam** Exchange scheme with Ohio University, USA; design and technology option available. **Stirling** Subject can be studied to minor, subsidiary or major level in Part I.

Study opportunities abroad: **Brighton** FR NL USA; **Cambridge (Hom)** (E); **Cardiff (IHE)** USA SW; **Cheltenham & Glos (CHE)** (E); **Chester (CHE)** USA; **Heriot-Watt/Moray House** (E) FR SP G B; **Leeds Met** USA GR; **Ripon & York St John (CHE)** (E); **Roehampton (IHE)** (E); **Sheffield Hallam** USA; **West Sussex (IHE)** NL CAN; **Westminster (CHE)** (E).

Work opportunities abroad: Brighton USA CAN; **Charlotte Mason (CEd)** USA FR G; **Greenwich** SP; **North East Wales (IHE)** USA SW; **Roehampton (IHE)** FR B NL; **West Sussex (IHE)** NL CAN; **Westminster (CHE)** FR USA.

ADMISSIONS INFORMATION

Number of applicants per place (approx): Aberystwyth 6; **Anglia (Poly Univ)** 3; **Bangor** 4; **Bath (CHE)** 6; **Bedford (CHE)** 4; **Bretton Hall (CHE)** 4; **Brighton (PE)** 6; **Cambridge (Hom)** 6 (Average for all courses); **Canterbury Christ Church (CHE)** 15; **Cardiff (IHE)** 3; **Charlotte Mason (CEd)** 4; **Cheltenham & Glos (CHE)** 4; **Chester (CHE)** 10; **Derby** 4; **Durham** 8; **Greenwich** 3; **Heriot-Watt/Moray House** (Primary) 3, (PE) 4; **Exeter** 10, (Sec/PE) 13; **Hertfordshire** 4; **Leeds Met** (Sec) 5; **Liverpool (IHE)** 5; **Loughborough** (Educ/Maths) 3; **Manchester Met** 16; **Middlesex** 7; **Nene (CHE)** 4; **Newman & Westhill (CHE)** 9; **North Riding (Coll)** 4; **Northumbria** 8; **Nottingham Trent** 3; **Oxford Brookes** 6; **Roehampton (IHE)** 5; **S Martin's** 5; **Strathclyde/St Andrews** 2; **St Mark & St John (CHE)** 5; **St Mary's (CHE)** 4; **Sheffield Hallam** 7; **Sunderland** 10; **Trinity Carmarthen (CHE)** 4; **West London (IHE)** (PE) 5, (P) 7, (S) 12; **Westminster (CHE)** 5; **Worcester (CHE)** 7.

General Studies acceptable: Bangor; Bath (CHE); Bedford (CHE) (2); Bradford & Ilkley (CmC); Bretton Hall (CHE) (2) not AEB; Bristol UWE (2); Canterbury Christ Church (CHE); Cardiff (IHE) (2); Chester (CHE); Derby; Exeter; Greenwich (2); Hertfordshire (2); Kingston; Lancaster; Liverpool (IHE); Liverpool John Moores; Loughborough; Manchester Met; Newman & Westhill (CHE) (2) not AEB/London; North Riding (Coll); Oxford Brookes; Plymouth (2); Ripon & York St John (CHE); Roehampton (IHE); S Martin's (CHE) (2); St Mark & St John (CHE) (2); Trinity & All Saints (CHE) (2); Trinity Carmarthen (2); Westminster (CHE) (2); West Sussex (IHE) (2); Wolverhampton; Worcester (CHE) (2); York (varies);

Selection interviews: Usually all institutions for teacher training courses.

Offers to applicants repeating A-levels: Higher Chester (CHE); **Possibly higher** Bath (CHE), Cambridge (Hom), Newman & Westhill (CHE), Ripon & York St John (CHE), S Martin's (CHE); **Same** Bangor, Bishop Grosseteste (CHE), Canterbury Christ Church (CHE), Derby, Durham, La Sainte Union (CHE), Liverpool John Moores, London (Gold), Loughborough (Educ/Maths), North London, Northumbria, West London (IHE), Wolverhampton, Worcester (CHE).

Admissions Tutors' advice: Cambridge (Hom) Most offers range between BCD and CD (the latter often for chemistry and physics). Applicants should be able to show evidence of interest in children and motivation towards teaching. Most applicants will be interviewed, especially if they have a reasonable GCSE record and 2 grade Cs at A-level (or the equivalent at A/AS-levels) are likely. Mature applicants and those with non-standard (but relevant) academic qualifications also considered.

Examples of interview questions: What do you think are important issues in education at the moment? Will your current spare-time activities help in a teaching career? How would you explain the miracles to a ten year-old? (RE applicant). Are you enjoying your A-levels? Why do you want to teach? What is important in the education of infants? How would you discipline children? Should teachers go on strike? How would you prepare for classroom management? What are the qualities required to be a good teacher? Why do you think you have these qualities? Name a popular author of children's books – why are the books popular? What other talents could you offer a school in addition to your chosen subject? How would you cope with slow learners? What do you think of the GCSE? How has your schooling affected your choice of a career? Explain the national curriculum. Applicants are strongly advised to have had some teaching practice prior to interview.

GAP YEAR ADVICE

Institutions accepting a Gap Year: Most institutions; **Bath (CHE)** Apply before gap year only if travelling abroad; **Cambridge (Hom)** Advises a well-organised programme involving some work with children/young people; **Greenwich** Work in a school if possible; **Oxford Brookes** Work in a school if possible; **Roehampton (IHE)** Give reasons for your gap year; **Sheffield Hallam** Work with children if possible; **Westminster (CHE)** Keep involved with your subject and gain experience in education.

Institutions willing to defer entry after A-levels (see Ch 5): Most institutions; Bishop Grosseteste (CHE); Brighton; Heriot-Watt/Moray House; King Alfred's; Kingston; Lancaster; Newman & Westhill (CHE) (No); Plymouth; Ripon & York St John (CHE) (No); Roehampton (IHE); South Bank; St Mark & St John (CHE) (Yes but not preferred); Swansea (IHE); Westminster (Coll) (No).

AFTER A-LEVELS ADVICE

Institutions which may accept the same points score after A-levels: Most institutions.

Institutions demanding the actual grades offered after A-levels: Chester (CHE); Newman & Westhill (CHE); North Riding (Coll); Ripon & York St John (CHE).

Institutions which may accept under-achieving applicants after A-levels: Most institutions will consider applicants whose A-level results do not quite match the offer made. (Two A-level passes and English and mathematics at GCSE (grades A-C) are the minimum requirements.)

Institutions with vacancies in Aug/Sept 1992 (see Ch 5): Most institutions; Aberystwyth; Brunel; Cheltenham & Glos (CHE); Heriot-Watt/Moray House; King Alfred's (CHE) 10-8 pts; Kingston EE; North London; Plymouth 8 pts; Roehampton (IHE) (varies depending on subjects); St Mark & St John (CHE) (Des/Tech); Westminster (CHE).

ADVICE FOR MATURE STUDENTS

Teacher training courses now attract more mature students than any other degree course. In a recent survey 86% quickly obtained employment following graduation compared with 58% for all subjects and 98% for Medicine. English and mathematics at GCSE or equivalent are required for entry to courses.

GRADUATE EMPLOYMENT

New Graduates' destinations (percentages) 1991:
Permanent employment: (Teacher training) U 94; P 92; C 93. (Education) U 100; P 64; C 71.
Unemployment: (Teacher training) U 3; P 4; C 4. (Education) U 0; P 15; C 22.
Further studies (all types): (Teacher training) U 2; P 1; C 1. (Education) U 15; P 24; C 28.
Main career destinations (approx): Teaching 95.

Anglia (Poly Univ) Most graduates had no problem securing primary teaching posts. However, one graduate joined a local health authority as a primary health care facilitator, one entered environmental health services as a technician and one was appointed as an account manager in marketing.

York (1989-91) Social work, creative and media work (journalism, theatre management, video work), teaching and careers in finance accounted for most graduates. 42% went on to further study.

This was one of the subjects with a good employment record in 1991–92.

ENGINEERING/ENGINEERING SCIENCES (including Enhanced Courses)

Special subject requirements: 2-3 A level passes in mathematics/physics subjects; GCSE (grades (A-C) English, chemistry or a language may be required for some courses.

NB Institutions may raise or lower the level of published offers depending either on the quality or otherwise of individual applications or the numbers of applications received; grades/points offered may be adjusted downwards after A-level results. The level of an offer is not indicative of the quality of a course.

30 pts.	**Cambridge/Oxford** - AAA potential recommended (Eng)
28 pts.	**Brunel** - AAB (Eng - Special Engineering Programme SEP; inc SEP/French and SEP/German) (BTEC M overall)
24 pts.	**Durham** - BBB (All courses)
	Lancaster - BBB (Mechatronics)
	UMIST - BBB (Eng Mnfr/Man)
22 pts.	**Bath** - BBC (BSc/BEng) (BTEC 2D+1M)
	Hull - BBC/BB (Eng Eur)
	Loughborough - 22 pts (Eng Sci 3/4)
	Southampton - 22 pts approx (Gen Eng - contact Admissions Tutor)
	Strathclyde - (Engineering Science)
	Surrey - BBC-CCC/BB (Eng Bus - H100/H101; Eng Bus Euro)
20 pts.	**Aston** - BCC/AA (Eng; Elmech Eng; Int Eng)
	Bradford - BCC/AB (Tech/Man)
	Lancaster - BCC-CCC (All Engineering courses except **24 pts**) (4 AS) (BTEC 2D inc maths +M)
	London (King's) - 20 pts approx (All courses - contact Admissions Tutor)
	Loughborough - 20 pts (Eng Des Tech)
	Manchester - 20 pts approx (Eng)
	Sussex - BCC-CCC (Eng/Eaps)
	Swansea - BCC (Eu Eng/Ger/Sp/Ital/Fr) (BTEC 5M)
	Ulster - BCC/BC (Eng) (AS des tech or any contrasting AS)
	UMIST - BCC/BB (Int Eng) (4 AS) (BTEC 5M)
	Warwick - BCC-CCC (All courses)
18 pts.	**Brunel** - CCC/BB (Ind Des Eng) (BTEC 4M)

Opportunities in Engineering

Are you considering engineering as a career? There is a national need for more engineering graduates, and career prospects are good.

The University offers a range of new undergraduate Honours courses in:

Chemical Engineering
Civil and Structural Engineering
Electrical and Electronic Engineering
Mechanical Engineering and Manufacturing Systems

Electronic Imaging and Media Communications
Environmental Management and Technology
Technology and Management
Manufacturing Management and Technology

Special features:

★   All our mainstream engineering courses are accredited by the relevant British Professional Institutions

★   Our courses apply academic theory to practical problems

★   Several courses integrate engineering with management or European studies

★   Courses are available either as four-year sandwich courses, which integrate practical training and experience with academic study, or as three-year continuous courses

★   European language support is available to all students, and industrial training placements may be available in Europe

★   For those who do not have the relevant science background, we offer programmes incorporating a foundation year. This gives the necessary grounding in mathematics and physics to enable students to follow mainstream engineering courses in later years

If you want to know more about our courses, we would be pleased to send you a Prospectus and relevant course booklet(s). Write to: Sheila Dobson, Schools Liaison Office, University of Bradford, FREEPOST, Bradford, West Yorkshire, BD7 1BR, or phone 0274 383081.

Cardiff - CCC/BB minimum (Int Eng) (BTEC 3M)
City - 18 pts (Man Des/Eng) (BTEC 1D+Ms)
Edinburgh - CCC (Engineer) (4 AS)
Exeter - CCC/BC (Op Eng; Eng Sci 3) (4 AS) (BTEC mainly M)
Hull - CCC/BC (Eng Des Mft)
Hull - BCD-CCD/BB (Eng Sci) (BTEC Ms)
Leicester - BCD-CCC (Engineer; Engin) (BTEC Ms)
Liverpool - CCC/BB (Eng Sci; Eng Sci/Man; Eng/Man/Eur; Eng Sci 4; Eng Sci/Man4) (4 AS)
London (QMW) - 18-14 pts (All courses) (BTEC 1D+4M)
Reading - CCC/BCD (Eng Sci)
Strathclyde - CCC (Eng/Bus)
Surrey - CCC-CCD/BC (Eng; Eng Bus Int - H105) (BTEC M overall)
Swansea - CCC-CCD/BB-CC (Eng Sci)

16 pts. **Bradford** - CCD/BB (Foundation Year)
Strathclyde - CCD (Pros/Orth)

12 pts. **Aberdeen** - CC (Eng Integ)
Bournemouth - 12 -8 pts (Eng Bus Dev) (BTEC 3M)
Brunel - CC (Foundation of Engineering) (BTEC Ms)
Manadon (RNEC) - CC (Naval Officer entry) (BTEC Ms)
Sheffield Hallam - 12-10 pts (Indust St; CAE/Des) (4 AS)

10 pts. **De Montfort** - 10 pts (Eng Tech)
Glamorgan - 10 pts (Tech/Bus St) (BTEC 3M)
Liverpool John Moores - DDE/DD (Tech Mgt; Comb Eng St)
Manchester Met - 10 pts (Eng) (BTEC 1D+1M+1P)
Portsmouth - 10 pts (Eng courses) (BTEC 3M)

8 pts. **Coventry** - (Comp Eng) (6 AS) (BTEC 2M+3P)
Manadon (RNEC) - CE (Eng)
Napier - (Tech Indust)
Nottingham Trent - 8 pts (Ind St; Int Eng)
Sheffield Hallam - 8 pts (Eng Bus; Eng Phys; Env Eng; Integ Eng Ext)
Staffordshire - DD (Tech Man) (BTEC Ms)
Westminster - (Ind Syst/Bus)
Wolverhampton - (Comb Eng St)

6 pts. **and below**
Bradford - EEE/EE (Foundation)
Brighton - (Foundation)
Central England - 6-4 pts (Eng; Export Eng) (4 AS)
De Montfort - (Eng/Tech - extended course requiring 5 GCSEs + further study or experience)
Derby - (Power Eng; Modular) (4 AS)
Greenwich - (BA/BEng - Eng/Bus)
Humberside - 6 pts (Eng/Air Frame/Electrical/Mechanical) (4 AS)
Liverpool John Moores - (Foundation course)
Loughborough - 4 pts (Foundation course)
Luton (CHE) - (Part-time course for HNC students)
Napier - (Eng Man; Energy Man; Eng Syst)
Paisley - (Ind Eng)
Plymouth - (Eng Sys; Ext Eng)
Robert Gordon - (Eng Tech)
Salford - (Eur Eng)
Salford (UC) - (Prod Des Dev)
Southampton (IHE) - E for Foundation - HITECC course (Eng Bus Syst) (4 AS)
South Bank - (All Engineering courses) (4 AS) (BTEC 3M)
Teesside - (Eng/Tech - foundation year)
Trinity & All Saints (CHE) - (Tech)
Westminster (CHE) - 1 pt (Foundation course)

Engineering
–It's your choice

So you're interested in science, technology and engineering. You see how they contribute to your daily life and the benefits they bring to society.

All around, you can see today's developments. You can imagine tomorrow's exciting world. What part will you play?

Are you looking for a career which will build on your current education, a career with high employment levels, team work, travel, intellectual demands?

If you have imagination, enterprise, scientific knowledge, and the ability to work with, and lead, others, you'd be ideally suited to Engineering.

And there are lots of opportunities for girls and boys in Engineering.

It's a highly competent profession. The Engineering Council awards the titles of Engineering Technician (Eng Tech), Incorporated Engineer (IEng) and Chartered Engineer (CEng) to those achieving the relevant standards in education, training and experience.

Don't leave it till it's too late. Act now and find out more about your future in Engineering.

Write to:
Marie-Noëlle Barton
Careers Executive
The Engineering Council
10 Maltravers Street
London WC2R 3ER

Franchised degree and HND courses (see Ch 5):

        Brighton - Brighton (CT); Chichester (CT); Crawley (CT); Hastings (CT); Northbrook (CDT).

        Central England - Handsworth (CFE).

        Cheltenham & Glos (CHE) - Gloucester (CAT).

        Plymouth - Cornwall (CFE); Somerset (CAT).

Diploma of Higher Education courses:
 10 pts.   Sheffield Hallam (Indust St) (4 AS)

EXTENDED ENGINEERING COURSES

Extended Engineering courses are available in institutions throughout the UK as listed below. The courses are open to applicants without the normal science A-levels. After the initial Foundation Year they move on to the degree course.

Franchised degree and HND courses (see Ch 5):

        Hertfordshire - Dunstable (CFE); Hertford Regional (CFE); North Herts (CFE); West Herts (CFE).

Acoustics: Southampton.

Aeronautical Engineering: Belfast, Bristol UWE, Hertfordshire, City, Loughborough, Southampton.

Chemical Engineering: Aston, Exeter, Glamorgan, Leeds (Fuel and Energy), Loughborough, Newcastle, Nottingham, Sheffield, Strathclyde, Swansea, Teesside.

Civil Engineering: Aston, Belfast, Brighton; City, Heriot-Watt, Leeds, Liverpool, Newcastle, Nottingham, Sheffield, Southampton, Strathclyde, Swansea.

Computer Engineering: Anglia (Poly Univ); Bradford (Elect/Comm/Comp Eng), Central England (Ind Inf Tech), Central London, Huddersfield, Kingston, Liverpool John Moores, Sheffield Hallam, South Bank, Staffordshire, Teesside, York (Comp Eng).

Control/Systems Engineering: Bristol UWE, City (Cont Eng), Huddersfield, Leeds Met, Plymouth, Sheffield (Cont Eng), South Bank, Sunderland.

Electrical/Electronic Engineering: Aston, Bangor, Bath, Belfast, Bolton (IHE), Bradford, Brighton (Environmental), Bristol UWE, Cardiff, Central England, Central Lancashire, City, Coventry, East London, Glamorgan, Hertfordshire, Heriot-Watt, Huddersfield, Hull, Kingston, Lancaster (Mechatronics), Leeds, Liverpool, Liverpool John Moores, Loughborough, Manchester Met, Middlesex, Newcastle, Northumbria, Nottingham, Nottingham Trent, Oxford Brookes, Plymouth, Portsmouth, Sheffield, Sheffield Hallam, Southampton, South Bank, Staffordshire, Strathclyde, Sunderland, Surrey, Teesside, UMIST, Warwick, Westminster, York.

General Engineering: Bolton (IHE) (HITECC Foundation), Brighton, Bristol UWE, Brunel, Central England (Foundation), Central London, Coventry, De Montfort, Durham, Exeter, Glamorgan, Hertfordshire, Huddersfield, Humberside, Kingston, Leeds Met, Liverpool, Liverpool John Moores, Manchester Met (Int Eng), Middlesex, North London, Northumbria, Nottingham Trent, Oxford, Oxford Brookes, Plymouth, Portsmouth, Sheffield Hallam, South Bank, Southampton (IHE), Staffordshire, Strathclyde, Sunderland, Teesside, Thames Valley London.

Manufacturing Engineering: Aston, Bristol UWE, Central England, East London, Hertfordshire, Portsmouth, Staffordshire; Sunderland.

Marine Engineering: Liverpool John Moores.

Mechanical Engineering: Aston, Belfast, Birmingham (Mech Eng/Econ), Brighton, Bristol, Bristol UWE, Central Lancashire, City, Hertfordshire, Heriot-Watt, Huddersfield, Kingston, Lancaster (Mechatronics), Leeds, Liverpool, Liverpool John Moores, Loughborough (Auto Eng), Manchester Met, Middlesex, Nottingham, Nottingham Trent, Plymouth, Portsmouth, Sheffield, Sheffield Hallam, South Bank, Southampton, Strathclyde, Sunderland, Swansea, Teesside, UMIST, Warwick, Westminster.

Mining Engineering: Nottingham.

Naval Architecture etc: Southampton (Ship Sci), Strathclyde (Naval Arch).

Production Engineering: Birmingham (Prod Eng/Econ), Cambridge, Hull, Loughborough, Newcastle, Nottingham.

Offers for Foundation, Certificate and Diploma courses (see Ch 5):

Higher National Diploma courses (England and Wales):
    4 pts.   **and below** Bristol UWE; Buckinghamshire (CHE); Cardiff (IHE); Central Lancashire (Eng Design); Cheltenham & Glos (CHE); De Montfort; East London; Glamorgan (Eng Design); Hastings (CAT); Hertfordshire; Huddersfield; Manchester Met; Nene (CHE); Oxford Brookes; Sheffield Hallam; Southampton (IHE); Sunderland; Swansea (IHE); Swindon (Coll); Thames Valley London; Westminster; Westminster (CHE) (Orthotics/ Prosthetics); Willesden (CT) (Gen Eng inc CAE).

Higher Diploma courses (Scotland):
    Bell (CT); Dundee (IT); Falkirk (CT); Glasgow Caledonian; Inverness (Coll); James Watt (Coll); Kirkcaldy (Coll); Napier EE; Robert Gordon.

Alternative offers:

IB offers: **Aberdeen** 24 pts; **Brunel** 30 pts. **Cambridge** H777; **Cardiff** 28 pts; **City** 26 pts; **Coventry** 24 pts; **Durham** H666; **Exeter** 30 pts; **Hull** 28 pts H55 in maths and physics; **Lancaster** 30 pts; **Leicester** 30 pts; **London (QMW)** 30 pts; **Loughborough** H66 in maths and physics; **Oxford** H777; **Surrey** 28 pts H555; **Swansea** 28 pts.

Irish offers: **Aberdeen** BBCCC; **Brunel** AABBB.

SCE offers: **Aberdeen** BBBC; **Edinburgh** BBBB; **Lancaster** ABBB; **Napier** CCC; **Oxford Brookes** International Foundation Programme available; **Robert Gordon** BBC; **Stirling** BBBC; **Strathclyde** BBBB, BBCC (Prosth/Orth).

Overseas applicants: Manadon (RNEC) Fluency in technical English required. **Liverpool** Foundation course offered. **Warwick** and **Coventry (TC)** offer a one-year preparatory course for international students who have failed to achieve the right entry grades. Details from The International Office at Warwick University.

CHOOSING YOUR COURSE (See also Ch 1)

> **Subject information:** These courses provide the opportunity to study two, three or four engineering specialisms and enable students to delay their choice of specialism. Mathematics and physics provide the foundation of engineering subjects. Several universities and colleges now offer one year foundation courses for applicants with non-science A-levels. Many sponsorships are available in engineering subjects. National Engineering Scholarships available - apply to the Department for Education.

Course highlights: Aston After common first year students have wide choice of options within the engineering and computer technologies. **Bath** Engineering offered with French or German. Choice between Aero/Mech/Man Engineering can be delayed until year 2. **Brunel** (SEP) Broad-based programme covering mechanical, electrical and manufacturing engineering with a significant management content. All students sponsored by one of 50 companies. **Cambridge** Two extra years of study are required for the Production and Chemical Engineering Tripos examination. **Central England** First year involves electrical, mechanical, electronic and manufacturing engineering together with computer programming. **Coventry** Course based on modules which the student selects to make up his/her degree. Choice includes mechanical, electrical, manufacturing and building services engineering, design, management and language. **Durham** Common course for first 5 terms; in final 4 terms students specialise in civil or mechanical or electrical or electronic engineering. **Edinburgh** Common first year with later specialism in one of 11 engineering subjects. **Exeter** Core course in year 1 then BEng or BSc in General Engineering or one from chemical, civil, electrical, electronic or mechanical engineering. **Greenwich** Language option and sandwich placements abroad. **Huddersfield** Common first year covers mechanical science and materials, electrical science, electronics, fluids and hydraulics. **Hull** 50% continuous assessment. All students eligible for bursary. 95% of all graduates find positions in industry. **Humberside** Course covers electrical and mechanical engineering. **Lancaster** Choice in year 2 from civil, environmental, electronic, mechanical, mechatronic engineering. **Leicester** Foundation year for all followed by specialisation in civil, mechanical or electrical engineering. **London (QMW)** Flexible programme leading to options in mechanical, aeronautical or civil engineering. **Loughborough** Years 1 & 2 common, then choice from electrical, production, mechanical or transport technology. **Manadon (RNEC)** Civilian students can apply with an LEA grant. **Manchester Met** Optical Fibre Communication VLSI, CAD. Continuous element to courses. **Newcastle** Course includes electronic and mechanical subjects with computer technology and business management. **Portsmouth** Electro-mechanical engineering with an emphasis on systems engineering. Integrated engineering programme. **Reading** Course tailored to achieve balanced approach between mechanical, electrical and electronic engineering. **Robert Gordon** (Eng Tech) Course covers mechanical, electro-mechanical and offshore engineering. (See also **Technology**). **Sheffield Hallam** (Eng Bus St) A broad-based engineering course in mechanical and manufacturing engineering. **Strathclyde** (Eng Sci) A 5-year general engineering course; covers electrical and electronic, mechanical and production engineering supported by mathematics, computing, management and possible foreign language classes.

Swansea Broad engineering course with options in civil, mechanical or electrical engineering and computer science or management science. **Ulster** Specialist studies in final year include electronics, engineering design and ship design and production. **Warwick** Course comprises common first year which then feeds into 2-year programmes in each of civil, mechanical, electrical and general engineering. **Wolverhampton** Computer-assisted learning, supportive tutorial system. Modular-based scheme gives considerable flexibility with business studies, languages etc. Options in manufacturing or product engineering and physical electronics. **Cambridge, Oxford, Warwick, Hull** High research ratings. NOW CHECK PROSPECTUSES FOR ALL COURSES.

Study opportunities abroad: Aberdeen (E); **Brunel** (E) D; **City** (E); **Coventry** (E) SP G FR; **Exeter** FR G; **Lancaster** USA; **London (QMW)** (E) FR G; **Portsmouth** (SEP) (E); **Strathclyde** EUR; **Surrey** (E); **Ulster** CAN; **Wolverhampton** (E).

Work opportunities abroad: Bournemouth (Eng Bus Dev) FR USA; **Bristol UWE** (Export Eng) G; **Brunel** FR G NL D USA; **Cardiff** G; **Central England** (E); **Exeter** (E); **Napier** FR G; **Nottingham Trent** G; **Oxford Brookes** EUR; **Plymouth** FR G; **Portsmouth** FR G NL USA CAN AUS NZ IT GR; **Surrey** EUR USA; **Ulster** USA CAN; **Warwick** (E).

ADMISSIONS INFORMATION

Number of applicants per place (approx): Aberdeen 6; **Aston** 8; **Bath** (Eng/Lang) 8; **Bournemouth** 5; **Brunel** 4; **Cardiff** 4; **City** 3; **Coventry** 4; **De Montfort** 5; **Durham** 5; **Edinburgh** 5; **Exeter** 7; **Glasgow Caledonian** 10; **Hull** 6; **Lancaster** 15; **Liverpool** 8; **Leicester** 15; **Loughborough** 9; **Manchester Met** 8; **Nottingham Trent** 5; **Robert Gordon** 2; **Sheffield Hallam** 3; **South Bank** 5; **Surrey** 7; **Warwick** 10.

General Studies acceptable: Aberdeen; Aston; Coventry; De Montfort; Exeter; Hull; Lancaster; Liverpool; Manchester Met; Portsmouth; South Bank; Surrey.

Selection interviews: Bath; Brunel (inc two selection tests); Cambridge; Coventry (T); Durham; Lancaster; Liverpool; Loughborough; Manadon (RNEC) (T); Manchester Met; Oxford; Oxford Brookes (English test for overseas students); Robert Gordon (some); Surrey.

Offers to applicants repeating A-levels: Higher Aston, Loughborough, Manchester Met; **Possibly higher** Coventry, De Montfort, Durham, Edinburgh, Lancaster, Manchester Met, Robert Gordon, Sheffield Hallam; **Same** Aston, Brunel (SEP) (Good reasons needed for repeating), Central England, Manadon (RNEC), South Bank.

Admissions Tutors' advice: Brunel (Sp Eng Prog) Looks for high intellectual abilities, creativity, substantial interests in engineering and in 'practical' things for example, making, designing. Apply early and ask for a visit before completing UCAS application. Two selection tests and two interviews and a group problem-solving exercise. **Liverpool** Unusual subject combinations at A-level are considered. An interest in broad-based engineering is important. Relevant work experience can be an advantage. **Manadon (RNEC)** Applicants wanting to join the Royal Navy as Engineering Officers selected by Admiralty Interview Board. Civilian students sponsored by defence contractor firms are interviewed by the college. **Loughborough** Interview consists of an introduction to department's activities, a tour of facilities, and an individual interview with member of academic staff. Parents and/or training managers are also invited to visit department at time of interview. Main purpose of interview is to provide conditions for free exchange of information and views between applicants and staff about basic academic and career objectives and requirements. Also it enables staff to become more keenly aware of motivation and aspirations of individual applicants who can also get some idea of social and physical environment of university. **Portsmouth** Students encouraged to take sandwich courses in view of excellent industrial placements.

Examples of interview questions: Why Engineering? What branch of engineering interests you the most? Define information technology. What do you think the power of the future will be? Questions on the applications of physics and applied maths to engineering, for example transmission of electricity, nuclear power and aeronautics. What practical engineering experience have you had? Applications of robots in industry. What did your art A-level course contain? What interests you in architecture? Explain the theory of an arch; what is its function? What is the connection between distance and velocity and acceleration and velocity? A wing-tip is vibrating; what device could we use to measure the velocity of the wing-tip? Instead of a wave we get a noise; if we integrate does noise increase or decrease? If we differentiate what happens? Do you have a record player? Does it have treble and bass controls? What do they do? How does a car ignition work? Questions on the viscosity of gases, the design factors of electrical cables and the magnetic and electrical effects on optical fibres. Technical problems involving a system of gears (for example, a cycle going uphill).

GAP YEAR ADVICE

Institutions accepting a Gap Year: Most institutions; **South Bank** Learn to use a computer; **Surrey** Preferably not. Prefer direct entry since the course is a sandwich with industrial placement. Gap students should try to get engineering experience. **Swansea** Obtain work experience in any aspect of engineering.

Institutions willing to defer entry after A-levels (see Ch 5): Bath (but give notice before April); Brunel; Plymouth; Robert Gordon; Salford (UC); South Bank; Staffordshire; Surrey; Swansea; UMIST; Westminster.

AFTER A-LEVELS ADVICE

Institutions which may accept the same points score after A-levels: Most institutions.

Institutions demanding the actual grades offered after A-levels: Brunel (SEP); Durham (usually); Stirling.

Institutions which may accept under-achieving applicants after A-levels: Most institutions.

Institutions with vacancies in Aug/Sept 1992 (see Ch 5): Aberdeen; Aston; Brunel (Ind Des Eng), (Foundation) 8 pts, (SEP) BBB; Glamorgan; Liverpool; London (QMW); Paisley; Plymouth; Portsmouth; RNEC Manadon; Robert Gordon; Salford (UC); Sheffield Hallam 4 pts; South Bank; Southampton (IHE); Staffordshire; Strathclyde; Sunderland; Surrey; Swansea 14 pts; Trinity & All Saints (CHE); Westminster; most institutions are likely to have vacancies in 1993 in this subject and in the various specialisms.

ADVICE FOR MATURE STUDENTS

Academic qualifications are important although industrial experience is also given serious consideration. An average of 3% of mature students are admitted to Engineering courses each year. Foundation and Access to Science and technology courses should be given serious consideration by mature students interested in these subjects. **Aston** 10%.

GRADUATE EMPLOYMENT

New Graduates' destinations (percentages) 1991:
Permanent employment: U 89; P 62; C 100.
Unemployment: U 8; P 30; C 0.
Further studies (all types): U 17; P 23; C 96.
Main career destinations (approx): Engineering 59; Computing 14; Finance/Business 22.

Surrey (Engineering with Business Management) 15 graduates went into full-time employment, most associated with engineering occupations. Apart from two who are studying for MSc degrees, the remaining two are in training as a lawyer and an accountant respectively.

The following institutions are perceived as above average in producing graduates for employment: Aston, Bath, Birmingham, Bradford, Brunel, Cambridge, Leeds, Loughborough,

Manchester, Nottingham, Sheffield Hallam, Southampton, UMIST, Warwick. (See PIP references in Chapter 5.)

ENGINEERING (ACOUSTICAL)

Special subject requirements: See **Engineering.**

NB Institutions may raise or lower the level of published offers depending either on the quality or otherwise of individual applications or the numbers of applications received; grades/points offered may be adjusted downwards after A-level results. The level of an offer is not indicative of the quality of a course.

18 pts.   **Salford** - CCC/BB (Elec Acous) (BTEC D maths + 2M)
            Southampton - CCC/CC approx (Acoustics)

CHOOSING YOUR COURSE (See also Ch 1)

> **Subject information:** Courses cover the measurement of sound, hearing, environmental health and legal aspects of acoustics and vibration. Acoustics topics are also involved in some music courses.

Course highlights: Salford Optional year in industry; 37% marks for continuous assesment in final exams. NOW CHECK PROSPECTUSES FOR ALL COURSES.

ADMISSIONS INFORMATION

Number of applicants per place (approx): Salford 4.

> **Examples of interview questions:** What interests you about this subject? What career have you in mind on graduating?

AFTER A-LEVELS ADVICE

Institutions with vacancies in Aug/Sept 1992 (see Ch 5): Salford 12 pts.

ADVICE FOR MATURE STUDENTS

See under **Engineering.**

ENGINEERING (AERONAUTICAL AND PROPULSION)

Special subject requirements: See **Engineering.**

NB Institutions may raise or lower the level of published offers depending either on the quality or otherwise of individual applications or the numbers of applications received; grades/points offered may be adjusted downwards after A-level results. The level of an offer is not indicative of the quality of a course.

30 pts.   **Cambridge** - AAA potential recommended (Aer Eng)
26 pts.   **Bristol** - ABB (AB in maths/phys/eng sci) (Aero Eng; Av Sys; Aero/Euro) (BTEC Ds +Ms)
            Southampton - 26 pts - B in maths (All courses)
24 pts.   **City** - BBB/AA (Aero Eng, MEng) (BTEC not considered)
            London (Imp) - ABC-BBC (H400; H401)

Loughborough - 24-22 pts/18-16 pts (Aero Eng) (BTEC maths 80%+4M)
UMIST - BBB (Aero Eng)
York - BBB/BB (Avionics) (BTEC Ds+Ms)
22 pts. **Bath** - BBC (Aero Eng; Aero Eng/Fr; Aero Eng/Ger) (BTEC 2D+1M)
Liverpool - 22 pts approx (Aero Eng)
Manchester - BBC approx (Aero Eng)
Salford - BBC/BB (Aero Eng; Aero Sys) (BTEC 3M))
20 pts. **Belfast** - BCC/BB (Aero Eng; Aero Extd)
City - BCC/BB (Aero Eng; Air Trans) (BEng courses) (BTEC Ds+Ms)
Cranfield (Shrivenham) - BCC/BB (Aero Mech Syst Eng) (BTEC 3M)
London (QMW) - BCC/BB (Aero Eng; Avion)
18 pts. **Salford** - CCC/BB (Aero Syst)
16 pts. **City** - CCD/CC (Air Trans) (BTEC Ds+Ms)
Glasgow - BB (1st yr entry) ABC (2nd yr entry) (Av/Aero)
14 pts. **Hertfordshire** - CDD-DDD/CC-CD (Aero Eng) (BTEC D maths +2M)
10 pts. **and below**
Bristol UWE - (Aero Man Eng) (6 AS)
Coventry - (Aero Sys Eng) (4 AS)
Kingston - 10 pts (Aero Eng)
North East Wales (IHE) - (Man Eng (Aero))
Salford (UC) - (2x2 course Man Eng Aero)

Offers for Foundation, Certificate and Diploma courses (see Ch 5):

Higher National Diploma courses:
 4 pts. **and below** Bristol UWE; Hertfordshire; North East Wales (IHE); Southall (CT).

Alternative offers:

IB offers: **Bath** 30 pts maths/phys 5; **Belfast** H655 S555; **Bristol** 32 pts; **Bristol UWE** 26 pts; **City** BEng 28 pts, MEng 30 pts inc H555, (Air Transport) 31 pts inc H655; **Coventry** 24 pts; **Cranfield (Shrivenham)** H655; **London (QMW)** 26 pts; **Loughborough** 24 pts; **Salford** 30 pts.

SCE offers: **Glasgow** AAA-BBBBB; **Salford** BBBB.

CHOOSING YOUR COURSE (See also Ch 1)

Subject information: Courses cover the manufacture of military and civil aircraft, theories of mechanics, thermodynamics, electronics, computing and engine design and manufacture.

Course highlights: Bath Choice between Aeronautical, Mechanical and Manufacturing Engineering can be delayed until year 2. **Belfast** Course covers manufacture and operation of civil and military aircraft. **Bristol** (Av Sys) Covers aeronautical engineering/electronics/computer science. (Aero/ Euro) Year 3 in Europe. Course includes languages and European Studies. **City** Continuous assessment for 50% of course. **Cranfield (Shrivenham)** Common year 1 with Mechanical and Electronic Systems Engineering. Transfers possible before year 2. Final year based around aircraft design project. Helicopter aerodynamics part of the course. Cranfield flight test course included in final year. Scholarships available for well-qualified candidates. **Glasgow** Course share similar subjects in years 1 and 2 with Mechanical Engineering, Naval Architecture and Ocean Engineering. **Hertfordshire** Common year 1 with Mechanical and Vehicle Engineering. Emphasis on engineering applications and design. Most able students can transfer to MEng in year 2. **Kingston** First year common with Mechanical and Manufacturing degree courses. **London (Imp)** Broadly based courses in engineering science, combined with specialist study of aerodynamics and advanced structural mechanics. **London (QMW)** Course unit system allows flexible choice of subjects studied within the Aeronautical and Electronics departments. **Loughborough** Year 1 common with Automobile Engineering; transfers possible. **Salford** Scholarships available for women. NOW CHECK PROSPECTUSES FOR ALL COURSES.

Study opportunities abroad: City (E) D IRE; **Coventry** (E) FR G; **Cranfield (Shrivenham)** USA; **London (QMW)** (E) FR.

Work opportunities abroad: Bath FR G; **Coventry** FR G SP; **London (Imp)** FR G.

ADMISSIONS INFORMATION

Number of applicants per place (approx): Bath 13; **Belfast** 6; **Bristol** 10; **City** 20; **Coventry** 20; **Cranfield (Shrivenham)** 4; **Hertfordshire** 15; **London (Imp)** 7; **London (QMW)** 8; **Loughborough** 18; **Salford** 12; **Southampton** 13.

General Studies acceptable: Salford.

Selection interviews: Bath; Bristol; Cambridge; Kingston (some) (T); Loughborough (some).

Offers to applicants repeating A-levels: Higher Belfast, Bristol, Loughborough; **Possibly higher** Hertfordshire; **Same** Bath, City, Kingston.

Admissions Tutors' advice: Loughborough GCSE grade B average preferred. **Cranfield (Shrivenham)** Contact Admissions Tutor for two A-level entry.

> **Examples of interview questions:** Why Aeronautical Engineering? Questions about different types of aircraft and flight principles of helicopters.

GAP YEAR ADVICE

Institutions accepting a Gap Year: Most institutions; **Bath** Preferably should be for industrial training; **London (QMW)** Apply for a sponsorship to GEC Avionics/British Aerospace; **Loughborough** Seek sponsorship for the 1:3:1 scheme. See under **Engineering (Mechanical)**.

Institutions willing to defer entry after A-levels (see Ch 5): Bath (But give notice before April); City; Cranfield (Shrivenham); Hertfordshire; Kingston; Loughborough; York (No).

AFTER A-LEVELS ADVICE

Institutions which may accept the same points score after A-levels: City; Coventry; Cranfield (Shrivenham); Hertfordshire; Kingston; Loughborough; North East Wales (IHE).

Institutions demanding the actual grades after A-levels: Belfast; Bristol.

Institutions which may accept under-achieving applicants after A-levels: Bath; Belfast; Bristol; City; Coventry; Cranfield (Shrivenham); Loughborough.

Institutions with vacancies in Aug/Sept 1992 (see Ch 5): Bath; City (MEng) 18 pts; Cranfield (Shrivenham) 14 pts; Hertfordshire 8 pts; Kingston 8 pts; Liverpool; London (QMW); York 14 pts; 12-14 pts secured places in the more popular universities. Lower scores could also be considered for other courses. See also under **Engineering Science**.

ADVICE FOR MATURE STUDENTS

See under **Engineering**.

GRADUATE EMPLOYMENT

New Graduates' destinations (percentages) 1991:
Permanent employment: U 75; P 48.
Unemployment: U 20; P 43.
Further studies (all types): U 22; P 19.

Main career destinations (approx): Engineering 69; Management/Admin 24; Finance 4; Computing 2; Marketing 5.

ENGINEERING (AGRICULTURAL) (See also **Agriculture** in Agricultural Sciences)

Special subject requirements: 2 A-levels in mathematics and/or science subjects. GCSE (grade A-C) physics required.

NB Institutions may raise or lower the level of published offers depending either on the quality or otherwise of individual applications or the numbers of applications received; grades/points offered may be adjusted downwards after A-level results. The level of an offer is not indicative of the quality of a course.

18 pts.   **Cranfield (Silsoe)** - CCC/CC (Agric Eng; Rur Env Eng) (BTEC Ms)
           Newcastle - CCC/CD (Agric Eng; Food Proc Eng; Env Eng) (BTEC varies)
14 pts.   **Cranfield (Silsoe)** - CDD/CC (Ag Tech/Management) (BTEC Ms)
12 pts.   **Harper Adams (CAg)** - DDD/CC (Agric Eng) (4 AS) (BTEC 3M)
10 pts.   **Harper Adams (CAg)** - DDE/CD (Rural Tech/BS) (BTEC 3M)

Offers for Foundation, Certificate and Diploma courses (see Ch 5):

Higher National Diploma courses (England and Wales):
     4 pts. **and below** Rycotewood (Coll); Harper Adams (CAg); Writtle (CAg).

Higher Diploma courses (Scotland):
     4 pts. **and below or equivalent** Bell (CT) and SAC (Au).

Alternative offers:

IB offers: **Harper Adams (CAg)** 24 pts; **Cranfield (Silsoe)** (Ag Eng) H555; **Newcastle** Individual basis.

Overseas applicants: Newcastle Induction courses.

CHOOSING YOUR COURSE (See also Ch 1)

> **Subject information:** This is a study of agricultural, food or environmental engineering systems.

Course highlights: Harper Adams (CAg) Strong emphasis on business studies and computer-aided engineering. **Newcastle** (Agric Food Env) Common first year for engineering subjects. Foundation year available for students who cannot meet entry requirements. NOW CHECK PROSPECTUSES FOR ALL COURSES.

Work opportunities abroad: Cranfield (Silsoe) USA AUS COL EUR K NI SWZ PA Z BZ CAM; **Harper Adams (CAg)** NL AF; **Newcastle** G.

ADMISSIONS INFORMATION

Number of applicants per place (approx): Cranfield (Silsoe) 1; **Harper Adams (CAg)** (Agric Tech) 3, (Agric Eng) 5; **Newcastle** 4.

> **Examples of interview questions:** What kind of work are you interested in after completing your degree course? What do you already know about agricultural engineering?

GAP YEAR ADVICE

Institutions accepting a Gap Year: Most institutions; **Harper Adams (CAg)** A year on a farm prior to entry is recommended. **Newcastle** Relevant experience useful.

Institutions willing to defer entry after A-levels (see Ch 5): Cranfield (Silsoe); Newcastle (No).

AFTER A-LEVELS ADVICE

Institutions with vacancies in Aug/Sept 1992 (see Ch 5): Cranfield (Silsoe) 14 pts; Harper Adams (CAg) 8-6 pts; Newcastle 16 pts.

ADVICE FOR MATURE STUDENTS

See under **Engineering**.

ENGINEERING (CHEMICAL)

Special subject requirements: 2-3 A-levels from mathematics/science subjects. Chemistry is usually essential; physics and mathematics also important for some courses.

NB Institutions may raise or lower the level of published offers depending either on the quality or otherwise of individual applications or the numbers of applications received; grades/points offered may be adjusted downwards after A-level results. The level of an offer is not indicative of the quality of a course.

30 pts.	**Cambridge** - AAA potential recommended (Chem Eng)
26 pts.	**Aston** - 26 pts (MEng - Chem Eng/App Eng; Chem Proc Eng)
	Bradford - ABB (Chem Eng - MEng)
24 pts.	**London (Imp)** - BBB-BBC (Chem Eng - MEng) (4 AS)
22 pts.	**Aston** - 22 pts (Chem Eng; Chem Eng/Eur)
	Bath - BBC or 22 pts (Ch Bio Pr Eng; Chem Eng)
	Birmingham - BBC/22 pts (All courses)
	Bradford - BBC-CCC (BEng Chem Eng; Chem Eng Man)
	Leeds - BBC-BCC (Math Chem Eng) (BTEC Ds or Ms)
	Loughborough - BBC-BCC (Chem Eng 3 and 4)
	Manchester - 22-20 pts approx (Nucl Eng)
	Nottingham - BBC-BCC (Chem Eng)
	Swansea - BBC/BB (MEng) (BTEC 3M)
	UMIST - BBC (All courses) (BTEC D maths +Ds+Ms)
20 pts.	**Belfast** - BCC (Chem Eng)
	Leeds - BCC (Env Chem Eng - new course; Chem Eng)
	London (Imp) - 20 pts minimum (MEng Petr Eng)
	London (UC) - BCC approx (Chem Eng; Chem Eng/Eur)
	Newcastle - BCC/BC (Chem Eng; Chem Proc Eng) (BTEC Ds or Ms)
	Nottingham - BCC-CCC (Chem Proc Mat)
	Sheffield - BCC (Chem Eng/Fuel; Chem Eng/Bio)
	Surrey - BCC (All courses - lower offers for Integrated Foundation Year) (BTEC Ms)
	Swansea - BCC/BB (All courses except under **22 pts**)
18 pts.	**Belfast** - CCC/BC (Chem/Food Eng; Chem Extd)
	Bradford - CCC/BB (Foundation Year/Chem Eng)
	Edinburgh - CCC (Chem Eng)
	Exeter - CCC/BC (Chem/Proc Eng; Engin) (4 AS) (BTEC Ms)
	Leeds - CCC/BB (Fuel Eng) (Any 4 AS)
	London (UC) - CCC (Biochem Eng)

16 pts. **Heriot-Watt** - CCD/CD (maths C, chem D) (O Eng/Ch Eng; Energy Res/ Ch Eng) (2 AS pref chem/phys C)
    London (Imp) - 16 pts (Eng Pet St)
    Strathclyde - CCD (BCC 2nd yr entry) (Chem Eng; Chem Eng Proc Biotech)

14 pts. **Heriot-Watt** - CDD (maths C, chem D)/CD (maths C) (O Eng) (2 AS pref chem/phys C)
    Huddersfield - 12 pts (Ap Chem)
    Teesside - 12-8 pts (Chem Eng) (4 AS) (BTEC 3M)

8 pts. **and below**
    Coventry - 8 pts (Energy st) (BTEC Ms)
    Glamorgan - DD (Chem Eng) (4 AS)
    Greenwich - (Poly Eng) (4 AS)
    Napier - DD (Energy Eng)
    North London - (Poly Eng)
    Paisley - (Chem Eng)
    South Bank - 8 pts (Chem Eng) (4 AS) (BTEC Ms - maths/phys/chem)

Franchised degree and HND courses (see Ch 5):
    South Bank - South Bank (CFE).

Offers for Foundation, Certificate and Diploma courses (see Ch 5):

Higher National Diploma courses (England and Wales):
4 pts. **and below** Farnborough (CT) (Energy Management); Glamorgan; Huddersfield; South Bank; Teesside.

Higher Diploma courses (Scotland):
2 pts. **or equivalent** Kirkcaldy (CT) (Petroleum Eng).

Alternative offers:

IB offers: **Bath** 30 pts inc 16 pts Highers; **Belfast** H655 S555; **Exeter** 30 pts; **Heriot-Watt** 26 pts; **Leeds** 30 pts; **Loughborough** 25 pts H555; **Newcastle** H555; **Surrey** 28 pts inc H555in maths, phys, chem; **Swansea** 28 pts; **Teesside** 24 pts H555; **UMIST** 32-31 pts.

SCE offers: **Edinburgh** BBBB; **Heriot-Watt** (1st yr) BBBC, (2nd yr) AABB + good SYS; **Leeds** (Fuel Eng) BBB; **Sheffield** BBBB; **Strathclyde** ABBC/BBBB.

Overseas applicants: Bath One month remedial English course. **Leeds** Foundation course available. **UMIST** Foundation course available.

CHOOSING YOUR COURSE (See also Ch 1)

> **Subject information:** Courses are based on maths, physics and chemistry and lead on to studies in energy resources, nuclear energy, pollution, petroleum engineering, bio-process engineering and biotechnology.

Course highlights: Aston MEng students in Chemical Process Engineering can take European Studies including French and German. **Bath** Flexible course choice in year 3, graduating in Chemical Engineering or Chemical and Bio Process Engineering. **Bradford** French and German options in year 1; 60% of students have at least one six-month placement abroad. **Heriot-Watt** Range of language and business studies electives in years 1 and 2. **Glamorgan** Bias towards energy studies, biotechnology and computer-aided process engineering; language studies possible. **Leeds** Strong chemistry content. (Math Chem Eng) Unique course for those who could follow Maths or Chemical Engineering courses. (Fuel Eng) Course covers all aspects of energy supply and conservation including major fuels, coal, oil, gas and nuclear as well as alternative sources such as solar, biomass, wind, wave etc. **London (Imp)** Years 3 and 4 options include management, nuclear chemical engineering, energy fuels and pollution biotechnology. Language options include Japanese. **London (UC)** First year of the 3-year course concentrates on science, with courses in chemistry, computing, mathematics and transport processes, experimental aspects. **Loughborough** All courses have common years 1 and 2; transfers possible up to end of year 2. Emphasis on plant safety, loss prevention, environmental protection, food and other bioprocessing. **South Bank** Specialisation in biochemical engineering, energy engineering and materials. **Teesside** Subjects covered include biotechnology, separation processes and process and systems design. **UMIST** Strong interest in chemical plant design. Optional year out. Environmental technology, biotechnology, French or German options. High research ratings at **Cambridge, London (Imp), (UC), UMIST. Teesside.** NOW CHECK PROSPECTUSES FOR ALL COURSES.

Study opportunities abroad: Bath (E); **Birmingham** (E); **Bradford** (E); **Exeter** (E); **Glamorgan** (E); **Heriot-Watt** (E); **Leeds** FR G; **London (Imp)** FR; **Loughborough** (E); **Newcastle** (E)FR SP IT GR; **Swansea** (E); **Teesside** (E); **UMIST** FR G.

Work opportunities abroad: Aston EUR; **Bath** EUR; **Bradford** (E) FR G; **Glamorgan** FR G IT SP AUS; **Leeds** (E); **London (Imp)** (E) EUR; **Loughborough** EUR FR G N IT USA; **Newcastle** AUS USA G CZ SA; **North London** EUR; **South Bank** EUR; **Surrey** FR G AUS USA CAN NZ SZ; **Teesside** BR EUR USA.

ADMISSIONS INFORMATION

Number of applicants per place (approx): Aston 6; **Bath** 10; **Bradford** 5; **Birmingham** 5; **Coventry** 2; **Glamorgan** 10; **Heriot-Watt** 8; **Huddersfield** 7; **Leeds** (Fuel) 2, (Chem) 9; **London (Imp)** 4, (MEng) 4; **Loughborough** 6; **Newcastle** 6; **Nottingham** 6; **Sheffield** 14; **South Bank** 6; **Strathclyde** 6; **Surrey** 5; **Swansea** 8; **Teesside** 4; **UMIST** 10.

General Studies acceptable: Aston; Exeter; Heriot-Watt (grade C); Leeds; Loughborough (2).

Selection interviews: Aston; Bradford; Cambridge; Glamorgan; Leeds (some); Newcastle; Nottingham; South Bank; Surrey; Swansea; Teesside; UMIST.

Offers to applicants repeating A-levels: Higher Swansea, UMIST; **Possibly higher** Bath, Belfast, Leeds, South Bank; **Same** Aston, Bradford, Exeter, Loughborough, Nottingham, Surrey, Swansea, Teesside, Ulster.

Admissions Tutors' advice: Aston MEng students need GCSE grades A-C in French or German. **Bath** Students taking A-level maths and chemistry may offer AS physics (not essential unless physics has not been taken at GCSE). **Coventry** Full-time or sandwich courses available. **Leeds** Standard offer can be made without interview to high achieving candidates taking usual subjects, but all are invited for a visit. An individual approach is taken to others in which the interview may be very important. **Newcastle** No decisions made before interview. **Nottingham** looks for high academic abilities, plus personality and temperament to make good professional engineers; interview important part of selection procedure. **UMIST** Course requires good grounding in mathematics and physics, and fair knowledge of chemistry. Offers rarely made for less than three A-levels. Candidates other than A-level students all treated as special cases on 'merit'.

> **Examples of interview questions:** Discuss some industrial applications of chemistry. How would you justify the processing of radioactive waste to people living in the neighbourhood? What is public health engineering? What is biochemical engineering? What could be the sources of fuel and energy in the year 2088?

GAP YEAR ADVICE

Institutions accepting a Gap Year: Most institutions; **Bradford** If working with a chemical firm discuss your arrangements with admissions tutor; **Glamorgan** Sandwich courses may provide a better experience; **Loughborough** Take a job in the process industries; **Newcastle** Year must have real purpose; **South Bank** No; **Surrey** Keep up with mathematics; **UMIST** Year out in the process industry is valuable.

Institutions willing to defer entry after A-levels (see Ch 5): Coventry; Glamorgan; Heriot-Watt; Leeds; Newcastle; Surrey; Swansea; UMIST.

AFTER A-LEVELS ADVICE

Institutions which may accept the same points score after A-levels: Aston; Bath; Bradford; Glamorgan; Leeds; Loughborough; Newcastle; South Bank; Strathclyde; Surrey; Teesside; UMIST.

Institutions demanding the actual grades offered after A-levels: Nottingham.

Institutions which may accept under-achieving applicants after A-levels: Bath; Belfast; Bradford; Glamorgan; Leeds; Loughborough; Newcastle; Surrey; Swansea; Teesside; UMIST; most new universities.

Institutions with vacancies in Aug/Sept 1992 (see Ch 5): Aston; Bath; Coventry; Glamorgan 8 pts; Heriot-Watt 14 pts; Leeds; Newcastle; Paisley; South Bank 8 pts; Swansea 14 pts.

ADVICE FOR MATURE STUDENTS

Coventry Mature students represent 10% of intake. Industrial experience in relevant areas in part compensates for lack of formal qualifications. Each application is treated on merit. See also under **Engineering**.

GRADUATE EMPLOYMENT

New Graduates' destinations (percentages) 1991:
Permanent employment: U 84; P 64.
Unemployment: U 13; P 35.
Further studies (all types): U 20; P 21.
Main career destinations (approx): Engineering 82; Finance 6; Admin 10; Computing 2.

Surrey The great majority of graduates went into various branches of chemical engineering (chemicals, air products, environmental, oil and petroleum, paint and water engineering).

Teesside All graduates moving into full-time employment secured work in the industry with major chemical firms.

ENGINEERING (CIVIL) (including Engineering (Environmental))

Special subject requirements: 2-3 A-levels from mathematics/science subjects. English and chemistry important at GCSE (grade A-C) for some courses.

NB Institutions may raise or lower the level of published offers depending either on the quality or otherwise of individual applications or the numbers of applications received; grades/points offered may be adjusted downwards after A-level results. The level of an offer is not indicative of the quality of a course.

30pts.	**Cambridge/Oxford** - AAA potential recommended (Eng)
24pts.	**Brunel** - BBB (Env Syst Des; Env Eng) (BTEC D+Ms)
	City - BBB/AA (Civ Eng) (MEng) (BTEC not considered)
	Durham - BBB (Eng)
	Southampton - 24 pts min (Civ Eng; Env Eng - MEng)
22pts.	**Surrey** - BBC (Civ Eng; Civ Lang; Civ Eng Comp; MEng)
	Warwick - BCC-CCC (Eng Civil)
20pts.	**Belfast** - BCC (Civil Eng; Civil Extd)

Birmingham - BCC-CCC (Civ Eng courses)
Bristol - BCC (Civ Eng)
London (Imp) - BCC/AB-BB (Civ Eng; Civ Eng/Eur)
Newcastle - BCC (Str Eng)
Nottingham - BCC-CCC (Civ Eng; Env Eng)
Southampton - 20-18 pts (Civ Eng; Env Eng - BEng)
Surrey - BCC-BCD/AB-BB (Civ Eng Comp; Civ Eur; Civ Eng BEng) (BTEC 2D inc maths+3M)

18 pts. **Aston** - CCC/AB (Civ Eng; Civ Eng/Eur) (BTEC D+M)
Bath - CCC/AB (Civil/Str; Build/Str)
Brighton - CCC/BC (Env Eng; Civ Eng; Arch Eng) (BTEC Ds or Ms)
Cardiff - CCC/BB (All courses) (BTEC 3M)
City - CCC/BB (Civil Eng - BEng) (BTEC 1D+Ms)
Cranfield (Shrivenham) - BCD/CC (Civ Eng)
Cranfield (Silsoe) - CCC (Env Eng)
Exeter - CCC/BC (Civ Eng) (4 AS) (See also **Engineering Sciences**)
Lancaster - CCC (Civ Eng)
Leeds - CCC/CC (Civ Eng)
Leeds - CCC (Civ Eng/Arch; Arch Eng - see **Admissions Tutors' advice**)
Liverpool - CCC/BB (Civil Eng 4; Civ/Str Eng; Civ/Mar Eng) (4 AS)
London (UC) - CCC (Civ Eng)
Loughborough - CCC/18 pts (Civil Eng courses) (BTEC D maths+3M)
Manchester - 18 pts approx (Civil Eng)
Newcastle - CCC/CC (Env Eng all courses) (BTEC average 70%)
Sheffield - CCC/BB (Civ/Str Eng) (6 AS) (BTEC D maths+Ms)
Strathclyde - CCC (2nd yr entry) (Civ Eng)
Strathclyde - CCC (BBC 2nd yr entry) (Env Eng)
Swansea - CCC/BC (Civ Eng; Civ Eng/Euro) (BTEC 5M)
UMIST - CCC/AB-BB (All courses) (BTEC 3D inc maths)

16 pts. **Bradford** - CCD/BB (Civ Eng Foundation course; BEng; MEng) (4 AS) (BTEC 4M)
Edinburgh - CCD (Civ Eng; St/Fire Eng)
London (QMW) - CCD (Civ Eng)
Nottingham Trent - 16 pts (Civ Eng)
Oxford Brookes - CCD-CDD/CC-CD (Civ Eng) (4 AS)
Salford - CCD/BB (Civil Eng/Euro St; Civ Eng) (BTEC 2D+3/4M)
Ulster - CCD/BC (Civil Eng) (AS des tech or contrasting subject)

14 pts. **Coventry** - 14-12 pts (Civ Eng; BEng/MEng; Env Eng - new course) (BTEC 4/5M)
Heriot-Watt - CDD maths C (1st yr entry) BCC maths B (2nd yr entry) (All courses inc O Eng/C Eng) (BTEC 1D+3M)
Hertfordshire - 14-12 pts (Civ Eng) (BTEC 2D or 5M)

12 pts. **Aberdeen** - CC (Civ Eng)
Dundee - DDD/CC (Civ Eng)
Glasgow - CC (Civil Eng; Civ Eng/Geol)
Greenwich - 12 pts (Eng Geol; Civ Eng)
Nottingham Trent - 12 pts (Eng Surv)
Portsmouth - 12 pts (Civ Eng) (4 AS) (BTEC 3M)
South Bank - 12 pts (Civ Eng; Env Eng) (4 AS) (BTEC 5M)
Westminster - 12 pts (Arch Eng) (BTEC M in maths)
Wolverhampton - (Civ Eng Man)

10 pts. **Coventry** - DDE/CD (Civ Eng Constr)
Dundee (IT) - CD (Civ Eng) (4 AS)
Glamorgan - 10 pts (Civ Eng) (4 AS) (BTEC 5M)
Kingston - 10 pts (Civil Eng)
Liverpool John Moores - (Civ Eng) (6 AS) (BTEC 3M)
Middlesex - 10-8 pts (Civ Eng; Con Eng Man) (BTEC 4M)
Plymouth - 10 pts (Civ Eng) (BTEC Ds+Ms)
Teesside - 10 pts (Civ Eng) (4 AS)
Westminster - 10-6 pts (Civ Eng) (4 AS)

8 pts. **and below**

Bolton (IHE) – 6 pts (Civ Eng; Cons Eng Man) (4 AS)
Derby – (Modular) (4 AS)
East London – (Civ Eng)
Glasgow Caledonian – (Civ Eng)
Napier – (Trans Eng; Civ Eng) (4 AS)
Paisley – (Civ Eng) (6 AS)
Sheffield Hallam – DD-DE (Civil Eng) (4 AS) (BTEC 5M)
Sunderland – 6 pts (Civ Eng) (BTEC 3M)

Franchised degree and HND courses (see Ch 5):
  South Bank – Guildford (CFE); Mid Kent (CFE); North East Surrey (CT); South Bank (CFE); Vauxhall (CFE); Waltham Forest (CFE); Westminster (CFE).

Offers for Foundation, Certificate and Diploma courses (see Ch 5):

Higher National Diploma courses (England and Wales):
4pts. **and below** Bolton (IHE); Cardiff (IHE); Doncaster (Coll); East London; Glamorgan; Greenwich; Hertfordshire; Kingston; Leeds Met; Liverpool John Moores; North East Wales (IHE); Nottingham Trent; Oxford Brookes; Plymouth; Portsmouth; Sheffield Hallam; South Bank; Stockport (CT); Teesside; Willesden (CT); Wolverhampton.

Higher Diploma courses (Scotland):
4pts. **and below or equivalent** Dundee (IT); Glasgow Caledonian; Napier EE.

Alternative offers:

IB offers: **Aberdeen** 24 pts; **Aston** 30 pts; **Bath** 28 pts H5 maths; **Belfast** H655 S555; **Bradford** 24 pts H655; **Brighton** 27 pts; **Bristol** 30 pts H66 in maths and physics; **Cardiff** 28 pts H555; **City** (MEng) 30 pts, (BEng) 28 pts; **Cranfield (Silsoe)** 30 pts inc H 15 pts; **Durham** H666; **Exeter** 30 pts; **Hertfordshire** 24 pts; **Heriot-Watt** 30 pts; **Liverpool** 28-24 pts; **Loughborough** 30 pts inc 15 pts Highers 5 pts in Maths; **Middlesex** 24 pts; **Sheffield** 30 pts inc 5 in maths; **Surrey** 26 pts H66; **Swansea** 28 pts; **UMIST** H666; **Westminster** 24 pts.

Irish offers: **Aberdeen** BBCCC; **Bristol** BBBCCC; **Glamorgan** CCCDD; **Sheffield** BBBCC inc English.

SCE offers: **Aberdeen** BBBC; **Dundee** BBB, B (maths) B (physics) CC (Civil); **City** AABB; **Durham** AAAAA; **Edinburgh** BBBB; **Glasgow** BBBB; **Heriot-Watt** BBBC; **Newcastle** BBB; **Paisley** BCC; **Sheffield** BBCC; **Sheffield Hallam** BBB; **Strathclyde** BBBC; **Sunderland** CCC.

Overseas applicants: Bath, Westminster, Competence in written and spoken English required. **Brighton** Two-week English language course available. **Liverpool John Moores, Newcastle** Foundation course offered. **City, Sheffield, Liverpool, Brighton, Westminster** and many other institutions: direct access possible to year two for some students.

CHOOSING YOUR COURSE (See also Ch 1)

Subject information: Specialist courses in this field may cover traffic and highway engineering, water and waste engineering, construction management, explosives and public health engineering. Essential elements in all courses, however, include surveying, design projects (eg, Channel Tunnel to suspension bridges) and building technology. Aesthetic design may also play a part in the design of some structures eg, motorway bridges.

Course highlights: Aston Course covers structural, public health and highway engineering and construction management. **Bradford** Strong emphasis on business, communication and design. **Brighton** Options in transportation, water, public health, river and coastal engineering, applied ecology. **Bristol** Third stage includes: The Engineer in Society as one of the core subjects with a range of options which may include water resources, traffic engineering, concrete technology, coastal engineering and

French. **Cranfield (Silsoe)** (Env Eng) Engineering for wildlife habitats, land restoration, waste treatment and erosion control. **Dundee** Three main options: building/management/civil; delayed choice until year three. **Hertfordshire** Options include civil engineering for developing countries, and water and environmental engineering. **Heriot-Watt** Opportunity to transfer between courses linking technology and management. **Glamorgan** Water, structural and highway engineering included as final year topics. **Liverpool** Fourth year specialisms in environmental, maritime and structural engineering. **London (Imp)** Unique in the number of options available including languages, management, earthquake engineering and water technology. **London (QMW)** Third year subjects include geotechnical and water engineering, transport studies and construction management. **Plymouth** Options include coastal, environmental, structural and highway engineering and a modern foreign language. **South Bank** Unit-based scheme offering five degree courses. **Strathclyde** Third year includes public health, traffic and highway engineering and the fourth year, practical design projects. **UMIST** Common first year for most Civil Engineering courses with option to select specialism in year two. **Westminster** (Arch Eng) Gives exemption from RIBA Part II. **Bristol, London (Imp), (UC), Newcastle, Surrey** High research ratings. NOW CHECK PROSPECTUSES FOR ALL COURSES.

Study opportunities abroad: Aston (E); **Birmingham** (E); **Bolton (IHE)** (E); **Brighton** (E); **Bristol** (E) FR G B SP IT (COMETT); **Cardiff** (E); **City** (E); **Coventry** (E) FR G SP; **Glamorgan** (E); **Heriot-Watt** (E); **Hertfordshire** (E); **Leeds** (E) FR; **Leeds Met**; **London (Imp)** (E) FR; **Loughborough** (E); **Middlesex** (E); **Newcastle** (Env Eng) (E); **Paisley** (E); **Plymouth** (E); **Salford** (E) FR; **Sheffield** (E) D; **Sheffield Hallam** (E); **Southampton** FR; **Strathclyde** (E) EUR; **Surrey**; **Swansea** (E); **Westminster** (E); **Wolverhampton** (E) G NL.

Work opportunities abroad: Aston FR G; **Bolton (IHE)** FR B IT; **Brighton** FR G; **Cardiff** EUR; **Coventry**; **Glamorgan** D P G FR IT SP; **Greenwich** B G FR; **Leeds Met**; **Newcastle** EUR USA; **Nottingham Trent**; **Oxford Brookes**; **Salford** FR G SP LUX; **South Bank**; **Surrey** FR G SZ SA IT HK.

ADMISSIONS INFORMATION

Number of applicants per place (approx): Aston 7; **Bath** 10; **Belfast** 6; **Bolton (IHE)** 6; **Bradford** (BEng) 6; **Brighton** 7; **Bristol** 9; **Cardiff** 12; **City** 5; **Coventry** (Civ Eng Constr) 8, (Civ Eng) 14; **Cranfield (Shrivenham)** 3; **Dundee** 8; **Dundee (IT)** 6; **Durham** 8; **Glamorgan** 5; **Glasgow Caledonian** 4; **Greenwich** 11; **Hertfordshire** 10; **Heriot-Watt** 7; **Leeds** 10; **Liverpool** 12; **Liverpool John Moores** 16; **London (Imp)** 4; **Loughborough** 8, (Civ/Ger) 3; **Middlesex** 3; **Napier** 6; **Newcastle** 11, (Env) 6; **Nottingham** 10; **Nottingham Trent** 11; **Oxford Brookes** 8; **Paisley** 4; **Plymouth** 16; **Portsmouth** 11; **Salford** 9; **Sheffield** 7; **Sheffield Hallam** 17; **South Bank** 5; **Strathclyde** 13; **Sunderland** 3; **Surrey** 5; **Swansea** 8; **Teesside** 15; **UMIST** 9; **Westminster** 8.

General Studies acceptable: Aston; Bradford; Brighton (2); Coventry (2); Cranfield (Shrivenham); Dundee; Exeter; Glamorgan; Greenwich; Hertfordshire; Leeds (some); Liverpool John Moores (2); Newcastle; Plymouth; Salford; Sheffield; South Bank (No); Teesside; Wolverhampton.

Selection interviews: Aston (some); Bath; Belfast (some); Bolton (IHE); Bradford (some); Brighton; Bristol; Cambridge; City; Coventry; Dundee (most applicants); Durham; Greenwich (some); Heriot-Watt (some); Kingston; Leeds; Liverpool; Loughborough (some); Newcastle (some); Nottingham (30%); Nottingham Trent; South Bank; Surrey; Swansea (some); UMIST; Westminster (some).

Offers to applicants repeating A-levels: Higher Belfast, Bolton (IHE), East London, Kingston, Liverpool John Moores, Nottingham, Oxford Brookes, Swansea, Teesside; **Possibly higher** Durham, Portsmouth, Southampton, UMIST; **Same** Aston, Birmingham, Bradford, Brighton, Bristol, City, Coventry, Greenwich, Leeds, Loughborough, Newcastle, Sheffield, South Bank.

Admissions Tutors' advice: Brighton All suitable applicants interviewed before decisions made. We look at predicted A-level or BTEC performance, motivation, knowledge of the construction industry and intuitive aptitude. **Greenwich** Applicants may receive 'dual' offers for degree and diploma courses with transfer from HND to BEng after 1-2 years' study. **Leeds** (Arch Eng) Not an Architecture course but covering important aspects of buildings and their structures. **Sheffield** A-level maths essential.

Sunderland A thin sandwich course so previous industrial experience (not generally applicable to A-level students) an asset and can counter-balance academic performance. **Westminster** (Arch Eng) Portfolio of sketches, photographs, technical drawings preferred.

Examples of interview questions: Why have you chosen Civil Engineering? Have you written to the Institute of Civil Engineers? How would you define the difference between the work of a civil engineer and the work of an architect? What would happen to a concrete beam if a load was applied? Where would it break and how could it be strengthened? The favourite question – why do you want to be a civil engineer? What would you do if you were asked to build a concrete boat? Do you know any civil engineers? What problems have been faced in building the Channel Tunnel?

GAP YEAR ADVICE

Institutions accepting a Gap Year: Most institutions; **Loughborough** Only if useful work is found; **Salford, Brighton** Extremely useful if time is spent in civil engineering or environmental industry; **Swansea** Obtain work experience; **Wolverhampton** Work in industry useful.

Institutions willing to defer entry after A-levels (see Ch 5): Aston; Bath; Bradford; Brighton; City; Coventry; Cranfield; Dundee; Glamorgan; Heriot-Watt; Hertfordshire; Newcastle; Plymouth; Portsmouth; Salford; South Bank, Surrey, Swansea; UMIST; Westminster (Arch Eng).

AFTER A-LEVELS ADVICE

Institutions which may accept the same points score after A-levels: Aston; Bolton (IHE); Bradford; Brighton; Bristol; City; Coventry; Dundee; Greenwich; Kingston; Leeds; Liverpool John Moores; Loughborough (usually); Manchester Met; Newcastle; Nottingham Trent; Oxford Brookes; Plymouth; Portsmouth; Salford; Sheffield; Sheffield Hallam; South Bank; Strathclyde; Sunderland; Surrey (perhaps); Swansea; Teesside; UMIST; Westminster.

Institutions demanding the actual grades offered after A-levels: Belfast; Bradford (BSc); Durham (usually); Liverpool; Nottingham; Southampton; Westminster.

Institutions which may accept under-achieving applicants after A-levels: Aberdeen; Aston; Belfast; Birmingham; Bradford; Brighton; City; Dundee; Heriot-Watt; Leeds; Liverpool; Liverpool John Moores; Loughborough; Newcastle; Nottingham; Salford; Sheffield; Surrey (perhaps); Swansea; Teesside; UMIST; Warwick; many other institutions.

Institutions with vacancies in Aug/Sept 1992 (see Ch 5): Aberdeen 14 pts; Aston 14 pts; Bath 16 pts; Bradford; Brighton 12 pts; Bristol; City (MEng) 18 pts, (BEng) 12 pts; Coventry; Cranfield (Shrivenham) (Civ Eng) 10 pts, Silsoe; Dundee; Glamorgan; Greenwich 10 pts; Heriot-Watt; Hertfordshire 10 pts; Kingston; Liverpool; London (QMW); Newcastle 16 pts, (Env Eng) 16 pts; Paisley; Plymouth 10-8 pts; Portsmouth 10 pts; Salford 10 pts; South Bank 10 pts; Strathclyde; Sunderland; Swansea 14 pts; UMIST 14 pts; Westminster (Arch Eng); see also under **Engineering Science.**

ADVICE FOR MATURE STUDENTS

See under **Engineering**.

GRADUATE EMPLOYMENT

New Graduates' destinations (percentages) 1991:
Permanent employment: U 87; P 76; C 100.
Unemployment: U 10; P 17; C 0.
Further studies (all types): U 14; P 8; C 0.
Main career destinations (approx): Environmental 91; Business 3; Finance 4.

Surrey 31 graduates entered full-time employment in 1990, 29 of whom entered civil engineering careers. The remaining two became a mini-cab driver and a trainee commercial pilot respectively.

Teesside All graduates entering full-time employment secured work in the industry as engineers.

The following institutions are perceived as above average in producing graduates for employment: Birmingham, Cambridge, Coventry, Leeds, Loughborough, Newcastle, Nottingham, Nottingham Trent, Portsmouth, Salford, Sheffield, Sheffield Hallam. (See PIP reference in Chapter 5.)

ENGINEERING (COMMUNICATIONS) (See also Electrical/ Electronic Engineering)

Special subject requirements: 2-3 A-levels in mathematics/science subjects.

NB Institutions may raise or lower the level of published offers depending either on the quality or otherwise of individual applications or the numbers of applications received; grades/points offered may be adjusted downwards after A-level results. The level of an offer is not indicative of the quality of a course.

26 pts.	**Bath** - ABB (Electron Eng)
	Bradford - ABB (ECCE; M Eng)
24 pts.	**Birmingham** - BBB-BBC (Commun)
22 pts.	**Kent** - BBC-BCC/BB (Comm/Eng)
18 pts.	**Bradford** - CCC/BB (ECCE; B Eng)
	Cranfield (Shrivenham) - CCC approx (Info Sys Eng; Comm Info Sys) (BTEC 4M)
	Essex - CCC (Co Co)
	Hull - BCD/BB (E Comm) (4 AS)
	London (QMW) - CCC/BC (Telecommun; Comm Eng)
12 pts.	**Leeds Met** - DDD/6 pts (Com Eng) (Ref EE)
	Napier - CC-EE (Comm Elect Eng)
10 pts.	**Northumbria** - CD (Comm Elect Eng) (4 AS) (BTEC Ms)
	Portsmouth - 10 pts (Comm Eng)
8 pts.	**and below**
	Anglia (Poly Univ) - EE (Telecom)
	Coventry - 8 pts (Comm Sys Eng)
	North London - DD (Elect/Com Eng)
	Plymouth - 6 pts (Com Eng) (BTEC M maths + Ms)

Offers for Foundation, Certificate and Diploma courses (see Ch 5):

Higher National Diploma courses:
  4 pts. and below Cardiff (IHE); Central England; East London; Liverpool John Moores; Luton (CHE); Plymouth; Ravensbourne (CDC).

Alternative offers:

IB offers: **Kent** 29 pts, H 13 pts.

CHOOSING YOUR COURSE (See also Ch 1)

> **Subject information:** This subject varies in content depending on the chosen course but it usually focuses on telecommunications and the design of systems.

Course highlights: Cranfield (Shrivenham) (Comm Info Sys) Open to beginners to computing. A-level maths not required. **Northumbria** Transfers possible to Elect/Electronic Engineering at end of year 1. NOW CHECK PROSPECTUSES FOR ALL COURSES.

Study opportunities abroad: Coventry FR G (optional); **London (QMW)** (E).

Work opportunities abroad: Coventry FR G SP.

ADMISSIONS INFORMATION

Number of applicants per place (approx): Bradford 9; **Coventry** 7; **Leeds Met** 8; **Northumbria** 10; **North London** 8; **Plymouth** 4.

General Studies acceptable: Coventry (No); London (QMW).

Selection interviews: Bradford; Kent; Leeds Met.

Offers to applicants repeating A-levels: Higher Leeds Met.

Admissions Tutors' advice: Leeds Met Looks for intellectual ability, interest in, and motivation towards, Communications Engineering. No offers made without interview.

> **Examples of interview questions:** See under **Electrical/Electronic Engineering**.

GAP YEAR ADVICE

Institutions accepting a Gap Year: Most institutions; **Anglia (Poly Univ)** Apply for place before taking gap year.

Institutions willing to defer entry after A-levels (see Ch 5): Coventry; Cranfield (Shrivenham); Plymouth.

AFTER A-LEVELS ADVICE

Institutions which may accept the same points score after A-levels: Bradford.

Institutions with vacancies in Aug/Sept 1992 (see Ch 5): Coventry; Cranfield (Shrivenham) 12 pts; Plymouth 4 pts.

ADVICE FOR MATURE STUDENTS

Coventry Maturity cannot replace qualifications. Access and Foundation courses giving entry to year 1 of the degree course available. See also under **Engineering**.

ENGINEERING (COMPUTER including CONTROL AND SYSTEMS) (See also under Computer Courses)

Special subject requirements: 2 A-levels in mathematics/physics subjects. Physics required at Hull and also GCSE (grade A-C) chemistry.

NB Institutions may raise or lower the level of published offers depending either on the quality or otherwise of individual applications or the numbers of applications received; grades/points offered may be adjusted downwards after A-level results. The level of an offer is not indicative of the quality of a course.

26 pts.   **Bradford** - ABB (ECC Eng) (MEng)
  Bristol - ABB (Comp/Euro)
  Southampton - ABB (Inf Eng)
  York - ABB/AB (Electro S Eng)

24 pts.   **Aberystwyth** - 24-18 pts (Soft Eng) (4 AS)
  Bangor - BBB (Comp/Sys; BEng/MEng)
  Bath - BBB-BBC (Syst Eng; Syst Eng/Fr; Syst Eng/Ger)
  Birmingham - BBB (Computer)
  Birmingham - BBB-BBC (Control)
  Durham - BBB (Eng)
  London (Imp) - BBB (Software Eng)
  Warwick - BBB-BBC (Comp Sys Eng)

22 pts.   **Bristol** - BBC (Comp Syst Eng)
  East Anglia - BBC (Comp Sys/NAM) (BTEC 5D)
  London (Imp) - BB maths/physics C (Inf Sys Eng)
  London (King's) - 22 pts approx (Comp Syst; Inf Sys courses)
  Newcastle - BBC/AB (Micro/Soft H690; MEng)
  Southampton - 22 pts C in maths (Comp Sys)
  Surrey - BBC-BCC (All courses) (BTEC 2D+Ms)
  UMIST - BBC (All courses) (BTEC Ds+Ms)
  York - 22 pts (Comp SS Eng; Info Eng) (See also **Computer Courses**)

20 pts.   **Birmingham** - BCC (Comp Software)
  Bradford - BCC/BB (ECC Eng) (BEng)
  Essex - BCC/BB (Int Bus Sys)
  Kent - BCC/BB (Comp Sys Eng)
  Lancaster - BCC (Inf Engin; Comp/Soft)
  Loughborough - BCC/BB (Syst Eng 3/4)
  Sheffield - BCC/BB (Software Eng; Control; Elec Con Syst; Electron/Info) (6 AS) (BTEC Ds+Ms)
  Stirling - BCC/DD (Soft Eng)

18 pts.   **Cranfield (Shrivenham)** - CCC (Inf Sys Eng)
  Edinburgh - CCC/BB (Comp Sci) (4 AS)
  Heriot-Watt - CCC (1st yr entry) BBB (2nd yr entry) (Info Sys)
  Hull - BCD/BB (Comp A Eng; Optel Sys; Con Robot;Inf Eng) (4 AS) (BTEC Ms and above)
  Liverpool - CCC/BC-CC (Comp/Micro Sys) (4 AS)
  London (QMW) - CCC (Comp Eng)
  Newcastle - CCC/BB-BC (Microelect; BEng)
  Strathclyde - CCC (Inf Eng)
  Sussex - CCC (CS Eng; C Eng)
  Ulster - CCC/BB (Elec Sys)

16 pts.   **City** - CCD/BC (Comp Sys Eng; Control) (BTEC 2D+3M)
  East Anglia - CCD/BB (Comp Syst Eng - see also **22 pts**) (BTEC 3M inc maths)
  Loughborough - BB-BC (Syst Eng)
  Manchester Met - 16-10 pts (Comb St)
  Reading - CCD (Cyb/Cont; Inf Sci Eng)

	Ulster - CCD (Comp Inf Sci)
12pts.	**Cranfield (Shrivenham)** - CC (CCCIS)
	De Montfort - 12 pts (Soft Eng) (BTEC 3D+3M)
	Glasgow - CC (Comp Int)
	Liverpool John Moores - 12 pts (Comp Aid Eng; Soft Eng - awaiting approval)
	Westminster - 12 pts (Con/Comp Eng) (BTEC D+Ms)
10pts.	**Glamorgan** - 10 pts (Soft Eng) (BTEC 4M)
8pts.	**and below**
	Anglia (Poly Univ) - (Eng Software; Comp Sci)
	Bangor - DD (Comp Sys Eng; Comp Sys/Maths) (BTEC Ms)
	Bournemouth - (Soft Eng Man; Comm Inf Syst) (BTEC 5M)
	Bristol UWE - (Dig Syst Eng) (6 AS) (BTEC Ds+Ms)
	Buckinghamshire (CHE) - (Comp Eng Euro)
	Central England - (ASE) (BTEC 5M)
	Coventry - 8 pts (All courses) (BTEC 3M)
	Glasgow Caledonian - DEE/DD (Comp Aid Eng)
	Huddersfield - (Comp Aid Eng; ESC)
	Kingston - DD (Comp Inf Sy)
	Leeds Met - DD (Man Sys Eng) (BTEC 6M)
	Manadon (RNEC) - 8 pts (Eng Sys)
	Napier - (Soft Eng; Eng Syst)
	Paisley - (Soft Eng)
	Salford (UC) - (Micro Con Eng)
	Sheffield Hallam - (CAE/Des; Elect Sy/Con Eng; Ins/Meas) (BTEC 3M)
	South Bank - (Eng Sys Des; Comp Inf Eng; Soft Eng) (BTEC 3M)
	Staffordshire - (Comp Aid Eng)
	Staffordshire - DD (Soft Eng) (4 AS) (BTEC 4M)
	Sunderland - 6 pts (Dig Sy Eng)
	Swansea (IHE) - EE (Comp Sys Eng) (4 AS)
	Teesside - 8 pts (Soft Eng; Instr/Con Eng; Comp Eng) (4 AS)
	Westminster - DD (Soft Eng - modular)

Franchised degree and HND courses (see Ch 5):

Liverpool John Moores - South Cheshire (CFE); Southport (CFE).
South Bank - South Bank (CFE).

Offers for Foundation, Certificate and Diploma courses (see Ch 5):

Higher National Diploma courses:

Computer Aided Engineering
4pts. **and below** Bournemouth (Eng); Cardiff (IHE); Central Lancashire (Eng); Glamorgan; Hertfordshire (Soft Eng); Liverpool John Moores; Luton (CHE); North East Wales (IHE); Norwich City (CHFE) (Eng); Salford (UC); Sandwell (CHFE) (Eng); Sheffield Hallam; South Bank; Swansea (IHE); Teesside.

Computer Technology
4pts. **and below** Mid-Kent (CHFE); Nottingham Trent (HITECC Diploma);Teesside; Thames Valley London; Westminster.

Control and Systems Engineering
4pts. **and below** Farnborough (CT); Huddersfield; North East Wales (IHE); Salford (UC).

Software Engineering
4pts. **and below** Anglia (Poly Univ); Coventry; Farnborough (CT); Hertfordshire; Leeds Met; Liverpool John Moores; Napier; Salford (UC) (Micro/Con/Soft).

Alternative offers:

IB offers: **Bangor** 28 pts; **Birmingham** 30 pts H5 in maths and another science; **Bristol** 30 pts H66; **City** 28 pts; **Cranfield (Shrivenham)** 28 pts inc H55 maths and physics; **Hull** 28 pts; **Kent** 27 pts, H 12 pts; **Lancaster** 30 pts H5 in maths; **Newcastle** H665 (MEng) Grades 5 (BEng); **South Bank** 24 pts; **UMIST** 30 pts H65 maths/phys; **York** 28 pts H5 maths.

Irish offers: **Edinburgh** BBBB; **Sheffield** BBBBB-BBCCC; **South Bank** CCCC.

SCE offers: **Aberdeen** BBBC; **City** AAAB; **Edinburgh** BBBB; **Glasgow** BBBB; **Heriot-Watt** BBBB; **Lancaster** ABBB; **Sheffield** BBBB; **Strathclyde** BBBBB; **Sunderland** CCC.

Overseas applicants: Surrey Sponsorship difficult. **East Anglia, Coventry** Language tuition available.

CHOOSING YOUR COURSE (See also Ch 1)

> **Subject information:** The design and application of modern computer systems is fundamental to all these courses which will also include electronic engineering, software engineering and computer-aided engineering. Several universities offer sufficient flexibility to enable final course decisions to be made in the second year.

Course highlights: Bristol (Comp Syst Eng) Course covers microelectronics, software design, communications, mathematics and computer architecture. **City** Emphasis on engineering design and management. **Coventry** At the end of year one transfers are possible to Electrical and Electronic Engineering or Information Systems Engineering. **East Anglia** (Comp Sys Eng) This degree programme combines training in both hardware and software engineering. **Liverpool John Moores** (Comp Aid Eng) The emphasis is on design and computer integrated manufacture. Management, business and applied industrial studies are included. **London (Imp)** During the third and fourth years, special emphasis is made on the principles and practice of software engineering. **London (QMW)** Course intended for students aiming for a career in the electronics industry dealing with digital and microprocessor-based systems. **Nottingham Trent** (Comp Aid Eng) The first two years are common with Electrical and Electronic and Mechanical Engineering, allowing a late decision about taking this degree course. **Oxford** (Eng/Comp) The first year of this four-ear course is common with Engineering Science and transfers may take place up to the end of the year. **Sheffield** (Software Eng) The first year is common with other courses and transfers are possible up to the end of that year. **Sheffield Hallam** Part II of the course can be studied in France (Bordeaux). **Surrey** Transfers possible to the Electrical/Electronic Engineering course. French and German offered as subsidiary subjects. **UMIST** Common first year for Elect Sys Eng/Micro Syst Eng/ Comp Sys Eng/Software Eng; transfers possible in year two. NOW CHECK PROSPECTUSES FOR ALL COURSES.

Study opportunities abroad: City (E); **Newcastle** (E) IT FR; **Sheffield** (E) EUR.

Work opportunities abroad: Aberystwyth EUR USA; **Coventry** EUR; **East Anglia** CAN; **Sheffield** EUR; **York** SZ IT G GR FR USA CAN.

ADMISSIONS INFORMATION

Number of applicants per place (approx): Aston 7; **Bangor** 5; **Bradford** 6; **Bristol** 9; **Bristol UWE** 4; **Central England** 6; **Coventry** 8; **Durham** 3; **East Anglia** 4; **Edinburgh** 3; **Huddersfield** 2; **Lancaster** 12; **London (Imp)** 5; **Loughborough** 17; **Middlesex** 3; **Sheffield** 10; **Sheffield Hallam** 17, 3 (Control); **Staffordshire** (Comp Aid Eng) 6; **Strathclyde** 7; **Sunderland** 10; **Surrey** (MEng, BEng) 3; **Swansea (IHE)** 1; **Teesside** 5; **Westminster** 5.

General Studies acceptable: Birmingham (Software); Coventry (No); Glamorgan (2); Huddersfield; Hull; Lancaster; Sheffield; Teesside; York.

Selection interviews: Aston; Bradford; City (some); East Anglia; Huddersfield; Liverpool John Moores; Sheffield; South Bank; Sussex; Teesside; Warwick (some); Westminster; York.

Offers to applicants repeating A-levels: Higher Bristol, Strathclyde, York (BBB); **Possibly higher** Aston, City, Huddersfield, Sheffield; **Same** Bath, Birmingham (Software), Coventry, East Anglia, Lancaster, Liverpool John Moores, South Bank, Teesside, Ulster, UMIST.

Admissions Tutors' advice: Bristol Offers also made on 2 A-levels and 2 AS-levels. **Teesside** All students interviewed by telephone. **York** (Comp SS Eng) A four-year sponsored MEng course. Early application advised; candidates interviewed by one of our regular sponsors. All applicants receive a bursary from their sponsoring company.

Examples of interview questions: See under **Computer Courses**.

GAP YEAR ADVICE

Institutions accepting a Gap Year: Most institutions.

Institutions willing to defer entry after A-levels (see Ch 5): Coventry; East Anglia; Glamorgan; Lancaster; Sheffield Hallam; South Bank; Staffordshire; Surrey; Swansea (IHE); UMIST; Westminster; York.

AFTER A-LEVELS ADVICE

Institutions which may accept the same points score after A-levels: Aberystwyth; Aston; Birmingham; Bradford; Central England; City; Coventry; De Montfort; Huddersfield; Liverpool John Moores; Sheffield; South Bank; Staffordshire; Sunderland; Teesside; UMIST; York.

Institutions which may accept under-achieving applicants after A-levels: Aberystwyth; Bangor; Birmingham; Central England; Coventry; De Montfort; East Anglia; Huddersfield; Liverpool John Moores; Sheffield; South Bank; Staffordshire; Strathclyde; Teesside; York.

Institutions with vacancies in Aug/Sept 1992 (see Ch 5): Anglia (Poly Univ); Bangor; Bristol; City; Coventry; East Anglia 14 pts; Glamorgan 8 pts; Greenwich; Heriot-Watt; Hull; Liverpool; London (QMW); Newcastle; Paisley; South Bank; Staffordshire 8 pts; Strathclyde; Sunderland; Surrey 14 pts; Swansea (IHE) 4 pts; Westminster; York 18 pts; see also under **Engineering Science**.

ADVICE FOR MATURE STUDENTS

Coventry Foundation and Access courses available prior to entry to year one. See also under **Engineering**.

GRADUATE EMPLOYMENT

Surrey Apart from a ski representative and a youth worker, all others who graduated went into various aspects of computer work.

Teesside Leading UK firms offered employment to graduates in computer engineering fields. (Control Engineering) All graduates entering full-time employment entered industry as engineers with a variety of firms in offshore, telecommunications and power engineering.

ENGINEERING (ELECTRICAL AND ELECTRONIC) (See also Micro-Electronics and Building Services Engineering)

Special subject requirements: 2-3 A-levels in mathematics/physics subjects. GCSE (grade A-C) chemistry required in some cases.

NB Institutions may raise or lower the level of published offers depending either on the quality or otherwise of individual applications or the numbers of applications received; grades/points offered may be adjusted downwards after A-level results. The level of an offer is not indicative of the quality of a course.

30 pts.	**Cambridge/Oxford** – AAA potential recommended (Eng)
28 pts.	**Brunel** – AAB (Springboard Prog)
	Southampton - 28-26 pts (Elect Eng)
26 pts.	**Bradford** – ABB (Elec Eng; ECCE; EEES) (BEng/MEng) (BTEC 1D maths +M overall)
	Bristol – ABB (Electron Eng/Eur)
	Loughborough – ABB (Elec Eng - extended)
24 pts.	**Aston** – BBB-BBC (Elec Sys Eng) (BTEC 2D+Ms)
	Bangor – BBB + sponsorship (Electron Eng - MEng; Comp Sys Eng) (4 AS)
	Bath – 24 pts (All courses, MEng, BEng) (BTEC 4D)
	Birmingham – BBB-BBC (Elec Eng)
	Cardiff – BBB (Elect Eng - MEng)
	City – BBB/AB (MEng - Elec Eng)
	Durham – BBB (Eng)
	Lancaster – BBB (Mechatronics)
	London (Imp) – ABC (Elect Eng - 3yr/4yr courses; EI/EI Eng Eur) (B maths; B phys + C)
	Loughborough – 24 pts (Elect Eng 3/4 standard) (BTEC 1D maths +M overall)
	Southampton – 24 pts B in maths and phys (Elec/Mech; Elec Eng)
	Strathclyde – BBC (Elec Mech)
	UMIST – BBB/AB (ME Eng)
	York – BBB/BBC (BB + 2 AS at BB) (All courses) (BTEC Ds+Ms)
22 pts.	**Bradford** – BBC/BB (EIMC H6P4)
	Bristol – BBC (Elec Eng; Electron Eng; Electron Comm)
	Brunel – BBC/BB (Elect Eng; Micro S Des) (BTEC Ms)
	East Anglia – BBC (E Eng/Nth Am)
	Essex – BBC (Elec Eng Euro)
	Kent – BBC-BCC/BB (Electron Eng; Elec Eng/Med; Comm Eng)
	London (UC) – BBC (Elect Eng; Elec/Comp; Elec/Optel; Elec/Med; Elec/Mgt St)
	Newcastle - BBC/AB (MEng courses)
	Nottingham – BBC-BCC (Elect Mat)
	Sheffield - BBC-BCC/BB (Elect Eng; Electron; Electron/Comp; Electron/Comm) (BTEC D maths +Ms)
	Strathclyde – BBC (E/M Eng)
	Surrey – BBC-BCC (All courses) (BTEC 2D)
	Sussex – BBC/AB (Eng/Eaps; EE/Eaps)
	Swansea – BBC-BCC/BB (Elec Comp Sci)
	UMIST – BBC-BCC/BB (All courses except under **24 pts**) (2 AS) (BTEC Ds+Ms)
20 pts.	**Aston** – BCC-CCC/BB (Elec Eng; Elmech Eng; Elec Comp; Ap Phys/Elec)
	Bath – 20 pts (All courses BEng) (BTEC Ds+Ms)
	Belfast – BCC (Elect Eng; Elect Extd)
	Cardiff – BCC/BB (Comp Syst)
	Essex – BCC/BB (3 yr scheme for BEng courses) (None at AS)
	Keele – BCC-CCC/BB-BC (Electron)
	Leeds – BCC/BC (Mechatronics) (BTEC 75% overall)
	London (King's) – 20 pts approx (Elect Eng courses)
	Loughborough – 20 pts (Elmech Power 3/4; Syst Eng 3/4) (BTEC 2D+3M)

THE UNIVERSITY *of* BATH

Top University *for* Graduate Employment in 1992

SCHOOL OF ELECTRONIC & ELECTRICAL ENGINEERING

Degree Courses in:

> **Electrical Engineering and Applied Electronics**
> **Electrical and Electronic Engineering**
> **Electronic and Communication Engineering**
> *All with a common first year*

Bath University offers degrees in Electronic and Electrical Engineering with choice, flexibility and variety.

3-year BEng or	**Study abroad and foreign language tuition**
4-year MEng degrees	**A friendly working environment**
Sandwich courses	**Large and attractive campus with excellent**
Certificate in Education option	**accommodation and sports facilities**

For further information please contact: The Admissions Tutor,
School of Electronic & Electrical Engineering,
University of Bath,
Claverton Down, BATH, BA2 7AY.
Telephone: (0225) 826309

Manchester – 20-18 pts approx (Elect Eng)
Reading – BCC (Elect Eng)
Southampton – 20 pts C in maths (Electro Eng; Inf Eng)
Swansea – BCC (MEng)
Warwick – BCC-CCC (Electronics courses)
18 pts.   **Bradford** – CCC (All courses except under **26 pts**)
Cardiff – CCC/BB (Elect; Electro) (BTEC 1D maths+M overall)
Cranfield (Shrivenham) – CCC (El Sys Eng)
Edinburgh – CCC/BB (4 AS) (All courses)
Exeter – CCC/BC (Elect Eng) (4 AS) (BTEC Ms)
Heriot-Watt – CCC (All courses) (6 AS)
Hull – CCC/BB (All courses) (BTEC Ds+Ms)
Lancaster – CCC (Engin Elec) (BTEC 2D+1M)
Leeds – CCC (Elec Eng; Electron Eng)
Leicester – BCD-CCC (Eng Elec)
Liverpool – CCC/BB-BC (Electr Eng; Elect Eng; Med Elect/Inst; Elec/El Eng) (4 AS)
London (QMW) – CCC/BC (Elect Eng)
Loughborough – 18-16 pts (Elec Phys 3/4) (BTEC 2D+3M)
Loughborough – CCC/BB (Elec/Manuf 3/4) (BTEC 2D+3M)
Newcastle – CCC/BB (BEng courses) (BTEC 4M)
Nottingham – CCC/CC (All courses except **22 pts**)
St Andrews – 18 pts (Electron)
Salford – CCC/BB (Elec Eng Int; Elec Eng FT; Elec Eng Eur; Electronics; Elec Comm; Elec
    Comm Sys) (6 AS)
Sheffield – CCC (Electron/Info) (2 AS) (BTEC D maths+Ms)
Southampton – CCC – C in maths (Elec Eng)
Sussex – CCC/BB (EM/Eaps)
Swansea – CCC/BB (All courses except under **20 pts**) (BTEC Ms)
16 pts.   **City** – CCD/BC (Elec Eng) (BTEC 2D+Ms)

Dundee - CC (maths + physics) D (Elect Eng)
East Anglia - CCD/BC (E Eng; El Eng/Eur) (BTEC 4M inc maths)
Glasgow - CCD/BC (All courses)
Hull - CCD/CC (Optel Laser; Electron)
Newcastle - CCD/BC (BEng)
Salford - 16 pts approx (Elect Eng; Biomed Elect)
Strathclyde - CCD (BCC 2nd yr entry) (Elec Eng courses)

14pts.   **Central England** - CDD/CC (Electron Eng) (BTEC 3M)
Central Lancashire - CDD/CD (Elect Eng) (4 AS)
East Anglia - CDD/CC (EDT; E Bus) (BTEC 4M inc maths)
Essex - CDD/CC (4 yr scheme for BEng courses)
Heriot-Watt - CDD (maths C, phys D)/CD (1st yr entry) CCC (2nd yr entry) All courses inc O Eng)
Northumbria - CDD/CC (maths C) (Elect Eng) (BTEC Ms)
Swansea - CDD/CC (Elect Mat Eng)

12pts.   **Aberdeen** - CC (Elect; Micro)
Central Lancashire - CC (Comb Hons) (4 AS)
Kingston - 12 pts (Elect Sy Eng)
Liverpool John Moores - DDD/CC (Elect Eng) (4 AS)
Manadon (RNEC) - CC (Naval Officer entry)
Oxford Brookes - CC (Electron) (BTEC 3M inc maths)

10pts.   **Bournemouth** - (Electro Sys Design) (4 AS)
Brighton - 10 pts (Elect Eng) (4 AS) (BTEC 5M)
Bristol UWE - 10 pts (Elec Eng) (BTEC 4M)
City - DDE-DEE (Wide access)
Hertfordshire - 10 pts (Elect Eng) (BTEC 3M)
Kingston - (Elec/Comp/Bus)
Manchester Met - DDE/CD (Elect Eng) (4 AS) (BTEC 1D maths+Ms)
Middlesex - DDE/CD (Electron Eng) (BTEC D+M)
Nottingham Trent - 10-8 pts (Elect Eng) (BTEC 3M)
Portsmouth - CD (Elect Eng) (4 AS) (BTEC 3M)
Staffordshire - 10 pts (All courses) (BTEC 3M)
York - No standard offer (Foundation)

8pts.   **and below**
Bangor - DD (Electron; Comp Sys Eng; Comp Sys Maths; Elec Eng) (4 AS)
Bell (CT) - (Elect Eng)
Bolton (IHE) - DD-EE (Electron Eng)
Bradford - EEE (Foundation course)
City - EE (Foundation course)
Coventry - (Elect Eng; Elec Comp Con) (4 AS)
De Montfort - (Electron)
Dundee - DD (All courses)
Dundee (IT) - (Elect Eng)
East Anglia - DD (Electronics; BSc Tech) (BTEC 3M inc maths)
East London - (Elect Eng) (4 AS - maths grade A required)
Glamorgan - DD (All courses) (4 AS)
Glasgow Caledonian - DEE/DD (Electron Eng)
Greenwich - 8 pts (Elect; Elect Mat)
Gwent (CHE) - (Elect/Inst Syst)
Huddersfield - 4 pts (Elect Eng) (4 AS)
Humberside - (EC) (BTEC Ms)
Inverness (Coll) - (Elec Eng)
Middlesex - (Elect Eng Man)
Napier - (Electronic/Elect Eng; Inf Tech/Elect)
North East Wales (IHE) - (Electron Eng)
North London - DD (Elect/Com Eng; Bus/Comp Electron)
Northumbria - DD (Op Elec Eng) (4 AS)
Paisley - DD-EE (Elect Electron Eng)
Plymouth - 6 pts (All courses) (BTEC Ms)

Robert Gordon – (Elect Eng)
Sheffield Hallam – DD (Elec Sys Con; Elec Sys Inf)
South Bank – (Elect Eng; Euro Eng – Fr/Ger/Sp) (4 AS)
Sunderland – 8 pts (Elect Eng) (BTEC Ms)
Swansea (IHE) – (Opto Elec/Laser; Mechatronics; Elec Eng)
Teesside – (Elect Eng)
Westminster – 8 pts (Elect Eng)
Wolverhampton – (Elect Con)

Franchised degree and HND courses (see Ch 5):
> **Brighton** – Brighton (CT); Chichester (CT); Crawley (CT); Hastings (CAT); Northbrook (CDT).
> **Central England** – East Birmingham (CFE); Stourbridge (CFE).
> **De Montfort** – Bedford (CFE); Broxtowe (CFE); Charles Keene (CFE); Milton Keynes (CFE).
> **Derby** – Newark & Sherwood (CFE).
> **Leeds Met** – Leeds (CM).
> **South Bank** – South Bank (CFE).

Diploma of Higher Education courses: Greenwich.

Offers for Foundation, Certificate and Diploma courses (see Ch 5):

Higher National Diploma courses (England and Wales):
8 pts. Leeds Met.
6 pts. Middlesex; Portsmouth.
4 pts. **and below** Anglia (Poly Univ); Bolton (IHE); Brighton (CT); Bristol UWE; Cardiff (IHE); Central England; Central Lancashire; Coventry; De Montfort; Derby; Doncaster (Coll); Durham-Tees (Coll); East London; Glamorgan; Greenwich; Gwent (CHE); Hastings (CT); Hertfordshire; Huddersfield; Kingston; Liverpool John Moores; Luton (CHE); Manchester Met; North East Wales (IHE) for BEng at Salford Univ; North London; Northumbria; Norwich (CHFE); Nottingham Trent; Oldham (CT); Oxford Brookes; Plymouth; Salford (UC) for BEng at Salford Univ; Sheffield Hallam (Electr/Elect; Electr/Micro; Opto/Elect); South Bank; Southall (CT); Southampton (IHE); Staffordshire; Stoke on Trent (Coll); Sunderland; Swansea (IHE); Swindon (Coll); Thames Valley London; Westminster; Willesden (CT) (Electrical/Electronic Eng).

Higher Diploma courses (Scotland):
> Bell (CT); Dumfries & Galloway (Coll); Dundee (IT) DE; Falkirk (CT); Glasgow Caledonian; Inverness (Coll); James Watt (Coll); Kilmarnock (Coll); Kirkcaldy (Coll); Napier EE; Robert Gordon.

Alternative offers:

EB offers: **Liverpool** 70%.

IB offers: **Aberdeen** 26 pts; **Aston** 30 pts inc 16 pts Highers; **Bath** (MEng) 30 pts inc H665, (BEng) 28 pts inc H555; **Belfast** H666 S555; **Birmingham** H666 S666; **Bristol** 32 pts inc H66 in maths, physics; **Brunel** 30-28 pts H65; **City** 30-26 pts; **Cranfield** 25 pts; **Durham** H666; **Essex** 30 pts inc 11 pts Highers; **Exeter** 30 pts; **Heriot-Watt** 28 pts; **Hertfordshire** 24 pts; **Hull** 27 pts inc H5 maths; **Lancaster** 31-29 pts inc H55 maths + physics; **Kent** 29 pts, H 13 pts; **Leeds** 30 pts; **Loughborough** H766, (El Mech) 26 pts; **Newcastle** (BEng) Grades 5, (MEng) Grades 6; **North London** 29 pts with 14 pts Highers; **Portsmouth** 28 pts inc 14 pts Highers; **Reading** 30 pts; **Staffordshire** 26 pts; **Swansea** 28 pts; **UMIST** 30 pts H65 in maths/phys. **York** 30 pts + H66 maths/physics.

Irish offers: **Aberdeen** BBCCC; **Bangor** BBCCC; **Liverpool** BBCCC.

SCE offers: **Aberdeen** BBBC; **Dundee** BBCC; **East Anglia** AAA; **Edinburgh** BBBB; **Glasgow** AABB; **Heriot-Watt** BBBB; **Lancaster** ABBB; **Robert Gordon** BCC; **Sheffield** BBCC; **Strathclyde** ABBB.

Overseas applicants: Sheffield Hallam, East Anglia, Leeds Language courses available. **Bath** Competence in English required. **Heriot-Watt** Some Norwegian scholarships available. **Newcastle** Foundation year offered. **Surrey** Direct entry to year two sometimes possible. Sponsorships can be difficult to arrange. **Hull** Living costs 30% lower than in London.

CHOOSING YOUR COURSE (See also Ch 1)

> **Subject information:** Options to specialise should be considered when choosing courses, so read the prospectuses carefully. In this field options could include opto-electronics and optical communication systems, microwave systems, radio frequency engineering and circuit technology.

Course highlights: Aston Specialisms in opto-electronics and telecommunications. **Bangor** First year common with Electronic, Computer Systems and Electrical Eng. Opportunity to transfer in year two. **Bath** The final year options allow specialisms in electronics, communications control engineering, electrical machines and power systems. **Belfast** Emphasis on application, design and professional studies. **Bradford** New course now offered in Electronic Imaging and Media Communication. **Bristol** Final year specialisations include communications, industrial economics and computer architecture. **Brunel** Choice of specialisation in communication, control and instrumentation, power and electron systems. **City** Because of a major joint programme of physics, electrical, electronic and control engineering, instrumentation and systems engineering, much of the first and second years is taken in common and transfers are possible at the end of the first year. **Coventry** Emphasis on electrical and electronic systems, development and sales. **Cranfield (Shrivenham)** First year common with Mechanical Engineering and Aeronautical Systems Engineering. **De Montfort** Optional route to study European language or Business Studies. **Dundee** Common first year within Electronics/Electrical/Mechanical/ Manufacturing Engineering and Management. **East Anglia** Common first year; opportunity to transfer to Computer Systems Engineering, Electronic Design and Technology or Electronics with Business Studies. **Hull** Transfer possible in first year between Opto-electronics and Laser Systems Engineering and Applied Physics in year 1. A four-year course with five final year options. **Kingston** Non-engineering subjects include business, foreign language, software applications, information systems. **Loughborough** Common first year with choice to transfer to other subjects. (Elec Eng/Phy) Balance between engineering and physics. Possible to transfer to either major subject in year two. (Electro/ Mech) Close links with industry, 85% of students on sponsorships. **Newcastle** Common first year for MEng/BEng students. MEng courses specially related to British Telecom sponsorship. **Northumbria** Transfer to Communication Engineering possible at the end of first year. **Robert Gordon** Choice in year two between Electrical/ Electronic or Electronic/Information Engineering. **Surrey** Transfers possible in first year to Information Systems Engine ering course possible. **York** (Elect Eng) Optional courses include music, technology, avionics and flight control and technical German or French. **Glasgow, London (Imp), (UC), Sheffield** High research ratings.

Study opportunities abroad: Aston (E) FR; **Bath** (E); **Bournemouth; Brighton** (E); **Bristol** (E); **Brunel** (E) IT F; **Cardiff** (E); **Central England** (E) D FR; **Central Lancashire** (E); **City** (E) S; **Coventry** (E) FR G; **De Montfort** (E); **Glamorgan** (E); **Heriot-Watt** (E); **Huddersfield** (E); **Hull**; **Kent** (E); **Leeds** (E) FR G IT SP; **Leeds Met** FR; **Liverpool John Moores** (E); **London (Imp)** EUR, **(QMW)** (E) FR G SP, **(UC)** (E) FR G; **Newcastle** (E) FR; **Nottingham** (E) FR G; **Nottingham Trent** FR G; **Salford** (E) FR; **Staffordshire; Surrey** F G; **Sussex** (E); **York** (E).

Work opportunities abroad: Bath; Bournemouth FR; **Brighton** EUR; **Bristol** FR G; **Brunel** FR G IT; **Central England** D NL G; **Central Lancashire** G FR SP; **Coventry** EUR; **De Montfort** G FR JAP; **East Anglia** USA; **Glamorgan** G SZ P; **Hull** G; **Loughborough** FR G; **Middlesex** HK JAP; **Nottingham Trent** FR G; **Salford** G; **South Bank** G; **Surrey** FR G; **York** USA FR G.

ADMISSIONS INFORMATION

Number of applicants per place (approx): Aston 10; **Bangor** (Electron Eng) 3, (Elec Eng) 5; **Bath** 12, (Electron) 6; **Bolton (IHE)** 3; **Bournemouth** 2; **Brighton** 20; **Bradford** (Elec Eng) 8, (ECCE Eng) 8; **Bristol** 10; **Brunel** 8; **Central England** 11; **Central Lancashire** 14; **City** 10; **Coventry** 8; **De Montfort** 5; **Dundee** 7; **Dundee (IT)** 3; **Glamorgan** 8; **Glasgow Caledonian** 5; **Greenwich** 10; **Gwent (CHE)** 1; **Hertfordshire** 9; **Huddersfield** 15; **Hull** 8; **Kent** 14; **Kingston** 8; **Leeds** 10; **Lancaster** 7; **Liverpool** 11; **Liverpool John Moores** 9; **Loughborough** (Elec/Phys) 8, (El/Mech Power) 4; **Newcastle** 17; **North London** 8; **Northumbria** 11, (Phys Elect) 12; **Nottingham** 4; **Nottingham Trent** 12; **Plymouth** 22; **Portsmouth** 17; **Robert Gordon** 3; **Salford** 5; **Sheffield** 15; **South Bank** 11; **Staffordshire** 7; **Strathclyde** 7; **Sunderland** 11; **Surrey** (BEng) 6. (MEng) 3; **Swansea** 5; **Teesside** 4; **UMIST** 14; **Westminster** 4; **York** 5.

General Studies acceptable: Aston; Bradford (Elec Eng; ECCE Eng); **Coventry** (No); **Derbyshire** (CHE); **East London; Exeter; Hertfordshire; Kent; Lancaster; Leeds; Loughborough; Manchester Met; Northumbria; Staffordshire; Teesside.**

Selection interviews: Aston; Bangor (Electron only); **Bath** (some); **Belfast** (some); **Bradford** (T); **Brighton; Bristol; Brunel; Cambridge; City; Cranfield** (Shrivenham); **De Montfort; Derby; Dundee** (most applicants); **Durham; East Anglia** (Electron) (T); **Essex; Greenwich** (some); **Gwent** (CHE); **Huddersfield** (some); **Hull; Kent; Kingston** (T); **Lancaster; Liverpool; Loughborough** (some); **Newcastle** (some); **Nottingham; Oxford; Plymouth** (some); **Robert Gordon; Sheffield; South Bank** (some); **Surrey; Swansea** (some); **Warwick** (some); **Westminster; York.**

Offers to applicants repeating A-levels: Higher Belfast, Brighton, Central Lancashire, Greenwich, Huddersfield, Kingston, Loughborough (Elec/Phys 3 and 4), Newcastle, Northumbria, South Bank, Staffordshire, Strathclyde, Swansea; **Possibly higher** Aston (Elmech Eng; Elec/Ap Phys), City, De Montfort, Derby, Glasgow, Hertfordshire, Manchester, North London, Portsmouth, Sheffield; **Same** Aston, Bangor, Bath, Birmingham, Bolton (IHE), Bradford, Brunel, Coventry, Gwent (CHE), Hull, Kent, Leeds, Liverpool, Loughborough, Northumbria (Phys Elect), Nottingham (usually), Robert Gordon, South Bank, Surrey, UMIST.

Admissions Tutors' advice: Aston MEng students need GCSE grades A–C in French or German; (Elmech Eng) University arranges sponsorships for those offered a place; students are interviewed by both the university and sponsor. **Bath** Motivation for career important. **Kingston** Good written and oral communication skills and academic potential needed for MEng course. Candidates assessed for ability to obtain industrial training during course. **Loughborough** Disregards A-levels in engineering drawing and general studies. **Northumbria** Non-UK nationals must guarantee their training via a UK-based company.

Examples of interview questions: How does a combustion engine work? How does a trumpet work? Why, being female, did you choose to study Electrical Engineering? What type of position do you hope to have attained in five to ten years' time? Could you sack an employee? What was your last physics practical? What did you learn from it? What are the methods of transmitting information from a moving object to a stationary observer? Wire bending exercise – you are provided with an accurate diagram of a shape that could be produced by bending a length of wire in a particular way. You are supplied with a pair of pliers and the exact length of wire required and you are given 10 minutes to reproduce the shape drawn as accurately as possible. How does a transistor work? A three-minute talk had to be given on one of six subjects (topics given several weeks before the interview); for example, the best is the enemy of the good? Is there a lesson here for British industry? I was asked to take my physics file and discuss some of my conclusions in certain experiments.

GAP YEAR ADVICE

Institutions accepting a Gap Year: Most institutions; **Bournemouth** (Prefer not - year three in industry; **Bradford** Work experience in gap year is unlikely to be counted towards industrial training; **De Montfort** Could be a danger in losing motivation; **Glamorgan** Seek advice on application; **Hull**

Apply as normal and request deferred entry; **London (QMW)** Students advised to work in industry; **Loughborough** Inform us as soon as possible and confirm if you do not wish to take up your place; **Salford** Some courses require applicant to select a relevant employer beforehand. Check with admissions tutor.

Institutions willing to defer entry after A-levels (see Ch 5): Aston; Bell (CT); Bradford; Brighton; Coventry; Cranfield; Dundee; Glamorgan; Heriot-Watt; Hull; Leeds (Mechatronics); Loughborough; Newcastle; Plymouth; Robert Gordon; South Bank; Staffordshire; Surrey; Swansea; UMIST; York.

AFTER A-LEVELS ADVICE

Institutions which may accept the same points score after A-levels: Aston; Bangor; Bath; Bolton (IHE); Bournemouth; Bradford (Elec Eng; ECCE Eng); Brighton; Brunel; Central Lancashire; De Montfort; Derby; Dundee; Durham; East Anglia; Essex; Glamorgan (provided mathematics is D or better); Gwent (CHE); Hertfordshire; Huddersfield; Hull; Kingston; Kent; Leeds; Liverpool; Liverpool John Moores; London (UC); Manchester Met (inc maths grade E); Newcastle; Northumbria; Nottingham; Oxford Brookes; Plymouth; Portsmouth; Salford; South Bank; Staffordshire; Strathclyde; Surrey; Swansea; UMIST; York.

Institutions demanding the actual grades offered after A-levels: Belfast; Birmingham; Bristol; Central Lancashire; Glasgow; Greenwich; Leeds; Loughborough (usually); North London; Robert Gordon; South Bank; Warwick.

Institutions which may accept under-achieving applicants after A-levels: Aston; Bangor; Bath; Bournemouth; Central Lancashire; City (Wide access and Foundation courses); Coventry; Glamorgan; Hull (overseas students 18-16 pts); Liverpool John Moores; London (UC); Manchester Met; Oxford Brookes; Salford; Sheffield; South Bank; Westminster; York.

Institutions with vacancies in Aug/Sept 1992 (see Ch 5): Aberdeen; Aston 16 pts; Bangor; Bath 18 pts; Bell (CT) 5 pts; Bournemouth DD; Bradford BEng/MEng 24 pts; Brighton 6 pts; Bristol 18 pts; Brunel 18 pts; City; Coventry; Cranfield 14 pts; De Montfort; Dundee; East Anglia 14-8 pts; Essex; Glamorgan 6 pts; Greenwich; Heriot-Watt 12 pts; Hull 12 pts; Humberside 6 pts; Kingston 6 pts; Leeds 12 pts, (Mechatronics) 18 pts; Liverpool; London (QMW); Loughborough 18 pts; Newcastle; Northumbria 10 pts; Oxford Brookes; Paisley; Plymouth 4 pts; Portsmouth; Robert Gordon; Sheffield Hallam 4 pts; Southampton (IHE); South Bank; Strathclyde; Sunderland; Surrey 14 pts; Swansea DDD; UMIST 16 pts; York; see also under **Engineering Science**.

ADVICE FOR MATURE STUDENTS

See under **Engineering**.

GRADUATE EMPLOYMENT

New Graduates' destinations (percentages) 1991:
Permanent employment: U 83; P 66; C 47.
Unemployment: U 13; P 29; C 49.
Further studies (all types): U 20; P 15; C 16.
Main career destinations (approx): Engineering 77; Computing 12; Finance 5.

Surrey Of 14 graduates on the MEng course in 1990, 13 entered various subject-related careers in design, research, development and management training; the 14th became an evangelical worker in a mission in India. The great majority of BEng graduates also entered electrical or electronic engineering in aeronautical, automotive and micro-electronics engineering. Two students went on to train as chartered accountants and several followed MSc courses.

York (1986-91) 80% of graduates went into employment, nearly all of them into scientific and engineering careers (electronics, design, development, systems and software engineering); 3% went into management careers, 2% into finance and 1% each into the armed services, media (disc jockey, production assistant BBC) and social work.

The following institutions are perceived as being above average in producing graduates for employment: Aston; Bath; Belfast; Bristol; Brunel; Cambridge; Heriot-Watt; Leeds; Manchester; Nottingham; Oxford; Southampton; UMIST; Warwick; see PIP reference in Chapter 5.

ENGINEERING (MANUFACTURING) (See also Production Engineering)

Special subject requirements: 2-3 A-levels in mathematics/science subjects; physics sometimes required at A-level and chemistry at GCSE (grade A-C).

NB Institutions may raise or lower the level of published offers depending either on the quality or otherwise of individual applications or the numbers of applications received; grades/points offered may be adjusted downwards after A-level results. The level of an offer is not indicative of the quality of a course.

30pts.	**Cambridge/Oxford** - AAA potential recommended (Eng)
24pts.	**Brunel** - BBB/AB (Mfg/Eng also with Fr or Ger) (BTEC D overall)
	Durham - BBB (Eng)
	Loughborough - BBB (MEng courses)
	UMIST - BBB (4 yr Enhanced Eng Mnfr/Man)
22pts.	**Bath** - BBC (Manuf courses) (BTEC 2D+M)
	Nottingham - BBC-BCC (Prod Eng; Prod Man; Man Eng Man)
20pts.	**Belfast** - BCC (Manuf Eng)
	Exeter - BCC (Op Eng) (4 AS)
	Leeds - BCC/BC (Man Sys Eng) (BTEC 75% overall)
	London (King's) - BCC-CCC (Man Sys Eng)
	Manchester Met - BCC/AB (All courses except under 16 pts)
	Strathclyde - BCC (Manuf/Eng Man)
	Ulster - BCC (Manu Eng)
	Warwick - BCC-CCC (All courses)
18pts.	**Aston** - CCC/AB (Manuf Eng; Manuf Eng/Euro)
	Birmingham - CCC (Manu Eng)
	Bradford - CCC/AB (Man/Mech Eng) (BTEC 3M)
	Cardiff - CCC/BB (Mech/Man Eng) (BTEC 75% overall)
	Hull - CCC/BC (Eng Des Mft)
	Loughborough - CCC/BB (Des/Manuf 3/4; Manuf/Man 3/4; Man/Comp) (BTEC 2D+3M)
16pts.	**Glasgow Caledonian** - CCD (Bus/Man Syst Eng)
	Manchester Met - 16-10 pts (Comb St)
14pts.	**Bradford** - CDD/BC (Mech Man Sys; Mech/Man Sys) (BTEC 3M)
	Hertfordshire - 14-10 pts (Man Syst Eng) (BTEC 3M)
12pts.	**Aberdeen** - CC (Eng Manuf)
	Glasgow - CC (Des Eng)
	Newcastle - 12 pts (Man Syst Eng) (4 AS)
	Nottingham Trent - 12 pts (Indust St)
	Plymouth - 12 pts (Eng Prod Des; Pro Tech/Mgt St)
	Westminster - 12 pts (Prod des) (BTEC 7 Ds/Ms)
10pts.	**Bristol UWE** - 10 pts (Man Syst Eng)
	Liverpool John Moores - DDE/DD (Man Eng)
	Plymouth - 10 pts (MSE Mech)
	Portsmouth - 10 pts (Man Sys Eng)
	Scottish (CText) - CD (Qual Man)
8pts.	**and below**
	Anglia (Poly Univ) - (Man Sys)
	Bolton (IHE) - (Man Syst Eng; Manuf Man)
	Central England - (Export Eng; Man Sys)

Coventry - (Man Bus Studs; Man Syst Eng; Prod Des) (4 AS) (BTEC 3Minc maths)
Dundee - DD (M Eng/Man)
East London - (Man Eng; Man Sys Man) (BTEC 3M)
Glamorgan - (Manuf Sys; Manuf/Env)
Huddersfield - (Eng Sys Man)
Kingston - (Manf Eng)
Leeds Met - DD (Man Sys Eng) (4 AS)
Manchester Met - (Man Man)
Middlesex - (Mech Eng Man)
North East Wales (IHE) - (Man Eng) (4 AS)
Nottingham Trent - 6 pts (Manuf Eng)
Salford - (2x2 course Man Eng)
Salford (UC) - (Comp Aid Man)
Suffolk (CFHE) - (Man Eng Sys)
Teesside - (Manuf Eng)

Offers for Foundation, Certificate and Diploma courses (see Ch 5):

Higher National Diploma courses:
2pts.   Anglia (Poly Univ); Bolton (IHE) transfers to Salford Univ; Brighton; Cardiff (IHE); Coventry (Manuf Man); Hertfordshire; Humberside; Leeds Met; Liverpool John Moores; Manchester Met; Middlesex; North East Wales (IHE) transfers to Salford Univ; Nottingham Trent; Sheffield Hallam; Stockport (CT); Stoke on Trent (TC); Southampton (IHE) Proc Eng.

Higher National Diploma courses (Scotland):
   SAC (Au) (Mech Plan/Man).

Alternative offers:

IB offers: **Bath** H55 overall 30 pts; **Bradford** 27 pts; **Cardiff** 554 + 13 pts; **Loughborough** H766-H655; **Manchester Met** 30 pts; **UMIST** H666.

Irish offers: **Bristol UWE** CCCC.

SCE offers: **Aberdeen** BBBC; **Bristol UWE** BCC; **Dundee** BBCC; **Cardiff** ABBB; **Loughborough** BBB; **Strathclyde** AAAB/ABBB; **UMIST** AAAA.

CHOOSING YOUR COURSE (See also Ch 1)

> **Subject information:** Manufacturing Engineering is sometimes referred to as Production Engineering. It is a branch of the subject concerned with management aspects of engineering such as industrial organisation, purchasing and the planning and control of operations, and at the same time provides an overview of engineering design systems. This is a shortage area - out of 18,000 applicants for Engineering, around 350 applied for Production Engineering.

Course highlights: Aston First year common with Mechanical Engineering; transfers possible at end of first year and also to and from sandwich course. (MEng Manufacturing Engineering) Students can take European Studies with French or German with placements abroad; common first year with Mechanical Engineering with choice of subject at end of year one. **Bath** Choice between Aeronautical, Mechanical or Manufacturing Engineering made at the end of year one. **Bradford** Language options available. **Brunel** Technical French and German offered. One third of students on placements abroad in third year. **Coventry** (Man Syst Eng) The course has a common first year with Mechanical Engineering and transfers are possible. The third year of this sandwich course may be spent in Europe, and Part II academic studies may be undertaken at a Spanish university. **Dundee** Common first year; transfers to Electrical/Electronic or Mechanical Engineering. **Hull** (Eng Des Mft) This is a broad course covering engineering science, materials, manufacturing processes and business management. **Northumbria** (Man Syst Eng) Covers electronics, mechanics, materials, power and energy, control engineering, computer-aided engineering, process technology and business and management. **Nottingham Trent** Emphasis on computer-aided manufacturing. Joint degree with Fachhochschule, Karlsruhe. NOW CHECK PROSPECTUSES FOR ALL COURSES.

Study opportunities abroad: Birmingham (E); **Brunel** (E); **Dundee** (E); **Hertfordshire** (E); **Leeds** (E); **Nottingham Trent** (E); **Strathclyde** (E).

Work opportunities abroad: Aston FR G; **Bath** FR G; **Brunel** EUR – 33% of students USA; **Cardiff** JAP; **Central England** EUR; **Coventry** EUR; **East London** G; **Hertfordshire** F G; **Leeds** G FR CAN USA; **Leeds Met** USA G; **Nottingham Trent** G; **Sheffield Hallam** G; **Ulster** G.

ADMISSIONS INFORMATION

Number of applicants per place (approx): Aston 10; **Bath** 5; **Birmingham** 2; **Bolton (IHE)** 2; **Bradford** 2; **Bristol UWE** 3; **Brunel** 5; **Coventry** 4; **Hertfordshire** 3; **Leeds Met** 5; **Loughborough** 6; **Middlesex** 2; **Nottingham Trent** 6; **Strathclyde** 4; **Teesside** 4; **UMIST** 5.

General Studies acceptable: Aston; Bolton (IHE); Bristol UWE; Brunel; Teesside.

Selection interviews: Aston (some); Bath; Brunel; Coventry; Dundee; Loughborough; Nottingham Trent; Strathclyde.

Offers to applicants repeating A-levels: Higher Strathclyde; **Possibly higher** Brunel, Hertfordshire; **Same** Aston, Nottingham.

Admissions Tutors' advice: Aston GCSE grades A-C in French or German for MEng course. **Coventry** Strength in mathematics and physics advisable, in addition to good communication skills and personality. Personal qualities as important as academic qualifications.

> **Examples of interview questions:** What is the function of an engineer? Describe something interesting you have recently done in your A-levels. What do you know about careers in engineering? Discuss the role of women engineers in industry. Why is a disc brake better than a drum brake? Would you be prepared to make people redundant to improve the efficiency of a production line?

GAP YEAR ADVICE

Institutions accepting a Gap Year: Most institutions; **Teesside** Prepare for course by studying maths/physics if necessary.

Institutions willing to defer entry after A-levels (see Ch 5): Bath (but advise before April); Dundee; Kingston; Leeds (Man Sys Eng); Manchester Met; Westminster.

AFTER A-LEVELS ADVICE

Institutions which may accept the same points score after A-levels: Aston; Brunel; Coventry; Dundee; Hertfordshire; Loughborough (Man/Eng); Leeds Met; Nottingham; Nottingham Trent; Strathclyde.

Institutions demanding the actual grades offered after A-levels: UMIST.

Institutions which may accept under-achieving applicants after A-levels: Aston; most institutions.

Institutions with vacancies in Aug/Sept 1992 (see Ch 5): All courses had vacancies for this undersubscribed subject, including Aberdeen; Aston; Bath; Dundee; East London; Glamorgan; Greenwich; Kingston 4 pts; Leeds (Man Sys Eng) 18 pts; Manchester Met 8 pts; Paisley; Sheffield Hallam; Strathclyde; Sunderland; Westminster 12 pts; see also under **Engineering Science**.

ADVICE FOR MATURE STUDENTS

See under **Engineering.**

GRADUATE EMPLOYMENT

New Graduates' destinations (percentages) 1991:

See under **Engineering (Production).**

ENGINEERING (MARINE)

Special subject requirements: 2 A-levels in mathematics/science subjects.

NB Institutions may raise or lower the level of published offers depending either on the quality or otherwise of individual applications or the numbers of applications received; grades/points offered may be adjusted downwards after A-level results. The level of an offer is not indicative of the quality of a course.

20 pts.	**Newcastle** - BCC/BB (Marine Tech - MEng) (4 AS)
	Surrey - BCC-CCC/BB (Mech/Mar)
16 pts.	**Newcastle** - CCD/BC (Marine Eng)
10 pts.	**Liverpool John Moores** - 10 pts (Marine Eng) (Also at HND level)

Franchised degree and HND courses (see Ch 5):
        Liverpool John Moores - South Cheshire (CFE); Southport (CFE).
        Plymouth - Plymouth (CFE).

Offers for Foundation, Certificate and Diploma courses (see Ch 5):

Higher National Diploma courses:
        Southampton (IHE) Marine Eng.

Alternative offers:

IB offers: **Surrey** 28 pts inc H555 maths/physics.

CHOOSING YOUR COURSE (See also Ch 1)

> **Subject information:** There is a shortage of applicants for these courses which cover all aspects of the marine industry eg, offshore engineering, small craft technology and naval architecture (a subject in its own right).

Study opportunities abroad: Newcastle NL.

ADMISSIONS INFORMATION

Admissions Tutors' advice: Intake at **Newcastle** is 19 with approximately 100 applicants. Average entry grade BC. See also **Naval Architecture. Liverpool John Moores** had vacancies after A-levels last summer. (For awards see under **Engineering.**) **Southampton (IHE)** 'Most students on the course are paid and sponsored by well-known shipping companies. However, we do accept non-sponsored students. No barrier to female applicants. We are also interested in potential students with BTEC National Diploma or Certificate in Engineering. The majority of the staff have sea-going experience. **Surrey** See under **Engineering (Mechanical).** NOW CHECK PROSPECTUSES FOR ALL COURSES.

Examples of interview questions: Why do you want to study Marine Engineering? What future career are you considering? Shipping world-wide is on the decrease: do you see this situation changing?

ADVICE FOR MATURE STUDENTS

See under **Engineering**.

GRADUATE EMPLOYMENT

New Graduates' destinations (percentages) 1991:
Permanent employment: U 79; P 75.
Unemployment: U 15; P 0.
Further studies (all types): U 13; P 60.

ENGINEERING (MECHANICAL)

Special subject requirements: 2-3 A-levels in mathematics/science subjects. Physics and mathematics often required at A-level. English, chemistry at GCSE (grade A-C) often specified.

NB Institutions may raise or lower the level of published offers depending either on the quality or otherwise of individual applications or the numbers of applications received; grades/points offered may be adjusted downwards after A-level results. The level of an offer is not indicative of the quality of a course.

30 pts.   **Cambridge/Oxford** - AAA potential recommended (Eng)
28 pts.   **London (Imp)** - AAB-BBB (Mech Eng - H301)
24 pts.   **Bradford** - BBB/AB (Mech Eng) (BEng - MEng H391)
          City - BBB (M Eng Mech Eng)
          Durham - BBB (Eng) (See **Engineering**)
          Lancaster - BBB (Mechatronics)
          Loughborough - BBB/AB (Auto Eng 3/4)
          Newcastle - ABC-BBB/AB (Mech/Manuf Eng - 4 yr)
          Southampton - 24 pts minimum (Mech Eng - H300 & H301)
22 pts.   **Bath** - BBC (Mech Eng; Mech Eng/Fr; Mech Eng/Ger)
          Bristol - BBC (Mech Eng; Mech Eng/Euro St; Mech Eng/Manuf Syst) (BTEC 75% average, D in maths)
          London (Imp) - BBC (Mech Eng - H300)
          Newcastle - BBC/AB (Power) (2 AS)
          Surrey - BBC-CCC/BB (All courses except under **18 pts**) (BTEC 75% average)
20 pts.   **Aston** - BCC/AA (Mech Eng; Elmech Eng; Mech Eng/Euro)
          Belfast - BCC (Mech Eng Extd; Mech Eng; Mech/Food Eng)
          Birmingham - BCC (Mech Eng)
          Cranfield (Shrivenham) - BCC/BB (Mech Eng) (BTEC 3M)
          Leicester - BCC-BCD (Eng Mech)
          Leeds - BCC/BC (Mech Eng; Mechatronics; Man MM Eng) (BTEC 75% average)
          Liverpool - BCC/BB (Mech Eng 3/4; Mech Eng/Man 3/4; Mech/Sys Des 3/4)
          London (UC) - BCC (Mech Eng)
          Loughborough - BCC (Mech Eng 3/4 - C in maths and physics) (BTEC D maths+ 3M)
          Manchester - 20 pts approx (Mech Eng)
          Newcastle - BCC-BCD/BB-BC (Mech Manuf Eng; Mech Eng/Euro)
          Nottingham - BCC-CCC (Mech Eng)
          Reading - BCC-CCC (Mech Eng)
          Sheffield - BCC (Mech Eng; Mech Eng/Mod Lang) (6 AS)

Strathclyde - BCC (ABB 2nd yr entry)(BEng/Dipl Eng; Mech Eng/Aero)
Sussex - BCC-CCC (Mech Eng courses)
Swansea - BCC/BB (Mech Eng/Euro)
UMIST - BCC/AB (Mech Eng)
Warwick - BCC-CCC (Mech courses)

18 pts.   **Brunel** - CCC/BB (All Mech courses; Mech/Auto Des; Mech E/EIS; Mech/BS) (AS) (BTEC D maths+M overall)
Cardiff - CCC/BB (Mech Eng) (BTEC D+M)
Edinburgh - CCC/BB (Mech Eng)
Exeter - CCC/BC (Eng Sci 3) (4 AS) (See **Engineering**) (BTEC M overall)
Lancaster - CCC (Engin Mech) (BTEC 2D inc maths+M overall)
Liverpool John Moores - CCC (Mech/Man Sys Eng)
London (QMW) - 18-14 pts (Mech Eng; Mech Eng Sp) (BTEC 1D+4M)
Newcastle - CCC/BC (Mech Eng)
Salford - CCC/BB (Mech Eng Int; Mech Eng FT) (4 AS) (BTEC 1D+3M)
Strathclyde - CCC (BBC 2nd yr entry) (All courses BEng)
Surrey - CCC-CCD (Mech/Foundation) (BTEC Ds+Ms)
Swansea - CCC/BC (Mech Eng)

16 pts.   **City** - CCD/BC (BEng) (BTEC Ds+Ms)
Liverpool John Moores - CCD (Mech/Man Eng – MEng)

14 pts.   **Bradford** - CDD/14 pts (Mech Eng Man) (BTEC 3M)
12 pts.   **Aberdeen** - CC (Mech Eng)
Glasgow - CC (1st yr entry) BCC (2nd yr entry) (See also **Ocean Engineering**)
Hertfordshire - DDD/CD (Mech Eng) (BTEC 3M)
Heriot-Watt - DDD/CC (1st yr entry) CCC (2nd yr entry) (Mech Eng; E Res/MEng; O Eng/M Eng) (4 AS)
Manadon (RNEC) - CC (Naval Officer entry)
Northumbria - 12 pts (Mech Eng) (6 AS)
Oxford Brookes - CC (Mech Eng)

10 pts.   **Brighton** - 10-8 pts (Mech Eng) (BTEC 3M)
Kingston - 10-8 pts (Mech Eng)
Liverpool John Moores - DDE/DD (Mech Manuf Syst Eng; Mech Eng)
Paisley - DDE/DD (Mech Eng)
Portsmouth - 10 pts (Mech Eng) (4 AS)

8 pts.   **and below**
Bradford - EEE (Foundation)
Bolton (IHE) - (Mech Eng; Auto Eng)
Bristol UWE - (Mech Eng)
Central Lancashire - 8 pts (Mech Eng)
Coventry - (Mech Eng; Auto Eng) (4 AS)
De Montfort - 6 pts (Mech Eng)
De Montfort - (Mech Eng extended - 5 GCSEs + experience)
Dundee - DD (Mech Eng)
Dundee (IT) - (Mech Eng)
East London - (Mech Eng)
Glamorgan - (Mech Eng; Mech/Man Syst Eng)
Greenwich - (Mech Eng)
Huddersfield - (Mech Eng)
Liverpool John Moores - (Mech/Prod)
Manchester Met - (All courses)
Middlesex - 6 pts (minimum) (Mech Eng)
North East Wales (IHE) - (Mech Eng)
Nottingham Trent - 8 pts (Mech Eng) (4 AS) (BTEC 80/75% average overall)
Plymouth - (Mech Eng)
Robert Gordon - (Mech Eng)
Sheffield Hallam - (Mech/Man Eng)
South Bank - (Mech Eng) (4 AS) (BTEC 3M)
Staffordshire - DD (Mech Eng) (BTEC Ms inc maths)
Sunderland - (Mech Eng)

Teesside – 6 pts (Mech Eng) (4 AS) (BTEC 60% average overall)
Westminster - (Mech Eng)
Wolverhampton - (Mech Eng)

Franchised degree and HND courses (see Ch 5):

Brighton – Brighton (CT); Chichester (CT); Crawley (CT); Hastings (CT); Northbrook (CDT).
Liverpool John Moores – Knowsley (CmC); South Cheshire (CFE); Southport (CFE).
Middlesex - Writtle (CAg).
South Bank – Guildford (CFE); South Bank (CFE); South Thames (CFE); Vauxhall (CFE).

Diploma of Higher Education courses: Greenwich.

Offers for Foundation, Certificate and Diploma courses (see Ch 5):

Higher National Diploma courses (England and Wales):
6 pts. Middlesex; Nottingham Trent; Swansea (IHE).
4 pts. and below Blackburn (CT); Bolton (IHE) transfers to Salford Univ (inc Auto Eng); Brighton; Cardiff (IHE); Central England; Central Lancashire; Cheltenham & Glos (CHE); Coventry (CT) (Auto); Coventry; De Montfort; Derby; Farnborough (CT); Glamorgan (Plant Eng, Mech/Man Eng); Greenwich; Gwent (CHE); Hastings (CT); Hertfordshire; Huddersfield; Humberside; Kingston; Liverpool John Moores; Loughborough (CT) (Motor Vehicle Management); Luton (CHE); Manchester Met; Mid-Kent (CHFE); Middlesex; North East Wales (IHE) transfers to Salford Univ; Northumbria; Norwich City (CHFE); Nottingham Trent; Oldham (CT); Plymouth; Portsmouth; Sheffield Hallam; Southall (CT); Southampton (IHE); Staffordshire; Stockport (CT); Stoke on Trent (CT) (Motor Vehicle Man); Suffolk (CFHE); Sunderland; Swansea (IHE) Auto Eng; Willesden (CT) (inc Motor Vehicle Management).

Higher National Diploma courses (Scotland):
4 pts. and below Robert Gordon.

Alternative offers:

EB offers: **Glamorgan** 60%; **Liverpool** 70%; **Surrey** 65%; **UMIST** 65%.

IB offers: **Aberdeen** 24 pts; **Bath** 30 pts Highers; **Belfast** 655+555; **Birmingham** 665; **Bradford** 30-24 pts; **Brighton** 24 pts; **Bristol** 32 pts; **Brunel** 28 pts 5/6 at Highers; **Cardiff** 28 pts; **City** (BEng) 28 pts; **Coventry** 24 pts; **Cranfield (Shrivenham)** H655; **Durham** 666; **Exeter** 30 pts; **Hertfordshire** 26 pts; **Leeds** 665; **Lancaster** 30 pts; **London (QMW)** 30 pts; **Loughborough** 6 maths 6 physics 30 pts total; **Salford** 28 pts; **Surrey** 28 pts + H555; **UMIST** 655.

Irish offers: **Aberdeen** BBCCC; **Brunel** BBCCC; **Lancaster** BBBBC; **Leeds** (Arch Eng) BBBC; **Liverpool** BBCCC; **Paisley** BCC; **Salford** BBCC; **Sunderland** CCC; **Westminster** DDD.

SCE offers: **Aberdeen** BBBC; **Birmingham** AAAB; **Belfast** BBBB/BBBC; **Cardiff** ABBB; **Dundee** BBB; **Edinburgh** BBBB; **Glasgow** BBBB; **Heriot-Watt** BBBC; **Lancaster** ABBB; **Newcastle** BBBB; **Northumbria** BB; **Paisley** BCC; **Salford** BBCC; **Sheffield** BBBCC; **Southampton** BBBBB; **Strathclyde** ABBB.

Overseas applicants: Some applicants (with appropriate diplomas) may be accepted for second year courses. **Hull** Living costs 30% lower than in London; **Loughborough** English language tuition pre-sessional or concurrent with courses.

CHOOSING YOUR COURSE (See also Ch 1)

Subject information: All courses involve the design, installation and maintenance of equipment used in industry. Thermodynamics, computer-aided design, fluid mechanics and materials science are subjects fundamental to this branch of engineering. Many universities offer students the opportunity to transfer to other engineering courses in year two.

Course highlights: Aston and **Belfast** There is a common first year with Manufacturing Engineering. **Birmingham** The course has a bias towards computer-aided engineering and engineering systems. **Bradford** Year one common with Manufacturing Engineering, transfers possible. A wide range of options including automotive engineering and languages. **Brighton** Option in forensic engineering. Final year options in either engineering production technology or mechanical engineering and design. **Bristol** End of first year transfers possible to Civil or Aeronautical Engineering, Engineering Mathematics or Manufacturing Systems Engineering (MSE) and at the end of year two to MSE; language options. **Cardiff** Common first year between Civil, Mechanical, Environmental and Architectural Engineering; course decision at 16 weeks. **Central Lancashire** Language tuition is available for students who wish to complete part of their course at an institution elsewhere in the EC. **Coventry** (Automotive Engineering) A design studio-based course targeted to the automotive industry. **Cranfield (Shrivenham)** Year one common with Aero Systems Engineering and Electronic Systems Engineering. Transfers possible. Final year possible in automotive or aeromechanical engineering. Scholarships available for well-qualified candidates. **Dundee** The first year is common with Manufacturing Engineering, Electrical and Electronic Engineering. **Glasgow** A common course is taken by all students initially opting for Aeronautical and Mechanical Engineering and naval Architecture and Ocean Engineering. Specialisation then follows in the third and fourth years. **Heriot-Watt** The first year is taken in common with Energy Resource and Mechanical Engineering. Flexibility between Mechanical Engineering and Energy Resource Engineering. Possible specialisation in Computer Aided Engineering in later years. Final year language option. **London (UC)** A modern language is an optional subject in the third year. **Loughborough** Common first year then choice between Mechanical, Aero and Systems Engineering. **Middlesex** Options in third year include robotics, fuels and energy, production management and materials engineering. **Plymouth** Options include thermal power and offshore engineering. **Portsmouth** Computer-aided engineering is included in all areas of the course. **Robert Gordon** Offshore Engineering is also offered with specialisms in operations management, petroleum exploration, transportation, drilling, geology and reservoir engineering. **Salford** Special emphasis is placed on the business and commercial aspects of manufacturing. Scholarships for women. **South Bank** Students may spend the sandwich year at Mannheim gaining dual qualifications. **Sussex** Specialised topics including robotics, computer-aided design, thermal power and microprocessors. Engineering management is studied throughout the second and third years. **UMIST** In the first two years it is possible to choose as an option one topic from modern languages (German or French) or history of science and technology. NOW CHECK PROSPECTUSES FOR ALL COURSES.

Study opportunities abroad: Bath (E); **Belfast** (E); **Birmingham** (E); **Brighton** (E); **Bristol** (E); **Brunel** (E); **Cardiff** (E); **Central Lancashire** (E); **City** (E); **Coventry** (E); **De Montfort** (E); **Glamorgan** (E); **Hertfordshire** (E); **Huddersfield** (E); **Leeds** (E) FR CAN; **London (Imp)** (E), **(QMW)** E; **Loughborough** (E) D G IT GR; **Newcastle** (E); **Nottingham** (E); **Northumbria** (E); **Nottingham Trent** (E); **Robert Gordon** (E); **Salford** (E); **Sheffield** (E) EUR; **South Bank** (E); **Strathclyde** (E); **Sunderland** (E); **Surrey** (E); **Sussex** (E) FR G; **Swansea** (E); **Teesside** (E).

Work opportunities abroad: Aston FR G NAM; **Bath** FR G; **Brighton** USA FR G IT; **Bristol** FR G; **Brunel** HK FR G IT USA GR; **Central Lancashire** FR G SP IT D LUX IRE NL B P GR; **Coventry** FR G SP; **Cranfield** USA; **De Montfort** FR G NL; **Glamorgan** G; **Hertfordshire** G; **Loughborough** D G IT; **Middlesex** G; **Manchester Met** G NL; **Northumbria**; **Portsmouth** EUR; **Sheffield** G; **Sheffield Hallam** FR G; **South Bank** J G AUS; **Sunderland** G; **Surrey** USA G; **Teesside** FR.

ADMISSIONS INFORMATION

Number of applicants per place (approx): Aston 11; **Bath** 13; **Bradford** 6; **Brighton** 10; **Bristol** 10; **Bristol UWE** 6; **Brunel** 6; **Cardiff** 20; **Central Lancashire** 13; **Coventry** 12; **City**

13; **Cranfield (Shrivenham)** 6; **Dundee (IT)** 6; **Durham** 8; **Glamorgan** 6; **Hertfordshire** 10; **Heriot-Watt** 6; **Huddersfield** 7; **Lancaster** 8; **Leeds** 9; **Liverpool** 6; **Liverpool John Moores** (Mech Prod) 2, (Mech) 10; **Loughborough** (Mech Eng) 10, (Auto Eng) 5; **Manchester Met** 10, (Man Man) 2; **Middlesex** 3; **Newcastle** 7; **Northumbria** 8; **Nottingham** 10; **Nottingham Trent** 6; **Portsmouth** 10; **Salford** 6; **Sheffield** 10; **South Bank** 4; **Staffordshire** 6; **Strathclyde** 6; **Surrey** 7; **Swansea** 6; **Teesside** 3; **UMIST** 8; **Westminster** 11.

General Studies acceptable: Aberdeen; Aston; Belfast; Bradford; Exeter; Heriot-Watt; Lancaster; Loughborough; Manchester Met; North East Wales (IHE); Northumbria; Nottingham; Nottingham Trent; South Bank; Surrey.

Selection interviews: Aston (some); Bath (some); Belfast (some); Brighton (some); Bristol; Brunel; Cambridge; Central Lancashire (some); City; Dundee (IT); Durham; Kingston; Lancaster; Leeds; Liverpool John Moores; Manchester Met; Newcastle (some); Nottingham; Oxford; Paisley; Salford (some); Sheffield; Strathclyde; Sunderland (some); Surrey (some); Swansea (some); UMIST (some); most new universities.

Offers to applicants repeating A-levels: Higher Belfast, Brighton, Kingston, Loughborough (22 pts), Newcastle, Swansea; **Possibly higher** City, Durham, Huddersfield; **Same** Aston, Bath, Bradford, Bristol, Brunel, Coventry, East London, Leeds (usually), Liverpool, Liverpool John Moores, Manchester Met, Northumbria, Nottingham, South Bank, Surrey, Teesside, UMIST.

Admissions Tutors' advice: Aston MEng students need GCSE grades A-C in French or German. **Loughborough** Apply early. This is a sandwich course - sponsorship is not essential. We also have an extended five-year MEng version of the course for which the DIS (Diploma in Industrial Studies) is also awarded. Usually certain students are invited to apply for this on completion of the first year but a very few are made conditional offers of ABB *ab initio*. Applicants for the five-year course are automatically considered for the four-year course also. We look for motivation and mathematical ability. **Portsmouth** Applicants must show some motivation, and in the case of sandwich courses, must be a saleable commodity to industry, since industrial training is part of the course. **Surrey** A good performance in maths is important.

> **Examples of interview questions:** What mechanical objects have you examined and/or tried to repair? How do you see yourself in five years' time? What do you imagine you would be doing (production, management or design engineering)? What engineering interests have you? What qualities are required to become a successful mechanical engineer? Do you like sixth form work? Describe the working of parts on an engineering drawing. How does a fridge work?

GAP YEAR ADVICE

Institutions accepting a Gap Year: Most institutions; **Bradford** If you are working in industry you will be visited by a member of staff. **Brunel** Not recommended: the four-year thin sandwich course is a better investment of time. **London (QMW)** For a list of industrial contacts and sponsors write to Mr G Sacks (Dept of Mech Eng). **Loughborough** Sympathetic if year-plan is organised. **Manchester Met, Newcastle** Seek sponsorship or relevant experience. **Surrey** 'Year in Industry' scheme useful.

Institutions willing to defer entry after A-levels (see Ch 5): Bradford; Brighton; City; Cranfield (Shrivenham) (No); Dundee; Heriot-watt; Loughborough; Manchester Met; Robert Gordon; Surrey; Swansea.

AFTER A-LEVELS ADVICE

Institutions which may accept the same points score after A-levels: Aston; Bradford; Brighton; Brunel; Cardiff; Central Lancashire; City; Coventry; Cranfield (Shrivenham); De Montfort; Dundee (IT); Kingston; Lancaster; Leeds; Liverpool; Liverpool John Moores; Loughborough; Manchester Met; Middlesex; Newcastle; Northumbria; Nottingham; Oxford Brookes; Portsmouth; Salford; Sheffield; South Bank; Staffordshire; Strathclyde; Sunderland; Surrey; Swansea; Teesside; UMIST.

Institutions demanding the actual grades offered after A-levels: Belfast; Bristol; Durham (usually); Hertfordshire.

Institutions which may accept under-achieving applicants after A-levels: Most institutions consider candidates who do not achieve target offers.

Hull Overseas students 18-16 pts.

Institutions with vacancies in Aug/Sept 1992 (see Ch 5): Aberdeen; Aston; Bath; Bradford 12 pts; Brighton 6 pts; Bristol; City 12 pts; Cranfield (Shrivenham) 14 pts; Dundee DD; Glamorgan 8 pts; Greenwich; Heriot-Watt 12 pts; Kingston 6 pts; Leeds; Liverpool; London (QMW); Loughborough (Auto Eng) 20 pts; Manchester Met; Newcastle; Paisley; Portsmouth; Robert Gordon; South Bank 8 pts; Strathclyde; Sunderland; Surrey 14 pts; Swansea 12 pts, (H302) 16 pts; York; see also under **Engineering Science.**

ADVICE FOR MATURE STUDENTS

See under **Engineering**.

GRADUATE EMPLOYMENT

New Graduates' destinations (percentages) 1991:
Permanent employment: U 82; P 66; C 100.
Unemployment: U 14; P 27; C 0.
Further studies (all types): U 20; P 14; C 0.
Main career destinations (approx): Engineering 80; Finance 5; Business 10; Computing 3.

Surrey The majority of the 27 graduates entered engineering careers with such organisations as the Road Research Laboratory, Unilever, British Aerospace, British Steel, Lucas Diesel Systems, GEC and London Underground. Two went on to take MSc degrees and one is an airline pilot trainee.

Teesside All graduates entering full-time employment secured employment as engineers.

ENGINEERING (MINING) (See also Geology)

Special subject requirements: See **Engineering.**

NB Institutions may raise or lower the level of published offers depending either on the quality or otherwise of individual applications or the numbers of applications received; grades/points offered may be adjusted downwards after A-level results. The level of an offer is not indicative of the quality of a course.

20 pts.	**London (Imp)** - BCC/BC (Min Eng/RM; Petr Eng - MEng)
18 pts.	**Cardiff** - 18-14 pts (Explor/Mining Geol)
	Nottingham - CCC-CDD/BC (Mining) (BTEC 65% overall)
16 pts.	**London (Imp)** - 16 pts (Petr Eng; Mining)
14 pts.	**Exeter (CSM)** - 14 pts (Mining Eng; Min Eng) (BTEC 3M)
	Leeds - CDD/CC (Mining Eng; Mineral Eng) (BTEC 4M)
12 pts.	**and below**
	Doncaster (Coll) - (Quarry Eng)

Offers for Foundation, Certificate and Diploma courses (see Ch 5):

Higher National Diploma courses (England and Wales):
Doncaster (Coll) (Road Surfacing); Exeter (CSM) Options in minerals engineering, mineral resource management, minerals surveying, plant-electro engineering; Glamorgan Mineral Surveying; Sheffield Hallam.

Higher Diploma courses (Scotland):
      Kirkcaldy (Coll).

Alternative offers:

EB offers: **Exeter (CSM)** 60%.

IB offers: **Exeter (CSM)** 26-24 pts.

SCE offers: **Exeter (CSM)** BBB; **Leeds** BBBB.

CHOOSING YOUR COURSE (See also Ch 1)

Subject information: This subject covers geology, surveying and mineral processing with opportunities to enter careers in petroleum engineering as well as coal and metalliferous mining. (Applicants should note that the Camborne School of Mines (CSM) has now merged with Exeter University. Applications are made through UCAS.) See also under **Geology**.

Course highlights: Exeter (CSM) International reputation. Minerals and Mining Engineering students have a common first year; vacation work at end of second year in UK or abroad. Scholarships and other awards are made each year: Apply to Anglo-American Corporation of South Africa Ltd/De Beers Consolidated Mines Ltd, c/o ACIS International Appointments Ltd, 40 Holborn Viaduct, London EC1P 1AJ. (See also under **Engineering**.) Also Consolidated Gold Fields Ltd, Shell International and the National Coal Board (contact admissions tutor). **Leeds** Minerals and mining students have separate programmes with some common modules. **London (Imp)** Third year students work at least 500 hours in industry during summer vacations in UK or abroad. (Petr Eng) Choice between Petroleum Engineering and Mining Engineering at end of first or second years. Optional sandwich placements. Quarry Engineering option on the Mining Engineering course. **Nottingham** Options enable students to specialise in petroleum engineering as well as coal and metalliferous mining. NOW CHECK PROSPECTUSES FOR ALL COURSES.

Study opportunities abroad: Exeter (CSM) (E); **Nottingham** (E).

Work opportunities abroad: Exeter (CSM) Worldwide.

ADMISSIONS INFORMATION

Number of applicants per place (approx): Exeter (CSM) 3; **Leeds** (Mining) 11, (Mineral) 2; **Nottingham** 7.

General Studies acceptable: Leeds (as a third subject).

Selection interviews: Exeter (CSM); Leeds; Nottingham.

Offers to applicants repeating A-levels: Same Leeds.

Admissions Tutors' advice: Exeter (CSM) Maths, physics, chemistry and English at GCSE grade C or above required. **Leeds** GCSE (grade C or above) in maths and physics required if not taken at A-level.

Examples of interview questions: Have you visited any mines? Describe them. Have you any relatives in the mining industry? What problems exist at present for the mining unions? Where are the largest coalfields in Britain? What other products are mined in Britain? What products are mined in other parts of the world?

GAP YEAR ADVICE

Institutions accepting a Gap Year: Leeds.

Institutions willing to defer entry after A-levels (see Ch 5): Leeds.

AFTER A-LEVELS ADVICE

Institutions which may accept the same points score after A-levels: Exeter (CSM); Leeds; Nottingham.

Institutions which may accept under-achieving applicants after A-levels: Most institutions consider applicants who have failed to achieve target A-levels.

Institutions with vacancies in Aug/Sept 1992 (see Ch 5): Exeter (CSM); Leeds 10 pts; see also under **Engineering Science**.

ADVICE FOR MATURE STUDENTS

See under **Engineering**.

GRADUATE EMPLOYMENT

New Graduates' destinations (percentages) 1991:
Permanent employment: U 80.
Unemployment: U 19.
Further studies (all types): U 26.

ENGINEERING (PRODUCTION) (See also Engineering (Manufacturing))

Special subject requirements: 2-3 A-levels in mathematics/science subjects. GCSE (grade A-C) in English and chemistry often required.

NB Institutions may raise or lower the level of published offers depending either on the quality or otherwise of individual applications or the numbers of applications received; grades/points offered may be adjusted downwards after A-level results. The level of an offer is not indicative of the quality of a course.

30 pts.	**Cambridge/Oxford** - AAA potential recommended (Eng)
24 pts.	**UMIST** - BBB (Eng Mnfr/Man) (Enhanced)
22 pts.	**Nottingham** - BBC-BCC (Prod Man)
20 pts.	**Loughborough** - BCC min 20 pts (Des) (BTEC 4M + maths 80%)
	Strathclyde - BCC 2nd yr entry only (Man Eng Man)
	Ulster - BCC (Manu Man)
18 pts.	**Aston** - 18 pts (Manuf Eng)
	Cardiff - CCC/BB (Tech Prod Man) (BTEC 75% overall)
	Warwick - CCC (Eng Manu)
12 pts.	**Nottingham Trent** - 12 pts (Indust St)
8 pts.	**and below**
	Bell (CT) - (Qual Man)
	Coventry - DD (Prod Des) (4 AS) (BTEC 3M inc 65% maths + Mech Sci + 1 other 75%)
	Middlesex - 8 pts (Mech Eng Man)
	South Bank - 8 pts (Eng Prod Des; Pro Tech/Mgt St) (BTEC 3M)

Franchised degree and HND courses (see Ch 5):
>   **South Bank** - South Bank (CFE); Waltham Forest (CFE).

Offers for Foundation, Certificate and Diploma courses (see Ch 5):

Higher National Diploma courses:
> **4 pts.   and below**
>   Blackpool (Coll); Brighton; Coventry (Manufacturing Systems); Farnborough (CT); Hertfordshire; Humberside; Leeds Met; Liverpool John Moores; Middlesex; Nottingham Trent; Sheffield Hallam; Stockport (CT);

Alternative offers:

IB offers: **Cardiff** 554 + 13 pts.

SCE offers: **Cardiff** ABBB; **Lougborough** (Man Syst) BBB; **Strathclyde** ABBB/AABC.

Overseas applicants: Hull Living costs 30% lower than in London.

CHOOSING YOUR COURSE (See also Ch 1)

***

Subject information: See under **Engineering (Manufacturing).**

***

Course highlights: Nottingham Trent (Prod Eng) Covers production operations, work design, quality and reliability, industrial relations, business accounting and manufacturing technology. See **Engineering (Manufacturing).** NOW CHECK PROSPECTUSES FOR ALL COURSES.

ADMISSIONS INFORMATION

Number of applicants per place (approx): Coventry 8; **Middlesex** 2; **Strathclyde** 8.

General Studies acceptable: Aston; Nottingham; Nottingham Trent.

Selection interviews: Aston (some); Coventry; Oxford; South Bank.

Offers to applicants repeating A-levels: Higher Strathclyde; **Same** Aston, Nottingham; Nottingham Trent; South Bank.

Admissions Tutors' advice: Aston GCSE grades A-C in French or German for MEng course. **Coventry** Strength in mathematics and physics advisable, in addition to good communication skills and personality. Personal qualities are as important as academic qualifications. **South Bank** (Eng Prod Des) Flair for inventive and creative design work (portfolio required) and qualities as an engineer are required.

***

Examples of interview questions: What is the function of an engineer? Describe something interesting you have recently done in your A-levels. What do you know about careers in engineering? Discuss the role of women engineers in industry. Why is a disc brake better than a drum brake? Would you be prepared to make people redundant to improve the efficiency of a production line?

***

GAP YEAR ADVICE

Institutions accepting a Gap Year: Most institutions.

Institutions willing to defer entry after A-levels (see Ch 5): Bell (CT); South Bank.

AFTER A-LEVELS ADVICE

Institutions which may accept the same points score after A-levels: Aston; Coventry; Nottingham; Nottingham Trent; Strathclyde.

Institutions which may accept under-achieving applicants after A-levels: Hull (Overseas students 18-16 pts); Strathclyde.

Institutions with vacancies in Aug/Sept 1992 (see Ch 5): Many vacancies were declared and all students with two A-level passes would be considered. The more popular universities initially were asking an average of 16 pts.

ADVICE FOR MATURE STUDENTS

See under **Engineering**.

GRADUATE EMPLOYMENT

New Graduates' destinations (percentages) 1991:
Permanent employment: U 80; P 76.
Unemployment: U 16; P 15.
Further studies (all types): U 20; P 7.

ENGLISH

Special subject requirements: A-levels in English and a language often 'required' or 'preferred'; GCSE (grade A-C) in English and a language.

NB Institutions may raise or lower the level of published offers depending either on the quality or otherwise of individual applications or the numbers of applications received; grades/points offered may be adjusted downwards after A-level results. The level of an offer is not indicative of the quality of a course.

30 pts.	**Cambridge/Oxford** - AAA potential recommended in most cases
28 pts.	**Edinburgh** - (Engl Lit)
26 pts.	**Edinburgh** – ABB (English)
24 pts.	**Cardiff** - BBB/AA (Eng Lit; Eng/Hist - Q308)
	Durham - ABC (All courses except under **22 pts**)
	East Anglia - BBB (EAS)
	Edinburgh - BBB-BBC (Engl/Hist; Engl/Lang; Eng/Scot Lit)
	Hull - BBB/BB (All courses) (4 AS) (BTEC Ds+Ms)
	Leeds - ABC (English)
	Leeds - BBB (Eng/Thea; Int Eng (Q301)) (BTEC Ds+Ms)
	Liverpool - BBB (English; Eng/Fr; Eng/Lit) (For Med H/Med E)
	London (King's) - 24-20 pts approx (English)
	London (RH) - ABC/AB (Eng/Drama; English; Eng/Fr)
	Loughborough - 24-16 pts (English) (NMI) (See **Admissions Tutors' advice**)
	Manchester - BBB-BCC approx (English)
	Newcastle - ABC minimum B in English (English; Eng Lit)
	Reading - BBB (English)
	St Andrews - BBB (English) (4 AS)
	Sheffield - BBB (English courses)
	Southampton - ABC B in English (English)
	Sussex - BBB/AB (All English courses)
	Warwick - BBB (Eng Thea)
	Warwick - BBB-BBC (Eng Euro; Eng Span; Am Lit; Eng Lit; Eng Fr)
	York - ABC (All coures except under **22/20 pts**)

22 pts.	**Aberdeen** - BBC (English; Eng/SL)
	Birmingham - BBC-BCC (English)
	Bristol - BBC/BB (Eng/Lat; Eng/Gk)
	Cardiff - BBC/AB (Eng Med)
	Cardiff - BBC/AB (Mod Engl)
	Durham - 22 pts (Eng/Ling; Mod Lang/Ling)
	Edinburgh - 22 pts (Engl/Fr)
	Essex - BBC/BB (E Lang EEL) (BTEC Ms)
	Exeter - BBC/AB (English) (6 AS)
	Exeter - BBC-BCD/BB (Engl/GRS) (6 AS)
	Glasgow - 22 pts (English)
	Keele - BBC-BCC/AB-BC (joint courses) (4 AS)
	Kent - BBC/AB (English; Eng St)
	Kingston - 22-20 pts (Modern Arts - Engl)
	Lancaster - BBC (English; Comb St courses) (BTEC Ms)
	Leeds - BBC-BCC/BB (Eng joint courses with Fr/Ger/Hist/Hist Art/ Sp/Phil)
	Leicester - BBC/AB (English)
	London (Gold) - BBC (Engl)
	London (RH) - BBC/BB (Eng/Ital; Eng/CS; Eng/Lat)
	London (UC) - BBC (English)
	Loughborough - BBC-CCC/BB-CC (Engl/PE) (See **Admissions Tutors' advice**)
	Newcastle - BBC (Eng Lang)
	Nottingham - BBC (English)
	Reading - BBC (All courses except under **24/20 pts**)
	Ripon & York St John (CHE) - BBC (All courses except under **20/18 pts**)
	Salford - BBC/AB (English)
	Southampton - BBC (Eng/Fr; Eng/Hist)
	Stirling - BBC (Engl; EFL; joint courses)
	Swansea - BBC/BB (English - single hons)
	Warwick - BBC (Eng Ital; Eng Lat)
	York - BBC (Engl/AH EQ; Eng Phil EQ; Engl/Hist EQ)
20 pts.	**Aberystwyth** - BCC/BB (English) (BTEC Ms)
	Central England - BCC-BCD/BB (Engl) (4 AS)
	Dundee - BCC (English) (BTEC 6M)
	Essex - BCC (ELL)
	Exeter - BCC (Engl/Art)
	Glasgow - BCC (Joint courses)
	Kent - BCC (Eng/Soc)
	Kingston - 20-16 pts (Eng)
	Lancaster - BCC (B in English) (Combined courses - except **22 and 14 pts**)
	Leeds - BCC (Eng joint courses with Gk Civ/Ital/Lat/Port/Rel St/ R Civ/Rus/Theol/ Soc) (See also **22 pts**)
	Leeds - BBD (Eng/Mus)
	Liverpool - BCC-CCC/AB-BB (Eng/Fr)
	London (RH) - (Eng/Ger)
	London (QMW) - BCC (English)
	Loughborough - BCC (Engl/Drama) (See **Admissions Tutors' advice**)
	Northumbria - BCC/BB (Eng/Hist)
	Reading - BCC (Contemp Eng/Man St; Eng/Class St; Eng/Latin) (See also **24/22 pts**)
	Ripon & York St John (CHE) - BCC/BB (Eng Lang/Lit; Eng/DT)
	Sheffield - BCC/BB (English courses except under **24 pts**)
	Sheffield Hallam - 20 pts B in English/BB (Engl St)
	Southampton - BCC (Eng/Span; Eng/Ger; Eng/Phil)
	Swansea - BCC/BB (English - joint hons)
	Warwick - BCC/BB B in English (Eng BA(QTS); Eng Ger) (See also **22 pts**)
	York - BCC/BB (Eng Lang/Ling)
18 pts.	**Anglia (Poly Univ)** - 18 pts (B in English)(Engl and joint courses)
	Bangor - BCD/BB-BC (English single and joint hons)

Belfast - CCC/BC (English)
Bristol - AB (English)
Bristol UWE - 18-14 pts (Hum)
Cambridge (Hom) - BCD (Eng/Ed) (4 AS) (See also **Education**)
Essex - CCC/BB (LEE)
Oxford Brookes - CCC/AB (Modular) (4 AS)
Plymouth - CCC (Comb Eng) (BTEC 5M)
Portsmouth - BCD/BB (Engl/Trans)
Ripon & York St John (CHE) - CCC (App S Sc/Eng)
Salford - BCD (Eng/Hist)
Southampton - BCD/BB-BC (Eng/Phil)
St David's - BCD/BB (English)
Strathclyde - CCC (BBD 2nd yr entry) (Eng)
West Sussex (IHE) - CCC/BC (Eng) (6 AS)

16 pts. **Bath (CHE)** - BB (Comb St with History)
Bristol - BB minimum offer (Engl/Phil)
Bristol - BB (Eng/Dr)
Buckingham - CCD/CC (English) (BTEC 3M)
Central Lancashire - CCD (Comb Hons)
London (Gold) - BB (Engl/Hist)
Manchester Met - BCE/BC (Engl St; Hum/Soc St)
Middlesex - 16-12 pts (Con Writing; Eng)
Nottingham - BB (Joint Honours)
Ulster - CCD/BC (Eng)

14 pts. **Brighton** - 14 pts (Hum)
Cheltenham & Glos (CHE) - 14-12 pts C in English (Engl St) (BTEC 3D+3M)
Lancaster - BC (Eng/Mus)
North London - BC-CC-CD (Hum) (4 AS)
Portsmouth - CCD/BC (Engl/Fr; Lit St)
S Martins (CHE) - BDE/BC (Eng)
Trinity & All Saints (CHE) - CDD (English; Eng/PM)
West Sussex (IHE) - 14 pts (BA)

12 pts. **Bath (CHE)** - CC (Comb St with Rel St or Sociol)
Bretton Hall (CHE) - CC-EE (Eng/Inter Arts; Eng/Social Studies) (4 AS) (See under Social Studies)
Canterbury Christ Church (CHE) - CC (Comb St) (4 AS)
Edge Hill (CHE) - CC (Eng)
King Alfred's (CHE) - 12 pts (Joint courses) (4 AS)
North London - BD approx (B in English) (Engl)
Roehampton (IHE) - CC (English + comb)
Sunderland - CC-EE (Comb St; Engl St)
Westminster - 12 pts (All courses)
Wolverhampton - (All courses)

10 pts. **Bedford (CHE)** - 10 pts (Comb St)
Middlesex - CD approx (Modular)
Worcester (CHE) - 10 pts and below inc Access (Comb Hons) (4 AS)

8 pts. and below
Bath (CHE) - (Creative Arts)
Central Lancashire - (Comb Hons)
Chester (CHE) - (Comb St)
Derby - (Modular; Comb St) (4 AS)
Greenwich - (Hum)
Hertfordshire - (Hum)
Huddersfield - (Comm Arts)
La Sainte Union (CHE) - Comb St
Liverpool (IHE) - (Comb St)
Liverpool John Moores - (Int Credit Scheme)
Luton (CHE) - (Eng/Hist)
Nene (CHE) - (Comb St)

North East Wales (IHE) - (Engl/Hist)
Nottingham Trent - (Hum; M Eur St)
St Mary's (CHE) - (Comb St)
South Bank - EE (English courses)
Staffordshire - (Mod St)
Swansea (IHE) - (Comb St)
Trinity Carmarthen (CHE) - (Hum)
West London (IHE) - 8 pts (Joint)

Diploma of Higher Education courses:
  2 pts.   Bath (CHE); Crewe & Alsager (CHE); Oxford Brookes; Westminster (CHE); Worcester (CHE).

Alternative offers:

IB offers: **Aberdeen** 30 pts; **Aberystwyth** 30 pts; **Anglia (Poly Univ)** 28 pts; **Bangor** 30-28 pts; **Bristol** 34-32 pts; **Buckingham** 24 pts; **Cardiff** H555 S444; **Central England** 30-28 pts H5 English; **Dundee** 29 pts; **Durham** H665; **Edinburgh** H665; **Exeter** 33 pts; **Hull** 30 pts; **Kent** 27 pts, H 12 pts; **King Alfred's (CHE)** 24 pts; **Lancaster** 32-30 pts; **Leeds** 30 pts inc H665; **London (QMW)** H655; **Loughborough** 28 pts Highers 14 pts; **Sheffield** 33 pts; **South Bank** 24 pts; **St Andrews** 30 pts; **Warwick** H76; **Swansea** 28 pts; **York** 30 pts H766 inc 6 in English.

Irish offers: **South Bank** CCCC.

SCE offers: **Aberdeen** BBBB; **Bangor** BBBB; **Dundee** BBBC; **Edinburgh** BBBB (Lang), ABBB (Lit); **Glasgow** BBBB; **Lancaster** ABBB; **Sheffield** AABB; **South Bank** CCC; **St Andrews** BBBB; **Stirling** BBBB; **Strathclyde** BBBB.

Overseas applicants: Hull Living costs 30% lower than in London; **Liverpool** Limited places: English language competence essential. **Oxford Brookes** International Foundation Programme available for overseas students.

CHOOSING YOUR COURSE (See also Ch 1)

> **Subject information:** These courses are an extension of school studies in literature and language and may cover topics ranging from Anglo-Saxon literature to the present day. Most courses, however, will focus on certain areas such as the Medieval or Renaissance periods of literature or English language studies. Admissions Tutors will expect students to have read widely outside their A-level syllabus. (Sunday newspapers' book reviews will give a useful introduction to modern literature.)

Course highlights: Aberystwyth Offers specialisation including old and middle English, 16th and 17th century literature, old Icelandic, American literature and literature in 20th century Wales. **Bangor** Emphasis on historical development of English literature, dramatic literature in performance. **Bristol** Sixteenth century to present day literature taught by tutorial system. **Buckingham** Specialist studies in 19th and 20th century literature. **Central England** Broad chronological and generic spread of courses in literature together with emphasis on language analysis and use, and computer-related skills. **Durham** Emphasis on modern English syntax and phonology, one third of course assessed by non-examination methods. **East Anglia** (Eng Lit) Special features: women's writing, modernism, post-modernism. **Edinburgh** English language covers pronunciation and grammar and examines the historical background to language through Anglo-Saxon English, medieval English, Elizabethan English and older Scots. **Hull** Course includes Renaissance, Commonwealth contemporary literature and Women's Studies. **Lancaster** In the second and third years a range of topics such as Victorian, 19th and 20th century literature, women writers of Britain and America, language, anthropology and psycho-linguistics. **Leeds** Wide range of specialities including Afro-Caribbean, Australian and Canadian literature. (Q301 Int Eng) One year abroad in an English department. **London (RH)** Topics from Old English to 20th century. **Loughborough** Emphasis on 20th century literature in year 3. **Newcastle** (Eng Lang) History of English language and early medieval literature. Theoretical and computational linguistics. (Eng Lit) Broad course covering Chaucer and Shakespeare to American literature of 19th and 20th centuries. **Sheffield Hallam** Creative writing compulsory for two years. **Sheffield** Course covers modern literature, drama, theatre and film studies. **Warwick** Course in European Literature provides students with the opportunity to extend their knowledge of a foreign language and literature (French, German or Latin). For those taking American Literature the balance between this subject and English is largely left to the student. **West Sussex (IHE)** Chichester Festival Theatre placements. Opportunity to combine 75% English with 25% other subjects eg, art, music, history, religious studies, education. **York** Exceptional range of options: students construct own courses by selecting nine out of 50 papers. Q300 students take foreign literature paper studied in original language. NOW CHECK PROSPECTUSES FOR ALL COURSES.

Study opportunities abroad: Aberdeen (E); **Bangor** (E); **Bristol** (E); **Dundee** (E); **Edinburgh** (E); **Hull** (E); **Lancaster** FR IT; **Leeds** (E); **Leicester** (E); **Liverpool** (E); **Manchester Met** (E) EUR; **Newcastle** (E) B NL SP; **Northumbria** (E); **Sheffield** (E); **Southampton** USA; **York** (E) FR IT G.

Work opportunities abroad: Leeds USA; **Roehampton (IHE)** USA; **Sheffield** USA FN; **Sheffield Hallam** SZ; **Worcester (CHE)** USA.

ADMISSIONS INFORMATION

Number of applicants per place (approx): Aberystwyth 7; **Anglia (Poly Univ)** 6; **Bangor** 9; **Birmingham** 11; **Bretton Hall (CHE)** 4; **Bristol** 27; **Buckingham** 3; **Cambridge (Hom)** 4 (All BEd courses); **Cardiff** 5; **Central England** 27; **Cheltenham & Glos (CHE)** 12; **Durham** (Q300) 12, (QQ13) 5; **East Anglia** 20; **Exeter** 13; **Kingston** 20; **Lancaster** 12; **Leeds** 10; **London (QMW)** 9, **(RH)** 5 average; **Loughborough** (Eng) 11, (Eng/PE/Sp Sci) 18, (Eng/Drama) 40; **Manchester Met** 70; **Middlesex** 8; **Newcastle** (Q300) 22, (Q302) 23; **North London** 10; **Nottingham** 33; **Oxford Brookes** 30; **Portsmouth** 5; **S Martins (CHE)** 8; **Salford** (Eng/Hist) 7; **Sheffield** 6; **Sheffield Hallam** 36; **St David's** 7; **Sunderland** 10; **Swansea** 7; **Swansea (IHE)** 4; **Teesside** 8; **Trinity & All Saints (CHE)** 7; **West London (IHE)** 9; **West Sussex (IHE)** 7; **York** 18.

General Studies acceptable: Aberdeen; Aberystwyth (JMB); Anglia (Poly Univ); Bangor; Bretton Hall (CHE) (not AEB); Buckingham; Central England; Cheltenham & Glos (CHE); East Anglia; Edge Hill (CHE); Exeter (2); Hull; Keele; Lancaster; Loughborough; Manchester Met; Newcastle; North London; Oxford Brookes; Portsmouth (2); S Martins (CHE); St David's; Sheffield; Sheffield Hallam (2); Swansea (IHE); Teesside; Trinity & All Saints (CHE); West Sussex (IHE) (2); Worcester (CHE) (2); York.

Selection interviews: Anglia (Poly Univ); Bangor (some); Bristol (sometimes written work); Cambridge; Cambridge (Hom); Durham; East Anglia; Edge Hill (CHE); Exeter; Hull (some); Kent; Lancaster (some); Liverpool (Eng Lit/Fr); London (Gold), (RH); Loughborough; Manchester Met; Newcastle (all courses; very important) (T); Oxford; Portsmouth; Sheffield; St David's; Stirling (some); Swansea (some); Trinity & All Saints (CHE); Warwick; York; Most new universities and colleges.

Offers to applicants repeating A-levels: Higher Newcastle (varies), Sheffield Hallam; **Possibly higher** Cambridge (Hom), Lancaster, Newcastle, Oxford Brookes; **Same** Aberystwyth, Anglia (Poly Univ), Bangor, Bretton Hall (CHE), Bristol, Durham, East Anglia, Edge Hill (CHE), Hull, Leeds, Liverpool, London (Gold), (RH), Loughborough (varies), Manchester Met, Nottingham, Portsmouth, S Martins (CHE), Sheffield, St David's; Swansea, Trinity & All Saints (CHE), Ulster, West Sussex (IHE), York.

Admissions Tutors' advice: Anglia (Poly Univ) Candidates required to bring examples of written work with interview reference and A-level grades; these are main criteria for selection. **Durham** We select applicants according to scholastic attainment and potential. School reports important as is evidence of strong motivation, facility with language, powers of concentration and intellectual curiosity. More applicants should consider the English/Latin combinations. **Lancaster** Interested in applicants with A-level English language as well as literature. **Leeds** Read voraciously! **London (RH)** (Eng/Drama) We do not make an offer before interviewing the candidate. At interview we are looking for students who are mentally agile and versatile - who enjoy reading as well as taking part in productions and who desire knowledge as well as opportunities for creative expression. **Loughborough** We look for enthusiasm for the subject, evidence of wide reading. Lucidity of expression both in speech and writing, some grasp of literary and critical problems. We do not set standard offers, preferring to treat each applicant as an individual. We are prepared to consider applicants with unconventional combinations of A-levels. Applications from mature students welcome. For (English/PE) candidates must be good academically and show good sporting achievement. (Engl/Drama) Offers are made on an individual basis. We consider mature candidates. Final selection is made on the basis of an interview and audition. **Newcastle** No applicant can be considered without an interview. Academic excellence and suitability for chosen course are of paramount importance. (Eng Lit) Motivation important eg, wide reading, creative writing, theatre experience. **Nottingham** Serious consideration can only be given to applicants with AAB grades achieved or predicted. **Portsmouth** (English Lit and Lit in Translation (Eng Eur)) This is a course in international literature including some non-European texts and should not be confused with the Engl/Fr course. **St David's** We encourage applicants to acquire additional appropriate experience before entering university. The College actively encourages mature applicants (11% of the intake). **Warwick** Selectors favour candidates with a foreign language interest but do not insist on A-level foreign language.

Examples of interview questions: Questions on set A-level texts. Which texts are you studying? Which modern writers do you read? Short verbal tests and a précis may be set. Do you enjoy prose or poetry (discuss)? Do you think that class discussion plays an important part in your English course? What do you hope to do after your degree? What do you read outside the syllabus? What is the value of studying a text in depth rather than just reading it for pleasure? What is the difference between satire and comedy?

GAP YEAR ADVICE

Institutions accepting a Gap Year: Most institutions; **Buckingham** Not appropriate; **London (QMW)** Keep in touch with admissions tutor during gap year; **Portsmouth** Spend some time in a French-speaking country; **Salford** Read widely.

Institutions willing to defer entry after A-levels (see Ch 5): Aberystwyth (No); Bangor; Buckingham; Cheltenham & Glos (CHE); Dundee; King Alfred's (CHE); Lancaster; Leeds; Newcastle (Prefer not); Northumbria; Plymouth; Roehampton (IHE); Ripon & York St John (CHE) (No); Salford; Sheffield Hallam; St Andrews; Swansea; York (Prefer not).

AFTER A-LEVELS ADVICE

Institutions which may accept the same points score after A-levels: Aberystwyth (including B in English); Anglia (Poly Univ); Bangor; Bretton Hall (CHE); Canterbury Christ Church (CHE); Central England; Central Lancashire; Durham; Kingston; Leeds; Liverpool; London (RH); Loughborough (most); Manchester; Newcastle (perhaps); Oxford Brookes; St David's; Sheffield; Sheffield Hallam; Swansea.

Institutions demanding the actual grades offered after A-levels: Bristol; Dundee; East Anglia; Glamorgan; Kent; London (Gold); Loughborough (Eng/Hist); Manchester Met; Newcastle; Northumbria (usually); Stirling; Sunderland; Warwick; York.

Institutions which may accept under-achieving applicants after A-levels: Aberystwyth; Anglia (Poly Univ); Bangor; Cambridge (Hom); Central England; Central Lancashire; Dundee; Durham; East Anglia; Exeter; Glasgow; Hull (overseas students 16-14 pts) Keele; Kent; Lancaster; Leeds; Leicester; London (Gold); Loughborough; Manchester Met; Newcastle; Nottingham; Sheffield; Stirling; Swansea; Ulster; Warwick; West Sussex (IHE); York; most new universities and colleges.

Institutions with vacancies in Aug/Sept 1992 (see Ch 5): Bangor B (English) CC; Bishop Grosseteste (CHE); Buckingham 8 pts; Essex 20 pts; King Alfred's (CHE) 12 pts; Kingston; Plymouth; Roehampton (IHE); Trinity & All Saints (CHE); Swansea Full by 20th August - 20 pts. This subject continues to be one of the most popular in all universities with a grade B or a C being sought by admissions tutors. Vacancies vary each year and most institutions will seek at least grade C passes in Clearing.

ADVICE FOR MATURE STUDENTS

This is a popular course for many mature students. Several universities seek recent study experience, some requiring A-levels. Some preference is given to applicants resident in the same locality as the degree awarding institution. **Bangor** Mature students will be interviewed and must be prepared to discuss literary works.

GRADUATE EMPLOYMENT

New Graduates' destinations (percentages) 1991:
Permanent employment: U 65; P 48; C 60.
Unemployment: U 23; P 38; C 26.
Further studies (all types): U 39; P 28; C 32.
Main career destinations (approx): Business/Secretarial 48; Finance 11; Teaching 5; Management 16; Legal 8; Creative 16; Social Work 8.

York (1989-91) 42% of graduates went into employment (education, management trainees (publishing, retail, technical recruitment) and media work (editorial, theatre, journalism, copywriting, TV research, video, news trainee); 11 graduates went into finance careers, 7 into public sector administration, 5 into social work, 3 into law and 3 into secretarial occupations (BBC and publishing); 36% went into further study (teacher training, law, acting and teaching English as a foreign language). Finally there were 29 graduates who went on to 9 other universties to take higher degrees.

ENVIRONMENTAL SCIENCE/STUDIES

Special subject requirements: variable depending on emphasis of course.

NB Institutions may raise or lower the level of published offers depending either on the quality or otherwise of individual applications or the numbers of applications received; grades/points offered may be adjusted downwards after A-level results. The level of an offer is not indicative of the quality of a course.

28 pts.	**East Anglia** - AAB (Env/USA)
24 pts.	**East Anglia** - BBB (Env)
	St Andrews - BBB-BBC (Env Biol)
22 pts.	**Leeds** - BBC (Env Man - new course)
	Southampton - BBC (Env Sci)
20 pts.	**Aberystwyth** - BCC/BC (Env Sci) (4 AS)
	Dundee - BCC (Env Sci)
	Edinburgh - (Eco/Env - new course, check with Admissions Tutor)
	Hull - BCC (Env/Earth R/M)
	Lancaster - BCC (Env Sci) (BTEC Ms)
	Leeds - BCC (Env Sci/Bio - new course)
	London (RH) - BCC-CCD/BB-BC (Env Ch/Man St)
	Newcastle - BCC-BCD (Env Biol)
	Reading - 20 pts (Env Sci)
	Sussex - BCC/BC (ES/Mols)
	Swansea - BCC-CCC (Env Biol)
	York - BCC (Env Econ)
18 pts.	**Aberdeen** - CCC-CCD/BC (Env Sci; Country/Env Man)
	Aberystwyth - 18-16 pts (Env Biol; Env Microb; Env Micro)(BTEC 3M)
	Belfast - CCC (Env Biol)
	Bradford - BCD-CCC/BB (Env; Env/Geog) (BTEC Ds+Ms)
	Bradford - CCC/BB (Env Man/Tech) (BTEC 3M)

East Anglia - CCC/BB (Env/Chem)
Lancaster - CCC (Env Chem)
Leeds - CCC (Env Sci/Env Chem; Env Sci/Energy - new courses)
Leeds Met - 18 pts (Env Health)
London (King's) - 18 pts approx (Env Health; App Env Sci)
London (RH) - 18-14 pts (Env E Sci; Env Geol; Env Geochem)
London (Wye) - CCC (Rural Env)
Reading - CCC (Env Biol)
Salford - CCC/BB (Env Sci; App Env) (BTEC 5M)
Sheffield - BCD-CCC (NES) (4 AS)
Stirling - CCC/BB (All courses)
Strathclyde - CCC-BCD (2nd yr entry) (Env Health)

16 pts. **Bedford (CHE)** - 16-14 pts (Modular)
Brunel - CCD (MAE Chem)
Central Lancashire - 16 pts (Comb Hons)
Coventry - CCd/BB-AC (2 sciences) (Env Sci) (BTEC Ds+Ms)
Hull - CCD/BC (Env Biol/Geog) (4 AS)
Kingston - CCD-DDE/CC-CD (Env Sci) (BTEC 3M)
Liverpool - CCD (Env Biol)
London (QMW) - CCD (Env Sci; Env Chem)
London (Wye) - CCD (Env Sci)
Manchester Met - 16 pts (Env Man; Env Sci; Env Health) (4 AS)
Middlesex - 16-12 pts (Env Soc)
Ulster - CCD/BC (Env Health)

14 pts. **Bangor** - CDD/CC (Ocean Sciences)
Cranfield (Silsoe) - CDD/CC (Rur Env Man)
Dundee - CDD (Env Man - new course)
Essex - CDD (El Chem) CCE (Env Biol) (BTEC 65%)
Glamorgan - 14 pts (En/Env Tech) (BTEC 3M)
Hertfordshire - 14-12 pts (Env St) (4 AS) (BTEC 3M)
Huddersfield - CDD-DDD/CC (Human Ec)
Newcastle - CDD/BC (Ag/Env Sci)
Nottingham - CDD/CC (Env Sci; Env Biol) (2 AS in science subjects)
Plymouth - CDD/CC (Env Sci) (6 AS)
Ulster - CDD-DDD/CC-CD (Env Sci)

12 pts. **Bangor** - 12 pts (Env Chem) (BTEC 3M)
Bournemouth - 12-10 pts (Env Prot)
Brighton - 12 pts (Env Sci modular; Energy St) (BTEC 3M)
Bristol UWE - 12 pts (Env Qual/RM)
Cheltenham & Glos (CHE) - 12 pts (Env Pol) (BTEC 3M)
Durham-Tees (Coll) - 12-8 pts approx (Env Man; Env Tech)(See Ch.3)
Greenwich - 12 pts (Env Earth Sci; Eng Geol)
Greenwich - CC (Env Health) (4 AS) (BTEC 5P)
Harper Adams (CAg) - DDD/CC (Rural Env Protect)
Kingston - 12 pts (Env Sci)
Northumbria - CDE/BD (Env St) (BTEC 3M)
Oxford Brookes - DDD/CC-DD (Modular)
South Bank - 12 pts (Env Eng)
Sunderland - DDD/CC (Env St) (BTEC 3M)

10 pts. **Central Lancashire** - DDE/CD (Env Man)
Glamorgan - CD-DD (Env Poll Sci) (4 AS)
Guildhall London - CD (Env Pol/Man)
Kingston - (Resources/Env)
Oxford Brookes - CD (Env Biol; Sci in Env; Env Biol)
Sheffield Hallam - 10 pts (Env Man) (BTEC 4M)
Southampton (IHE) - (Env Man - subject to approval)
Staffordshire - 10 pts (All courses)
Sunderland - 10 pts standard offer (Env Tech)
Wolverhampton - 10-8 pts (Env Sci)

Worcester (CHE) - 10 pts approx inc Access (Comb St; Env Sci)

8 pts. **and below**

Anglia (Poly Univ) - (Env Sci)
Bangor Normal (CHE) - (Env St)
Bath (CHE) - (Comb St)
Bristol UWE - DD-DE (Env Sci; Env Health)
Cardiff (IHE) - (Env Health)
Cheltenham & Glos (CHE) - EE (Earth Res)
Coventry - (Comb Sci)
Crewe & Alsager (CHE) - (Env St)
De Montfort - (Sci/Env) (BTEC 3M)
East London - EE minimum (Env Man) (BTEC 3M)
Glamorgan - (Env Sci/Geol; Biol/Env Sci; Env Pol Sci)
Greenwich - EEE/DE (Env Biol; Env Sci) (4 AS)
Gwent (CHE) - (Env Sys)
Humberside - (Env St)
Liverpool (IHE) - (Comb St)
Middlesex - (Env Tech; Env Health)
Nene (CHE) - (Comb St)
North East Wales (IHE) - (Env St; Comb St)
North London - (Env Sci)
North Riding (Coll) - (Env Sci Con)
Portsmouth - (Env Sci)
Robert Gordon - DD (Env Sci Tech)
Roehampton (IHE) - (Env St courses)
SAC (Au) - (Rural Resources)
St Mary's (CHE) - (Env Biol; Env Sci)
South Bank - DD (Env Biol courses) (BTEC 3M)
Teesside - 8 pts minimum (Env Man; Env Tech)
Trinity Carmarthen (CHE) - (Rural Env)
West Sussex (IHE) - (Env Sci)
Westminster - DD (Env Sci)

Franchised degree and HND courses (see Ch 5):
South Bank - South Bank (CFE); Waltham Forest (CFE).

Diploma of Higher Education courses:
4 pts. Bath (CHE); Crewe & Alsager (CHE); Doncaster (Coll); King Alfred's (CHE); Middlesex; Oxford Brookes; Wolverhampton; Worcester (CHE).

Offers for Foundation, Certificate and Diploma courses (see Ch 5):

Higher National Diploma courses (England and Wales):
2 pts. Farnborough (CT); Seale Hayne (CAg); Writtle (CAg) Rural Man.

Higher National Diploma courses (Scotland):
SAC (Au) Rural Resources.

Professional Diploma courses:
Enviromental Health Nottingham Trent; Tottenham (CT).

Alternative offers:

EB offers: **Aberystwyth** 75%; **East Anglia** 70%; **London (RH)** 75%; **Sheffield** 65%.

IB offers: **Aberdeen** 26 pts; **Aberystwyth** 30-28 pts; **Bedford (CHE)** 26 pts; **Bradford** 28 pts; **Coventry** 24 pts; **East Anglia** H555 inc 28 pts; **Essex** 28 pts inc 10 pts Highers chem, biol; **Hertfordshire** 24 pts; **Lancaster** 30 pts; **Liverpool** H555; **London (RH)** 25 pts; **Nottingham** 28 pts 7 subjects 24 pts 6 subjects; **Sheffield** H555; **Swansea** 28 pts.

Irish offers: **Aberdeen** BBCC/BCCCC; **Aberystwyth** BBBCC; **East Anglia** BBBBB; **London (RH)** BBCCC; **Sheffield** BBBCC; **South Bank** CCCC.

SCE offers: **Aberdeen** BBBB; **Dundee** BBCC/BBB; **East Anglia** BBBB; **Essex** BCCC; **Lancaster** BBBB; **Liverpool** BBBB; **Northumbria** BBB; **Sheffield** BBBC; **St Andrews** BBBC; **Stirling** BBCC; **Strathclyde** ABBC/BBBB.

CHOOSING YOUR COURSE (See also Ch 1)

Subject information: Environmental Health courses usually lead to qualification as an environmental health officer. Environmental Science, however, can cover a range of subjects with options to specialise which may include biology, geography, geology, oceanography or chemistry. The new Environmental Science course at **Salford** also includes legal, social and political issues. Several new courses will be offered by **Leeds**. Environmental Science/Studies courses need to be considered with care. They may, for example, include town and country planning or environmental health options thus leading to two quite different careers. For example, **Aberystwyth** and **Sheffield** emphasise biology and geography whereas at **East Anglia** the emphasis is on the physical, biological and social sciences, at **London (RH)** on geology and geography, and at **Sussex** on chemistry, biology and geography. At **Lancaster** the course focuses on aquatic and atmospheric systems, environmental assessment and management and applied earth science (see also **Admissions Tutors' advice**).

Course highlights: Aberdeen (Country/Env Man) Agricultural bias. (Env Sci) Covers the sciences, population communities, land management and forest ecology. **Bradford** Integrated course covering chemistry, ecology, physical and economic geography, applied economics and biology. **Brighton** Course covers five themes: human environment, soil studies, ecology, pollution and energy management. **Central Lancashire** The course includes environmental policy, chemistry, land management and ecology. Opportunities for placements with environmental agencies and residential field work. **Coventry** Transfers possible at end of year 1 to Applied Biology, Geography. Language options in year 2. Sandwich placements in France. **Crewe & Alsager (CHE)** Options include water pollution, conservation, ecology and energy studies. **East Anglia** The course brings together subjects such as geology, geography, ecology, oceanography, economics, politics, planning, meteorology, soil science, geophysics, resource management, environmental pollution. **Guildhall London** Course covers geography, sociology, economics and politics. **Hertfordshire** This is a study of environmental planning, landscape development and pollution issues. **Hull** Multi-disciplinary courses covering management, environment, law, social studies, physical and economic sciences. **London (QMW)** Course includes physical geography, geology, environmental biology and chemistry. **London (RH)** The course covers geographical environment, nature of rocks, remote sensing, geochemistry and a study of earth resources. **Manchester Met** (Env Health) Study areas cover food, housing, pollution, occupational health and safety. (Env Man) The course focuses on the physical, social. scientific, political and economic aspects. **Newcastle** (Nat Res) First year students take a course in numerical methods and two options chosen from applied biology, soil and land resources, environmental chemistry, economic principles and engineering science. **North East Wales (IHE)** All students can spend part of course at one of the faculty links in USA or Sweden. **Plymouth** The course includes a study of environmental biology, chemistry, geology and the human environment. **Salford** Common first year programme for all students who then opt for the environmental health or the housing option. **Sheffield** In the third year there are four compulsory courses covering botany, geography and geology. **Southampton** The course covers the physical and the biological environments, chemistry and human sciences within the environment and water in the environment, hydrology and hydrobiology. **Stirling** Final year options include countryside management, deserts, environmental hazards, rivers and tropical environments. **Trinity Carmarthen (CHE)** Course covers conservation, geology, ecology, pollution and planning. NOW CHECK PROSPECTUSES FOR ALL COURSES.

Study opportunities abroad: Coventry (E) IRE FR; **East Anglia** USA; **Hertfordshire** (E) CIS; **Leeds Met** (E) EUR; **Manchester Met** (E) G NL; **Nottingham** (E); **Salford** (E) FR G.

Work opportunities abroad: Coventry; Greenwich (Earth Sci) SP FR IT; **Greenwich** (E); **Hertfordshire** F H G NL; **Manchester Met** J K; **Salford** AUS; **South Bank** EUR; **Worcester (CHE)** USA.

ADMISSIONS INFORMATION

Number of applicants per place (approx): Aberystwyth 7; **Bradford** 10; **Cardiff (IHE)** 5; **Coventry** 10; **De Montfort** 9; **East Anglia** 8; **East London** 2; **Glamorgan** 3; **Hertfordshire** 8; **Hull** 8; **Lancaster** 11; **Leeds Met** 10; **London (RH)** 8; **Manchester Met** (Env Man) 16; **Oxford Brookes** 13; **Plymouth** 8; **Salford** 8; **Strathclyde** 5; **Sunderland** 10; **Trinity Carmarthen (CHE)** 2; **Westminster** 3; **Wolverhampton** 10.

General Studies acceptable: Aberystwyth; Bedford (CHE) (2); Bradford (possibly); Brighton (2); Bristol UWE; Cardiff (IHE); Cheltenham & Glos (CHE); Coventry; Cranfield (Silsoe); Crewe & Alsager (CHE); De Montfort; East Anglia (usually); East London; Essex; Glamorgan (2); Harper Adams (CAg); Huddersfield; Hull; Manchester Met; Oxford Brookes; St Mary's (CHE); South Bank (No); Sunderland; Trinity Carmarthen (CHE) (2); Wolverhampton (2); Worcester (CHE) (2).

Selection interviews: Bradford; Bristol UWE; East Anglia (some); Liverpool (some); London (RH); Newcastle; Plymouth; Sheffield (some); South Bank; Southampton; Strathclyde; Sussex; Warwick.

Offers to applicants repeating A-levels: Higher Greenwich, Lancaster, Nottingham, Strathclyde, Swansea; **Possibly higher** Aberystwyth, Bradford, Northumbria, Salford; **Same** Cardiff (IHE), East Anglia, Leeds Met, London (RH), Manchester Met, South Bank, Ulster.

Admissions Tutors' advice: Aberystwyth GCSE (grade A–C) English and mathematics are required. **Bangor** (Ocean Sciences) We look for students with a good science background (physics, chemistry, maths, biology, geography, geology). **Cardiff (IHE)** All students must be sponsored by a local authority which will provide professional practice facilities for a minimum of 32 weeks during the third year of the course. **Greenwich** All students must be sponsored by a local authority which will provide professional training facilities for 18 months of the four-year course. **Lancaster** We would emphasise the word 'science' in the title of our degree: this is a rigorous experimental science discipline. A-levels in subjects such as mathematics, physics and chemistry form the best preparation although able students with other A-levels (eg geography and geology) may be considered provided that they have adequate background. **Salford** Students need not find a sponsor before applying. Clear commitment to housing administration or environmental health expected.

> **Examples of interview questions:** How would you cope with pollution in cities? Do you think environmental health officers should be employed by industry? What are the environmental problems in the area in which you live? How would you solve them? What qualities are required to be a successful environmental health officer? Have you been to an abattoir? (Environmental Health applicant)

GAP YEAR ADVICE

Institutions accepting a Gap Year: Most institutions; **Aberystwyth** Environmentally related experience preferred; **De Montfort** Plan of action necessary; **London (RH)** Strongly encouraged; **South Bank** Try to retain study habits; **Westminster** Apply for a place as normal but mark it for a year later.

Institutions willing to defer entry after A-levels (see Ch 5): Aberystwyth (contact Admissions Tutor as soon as possible); Bangor; Bradford; Cheltenham & Glos (CHE); Coventry; Dundee; Glamorgan; Harper Adams (CAg); Humberside; Kingston; Lancaster; Leeds (No); London (RH); Northumbria; Plymouth; Robert Gordon; Roehampton (IHE); South Bank; Swansea (last minute deferrals discouraged); Westminster; York.

AFTER A-LEVELS ADVICE

Institutions which may accept the same points score after A-levels: Aberystwyth; Bradford; Bristol UWE; East Anglia; Essex; Greenwich; Hertfordshire; Humberside; Lancaster; Liverpool; London (RH); Manchester Met; Newcastle (Agric Env); Northumbria; Nottingham; Plymouth (perhaps); Roehampton (IHE); South Bank; Strathclyde; Sunderland; Swansea; Ulster.

Institutions demanding the actual grades offered after A-levels: Stirling; Southampton.

Institutions which may accept under-achieving applicants after A-levels: Aberystwyth; Bradford; East Anglia; Hertfordshire; Humberside; Lancaster; London (RH); Northumbria; Nottingham (Env Biol); Plymouth (perhaps); Roehampton (IHE); Salford; Stirling; Swansea; Ulster; most new universities.

Institutions with vacancies in Aug/Sept 1992 (see Ch 5): Aberdeen; Aberystwyth; Anglia (Poly Univ); Bangor 10 pts; Bournemouth 8 pts; Cranfield (Silsoe); Glamorgan 10-8 pts; Greenwich 8 pts; Humberside 6 pts; King Alfred's (CHE); London (QMW), (RH) 14 pts; Northumbria 12 pts; Paisley; Robert Gordon 4 pts; Roehampton (IHE) 10 pts; Salford 18 pts; Sheffield Hallam; South Bank DD; Sunderland 10 pts; Teesside; West Sussex (IHE); Westminster. Point scores from 10 to 16 pts could achieve the required entry level in some of the more popular universities. Most institutions, however, were prepared to consider applicants in Clearing for this subject. See also under **Occupational Hygiene**.

ADVICE FOR MATURE STUDENTS

About 10% of students come into the mature category on these courses for which science or geography A-levels could be advantageous.

GRADUATE EMPLOYMENT

New Graduates' destinations (percentages) 1991:
Permanent employment: U 64; P 83; C 50.
Unemployment: U 24; P 14; C 25.
Further studies (all types): U 43; P 3; C 20.
Main career destinations (approx): Scientific 34; Business 23; Finance 9; Computing 2.

EUROPEAN STUDIES (See also **Business Courses**)

Special subject requirements: 2-3 A-levels, at least one in a modern language for language courses.

NB Institutions may raise or lower the level of published offers depending either on the quality or otherwise of individual applications or the numbers of applications received; grades/points offered may be adjusted downwards after A-level results. The level of an offer is not indicative of the quality of a course.

24 pts. **Aston** - BBB-BBC (Int Bus/Fr; Int Bus/Ger)
Bath - ABC (Europ/Mod Lang)
Lancaster - BBB-BBC (ELS)
London (King's) - BBB approx (Euro St)
London (RH) - BBB-BBC (Eur St)
Manchester - BBB approx (Euro St courses)
22 pts. **Aberdeen** - BBC (Europ)
Bradford - BBC-BCC/BB (Fr/Ger/Sp Europ; Europ; Eur Ar St)
Edinburgh - BBC (Euro C St/Lang)
Glasgow - 22 pts (Euro)
Hull - BBC/AA (Europ St 4; Sp Europ St)

Lancaster – BBC (Psy/MES)
Leeds – BBC (Eur St)
Leicester – BBC (Eur St)
London (RH) – BBC/BB (Eur St/Ital; Eur Studs) (6 AS) (BTEC 3M)
Nottingham – BBC (Eur/Studs)
Sheffield – BBC (E Eur St)

20 pts. **Aberystwyth** – BCC/BB (Eur Int)
Aston – BCC (Comp/Eur St; Eng/Eur St)
Cardiff – BCC-CCC/BB-BC (Eur Comm St)
Dundee - BCC (Euro St)
East Anglia – BCC (Eur/Soc)
Essex – BCC/BC (Euro SS; Euro Com)
Hull - BCC/BB-BC (Europ St)
Keele – BCC (All courses)
Kent – BCC-CCC/BC (All courses)
Leicester – BCC (Euro St)
London (SSEES) – BCC-CCC/BC (Con EE St)

18 pts. **Aberystwyth** – CCC/BB (Euro)
Brighton – 18-14 pts (Eur Bus)
Brunel – CCC/BC (Comp/Eur St; Euro 3)
Guildhall London – CCC/BB (Euro/Legal/Econ)
London (QMW) – 18 pts/BC (All courses)
Loughborough – BCD-CCC/BB (Europ) (4 AS)
Manchester Met – 18 pts (Bus Europ)
Strathclyde – CCC (BBD 2nd yr entry) (Euro St; Arts/Soc St)
Ulster – CCC (Hum)

16 pts. **Bedford (CHE)** – 16-14 pts (Modular)
Durham-Tees (Coll) – 16-10 pts approx (Euro St)
Northumbria – CCD (Euro St)

14 pts. **Central Lancashire** – CCE (EBAL)
Middlesex – CDD/CC (Eur Econ; Eur Soc)
Nottingham Trent – 14-12 pts (Eur Bus/Fr; Eur Bus/Ger)
Plymouth – 14 pts (Euro St)

12 pts. **Anglia (Poly Univ)** – 12 pts (ETL courses)
Coventry – 12 pts (Euro Bus/Tech; Eur St) (BTEC Ms)
Humberside – 12 pts (Eur Admin; Euro Contemp St)
Leeds Met – CC (Eur Lang/Bus courses)
North London – CC-CD (CES) (4 AS)
Thames Valley London – 12 pts average (Mod Euro St)
Wolverhampton – DDD/CD (Euro St) (6 AS)

10 pts. **Liverpool (IHE)** – 10 pts (Euro St)
Nene (CHE) – CD (Euro Bus Fr/Ger/Sp)
Oxford Brookes – 10 pts (Euro Bus St)
South Bank – CD/DD (Euro St courses) (BTEC D in lang + Ms)
Sunderland – 10 pts (ESME)

8 pts. **and below**
Cardiff (IHE) – (Euro Admin)
Derby – (Modular) (4 AS)
Humberside – (Euro Tourism; Euro Audio Vis St)
Southampton (IHE) – (Eur Pol) (4 AS)

Alternative offers:

EB offers: **North London** 60%.

IB offers: **Aberdeen** 30 pts; **Aberystwyth** 32-30 pts; **Anglia (Poly Univ)** 28 pts; **Brunel** 28 pts; **Dundee** 29 pts H 15 pts; **Hull** 31 -30 pts; **Kent** 27 pts, H 12 pts; **Lancaster** 32-30pts; **London (RH)** 28 pts, **(SSEES)** 26 pts.

SCE offers: **Aberdeen** BBBB; **Dundee** BBBC; **Edinburgh** BBBB; **Essex** BBBB; **Kent** ABBB; **Lancaster** (ELS) BBB, (Psy/MES) BBBB; **Strathclyde** BBBB.

CHOOSING YOUR COURSE (See also Ch 1)

> **Subject information:** This is an increasingly popular subject and offers the language student the opportunity to study modern languages within the context of a European country (eg, economics, politics, legal, social and cultural aspects). On these courses there is usually a strong emphasis placed on the written and spoken word.

Course highlights: Bath Course combines practical language work with politics, history, economics and cultural studies. **Bradford** (Eur Ar Stud) Course combines a language plus economics for history/geography/ politics/sociology. **Brunel** Combination of European politics and history plus French or German. **Cardiff** (Eur Comm St) A unique course in which students can study one or two modern European languages in the context of the contemporary, political, economic, legal and social structure of Western Europe. **Hull** (Europ St) Core courses with a European perspective combining the study of either Dutch, French, German, Italian, Spanish or Swedish. **Leeds** (Euro St) New course with broad overview of Europe (social, political, cultural, economic) with option to specialise in a modern language. **London (QMW)** Course involves a language course in French, German, Russian or Spanish. **(RH)** Course includes the study of French, German or Italian. **(SSEES)** Opportunity to study one East European language from scratch. **Sheffield** Two separate courses in the first year - one for those with A-level Russian and one for those without. **Strathclyde** Students take one foreign language from French, German, Italian, Russian or Spanish. NOW CHECK PROSPECTUSES FOR ALL COURSES.

Study opportunities abroad: Bath (E) FR G IT; **Bradford** (E); **Brunel** (E) FR G; **Cardiff (IHE)** FR G SP; **Central Lancashire** (E); **East Anglia** (E); **Essex** (E); **Hull** (E); **Kent** (E); **Lancaster** EUR; **Leicester** (E); **London (RH)** FR G IT; **Nottingham Trent** USA; **Surrey** (E); **Thames Valley London** (E) FR G SP B NL.

Work opportunities abroad: Brunel FR G; **Hull** FR G IT SP B NL SW; **Southampton (IHE)** FR G; **Wolverhampton** (Eur Bus Ad)).

ADMISSIONS INFORMATION

Number of applicants per place (approx): Anglia (Poly Univ) 8; **Bath** 10; **Bradford** (Europ) 9; **East Anglia** 11; **Hull** 11; **Kent** 11; **Lancaster** 9; **Leeds Met** 25; **London (RH)** 6, **(SSEES)** 2; **Loughborough** 10; **Nottingham Trent** 12; **South Bank** 6; **Thames Valley London** 5; **Wolverhampton** 7.

General Studies acceptable: Aberdeen; Anglia (Poly Univ); Bradford; Buckingham; East Anglia; Hull; Liverpool John Moores; London (RH) (2), (SSEES) (2); Northumbria; South Bank; Thames Valley London (2); Wolverhampton.

Selection interviews: Bath; Bradford; East Anglia; Hull (some); Kent (frequently); Leeds Met (T); Loughborough (some, eg mature students); South Bank; Southampton (IHE); Surrey; Sussex; Thames Valley London.

Offers to applicants repeating A-levels: Higher Aberystwyth, East Anglia, Leeds Met; **Same** Bradford, Loughborough, North London, South Bank, Southampton (IHE), Wolverhampton.

Admissions Tutors' advice: Bath Individual offers made after selection interview. Applicants must show enthusiasm for language and cultural studies and have serious, wide-ranging interest in contemporary scene of countries concerned. Evidence of time spent abroad welcomed. **Buckingham** Apply early. As there are five options within the School, individual interests will receive particular attention. There is an initial compulsory term abroad. **Leeds Met** We are looking for well-motivated students with the maturity and intellectual ability to be able to study abroad successfully.

> **Examples of interview questions:** Questions will relate to the politics, commerce and culture of the chosen country. A language test will occupy part of the interview. (See also under the appropriate language, for example **French, German.**)

GAP YEAR ADVICE

Institutions accepting a Gap Year: Most institutions (suggesting travel); **Bath** Discuss at interview; **Brunel** Spend part of year in French or German speaking country; **London (RH)** Travel as much as possible. **Thames Valley London** Try to learn a language for your degree course.

Institutions willing to defer entry after A-levels (see Ch 5): Aberystwyth (Prefer not); Bradford; Brunel; Coventry; Dundee; Hull; Humberside; London (RH); Northumbria (Prefer not); Plymouth; South Bank (No); Thames Valley London.

AFTER A-LEVELS ADVICE

Institutions which may accept the same points score after A-levels: Bradford; Buckingham; Cardiff (IHE); Hull; Leeds Met; Southampton (IHE); South Bank (perhaps); Thames Valley; Wolverhampton.

Institutions demanding the actual grades offered after A-levels: Bath.

Institutions which may accept under-achieving applicants after A-levels: Anglia (Poly Univ); Bath; Bradford; Brighton; Cardiff (IHE); Kent; Hull; Loughborough; Middlesex; North London; Southampton (IHE); South Bank; Thames Valley London; Wolverhampton.

Institutions with vacancies in Aug/Sept 1992 (see Ch 5): Bradford 18 pts; Coventry CD; Essex 18-16 pts; Humberside; Plymouth; South Bank; Thames Valley London.

ADVICE FOR MATURE STUDENTS

Ability in languages is a pre-requisite for these courses whose students include some 10% mature students.

FILM AND VIDEO STUDIES (See also **Photography**)

Special subject requirements: variable.

NB Institutions may raise or lower the level of published offers depending either on the quality or otherwise of individual applications or the numbers of applications received; grades/points offered may be adjusted downwards after A-level results. The level of an offer is not indicative of the quality of a course.

26 pts.	**Glasgow** - ABB (All Film/TV courses)
	Stirling - 26 pts (All Media courses)
24 pts.	**Canterbury Christ Church (CHE)** - BBB-CCC/AA-CC (Radio/Film/TV)
	East Anglia - BBB/BB (EAS/FES) (BTEC Ms)
	Warwick - BBB (Film Lit) (2 AS except des tech and gen stds)
22 pts.	**Bradford** - BBC/BB (Elec/Med H6P4) (BTEC 4D+2M)
	Kent - BBC/BB (Drama/Film; Film St)
	Reading - BBC (Film/Drama; F + D/Ital; F + D/Soc)
18 pts.	**Bradford** - CCC (Elec/Med H6PL) (BTEC 2D+2M)
	Sheffield Hallam - CCC/18 pts (Film/Media)
16 pts.	**Sheffield Hallam** - 16 pts (Hist Art)
14 pts.	**West London (IHE)** - (FTV)
12 pts.	**Salford (UC)** - 12 pts (Film/TV)

10 pts.	**Staffordshire** – 12 pts (Film/TV) (BTEC 5M)

Staffordshire – 12 pts (Film/TV) (BTEC 5M)
10 pts. **East London** – 10 pts approx (MF)
8 pts. **and below**
    Bournemouth – (Scriptwriting – see **Course highlights**)
    Buckinghamshire (CHE) – (Film/Media/Cult – Contact Admissions Tutor)
    Derby – (Modular) (4 AS)
    London Inst (CP) – No standard offer (Film and Video)
    Napier – (Photo/Film/TV)
    North London – (Comb Hum)
    Ripon & York St John (CHE) – (Modular)
    Salford (UC) – (TV/Radio)
    Swansea (IHE) – (Comb St)
    Westminster – (Film) (4 AS)

Diploma of Higher Education courses:
4 pts. Ripon & York St John (CHE)

Offers for Foundation, Certificate and Diploma courses (see Ch 5):

Higher National Diploma courses:
4 pts. **and below** Bournemouth (CFE); Gwent (CHE); Northumberland (CFE); Ravensbourne (CDC); Salisbury (CFE).

Alternative offers:

IB offers: **East Anglia** 28 pts.

Irish offers: **Westminster** CCCCC.

SCE offers: **Glasgow** AAAB (Film/TV); **Kent** ABBB; **Stirling** ABBB (Film & Media).

CHOOSING YOUR COURSE (see also Ch 1)

Subject information: These courses vary between institutions and may cover film studies (history and/or practical aspects), TV studies, the media in general and video work. See also under **Media Studies** and **Communications Studies,**

Course highlights: Bournemouth (Scriptwriting for Film & TV) Unique new degree course very suitable for mature students. **East Anglia** Theoretical and practical approaches to film complemented by cultural studies. **Ravensbourne (CDC)** Unique courses in UK. Recognised route into independent broadcasting sector. **Reading** The course covers the history of the cinema and drama during the last century with practical work in drama, film and video. **Westminster** Integrated approach to media practice. NOW CHECK PROSPECTUSES FOR ALL COURSES.

ADMISSIONS INFORMATION

Number of applicants per place (approx): Canterbury Christ Church (CHE) 50; **Kent** 8; **East Anglia** 50; **London (CP)** 12; **Ravensbourne (CDC)** 9; **Warwick** 17; **West London (IHE)** 17; **Westminster** 41.

General Studies acceptable: East Anglia; Kent.

Admissions Tutors' advice: London Inst (CP) We look for an interest in theory and practice, group skills and evidence of practical experience in film and video. A general interest in social, political and cultural issues, women's cinema and Third World cinema is also sought.

Examples of interview questions: What films have you seen recently? Discuss the work of Stephen Spielberg, Cecil B de Mille etc. Who is your favourite producer? (Questions on the films by this producer will develop from this question.) Who are your favourite actors, actresses? Why?

GAP YEAR ADVICE

Institutions accepting a Gap Year: Bradford; most institutions.

Institutions willing to defer entry after A-levels (see Ch 5): Bradford.

AFTER A-LEVELS ADVICE

Institutions demanding the actual grades offered after A-levels: East Anglia.

ADVICE FOR MATURE STUDENTS

Experience in media work can be a considerable advantage for mature students seeking entry to these courses.

GRADUATE EMPLOYMENT

New Graduates' destinations (percentages) 1991:
Permanent employment: P 47.
Unemployment: P 41.
Further studies (all types): P 11.

FINE ART (See also Art)

Special subject requirements: none. Foundation Art courses are normally needed for entry to courses listed below but not for university Fine Art courses. Only about eight per cent of entrants are admitted with A-levels, direct from school or college.

Selection for degree courses is by interview when applicant's portfolio of work is scrutinised. Applications are submitted through the Art and Design Admissions Registry (ADAR) scheme (see Chapter 2).

Institutions offering degree courses: Bath (CHE); Bradford & Ilkley (CmC); Brighton; Bristol UWE; Cardiff (IHE); Central England; Central Lancashire; Cheltenham & Glos (CHE); Cornwall (CFHE Falmouth); Coventry; De Montfort; Dundee (CA); East London; Edinburgh (CA); Glasgow (SA); Gwent (CHE); Hertfordshire (CAD); Humberside; Kent (IAD) (Canterbury); Kingston; Leeds Met; Liverpool John Moores; London (Goldsmiths' Coll), London Inst (Camberwell SA), (Chelsea SA), (St Martin's SA); Loughborough (CA); Manchester Met; Middlesex; Norfolk (IAD); Northumbria; Nottingham Trent; Plymouth; Portsmouth; Robert Gordon; Sheffield Hallam; Staffordshire; Stourbridge (CAT); Sunderland; Ulster; Westminster; West Surrey (CAD); West Sussex (IHE); Wimbledon (SA); Winchester (SA); Wolverhampton.

Diploma of Higher Education:

4 pts.   Cumbria (CAD); Southampton (IHE).

Higher National Diploma courses:
2 pts.   London Inst (Camberwell SA); Lincolnshire (CA) (Conservation/ Restoration).

Overseas applicants: Good photographs or transparencies may be acceptable for applicants unable to attend for interview. Original work helpful.

CHOOSING YOUR COURSE (See also Ch 1)

> **Subject information:** These are usually specialised studies in painting and almost always follow a Foundation Art course.

Course highlights: Brighton Placements in Europe and USA. **Bristol UWE** Exchange system funded by EC with placements in Europe. **Cornwall (CFHE Falmouth)** Optional areas cover painting, printmaking and photographic media. **Staffordshire** A critical/theoretical course which includes a 'writing for mass media' course. NOW CHECK PROSPECTUSES FOR ALL COURSES.

ADMISSIONS INFORMATION

Number of applicants per place (approx): Bath (CHE) 5; **Brighton** 5; **Bristol UWE** 3; **Cardiff (IHE)** 3; **Central Lancashire** 4; **Cheltenham & Glos (CHE)** 4; **Cornwall (CFHE Falmouth)** 5; **De Montfort** 5; **Dundee (CA)** 5; **Gwent (CHE)** 2; **Humberside** 4; **Kent (IAD)** 3; **Leeds Met** 6; **Manchester Met** 4; **Middlesex** 3; **Norfolk (IAD)** 3; **Northumbria** 4; **Nottingham Trent** 3; **Robert Gordon** 5; **Sheffield Hallam** 4; **Staffordshire** 4; **West Surrey (CAD)** 2; **Winchester (SA)** 4.

Selection interviews: All institutions.

Admissions Tutors' advice: Winchester (SA) First and second choice applicants interviewed with folio of work.

Examples of interview questions: Questions asked on portfolio of work. (See under **Art (Fine, History, Design)**).

ADVICE FOR MATURE STUDENTS

Mature students account for about 5% of the student total on these courses. Selection is invariably by portfolio.

GRADUATE EMPLOYMENT

New Graduates' destinations: See under **Art**.

FISHERY SCIENCE

Special subject requirements: English and mathematics at GCSE (grade A-C).

NB Institutions may raise or lower the level of published offers depending either on the quality or otherwise of individual applications or the numbers of applications received; grades/points offered may be adjusted downwards after A-level results. The level of an offer is not indicative of the quality of a course.

12pts. **Plymouth** – 12 pts (Marine St; Fish Sci)
10pts. **SAC (Au)** – (Aquaculture)

Higher National Diploma courses:
2pts. **Hampshire (CAg)** – (Fish Farming).

Alternative offers:

SCE offers: **Plymouth** BBB.

CHOOSING YOUR COURSE (See also Ch 1)

> **Subject information:** This is a specialist study as part of the Marine Studies course at Plymouth University. NOW CHECK PROSPECTUSES FOR ALL COURSES. See also **Marine Biology**.

> **Examples of interview questions:** Why have you chosen this course? (Questions will then develop from this.) Discuss fish farming in Britain today. Is there a future in fish farming? What are the limitations?

FOOD SCIENCE AND TECHNOLOGY

Special subject requirements: usually chemistry and one or two other science or mathematics subjects at A-level.

NB Institutions may raise or lower the level of published offers depending either on the quality or otherwise of individual applications or the numbers of applications received; grades/points offered may be adjusted downwards after A-level results. The level of an offer is not indicative of the quality of a course.

18 pts.	**Newcastle** - CCC/CC (Food Eng)
	Strathclyde - CCC-BCD (2nd yr entry) (Food Sci/Micro)
	Surrey - CCC/BB (Nutr/Food Sc; Food/Micro) (BTEC 4M)
16 pts.	**Belfast** - CCD (Food Sci; Food Tech)
	Leeds - CCD (Food Sci; Food/Micro; Bioch/Food; Food Sci (Euro))
	London (King's) - CCD (Food Sci)
	Reading - CCD/BB (All courses)
	Ulster - CCD/BC (Food T Mgt)
14 pts.	**Cranfield (Silsoe)** - CDD/CC (Food Mar/Dist)
	Dundee - CDD (Food Welf) (BTEC 6M)
	Newcastle - CDD/CC (Food Q Prod; Food/Hum Nut)
	Nottingham - CDD/CC (Food Sci)
12 pts.	**Bath (CHE)** - 12 pts (Food Man)
	Humberside - 12 pts (All courses) (4 AS)
	Manchester Met - 12 pts (Ap Con Sci)
10 pts.	**Bournemouth** - DDE-CEE (Food Qual) (BTEC Ms)
	Sheffield Hallam - 10 pts (Food Market)
8 pts.	and below
	Manchester Met - EEE/EE (Food Man; Con Pro (see also Bus St)) (4 AS) (BTEC 3M)
	North East Wales (IHE) - 6 pts (Food Sci)
	North London - (Food/Con St)
	Oxford Brookes - DD (Modular; Food/Cons St)
	Plymouth - (Food/Ag; Food Sys Man; FQPD)
	Queen Margaret (Coll) - (App Food Sci/Mkt; Food Prod Man) (4 AS)
	South Bank - DEE/DD (Food Sci; Baking Tech) (4 AS) (BTEC 3M)
	Robert Gordon - (FTCS) (4 AS)
	SAC (Au) - (Food Prod/Man/Mark - provisional new course)

Offers for Foundation, Certificate and Diploma courses (see Ch 5):

Higher National Diploma courses (England and Wales):
4 pts. and below Birmingham (CFT & CS); Blackpool (CFE); Bristol UWE; Cardiff (IHE); Harper Adams (CAg); Humberside; Manchester Met; North East Wales (IHE); Plymouth; South Bank.

Higher Diploma courses (Scotland):
4 pts. or equivalent Glasgow (CFood); Queen Margaret (Coll); Robert Gordon; SAC (Au).

Alternative offers:

EB offers: **South Bank** 70%.

IB offers: **Bournemouth** 24 pts; **Dundee** 24 pts; **Leeds** H6 chem H55 in science subjects; **Nottingham** 28 pts 7 subjects 24 pts 6 subjects; **South Bank** 24 pts; **Surrey** 28 pts.

Irish offers: **Manchester Met** 4 Ds or Cs; **South Bank** CCCC.

SCE offers: **Strathclyde** BBB.

CHOOSING YOUR COURSE (See also Ch 1)

> **Subject information:** Biochemistry, microbiology, human nutrition, food processing and technology are components of these courses. The study depends for its understanding on a secure foundation of several pure sciences – chemistry and two subjects from physics, mathematics, biology, botany or zoology. Only students offering such a combination can be considered. Food Technology covers the engineering aspects of food processing and management.

Course highlights: Belfast Course covers human nutrition, food process engineering, economics and marketing, quality and safety. **Bournemouth** (Food Qual) Covers the science, technology and management aspects of the food industry. **Leeds** Pure science base applied to food and its processing. **Manchester Met** (Con Pro) Main options: food, catering, housing. **Newcastle** (Food Eng) Common first year with Agricultural Engineering and Environmental Engineering options. **North London** Includes food, nutrition, home studies, consumer studies and marketing. **Nottingham** In the first two terms students take agriculture, biochemistry, biology and physical science. **Queen Margaret (Coll)** Technical and commercial aspects of food and beverage manufacture. **Reading** Part I (two terms) deals with the agricultural and fisheries backgrounds, dairy and cereal products, physiology and biochemistry. In Part II (three terms) food processing, the chemistry, biochemistry and physics of food are covered as well as human nutrition and microbiology. **Sheffield Hallam** Course covers marketing, consumer behaviour, biotechnology and quality control, food packaging and product development. **South Bank** BSc Food Science and HND Food Technology have a common first year. Transfers possible. NOW CHECK PROSPECTUSES FOR ALL COURSES.

Study opportunities abroad: Bath (CHE) (E); **Humberside**; **Leeds** (E) FR NL G P IRE; **Newcastle** (E); **Reading** EUR.

Work opportunities abroad: Humberside GK SP P G B FR HG; **Newcastle** G; **Reading**; **South Bank** FR G M.

ADMISSIONS INFORMATION

Number of applicants per place (approx): Belfast 10; **Birmingham (CFood)** (HD) 3; **Blackpool (CFE)** 1; **Leeds** 10; **Manchester** 4; **Oxford Brookes** 20; **Robert Gordon** 2; **Sheffield Hallam** 7; **Strathclyde** 10; **South Bank** 8; **Surrey** 17.

General Studies acceptable: Manchester Met; North East Wales (IHE); Oxford Brookes; Robert Gordon; Surrey.

Selection interviews: Belfast (some); Leeds (some); Manchester Met; Reading.

Offers to applicants repeating A-levels: Higher Leeds, Nottingham CCD; **Possibly higher** Manchester Met; **Same** Belfast, Sheffield Hallam, Surrey.

> **Examples of interview questions:** What type of work do you expect this course to lead to? What made you choose this subject? Have you any experience of the food industry?

GAP YEAR ADVICE

Institutions accepting a Gap Year: Most institutions; **Bath (CHE)** Candidates should apply in academic year immediately prior to college entry unless travelling abroad.

Institutions willing to defer entry after A-levels (see Ch 5): Bournemouth; Cranfield (Silsoe); Dundee; Humberside; Leeds; Manchester Met; Plymouth; Queen Margaret (Coll); Robert Gordon; South Bank; Surrey.

AFTER A-LEVELS ADVICE

Institutions which may accept the same points score after A-levels: Belfast; Humberside; Leeds; Manchester Met; Newcastle; Nottingham; Oxford Brookes; Robert Gordon; Sheffield Hallam; South Bank; Strathclyde; Surrey.

Institutions demanding the actual grades after A-levels: Leeds (or better points score usually).

Institutions which may accept under-achieving applicants after A-levels: Humberside; Leeds; Manchester Met; Newcastle; Sheffield Hallam; South Bank; Surrey.

Institutions with vacancies in Aug/Sept 1992 (see Ch 5): Bath (CHE); Bournemouth; Cranfield (Silsoe) 14 pts; Humberside 4 pts; Leeds 12 pts; Manchester Met 4 pts; Newcastle 16 pts; Plymouth 4 pts; Queen Margaret (Coll) EE; Robert Gordon; South Bank 6 pts; Surrey CDD.

ADVICE FOR MATURE STUDENTS

Previous qualifications are considered important for these courses.

GRADUATE EMPLOYMENT

New Graduates' destinations (percentages) 1991:
Permanent employment: U 87.
Unemployment: U 10.
Further studies (all types): U 25.

FORESTRY

Special subject requirements: A-levels in mathematics or science.

NB Institutions may raise or lower the level of published offers depending either on the quality or otherwise of individual applications or the numbers of applications received; grades/points offered may be adjusted downwards after A-level results. The level of an offer is not indicative of the quality of a course.

18 pts.	**Bangor** - CCC-CDD/BC-CD (Forestry; For/App Zoo; Agro For) (BTEC 3M)
	Edinburgh - CCC/BB (Forestry) (4 AS)
16 pts.	**Edinburgh** - CCD (Ecol Sci)
14 pts.	**Aberdeen** - CDD/BC (Forestry)
	Bangor - CDD (For/Wood Sci) (BTEC 65% average)
12 pts.	**Bangor** - DDD/CD (Wood Sci) (4 AS)

Alternative offers:

IB offers: **Bangor** 28 pts.

SCE offers: **Aberdeen** BBBC; **Edinburgh** BBBB.

Overseas applicants: Bangor Good proportion of overseas students on course.

CHOOSING YOUR COURSE (See also Ch 1)

> **Subject information:** Forestry is concerned with the establishment and management of forests for timber production, environmental, conservation and amenity purposes.

Course highlights: Aberdeen Two programmes - aboriculture (production of oriental trees/shrubs and seed nursery production) and amenity forestry or forest management. **Bangor** Specialisms in tropical forestry and environmental studies in forestry. Supervised year of industrial experience between years 2 & 3. (Agroforestry) The programme covers both agriculture and forestry in tropical and temperate fields. NOW CHECK PROSPECTUSES FOR ALL COURSES.

Study opportunities abroad: Aberdeen (E); **Bangor** (E).

Work opportunities abroad: Bangor USA FN.

ADMISSIONS INFORMATION

Admissions Tutors' advice: Aberdeen Eighteen weeks of practical experience necessary before entering year 2. **Bangor** Intake is 20 with about 150 applicants. Actual grades, post A-level will be asked for. Mature students account for 20% of students on the course. Two science A-levels or equivalent required. **Edinburgh** Eight places and approximately 70 applicants. **Aberdeen** and **Bangor** interview for selection and both had vacancies after A-levels.

> **Examples of interview questions:** Analyse a piece of diseased wood and say what is wrong with it (Dutch Elm Disease). What experience of forestry do you have? What is wood science? What does visco-elasticity mean? What type of a career are you aiming for? On a desert island how would you get food from wood? How do you see forestry developing in the next hundred years? What aspects of forestry are the most important?

GAP YEAR ADVICE

Institutions willing to defer entry after A-levels (see Ch 5): Bangor.

AFTER A-LEVELS ADVICE

Institutions with vacancies in Aug/Sept 1992 (see Ch 5): Aberdeen; Bangor 12 pts.

GRADUATE EMPLOYMENT

New Graduates' destinations (percentages) 1991:
Permanent employment: U 70.
Unemployment: U 21.
Further studies (all types): U 15.

FRENCH (See also **Modern Languages, Language** and **European Studies**)

Special subject requirements: A-levels in French and one other subject.

NB Institutions may raise or lower the level of published offers depending either on the quality or otherwise of individual applications or the numbers of applications received; grades/points offered may be adjusted downwards after A-level results. The level of an offer is not indicative of the quality of a course.

30 pts.	**Cambridge/Oxford** - AAA potential recommended (Mod Lang)
24 pts.	**Aston** - BBB-BBC (Fr; Int Bus/Fr)
	Bath - ABC (Mod Lang/Europ)
	Bristol - BBB/AB-BB (Fr/Ger; Fr/Ital; Fr/Sp; Fr/Russ; Fr/Phil)
	Hull - BBB (Fr/Bus St; Fr/Eng)
	Leeds - BBB/AB (French; Fr/Man St) (4 AS)
	London (King's) - 24 pts approx (French)
	London (RH) - ABC-BBC/18-16 pts (French; Fr Comb)
	London (SSEES) - BBC/BC (Fr/Rom)
	Newcastle - BBB/AA-AB (All French courses)
	St Andrews - BBB (French)
	Swansea - ABC-CCC (Russ/Welsh)
	Swansea - ABC-BBC/BB (Mod Lang/Bus; EBS Fran)
22 pts.	**Aberdeen** - BBC (French)
	Aston - 22 pts (Fr/Ger; Fr/Jap)
	Birmingham - BBC-CCC (All French joint courses - See also under **20 pts**)
	Bristol - BBC/BB (French; Comp Sci/Fr; Fr/Lat)
	Cardiff - BBC-CCC/AB-BB (French; Fr/Hist)
	Durham - BBC (Mod Lang/Ling; Mod Lang/Mus)
	East Anglia - BBC-BCC/BB (Fr/Ger; Fr Ling; Fr; Fr St; F/G Bus; F/G/Lang)
	Edinburgh - BBC (French)
	Exeter - BBC-BCC/BB (Fr/GRS) (See also **20 pts**)
	Glasgow - BBC (French)
	Heriot-Watt - BBC inc BB in languages (Comb courses)
	Hull - BBC-BCC/BB (Sp/Fr)
	Hull - BBC (Fr/Pol; Fr/Phil; Fr/Hist; Fr/Mus; Fr/Sp; Fr/Germ)
	Keele - BBC-BCD/BB-BC (Double Lang Comb) (4 AS)
	Lancaster - BBC (Acc/Fr; Mktg/Fr; Econ/Fr; Eng/Fr)
	Leeds - BBC (Fr/Hist; Fr/Sp)
	London (QMW) - BBC/BB (Fr/Ling/Comp Sci)
	Manchester - 22 pts approx (French courses)
	Nottingham - BBC-BCE (French and combined courses)
	Reading - BBC (French courses)
	Sheffield - BBC-BCD/BB (French and dual degrees, offer varies)
	Southampton - BBC-BCC (French)

Surrey – BBC/AB (French – RM13; R11) (4 AS)
Surrey – BBC-BCC/AB (RT12; RQ11)
Swansea – BBC/BB-BC (French/BS) (BTEC 1D+Ms)
Warwick – BBC (Fr Film; Eng Fr)
Warwick – BBC-BCC (Fr Hist; Fr Thea; French)

20 pts. Aston – BCC/AA (Comb Hons)
Bangor – BCC-CCC/BC (French; Joint Hons) (See **Admissions Tutors' advice**)
Birmingham – BCC (French)
Bradford – BCC/BB (French with Ger/Russ/Sp)
East Anglia – BCC-BCD/BC (Fr/Scand)
Essex – BCC (French; Fr/Ling)
Exeter – BBD (French) (4 AS)
Exeter – BCC (Fr/Ital)
Hull – BCC-BBD/BB-BC (Fr/Drama; Fr/Scand; Fr/Ital; Fr/Philos)
Keele – BCC-BCD/BB-BC (All courses except **22 pts**) (4 AS)
Kent – BCC/BB (French – unless combined with a subject having a higher level offer)
Lancaster · BCC (French and all other courses except under **22 pts**)
Leeds · BCC/BB (Fr/Ger)
London (**QMW**) – BCC/BC (French; French Comb)
Salford – 20 pts approx (Joint courses)
Southampton – BCC-CCC/BB (All courses except under **22 pts**)
Sussex – BCC/BB (Approx offer for French courses) (Fr/Euro; Fr/Afras)
Swansea – BCC-BCD/BC (Fr; French plus science or engineering subjects)
UMIST – BCC/AA (Fr; Fr/Comp L) (BTEC Ms)
York – BCC/BB (All Language courses inc **Language**) (B in French)

18 pts. Aberystwyth – CCC (French)
Belfast – CCC/BB (Approx offer for French courses)
Leicester – BCD (French; Fr/Ger)
Leicester – CCC/BC (Mod Langs; Fr/Pol)
Leeds – BCD/BB (Fr/Lat; Fr/Rus) (See also **22/24 pts**)
Liverpool – BCD-CCC/BB (French; Fr/Ger; Fr/Hisp St; Fr/Maths)
Nottingham – CCC (Fr/Lat)
Stirling – CCC/BB (All courses)
Strathclyde – CCC/BC (BBD 2nd yr entry) (French)
Ulster – CCC-CCD/BC (Hum Comb)

16 pts. Bristol – BB (Fr/Phil)
Central Lancashire – 16 pts (Comb Hons)
Durham – BB (French)
Kingston – CCD-CEE/CD (Fr/Econ/Pol)
London (**SSEES**) – BB (Fr/Russ)
Middlesex – 16-12 pts (Modular)
Nottingham Trent – 16 pts (Eur Bus/Fr)
St David's – CCD/CD (French)

14 pts. Brighton – 14 pts (Ap Lang)
Central Lancashire – CCE/CC (OCL) (4 AS)
London (**Gold**) – BC (Fr Studs)
Portsmouth – CDD (Fr St)

12 pts. Bristol UWE – DDD/CC (Fr/Ger; Fr/Sp; FGIS; FSIS)
Buckingham – DDD (Fr/Euro Pol)
Coventry – CC (Fr/Sp *ab initio*)
Liverpool John Moores – CC-EE (Fr/Ger; Fr/Rus; Fr/Sp)
North London – CC-CD (French; Hum)
Oxford Brookes – DDD/CC (Fr Modular) (4 AS)
Portsmouth – CDE/BC (Engl/Fr)
Westminster – CC-CD (All French Mod Lang options)

10 pts. Bedford (**CHE**) – 10 pts (Comb St)
Cheltenham & Glos (**CHE**) – 10 pts (Mod Lang Fr) (BTEC French A-level required)
Coventry – CD (Fr/Ger; Fr/Sp)
Derby – 10 pts (Comb St)

Kingston - CD (French) (4 AS)
Manchester Met - CEE/DD (Fr/Ger; Fr/Sp)
North London - CD (Comb St)
Northumbria - 10 pts (All courses)
Wolverhampton - 10 pts (Hum; Mod Lang courses)

8 pts. **and below**
Anglia (Poly Univ) - (Joint courses)
Bournemouth - (Comb St)
Central Lancashire - (Comb St)
Coventry - (Modular)
Guildhall London - DD (French - Modular) (BTEC 4M)
Hertfordshire - (Hum)
Huddersfield - (Comm Arts)
Leeds Met - (ELI/Fr)
London (UC) - EE (French)
Nottingham Trent - (M Eur St)
Ripon & York St John (CHE) - (Modular)
Roehampton (IHE) - D in French (French courses)
Southampton (IHE) - (Comb St)
South Bank - (MLIS; MLIB - Fr/Ger/Sp)
Staffordshire - (Mod St)
Sunderland - (Comb St)
Teesside - (Hum)
Thames Valley London - (All App Lang courses; Fr/Gr)
Trinity & All Saints (CHE) - DD (French)

Diploma of Higher Education courses:
4 pts. Crewe & Alsager (CHE); Guildhall London; Middlesex; Oxford Brookes; Westminster (Office Inf Tech with French); Westminster (CHE).

Offers for Foundation, Certificate and Diploma courses (see Ch 5):

Higher National Diploma courses (with Business Studies):
4 pts. **and below**
Bristol UWE; Central Lancashire; Crewe & Alsager (CHE); Gwent (CHE); Glamorgan; Humberside; Loughborough (CT); Northumbria; Norwich City (CHFE); Plymouth; Salford (UC); Stockport (CT); Swansea (IHE).

Alternative offers:

EB offers: **Keele** 65%; **Leeds** 65%; **Surrey** 60%.

IB offers: **Aberdeen** 30 pts; **Aston** 31 pts; **Bradford** 30 pts inc H666; **Bristol** 32-30 pts inc H555; **Buckingham** 26 pts; **East Anglia** 30-28 pts inc 15 pts Highers; **Exeter** 30 pts; **Guildhall London** 28 pts 7 subjects 24 pts 6 subjects; **Hull** 30 pts; **Kent** 27 pts, H 12 pts; **Lancaster** 30 pts; **Leeds** 30 pts inc H666; **London (QMW)** 24 pts, **(RH)** 30 pts; **North London** H555; **St Andrews** 30 pts; **Sheffield** 33-30 pts; **Surrey** 30 pts; **Swansea** 27 pts; **York** H655.

Irish offers: **Aberdeen** BBBB; **Bristol UWE** CCCC; **Guildhall London** CCCCC; **Keele** BBBCC; **Liverpool** BBBCC; **Manchester Met** ABBBB; **Newcastle** BBCCC; **Sheffield** BBBBB; **Surrey** ABBBCC.

SCE offers: **Aberdeen** BBBB; **Aberystwyth** BBBB; **Edinburgh** BBBB; **Essex** BBBB; **Glasgow** ABBB-BBBB; **Guildhall London** BBCCC; **Heriot-Watt** AABB + interview; **Keele** BBBCC-BCCC; **Lancaster** BBBBB; **Sheffield** BBBB; **St Andrews** BBBB; **Stirling** BBCC; **Strathclyde** AABB-BBBB **Surrey** BBBC.

Overseas applicants: North London French nationals accepted (essays written in French and English). **Sheffield** Applicants should state if French is their first language. **Surrey** High level of competence in French required.

CHOOSING YOUR COURSE (See also Ch 1)

> **Subject information:** Courses could include an emphasis on literature and linguistics, the written or spoken word or a wider study of France and her culture as in European Studies courses. Check prospectuses before choosing courses.

Course highlights: Bangor Options include French commercial language and business practice. **Bristol** Students take subsidiary subject from 10 options in years 1 & 2. Traditional literary or historical emphasis. **Durham** The first year of the course covers the study of language, translation and history, phonetics and medieval and 17th century literature. **East Anglia** The subject is studied with an emphasis on linguistic proficiency. **Exeter** Emphasis on fluency - oral and written work. **Heriot-Watt** (French: Translating and Interpreting) Strong bias towards written and spoken word. **Hull** Communication skills, modern French culture (including literature) art, music, drama, film covered in course. Wide range of topics include literature, lexicology, linguistics, politics, sociology and new technology. Other languages or additional subjects as options in years 1/2/4. **Lancaster** Emphasis on practical language work. **Leeds** Option-based flexible course with few compulsory subjects. Practical language teaching. All tuition in French. **London (RH)** All areas of French literature, institutions and computer-assisted language learning. Wide range of options, linguistic, literary, political, economic. **Newcastle** Emphasis on oral and aural communication. Options in literature and film in the 20th century. **Portsmouth** This is a course with a strong bias towards modern French and modern France. **Reading** Strong emphasis on written and spoken French. Choice between traditional literary studies and history and institutions. **St David's** Flexible course offering students opportunity to tailor own course (linguistic, literary, contemporary society, history of ideas). **Sheffield** Wide range of French topics - historical and modern. **Swansea** (French/BS) Common core of post A/AS-level general language plus specialised business language courses. Study of political, social, economic, life of France plus other options. NOW CHECK PROSPECTUSES FOR ALL COURSES.

Study opportunities abroad: Aberystwyth (E); **Aston** (E); **Bangor** (E); **Birmingham** (E); **Bournemouth** (E); **East Anglia** (E); **Hull** (E); **Leeds** (E); **London (QMW)** (E), **(RH)** (E); **Newcastle** (E); **Portsmouth** (E); **Reading** (E); **Sheffield** (E); **Surrey** (E).

Work opportunities abroad: Leeds; London (RH) FR B SW CAN G IT; **Roehampton (IHE)** FR B CAN; **Sheffield** FR CAN SZ B; **Surrey** FR B CAN AU G.

ADMISSIONS INFORMATION

Number of applicants per place (approx): Aston 6 pts; **Birmingham** 8; **Bradford** (Fr/Sp) 14, (Fr/Ger) 8, (Fr/Russ) 4; **Bristol** 9; **Central Lancashire** 5; **Durham** 8; **Exeter** 8; **Kent** 16; **Lancaster** 19; **Leeds** 6; **Liverpool** 5; **London (RH)** 3; **Manchester Met** 13; **Middlesex** 6; **Newcastle** 25; **Nottingham** (Fr/Ger) 3; **Oxford Brookes** 24; **Portsmouth** 18; **Swansea** 5; **Trinity & All Saints (CHE)** 3; **York** 8.

General Studies acceptable: Aberdeen; Aberystwyth; Aston; Birmingham; Bradford; East Anglia; Exeter (2); Hull (2); Keele; Kingston; Lancaster; Leeds (JMB); Liverpool; London (QMW) (2); North London; Nottingham; Oxford Brookes; Roehampton (IHE); Southampton; St Andrews; Stirling; Surrey; Swansea; Trinity & All Saints (CHE); Wolverhampton; most other new universities and colleges.

Selection interviews: Birmingham; Cambridge; Durham; East Anglia (after offer); Essex; Guildhall London (some); Heriot-Watt; Hull (some); Kent; Lancaster (some); Leeds (some); Liverpool (T); London (RH) (T); Nottingham (some); Oxford Brookes (some); Portsmouth (some); Reading; St David's; Sheffield; South Bank; Stirling (some); Sussex; Swansea (some); Trinity & All Saints (CHE); Warwick; York (some); most new universities and colleges.

Offers to applicants repeating A-levels: Higher Aberystwyth (1 pt), Bristol (Fr; Fr/Pol), Newcastle ABD-BBC, Oxford Brookes; **Possibly higher** Aston (Fr; Fr/Ger); **Same** Aston, Bradford, Bristol (Fr/Phil; Fr/Lat), Durham, East Anglia, Lancaster, Leeds, Liverpool, London (RH), North London, Nottingham (Fr/Germ; Fr; Fr/Lat), St David's (most), Sussex, Swansea, Ulster.

Admissions Tutors' advice: Bangor (Joint Courses) A-level results are not the most important factor when decisions are made. There is no such thing as a 'normal' offer. Currently we would be most unlikely to consider a candidate with less than grade C in French. **Bath** See **European Studies**. **Durham** Takes about as many Joint Honours as Single Honours students. Numbers of places and applicants and the policies relating to different joint courses vary. Further details from admissions tutor. (Fr/Russ) Applications considered on their merits. (Fr/Span) In addition to grades indicated we look for evidence of wide reading, intellectual initiative and curiosity. No candidates are admitted without an interview. **Leeds** Make the most of yourself on your UCAS application. **London (RH)** We welcome non-standard applications (mature and overseas students) and also well- qualified late applicants. **Newcastle** Our practice is to make an offer to almost all applicants and to invite them for an open day. **Nottingham** Candidates receiving offers are invited to an open day. Candidates re-applying but who performed poorly in languages at the first A-level sitting may be rejected. **Oxford Brookes** (Fr Lang; Comb St) Motivation is more important than A-level predictions. Students with post A-level experience preferred. Few offers after February due to pressure on places. **Surrey** Preference for candidates with history, politics, economics among A-levels. Candidates must be aware that this is not a traditional language and literature course, and must have a positive interest in the history, politics and sociology field as well as linguistic aspects. **UMIST** No knowledge of computing required for Fr/Comp L courses.

> **Examples of interview questions:** Questions on A-level syllabus, and at Oxford on the entrance examination. Part of the interview will be conducted in the language. What foreign newspapers and/or magazines do you read? What are your favourite authors? Compare Molière to Flaubert. Discuss your personality. What do you do in your spare time? 'I was asked to speak in both French and German (Joint Hons **Lancaster**) about a French holiday and was questioned on a German set book.' 'What offer do you think I should make to you?' Questions on French current affairs/politics, travel abroad, books read outside the course etc.

GAP YEAR ADVICE

Institutions accepting a Gap Year: Most institutions - all recommend part or all of the year in French-speaking environment; **Leeds** We encourage a year out (ideally in France) providing the student keeps in touch with French; **Newcastle** We encourage a year out, particularly if there is a French connection; **Portsmouth** Don't neglect the written language.

Institutions willing to defer entry after A-levels (see Ch 5): Aston; Hull; Leeds; Newcastle; Portsmouth; Roehampton (IHE); South Bank (Prefer not); Swansea; UMIST; York.

AFTER A-LEVELS ADVICE

Institutions which may accept the same points score after A-levels: Aberystwyth; Aston; Birmingham; Bristol; Durham; East Anglia; Leeds (B in French); Liverpool; London (RH); Newcastle; North London; Oxford Brookes; Nottingham (French); Swansea (but actual grade in French); York.

Institutions demanding the actual grades offered after A-levels: Bradford; Guildhall London; Hull; Kent; Nottingham (Fr/Germ), (Fr/Russ), (Fr/Lat); St David's; Southampton; Stirling.

Institutions which may accept under-achieving applicants after A-levels: Aston; Belfast; Birmingham; Bradford; Durham; East Anglia; Essex; Exeter; Glasgow; Hull; Kent; Lancaster; Leeds; Liverpool; London (RH); Newcastle; Nottingham; Reading; Swansea; York.

Institutions with vacancies in Aug/Sept 1992 (see Ch 5): Anglia (Poly Univ); Aston BBC; Bradford 20 pts; Buckingham; Essex 20 pts; Glamorgan; Greenwich; Lingston; London (QMW), (RH),

(SSEES) 20-18 pts; Portsmouth 12 pts; Roehampton (IHE) 2 pts; South Bank DE; Sunderland; Surrey; Swansea 22-18 pts; UMIST 16 pts.

ADVICE FOR MATURE STUDENTS

Previous qualifications particularly in languages are important for these courses, which usually attract about 5% of mature students.

GRADUATE EMPLOYMENT

New Graduates' destinations (percentages) 1991:
Permanent employment: U 75; P 71.
Unemployment: U 14; P 7.
Further studies (all types): U 34; P 38.
Main career destinations (approx): Finance 19; Admin/Managerial 16; Marketing etc 27; Secretarial 15; Social 5; Teaching 4; Legal 5.

Surrey Students entered a wide range of careers from Assistante a la Direction with Electricité de France in Paris and ship broking to public relations, publishing, chartered accountancy, law and teaching.

See also under **Modern Languages**.

FURNITURE DESIGN AND PRODUCTION

Special subject requirements: none. Foundation Art course required.

All candidates for degree courses are interviewed and their portfolios scrutinised. Applications are submitted through the Art and Design Admissions Registry (ADAR Scheme). (See Chapter 3.)

NB Institutions may raise or lower the level of published offers depending either on the quality or otherwise of individual applications or the numbers of applications received; grades/points offered may be adjusted downwards after A-level results. The level of an offer is not indicative of the quality of a course.

6 pts.	**Buckinghamshire (CHE)** - (Furn Prod)
4 pts.	**Bournemouth** - (Furn Des)
	Buckinghamshire (CHE) - (Furn Des/Crafts; Rest/Craft)
	De Montfort - (3D Des Furn)
	Guildhall London - (Furn)
	Kingston - (3D Des Furn)
	Leeds Met - (3D Des Furn)
	Loughborough (CA) - (3D Des Furn)
	Middlesex - (3D Des Furn)
	Nottingham Trent - (3D Des Furn)
	Ravensbourne (CDC) - (3D Des Furn)
	Westminster - (Furn Des/Tech)

Offers for Foundation, Certificate and Diploma courses (see Ch 5):

Higher National Diploma courses:
   2 pts.   **and below** Guildhall London.

CHOOSING YOUR COURSE (See also Ch 1)

Subject information: Some of these courses will require a preparation by way of a Foundation Art course. Check prospectuses for details.

Course highlights: Buckinghamshire (CHE) (Furn Des/Crafts) One of the first craftsman/designer business courses world-wide aimed at small businesses involved in furniture restoration to museum standard. Every year students win highest national awards. NOW CHECK PROSPECTUSES FOR ALL COURSES.

Study opportunities abroad: Buckinghamshire (CHE) (E).

Work opportunities abroad: Buckinghamshire (CHE) AF AS.

ADMISSIONS INFORMATION

Number of applicants per place (approx): Buckinghamshire (CHE) 2; **Nottingham Trent** 4; **Westminster** 4.

Examples of interview questions: Why have you chosen this course? You will be expected to discuss the work of at least one modern designer. Questions on history of furniture design and on modern designers.

GENETICS

Special subject requirements: 2 or 3 A-levels in science and mathematics subjects.

NB Institutions may raise or lower the level of published offers depending either on the quality or otherwise of individual applications or the numbers of applications received; grades/points offered may be adjusted downwards after A-level results. The level of an offer is not indicative of the quality of a course.

30 pts.	**Cambridge** - AAA potential recommended (Nat Sci)
20 pts.	**Manchester** - 20 pts approx (Genetics)
	Nottingham - BCC or BC + CC grades at AS-level (Genetics)
	St Andrews - BCC-CCC (Genetics) (4 AS)
	York - BCC-CCC (Genetics) (BTEC 4M)
18 pts.	**Aberdeen** - CCC-CCD/BC (Genetics)
	Birmingham - BCD (Bio Sc Genet)
	Cardiff - BCD (Gen)
	Edinburgh - 18 pts (Genetics)
	Glasgow - CCC-CCD/BC (Genetics)
	Leeds - CCC (Gen) (4 AS)
	Leicester - BCD (BSc Gen)
	Liverpool - CCC (Genet) (4 AS)
	Newcastle - CCC/AB (Genet)
	Sheffield - CCC-BCD (Genetics courses) (BTEC Ms)
	Sussex - BCD/CC (M Gen T/Biols)
	Swansea - CCC/BB (Genetics) (BTEC 1D+Ms)
16 pts.	**Belfast** - CCD (Gen)
	London (QMW) - CCD (Genetics)
	London (UC) - CCD (Genetics)
14 pts.	**Aberystwyth** - CDD/CC (Genetics; Genet Biochem) (BTEC 3M)

Alternative offers:

IB offers: **Aberdeen** 26 pts; **Aberystwyth** 27 pts; **Leeds** H655; **Liverpool** 30 pts; **Nottingham** 33 pts; **St Andrews** 28 pts; **Swansea** 28 pts.

Irish offers: **Aberdeen** BBCC; **Liverpool** BBCCC.

SCE offers: **Aberdeen** BBCC; **Edinburgh** BBBB; **Glasgow** BBBB; **Leeds** AAAA; **Liverpool** AABB; **Newcastle** AAAAA; **St Andrews** BCCC.

CHOOSING YOUR COURSE (See also Ch 1)

> **Subject information:** This is an appropriate course of study for those aimimg to follow careers in such areas as biological and medical research, biotechnology, plant or animal breeding. See also under **Biotechnology** and **Microbiology**.

Course highlights: Aberdeen The course involves animal, plant and human biology. **Aberystwyth** Biology, biochemistry and a computer science option. Strong research base in plant genetics. **Swansea** Wide choice of specialisms in year 2 and specialisation in year 3. **York** Strong research department (population and evolutionary genetics). NOW CHECK PROSPECTUSES FOR ALL COURSES.

Study opportunities abroad: Swansea (E).

Work opportunities abroad: Aberystwyth EUR.

ADMISSIONS INFORMATION

Number of applicants per place (approx): Leeds 7; **Newcastle** 8; **Swansea** 5; **York** 11.

General Studies acceptable: Aberdeen; Aberystwyth; Liverpool (JMB or Camb only).

Selection interviews: Cambridge; Leeds (some); Liverpool; Newcastle (some); Nottingham; York.

Offers to applicants repeating A-levels: Higher Aberystwyth, Leeds, Newcastle, Nottingham, Swansea, York (1 pt).

> **Examples of interview questions:** What has fired your interest in genetics? What books have you read on the subject? What future career have you considered? What areas of genetics most interest you?

GAP YEAR ADVICE

Institutions accepting a Gap Year: Most institutions; **Aberystwyth** Try to work in a related area. **York** Try to learn a foreign language.

Institutions willing to defer entry after A-levels (see Ch 5): Aberystwyth; York.

AFTER A-LEVELS ADVICE

Institutions which may accept the same points score after A-levels: Aberystwyth; Leeds; Liverpool; Newcastle (usually); Swansea; York.

Institutions which may accept under-achieving applicants after A-levels: Aberdeen; Lancaster; Leeds; Liverpool; London (RH Bed); Newcastle.

Institutions with vacancies in Aug/Sept 1992 (see Ch 5): Aberdeen; Aberystwyth 10 pts; Leeds; London (QMW); Newcastle; Swansea 16-14 pts; York 18 pts; most institutions are likely to have vacancies in 1993.

ADVICE FOR MATURE STUDENTS

Newcastle offers courses for students over age 25.

GRADUATE EMPLOYMENT

New Graduates' destinations (percentages) 1991:
Permanent employment: U 57.
Unemployment: U 32.
Further studies (all types): U 54.
Main career destinations (approx): No information available.

GEOGRAPHY

BA COURSES

Special subject requirements: usually geography at A-level and mathematics at GCSE (grade A-C).

NB Institutions may raise or lower the level of published offers depending either on the quality or otherwise of individual applications or the numbers of applications received; grades/points offered may be adjusted downwards after A-level results. The level of an offer is not indicative of the quality of a course.

30 pts.	**Cambridge/Oxford** - AAA potential recommended (Geography)
24 pts.	**Exeter** - BBB-BBC/AB (Geog Arts)
	Leeds - BBB/22 pts + 2 AS (Geog Arts)
	Nottingham - BBB-BBC (Geog; Geog/Arch)
	St Andrews - BBB (Geog MA) (4 AS)
	Sheffield - BBB (Geog/Jap)
22 pts.	**Aberdeen** - BBC (MA)
	Birmingham - BBC (Geog Arts)
	Durham - BBC (All courses)
	Edinburgh - 22 pts (Geog MA)
	Glasgow - BBC (MA)
	Lancaster - BBC (Geog; Econ/Geog)
	Liverpool - BBC-CCD/AB-BB (Geog Arts) (4 AS)
	London (LSE) - BBC potential recommended (Geog Arts)
	London (RH) - BBC-BCC/AB-BB (B in geog) (Geog/Hist; Geog Arts)
	Newcastle - BBC (Geog)
	Manchester - 22 pts approx (Geog courses)
20 pts.	**Aberdeen** - BCC (Geog Arts)
	Aberystwyth - BCC/BB (Geog A) (BTEC 3M)
	Dundee - 20 pts (Geog)
	Hull - BCC/AB (Geog Arts) (4 AS) (BTEC Ds+Ms)
	Kent - BCC/BC (Geog)
	Leeds - BCC/AB (All joint courses)
	Leicester - BCC/BB (Geog Arts; Geog Soc)
	London (QMW) - BCC/BB (Geog; Geog Arts; Hum Geog; Geog/Pol; Geog/Fr; Geog/Ger; Geog/Russ)
	Ripon & York St John (CHE) - BCC/BB (Geog/Am St)
	Salford - BCC-BCD/AB-BB (Geog Arts) (BTEC 5D)

Sheffield - BCC/BC-CC (Geog SS; Geog/Pol; Geog/Soc) (BTEC M geog +65% average)

Southampton - BCC (B in Geog) (Geog Arts)

Strathclyde - BCC/BB (BA Bus Sch)

Sussex - BCC/BB (Geog Soc; other BA Geography courses)

Swansea - BCC/AB-BB (Geog Arts)

18 pts. Belfast - CCC/BB (Geog Arts)

Bristol UWE - 18 pts (Hum)

Keele - BCD-CCC/BB-BC (Joint Hons) (4 AS)

Lampeter - BCD/BC (Geography; Hu Geog - Single Hons)

Leicester - CCC/BC (Geog/ESH)

London (King's) - 18 pts approx (Geog)

London (QMW) - CCC (Geog/Hisp St)

London (UC) - BCD (Geog Arts)

Manchester Met - CCC/CD (Comb)

Portsmouth - 18 pts (Geog)

Ripon & York St John (CHE) - CCC/BB (Geog/PE; Geog/Hist; Geog/App Soc Sci)

Strathclyde - CCC (1st yr entry) (BA Arts; Soc Sci) BBD (2nd yr entry) (Geog)

16 pts. Cambridge (Hom) - CCD (Geog/Ed) (4 AS) (See also **Education**)

Central Lancashire - 16 pts (Comb Hons)

Kingston - 16 pts (Geog) (BTEC 3M)

London (SOAS) - BB (BC for certain combinations) (Geog Asia/Af)

Middlesex - 16-12 pts (Geog; Modular) (4 AS)

Northumbria - CCD/BC-CC (Geography)

Oxford Brookes - CCD/BB (Geog) (4 AS)

St David's - 16-12 pts (C in geog) (All courses)

Staffordshire - CCD (Geog)

14 pts. Anglia (Poly Univ) - CDD/BC (Geog)

Cheltenham & Glos (CHE) - 14-10 pts (Phy Geog)

Kingston - 14 pts (Geog Inf Sys) (4 AS) (BTEC 2D+2M)

Portsmouth - CDD/BD (Econ/Geog)

West Sussex (IHE) - CDD/CC (Comb Hons)

12 pts. Anglia (Poly Univ) - DDD/CD (Joint courses)

Brighton - 12-8 pts (Hum) (BTEC 3M)

Canterbury Christ Church (CHE) - CC-EE (Comb St)

Cheltenham & Glos (CHE) 12 pts (Hum Geog)

Greenwich - 12 pts (Geog)

Kingston - 12 pts (Geog/French) (4 AS)

Liverpool John Moores - 12 pts (Hum Geog)

North London - CDE/CD (Geography) (4 AS)

Oxford Brookes - DDD/CC (Cart)

S Martins (CHE) - CDE/CC (Geog) (BTEC 3M)

Trinity & All Saints (CHE) - CC (Geog BMA; Geog PM)

Warwick - CDE/CC (BA(QTS))

10 pts. Guildhall London - CD (Geog; Geog/Licence) (BTEC 4M)

Portsmouth - 10 pts (Econ Geog)

Ripon & York St John (CHE) - CD (Geog/Biol; Geog/Env Sci)

Worcester (CHE) - 10 pts approx inc Access (Comb St) (4 AS)

8 pts. and below

Chester (CHE) - (Comb Hons)

Derby - (Comb St - Modular) (4 AS)

Edge Hill (CHE) - (Geog)

Glamorgan - (Hum)

La Sainte Union (CHE) - (Comb St)

Liverpool (IHE) - (Comb St)

Nene (CHE) - (Comb St)

Nottingham Trent - (M Eur St; Hum)

Roehampton (IHE) - (Comb St)

St Mark & St John (CHE) - (Geog)
Sunderland - (Comb St)
Trinity Carmarthen (CHE) - (Geog)
West London (IHE) - (Joint)
Westminster - (Soc Sci)
West Sussex (IHE) - (Geog; BEd Geog)
Wolverhampton - (All courses)

Diploma of Higher Education courses:
4 pts.　Bath (CHE); Crewe & Alsager (CHE); Guildhall London; Middlesex; Oxford Brookes; Ripon & York St John (CHE); Westminster (CHE); Worcester (CHE).

GEOGRAPHY

BSc/BSc(Soc Sci) COURSES

Special subject requirements: usually geography at A-level with mathematics at GCSE (grade A-C).

NB Institutions may raise or lower the level of published offers depending either on the quality or otherwise of individual applications or the numbers of applications received; grades/points offered may be adjusted downwards after A-level results. The level of an offer is not indicative of the quality of a course.

24 pts.　**Birmingham** - BBB-BCC (Geog/Soc Sci)
　　　　　Bristol - BBB-BBC/AB (Geog Sci; Geog Soc Sci)
22 pts.　**Birmingham** - BBC (Geog Sci)
　　　　　Bristol - BBC (Geog Soc Sci)
　　　　　Durham - BBC-BCC (All courses)
　　　　　Exeter - BBC (Geog Soc St; Geog Sci) (4 AS)
　　　　　Lancaster - BBC (Geog)
　　　　　Leeds - BBC-BCC/AA-AB (Geog Sci)
　　　　　London (RH) - BBC/BB (Geog Sci)
　　　　　Newcastle - BBC (Geog Sci)
　　　　　Nottingham - BBC-BCC (Geog Sci)
　　　　　St Andrews - BBC (Geog courses)
20 pts.　**Aberystwyth** - BCC/BB (Geog Sci) (A or AS geog acceptable)(BTEC 3M)
　　　　　Belfast - 20 pts (Pal/Geog)
　　　　　Birmingham - BCC/AB-BB (Geog/Plan)
　　　　　Cardiff - BCC-CCC/BB (Mar Geog)
　　　　　East Anglia - BCC-CCC (Env)
　　　　　Edinburgh - BCC (BBB for 3 yr course)/AB (Geog/Soc) (4 AS)
　　　　　Glasgow - BCC (Geog)
　　　　　Hull - BCC/AB (Geog Sci)
　　　　　Leeds - BCC/BB (All Combined courses)
　　　　　Leicester - BCC (Geog Sci)
　　　　　Liverpool - BCC (Geog/Comp Sc)
　　　　　London (QMW) - BCC/BB (Geog Sci; Geog/Maths; Env Geog; Phys Geog; Geog SS; Geog/Bus Ec)
　　　　　Loughborough - B in Geog + 12 pts (Geog/PE; Geog; H Geog/Econ)
　　　　　Manchester - 20-18 pts approx (Geog)
　　　　　Newcastle - (Geog) Contact Admissions Tutor (new joint courses)
　　　　　Reading - BCC-BCD (Hum Geog; Geog H and P; Reg Sci)
　　　　　Salford - BCC-BCD/AB (Geog) (BTEC 5D)
　　　　　Sheffield - BCC-CCC/AB-BB (Geog Sci; Ecol/Geog; Arch/Geog; Geol/Ph Geog) (4 AS) (BTEC 1D+2M)
　　　　　Southampton - BCC (B in geog) (Geog/Ocean)
　　　　　Swansea - BCC/BB (Geog Sci; Geog)
　　　　　Swansea - BCC-CCC/Bc (Joint courses with Topographical Science)
18 pts.　**Aberdeen** - CCC-CCD/BC (BSc)

Bradford - CCC-BCD/BB (Env Geog)
Bristol - CCC (Geog/Geol)
Glasgow - CCC-CCD/BC (Topog Sci)
Liverpool - CCC (Geog Comb; Geog Sci) (5 AS)
London (King's) - 18 pts approx (Geog)
London (UC) - BCD (Geog Sci)
Loughborough - 18 pts (B in Geog minimum) (Geog)
Manchester Met - 18-10 pts (Comb St)
Reading - BCD (Phys Geog; Meteorol)
St David's - BCD/BC (Ph Geog – Single Hons)
Southampton - BCD-CCC (Geog/Geol)
Strathclyde - CCC/BC (1st yr entry) BBD (2nd yr entry) (Geog/Biol)
Sussex - CCC/BB (G/Biols)
Swansea - CCC/BB (Dev St/Geog)

16 pts. **Edinburgh** - CCD (BSc)
Middlesex - 16-12 pts (Geog; Modular) (4 AS)
Oxford Brookes - CCD/BB (Geog)
Plymouth - CCD/BC (Geog Sci) (4 AS)
St David's - CCD (Ph Geog - Joint Hons)

14 pts. **Anglia (Poly Univ)** - 14 pts (Geog)
Cheltenham & Glos (CHE) - 14-10 pts (Phy Geog)
Coventry - 14 pts (C in geog) (Geog Modular) (4 AS) (BTEC 2M)
Coventry - 14 pts (Geog Sci) (BTEC 2M)
Dundee - CDD/BC (Geog/Bot)
Huddersfield - CDD/CC (Geography) (4 AS)
Newcastle - CDD/CC (Map Inf Sci)
Portsmouth - 14-12 pts (Geog Sci)
Ulster - CDD-DDD/CC-CD (Geog; Reg Anal/Dev)

12 pts. **Belfast** - CC (Geog Sci)
Canterbury Christ Church (CHE) - CC-DE (Comb Hons)
Greenwich - 12 pts (Geog Sci)
Kingston - 12 pts (All courses)
North London - 12 pts (Geography)
Warwick - CDE/BC (QTS Geog)

10 pts. **Central Lancashire** - 10 pts (Comb St)
Cheltenham & Glos (CHE) - 10 pts (Geog/Geol) (4 AS)
Guildhall London - CD (Geog; Geog/Licence) (BTEC 4M)
Liverpool John Moores - 10 pts (Geog)

8 pts. and below
Bath (CHE) - (Comb St)
Chester (CHE) - (Geog Inf Sys)
Coventry - (Comb Sci) (BTEC 2M)
Derby - (Comb St - Modular; Earth/Life St) (4 AS)
Edge Hill (CHE) - (Geog)
Luton (CHE) - (Geog/Geol; Mapping Sci)
Nene (CHE) - (Comb St)
North London - (Comb Sci)
St Mary's (CHE) - (Geog) (BTEC 3M)
West London (IHE) - (Joint)
Worcester (CHE) - (Comb St)

Diploma of Higher Education courses:
  4 pts. Guildhall London; Worcester (CHE).

Offers for Foundation, Certificate and Diploma courses (see Ch 5):

Higher National Diploma courses:
  4 pts. and below Luton (CHE).

Alternative offers:

EB offers: **Aberystwyth** 75%; **Keele** 70%; **Sheffield** 60%.

IB offers: **Aberdeen** (Arts) 30 pts, (Sci) 26 pts; **Aberystwyth** 30 pts; **Bristol** 32 pts H655; **Durham** 30 pts inc Geog H6; **Edinburgh** 32 pts; **Exeter** 33 pts; **Guildhall London** 24 pts; **Hull** 28 pts; **Kent** 27 pts, H 12 pts; **Lancaster** 30 pts; **Leeds** 28 pts; **Leicester** 28 pts; **Liverpool** 30 pts inc 5/6 in 2 science subjects; **London (QMW)** 30 pts, **(RH)** 30 pts; **Newcastle** 24 pts; **Nottingham** H655; **St Andrews** 28 pts; **Salford** 35 pts inc 16 pts Highers; **Sheffield** (BA) H655, (BSc) 555 opverall 24 pts; **South Bank** 24 pts; **Southampton** 30 pts; **Swansea** (BSc) H 17 pts.

Irish offers: **Aberdeen** (Arts) BBBB, (Sci) BBCC; **Aberystwyth** BBBBC; **Edge Hill (CHE)** BBBB; **Edinburgh** ABBB; **Guildhall London** CCCCC; **Keele** BBBCC; **Liverpool** BBCCC; **London (RH)** BBBCC; **Oxford Brookes** CCCCC; **Plymouth** BCCCC; **Sheffield** BBBCC; **South Bank** CCC; **Swansea** H665.

SCE offers: **Aberdeen** (Arts) BBBB, (Sci) BBBC; **Belfast** BBBB; **Dundee** BBBC (Joint Hons), BBCC (Geog/Bot); **Edinburgh** BBBB or BBBC; **Glasgow** BBBB (MA), BBB (BSc); **Guildhall London** BBBC; **Lancaster** BBBBB; **Leeds** ABB; **Liverpool** AABB; **Newcastle** AABBB; **St Andrews** BBBB; **Sheffield** BBBB; **Strathclyde** BBBB or AABB (Business School); **Sussex** ABBB.

Overseas applicants: Durham Interview essential. **Oxford Brookes** Orientation course prior to autumn and spring terms.

CHOOSING YOUR COURSE (See also Ch 1)

> **Subject information:** These courses cover the human, physical, economic and social aspects of the subject. Each institution offers its own particular emphasis. Check the prospectuses for all courses, with particular attention to the specialist options in years 2 & 3.

Course highlights: Aberystwyth Courses in human and physical geography; freedom of choice between faculties. **Anglia (Poly Univ)** Covers the subject by way of social science as physical geography or with 'green' topics. **Belfast** Final year options in human or physical geography. **Birmingham** Wide range of year 2 and 3 options embracing both human and physical geography. **Bristol** Option to specialise at end of year 1 in human or physical geography or both. **Cardiff** (Mar Geog) This course focuses on the ocean as a maritime frontier, Man's socio-economic relationship with the physical environment and the principles of maritime transport. Topics covered include geology, cartography, coastal hydrography and coastal zone management. **Greenwich** BA or BSc options chosen at end of year 2. BA covers urban studies, third world development; BSc, environmental management. **Huddersfield** This course focuses on rural geography, commercial activities, recreation studies, transport and urban studies and water resources. **Hull** Geography can be taken with science or social science emphasis with specialisations in year 3. **Kingston** (Geographical Information Systems) First course of its kind in UK. **Leeds** After year 1 students specialise in either human or physical courses or a combination. Third year options include hydrology, water quality, energy resources, soils, conservation, environmental risk assessment, climatic change and glacial processes. **London (LSE)** BA course in the first year covers physical geography, geographical perspectives on modern society, geographical analysis. **London (RH)** Strong interests in third world and environmental change. Free choice of courses in years 2 and 3. Purpose-built accommodation. **Loughborough** Economic Geography, development and planning studies. **Newcastle** Environmental studies available to all students plus urban and regional development and water resource management. Language options. **Oxford Brookes** Offers cartography as a modular course option. **Portsmouth** Very large range of option studies including remote sensing, computer-assisted cartography, urban and rural studies, fluvial studies, biogeography, medical geography, economic geography and development studies. **Salford** The first year of this course concerns environmental analysis and human ecology. Third year specialities range from geomorphology and climatic change to transport and urban geography. **Staffordshire** Applied, social, political geography with leisure and recreational issues. **Sussex** Geography in School of Biological Science has strong environmental emphasis. **Swansea** Options between human or physical geography or topographical science/cartography. **West Sussex (IHE)** 'Green' issues. Field courses in

Africa (Sahara) and Eastern Europe. **Cambridge, Leeds, Oxford, London (UC)** High research ratings. NOW CHECK PROSPECTUSES FOR ALL COURSES.

Study opportunities abroad: Bristol (E); **Cardiff** (Mar Geog) SP GR FR; **Durham** (E) EUR; **Edinburgh** (E); **Exeter** (E); **Glasgow** (E); **Hull** FR G IT; **Keele** (E); **Lancaster** USA EUR; **Leeds** (E) USA CAN FR SP B; **Leicester** (E); **Middlesex** (E); **London (QMW)** (E); **Plymouth** (E) SP F B USA; **St David's** CAN (Student exchange); **Salford** (E); **West Sussex (IHE)** (E) FR G CAN NL.

Work opportunities abroad: Aberystwyth USA EUR; **Coventry** EUR; **London (RH)** SP; **Plymouth** SP F B USA; **Worcester (CHE)** USA.

ADMISSIONS INFORMATION

Number of applicants per place (approx): Aberystwyth 25; **Anglia (Poly Univ)** 10; **Bristol** 9, (Soc Sci) 18; **Birmingham** 15; **Cambridge (Hom)** 4; **Cheltenham & Glos (CHE)** 4; **Coventry** 17; **Durham** 8; **Edinburgh** (Geog Sci) 8; **Exeter** 10; **Greenwich** 2; **Huddersfield** 22; **Hull** 30; **Kent** 15; **Kingston** 33; **Lancaster** 13; **Leeds** 17; **Liverpool** (BA) 10, (BSc) 8; **London (RH)** 7, **(SOAS)** 8; **Loughborough** 17, (Geog/PE) 30; **Luton (CHE)** 4; **Middlesex** 20; **Newcastle** 17; **North London** 8; **Northumbria** 50; **Nottingham** 13; **Oxford Brookes** (Cart) 9; **Plymouth** 10; **Portsmouth** 28, (Geog Sci) 28; **S Martins** 9; **Salford** 10; **St David's** 6; **Sheffield** (BA) 13, (BSc) 10; **South Bank** 6; **Staffordshire** 15; **Swansea** 12; **Trinity & All Saints (CHE)** 5; **West London (IHE)** 5; **West Sussex (IHE)** 1.

General Studies acceptable: Aberdeen; Aberystwyth (varies); Anglia (Poly Univ); Bedford (CHE); Belfast; Birmingham; Cheltenham & Glos (CHE); Hull (high grade GS - B); Exeter; Greenwich (2); Leeds (JMB); Leicester; Liverpool (JMB); London (RH) (2); Loughborough; Newcastle; Oxford Brookes; Plymouth; S Martins (CHE); Salford; St Andrews; St David's (2); Salford (2); Sheffield (Not AEB); South Bank (some); Staffordshire; Trinity & All Saints (CHE); West Sussex (IHE) (2); Worcester (CHE) (2).

Selection interviews: Aberystwyth (some); Anglia (Poly Univ) (some); Birmingham (some); Bristol; Cambridge; Cambridge (Hom); Coventry; Durham; Edge Hill (CHE); Guildhall London (some); Huddersfield (some); Hull; Kingston; Liverpool (90%); Liverpool (IHE); London (RH), (SOAS); Loughborough; Newcastle (50%); Northumbria; Nottingham; Plymouth (some); St David's (some); Southampton (some); South Bank (some); Warwick (BA (QTS)).

Offers to applicants repeating A-levels: Higher Bournemouth, Durham, Hull, Kingston, London (Gold), Nottingham, Sussex (Geog/Lang); **Possibly higher** Aberystwyth, Edinburgh, Leeds, Plymouth; **Same** Birmingham, Bristol, Coventry, Edge Hill (CHE), Huddersfield, Lancaster, Leeds (applicants consider which A-levels to resit for the BSc course), Liverpool, London (RH), (SOAS), Loughborough, Manchester Met, Newcastle, North London, Northumbria, Oxford Brookes, S Martins (CHE), Salford, St David's, South Bank, Staffordshire, Swansea, Ulster.

Admissions Tutors' advice: Durham Interviewers seek sound all-round ability, enthusiasm and interest for subject and a lively, flexible mind, to handle diversity of course. **Liverpool** A-level geography not required. Interview allows us to assess a student's academic background and any difficulties they could have on our courses. Preference given to candidates with two sciences at A-level for Geog BSc courses. **Newcastle** Candidates for BSc course should offer one or two science subjects at A-level in addition to geography. Applicants with a science background but without A-level geography may apply for course L803 (a four year course. (Map Inf Sci) Mathematical ability important. **Oxford Brookes** (Cartography) Applicants should have studied geography and mathematics beyond GCSE. Colour blindness should be notified. **St David's** Operates flexible admissions policy and as far as possible, each application is considered on merit. Hence an offer below the standard offer may be made in certain circumstances.

Examples of interview questions: What fieldwork have you done? What are your views on ecology? What changes in the landscape have you noticed on the way to the interview? Explain in simple meteorological terms today's weather. Why are earthquakes almost unknown in Britain? What is the value of practical work in geography to primary school children? (BEd course). How important is it to be able to judge the history of towns when studying settlement patterns? What do you enjoy about geography and why? Are there any stories of geographical importance in the news at present? Identify certain features from a satellite picture of Canada and America. Why is the tower called 'Old Joe' (Birmingham)? Preference between human and physical geography. Discuss the current economic situation in Britain and give your views. What do you think about underdevelopment in India? What could be the solution – increased agriculture or industry? Questions on the third world, on world ocean currents and drainage and economic factors world-wide. Expect to comment on local geography and on geographical photographs and diagrams.

GAP YEAR ADVICE

Institutions accepting a Gap Year: Most institutions; **Birmingham** Reading list available. **Newcastle** Year out must be put to positive use; (Map Inf Sci) No. **Northumbria** Travel abroad. **Plymouth** Advisable. **St David's** Take a book and see the world.

Institutions willing to defer entry after A-levels (see Ch 5): Bristol (No); Bristol UWE; Cheltenham & Glos (CHE); Coventry; Kingston; Leeds (Tell us before your results are known if possible); London (RH); Newcastle (Prefer not), (Map Inf Sci) We prefer them to apply when the A-level results are known; Northumbria; Plymouth (No); Ripon & York St John (CHE) (No); Roehampton (IHE); St Andrews; St David's; St Mary's (CHE); South Bank; Swansea.

AFTER A-LEVELS ADVICE

Institutions which may accept the same points score after A-levels: Aberystwyth; Cheltenham & Glos (CHE); Coventry; Edinburgh; Huddersfield; Hull; Kingston; Leeds; Liverpool; London (RH); Loughborough; Middlesex; Newcastle; North London; Northumbria; Oxford Brookes; Plymouth (Grade C in geog); Portsmouth; S Martins (CHE); St David's; Salford; Sheffield; South Bank; Staffordshire; Swansea; West Sussex (IHE).

Institutions demanding the actual grades offered after A-levels: Anglia (Poly Univ); Birmingham; Dundee; Durham; London (SOAS); Nottingham.

Institutions which may accept under-achieving applicants after A-levels: Aberdeen; Aberystwyth (1 pt); Belfast; Bristol; Cambridge (Hom); Durham (very few); Edinburgh; Exeter; Glasgow; Hull; Huddersfield; Kent; Kingston; Leeds (1 pt); Leicester; Liverpool; London (RH), (SOAS); Loughborough; Luton (CHE); Plymouth; Salford; South Bank; Staffordshire; Swansea; Trinity & All Saints (CHE).

Institutions with vacancies in Aug/Sept 1992 (see Ch 5): Aberdeen; Anglia (Poly Univ); Bishop Grosseteste (CHE); Bristol UWE; Cheltenham & Glos (CHE); Derby; Glamorgan; Greenwich 6 pts; King Alfred's (CHE); Kingston; London (QMW), (RH) 20 pts; Newcastle (Map Inf Sci) 10 pts; Northumbria 16-14 pts; Oxford Brookes; Portsmouth; Roehampton (IHE); S Martin's (CHE); St David's 14-12 pts; St Mary's (CHE) >8 pts; South Bank EE.

ADVICE FOR MATURE STUDENTS

Applicants are often considered on merit for these courses for which motivation could be regarded as more important than academic qualifications.

GRADUATE EMPLOYMENT

New Graduates' destinations (percentages) 1991:
Permanent employment: U 62; P 56; C 60.
Unemployment: U 18; P 24; C 20.
Further studies (all types): U 34; P 21; C 33.

Main career destinations (approx): Finance (Univ) 27, (Poly) 12, (Coll) 11; Admin/Managerial (Univ) 18, (Poly) 22, (Coll) 30; Secretarial (Univ) 7, (Poly) 6, (Coll) 12. For all sectors approximately 15% go into Marketing and 8% into Computing and 7% into Social/Welfare work.

GEOLOGY/GEOLOGICAL SCIENCES (See also Engineering (Mining))

Special subject requirements: 2-3 A-levels. Some courses require science and/or mathematics subjects at A-level and GCSE (A-C).

NB Institutions may raise or lower the level of published offers depending either on the quality or otherwise of individual applications or the numbers of applications received; grades/points offered may be adjusted downwards after A-level results. The level of an offer is not indicative of the quality of a course.

30 pts.	**Cambridge** (Nat Sci)/**Oxford** (Geol) – AAA potential recommended
20 pts.	**East Anglia** – BCC/AA (Env)
	London (Imp) – BCC-CCC (All courses)
	London (RH) – BCC/BB (Geol/Maths) (4 AS)
18 pts.	**Aberystwyth** – CCC/BB (Geology)
	Belfast – CCC (Geol)
	Birmingham – CCC (Geology; App Env Geol)
	Bristol – CCC (Geol/Biol; Geology)
	Cardiff – CCC/BC (Geol; Exp/Min Geol)
	Durham – CCC (Geolology courses)
	East Anglia – CCC (Geophys Sci)
	Edinburgh – CCC (Geology) (4 AS)
	Keele – BCD-CCC/BC-CC (Geology)
	Leeds – CCC (Geol Sci; Geoph Sci)
	Leicester – CCC (Geology; Geophys)
	London (QMW) – BCD (Geol Eng)
	London (RH) – CCC/BC (Geology; Geol/Zool; Env Geol) (6 AS)
	London (UC) – CCC/BB (Geology)
	Manchester – CCC approx (Geology)
	St Andrews – CCC (Geoscience; Geol)
	Southampton – CCC (Geology; Geophys Sci)
16 pts.	**Aberdeen** – CCD/BC (Geol)
	Glasgow – 16 pts (Geol)
	Liverpool – CCD (Geol; Geol Comb) (5 AS)
14 pts.	**Bangor** – CDD/CC (Geol Oc)
	Portsmouth – CDD/BC (Geol) (4 AS) (BTEC 3M)
	Sheffield Hallam – 14 pts (Min Est Man)
12 pts.	**Coventry** – CC-CD (Modular)
	Greenwich – 12 pts (Eng Geol; Geol) (4 AS)
	Kingston – 12 pts (Geol) (4 AS)
	Plymouth – 12 pts (App Geol; Env Geol) (4 AS)
	Portsmouth – 12 pts (Env Geol)
	Strathclyde – CC (1st yr entry) CCC (2nd yr entry)
10 pts.	**Cheltenham & Glos (CHE)** – 10-8 pts (Geology)
	Exeter (CSM) – 10 pts (Ind Geol)
	Kingston – CEE/CD (Geol/Comp; Geol/App Phys; Geol/Fr)
	Portsmouth – DDE/CD (Eng Geol/Geotech; App Env Geol) (4 AS)
	Sunderland – 10 pts (Ap Geol)
8 pts.	**and below**
	Anglia (Poly Univ) – (Earth Sci)
	Buckinghamshire (CHE) – (Ind Geol)

Derby - (Earth/Life St - Modular) (4 AS)
Glamorgan - (Geol/Phys; Geol/MIS)
Guildhall London - DEE-EEE/DD-EE (Modular)
Hertfordshire - (Comb St)
Liverpool John Moores - (Comb St; Earth Sci)
Luton (CHE) - (Geol courses) (4 AS)
North London - (Geol/Geog)
Oxford Brookes - (Geol; Geol Sci; App Geol)
Staffordshire - (Comb Sci)
Sunderland - (Geol/Mat Sci; Geol/Phys)
West London (IHE) - (Joint)
Worcester (CHE) - (Comb St/Earth St)

Diploma of Higher Education courses:
4 pts. Guildhall London; Oxford Brookes.

Offers for Foundation, Certificate and Diploma courses (see Ch 5):

Higher National Diploma courses:
4 pts. **and below** Exeter (CSM) (Ind Geol); Luton (CHE) (Geological Technology).

Alternative offers:

EB offers: **London (RH)** 70%.

IB offers: **Aberdeen** 26 pts; **Aberystwyth** 30-28 pts; **Bristol** 27 pts; **Durham** H555; **Exeter** 30 pts; **Guildhall London** 28 pts 7 subjects 24 pts 6 subjects; **Liverpool** H555 30 pts average; **London (RH)** 27 pts; **Portsmouth** 12 pts Highers.

Irish offers: **Aberdeen** BBCC/BCCCC; **Edinburgh** BBBBC; **Leeds** BBBCC; **Liverpool** BBCCC; **London (RH)** BBBCC.

SCE offers: **Aberdeen** BBBC; **Edinburgh** BBBB; **Liverpool** BBBB; **Newcastle** BBB; **St Andrews** BBBC; **Strathclyde** BBBB.

Overseas applicants: Leeds Solid maths and science background required.

CHOOSING YOUR COURSE (See also Ch 1)

Subject information: Topics covered include the physical and chemical constitution of the earth, exploration geophysics, oil and marine geology (oceanography) and seismic interpretation. Civil and Mining Engineering, Earth Science, Soil Science and Environmental Science could also be considered as alternative courses.

Course highlights: Aberdeen Geology or petroleum geology options. **Aberystwyth** Final year option schemes: oil geology, marine geology and mineral exploitation. **Bangor** Students specialise in one or two main disciplines from marine biology and biological oceanography, geological and physical oceanography. **Cardiff** Opportunity to defer final course decision until end of year 1, to learn a European language and to study in Europe. **Exeter (CSM)** Strongly vocational course. A modern European language is an essential part of the course. Contacts with Schools of Mines in France. **London (RH)** In the second and third years a selection of optional courses include marine geology, fossil fuels, mineral deposits and engineering geology. **Southampton** In the first year students take four units in geology. These include geochemistry, map interpretation, mineralogy and petrology and paleontology. NOW CHECK PROSPECTUSES FOR ALL COURSES.

Study opportunities abroad: Cheltenham & Glos (CHE) (E); **Sheffield** (E) G AU SZ NL B FN; **Surrey** (E).

Work opportunities abroad: Bristol G AU SZ; **Cardiff** EUR (West and East) USA AUS AF; **Exeter (CSM)** FR; **Greenwich** SP FR IT; **Hull** G AU SZ; **London (Imp)**; **London (RH)** SP IT; **Plymouth** USA; **Portsmouth** (Eng Geol/Geotech) SP SW.

ADMISSIONS INFORMATION

Number of applicants per place (approx): Bangor 4; **Birmingham** 4; **Bristol** 8; **Cheltenham & Glos (CHE)** 6; **Durham** 4; **Edinburgh** 5; **Greenwich** 2; **Kingston** 19; **Leeds** 6; **Liverpool** 5; **London (Imp)** 5, **(RH)** 3; **Luton (CHE)** 4; **Oxford Brookes** 30; **Portsmouth** (Eng Geol) 8, (Geol) 28; **West London (IHE)** 6.

General Studies acceptable: Cheltenham & Glos (CHE).

Selection interviews: Aberystwyth; Birmingham (promising candidates who would normally receive offers); Bristol; Cardiff; Durham; Edinburgh (some); Guildhall London (some); Liverpool (some); London (RH); Oxford; Southampton; Swansea (some); most new universities and colleges.

Offers to applicants repeating A-levels: Higher Aberystwyth, Bristol, Nottingham, Swansea; **Possibly higher** Portsmouth; **Same** Birmingham (BBC-CCC), Durham, East Anglia, Leeds, London (RH), Nottingham (Geog/Geol).

Admissions Tutors' advice: Durham Geology/Geophysics requires very good maths.

Examples of interview questions: Questions on the field courses attended, and the geophysical methods of exploration in the detection of metals. The differences between Geology courses at the various institutions to which candidates have applied. How would you determine the age of this rock (sample shown)? Can you integrate a decay curve function and would it help you to determine the age of rocks? How many planes of crystallisation could this rock have? What can you offer the department as a Geology student? What do you know about Stonehenge? What is your local geology? Most universities do not seem to ask specific geology questions but try to find out why a student is interested in Geology, why they have chosen that particular institution, what other offers have been received and their impressions of other universities.

GAP YEAR ADVICE

Institutions accepting a Gap Year: Most institutions; **Bristol** Your year off ideally should include some experience related to the course. Get your place before taking your gap year. **Cardiff** and **Greenwich** Discuss your plans with the admissions tutor beforehand.

Institutions willing to defer entry after A-levels (see Ch 5): Kingston; Plymouth.

AFTER A-LEVELS ADVICE

Institutions which may accept the same points score after A-levels: Aberystwyth; Bristol; Cardiff; Durham; Kingston; Leeds; Liverpool; London (RH); Nottingham; Plymouth; Portsmouth; Southampton; Swansea.

Institutions demanding the actual grades offered after A-levels: Guildhall London; Hull.

Institutions which may accept under-achieving applicants after A-levels: Aberdeen; Birmingham; Cardiff; Cheltenham & Glos (CHE); Derby; Durham; Exeter; Keele; Leeds; Leicester; Liverpool; London (RH); Luton (CHE); Nottingham; Plymouth; Portsmouth; Swansea.

Institutions with vacancies in Aug/Sept 1992 (see Ch 5): Aberdeen; Aberystwyth; Anglia (Poly Univ); Bristol; Cheltenham & Glos (CHE) 8 pts; Exeter (CSM); Glamorgan; Greenwich 4 pts; Kingston 10-4 pts; Leeds; London (QMW), (RH); Oxford Brookes; Plymouth 10 pts; St Andrews; Sunderland 4 pts; most institutions are likely to have vacancies in 1993.

ADVICE FOR MATURE STUDENTS

Mature students usually represent about 5% of the student total for these courses for which recent successful academic study is usually required.

GRADUATE EMPLOYMENT

New Graduates' destinations (percentages) 1991:
Permanent employment: U 67; P 63.
Unemployment: U 25; P 20.
Further studies (all types): U 46; P 22.
Main career destinations (approx): Scientific 53; Finance 6; Computing 5; Admin/Business 15; Finance 6.

GEOPHYSICS

Special subjects requirements: 2 or 3 A-levels from science or mathematics subjects. Physics often required.

NB Institutions may raise or lower the level of published offers depending either on the quality or otherwise of individual applications or the numbers of applications received; grades/points offered may be adjusted downwards after A-level results. The level of an offer is not indicative of the quality of a course.

30 pts.	**East Anglia** – 30 pts approx (Geophys/USA)
18 pts.	**East Anglia** – CCC/BC (Geophys Sci) (4 AS)
	Edinburgh – CCC/BB (Geophysics) (4 AS)
	Lancaster – BCD (Geophys)
	Leicester – CCC (Geophys)
	Leeds – CCC/BB (Geoph Sci; Comb Hons)
	Liverpool – BCD-CCC (Geophys P; Geophys G)
	London (UC) – CCC/BB (Ex Geophys)
	Newcastle - CCC/BC (Geoph/Planet)
	Southampton – BCD (Geophys Sci)
	St Andrews – 18 pts (Geo Science)

Alternative offers:

IB offers: **East Anglia** H555 ; **Liverpool** H555; **Newcastle** H655.

SCE offers: **East Anglia** BBBB; **Edinburgh** BBBB; **St Andrews** BBB.

CHOOSING YOUR COURSE (See also Ch 1)

> **Subject information:** This is a study of the techniques of physics and mathematics relating to earth systems which include meteorology, oceanography, climatic change, hydrology and sedimentology.

Course highlights: Edinburgh Very flexible course - years 1,2 & 3 curricula compatible with Maths, Physics, Geology and Astronomy courses. **East Anglia** Study of atmosphere, oceans and solid earth; wide range of specialist subjects. Good contacts with leading oil companies, the Meteorological Office, water authorities and environmental consultants. **Newcastle** The course is relevant to students with maths/physics A-levels and an interest in geology/earth sciences. NOW CHECK PROSPECTUSES FOR ALL COURSES.

ADMISSIONS INFORMATION

Number of applicants per place (approx): East Anglia 7; **Edinburgh** 4; **Lancaster** 10; **Liverpool** 9; **Newcastle** 10; **Southampton** 9.

Selection interviews: Newcastle; Southampton.

Offers to applicants repeating A-levels: Same East Anglia.

Examples of interview questions: Why do you want to study Geophysics? Explain what you think a study of Geophysics will involve. What future career do you have in mind? What other careers could geophysicists consider?

GAP YEAR ADVICE

Institutions willing to defer entry after A-levels (see Ch 5): Leeds.

AFTER A-LEVELS ADVICE

Institutions which may accept the same points score after A-levels: Edinburgh; Lancaster; Liverpool; Newcastle; Southampton.

Institutions with vacancies in Aug/Sept 1992 (see Ch 5): Leeds 16-12 pts; Newcastle 10 pts.

GERMAN (See also Modern Languages, Languages, European Studies)

Special subject requirements: German at A-level.

NB Institutions may raise or lower the level of published offers depending either on the quality or otherwise of individual applications or the numbers of applications received; grades/points offered may be adjusted downwards after A-level results. The level of an offer is not indicative of the quality of a course.

30 pts.	**Cambridge/Oxford** - AAA potential recommended in most cases (Mod Lang)
26 pts.	**Bristol** - ABB-BBB/AB (Ger/Ital; Ger/Sp)
24 pts.	**Aston** - BBB-BBC (Int Bus/Ger)
	Bath - ABC (Europ/Fr/Ger)
	Bristol - BBB (Ger/Span; Ger/Ital; Ger/Russ; Ger/Pol)
	Cardiff - BBB-BCC/AB-BB (German - Joint Hons)
	St Andrews - BBB (German) (4 AS)
	Swansea - ABC-BBC (EMS(Ger))
	Warwick - BBB (Ger Bus) (or BBB in 2As + 2AS or BB in 2As + C in 1A + C in 2 AS)
22 pts.	**Aberdeen** - BBC (German)
	Aston - BBC-BCC (Ger; Ger/Fr; Ger/Jap)
	Birmingham - BBC (General Hons)
	Bradford - BBC-BCC (Europ)
	Bradford - BBC/BB-BC (Ger/Fr; Ger/Sp)
	Bristol - BBC/BB (German; Ger/Phil; Ger/Russ)
	Cardiff - BBC-CCC (German)
	East Anglia - BBC-BCC/BB-BC (All courses)
	Edinburgh - BBC (German)
	Glasgow - BBC (German)
	Heriot-Watt - BBC inc BB in languages (Comb courses)

Lancaster - BBC-BCC (German St combined majors)
Leeds - BBC (Ger/Hist)
London (RH) - BBC (Joint Hons courses)
Manchester - 22 pts approx (Ger St)
Reading - BBC (German/Film and Drama)
Surrey - BBC/AB (Ger/Law)
Swansea - BBC-BCD/BB-BC (German/BS)
Warwick - BBC-BCC (Ger/Pol)

20 pts. **Aston** - BCC/AB (Comb Hons)
Bradford - BCC/BB (Ger/Russ; Ger/Fr; Ger/Sp; Europ)
Essex - BCC (German)
Hull - BCC/BB (Joint courses except under **18 pts**)
Keele - BCC-CCC/BB-BC (Joint courses) (4 AS)
Kent - BCC-CCC/BC (German)
Lancaster - BCC (Fr/Germ; Germ/Hist; Germ/Ital; ML/Mktg; ML/Pol; ML/Theatre)
Leeds - BBD (Ger/Mus)
Leeds - BCC/BB (Ger/Ital)
Liverpool - BCC/BC (German) (4 AS)
London (King's) - BCC (German)
London (QMW) - BCC/BC (German)
London (RH) - BCC/BB (German)
Newcastle - 20 pts (B in german) (All courses)
Reading - BCC/BB (Ger/Man St)
Sheffield - BCC/BB (German) (Single Hons 4 AS; Dual Hons 2 AS)
Stirling - BCC/BB (Engl/Ger)
Surrey - BCC (Ger/Econ)
Swansea - BCC-BCD/BC (German/CS; German joint courses with science and engineering)
UMIST - BCC-CCC/AB (Ger/Comp L; Ger) (BTEC Ms inc german)
York - BCC/BB (Germ/Ling) (4 AS)

18 pts. **Aberystwyth** - CCC/BC (Joint courses with German)
Belfast - CCC/BB (All courses)
Birmingham - BCD (German St - single hons)
Exeter - BCD (Ger/Ital)
Hull - CCC (German; Ger/Fr; Ger/Eng; Ger/Scand) (6 AS) (See also under **20 pts**)
Leeds - BCD/BB (German; Ger/Sp)
Leicester - BCD/BC (Fr/Ger; German)
Leicester - CCC/BC (Mod Langs)
Liverpool - CCC/CC (Ger/Dutch) (4 AS)
London (King's) - 18-16 pts approx (German)
Nottingham - BBE-CDE (German and combinations)
Reading - CCC/BC (German and combinations except under **20/22 pts**)
Salford - 18 pts approx (Joint courses)
Southampton - BCD-CCC (Ger/Span; Ger/Phil; Ger/Mus)
Stirling - CCC/BB (German)
Strathclyde - CCC/BC (BBD 2nd yr entry) (German)
Sussex - CCC (Ger/Eur) (BTEC Prefer not)
Ulster - CCC/BB (Hum Comb)
Warwick - CCC (Ger)

16 pts. **Birmingham** - BDD (German St)
Central Lancashire - 16 pts (Comb Hons)
Durham - BB (German; Ger/Russ; Fr/Ger; Ger/Sp)
Middlesex - 16-12 pts (Modular)
Nottingham Trent - 16 pts (Eur Bus/Ger)

14 pts. **Exeter** - BC-BD (German) (4 AS) (BTEC Ms)
Lancaster - BC (German courses)

12 pts. **Liverpool John Moores** - CC minimum (Ger/Rus; Ger/Sp)
London (Gold) - CC (German Studs)

London (UC) - CC (German)
North London - CC-CD (Hum Comb)
Oxford Brookes - DDD/DD (German courses) (4 AS)
Portsmouth - CDE/CD (Ger/Fr St)
Southampton - CC (German)
Westminster - CC (All German courses)
Wolverhampton - 12 pts (Mod Langs; GS)

10 pts. **Coventry** - CD (Ger/Sp)
Manchester Met - DDE/DD (Sp/Ger; Fr/Ger)
Portsmouth - 10 pts (Ger St; Rus/Ger St)
St David's - CEE/CD (German)

8 pts. and below
Anglia (Poly Univ) - (Comb Hons)
Brighton - (App Lang/Ger)
Bristol UWE - DD (Ger/Sp; GSIS)
Coventry - DD (Ger/Sp *ab initio*; Modular)
Derby - (Modular) (4 AS)
Guildhall London - DEE/DD-CE (Modular)
Hertfordshire - (Hum)
Kingston - (Ger/Econ/Pol)
La Sainte Union (CHE) - (Comb St)
Leeds Met - (Eur Lang Bus)
Northumbria - Ger/Rus; Ger/Sp)
Nottingham Trent - (M Eur St)
South Bank - DD (MLIS; MLIB - Fr/Ger/Sp) (BTEC D in lang)
Staffordshire - (Mod St)
Sunderland - (Comb St)
Thames Valley London - (All App Lang St courses)

Diploma of Higher Education courses:
4 pts.   Guildhall London; Oxford Brookes.

Offers for Foundation, Certificate and Diploma courses (see Ch 5):

Higher National Diploma courses (with Business Studies):
4 pts.   and below Humberside; Loughborough (CT); Northumbria; Norwich City (CHFE); Salford (UC); Swansea (IHE); Thames Valley London.

Alternative offers:

IB offers: **Aberdeen** 30 pts; **Aston** 31-28 pts; **Bradford** 24 pts; **Bristol** 26 pts; **Durham** H555; **Exeter** 30 pts; **Kent** 27 pts, H 12 pts; **Lancaster** 30-28 pts; **London (QMW)** 30-28 pts, **(RH)** 30 pts; **Reading** 30-29 pts; **St Andrews** 30 pts; **Swansea** 33 pts H645; **York** H655.

Irish offers: **Aberdeen** BBBB; **Keele** BBBCC; **Liverpool** BBBB; **London (RH)** BBBCC.

SCE offers: **Aberdeen** BBBB; **Bradford** AAAB/ABCC; **Edinburgh** BBBB; **Glasgow** ABBB/BBBB; **Heriot-Watt** AABB inc AA in languages + interview; **Hull** AAA; **Keele** BBBC/BBCC; **Lancaster** BBBB; **Sheffield** BBBB; **St Andrews** BBBB; **Strathclyde** BBBB.

CHOOSING YOUR COURSE (See also Ch 1)

Subject information: Language, literature, practical language skills or a broader study of Germany and its culture (European Studies) are alternative study approaches.

Course highlights: Aberdeen Emphasis on practical language skills. **Bangor** Students opt for one of two courses (a) German Literature (b) German Language and Modern German. **Bristol** A subsidiary subject is taken in the first two years. **Cardiff** Course decisions finalised end of year 1. Options include emphasis on present-day language. **Durham** The course is focused on proficiency in written and spoken German and on literature of the 18th, 19th and 20th centuries. **Edinburgh** The course is divided equally between German language and literature. **Leeds** Study of main features of German political, social and economic life. **London (QMW)** Students also take a subsidiary subject, for example English, French, Latin, Russian, Spanish, history, geography, economics or politics. **Newcastle** Wide range of final year German options including business German. **Portsmouth** Options include economics, business studies. **Sheffield** Special options are available in Dutch and Swedish. **St David's** Modular; large amount of continuous assessment; broad range of options. Study in German leads to British and German qualifications. **Swansea** Specialised business courses; study of politics, social and economic life of Germany. **York** (Germ/Ling) Involves 50% German, 30% linguistics and 20% a non-European language. NOW CHECK PROSPECTUSES FOR ALL COURSES.

Study opportunities abroad: Birmingham (E); **Cardiff** (E); **Lampeter** (E) G SZ AU; **Newcastle** (E) EUR; **Reading** (E) EUR; **Surrey** (E).

Work opportunities abroad: Birmingham G AU SZ; **Cardiff** AU G; **Reading** G AU; **Surrey** FR G AU SZ USSR.

ADMISSIONS INFORMATION

Number of applicants per place (approx): Aston 6; **Birmingham** 5 (Single Hons), 10 (Comb Hons); **Bradford** 5; **Bristol** 23; **Cardiff** 6; **Durham** 4; **Exeter** 4; **Kent** 10; **Lancaster** 7; **Leeds** 6; **London (QMW)** 6, **(RH)** 5; **Newcastle** 13; **Oxford Brookes** 12; **Portsmouth** 8; **St David's** 3; **Swansea** 5; **York** 6.

General Studies acceptable: Aberdeen; Aston; Birmingham; Bradford; East Anglia; Essex; Exeter (2); Hull; Kent; Lancaster; Leeds; Newcastle; Oxford Brookes; St David's (2); Surrey (No); York.

Selection interviews: Bangor; Birmingham; Bradford (some); Bristol; Cambridge; Durham; East Anglia (some); Exeter; Heriot-Watt; Hull; Kent (frequently); Leeds (some); Leicester (some); Liverpool; London (RH); Newcastle (some); Nottingham (T); Oxford; St David's (some); Sheffield (some); South Bank; Southampton; Surrey (always); Warwick; most new universities and colleges.

Offers to applicants repeating A-levels: Higher Birmingham, Essex, Leeds (2 pts), Oxford Brookes; **Same** Aston, Bradford, Durham, East Anglia, London (RH), Newcastle (not always), Nottingham, Surrey, Swansea, Ulster, York.

Admissions Tutors' advice: Bath See **European Studies**. **Nottingham** We look for a high degree of competence in using and understanding the German language, skills in linguistic comprehension and analysis, and a love of literature. **UMIST** No prior knowledge of computing required for Ling/Comp courses.

> **Examples of interview questions:** Questions asked on A-level syllabus, and at Oxford on the entrance examination. Part of interview may be in German. What foreign newspapers and/or magazines do you read? Questions on German current affairs, books read outside the course, etc.

GAP YEAR ADVICE

Institutions accepting a Gap Year: Most institutions; **Cardiff** Any kind of residence abroad useful.

Institutions willing to defer entry after A-levels (see Ch 5): Aston; Bradford; Bristol; Lancaster; London (RH) No; Newcastle; St David's; South Bank (Prefer not); Surrey; Swansea; UMIST.

AFTER A-LEVELS ADVICE

Institutions which may accept the same points score after A-levels: Aston; Birmingham; Durham; East Anglia; Lancaster; Newcastle; Nottingham; Oxford Brookes; Reading; Salford; St David's; Swansea; York.

Institutions demanding the actual grades offered after A-levels: Bristol; Dundee; Guildhall London; Kent; London (SSEES); South Bank; Southampton; Stirling; Surrey.

Institutions which may accept under-achieving applicants after A-levels: Aston; Birmingham; Durham; Exeter; Glasgow; Hull; Kent; Leeds; Leicester; London (RH); St Andrews; St David's; Swansea.

Institutions with vacancies in Aug/Sept 1992 (see Ch 5): Anglia (Poly Univ); Aston BCC; Bradford 20 pts; Buckingham; De Montfort; Essex; Glamorgan; Greenwich; Kingston; London (QMW), (RH) 18 pts, (SSEES); Newcastle 20 pts; St David's; South Bank DE; Sunderland; Surrey (Ger/Law) B in German + CC; UMIST 16 pts.

ADVICE FOR MATURE STUDENTS

Linguistic competence and evidence of it are obviously important for these courses which attract a small number of applicants each year.

GRADUATE EMPLOYMENT

New Graduates' destinations (percentages) 1991:
Permanent employment: U 74; P 80.
Unemployment: U 16; P 7.
Further studies (all types): U 30; P 25.
Main career destinations (approx): Admin/Managerial 20; Finance 22; Marketing etc 21; Secretarial 7; Legal 5; Creative 3; Social/Welfare 10; Teaching 4.

Surrey Teaching was a popular destination although other graduates found full-time employment in publishing (proof-reading), marketing information work (Citizens' Advice Bureau). Library work and law also attracted some students.

GOVERNMENT (See also POLITICS)

Special subject requirements: GCSE (grade A-C) mathematics in most cases.

NB Institutions may raise or lower the level of published offers depending either on the quality or otherwise of individual applications or the numbers of applications received; grades/points offered may be adjusted downwards after A-level results. The level of an offer is not indicative of the quality of a course.

24 pts.	**London (LSE)** - BBB-ABC (Gov)	
22 pts.	**Newcastle** - BBC/AB-BB (Gov/Eur C St)	
20 pts.	**Aberystwyth** - BCC (Govt/For)	
	Aston - BCC (Comb Hons)	
	Brunel - BCC/AB (Gov)	
	Essex - BCC/BB-BC (GS Com; Ph Gv; G Soc; EG; WEP; GSS)	
16 pts.	**Central England** - CCD-CDD/CC (Govt) (4 AS)	
	Northumbria - 16 pts (Govt/PP)	
12 pts.	**Teesside** - 12-10 pts (Euro Gov)	

Alternative offers:

IB offers: **Essex** 28 pts inc 10 pts in 2 Highers.

SCE offers: **Aberystwyth** BBBB.

Overseas applicants: Northumbria Strong bias towards British political institutions.

CHOOSING YOUR COURSE (See also Ch 1)

> **Subject information:** The history of political thought, analysis and institutions covering major foreign countries and also British politics and government will be covered on these courses.

Course highlights: Brunel Strong commitment to teaching contemporary European and British history and politics. Close attention to European Community affairs. **Newcastle** Language element essential. Options in European law, economics and agricultural policy. Year 3 abroad. **Northumbria** Strong bias towards British socio-political systems and institutions. NOW CHECK PROSPECTUSES FOR ALL COURSES.

Study opportunities abroad: Newcastle EUR; **Northumbria** USA.

Work opportunities abroad: Brunel G USA.

ADMISSIONS INFORMATION

Number of applicants per place (approx): Central England 9; **Newcastle** 6; **Northumbria** 13.

General Studies acceptable: Aston; Central England; Essex; Newcastle.

Selection interviews: Central England (some); Essex; Northumbria (occasionally).

Offers to applicants repeating A-levels: Higher Essex, Northumbria; **Possibly higher** Central England; **Same** Aston, Newcastle.

Admissions Tutors' advice: Central England Keen interest in politics and public administration important. We encourage students to have a year off after A-levels since they come to us much more mature.

> **Examples of interview questions:** What does a course in Government involve? Why do you wish to study this subject? What career would you like to enter on completing this course?

GAP YEAR ADVICE

Institutions accepting a Gap Year: Most institutions.

Institutions willing to defer entry after A-levels (see Ch 5): Northumbria.

AFTER A-LEVELS ADVICE

Institutions which may accept the same points score after A-levels: Aston; Central England; Essex; Northumbria.

Institutions which may accept under-achieving applicants after A-levels: Central England.

Institutions with vacancies in Aug/Sept 1992 (see Ch 5): Northumbria 14 pts.

ADVICE FOR MATURE STUDENTS

These courses attract a number of applicants each year, many of whom are selected on merit and who may not hold formal academic qualifications.

GRADUATE EMPLOYMENT

New Graduates' destinations (percentages) 1991: See under **Politics**.

GRAPHIC DESIGN (See also Art, Education (B Ed), Visual Communications Studies)

Special subject requirements: none. Foundation Art course normally required for entry to courses listed below. Only about eight per cent of entrants are admitted with A-levels, direct from school or college. All candidates are interviewed and their portfolios of work are scrutinised. Applications are submitted through the Art and Design Admission Registry (ADAR) Scheme (Chapter 3).

NB Institutions may raise or lower the level of published offers depending either on the quality or otherwise of individual applications or the numbers of applications received; grades/points offered may be adjusted downwards after A-level results. The level of an offer is not indicative of the quality of a course.

Institutions offering degree courses: Anglia (Poly Univ) (Illustration); Bath (CHE); Blackpool (CFE); Brighton; Bristol UWE (Illustration); Buckinghamshire (CHE); Camberwell (Coll) (Hist Drg/Prtg); Central England; Central Lancashire; Central London (Illustration); Cornwall (CFHE (Falmouth)) (Sci/Tech Graph); Coventry; Cumbria (CA); De Montfort; Derby; Glasgow (SA); Gwent (CHE); Humberside; Kent Inst (IAD); Kingston; Leeds Met; Liverpool John Moores; London Inst (CP) (also Film and Video, Photography); London (Central Sch); Manchester Met; Middlesex (including Scientific and Technical Illustration); Norfolk (IAD); Northumbria; North Wales (IHE) (Medical Illust); Nottingham Trent (Information Graphics); Plymouth; Plymouth; Portsmouth; Ravensbourne (CDC); Reigate (Coll) (Calligraphy); Salford (UC) (Des Practice); Staffordshire; Suffolk (CFHE); Teesside; Trinity Carmarthen (CHE) (Wild Life Illus); Ulster; West Herts (CFE); Westminster/Harrow (Graph Inf Des); Wolverhampton.

Offers for Foundation, Certificate and Diploma courses (see Ch 5):

Higher National Diploma courses:
  4 ptse   and below Amersham (CFE); Anglia (Poly Univ) (Illustration); Barnet (Coll); Berkshire (CA); Birmingham (Coll); Blackpool (CFE); Bolton (IHE); Bournemouth (CA); Bradford & Ilkley (CmC); Buckinghamshire (CHE); Central Lancashire; Cheltenham & Glos (CHE) (Des Electron Media); Colchester (Inst); Croydon (Coll); Cumbria (CA); Derby; Dewsbury (CA) (Communications); Doncaster (Coll); Dunstable (Coll); East Ham (CT); Epsom (SA); Falmouth (SA); Hounslow Borough (Coll); Kent (Inst); Kingston; Lincolnshire (CA); London Inst (Chelsea SA), (CP); Loughborough (CT); Medway (CD); Nene (CHE); Newcastle (SA); Newham (CCom); Norfolk (IAD); North East Wales (IHE); Northumberland (CA); Norton (Coll); Plymouth; Plymouth (CA); Portsmouth; Ravensbourne (CDC) (Design Communications); Reigate (SA); Richmond-on-Thames (Coll); Salford (CT); Salisbury (CAD); Sheffield Hallam (Communications); Somerset (CA); Southampton (IHE); Staffordshire (Electronic Instructional Media); Stockport (CFE); Stourbridge (CT); Suffolk (CFHE); Sunderland; Swansea (IHE); Swindon (Coll) (Graph Des; Pack Des); West Herts (CFE); West Surrey (CAD); York (CAT).

Overseas applicants: De Montfort 12 examples of work on transparencies required.

CHOOSING YOUR COURSE (See also Ch 1)

Subject information: Specialised studies in advertising art, book design, TV graphics etc, almost always preceded by a Foundation art course.

Course highlights: Brighton Exchange programmes with USA and Australia. **Westminster/ Harrow** Work experience in studios in year 2. NOW CHECK PROSPECTUSES FOR ALL COURSES.

Study opportunities abroad: Bath (CHE) USA SZ G; **Central Lancashire** G GR USA SP; **De Montfort** FR USA NL; **Humberside** G.

ADMISSIONS INFORMATION

Number of applicants per place (approx): Anglia (Poly Univ) 5; **Bath (CHE)** 9; **Brighton** 5; **Bristol UWE** 4; **Central Lancashire** 3; **Coventry** 6; **Falmouth (CA)** 2; **Kingston** 8; **Humberside** 7; **Leeds Met** 6; **Liverpool John Moores** 7; **London (Central Sch)** 5; **London (CP)** 4; **Loughborough (CT)** 5; **Manchester Met** 8; **Middlesex** 3; **Northumbria** 8; **Nottingham Trent** 6; **Ravensbourne (CD)** 3; **Wolverhampton** 5.

Examples of interview questions: Discuss recent trends in graphic design from the points of view of methods and designers. Questions asked on applicant's portfolio of work.

AFTER A-LEVELS ADVICE

Institutions with vacancies in Aug/Sept 1992 (see Ch 5): Only a small number of vacancies were declared including one in Animation at **Bournemouth**.

ADVICE FOR MATURE STUDENTS

Selection for these courses is by portfolio.

GRADUATE EMPLOYMENT

New Graduates' destinations (percentages) 1991: See under **Art (Design)**.

GREEK (See also **Classics**)

Special subject requirements: Most courses require Greek and some require Latin at A-level, and Greek and Latin GCSE (grade A-C). At Exeter, Leeds and Newcastle there are no special requirements.

NB Institutions may raise or lower the level of published offers depending either on the quality or otherwise of individual applications or the numbers of applications received; grades/points offered may be adjusted downwards after A-level results. The level of an offer is not indicative of the quality of a course.

30 pts.	**Cambridge/Oxford** - AAA potential recommended (Classics)
22 pts.	**Bristol** - BBC-BCC/BC (Gk/Phil)
	Edinburgh - BBC (Gk)
	Exeter - BBC-BCD/BB (GRS/Ital)
	Glasgow - BBC (Greek)
	Liverpool - BBC-CDD/BB-CC (All Classics courses)
	Newcastle - BBC/AB (Greek; Anc Hist; Class Studs; Classics; Latin)
	St Andrews - BBC (Greek) (4 AS)

20 pts. **Birmingham** - BCC-CCC (Greek; Gr/Rom St)
 Durham - BCC (Gk/Phil)
 Leeds - BCC (Greek)
 London (RH) - BCC/BC (Greek)
 Manchester - 20 pts approx (Gk)
 Reading - BCC (Gk/Engl)
18 pts. **Belfast** - CCC/BB (Greek and joint courses; Gr/Rom Civ (M))
 Bristol - CCC/CC (Gk/Phil)
 Kent - CCC (Greek unless combined with a subject with higher level offer)
 London (King's) - CCC approx (Greek)
 London (UC) - CCC/CC (Gk/Lat)
 Nottingham - CCC/BC (Gk/Phil; Gk/Theol)
 Reading - BCD-CCC (Gk/Phil)
 Swansea - BCD-CCC/BB-BC (GRS courses)
14 pts. **St David's** - CDD/CC (Greek)

Alternative offers:

IB offers: **Exeter** 30 pts; **Kent** 25 pts, H 11 pts; **St Andrews** 30 pts.

SCE offers: **Edinburgh** BBBB; **Glasgow** BBBB; **St Andrews** BBBB.

CHOOSING YOUR COURSE (See also Ch 1)

> **Subject information:** Courses are offered in Ancient and Modern Greek covering the language and literature from ancient times to present day.

Course highlights: Leeds One of the largest departments. **London (RH)** Options include art and archaeology, philosophy and history. **Swansea** Possibility of deferring decisions on some courses to year 2. NOW CHECK PROSPECTUSES FOR ALL COURSES.

Study opportunities abroad: Birmingham (E).

ADMISSIONS INFORMATION

Number of applicants per place (approx): Birmingham 2; **Bristol** 5; **Kent** 5; **Newcastle** 20.

General Studies acceptable: Birmingham; Kent; Leeds; Liverpool.

Selection interviews: Bangor; Birmingham; Leeds; Liverpool; London (RH); Newcastle; Sheffield.

Offers to applicants repeating A-levels: Same Birmingham, Bristol, Kent, Leeds, Newcastle.

> **Examples of interview questions:** Questions asked on A-level syllabus. Why do you want to study Greek? What aspects of this course interest you? (Questions will develop from answers.)

GAP YEAR ADVICE

Institutions accepting a Gap Year: Most institutions; **Birmingham** Don't just study - see life!

Institutions willing to defer entry after A-levels (see Ch 5): Leeds; St Andrews; Swansea.

AFTER A-LEVELS ADVICE

Institutions which may accept the same points score after A-levels: Birmingham; Leeds; Liverpool; London (RH).

Institutions demanding the actual grades offered after A-levels: Kent; Newcastle (some flexibility).

Institutions which may accept under-achieving applicants after A-levels: Exeter; Kent; Leeds.

Institutions with vacancies in Aug/Sept 1992 (see Ch 5): Leeds 18 pts.

HEBREW

Special subject requirements: A language at GCSE (grade A-C).

NB Institutions may raise or lower the level of published offers depending either on the quality or otherwise of individual applications or the numbers of applications received; grades/points offered may be adjusted downwards after A-level results. The level of an offer is not indicative of the quality of a course.

30 pts.	**Cambridge** - AAA potential recommended (Oriental)
24 pts.	**St Andrews** - BBB (Hebrew) (4 AS)
22 pts.	**London (SOAS)** - BBC-BCC/BB-BC (All courses inc Semitic langs)
	Glasgow - 22 pts (Hebrew)
20 pts.	**Liverpool** - BCC/BC (Hebrew)
16 pts.	**Belfast** - CCD (Joint courses)
12 pts.	**London (UC)** - (Hebrew)

Alternative offers:

IB offers: **St Andrews** 30 pts.

SCE offers: **St Andrews** BBBB.

CHOOSING YOUR COURSE (See also Ch 1)

> **Subject information:** This subject attracts the occasional student of languages and at **Bangor** may be taken as one of three first year subjects. It is often a useful preparation for Biblical Studies courses.

Course highlights: St Andrews See under **Arts**. NOW CHECK PROSPECTUSES FOR ALL COURSES.

ADMISSIONS INFORMATION

Number of applicants per place (approx): Liverpool 2; **London (SOAS)** 1.5.

> **Examples of interview questions:** Discuss your interest in Hebrew. What are your reasons for choosing this course? What do you hope to do at the end of the course?

AFTER A-LEVELS ADVICE

Institutions which may accept the same points score after A-levels: Liverpool.

Institutions demanding the actual grades offered after A-levels: London (SOAS).

HISTORY (including **Medieval Studies**)

Special subject requirements: history preferred in most cases at A-level; a language usually required at GCSE (grade A-C).

NB Institutions may raise or lower the level of published offers depending either on the quality or otherwise of individual applications or the numbers of applications received; grades/points offered may be adjusted downwards after A-level results. The level of an offer is not indicative of the quality of a course.

30 pts.	**Cambridge/Oxford** - AAA potential recommended (History; Hist/Ec)
26 pts.	**Birmingham** - ABB-BCC (Med St)
	Warwick - ABB-BBB (Hist)
24 pts.	**Cardiff** - BBB (Eng/Hist)
	Durham - ABC (History; Soc/Hist; Econ/Hist; Med St)
	Durham - BBB (Pol/Hist)
	East Anglia - BBB/BB (EAS/AH)
	Edinburgh - BBB (History)
	Exeter - BBB (Hist/Pol)
	Hull - BBB (Hist/Engl)
	Leeds - BBB-BBC/BB (History) (4 AS)
	Leeds - BBB/AB-BB (Int H/Pol)
	Manchester - 24-22 pts approx (All History courses)
	Newcastle - BBB/AB (History) (4 AS but A-level history)
	Sheffield - BBB (History)
	St Andrews - BBB (All History courses)
	Warwick - BBB (Hist Pol)
22 pts.	**Aberdeen** - BBC (All History courses)
	Birmingham - BBC-BCC/AB-BB (E Med; History)
	Bristol - BBC/AB-BB (All History courses except **20 pts**)
	Cardiff - BBC (B in hist/French) (Econ/Hist; Fr/Hist; Hist/Phil)
	Durham - BBC (Arch/Hist)
	East Anglia - BBC/BB-BC (Range of offers for most History courses; see also **24 pts**)
	Edinburgh - BBB-BBC (All History courses except under **24 pts**)
	Exeter - BBC (History; Hist/Ger) (4-6 AS)
	Glasgow - BBC (All History courses)
	Hull - BBC (Hist/Fr; Hist/Pol)
	Keele - BBC-CCC/AB-BC (Hist - Joint Hons) (4 AS) (BTEC 3M)
	Lancaster - BBC (All History courses)
	Leeds - BBC (Hist/Sp)
	Liverpool - BBC-BCC/AB-BB (History)
	London (LSE) - 22 pts approx (History and joint courses)
	London (RH) - BBC/BB (All History courses)
	London (SSEES) - BBC-BCC (History; Hist/Jew)
	Nottingham - BBC (All History courses)
	Warwick - BBC-BCC (Hist Soc)
	York - BBC/BB (All History courses)
20 pts.	**Aberystwyth** - BCC (All History courses inc Pol/Mod Hist V135 new course)
	Birmingham - BBD-BCC (Hist ES)
	Birmingham - BCC (Anc/Med Hist)
	Bristol - BCC (History II)
	Cardiff - BCC/AB (Anc/Med Hist; Archaeol/MH; Archaeol/AH; History)
	Dundee - BCC (Hist)
	Essex - BCC/BB (All History courses)
	Hull - BCC/BB (History and joint courses except under **24/22 pts**) (4 AS)
	Kent - BCC/BB (All History courses)
	Leeds - BCC (All other joint courses except under **22/24 pts**)

Leicester - BCC/BB (History; Hist/Pol)
Liverpool - BCC/BB (M Hist/Pol)
London (King's) - 20 pts approx (History; Anc Hist)
London (QMW) - BCC/BB (Mod Hist; History)
Portsmouth - BCC-CCC/BC (Hist St) (4 AS)
Reading - BCC (Hist and other courses except under 18 pts)
Reading - BBD (Hist/Eng - incl B in English and history)
Ripon & York St John (CHE) - BCC/BB (Hist/Eng; Hist/Theol; Hist/Amer St)
Southampton - BCC-ACD/BB (Mod H/Pol; Hist/Soc)
Stirling - BCC/BB (All History courses)
Strathclyde - BCC/BB (Hist - Bus Sch)
Sussex - BCC/BB (All History degree schemes; Econ H/Soc)
Swansea - BCC/BB (History; Med St) (BTEC 4D+Ms)

18 pts. Bangor - 18 pts (History; Hist/Naut St; Welsh Hist; Hist/Soc Pol) (4 AS) (No standard offer)
Belfast - CCC/BB (Hist)
Bradford - CCC/BB (Pol/Hist)
Bristol UWE - 18 pts (Hum)
Leicester - BCD (Hist/Arch)
Liverpool - 18 pts approx (Arts Comb) (See **Admissions Tutors' advice**)
London (Gold) - CCC/CC (All History courses)
London (UC) - CCC/EE (History)
Oxford Brookes - CCC/AB (Modular; maximum depending on 2nd field)
Reading - BCD (Hist/Arch; Hist/A Hist)
Salford - BCD (Hist/Eng)
St David's - BCD/BC (Vict Stds; Comb St)
Sheffield Hallam - 18-16 pts (Hist St)
Southampton - BB (Hist)
Strathclyde - CCC/BC (BBD 2nd yr entry)(Hist courses; Arts Soc St)
Swansea - CCC/BC (Joint courses)
Warwick - CCC-CCD (QTS Hist) (Any 2 AS except hist/des tech/ gen stds)
West Sussex (IHE) - CCC/BB (Hist - BEd)

16 pts. Bath (CHE) - BB (Comb St with English)
Bedford (CHE) - 16-14 pts (Modular)
Belfast - CCD/BC (Byz joint courses)
Cambridge (Hom) - CCD (Hist/Ed) (See also **Education**)
Cardiff - CCD (Welsh History - joint courses)
Central Lancashire - CCD (Comb Hons)
London (SOAS) - BB (All History courses)
Middlesex - 16-12 pts (Hist; HI; TU; TW) (4 AS)
Plymouth - CCD/BC (Land/Design Heritage) (BTEC 5M)
Southampton - BB (History)
Ulster - CCD/BC (Hist)

14 pts. Anglia (Poly Univ) - 14-12 pts (All History courses)
Kingston - CDD/CC (Hist) (4 AS)
Manchester Met - BC-BD (B in history) (Hum/Soc St; Hist St)
North London - CDD/CC (History)
St David's - 14 pts (Single/Joint courses) (4 AS)
Trinity & All Saints (CHE) - BC (Hist/BMA; Hist/PM)
West Sussex (IHE) - CDD/CC (Hist - BA)

12 pts. Bath (CHE) - CC (Comb St with Rel St or Sociol)
Bolton (IHE) - DDD/CD (History courses)
Bournemouth - 12 pts (1 subject at grade C) (Her Con)
Canterbury Christ Church (CHE) - CC-EE (Comb St)
Cheltenham & Glos (CHE) - 12 pts (Hist; Modular)
Coventry - BD-CD (Mod St)
King Alfred's (CHE) - 12 pts (Hist Comb)
North London - CC (Comb Hum) (4 AS)
S Martins (CHE) - CDE/CC (Hist) (BTEC 1D+3M)

Staffordshire - CC-CD (Lit/Hist)
Sunderland - CC (Hist St)
Wolverhampton - 12 pts (Hum; Comb St)
10 pts. **Buckingham** - DDE/DD (All History courses)
Worcester (CHE) - 10 pts approx inc Access (Comb St) (4 AS)
8 pts. and below
Chester (CHE) - (Comb St)
De Montfort - (Comb Arts Hum)
Derby - 8 pts (Modular)
Edge Hill (CHE) - (Hist)
Glamorgan - (Hum)
Greenwich - (Hum)
Guildhall London - (Modular)
Hertfordshire - (Hum)
Huddersfield - (Hist/Pol St)
La Sainte Union (CHE) - (Comb St)
Liverpool John Moores - (Integrated Credit Scheme)
Liverpool (IHE) - (Comb St)
Nene (CHE) - (Hist)
North East Wales (IHE) - (Engl/Hist)
Northumbria - (Engl/Hist)
Nottingham Trent - (Hum; M Eur St)
Roehampton (IHE) - (Comb St)
St Mark & St John (CHE) - (Hist)
St Mary's (CHE) - (Comb St)
Sunderland - (All History courses)
Teesside - (Hum)
Trinity Carmarthen (CHE) - (Hum)
West London (IHE) - (Joint)
Westminster - (Soc Sci)

Diploma of Higher Education courses:
4 pts. Bath (CHE); Bradford & Ilkley (CmC); Crewe & Alsager (CHE); East London; Edge Hill (CHE); Guildhall London; Middlesex; Oxford Brookes; Ripon & York St John (CHE); Westminster (CHE); Worcester (CHE).

Higher National Diploma courses:
Cumbria (CA) - (Heritage Management).

Alternative offers:

EB offers: **Aberystwyth** 65% overall or 70% in 2 specified subjects.

IB offers: **Aberdeen** 30 pts; **Aberystwyth** 28 pts H555; **Bangor** 30-28 pts; **Bristol** 33 pts; **Buckingham** 24 pts; **Cardiff** 28 pts; **Dundee** 29 pts H 15 pts; **Durham** H666; **East Anglia** 30-28 pts; **Exeter** 30 pts; **Hull** 30 pts; **Kent** 27 pts; **Kingston** 25 pts; **Lancaster** 32-30 pts; **Leeds** 30 pts inc 15 pts Highers (history 5 or 6); **Leicester** 30-28 pts; **London (QMW)** 30 pts, **(RH)** 30 pts, **(SSEES)** 30 pts; **Newcastle** 30 pts; **St Andrews** 30 pts; **Swansea** 30 pts; **Warwick** H655; **York** 30 pts H6 hist.

Irish offers: **Aberdeen** BBBB; **Aberystwyth** BBCC; **Keele** BBBCC; **North London** CCCC; **Sheffield** ABBB.

SCE offers: **Aberdeen** BBBB; **Aberystwyth** BBBB; **Birmingham** BBC; **Durham** AABB; **Edinburgh** BBBB; **Essex** BBBB; **Glasgow** ABBB/BBBB; **Leeds** BBBB; **Newcastle** AABB; **St Andrews** BBBB; **Stirling** BBBB; **Strathclyde** BBBB; **York** BBBBB.

Overseas applicants: Oxford Brookes Access course and English language teaching available.

CHOOSING YOUR COURSE (See also Ch 1)

> **Subject information:** This is a very broad subject with most courses covering British and European history. There are, however, a wide range of specialist topics on offer, eg American, Scottish, East European and Far Eastern history. Degree courses International Relations, Politics, Economic and Social History could also be considered.

Course highlights: Aberdeen (Cult Hist) An interdisciplinary course covering art, commerce, international relations, race and religion. **Aberystwyth** Extensive course options cover medieval, modern and Welsh history (also offered by **Bangor**). Wide range of courses including Welsh, Irish, American and African history. Various methods of assessment – unseen and 'take-away' exams, projects, dissertations. **Anglia (Poly Univ)** Early modern history, post 1800, of Latin America, USA, Britain, Russia and Eastern Europe. **Bangor** Part I covers Welsh history, archaeology and classical studies. **Birmingham** Courses on medieval, modern and world history, and economic and social history. **Bournemouth** (Her Con) Balance between sciences, humanities and management studies. Focus on historic buildings, monuments, landscapes and artefacts. **Bristol** Courses in ecological history. High national research rating and employment record. (Hist I) Political focus. Medieval or economic history options in year 1. (Hist II) Modern economic and social history with computer skills. (Hist III) bias towards modern (post 1800) European History). **Buckingham** A common course exists for all students in the first four terms after which students opt for their choice of course from History and English, History and Politics or English and Politics. **Cardiff** Specialist topics offered in the second and third years include medieval Britain, American and European history. **Leeds** Main emphasis on British (including local) history and modern European history. Wide range of optional courses. (Int H/Pol) A unique course placing contemporary international affairs in the context of international events of the 19th and 20th centuries. **London (RH)** The course is divided into two branches: (1) Ancient and Medieval History, (2) Medieval and Modern History. **London (SSEES)** Teaching and research strengths related to modern Soviet and East European history. Course unit system gives students maximum flexibility in course choice. **Newcastle** Emphasis on British, European and North American History. **Portsmouth** Social history, modern and early modern, British and European history, cultural history. **St David's** 19th and 20th century British, European and overseas history; French, German, Swedish, Arabic offered in year 1. **Sheffield Hallam** 19th and 20th century history, including new developments in women's history, Eastern European history and information technology for historians. **Southampton** Nineteen units are avaulable in the second year including European and British history, economic, social, political, religious, intellectual and art history. American civilisation and the history of particular countries for example, France, the Balkans and Latin America. **York** Individual course choice after year 1 includes British, European, non-European art, social and cultural history. NOW CHECK PROSPECTUSES FOR ALL COURSES.

Study opportunities abroad: Bristol (E); **Dundee** FR; **Hull** (E); **Lancaster** USA FR G IT; **Leicester** (E); **London (QMW)** (E), **(RH)** (E); **Manchester Met** (E); **Middlesex** EUR; **Swansea** (E); **West Sussex (IHE)**; **York** (E) G FR USA CAN.

ADMISSIONS INFORMATION

Number of applicants per place (approx): Aberystwyth 6; **Anglia (Poly Univ)** 4; **Bangor** 6; **Birmingham** 11; **Bournemouth** (Her Con) 3; **Bristol** (Hist I) 18, (Hist II) 3; **Durham** 8; **East Anglia** (EAS/H) 5, (Eur H) 14; **Exeter** 9; **Hull** 11; **Kent** 12; **Kingston** 15; **Lancaster** 11; **Leeds** 12, (Int H/Pol) 10 ; **Leicester** 16; **Liverpool** 15, (Med/Mod Hist) 7, (Mod Hist Pol) 12; **London (QMW)** 3, **(RH)** 3; **Manchester Met** 25; **Middlesex** 10; **Newcastle** 27; **Nottingham** 15; **Oxford Brookes** 25; **Portsmouth** 26; **Roehampton (IHE)** 6; **St David's** 3; **S Martin's (CHE)** 9; **Sheffield Hallam** 21; **Swansea** 7; **Trinity & All Saints (CHE)** 29; **West London (IHE)** 6; **West Sussex (IHE)** 3; **York** 18.

General Studies acceptable: Aberdeen; Aberystwyth; Anglia (Poly Univ); Bangor; Birmingham; Bournemouth (2); Bristol; Cheltenham & Glos (CHE); East Anglia; Essex; Exeter (2); Hertfordshire; Hull; Lancaster; Leeds (JMB, Oxford or Camb); Liverpool; Newcastle; Nottingham; Oxford Brookes; St David's (2); S Martin's (CHE); Sheffield; Sheffield Hallam; Teesside (2); Trinity & All Saints (CHE); West Sussex (IHE); Worcester (CHE) (2); York.

Selection interviews: Aberystwyth (some); Bangor; Birmingham; Bristol; Durham (challenging); Essex; Hull (some); Lancaster (some); Leicester; Liverpool; London (RH); Manchester Met (minority); Newcastle; Nottingham (T); Oxford; Oxford Brookes; Portsmouth (some); St David's (some); Sheffield; Swansea (50%); Trinity & All Saints (CHE); Warwick; York (T).

Offers to applicants repeating A-levels: Higher East Anglia (EAS/H), Exeter, Leeds (2 pts), Liverpool, St David's, Swansea; **Possibly higher** Aberystwyth, Birmingham, Cambridge (Hom), Durham, Portsmouth, York; **Same** Anglia (Poly Univ), Bangor, Bristol, Edge Hill (CHE), Hull, Lancaster, London (RH), (SOAS), Newcastle, Oxford Brookes, S Martin's (CHE).

Admissions Tutors' advice: Bangor Attend interview if invited. Department prefers to operate on basis of personal contacts and direct links with schools, looking favourably on applicants from them. No standard offer. **Bournemouth** (Her Con) Preferred A-levels: archaeology, geography, geology, chemistry, environmental science. All applicants must have four weeks' practical experience before starting the course. **Durham** Candidates do not need history at A-level but if they do we usually ask for a B. GCSE (grade A-C) language is required and great emphasis placed on the interview. **Leeds** Demand for places heavy and growing. (International History and Politics - single subject) has always attracted applications from mature students and from those educated abroad. With very few exceptions, the most common offer is BBC. Between a third and a half of all applicants are interviewed. The School pays very careful attention to headteachers' reports. Interest in world outside Britain is essential for the course since it covers domestic history or politics of Britain only in relation to foreign policy. **Liverpool** Offers vary depending on candidates and interview. **London (RH)** We attach some importance to candidate's ability to read historical literature in a modern language other than English, although A-level history is not essential. Interviews usually held; we look for genuine intellectual interests, imagination and willingness to keep up, or acquire, ancilliary skills such as languages or statistics. **Newcastle** Early application advised. We try to interview as many applicants as possible. **Swansea** For Medieval History, candidates should show strong interest in medieval civilisation. **York** Very few candidates admitted without interview for which evidence of written work is needed. Department seeks evidence of ability to think in historical terms, to identify important facts, to ask relevant questions and to tackle historical problems effectively. High degree of commitment is expected. Policy on offers is flexible: no standard offer. A GCSE (grade A-C) in a foreign language is not a requirement for entry as tuition is provided.

Examples of interview questions: Interview questions are often asked on the A-level syllabus, and at Oxford from the entrance exam paper. Why did the Liberal Party win the 1906 election? Is there any parallel between the decline of the Liberal Party and the disputes within the Labour Party? Why did Imperialism happen? If a Martian arrived on Earth what aspect of life would you show him to sum up today's society? Has the role of class been exaggerated by Marxist historians? What historical topics would you like to discuss? - followed by questions. What history books have you read and what are your opinions of them? Is there such a thing as historical fact? What is the difference between power and authority and between patriotism and nationalism? Did Elizabeth I have a foreign policy? What would you look for in a good history book? (BEd course). What is the relevance of history in modern society? Who are your favourite monarchs? How could you justify your study of history to the taxpayer? Which newspapers do you read? What do you think are the similarities between Oliver Cromwell and Mussolini? Questions on the Arab-Israeli conflict.

GAP YEAR ADVICE

Institutions accepting a Gap Year: Most institutions; **Aberystwyth** Prefers it to be relevant, possibly gaining a foreign language. **Birmingham** (EM Hist) Improve your knowledge of one foreign language and of modern Middle East. **Bournemouth** (Her Con) Very keen; can advise prospective applicants on relevant experience. **Buckingham** Master another language. **London (RH)** Be prepared to justify your gap year. **Manchester Met** Apply for your place during the gap year. **Swansea** Request reading lists. Early decision preferable.

Institutions willing to defer entry after A-levels (see Ch 5): Bangor; Bournemouth (Her Con); Bristol UWE; Buckingham; Cheltenham & Glos (CHE); Dundee; Hull; King Alfred's (CHE); Lancaster;

London (RH); Manchester Met (No); Newcastle (No); Portsmouth; Ripon & York St John (CHE) (No); Roehampton (IHE); St David's (No); St Mary's (CHE); Salford; Sunderland; Swansea.

AFTER A-LEVELS ADVICE

Institutions which may accept the same points score after A-levels: Aberystwyth; Anglia (Poly Univ); Bangor; Birmingham; Bristol; Durham (varies); East Anglia (varies); Essex; Exeter; Hull; Kent; Lancaster; Leeds; Liverpool; London (RH), (SSEES); Manchester Met; Oxford Brookes; St David's; S Martin's (CHE); West Sussex (IHE); Warwick.

Institutions demanding the actual grades offered after A-levels: East Anglia (EAS/H); Kingston; London (SOAS); Newcastle; Nottingham; Portsmouth; Stirling; Swansea; York (varies).

Institutions which may accept under-achieving applicants after A-levels: Aberystwyth; Bangor; Birmingham; Bristol; East Anglia; Essex; Exeter; Glasgow; Hull; Kent; Lancaster; Liverpool (Mod Hist Pol); London (RH), (SOAS); Manchester Met; Portsmouth; St David's; S Martin's (CHE); Trinity & All Saints (CHE); West Sussex (IHE).

Institutions with vacancies in Aug/Sept 1992 (see Ch 5): Bangor; Bristol UWE; Buckingham; Cheltenham & Glos (CHE) 12 pts; Essex 20-18 pts; King Alfred's (CHE) 12 pts; Kingston; Leeds; London (QMW), (RH), (SSEES) 20 pts (excl gen st); Oxford Brookes; Roehampton (IHE) EE; St David's; Sunderland 16 pts; Trinity & All Saints (CHE) some courses; institutions with vacancies in this subject will vary each year.

ADVICE FOR MATURE STUDENTS

Some evidence of recent academic study is important for these courses. Some universities will require A-level history. **Bournemouth** (Her Con) One third of the intake is made up of mature students. Part-time study possible.

GRADUATE EMPLOYMENT

New Graduates' destinations (percentages) 1991:
Permanent employment: U 65; P 47; C 75.
Unemployment: U 24; P 36; C 17.
Further studies (all types): U 36; P 26; C 22.
Main career destinations (approx): Finance (Univ) 31, (Poly) 13, (Coll) 5; Legal (Univ) 5, (Poly) 8, (Coll) 14; Marketing (average) 17; Teaching 2; Creative 5; Social Work 10; Secretarial 15; Admin/Managerial 20.

York (1988-91) Graduates from this non-vocational degree moved to a wide range of careers; 11% went into finance (accountancy, banking, insurance, public finance) and 6% into management, catering, retail management, advertising and auctioneering. Public relations, journalism and editorial work attracted 15 graduates. Education, social work, museum and archive work (5 students), computing, law, nursing, radiography and secretarial work accounted for the remainder going into full-time employment. A total of 68 students went on to further study for teaching (25), law (solicitor), (24) journalism (3), and other careers included teaching English as a foreign language and radio journalism.

HISTORY (ANCIENT)

Special subject requirements: often a language at GCSE (grade A-C).

Institutions may raise or lower the level of published offers depending either on the quality or otherwise of individual applications or the numbers of applications received; grades/points offered may be adjusted downwards after A-level results.

NB The level of an offer is not indicative of the quality of a course.

24 pts.   **St Andrews** – BBB (Anc Hist) (4 AS)
22 pts.   **Bristol** – BBC-BCC/BC (Med Studs)
         Durham – BBC (A Hist/Arch)
         Edinburgh - BBC (Joint courses)
         London (RH) – BBC/BB (Anc Hist)
         Nottingham – BBC-CCC (Anc Hist courses)
         Warwick – BBC (Anc Hist Arch)
20 pts.   **Birmingham** – BCC/BB (Anc/Med Hist)
         Cardiff – BCC-CCC/BB-BC (Anc Hist; Anc/Med Hist)
         Durham – BCC/BC (Anc H/Gk; Anc H/Lat)
         Exeter – BCC/BB (Anc Hist)
         London (King's) – 20 pts approx (Anc Hist)
         London (RH) – BCC/BC (Anc Hist)
         Newcastle – BCC/BB (Anc Hist; Anc H/Arch)
         Swansea – BCC/BB (An Med Hist)
18 pts.   **Belfast** – CCC (Anc Hist and joint courses; Byz joint courses)
         Birmingham – BCD/BB (Archaeol)
         Leeds – CCC/BB (Lat/Anc Hist)
         Leicester – BCD-CCC/BC (Arts Comb)
         Liverpool – CCC/BC (Arts Comb)
         Liverpool – CCC (Hist/Arch)
         Reading – CCC (Anc Hist/Arch)
         Swansea – BCD-CCC/BC (Anc H/Civ and joint courses)
16 pts.   **Reading** – CCD (Anc Hist/Soc)
         St David's – CCD/BC (Anc Hist; A Hist/Arch)

Alternative offers:

IB offers: **Bristol** H555; **Exeter** 30 pts; **London (RH)** 30 pts.

SCE offers: **Birmingham** BBBC/BBCC; **St Andrews** BBBB.

CHOOSING YOUR COURSE (See also Ch 1)

> **Subject information:** Ancient History covers the classical world and the social, political and economic changes which took place in the Byzantine period and the medieval era which followed.

Course highlights: See also under **History. Birmingham** Many specialist options, eg classical history, Egyptology, environmental and practical archaeology. **Newcastle** (Anc H/Arch) Option in Greek or Latin for beginners; also museum studies. Practical experience of archaeology desirable. NOW CHECK PROSPECTUSES FOR ALL COURSES.

Study opportunities abroad: Cardiff IT GR T.

ADMISSIONS INFORMATION

Number of applicants per place (approx): Birmingham (Anc/Med Hist) 7, (Archaeol) 5; **Bristol** 11; **Cardiff** 3; **Durham** 4; **Newcastle** 17; **St David's** 6; **Swansea** 5.

General Studies acceptable: Birmingham; Exeter (2); Leeds.

Selection interviews: Birmingham; Bristol (Med Studs); Durham; Leeds; Newcastle; Swansea.

Offers to applicants repeating A-levels: Same Birmingham, Durham, Newcastle, Swansea.

Admissions Tutors' advice: Newcastle (Anc Hist/Arch) Prior experience of archaeology desirable but not essential.

> **Examples of interview questions:** Applicants taking ancient history at A-level likely to be questioned on their course; others probably will be questioned on their interest in the subject and how it developed. Since it is not a vocational subject, questions relating to future career interests are often asked.

GAP YEAR ADVICE

Institutions accepting a Gap Year: Most institutions; **Birmingham** Practical archaeological experience and foreign language study useful. **Cardiff** Secure university place before taking gap year.

Institutions willing to defer entry after A-levels (see Ch 5): Bristol (No); Newcastle (Anc Hist/Arch); Swansea.

AFTER A-LEVELS ADVICE

Institutions which may accept the same points score after A-levels: Birmingham; Durham; Leeds; Newcastle; Swansea.

Institutions demanding the actual grades offered after A-levels: Newcastle (some flexibility).

Institutions which may accept under-achieving applicants after A-levels: Durham; Leeds; Swansea.

Institutions with vacancies in Aug/Sept 1992 (see Ch 5): Bristol.

ADVICE FOR MATURE STUDENTS

See under **History**.

HISTORY (ECONOMIC and SOCIAL)

Special subject requirements: usually GCSE (grade A-C) mathematics.

NB Institutions may raise or lower the level of published offers depending either on the quality or otherwise of individual applications or the numbers of applications received; grades/points offered may be adjusted downwards after A-level results. The level of an offer is not indicative of the quality of a course.

24 pts.	**Sheffield** - BBB (Soc Hist)
	St Andrews - BBB (Ec/Soc Hist)
22 pts.	**Bristol** - BBC/BB (Econ/Ec Hist)
	Edinburgh - BBC (Ec Hist)
	Lancaster - BBC (Soc Hist)
	London (RH) - BBC/BC (Hist/Pol)
	Nottingham - BBC (Econ/Soc Hist)
	Warwick - BBC (Econ Hist)
20 pts.	**Aberdeen** - BCC (Hist)
	Aberystwyth - BCC (Joint courses)
	Birmingham - BCC/AB-BB (Soc/Ec Hist; Ec Hist Pol)
	East Anglia - BCC/BB (Econ Hist; approx offer for ESH courses)
	Exeter - BCC/BB (Ec/Soc Hist) (6-4 AS)
	Glasgow - BCC (Econ Hist)
	Kent - BCC (Hist/Ec Hist)
	Leicester - BCC (Ec Soc Hist; Ec/Ec Hist; Pol Ec Hist)
	Liverpool - BCC-CCD/BB-CD (Ec Hist)
	Sussex - BCC/BC (Econ H/Soc; EcEcH/Soc)
18 pts.	**Belfast** - CCC-CCD/BB-BC (Econ Hist Arts)
	Hull - BCD-CCC/BC (Ec/Soc Hist and joint courses)
	Kent - CCC (Ec Hist)
	Strathclyde - CCC (BBD 2nd yr entry) (Econ/Soc Hist)
	York - CCC/BB (Econ/E Hist EQ; E Hist and in combination)
16 pts.	**Leeds** - CCD/BC (ES Hist; ES Hist/Geog)
	Swansea - CCD/BC (Econ Hist/RS; Econ/Soc Hist)
14 pts.	**Manchester Met** - CDD/CC-CD (Hum/Soc St)
	Portsmouth - CDD/BC (Econ Hist) (NMI) (6 AS)

Alternative offers:

IB offers: **Aberdeen** 30 pts; **East Anglia** 30 pts; **Exeter** 30 pts; **Hull** 28 pts inc scores of 5; **Kent** 25 pts, H 11 pts.

SCE offers: **Aberdeen** BBBB; **Dundee** BBBC; **Edinburgh** BBBB; **Glasgow** ABBB-BBBB; **Liverpool** BBCC; **Sheffield** ABBB; **St Andrews** BBBB; **Stirling** BBBC; **Strathclyde** BBBB.

CHOOSING YOUR COURSE (See also Ch 1)

Subject information: Students will follow courses covering economics and the historical changes in Britain, Europe and other major powers.

Course highlights: See under **History. Hull** Large choice of options in years 2 and 3 covering economic and/or social history and a range of countries (Germany, Soviet Union, USA, India). NOW CHECK PROSPECTUSES FOR ALL COURSES.

ADMISSIONS INFORMATION

Number of applicants per place (approx): Birmingham 10; **East Anglia** 10;

Liverpool 3; **Portsmouth** 10; **York** 7.

General Studies acceptable: Aberdeen; Exeter (2); Lancaster; Liverpool; Portsmouth; York.

Selection interviews: Birmingham (some); Bristol; Durham; Exeter (for borderlines); Liverpool; Sheffield; Warwick (some); York (important).

Offers to applicants repeating A-levels: Higher Portsmouth, York; **Possibly higher** Liverpool; **Same** Exeter, Hull.

Admissions Tutors' advice: Warwick Course includes substantial amount of economics so selectors look for evidence of mathematical ability (for example GCSE mathematics grade B).

Examples of interview questions: Why are you interested in Economic and Social History?

GAP YEAR ADVICE

Institutions accepting a Gap Year: Most institutions; Exeter.

Institutions willing to defer entry after A-levels (see Ch 5): Bristol (No).

AFTER A-LEVELS ADVICE

Institutions which may accept the same points score after A-levels: Birmingham; Exeter; Hull; Kent; Liverpool; Portsmouth.

Institutions demanding the actual grades offered after A-levels: York.

Institutions with vacancies in Aug/Sept 1992 (see Ch 5): Few vacancies were advertised. Approximately 18 pts was the required entry level.

ADVICE FOR MATURE STUDENTS

See under **History**.

GRADUATE EMPLOYMENT

New Graduates' destinations (percentages) 1991:
Permanent employment: P 57.
Unemployment: P 43.
Further studies (all types): P 30.

York (1986-91) This is not a vocational course. Career destinations were equally divided between careers in finance (accountancy, banking, finance, insurance) and the various spheres of management (personnel, retail advertising), computing, law catering and nursing. Destinations also reflect the way in which graduates form their career decisions during their degree courses.

HOME ECONOMICS and INSTITUTIONAL MANAGEMENT (See also FOOD SCIENCE AND TECHNOLOGY and HOTEL AND CATERING MANAGEMENT)

Special subject requirements: science subjects at GCSE (grade A-C).

NB Institutions may raise or lower the level of published offers depending either on the quality or otherwise of individual applications or the numbers of applications received; grades/points offered may be adjusted downwards after A-level results. The level of an offer is not indicative of the quality of a course.

18 pts.	**Cardiff** - CCC/BB (Htl/Inst Man) (BTEC 3D+2M) (Home Ec) (BTEC 5M)
12 pts.	**Bath (CHE)** - 12 pts (inc one grade C) (Home Econ) (4 AS)
	Cardiff - DDD/CC (Home Ec/Tech) (BTEC 5M)
	Trinity & All Saints (CHE) - DDD/CD (HEc/BMA; HEc/PM)
10 pts.	**Cardiff** - CD (Home Ec - BEd)
	Northumbria - 10-8 pts (Ap Con Sci)
8 pts.	**and below**
	Leeds Met - (Con Serv Man)
	Liverpool John Moores - (Home Econ)
	Manchester Met - DD (Home Econ; App Cons Sci)
	Queen Margaret (Coll) - EE (App Con St)
	Robert Gordon - (Cons Prod Man)
	Sheffield Hallam - (Home Ec)
	South Bank - 8 pts (Home Econ/Resource Man) (4 AS) (BTEC 3M)

Offers for Foundation, Certificate and Diploma courses (see Ch 5):

Higher National Diploma courses (England and Wales):
4 pts. **and below** Birmingham (CFT & CS); Croydon (Coll); North London; Salford (UC); Sheffield Hallam.

College Diploma (Scotland):

4 pts. **and below or equivalent** Duncan of Jordanstone (CA).

Alternative offers:

IB offers: **Bath (CHE)** H444 + 3 Subsids; **Cardiff** 26 pts.

Overseas applicants: Bath (CHE) Linguistic ability required.

CHOOSING YOUR COURSE (See also Ch 1)

> **Subject information:** This subject involves food and nutrition, shelter, clothing, community studies and consumer behaviour and marketing. Other alternative courses could include Dietetics, Nutrition, Community Studies and Hotel and Catering Management.

Course highlights: Cardiff Subject options not made until year 2. Work experience part of course. Students entering teaching study technology as related to the National Curriculum in the Home Ec/Tech course. **Leeds Met** Core studies throughout the course cover food, shelter and clothing studies with the emphasis on consumer studies, marketing, management services and lifestyles. **Manchester Met** (App Cons Sci) Main options are food, clothing and housing. **Northumbria** Food technology, textiles and clothing form the basis of the third year. **Robert Gordon** (Cons Prod Man) Covers food textiles and finance. **South Bank** Students choose between the teaching route enabling them to qualify as teachers or the resource management route. NOW CHECK PROSPECTUSES FOR ALL COURSES.

Study opportunities abroad: Cardiff (E) G NL.

ADMISSIONS INFORMATION

Number of applicants per place (approx): Bath (CHE) 5; **Cardiff** 5; **Liverpool John Moores** (BA) 7; **Manchester Met** (BSc) 8, (BEd) 2; **Northumbria** 6; **South Bank** 5.

General Studies acceptable: Cardiff (2); Manchester Met; South Bank; Trinity & All Saints (CHE) (2).

Selection interviews: Bath (CHE); South Bank; Trinity & All Saints (CHE).

Offers to applicants repeating A-levels: Possibly higher Manchester Met (BSc); **Same** Bath (CHE), Liverpool John Moores, Trinity & All Saints (CHE), Ulster.

Admissions Tutors' advice: Bath (CHE) Early application strongly advised.

Examples of interview questions: Why have you applied for this course? What do you want to do in the future? What new developments are taking place in cookery techniques? What are the advantages and disadvantages? What is a home economist? What advice would you give to the designers of cookers? What are the future prospects of a home economist? Why do you want to teach? What teaching methods do you dislike? (BEd course). What is ergonomics? What interests you in current affairs? What world or national news has annoyed, pleased or upset you? What relevance do textiles and dress have to home economics? How would you react in a room full of fools?

GAP YEAR ADVICE

Institutions accepting a Gap Year: South Bank; most institutions.

Institutions willing to defer entry after A-levels (see Ch 5): Northumbria; Queen Margaret (Coll); Sheffield Hallam; South Bank; Trinity & All Saints (CHE).

AFTER A-LEVELS ADVICE

Institutions which may accept the same points score after A-levels: Cardiff; Liverpool John Moores; Manchester Met; Northumbria; South Bank; Trinity & All Saints (CHE).

Institutions which may accept under-achieving applicants after A-levels: Bath (CHE); Cardiff; Manchester Met.

Institutions with vacancies in Aug/Sept 1992 (see Ch 5): Edinburgh (QM) 4 pts; Northumbria 6 pts; Trinity & all Saints (CHE) 6 pts.

ADVICE FOR MATURE STUDENTS

Mathematics and English qualifications are important for some courses.

HORTICULTURE

Special subject requirements: A-levels in chemistry and 1 or 2 other subjects from mathematics or science. Similar GCSE (grade A-C) requirements.

NB Institutions may raise or lower the level of published offers depending either on the quality or otherwise of individual applications or the numbers of applications received; grades/points offered may be adjusted downwards after A-level results. The level of an offer is not indicative of the quality of a course.

18 pts.	**Bath** - CCC (Crop T/R Man)
14 pts.	**London (Wye)** - CDD/CC (Horticul; Hort/Bus Man)
	Nottingham - CDD/CC (Horticul)
	Reading - CDD/BC (Hortic)
12 pts.	**and below**
	Central England/Pershore (CHort) - (Hort)
	Central Lancashire - (Hort Mgt; Comb Hons) (4 AS)
	Greenwich - (Hort)
	Harper Adams (CAg) - DDD/CC (Hort) (BTEC Ds+Ms)
	Hertfordshire/Writtle (CAg) - 8 pts (Hort)
	SAC (Au) - (Hort; Hort/Man)
	Strathclyde - CD (CCD 2nd yr entry) (All Horticulture courses)

Offers for Foundation, Certificate and Diploma courses (see Ch 5):

Higher National Diploma courses (England & Wales):
   4 pts.   **and below** Askham Bryan (CAg); Greenwich; Harper Adams (CAg) (Golf Course Management); Pershore (CHort); Writtle (CAg) (Amenity/ Commercial Hort).

Higher National Diploma courses (Scotland):
   SAC (Au)

Alternative offers:

IB offers: **Nottingham** 28-24 pts.

SCE offers: **Strathclyde** BBB.

CHOOSING YOUR COURSE (See also Ch 1)

> **Subject information:** This is a broad course which covers commercial horticulture and the provision of recreational and leisure facilities (amenity horticulture). See also under **Botany**.

Course highlights: Central Lancashire (Hort Mgt) Strong links with horticultural industry through research and development work. **Hertfordshire/Writtle (CAg)** Emphasis on practical skills and management techniques. Amenity or commercial horticulture options in year 2. NOW CHECK PROSPECTUSES FOR ALL COURSES.

Study opportunities abroad: Askham Bryan (CAg) (HND) FR NL G IRE; **Bath**.

Work opportunities abroad: Bath FR USA.

General Studies acceptable: Hertfordshire/Writtle (CAg).

ADMISSIONS INFORMATION

Number of applicants per place (approx): Hertfordshire 4; **Strathclyde** 12.

Offers to applicants repeating A-levels: Higher Strathclyde.

> **Examples of interview questions:** How did you become interested in horticulture? How do you think this course will benefit you? Could you work in all weathers? What career are you aiming for? Are you interested in gardening? Describe your garden. What plants do you grow? How do you prune rose trees and fruit trees?

GAP YEAR ADVICE

Institutions accepting a Gap Year: Harper Adams (CAg).

Institutions willing to defer entry after A-levels (see Ch 5): Harper Adams (CAg).

AFTER A-LEVELS ADVICE

Institutions which may accept the same points score after A-levels: Strathclyde.

Institutions with vacancies in Aug/Sept 1992 (see Ch 5): Greenwich 4 pts; Strathclyde; most institutions are likely to have vacancies in 1993.

HOTEL AND CATERING MANAGEMENT (See also HOME ECONOMICS & INSTITUTIONAL MANAGEMENT)

Special subject requirements: GCSE (grade A-C) in mathematics and science.

NB Institutions may raise or lower the level of published offers depending either on the quality or otherwise of individual applications or the numbers of applications received; grades/points offered may be adjusted downwards after A-level results. The level of an offer is not indicative of the quality of a course.

20 pts.	**Surrey** - BCC-CCC/AB-BB (Hotel Man) (6 AS) (BTEC 3D + 3M)
18 pts.	**Cardiff** - CCC/BB (Htl/Inst Man) (BTEC 3D + 3M)
	Glasgow Caledonian - CCC (Htl/Cat Man; Hosp Man)
16 pts.	**Buckingham** - 16-14 pts (Bus St/IHM) (BTEC 3D)
	Robert Gordon - CCD/BC (Hosp Mgt)
	Strathclyde - CCD/BC (HCM) (4 AS)
	Ulster - CCD/BC (Htl/Tour) (AS maths/hum biol/mod lang/eng)
14 pts.	**Dundee** - CDD/CC (HCM; Food Welf)
	Surrey - CDD/CC (H & C Man) (6 AS) (See **Admissions Tutors' advice**)
12 pts.	**Brighton** - 12 pts (IHM; Int Tour Mgt)
	Huddersfield - DDD/CC (HCB) (4 AS)
	Oxford Brookes - DDD/CC (HCM; Modular) (4 AS) (BTEC 1D + Ms)
	Portsmouth - 12 pts approx (HCM)
	South Bank - CC (Hotel Mgt) (BTEC 6M)
10 pts.	**Central England** - 10 pts (Hotel/Cate)
	Cheltenham & Glos (CHE) - 10 pts (Hotel Man; Cat Mgt)
	Leeds Met - 10 pts (Hosp Man) (BTEC 4M)
	Manchester Met - 10 pts (HCM; Int Hot Mgt) (4 AS) (BTEC 75% overall)
	Middlesex - CD (HRM)
	Napier - DDE/CD (Hosp Mgt)
	North London - 10 pts (Int Hot Cate)
	Norwich City (CFHE) - 10 pts (Hosp Man)
	Nottingham Trent - 10 pts approx (IHM)
	Sheffield Hallam - 10 pts (HCM; HTM) (4 AS)
8 pts.	and below
	Bell (CT) - (Hosp Man)

Bournemouth - 8 pts (Hosp Mgt; Food/Cat Mgt) (BTEC Ms)
Cardiff (IHE) - (Hotel Man)
Central Lancashire/Blackpool (CFHE) - 8 pts (Hosp Mgt) (BTEC 3M)
Glasgow Caledonian - EE (Hosp Man)
Huddersfield - 8 pts (Cate/Ap N)
Humberside - (Cate St)
Plymouth/Seale Hayne (CAg) - (Hosp Man)
Queen Margaret (Coll) - CE-EE (Hosp Ent/Tourism)
Robert Gordon - (Hosp man)
Thames Valley London - DEE/DD (Hosp/Mgt)

Offers for Foundation, Certificate and Diploma courses (see Ch 5):

Higher National Diploma courses (England and Wales):
6 pts. Blackpool (CFHE); Huddersfield; Norwich City (CFHE).
4 pts. and below Birmingham (CFT & CS); Bournemouth; Brighton (CT); Cardiff (IHE); Central Lancashire; Cheltenham & Glos (CHE);Colchester (Inst); Colwyn Bay (Llandrillo Coll); Coventry (Henley Coll); Derby; Farnborough (CT); Leeds Met; London (West); Manchester Met (Hotel Man, Tourism Man); Middlesex; Newcastle (CFE); North London 2pts; Nottingham Trent; Salford (UC); Sheffield Hallam; South Devon (CAT); Stafford (CFE); Stoke on Trent (Coll); Thames Valley London.

Higher Diploma courses (Scotland):
4 pts. and below or equivalent Duncan of Jordanstone (CA); Edinburgh (QM); Glasgow (CFood); Glasgow Caledonian; Napier EE; Robert Gordon.

Professional courses (England and Wales):

4 pts. and below Brighton (CT); Eastbourne (Coll); Leeds Met; Middlesex; Norwich City (CFHE); Oxford Brookes; Thames Valley London.

Professional courses (Scotland):

4 pts. and below or equivalent Glasgow (CFood); Glasgow Caledonian; Napier; Queen Margaret (Coll); Robert Gordon.

Alternative offers:

IB offers: **Bournemouth** (Food/Cat Mgt) 24 pts; **Brighton** 26 pts; **Buckingham** 24 pts; **Cardiff** 28 pts; **Central England** 24 pts; **Manchester Met** 24 pts; **Oxford Brookes** 26 pts; **South Bank** 24 pts; **Surrey** 30 pts.

Irish offers: **Brighton** BBBB; **Glasgow Caledonian** CCC; **Huddersfield** CCCC; **Sheffield Hallam** CCCC; **Surrey** BBBBB.

SCE offers: **Dundee** BCCC/BBC (Food Welf); **Huddersfield** BB; **Leeds Met** BBB; **Strathclyde** BBBB/BBBCC.

Overseas applicants: Central England Interviews usually in home country. **Central Lancashire** EFL provision available. **Huddersfield** English language teaching available. **North London, Bournemouth, Middlesex, Central England** Ability required in spoken and written English.

CHOOSING YOUR COURSE (See also Ch 1)

Subject information: All courses provide a comprehensive preparation for entry into hotel, catering, tourism and leisure industries. Alternative courses could include Food Science, Home Economics and Dietetics.

Course highlights: Bournemouth (Hosp Mgt) Students involved in industrial projects at early stage commissioned by hotel, tourism and leisure groups. (Food/Cat Mgt) Specialist studies in tourism, facilities management, small business management, microbiology and nutrition Operations management with marketing and IT. **Brighton** (IHM) Six months is spent on placements abroad in Europe, USA, Far East or Australia. **Huddersfield** (Cate Ap N) The course focuses on large-scale catering and the scientific, nutritional and management aspects of a modern catering operation. **Leeds** The sandwich course covers all aspects of the industry - food and accommodation studies, management and manpower studies, finance, law and business policy. **Nottingham Trent** (IHM) Language study is mandatory in French, German, Italian or Spanish. **Oxford Brookes** Catering Management must be taken with a second subject. Hotel and Catering Management is a four-year course with year 2 on work experience. **Portsmouth** The course covers catering and accommodation studies, behavioural science, personnel work, law, marketing and finance. **Robert Gordon** Options are offered in modern languages. **Strathclyde** International recognition. Large number of overseas students. **Surrey** There are four main areas of study in the first two years - management studies, quantitative studies (accounting), food and beverage management and business studies. French and German language study available. **Wolverhampton** Final year students may specialise in tourism, hotel management, licensed retail management or international hospitality. NOW CHECK PROSPECTUSES FOR ALL COURSES.

Study opportunities abroad: Bournemouth (E); **Oxford Brookes** USA; **Strathclyde** (E); **Thames Valley London** (E).

Work opportunities abroad: Bournemouth EUR USA; **Brighton** USA HK CAN FR B SZ C K AUS NZ BZ; **Cardiff** AUS USA CAN HK SP FR; **Central England** USA EUR HK; **Central Lancashire; Cheltenham & Glos (CHE)** USA NL G IT GR; **Huddersfield; Leeds Met** CAN HK USA EUR; **Manchester Met** EUR USA HK; **Middlesex; Portsmouth** NL USA AUS; **Queen Margaret (Coll)** CAN USA FR SZ IRE FE; **Robert Gordon** FR SP G IT USA CAN AUS HK S BR AF SA; **South Bank** EUR; **Surrey** FR B NL G USA CAN.

ADMISSIONS INFORMATION

Number of applicants per place (approx): Bournemouth 4; **Brighton** 20; **Buckingham** 8; **Cardiff** 15; **Central England** 8; **Central Lancashire** 5; **Dundee** 9; **Huddersfield** (Cate/Ap N) 6, (HCB) 17; **Leeds Met** 10; **Manchester Met** 18; **Middlesex** 26; **Napier** 5; **Oxford Brookes** 9; **Portsmouth** 23; **Robert Gordon** 5; **Sheffield Hallam** 10; **South Bank** 6; **Strathclyde** 14; **Surrey** (Hotel Man) 12; **Thames Valley London** 6.

General Studies acceptable: Brighton; Buckingham; Cardiff (2); Cardiff (IHE) (2); Central England; Cheltenham & Glos (CHE) (2); Dundee (2); Glasgow Caledonian; Leeds Met; Manchester Met (2); Oxford Brookes (2); Surrey; Thames Valley London.

Selection interviews: South Bank; Surrey; most institutions.

Offers to applicants repeating A-levels: Higher Bournemouth, Huddersfield, Oxford Brookes, Surrey; **Same** Brighton, Manchester Met, South Bank, Strathclyde, Surrey (BSc Ord), Ulster.

Admissions Tutors' advice: Brighton Work experience in catering industry extremely important. **Buckingham** Course starts in January. **Central Lancashire/Blackpool (CFHE)** (Hospitality Man) English and maths GCSE (grade A-C) required. **Huddersfield** Students considered on academic ability, motivation to industry and verbal and visual impact on others. (Cate/Ap N) Initially we are looking for candidates with a science bias (but not obligatory) well motivated to career in catering and allied industries. **Leeds Met** Candidates must have recently discussed the career with a professional in the field and must demonstrate inter-personal skills essential to the service industry. Highly desirable/ almost essential that they have worked in the industry; must have worked with people. Hospitality Management course designed for BTEC entry. **Manchester Met** Attention paid to academic potential and knowledge of, and motivation for, a career in this field. Some work experience associated with the course is regarded favourably. **Middlesex, Portsmouth** Experience in the hotel or catering industry is beneficial. **Surrey** Home students are not normally considered for this course.

Examples of interview questions: What books do you read? What do you know about hotel work and management? What experience have you had? What kind of job do you have in mind when you have qualified? How did you become interested in this course? What do your parents think about you entering the profession? In what ways would you adapt yourself to industrial training? Do you eat in restaurants? What types of restaurants? Discuss examples of good and bad restaurant organisation. What foods do you like? What qualities do you have which make you suitable for management? What is the difference between a hotel manager and an ordinary manager? What quality do you possess which would make you a poor hotel manager? (All applicants are strongly recommended to obtain practical experience in catering or hotel work.)

GAP YEAR ADVICE

Institutions accepting a Gap Year: Most institutions; **Cardiff** Gain work experience and travel; **Oxford Brookes** Be in the UK in the following August to receive enrolment package.

Institutions willing to defer entry after A-levels (see Ch 5): Bournemouth; Buckingham; Cheltenham & Glos (CHE); Dundee (No); Manchester Met (But clarify your intentions as soon as possible); Oxford Brookes; Plymouth/Seale Hayne (CAg); Queen Margaret (Coll); Robert Gordon; Surrey (Contact before February).

AFTER A-LEVELS ADVICE

Institutions which may accept the same points score after A-levels: Bournemouth; Central England; Edinburgh (QM); Huddersfield; Manchester Met; North London; Portsmouth; Sheffield Hallam; South Bank; Strathclyde; Surrey.

Institutions which may accept under-achieving applicants after A-levels: Bournemouth; Central England; Manchester Met; North London; Portsmouth; Queen Margaret (Coll).

Institutions with vacancies in Aug/Sept 1992 (see Ch 5): Bournemouth 8 pts; Brighton 8 pts; Buckingham; Cardiff (IHE); Cheltenham & Glos (CHE); Dundee 10 pts; Manchester Met; Plymouth/ Seale Hayne (CAg); Robert Gordon; Strathclyde; Surrey 18 pts (contact Department Head).

ADVICE FOR MATURE STUDENTS

Up to 15% of the student total of some institutions is represented by mature students. In many cases, applicants are treated individually and experience may count more than previous academic qualifications.

GRADUATE EMPLOYMENT

New Graduates' destinations (percentages) 1991:
Permanent employment: U 88; P 79; C 69.
Unemployment: U 7; P 12; C 18.
Further studies (all types): U 26; P 9; C 13.

Surrey 48 Students graduated and entered full-time employment. By far the largest proportion entered the hotel industry with manager or trainee manager status. Graduates joined hotels in the UK and abroad, eg San Fransisco, Florida, New York, Nicosia, Jerusalem, Oslo, Amsterdam and Mauritius. Other graduates joined British Airways, Scandinavian Air Services, the Royal Navy, Sealink Ferries, Whitbreads, Marks and Spencer plc and even HM Prison Service. Seven students went in to accountancy and a small number into publishing and personnel management.

HOUSING

Special subject requirements: GCSE (grade A-C) English and mathematics.

NB Institutions may raise or lower the level of published offers depending either on the quality or otherwise of individual applications or the numbers of applications received; grades/points offered may be adjusted downwards after A-level results. The level of an offer is not indicative of the quality of a course.

20 pts.	**Heriot-Watt/Edinburgh** - BCC (House Stud)
12 pts.	**Bristol UWE** - 12-10 pts (Housing) (BTEC 4/5M)
	Sheffield Hallam - DDD/CC (Housing St) (BTEC 3M)
	South Bank - CC (Housing)
8 pts.	**and below**
	Anglia (Poly Univ) - (Housing St)
	Manchester Met - (Ap Con Sci)
	Westminster - 12 pts (Housing)

Offers for Foundation, Certificate and Diploma courses (see Ch 5):

Higher National Diploma courses:
   4 pts. **and below** Nottingham Trent; Sheffield Hallam (Land Admin).

Alternative offers:

Irish offers: **Bristol UWE** BBCC.

SCE offers: **Heriot-Watt/Edinburgh** BBBB.

CHOOSING YOUR COURSE (See also Ch 1)

Subject information: More applicants are sought for these courses, which provide a preparation for careers involving housing management allied to social needs and also economic and political considerations. Topics covered will include housing law, planning policy, finance and construction. **South Bank** Work experience or observation is important. Intending applicants advised to contact local authority housing departments, housing associations and estate agents to see something of their work.

Course highlights: Anglia (Poly Univ) Studies in private and social housing with exemptions from RICS examinations (most courses will give these exemptions). **Heriot-Watt** Curriculum a blend of lecture-based teaching, project and placements. Course run with the Department of Social Policy and Social Work at Edinburgh University (uniform entry requirements with the Social Science faculty). **Manchester Met** Main options in food, housing and clothing. NOW CHECK PROSPECTUSES FOR ALL COURSES.

Study opportunities abroad: Manchester Met.

Work opportunities abroad: South Bank EUR.

ADMISSIONS INFORMATION

Number of applicants per place (approx): Anglia (Poly Univ) 2; **Bristol UWE** 2; **Sheffield Hallam** 4.

General Studies acceptable: Anglia (Poly Univ); Bristol UWE; Heriot-Watt/Edinburgh; Sheffield Hallam.

Examples of interview questions: What is a housing association? Why were housing associations formed? In which parts of the country would you expect private housing to be expensive and by comparison, cheap? What is the cause of this? Have estates of multi-storey flats fulfilled their original purpose? If not, why not? What causes a slum? **Sheffield Hallam** An informal discussion of the course focussing on the student's interest in housing and any experience of working with the public.

GAP YEAR ADVICE

Institutions accepting a Gap Year: Westminster; most institutions.

Institutions willing to defer entry after A-levels (see Ch 5): Sheffield Hallam; South Bank (Prefer not).

AFTER A-LEVELS ADVICE

Institutions which may accept the same points score after A-levels: Bristol UWE; Sheffield Hallam; South Bank.

Institutions with vacancies in Aug/Sept 1992 (see Ch 5): Vacancies were numerous for these courses at relatively low grades. Westminster EE.

ADVICE FOR MATURE STUDENTS

At **Sheffield Hallam** a significant number of mature students have applied for the course. For most courses evidence of literacy and numeracy is required.

HUMAN MOVEMENT STUDIES (See also Physical Education)

Special subject requirements: GCSE (grade A-C) English and mathematics.

NB Institutions may raise or lower the level of published offers depending either on the quality or otherwise of individual applications or the numbers of applications received; grades/points offered may be adjusted downwards after A-level results. The level of an offer is not indicative of the quality of a course.

12 pts.	**Cardiff (IHE)** - 12 pts (SHMS)
	Leeds Met - 12 pts (Hum Mov St)
10 pts.	**Bath (CHE)** - 10 pts (BEd)
8 pts.	**and below**
	Canterbury Christ Church (CHE) - (Mov St)
	Nene (CHE) - (Movement Studies BEd)
	Ripon & York St John (CHE) - (Modular)
	St Mary's (CHE) - EEE/EE (Comb St)

Diploma of Higher Education courses:
    4 pts.   **and below** Ripon & York St John (CHE).

Alternative offers:

IB offers: **Leeds Met** H665.

SCE offers: **Bath (CHE)** BBC.

CHOOSING YOUR COURSE (See also Ch 1)

> **Subject information:** This is a study comprising two main areas involving practical activities such as aquatics, athletics games, dance, gymnastics and outdoor activities and theoretical studies in physiology, psychology and sociology. NOW CHECK PROSPECTUSES FOR ALL COURSES.

ADMISSIONS INFORMATION

Number of applicants per place (approx): Cardiff (IHE) 6; **Leeds Met** 16.

General Studies acceptable: Cardiff (IHE); Leeds Met.

Selection interviews: All institutions.

Offers to applicants repeating A-levels: Same Cardiff (IHE), Leeds Met.

> **Examples of interview questions:** Why do you think you will make a good teacher? What problems would you expect to face on teaching human movement? Questions relating to sport, your own activities, preferences and attitudes towards sport.

AFTER A-LEVELS ADVICE

Institutions which may accept the same points score after A-levels: Cardiff (IHE).

Institutions which may accept under-achieving applicants after A-levels: Cardiff (IHE).

HUMAN SCIENCES/HUMAN STUDIES

Special subject requirements: mathematics and science A-levels at Oxford and Sussex, and GCSE (grade A-C) only for Bradford and London (UC).

NB Institutions may raise or lower the level of published offers depending either on the quality or otherwise of individual applications or the numbers of applications received; grades/points offered may be adjusted downwards after A-level results. The level of an offer is not indicative of the quality of a course.

30 pts.	**Oxford** - AAA potential recommended (Hum Sci)
20 pts.	**Bradford** - BCC/BB (Int Hum) (BTEC 2D+3M)
	Sussex - BCC/BB (Hums/Biols)
	London (UC) - BCC (Hum/Sci)
16 pts.	**Durham-Tees (Coll)** - 16 approx (Hum Sci)
12 pts.	**Bretton Hall (CHE)** - CC-EE (Eng/Social St)
	Worcester (CHE) - 12 pts (Comb St)

Alternative offers:

SCE offers: **Bradford** BBBBC; **Sussex** ABBB.

CHOOSING YOUR COURSE (See also Ch 1)

> **Subject information:** This is a multi-disciplinary study relating to biological and social sciences. Topics range from genetics and evolution to health, disease, social behaviour and industrial societies.

Course highlights: Bradford The course covers communication studies, human nature, human society and logic and thought. NOW CHECK PROSPECTUSES FOR ALL COURSES.

ADMISSIONS INFORMATION

Examples of interview questions: What do you expect to get out of a degree in this subject? Why are you interested in this subject? What problems do you think you will be able to tackle after completing the course?

INDUSTRIAL DESIGN (including Engineering and Transportation) (See also Three Dimensional Design)

Special subject requirements (Brunel): maths and physics at A- or AS-level.

NB Institutions may raise or lower the level of published offers depending either on the quality or otherwise of individual applications or the numbers of applications received; grades/points offered may be adjusted downwards after A-level results. The level of an offer is not indicative of the quality of a course.

18 pts.   **Bournemouth** - CCC (Prod Des)
        Brunel - CCC/BC (Ind Des) (4 AS)
        Loughborough - CCC/BB (Prod Des)
        Strathclyde - CCC (BCC 2nd yr entry) (Prod Des)
12 pts.   **Coventry** - CC (Ind Des/Trans; Cons Prod Des) (4 AS)
8 pts.   **and below**
        Anglia (Poly Univ) - EE (Prod Des/Bus Man)
        East London - DD + aptitude for design (Prod Des)

Entry to the following degree courses is via the ADAR application scheme: Bath (CHE) (Prod Des); Cardiff (IHE); Central England; Coventry; De Montfort; Gwent (CHE); Huddersfield; Leeds Met; London Inst (Central SA); Manchester Met; Napier (Ind Des/Tech); Northumbria; Plymouth; Ravensbourne (CDC); Sheffield Hallam; Staffordshire; Swansea (IHE); Teesside; Ulster.

Higher National Diploma courses:
4 pts.   **and below** (Industrial/Product Design): Berkshire (CA); Bournemouth (Coll); Colchester (Inst); Hertfordshire; Huddersfield (Product Design); London (Chelsea). (Model Making): Hertford (Coll); Kent (IAD); London (Central St Martins); Sunderland.

CHOOSING YOUR COURSE (See also Ch 1)

Subject information: These are product design courses (eg the design of cars, telephones, cookers, radios) and they are almost always preceded by a Foundation Art course.

Course highlights: Brunel French or German compulsory in years 2, 3 & 4. Some placements abroad. Blend of science and art in context of design. NOW CHECK PROSPECTUSES FOR ALL COURSES.

Work opportunities abroad: Coventry FR G NL - regularly, USA JAP - occasionally.

ADMISSIONS INFORMATION

Number of applicants per place (approx): Bournemouth 3; **Brunel** 5; **Cardiff (IHE)** 4; **Central England** 5; **Coventry** 5; **London (Central SA)** 2; **Loughborough** 9; **Manchester Met** 2; **Napier** 6; **Northumbria** 4; **Sheffield** 5; **South Bank** 3; **Teesside** 2.

General Studies acceptable: Anglia (Poly Univ); East London.

Selection interviews: All institutions.

Admissions Tutors' advice: Brunel GCSE grade A in maths and English preferred.

Examples of interview questions: Applicants' portfolios of art work form an important talking point throughout the interview. In what aspects of industrial design are you interested? Applicants should be able to discuss examples of current design and new developments in the field.

GAP YEAR ADVICE

Institutions accepting a Gap Year: Most institutions; but Coventry (No).

AFTER A-LEVELS ADVICE

Institutions with vacancies in Aug/Sept 1992 (see Ch 5): Brunel 16-12 pts.

GRADUATE EMPLOYMENT

New Graduates' destinations (percentages) 1991: See under **Art (Design)**.

Teesside The majority of graduates secured employment in the design field.

INTERIOR DESIGN

Special subject requirements: none. Entry is usually via a Foundation Art course. Applicants for degree courses are interviewed and have to submit a portfolio of art work for inspection. Applications are made through the Art and Design Admissions Registry (ADAR) scheme (See Chapter 3).

NB Institutions may raise or lower the level of published offers depending either on the quality or otherwise of individual applications or the numbers of applications received; grades/points offered may be adjusted downwards after A-level results. The level of an offer is not indicative of the quality of a course.

Institutions offering degree courses: Bournemouth; Brighton; Cardiff (IHE); Central England; De Montfort; Duncan of Jordanstone (CA); Glasgow (CB); Buckinghamshire (CHE); Kingston; Leeds Met; Manchester Met; Middlesex; Napier; North London; Nottingham Trent; Ravensbourne (CDC); Scottish (CText); Suffolk (CFHE); Teesside.

Higher National Diploma courses (England):
    4 pts.   and below Berkshire (CA); Bournemouth (Coll); Dewsbury (Coll); Kent (IAD); London (Chelsea); Newcastle (CAT); Suffolk (CFHE).

College Awards (Scotland):
        Glasgow (CB); Napier.

CHOOSING YOUR COURSE (See also Ch 1)

Subject information: A Foundation Art course is usually taken followed by this specialised study of interiors (historical and modern) and their design. NOW CHECK PROSPECTUSES FOR ALL COURSES.

Study opportunities abroad: Middlesex.

ADMISSIONS INFORMATION

Number of applicants per place (approx): Cardiff (IHE) 4; **Duncan of Jordanstone (CA)** 6; **Glasgow (CB)** 7; **Leeds Met** 3; **Middlesex** 3; **Napier** 2; **Nottingham Trent** 3; **Scottish (CText)** 5; **Teesside** 3.

Selection interviews: All institutions.

> **Examples of interview questions:** Questions and discussion topics arise from inspection of work portfolios. Applicants should have a knowledge of the history of interiors and of more recent developments, and should be able to give examples.

GRADUATE EMPLOYMENT

New Graduates' destinations (percentages) 1991: See under **Art (Design)**.

INTERNATIONAL RELATIONS (See also **Politics**)

Special subject requirements: occasionally GCSE (grade A-C) mathematics.

NB Institutions may raise or lower the level of published offers depending either on the quality or otherwise of individual applications or the numbers of applications received; grades/points offered may be adjusted downwards after A-level results. The level of an offer is not indicative of the quality of a course.

26 pts.	**St Andrews** - ABB (All IR courses)
24 pts.	**London (LSE)** - 24 pts approx (Int Rel)
20 pts.	**Aberdeen** - 20 pts (IR courses)
	Aberystwyth - BCC/BB (All IR courses) (BTEC 3D+3M)
	Bradford - BCC/BB (Peace options)
	Birmingham - BCC/BB (Int Studs; Int Std Econ)
	Kent - BCC (Pol/IR; IR/Fr)
	Lancaster - BCC (Pol/IR; IRSS)
	Leeds - BCC/BB (Int St)
	Reading - BCC/BB (Int Rel/Econ) (BTEC 2D+Ms)
	Sussex - BCC/BB (All Int Rel courses)
	Warwick - 20 pts approx (Int Rel - joint courses)
18 pts.	**Keele** - BCD-CCC/BB-BC (Int Rls 3 and 4) (4 AS)
14 pts.	**Coventry** - 14 pts (Int St/Bus St)
	Staffordshire - 14 pts (Int Rel) (BTEC 1D+3M)
12 pts.	**Coventry** - 12 pts CC (Mod St)
10 pts.	**Nottingham Trent** - 10 pts (M Eur St)

Alternative offers:

IB offers: **Birmingham** 33 pts; **Kent** 27 pts, H 12 pts; **Reading** 28 pts; **St Andrews** 32 pts; **Staffordshire** 26 pts.

SCE offers: **St Andrews** BBBB.

CHOOSING YOUR COURSE (See also Ch 1)

> **Subject information:** A strong interest in international affairs is a prerequisite for these courses which often allow students to specialise in a geographical area such as African, Asian, West European politics etc. See also under **Politics** and **Peace Studies**.

Course highlights: Aberdeen (IR courses) Cover Europe, USA, Britain, politics and the history of international relations. **Birmingham** Offered with politics. **Staffordshire** Study visits to Western and Eastern Europe. NOW CHECK PROSPECTUSES FOR ALL COURSES.

ADMISSIONS INFORMATION

Number of applicants per place (approx): Birmingham 11; **Reading** 5; **Staffordshire** 5.

General Studies acceptable as one of two A-levels: Birmingham; Reading; Staffordshire.

> **Examples of interview questions:** Discuss the problems in nuclear disarmament between America and the former Soviet Union. Would you trust the Russians? Would you trust the Americans? Would you trust the French? What problems between France and England are likely to occur as a result of the Channel Tunnel?

GAP YEAR ADVICE

Institutions accepting a Gap Year: Leeds; most institutions.

Institutions willing to defer entry after A-levels (see Ch 5): Aberystwyth; Bradford; Leeds (No); St Andrews; Staffordshire.

AFTER A-LEVELS ADVICE

Institutions which may accept the same points score after A-levels: Staffordshire.

Institutions which may accept under-achieving applicants after A-levels: Staffordshire.

Institutions with vacancies in Aug/Sept 1992 (see Ch 5): Aberystwyth 18 pts; Staffordshire.

ADVICE FOR MATURE STUDENTS

This is a subject which attracts some mature students every year and for which specific A-levels or equivalent are required.

ITALIAN

Special subject requirements: A-level Italian sometimes 'required' or 'preferred'.

NB Institutions may raise or lower the level of published offers depending either on the quality or otherwise of individual applications or the numbers of applications received; grades/points offered may be adjusted downwards after A-level results. The level of an offer is not indicative of the quality of a course.

30 pts.	**Cambridge/Oxford** - AAA potential recommended (Mod Lang)
26 pts.	**Bristol** - ABB-BBB/AB (Sp/Ital)
24 pts.	**Bath** - ABC (Mod Lang/Europ)
	Hull - BBB (Engl/Ital)
22 pts.	**Bristol** - BBC/BB (Ital St)
	Edinburgh - BBC (Ital)
	Glasgow - BBC (Italian)
	Hull - BBC-BCC (Fr/Ital; Hist/Ital; Drama/Ital)
	London (RH) - BBC-BCC/BB (All courses)
	London (SSEES) - BBC-BCC (Ital/Rom)
	Manchester - 22 pts approx (Ital St)
20 pts.	**Birmingham** - BCC (Ital - joint courses)

Cardiff - BCC/BB (Ital and joint courses) (BTEC 2D+2M)
Exeter - BCC (GRS/Ital) (4 AS)
Kent - BCC-CCC (Comb courses)
Leicester - BCC-CCC/BC (Arts Comb)
Reading - BCC (Ital/Art Hist; Ital/Man St)
Swansea - BCC/BC (Joint courses; see under **18 pts**)
Warwick - BCC/BC (All courses)

18 pts. **Aberystwyth** - CCC/BB (Joint courses)
Belfast - CCC/BB (Arts Comb; Ital (M))
Hull - CCC (Italian; Germ/Ital; Bus St/Ital)
Leeds - BCD-CCC/BB (Ital; other joint courses)
Leicester - CCC/BC (Mod Langs; Ital/Pol)
London (UC) - CCC/BC (All courses)
Reading - CCC/BB (All courses except under **20 pts**)
Stirling - CCC approx (Ital)
Strathclyde - CCC/BC (BBD 2nd yr entry) (Ital)
Sussex - CCC/BC (P Ital/Maps; Ital/Euro; It/Fr/Euro)
Swansea - CCC/BC (Italian) (BTEC 3D+4M)
16 pts. **Lancaster** - BCE/BB (Ital)
12 pts. **Westminster** - CC-CD (Ital/Rus; Ital/Sp)
8 pts. **Anglia (Poly Univ)** - (Joint courses)

Diploma of Higher Education courses:
Leeds Met (EBC)

Higher National Diploma courses (with Business Studies):
8 pts. **and below** South Bank.

Other Diploma courses:
4 pts. **and below** Anglia (Poly Univ).

Alternative offers:

IB offers: **Bristol** 32 pts; **Cardiff** 30 pts, H 15 pts; **Hull** 30-28 pts; **Kent** 27 pts, H 12 pts; **Lancaster** 28 pts; **Leeds** 28 pts; **Leicester** 28 pts; **London (RH)** 28 pts; **Swansea** 28 pts.

SCE offers: **Edinburgh** BBBB; **Glasgow** ABBB/BBBB; **Lancaster** BBBB; **Leeds** BBBB; **Strathclyde** BBBB; **Sussex** BBBB.

CHOOSING YOUR COURSE (See also Ch 1)

Subject information: The language and literature of Italy will feature largely on most of these courses. The majority of applicants have no knowledge of Italian. They will need to give convincing reasons for their interest and to show that they have the ability to assimilate language quickly.

Course highlights: Anglia (Poly Univ) The course includes the language, culture, history and contemporary society in Italy. **Bath** See under **European Studies**. **Bristol** Equal emphasis on art history, language and literature. **Cardiff** Opportunity to start beginners' course in Italian in year 1. **Hull** Emphasis on language skills; options in years 2 and 3. **Leeds** Broad-based course covering literature and society. Extra year for beginners in Italian. **London (RH)** Wide choice of subjects available in new course system. **Swansea** Emphasis on language skills for beginners. NOW CHECK PROSPECTUSES FOR ALL COURSES.

Study opportunities abroad: Cardiff (E); **London (RH)** (E).

Work opportunities abroad: Leeds IT.

ADMISSIONS INFORMATION

Number of applicants per place (approx): Birmingham 10; **Bristol** 8; **Cardiff** 2; **Coventry** 28; **Hull** 10; **Lancaster** 8; **Leeds** 6; **London (RH)** 3.

General Studies acceptable: Hull; Lancaster.

Selection interviews: Cambridge; Hull; Kent (frequently); Leeds (some); London (RH); Oxford; Westminster.

Offers to applicants repeating A-levels: Higher Birmingham; **Same** Hull, Leeds, Swansea.

Admissions Tutors' advice: Lancaster We take students with or without A-level Italian. **Leeds** Because of the pressure on French places, unsuccessful modern language candidates are sometimes invited for Single Italian. **London (RH)** We do not make an offer without an interview. Keen candidates without A-level Italian take a summer course in Italy before entry.

> **Examples of interview questions:** Why do you want to learn Italian? What foreign newspapers or magazines do you read (if the applicant has taken A-level Italian)? Have you visited Italy? What do you know of the Italian people, culture, art etc?

GAP YEAR ADVICE

Institutions accepting a Gap Year: Most institutions; **Cardiff** Spend some time in Italy.

Institutions willing to defer entry after A-levels (see Ch 5): Bristol; London (RH); Swansea.

AFTER A-LEVELS ADVICE

Institutions which may accept the same points score after A-levels: Birmingham (usually); Hull; Kent; Lancaster; Leeds; Swansea.

Institutions which may accept under-achieving applicants after A-levels: Glasgow; Hull; London (RH).

Institutions with vacancies in Aug/Sept 1992 (see Ch 5): Anglia (Poly Univ); Bristol 22 pts; London (RH) CCC/18 pts, (SSEES) 20-18 pts; Swansea 16 pts. A number of single and joint course vacancies were declared requiring an average score of 16 pts.

GRADUATE EMPLOYMENT

New Graduates' destinations (percentages) 1991:
Permanent employment: U 70.
Unemployment: U 18.
Further studies (all types): U 44.

JAPANESE

Special subject requirements: A-level modern language preferred.

NB Institutions may raise or lower the level of published offers depending either on the quality or otherwise of individual applications or the numbers of applications received; grades/points offered may be adjusted downwards after A-level results. The level of an offer is not indicative of the quality of a course.

30 pts.	**Cambridge/Oxford** – AAA potential recommended (Oriental)
24 pts.	**Edinburgh** – 24 pts (Jap/Ling)
	London (SOAS) – BBB/BB (All courses)
	Newcastle – BBB-BCC (Pol/EAS – Japanese; Comb St)
	Sheffield – BBB (All courses)
22 pts.	**Aston** – BBC/AA (Japanese – subsidiary language)
	Durham – BBC (Japanese courses)
	Leeds – BBC (Japanese)
18 pts.	**Stirling** – CCC/BC (Japanese)

Alternative offers:

EB offers: **Sheffield** 75% average.

IB offers: **Leeds** 17 pts at Highers; **London (SOAS)** 34 pts; **Sheffield** 33 pts.

Irish offers: **Sheffield** AABBB.

SCE offers: **Edinburgh** BBBB; **Sheffield** AABBB; **Stirling** BBCC.

CHOOSING YOUR COURSE (See also Ch 1)

Subject information: A strong interest in Japan and Japanese culture is expected of applicants. A number of four-year joint courses are now offered, all of which include a period of study in Japan. Potential employers are showing an interest in Law/Japanese. Students report that 'it is not a soft option'. They are expected to be firmly dedicated to a Japanese degree (ie Japanese only on the UCAS application form), to have an interest in using their degree in employment, and 'to work their rear ends off'! NOW CHECK PROSPECTUSES FOR ALL COURSES.

Admissions Tutors' advice: Sheffield Japanese can be taken only as one half of a four-year dual degree course with the first year given entirely to an intensive study of basic Japanese grammar and the writing system. Fifteen per cent of students are 'mature' (over 21) and there is an upper age limit of 35. We will accept the same points score and general studies. There are 25 places with 250 applicants. **London (SOAS)** All candidates should have all-round, above-average GCSE results and should have taken a foreign (including classical) language at A-level. Interviews determine whether or not offers are made. Mature students usually have spent some time in Japan. There are 20 places and 180 applicants each year.

Examples of interview questions: Why do you wish to study Japanese? What do you know of Japanese history, culture etc? What do you hope to do when you leave university?

AFTER A-LEVELS ADVICE

Institutions with vacancies in Aug/Sept 1992 (see Ch 5): Leeds; Sheffield.
Some vacancies existed for students with 18 to 14 pts.

LANDSCAPE ARCHITECTURE (including Landscape Management)

Special subject requirements: GCSE (grade A-C) in English/mathematics/science. A-levels preferred in art/biology/geography.

NB Institutions may raise or lower the level of published offers depending either on the quality or otherwise of individual applications or the numbers of applications received; grades/points offered may be adjusted downwards after A-level results. The level of an offer is not indicative of the quality of a course.

20 pts.	**Reading** - BCC/BB (Land Man)
	Sheffield - BCC-CCC (LD/P Sci)
18 pts.	**Heriot-Watt** - CCC (Land Arch) (BTEC Ms)
16 pts.	**Manchester Met** - CCD/BC (Lands Des) (BTEC 3M)
14 pts.	**Kingston** - 14 pts (Land Arch)
12 pts.	**Cheltenham & Glos (CHE)** - 12 pts (geog/art/biol) (Modular)
	Greenwich - 12 pts (Land Arch) (BTEC 5M)
10 pts.	**Leeds Met** - CD (Land Arch)

For these courses a portfolio of art work must be presented at interview.

Alternative offers:

IB offers: **Greenwich** 24 pts inc 12 pts Highers.

Irish offer: **Heriot-Watt** ABBCC.

SCE offers: **Greenwich** BBB; **Heriot-Watt** ABBB + interview; **Sheffield** BBBB.

Overseas applicants: Cheltenham & Glos (CHE) Fluency in English required. **Manchester Met** Some interviews held in Malaysia. English courses availble.

CHOOSING YOUR COURSE (See also Ch 1)

> **Subject information:** A relatively recent specialised branch of architecture in which an ability in art and design is sought. It focuses on the design of the environment surrounding buildings. (It should not be confused with the work of a garden centre.)

Course highlights: Greenwich Credit/semester/unit system. Entry with advanced standing for applicants with experience. **Heriot-Watt** Course covers design, rural land use, ecology and construction. **Manchester Met** Strong environmental bias. Close ties with local professionals. **Sheffield** Science, ecology and environmental design leading to professional qualification as landscape architect. NOW CHECK PROSPECTUSES FOR ALL COURSES.

Study opportunities abroad: Greenwich (E) G B NL FR P.

Work opportunities abroad: Heriot-Watt.

ADMISSIONS INFORMATION

Number of applicants per place (approx): Cheltenham & Glos (CHE) 5; **Greenwich** 10; **Heriot-Watt** 9; **Leeds Met** 9; **Manchester Met** 9.

General Studies acceptable: Cheltenham & Glos (CHE); Greenwich; Manchester Met.

Selection interviews: Cheltenham & Glos (CHE); Heriot-Watt; Leeds Met; Manchester Met.

Offers to applicants repeating A-levels: Possibly higher Manchester Met; **Same** Greenwich, Heriot-Watt, Leeds Met.

Admissions Tutors' advice: Greenwich Students should be proficient in freehand drawing and written English, and well informed about landscape architecture. **Leeds Met** Interest, initiative, motivation for the work and a good portfolio are important. Lower offers to good applicants.

Examples of interview questions: Discuss your favourite example of landscaping. What is the role of the landscape architect in society? Have you read any books on the subject? Have you visited any historical landscape sites? Questions will follow on this answer. Are there any good examples of landscaping in your area? What contribution did Capability Brown make to landscaping?

GAP YEAR ADVICE

Institutions accepting a Gap Year: Most institutions; **Greenwich** Travel, sketch, but preferably in a landscape architect's office or similar.

Institutions willing to defer entry after A-levels (see Ch 5): Cheltenham & Glos (CHE); Greenwich; Heriot-Watt; Kingston.

AFTER A-LEVELS ADVICE

Institutions which may accept the same points score after A-levels: Greenwich; Heriot-Watt; Leeds Met; Manchester Met.

Institutions which may accept under-achieving applicants after A-levels: Manchester Met.

Institutions with vacancies in Aug/Sept 1992 (see Ch 5): Kingston 12 pts; Six institutions declared vacancies in this subject.

ADVICE FOR MATURE STUDENTS

Formal qualifications may not be required for these courses but design potential is usually important. A portfolio of art work would be very advantageous.

LANGUAGE

Special subject requirements: variable; some courses require a modern language at A-level.

NB Institutions may raise or lower the level of published offers depending either on the quality or otherwise of individual applications or the numbers of applications received; grades/points offered may be adjusted downwards after A-level results. The level of an offer is not indicative of the quality of a course.

24 pts.	**Heriot-Watt** - BBB/BB (Langs Int/Trans: Fr Ger Russ Sp)
22 pts.	**Hull** - BBC (Comb Lang)
20 pts.	**Essex** - BCC/BB (LSC; LTE)
	Lancaster - BCC (Educ/MEL)
	UMIST - BCC-CCC/AB-BB (All Comp Ling courses)
	York - BCC/BB (Lang/Ling)
18 pts.	**Manchester Met** - 18-14 pts (Comb St)
16 pts.	**Bedford (CHE)** - 16-14 pts (Modular)
14 pts.	**Oxford Brookes** - CDD (French)/CC (German) (Lang Bus)
	Ulster - 14 pts (App Lang)
12 pts.	**Ripon & York St John (CHE)** - 12 pts (Modular)

	Wolverhampton - CC (Lang Bus)
10pts.	**Anglia (Poly Univ)** - CD (Languages)
	Guildhall London - CD (Lang)
	Plymouth - 10 pts (Lang)
	Thames Valley London - CD (App Lang courses; App Lang Euro courses)
4pts.	**Brighton** - (Ap Lang)
	Cheltenham & Glos (CHE) - EE (Mod Lang)

Diploma of Higher Education courses:
12pts.   **Wolverhampton** - 12 pts (Soc Cult)

Alternative offers:

IB offers: **Brighton** 24 pts inc 12 pts Highers; **Essex** 32 pts inc 10 pts Highers; **Heriot-Watt** 34 pts; **Hull** 30 pts; **Lancaster** 30 pts; **Manchester Met** 30-26 pts; **York** H665.

SCE offers: **Heriot-Watt** AABB (AA in languages to be studied); **Lancaster** BBBBB.

CHOOSING YOUR COURSE (See also Ch 1)

> **Subject information:** Refer to individual language subject tables.

Course highlights: Essex The course in language and linguistics has 50% language, 50% linguistics and one year abroad. **Heriot-Watt** Unique course; work placements in translating companies, commerce and journalism. **Lancaster** Courses involve language studies and educational methods. **Thames Valley London** Course runs jointly with institutions in France, Germany and Spain. **York** Focuses on use of language – phonetics, computer synthesis of speech, structure and history of seven languages. Choice of up to three languages including Chinese, Swedish, Hindi and Swahili. NOW CHECK PROSPECTUSES FOR ALL COURSES.

Study opportunities abroad: Anglia (Poly Univ) (E); **Heriot-Watt** (E); **Wolverhampton** (E).

Work opportunities abroad: Heriot-Watt; York CH G FR IN USA AF WI.

ADMISSIONS INFORMATION

Number of applicants per place (approx): Anglia (Poly Univ) 5; **Brighton** 5; **Thames Valley London** 5; **UMIST** 8; **Wolverhampton** 4; **York** 8.

General Studies acceptable: Brighton; Essex; Lancaster; Thames Valley London; Wolverhampton (2); York.

Selection interviews: Brighton; Essex; Thames Valley London (T); UMIST; York (some).

Offers to applicants repeating A-levels: Higher Essex; **Same** Brighton, York.

Admissions Tutors' advice: York Applicants complete questionnaire; offers are made to majority of applicants and followed by invitation to visit department. We welcome students who have taken a year out, and those with unorthodox qualifications and backgrounds. Course videos available to schools.

> **Examples of interview questions:** See under the various language subject tables.

GAP YEAR ADVICE

Institutions accepting a Gap Year: Most institutions; **Thames Valley London** Students recommended to spend part of year abroad.

Institutions willing to defer entry after A-levels (see Ch 5): Heriot-Watt; Plymouth; Thames Valley London; York (No).

AFTER A-LEVELS ADVICE

Institutions which may accept the same points score after A-levels: Brighton; Essex; York.

Institutions demanding the actual grades offered after A-levels: UMIST.

Institutions which may accept under-achieving applicants after A-levels: Essex; York.

Institutions with vacancies in Aug/Sept 1992 (see Ch 5): Essex 20 pts; Plymouth; Thames Valley London 8 pts.

GRADUATE EMPLOYMENT

New Graduates' destinations (percentages) 1991:
Permanent employment: U 70; P 59; C 90 (Comb Lang).
Unemployment: U 19; P 19; C 9 (Comb Lang).
Further studies (all types): U 36; P 15; C 42 (Comb Lang).

LATIN (See also Classics)

Special subject requirements: A-level in Latin.

NB Institutions may raise or lower the level of published offers depending either on the quality or otherwise of individual applications or the numbers of applications received; grades/points offered may be adjusted downwards after A-level results. The level of an offer is not indicative of the quality of a course.

30 pts.	**Cambridge/Oxford** - AAA potential recommended (Classics)
24 pts.	**Durham** - ABC (Eng/Lat)
	Newcastle - 24-22 pts/10 pts (Latin)
22 pts.	**Durham** - BBC (Lat/Mus)
	Edinburgh - BBC (Lat St)
	Glasgow - BBC (Latin)
	Keele - BBC-CCD/BB-CD (Latin Joint courses) (4 AS)
	St Andrews - BBC (Latin) (4 AS)
20 pts.	**Birmingham** - BCC-CCC/BC (Latin)
	Durham - BCC (Latin; Anc H/Lat)
	Exeter - BCC-BDD (Latin)
	Kent - BCC-CCC/BB-BC (Latin and Combined courses)
	Leeds - BCC (Latin and joint courses)
	London (RH) - BCC/BC (Latin)
	Manchester - 20 pts approx (Latin)
	Nottingham - BCC-CCD (All Latin courses)
	Reading - BCC (Latin)
18 pts.	**Belfast** - CCC/BB (Latin and Combined courses)
	London (King's) - 18 pts approx (Latin)
	London (RH) - CCC/CC (All Latin courses except **20 pts**)
	Swansea - CCC-BCD/BC (Latin)
	Warwick - BCD (Eng Lat)

16 pts. **St David's** - CCD/BC (All Latin courses)
12 pts. **London (UC)** - CC (All Latin courses)
         Reading - CC (Latin/Germ; Latin/Ital)

Alternative offers:

EB offers: **Keele** 60%.

IB offers: **Bristol** H665/655; **Exeter** 30 pts; **Kent** 25 pts, H 11 pts; **St Andrews** 30 pts.

Irish offers: **Keele** BBBCC.

SCE offers: **Edinburgh** BBBB; **Glasgow** BBBB; **Kent** ABBBB; **Newcastle** BBB; **St Andrews** BBBB.

CHOOSING YOUR COURSE (See also Ch 1)

Subject information: This is a study of the language, art, religion and history of the Roman world. This table should be read in conjunction with the **Classical Studies** and **Classics** tables.

Course highlights: Belfast The study of Latin is not restricted to the ancient world but extends into the history of Latin in medieval and Renaissance periods. **Birmingham** Funded study tour in second year vacation. **St Andrews** See under **Arts**. NOW CHECK PROSPECTUSES FOR ALL COURSES.

Study opportunities abroad: Birmingham (E).

ADMISSIONS INFORMATION

Number of applicants per place (approx): Birmingham 3.

General Studies acceptable: Birmingham; Exeter (2).

Selection interviews: Birmingham; Cambridge; Durham; Exeter; Hull; Leeds; London (RH); Newcastle; Nottingham; Oxford; Reading; Swansea (some).

Offers to applicants repeating A-levels: Higher Durham; **Same** Leeds, Newcastle, Swansea.

Admissions Tutors' advice: Durham Students interested in studying Latin are invited to come and discuss the course with us and see something of the University. For this degree course we welcome all applicants regardless of the type of school they have attended.

Examples of interview questions: (See also under **Classics**) Applicants offering A-level Latin will be questioned on their course and usually will be asked what aspects of it they enjoy.

GAP YEAR ADVICE

Institutions accepting a Gap Year: Most institutions; **London (RH)** We send a reading list and request that intending students attend a summer school.

Institutions willing to defer entry after A-levels (see Ch 5): Leeds; Newcastle; St Andrews; Swansea.

AFTER A-LEVELS ADVICE

Institutions which may accept the same points score after A-levels: Birmingham; Durham; Leeds; London (RH); Swansea.

Institutions demanding the actual grades offered after A-levels: Kent; Newcastle (some flexibility).

Institutions which may accept under-achieving applicants after A-levels: Birmingham; Kent; Leeds; London (RH); Swansea.

Institutions with vacancies in Aug/Sept 1992 (see Ch 5): Leeds 18 pts; Swansea.

LATIN AMERICAN STUDIES

Special subject requirements: A-level in Spanish.

NB Institutions may raise or lower the level of published offers depending either on the quality or otherwise of individual applications or the numbers of applications received; grades/points offered may be adjusted downwards after A-level results. The level of an offer is not indicative of the quality of a course.

24 pts.	**Newcastle** - BBB/BB (Lat Amer)
20 pts.	**Aberdeen** - BCC (Hisp LA)
	Essex - BCC/BB (Lat)
	Glasgow - BCC (Hisp St)
	Leeds - BCC (Iber/Am St)
18 pts.	**Birmingham** - CCC (Hisp St)
	Liverpool - CCC/BC-CC (Lat Am St)
	Southampton - BCD-CCC (All courses)
12 pts.	**London (UC)** - CC (MILARS)
	Portsmouth - 12-10 pts (Lat Am St) (See **Admissions Tutors' advice**)

NB: At **Liverpool** offers normally require at least grade C in Latin; for other subjects taken at A-level similar grades may be required.

Alternative offers:

IB offers: **Aberdeen** 30 pts; **Essex** 28 pts inc 10 pts 2 Highers; **Portsmouth** 25 pts.

SCE offers: **Aberdeen** BBBB; **Essex** BBBB; **Glasgow** ABBB; **Newcastle** BBB.

CHOOSING YOUR COURSE (See also Ch 1)

> **Subject information:** On these courses there will be an emphasis on the study of Spanish alongside that of Latin American republics covering both historically and including present-day conditions and problems. Normally a year is spent in Latin America.

Course highlights: Portsmouth Course options can lead to humanities or social science or to spending year 2 in Latin America or to starting Spanish *ab initio* or adding Portuguese from year 3. NOW CHECK PROSPECTUSES FOR ALL COURSES.

ADMISSIONS INFORMATION

Number of applicants per place (approx): Essex 3; **Liverpool** 3; **Newcastle** 4; **Portsmouth** 5.

Study opportunities abroad: Newcastle SP; **Portsmouth** (E) P SP.

General Studies acceptable: Aberdeen; Essex.

Offers to applicants repeating A-levels: Higher Essex; **Same** Newcastle, Portsmouth.

Admissions Tutors' advice: Portsmouth Each applicant considered individually in context of academic profile and related work/travel experience. Offers approximate. Some A-levels are better predictors of performance than others: those for languages notoriously unreliable.

> **Examples of interview questions:** Why are you interested in studying this subject? What countries related to the degree course have you visited? What career are you planning when you have finished your degree? Applicants taking Spanish will be asked questions on their A-level syllabus and should also be familiar with some Spanish newspapers and magazines.

GAP YEAR ADVICE

Institutions accepting a Gap Year: Most institutions.

AFTER A-LEVELS ADVICE

Institutions which may accept the same points score after A-levels: Essex; Portsmouth.

Institutions with vacancies in Aug/Sept 1992 (see Ch 5): Essex 18 pts.

GRADUATE EMPLOYMENT

New Graduates' destinations (percentages) 1991:
Permanent employment: U 82.
Unemployment: P 12.
Further studies (all types): P 39.

LAW

Special subject requirements: English A-level and mathematics GCSE (grade A-C) very occasionally required.

NB Institutions may raise or lower the level of published offers depending either on the quality or otherwise of individual applications or the numbers of applications received; grades/points offered may be adjusted downwards after A-level results. The level of an offer is not indicative of the quality of a course.

30 pts.	**Cambridge/Oxford** - AAA potential recommended (Law)
28 pts.	**London (King's)** - AAB approx (Law courses)
	Warwick - AAB (Fr + ICP)/ABB (German) (Euro Law)
26 pts.	**Belfast** - ABB (Law; Law/Acctg)
	Birmingham - ABB (Law; Law Euro) (BTEC 5D+2M)
	Bristol - ABB (Law; Law/Fr; Law/Pol; Law/Bus St; Law/Ger)(BTEC 4D)
	Cardiff - ABB/AA (Law/French)
	Durham - ABB (All courses) (4 AS)
	Edinburgh - ABB (Law) (Ref BBC) (6 AS)
	Exeter - ABB/AA (Law; Law Eur; Law/Soc) (6-4 AS) (BTEC Ds+Ms)
	Glasgow - ABB (Law)
	Keele - ABB-BBC/AB-BB (All courses)
	Kent - ABB (Law)
	Kent - ABB-BBB (Eng (Fr/Ger/Sp) Law; Eur/Legal)
	Lancaster - ABB-BBC/AB (BB-CC mature students) (Law; ELS)(BTEC 4D)
	Leeds - ABB (Law)
	Leicester - ABB (Law/French)
	London (UC) - ABB (Law/Fr/Ger/Ital Law)

        Manchester - 26 pts approx (Law)
        Newcastle - ABB (Law) (BTEC Ds or Ms)
        Nottingham - ABB (Law)
        Reading - ABB (Law/Fr Law)
        Sheffield - ABB-BBB (Law)
        Warwick - ABB (Law) (Any AS except tech des/gen stds)

24 pts.   **Aberdeen** - BBB (Law)
        Aberystwyth - BBB-BBC/AB (Law; Law/Bus) (BTEC 4D+2M)
        Birmingham - BBB (Law/Soc)
        Brunel - BBB (Law; Bus Law) (BTEC 3D+Ms)
        Cardiff - BBB/AA (Law; Law/Jap; Law/Ital; Law/Germ)
        City - BBB (Bus Law)
        Dundee - BBB (Law)
        East Anglia - BBB (Law/German; Law/French; Law/Eur; Law) (BTEC 4D+1M)
        Essex - BBB (All Law courses)
        Hull - BBB (Law)
        Leeds - BBB (Law/Chinese; Law/Jap)
        Leicester - BBB (Law)
        Liverpool - BBB (Law)
        London (LSE) - 24 pts approx (Law; Engl/Fr Law; Engl/Ger Law)
        London (QMW) - BBB-BBC approx (Law)
        London (UC) - BBB (Law)
        Nottingham - BBB (Law/Pol)
        Oxford Brookes - BBB (Law - single field modular) (4 AS)
        Reading - ABC (Law)
        Southampton - BBB (Law)
        Strathclyde - BBB (Law)
        Sussex - BBB/AB (All Law courses)
        Warwick - BBB (Law Soc)

22 pts.   **Aberdeen** - BBC (Juris - MA)
        Bristol UWE - BBC (Eur Law/Lang)
        Cardiff - BBC/BB (Law/Pol; Law/Soc)
        Hull - BBC (Law/Soc; Law/Pol; Law/Phil)
        London (SOAS) - BBC (All courses)
        Northumbria - BBC/BB (Law)
        Oxford Brookes - BBC (Law - double field modular) (4 AS)
        Swansea - BBC/BB (Law) (BTEC Ds preferred)

20 pts.   **Bristol UWE** - 20 pts (Law)
        De Montfort - BCC/BB-CC (Law) (BTEC 4D)
        Glamorgan - 20 pts at one sitting; not gen studs (Law) (BTEC 5D+Ms)
        Greenwich - 20 pts (Law)
        Hertfordshire - BCC/BB (Law) (BTEC Ds+Ms)
        Kingston - BCC/AA (Law) (4 AS) (BTEC 6D)
        Liverpool John Moores - BCC/BB (Law) (6 AS) (BTEC 3D+2M)
        Sheffield Hallam - 20 pts from 3 A-levels (Law courses)
        Stirling - BCC/BB-BC (Bus Law; Bus Law/Econ)
        Thames Valley London - BCC-CCC (Law/Lang; Eur Law) (BTEC 3D+Ms)
        Wolverhampton - BCC/BB (Law)

18 pts.   **Anglia (Poly Univ)** - CCC/BC (Law)
        Bournemouth - 18 pts (Bus Law) (6 AS)
        Buckingham - CCC-DDD/BB-CC (Law; L/B/Env)
        Central England - CCC/BB-BC (Law)
        Central Lancashire - CCC/CC (Law) (4 AS)
        Coventry - CCC/BC (Bus Law) (4 AS)
        Guildhall London - CCC/BC (Bus Law) (BTEC 2/3D+Ms)
        Huddersfield - 18-14 pts (Bus Law) (4 AS)
        Humberside - 18-14 pts (Law/Bus)
        Leeds Met - CCC (Law)
        Luton (CHE) - 18 pts (Law) (4 AS)

Manchester Met - CCC (All Law courses) (BTEC No)
Middlesex - CCC/BB (Law) (BTEC M overall)
North London - CCC/BB (Law)
Nottingham Trent - CCC (Law)
Plymouth - 18 pts (Law) (6 AS)
South Bank - CCC (Law)
Teesside - CCC/BB (Law)
Thames Valley London - CCC/BC (Law; Crim; Bus Law - sandwich course)

16 pts. Anglia (Poly Univ) - BCE minimum/BC (Law Comb) (4 AS)
Central Lancashire - CCD (Comb Hons)
East London - 16-14 pts (Law)
Guildhall London - CCD (Modular)
Middlesex - 16 pts (Modular)
Staffordshire - 16-14 pts (Law)

14 pts. Buckingham - 14 pts (Law/Biol)
Southampton (IHE) - 14 pts approx (LLB)
Swansea (IHE) - BC (Law)
Teesside - 14 pts (Criminology)
Westminster - BC (average) (Law)

12 pts. Buckingham - DDD/CC (Eng/EL/Langs)
Guildhall London - CC (Law/Acc)
Holborn (Coll) - CC-EE (Law - LLB London) (4 AS)
Manchester Met - 12 pts (Con Pro)

10 pts. **and below**
Central England - (Police Studies - contact Admissions Tutor)
De Montfort - (Comb St)
Derby - (Modular) (4 AS)
Liverpool John Moores - (Crim Just)
Robert Gordon - DDE/CD (Legal/Admin St)
Nene (CHE) - (Comb St)
Nottingham Trent - Access (Law - part-time)
Wolverhampton - (Comb Studs (LA) - part-time course for mature students)

Diploma of Higher Education courses:
4 pts. **and below** East London; Guildhall London.

Higher National Diploma courses (England and Wales):
8 pts. **and below** Farnborough (CT).

Higher Diploma courses (Scotland):
8 pts. **and below or equivalent** Aberdeen (CC); Dundee (CC); Glasgow Caledonian; Napier EE.

Alternative offers:

EB offers: **East Anglia** 70%; **Edinburgh** 80%; **Glamorgan** 75%; **Keele** 70%; **Lancaster** 75%; **Leeds** 70%.

IB offers: **Aberdeen** 34 pts; **Aberystwyth** 32 pts; **Anglia (Poly Univ)** 28 pts; **Belfast** H666 S555; **Birmingham** 33 pts over 5 subjs inc grade 7 in English; **Bournemouth** (Bus Law) 26 pts; **Bristol** 34 pts H665; **Brsitol UWE** 26 pts; **Brunel** 32 pts inc H66; **Buckingham** 26 pts; **Cardiff** 31-30 pts; **Dundee** 31 pts; **Durham** H7 average; **East Anglia** 30 pts; **Essex** 30 pts inc 11 pts 2 Highers; **Exeter** 33 pts; **Guildhall London** 24 pts; **Hull** 33-31 pts, 18 at Highers; **Kent** 31 pts, H 13 pts; **Lancaster** 32 pts; **Leeds** 30 pts; **Leicester** 30 pts inc H66; **London (QMW)** H655, **(UC)** H666 S555 (Eng/Germ Law); **Manchester Met** 30 pts approx; **Middlesex** 30 pts; **Newcastle** 32 pts; **Reading** 30 pts; **Robert Gordon** (Legal/Admin St) 22 pts; **Southampton** 30 pts overall inc H55.

Irish offers: **Aberdeen** ABBB; **Aberystwyth** BBBBCC; **Bristol UWE** CCCC; **Brunel** AABBB; **East Anglia** CCCCC; **Edinburgh** AAAAB; **Guildhall London** CCCCC; **Holborn (Coll)** BBBCC; **Keele** BBBBCC; **Leeds** BBBBBCC; **Middlesex** BBBCC.

SCE offers: **Aberdeen** AAAB, BBBB (MA); **Birmingham** AAAAB/AAABB; **Bristol** AAABB; **Bristol UWE** AAB; **Cardiff** AABB/BBBB; **De Montfort** BBBB; **Dundee** ABBBB; **East London** BBBB; **Edinburgh** AAABB; **Glamorgan** CCCCC; **Glasgow** AAAAB, AAABBB at 2 sittings; **Guildhall London** CCCCC; **Holborn (Coll)** BBBBB; **Keele** BBBC; **Lancaster** AABBB; **Liverpool** AAABB; **Middlesex** BBBB; **Newcastle** ABBBB; **Nottingham** AAABB; **Nottingham Trent** BBBB; **Sheffield** AABBB; **Southampton** BBBBB; **Strathclyde** AAABB.

Overseas applicants: Bournemouth Good command of English required. **Brunel** Intermediate London external LLB may enable direct entry to year 2. **Glamorgan** Fluency in English required. **Holborn College** Help given in English and essay writing. **Hull** Living costs 30% lower than in London. **Leeds** Some scholarships available. **Manchester Met** Stay in touch with us by fax. **Middlesex** No foundation course. **Newcastle** Intensive pre-sessional English course.

CHOOSING YOUR COURSE (See also Ch 1)

> **Subject information:** Law courses are usually divided into two parts. Part 1 occupyies year 1 and introduces the student to criminal and constitutional law and the legal process. Thereafter many different specialised topics can be studied in years 2 and 3. The course content is very similar for most courses.

Course highlights: Aberdeen The course in private law involves the legal relationship between the private individual and domestic/commercial employment. **Aberystwyth** Outstanding library facilities. Particular research strengths in criminal law, criminal justice and environmental issues. **Belfast** This is now a 3-year course. **Birmingham** Good range of year 3 options. Emphasis on constant monitoring of academic progress. Affiliated to specialist institutes eg, Judicial Administration and European Law. **Bristol UWE** (Euro Law/Lang) Majority of staff are native speakers of the European languages offered. One of the very few courses in which you can get the CPE (Common Professional Exam) exemption and study two languages. **Bristol** Year 3 options include politics, accounting and economics. **Brunel** Broad study of law in a social science context; placements in industry, commerce and the professions; recognized by Law Society. Strength in commercial law and criminal justice. The only thin sandwich Law course in UK. Outstanding record of graduate employment placements. **Buckingham** A two-year course. **Cardiff** 33 options in years 2 and 3. Students taking straight Law also cover foreign legal systems (France, Italy, Germany, Japan). (Law/Languages) Extended provision for language training. **Central England** All students experience classical (practical) legal education. Option available to represent and advise clients. **Central Lancashire** Mini-placement scheme with all aspects of the legal profession. **City** (Bus Law) Graduates obtain same qualifications as those taking law courses but acquire business knowledge. **Glamorgan** Innovative teaching strategy, strong links with legal profession in South Wales; some sponsorships. Formal examinations and assessed coursework. **Holborn College** London University (External) degree: full-time course with very highly structured teaching system. College publishes its own teaching material. Also Law courses via **Wolverhampton**. **London (QMW)** Good contacts with City solicitors and the commercial bar. **Manchester Met** (Con Pro) Exemption from trading standards officers' qualification. **Newcastle** Wide range of options and half options in years 2 and 3 and dissertation option in year 3. **Robert Gordon** (Legal/ Admin St) This is a new and unique course in Scotland for para-legals. **Sheffield Hallam** Legal skills elements incorporated into both the BA and LLB degrees, with third year sandwich placements (only one of three sandwich degree courses in the UK). Languages offered. **Wolverhampton** One of the widest range of options available on a degree course including languages. Training in use of information systems. High research ratings for **Bristol, Cambridge, Oxford, London (King's), (LSE), (QMW), (UC), Leicester, Manchester, Nottingham, Sheffield, Southampton, Warwick.** NOW CHECK PROSPECTUSES FOR ALL COURSES.

Study opportunities abroad: Aberystwyth (E); **Bristol** (E); **Cardiff** (E); **East Anglia** (E); **Edinburgh** (E) F G NL SP USA; **Glamorgan** (E) FR IT G NL; **Lancaster** EUR; **Leeds** (E); **Leicester**

(E); **Sheffield** (E); **South Bank** USA; **Thames Valley London** (E); **Wolverhampton** (E); **York** (E).

Work opportunities abroad: Brunel EUR; **Cardiff** FR G IT SP P JAP; **Exeter** (Law/Eur) FR G; **Leeds** FR SP B NL G; **Wolverhampton** FR.

ADMISSIONS INFORMATION

Number of applicants per place (approx): Aberystwyth 10; **Anglia (Poly Univ)** 10; **Birmingham** 15; **Bournemouth** (Bus Law) 8; **Bristol** 19; **Bristol UWE** 27; **Brunel** 18; **Buckingham** 12; **Cardiff** (Law) 28, (Law/Fr) 8, (Law/Jap) 10, (Law/Ital) 7, (Law/Ger) 10; **Central England** 31; **Central Lancashire** 12; **City** 9; **Coventry** 21; **De Montfort** 25; **Dundee** 8; **Durham** 14; **East Anglia** 25; **East London** 13; **Edinburgh** 5; **Essex** 26; **Exeter** 15; **Glamorgan** 11; **Glasgow** 8; **Guildhall London** 13; **Holborn (Coll)** no quotas; **Huddersfield** 11; **Hull** 22; **Kent** 31; **Kingston** 25; **Lancaster** 26; **Leeds** 35; **Leeds Met** 42; **Leicester** 18; **Liverpool** 10; **Liverpool John Moores** 27; **London (QMW)** 17; **Manchester Met** 28; **Middlesex** 25, (Law/Soc) 17; **Newcastle** 27; **North London** 27; **Northumbria** 22; **Nottingham** 25 (Law/Pol) 22; **Nottingham Trent** 60; **Oxford Brookes** 58; **Sheffield** 16; **South Bank** 22; **Staffordshire** 15; **Strathclyde** 12; **Teesside** 5; **Thames Valley London** 18; **Westminster** 29; **Wolverhampton** 12.

General Studies acceptable: Aberdeen; Aberystwyth; Bournemouth (2); Bristol UWE; Coventry; Essex; Greenwich; Hertfordshire (2 if first subject is a 'heavy' academic study); Huddersfield; Hull; Kingston (No); Lancaster; Leeds; Leeds Met; Leicester; Manchester Met (No); North London; Oxford Brookes; Sheffield; Thames Valley London (Crim); Wolverhampton.

Selection interviews: Aberystwyth (some); Anglia (Poly Univ) (some); Belfast (some); Birmingham (some); Bristol (very few); Bristol UWE (some); Brunel (some); Cambridge; Central Lancashire; Coventry (some); Durham; East Anglia (very occasionally); Essex (some); Glasgow (some); Guildhall London (some); Holborn (Coll); Huddersfield (T); Kingston (some); Lancaster; Leeds; Leicester; Liverpool (some); Liverpool John Moores (some); Newcastle; Northumbria; Nottingham (T); Oxford Brookes (all mature applicants and some others); Sheffield; Warwick (occasionally).

Offers to applicants repeating A-levels: Higher Aberystwyth, Belfast, Birmingham (ABB/AAB), Bristol UWE, Coventry, De Montfort, Essex, Glamorgan, Glasgow, Guildhall London, Hull, Leeds (BBB), Leeds Met, Liverpool (unlikely), Manchester Met, Newcastle, North London, Nottingham, Oxford Brookes, Sheffield, Staffordshire, Strathclyde; **Possibly higher** Anglia (Poly Univ), Cardiff, Durham; **Same** Bristol, Brunel, Holborn (Coll), Huddersfield, Kingston, Liverpool John Moores, Northumbria, Wolverhampton.

Admissions Tutors' advice: Aberystwyth We expect to make some offers at BCC for candidates with particularly good GCSEs. **Durham** In an average year we will have between 500-600 applications from candidates with grades or predictions of ABC or better. **Holborn (College)** Since we accept applicants to study for the LLB (External) degree of the University of London, students are required to fulfil the University's registration requirements. We can accept students who meet these requirements, ie 2 A-level passes and 3 subjects at GCSE (grade A-C). **Lancaster** A-level repeaters not normally considered. **Sheffield** As and Bs at GCSE are preferred in a good range of subjects. **Newcastle** No offers made without interview.

Examples of interview questions: What interests you in the study of Law? What would you do to overcome the problem of prison overcrowding if you were (a) a judge (b) a prosecutor (c) the prime minister? What legal cases have you recently read about? What are your opinions of the 'closed shop'? What is jurisprudence? Should religion be involved in politics? What are the causes of violence in society? A friend bought a bun which unknown to him contained a rock. He gave it to you to eat and you broke a tooth. Could you sue anyone? A motor cyclist is going down a one-way street the wrong way and a chimney falls on him. What legal proceedings should take place? Have you visited any law courts? What cases did you see? A person arrives in England unable to speak the language. He lights a cigarette in a non-smoking compartment of a train? Can he be charged and convicted? Questions on current affairs and current legal cases. What should be done in the case of an elderly person who steals a bar of soap? What in your opinion would be the two basic laws in Utopia? How can we incorporate different ethnic backgrounds into the English culture? Should people of different backgrounds adopt the English culture? Describe without using your hands how you would do the butterfly stroke. What would happen if there were no law?

GAP YEAR ADVICE

Institutions accepting a Gap Year: Most institutions; **Cardiff** Get work experience. **Glamorgan** Initial application must make this clear. **Manchester Met** No. **Thames valley London** Not acceptable. **Wolverhampton** We favour a year out. Try to obtain work experience also work abroad.

Institutions willing to defer entry after A-levels (see Ch 5): Aberystwyth; Bournemouth; Brunel (only with a good reason); City; Dundee; East Anglia; Glamorgan; Hull; Humberside; Lancaster (No); Manchester Met (Con Pro); Plymouth; Robert Gordon; South Bank (Prefer not); Swansea (IHE); Thames Valley London.

AFTER A-LEVELS ADVICE

Institutions which may accept the same points score after A-levels: Aberystwyth; Anglia (Poly Univ); Belfast; Birmingham; Bristol UWE (perhaps); Brunel; Cardiff; Central England; Coventry; East Anglia; East London; Essex; Glamorgan; Glasgow; Guildhall London; Holborn (Coll); Hull; Lancaster; Leeds; Leeds Met; Liverpool; Liverpool John Moores; Luton (CHE); Middlesex; Newcastle; Nottingham Trent; Oxford Brookes; Sheffield Hallam; South Bank; Staffordshire; Strathclyde; Teesside; Thames Valley London.

Institutions demanding the actual grades offered after A-levels: Durham; Kent; North London; Nottingham; Sheffield; Southampton; Warwick.

Institutions which may accept under-achieving applicants after A-levels: Aberdeen; Aberystwyth (perhaps); Anglia (Poly Univ); Bristol UWE (perhaps); Brunel; Buckingham; Cardiff (perhaps); Central Lancashire; Coventry; Dundee; Essex; Exeter; Holborn (Coll); Huddersfield; Hull (overseas applicants 18 pts); Lancaster; Leeds; Liverpool; Luton (CHE); Sheffield Hallam; South Bank; Staffordshire; Teesside; Thames Valley London.

Institutions with vacancies in Aug/Sept 1992 (see Ch 5): Buckingham 18–10 pts; Brunel 24 pts; City 22 pts; Dundee 22 pts; Newcastle 24 pts; Robert Gordon; Sheffield Hallam 18 pts; South Bank 16 pts; Swansea (IHE) 14 pts; Thames Valley London 16 pts, (Euro Law, German and Spanish Law with Lang) 14 pts. Thirty-three institutions declared vacancies, the highest scores required ranging from 24-22 pts.

ADVICE FOR MATURE STUDENTS

A-levels are required for most courses. Distance-learning courses are offered by **Holborn College**.

GRADUATE EMPLOYMENT

New Graduates' destinations (percentages) 1991:
Permanent employment: U 76; P 49.
Unemployment: U 16; P 33.
Further studies (all types): U 77; P 75.
Main career destinations (approx): Legal 33; Finance 27; Admin/Managerial 12; Social/Welfare 7; Business 9; Secretarial 8.

Anglia (Poly Univ) Nine students entered full-time employment. These included four who entered law practices, one went into accountancy, one into insurance and one became a trainee manager with a bookshop chain. A large number of graduates went on to Law Society Part II examinations at Colleges of Law, nine proceeded to Bar finals and six went on to take Master's degrees.

The following institutions are perceived as being above average in producing graduates for employment: Birmingham, Bristol, Cambridge, Durham, Exeter, London (individual colleges not listed in the research project), Manchester, Nottingham, Oxford, Southampton. (See PIP reference in Chapter 5.)

Graduate employment prospects during the period of recession in 1992 proved excellent.

LEISURE and RECREATIONAL STUDIES

Special subject requirements: GCSE (grade A-C) mathematics.

NB Institutions may raise or lower the level of published offers depending either on the quality or otherwise of individual applications or the numbers of applications received; grades/points offered may be adjusted downwards after A-level results. The level of an offer is not indicative of the quality of a course.

22 pts.	**Loughborough** - 22-20 pts (PE/Rec Man) (BTEC mainly Ds)
	Manchester - 22 pts approx (Leis Man)
18 pts.	**Canterbury Christ Church (CHE)** - CCC-EEE (TRLS)
16 pts.	**Bedford (CHE)** - 16-14 pts (Modular)
	Bournemouth - 16-14 pts (Leis Mark)
	West London (IHE) - 16 pts (Leis Man)
14 pts.	**Leeds Met** - 14 pts (Leisure St)
	North London - 14 pts (Leis/Tour)
	Sheffield Hallam - 14 pts (Rec Man; Rec/Tour Man) (BTEC 1D+4M)
12 pts.	**Brighton** - CC (Leis/Pol)
	Cheltenham & Glos (CHE) - 12 pts (Leis Mgt/Rec St) (BTEC 3D or 4M)
	North Cheshire (CHE) - 12-10 pts (LRBM)
	Salford (UC) - (Leisure Man - Contact Admissions Tutor)
	Thames Valley London - DDD/CC (Leis) (4 AS)
10 pts.	**Bolton (IHE)** - CD (Comb St)
8 pts.	**and below**
	Bradford & Ilkley (CmC) - (Comm St)
	Coventry - 8 pts (Rec Country; Comb Sci)
	Heriot-Watt/Moray House - (Rec) (See **Admissions Tutors' advice**)
	St Mark & St John (CHE) - DD (Recreation and Community)
	Trinity & All Saints (CHE) - (Coll Hons)

Diploma in Higher Education:
Cheltenham & Glos (CHE).

Higher National Diploma courses (in Business Studies):
4 pts.   **and below** Birmingham (CFood); Buckinghamshire (CHE); Central Lancashire; Crewe & Alsager (CHE); Cumbria (CA) (Heritage Man); Farnborough (CT); Herefordshire (CT); Leeds Met; Loughborough (Coll); Newcastle (Coll); North London; Salford (UC); Southampton (IHE) (Water Leisure); Thames Valley London; West Herts (Coll).

Higher National Diploma courses (Scotland):
SAC (Au) (Leisure Man; Countryside/Rec/Conservation).

Alternative offers:

IB offers: **Loughborough** 30 pts; **Sheffield Hallam** 24 pts.

SCE offers: **Loughborough** BBBB.

CHOOSING YOUR COURSE (See also Ch 1)

Subject information: The courses cover various aspects of leisure and recreation. Specialist options include recreation management, tourism, countryside management, and the arts and other cultural pursuits.

Course highlights: Cheltenham & Glos (CHE) Long tradition of provision for sport and Physical Education at a national level. **Heriot-Watt/Moray House** Integration of arts, sport and countryside. **Leeds Met** The course focuses on the study of leisure. Options (a choice of two) include countryside recreation, urban recreation and the community, theraputic recreation, environmental education, tourism, play in contemporary society and sports and society. **Loughborough** Largest established department in any university. Excellent links with leisure industry and European links with a 'winter university'. Wide range of specialisations. **St Mark & St John (CHE)** Course combines social sciences with special skills and interests in sport or creative design. **Thames Valley London** Pan-European orientation of course. Flexible study programme with employers involved in organising and teaching. Students work on industrially sponsored projects and briefs; 50% of students are over 21. **West Herts (Coll)** (HND) Options in arts, entertainment, health and fitness, countryside management, European studies, foreign languages and playwork. NOW CHECK PROSPECTUSES FOR ALL COURSES.

Study opportunities abroad: Cheltenham & Glos (CHE) (E); **Leeds Met** (E); **Loughborough** (E); **St Mark & St John (CHE)** (E) USA P; **Thames Valley London** (E).

Work opportunities abroad: Thames Valley London FR IT SP G D SZ.

ADMISSIONS INFORMATION

Number of applicants per place (approx): Cheltenham & Glos (CHE) 5; **Heriot-Watt/Moray House** 4; **Leeds Met** 30; **Loughborough** 25; **North Cheshire (CHE)** 10; **St Mark & St John (CHE)** 8; **Sheffield Hallam** 12; **Thames Valley London** 5; **West London (IHE)** 16.

General Studies acceptable: Cheltenham & Glos (CHE); Leeds Met; Thames Valley London (JMB only) (2).

Admissions Tutors' advice: Heriot-Watt/Moray House Interview critical.

Examples of interview questions: Why are you interested in this subject? What indoor/outdoor activities are you involved in? Why are leisure activities important? How can recreational activities help old people? What is the difference between leisure and unemployment?

GAP YEAR ADVICE

Institutions accepting a Gap Year: Most institutions; **Loughborough** Use your time for general enrichment, travel etc, rather than spend it gaining relevant experience as, eg swimming pool attendant! **Thames Valley London** Try to work in leisure industry.

Institutions willing to defer entry after A-levels (see Ch 5): Brighton; Cheltenham & Glos (CHE); Heriot-Watt/Moray House; North Cheshire (CHE); Sheffield Hallam.

AFTER A-LEVELS ADVICE

Institutions with vacancies in Aug/Sept 1992 (see Ch 5): Cheltenham & Glos (CHE) 12 pts; North Cheshire (CHE); Sheffield Hallam 12 pts; Thames Valley London 10 pts. There was no shortage of vacancies on these courses.

LIBRARIANSHIP/LIBRARY STUDIES (including **Information Studies**)

Special subject requirements: GCSE (grade A-C) English and mathematics and a foreign language are sometimes required. A-levels specified dependent on the subject option.

NB Institutions may raise or lower the level of published offers depending either on the quality or otherwise of individual applications or the numbers of applications received; grades/points offered may be adjusted downwards after A-level results. The level of an offer is not indicative of the quality of a course.

20 pts.	**Aberystwyth** - BCC (Inf Acc/Fin)
18 pts.	**Aberystwyth** - 18 pts (Joint Hons + B or C in one subject)(BTEC Ms)
	Loughborough - CCC/BC (All Library Studies courses)
16 pts.	**Aberystwyth** - 16 pts (Single Hons) (BTEC 3M)
	Belfast - 16 pts (Inf Arts)
12 pts.	**Brighton** - CC/DD (Lib/Infor) (4 AS)
	Central England - 12 pts/CC minimum (Lib/Infor)
	Leeds Met - CC (varies) (Infor St)
	Manchester Met - CC (Lib/Infor)
	North London - CC (Inf/Comm)
	Queen Margaret (Coll) - 12 pts (Inf Man)
10 pts.	**Liverpool John Moores** - CD (Infor/Lib)
	Northumbria - 10 pts (Inf/Lib Mgt) (4 AS)
	Scottish (CText) - DDE/DD (Inf St)
	Thames Valley London - CD (IM/LIS)
8 pts.	**and below**
	Robert Gordon - DD (Lib/Inf St)

Diploma of Higher Education courses:

4 pts.	**Loughborough (CT)** - EE

Alternative offers:

IB offers: **Aberystwyth** 30-28 pts; **Brighton** 24 pts inc 12 pts Highers.

SCE offers: **Aberystwyth** BBBB; **Loughborough** BBBC; **Northumbria** BBC; **Robert Gordon** BBC.

Overseas applicants: Robert Gordon, Manchester Met Good command of written and spoken English required.

CHOOSING YOUR COURSE (See also Ch 1)

> **Subject information:** This subject covers the very wide field of information. Its organisation, retrieval, indexing, computer and media technology, classification and cataloguing are all included in these courses.

Course highlights: Aberystwyth BLib degree now changed to BA, BSc or BSc (Econ) depending on other half of Information and Library Studies degree. Extensive computer support for retrieval systems and word processing. Course decisions can be delayed until start of year 2. **Brighton** Course has large computing, media and communications element. **Central England** Four specialisms available: business information, information management, libraries in education, public libraries. **Loughborough** Options include the study of a foreign language and a minor subject from a wide range which includes music, geography, chemical engineering and human biology. **Manchester Met** Exams and continuous assessment, two periods fieldwork placement; information management skills in year 3. **Northumbria** Students follow own pathway (no compulsory subjects in year 3). Options in year 2: French, German,

Russian, Spanish *ab initio* . Strengths in information technology, work with young people and history of the book/archive. NOW CHECK PROSPECTUSES FOR ALL COURSES.

Study opportunities abroad: Northumbria (E).

ADMISSIONS INFORMATION

Number of applicants per place (approx): Aberystwyth 6; **Brighton** 8; **Central England** 6; **Liverpool John Moores** 4; **Loughborough** 7; **Manchester Met** 4; **Northumbria** 5; **North London** 4; **Robert Gordon** 3; **Thames Valley London** 3.

General Studies acceptable: Aberystwyth; Central England; Leeds Met; Liverpool John Moores; Manchester Met; Northumbria; Robert Gordon.

Selection interviews: Aberystwyth (some); Leeds Met; Liverpool John Moores; Loughborough; North London (very important, essay included); Northumbria; Robert Gordon; Thames Valley London.

Offers to applicants repeating A-levels: Higher Central England, Leeds Met; **Same** Liverpool John Moores, Loughborough, North London; Northumbria.

Admissions Tutors' advice: Brighton All applicants interviewed – we seek outgoing students with initiative. **Central England** We look for applicants who are slightly extrovert, alert and quick, a reasonable conversationalist, a good communicator prepared to think, with capacity to work. **Leeds Met** Good A-levels on their own are no guarantee of favourable consideration. Exact knowledge of the particular requirements of our uniquely structured programme and a favourable interview report is important.

> **Examples of interview questions:** What is it about librarianship which interests you? Why do you think you are suited to be a librarian? What does the job entail? What is the role of the library in school? What is the role of the public library? What new developments are taking place in libraries? Which TV programmes do you like and dislike? Which books do you read? How often do you use a library? What is the Dewey number for the history section in the library? *(Applicant studying A-level History)*

GAP YEAR ADVICE

Institutions accepting a Gap Year: Most institutions; **Aberystwyth** Seek relevant practical experience. **Manchester Met** Experience in library or information centre useful. **Northumbria** Experience in information or library environment or dealing with people in general. **Robert Gordon** No.

Institutions willing to defer entry after A-levels (see Ch 5): Aberystwyth (Preferred); Brighton; Robert Gordon; Thames Valley London.

AFTER A-LEVELS ADVICE

Institutions which may accept the same points score after A-levels: Aberystwyth; Brighton; Central England; Leeds Met; Liverpool John Moores; Loughborough; Manchester Met; North London; Northumbria; Robert Gordon; Thames Valley London.

Institutions which may accept under-achieving applicants after A-levels: Central England; Liverpool John Moores; Loughborough; Northumbria; Robert Gordon.

Institutions with vacancies in Aug/Sept 1992 (see Ch 5): Aberystwyth (Single Hons) 14 pts, (Joint Hons) 18-16 pts depending on subject; Brighton 10 pts; Queen Margaret (Coll) 12 pts; Thames Valley London.

ADVICE FOR MATURE STUDENTS

Some academic qualifications are sought for these courses which can attract up to 30% of mature students in the overall student total.

GRADUATE EMPLOYMENT

New Graduates' destinations (percentages) 1991:
Permanent employment: U 83; P 78.
Unemployment: U 17; P 19.
Further studies (all types): U 27; P 8.

LIFE SCIENCES

Special subject requirements: A-level chemistry preferable; other A-levels from biology/ physics/science/mathematics.

NB Institutions may raise or lower the level of published offers depending either on the quality or otherwise of individual applications or the numbers of applications received; grades/points offered may be adjusted downwards after A-level results. The level of an offer is not indicative of the quality of a course.

20 pts.	**Liverpool** - BCC-CCC (Life Sci courses)
	London (Imp) - BCC (Approx offer for the Life Sci Group)
	Manchester - 20 pts approx (Life Sci)
16 pts.	**Aberdeen** - CCD/BC (Health Sci)
14 pts.	**Salford (UC)** - 14 pts (Prosth/Orth)
12 pts.	**Northumbria** - 12 pts (Eur Health Sci)
	Ripon & York St John (CHE) - DDD/CC (Health Sci)
10 pts.	**and below**
	Cardiff (IHE) - (Biomed Sci)
	Derby - 10 pts (Earth/Life St)
	Leeds Met - (Health Sci)
	North London - 10 pts (Life Sci/Fr)
	Westminster - DD offers vary (Sci/Life)
8 pts.	**South Bank** - (Health Sci) (BTEC 3M)

Diploma of Higher Education courses:
4 pts. **and below** Westminster

Alternative offers: *IB offers:* **South Bank** 24 pts.

Irish offers: **South Bank** CCCC.

CHOOSING YOUR COURSE (See also Ch 1)

Subject information: This subject area is one of considerable breadth and may include biochemistry, biology, biological and environmental sciences. Students are advised to check each course and select the emphasis they seek. The prosthetist/orthotist requires a wide range of theoretical and practical knowledge and skills and prospective students are rarely strong in all of the relevant subjects, therefore weeks 2-5 of the course are dedicated to balancing studies which comprise: fundamentals of mathematics, fundamentals of life sciences and introductory workshop practice. This allows students who are weak in any of these areas to quickly bring themselves up to the standard required at the start of the course itself.

Course highlights: London (Imp) Subject provided by three departments: biochemistry, botany and zoology. **Salford (UC)** (Prosth/Orth) This course is run jointly between University of Salford and University College Salford. **Westminster** Course decisions can be delayed to year 2 with transfer to other degrees eg, Biotechnology. NOW CHECK PROSPECTUSES FOR ALL COURSES.

ADMISSIONS INFORMATION

Number of applicants per place (approx): Westminster 4.

General Studies acceptable: Cheltenham & Glos (CHE).

Admissions Tutors' advice: Cardiff (IHE) may accept applicants who fail to achieve their offer grades. They look for candidates with career interests in biological sciences.

Examples of interview questions: See under **Biochemistry, Botany, Biology** and **Zoology.**

GAP YEAR ADVICE

Institutions accepting a Gap Year: Salford (UC).

Institutions willing to defer entry after A-levels (see Ch 5): Salford (UC); South Bank; Westminster.

AFTER A-LEVELS ADVICE

Institutions with vacancies in Aug/Sept 1992 (see Ch 5): Salford (UC) 12 pts; South Bank; Westminster.

LINGUISTICS (See also LANGUAGE)

Special subject requirements: very occasionally an A-level in a modern language.

NB Institutions may raise or lower the level of published offers depending either on the quality or otherwise of individual applications or the numbers of applications received; grades/points offered may be adjusted downwards after A-level results. The level of an offer is not indicative of the quality of a course.

24 pts.	**Nottingham** – ABC-ACC (Ling/Maths)
	Sheffield – BBB (Ling/Japan)
22 pts.	**Edinburgh** – BBC (Linguist)
	Lancaster – BBC-BCC (Ling/Psy)
	Nottingham – BBC-CCC (Linguistics courses except under **24 pts**)
	Southampton – BBC (Mod L/Comp)
	UMIST – BBC (Ling/Comp; Comp L: Fr/Ger/Sp)
20 pts.	**East Anglia** – BCC/BC (EAS/Ling; Ling/Phil)
	Essex – BCC/BB (Linguistics courses)
	Kent – BCC approx (Ling)
	Lancaster – BCC-BCD (All courses except under **22 pts**)
	Leeds – BCC-CCC (Ling/Rus; Ling/Sp; Ling/Comp)
	London (UC) – BCC-CCC (Ling)
	Manchester – 20 pts approx (All courses)
	Newcastle – BCC/BB (Ling)
	Reading – BCC (Ling/Lang P)
	Sheffield – BCC (Linguistics courses except under **24 pts**)
	York – BCC/BB (B in lang) (All courses) (4 AS)
18 pts.	**Bangor** – CCC-BCD/BC (Ling/Engl; Ling/PE; Ling/Soc)

	Reading - 18 pts (Ling)
	Sussex - CCC/BB (All courses)
16 pts.	**Bangor** - CCD/BB (Ling)
	Central Lancashire - 16 pts (Comb Hons)
	London (SOAS) - BB (Linguistics)
8 pts.	**and below**
	Brighton - (Ap Lang)
	Hertfordshire - (Hum)

Diploma of Higher Education courses:
  4 pts.   Bradford & Ilkley (CmC); Central Lancashire; East London; Ripon & York St John (CHE).

Alternative offers:

EB offers: **UMIST** 70%.

IB offers: **Bangor** 32-28 pts; **East Anglia** 31 pts; **Essex** 28 pts; **Kent** 27 pts, H 12 pts; **Lancaster** 30 pts; **Leeds** 26 pts; **UMIST** 28 pts 7 subjects 24 pts 6 subjects; **York** H655.

Irish offers: **UMIST** BBBBC.

SCE offers: **Edinburgh** BBBB; **Lancaster** BBBBB; **Sussex** AABB.

CHOOSING YOUR COURSE (See also Ch 1)

Subject information: This subject covers the study of language in general including areas such as children's language, slang, language handicap, advertising language, styles of language and the learning of foreign languages.

Course highlights: Bangor Emphasis on assessment by practical course work rather than examinations. Course includes 'learning to talk', authors' styles, women and men's language. **Newcastle** Variety of exam arrangements, possibility of studying more than one foreign language including Chinese, Korean, Sanskrit or Japanese. High research rating. NOW CHECK PROSPECTUSES FOR ALL COURSES.

Study opportunities abroad: Lancaster FR G EUR; **Newcastle** (E) B SP NL.

ADMISSIONS INFORMATION

Number of applicants per place (approx): East Anglia 6; **Essex** 1; **Lancaster** 12; **Leeds** (L/P) 8; **Nottingham** 14; **UMIST** 3; **York** 7.

General Studies acceptable: Bangor; Brighton; East Anglia; Essex; Hull; Lancaster; Leeds (JMB only); Newcastle (providing the grade Bs are in other subjects).

Selection interviews: Brighton; Essex; Hull (some); Lancaster (some); Liverpool; Newcastle; Nottingham (70%); Reading (some).

Offers to applicants repeating A-levels: Higher Essex, Hull, Sussex; **Same** Brighton, East Anglia, Leeds, Newcastle, Nottingham, UMIST, York.

Admissions Tutors' advice: Leeds Video available for schools. GCSE grades A-C required in English language or foreign language. **Newcastle** Applicants with arts and science A-levels welcome. **UMIST** We are looking particularly, though not exclusively, for candidates taking mixed arts and science A-levels and showing an interest in an analytical approach to language. When A-level results are published, we try to be as humane as possible and allow, where feasible, points equivalent for the particular offer made. Certain restrictions must be met (for example candidates for English and

Linguistics or Linguistics with French must have a B in English or French respectively: good results in other subjects cannot compensate for a C). For the main German course the offer would be CCC. Candidates are recommended to have done some elementary reading before coming to interview (eg *Language and Linguistics* Lyons (Cambridge University Press) or *Linguistics* Crystal (Penguin)). **York** Course combines linguistics and study of a language (French, German or English). We are looking for students with keen interest in analysing how language works.

> **Examples of interview questions:** Why do you want to study Linguistics? What does the subject involve? What do you intend to do at the end of your degree course? What answer do you give to your parents or friends when they ask why you want to study the subject?

GAP YEAR ADVICE

Institutions accepting a Gap Year: Most institutions; **Newcastle** Time spent abroad useful.

Institutions willing to defer entry after A-levels (see Ch 5): Bangor; Newcastle (Prefer not); York (No).

AFTER A-LEVELS ADVICE

Institutions which may accept the same points score after A-levels: Bangor; Brighton; Essex; Hull; Leeds; UMIST; York.

Institutions demanding the actual grades offered after A-levels: Newcastle; Nottingham.

Institutions which may accept under-achieving applicants after A-levels: Bangor; Essex; Leeds; UMIST; York.

Institutions with vacancies in Aug/Sept 1992 (see Ch 5): There were a number of vacancies for these courses; Essex 20 pts.

GRADUATE EMPLOYMENT

New Graduates' destinations (percentages) 1991:
Permanent employment: U 83.
Unemployment: U 9.
Further studies (all types): U 41.

York (1988-91) Teaching English as a foreign language attracted the most students (15 out of a total of 80 going into employment). Others chose a range of destinations, management training, advertising, export sales, travel agency work, European Commission (Brussels), GCHQ, Foreign and Commonwealth Office, accountancy, publishing, MENCAP, computing, library work, reader/braillist (National Institute for the Blind), air hostess and conservation work in Ecuador.

LITERATURE

Special subject requirements: modern language at A-level.

NB Institutions may raise or lower the level of published offers depending either on the quality or otherwise of individual applications or the numbers of applications received; grades/points offered may be adjusted downwards after A-level results. The level of an offer is not indicative of the quality of a course.

22 pts.	**Essex** - BBC/BB (Lit courses; LEE; LUS)
20 pts.	**Bradford** - BCC/BB (Lit)
	Bristol UWE - 20 pts (Lit St)
	East Anglia - BCC/BB (CL/DH; CL/Phil; CL/Phil 4)
16 pts.	**Middlesex** - 16 pts (Lit/Phil) (4 AS)
	Portsmouth - CCD/BC (Lit St)
12 pts.	**Bolton (IHE)** - DDD/CD (Comb St)
	Liverpool John Moores - 12 pts (Comb St) (4 AS)
	Staffordshire - CC-CD (Lit/Hist)
10 pts.	**and below**
	Glamorgan - (Hum)
	Humberside - (Hum)
	Teesside - (Hum)
	West Sussex (IHE) - (Rel Arts/Engl)
	Worcester (CHE) - (Comb St)

Diploma of Higher Education courses:
 4 pts. Bradford & Ilkley (CmC); Doncaster (Coll); Edge Hill (CHE); Humberside.

Alternative offers:

IB offers: **Essex** 28 pts inc 10 pts 2 Highers.

CHOOSING YOUR COURSE (See also Ch 1)

> **Subject information:** This is a very broad subject which introduces many aspects of the study of literature and aesthetics. Courses will vary in content.

Course highlights: Staffordshire Option to follow Cultural Studies courses in video production, desk-top publishing etc. NOW CHECK PROSPECTUSES FOR ALL COURSES.

ADMISSIONS INFORMATION

Number of applicants per place (approx): East Anglia 12; **Essex** 4; **Liverpool John Moores** (Lit/Hist) 15, (Lit/Life) 2; **Middlesex** 8; **Portsmouth** 24; **Staffordshire** 8.

> **Examples of interview questions:** Questions asked about applicants' A-level syllabuses. They will be expected to discuss favourite authors and books read outside the syllabus.

AFTER A-LEVELS ADVICE

Institutions which may accept the same points score after A-levels: Staffordshire.

Institutions with vacancies in Aug/Sept 1992 (see Ch 5): Bristol UWE.

GRADUATE EMPLOYMENT

New Graduates' destinations (percentages) 1991:
Permanent employment: P 36.
Unemployment: P 33.
Further studies (all types): P 50.

MARINE (MARITIME) STUDIES

Special subject requirements: 2 A-levels from geography/mathematics/physics; geography/ mathematics at GCSE (grade A-C) for Maritime Geography.

NB Institutions may raise or lower the level of published offers depending either on the quality or otherwise of individual applications or the numbers of applications received; grades/points offered may be adjusted downwards after A-level results. The level of an offer is not indicative of the quality of a course.

24 pts.	**St Andrews** - BBB (Mar Env Biol)
22 pts.	**Bangor** - BBC/AB (Naut St) (BTEC 3D+Ms)
20 pts.	**Cardiff** - BCC-CCC/BB (Mar Stud; Mar Comm; Int Tran; Mar Geog)
	Newcastle - BCC/BB (Marine Tech - MEng)
18 pts.	**Newcastle** - CCC-CCD/BC (Marine Tech - BEng) (BTEC Ms)
	Southampton - CCC (Marine Science courses)
14 pts.	**Bangor** - CDD-DDD (Geol Oc) (See **Oceanography**)
12 pts.	**Manadon (RNEC)** - EE + Access course (see below) (Mar Defence/Man/Tech)
10 pts.	**Plymouth** - 10 pts (All Marine St courses; Hydrog)
8 pts.	**Liverpool John Moores** - 8 pts (Comb St)
	Robert Gordon - (Mar Res Man)
	Southampton (IHE) - (Mar Stud)

Offers for Foundation, Certificate and Diploma courses (see Ch 5):

Higher National Diploma courses:

Entry to HND courses in Nautical Studies and Maritime Technology is restricted to Merchant Navy Deck Officer cadets employed and sponsored by a shipping company.

Alternative offers:

IB offers: **Cardiff** 30 pts; **Newcastle** 35 pts.

CHOOSING YOUR COURSE (See also Ch 1)

> **Subject information:** This topic can involve a range of subjects such as marine business, technology, navigation, nautical studies, underwater rescue and transport.

Course highlights: Bangor (Naut St) Unique course combining history, maritime archaeology and ship archaeology. **Cardiff** The only course in Maritime Commerce and Maritime Studies in the United Kingdom. Good links with industry. (Mar Geog) There is a large marine resource management unit in the Department. **Plymouth** Topics offered include ocean sciences, fisheries, navigation and hydrography, marine technology, maritime history, marine business, law and transport. **Robert Gordon** The physical and biological processes relevant to the marine and coastal environment. NOW CHECK PROSPECTUSES FOR ALL COURSES.

ADMISSIONS INFORMATION

General Studies acceptable: Cardiff; Liverpool John Moores.

Admissions Tutors' advice: Liverpool John Moores Approximately 120 applicants for 48 places. Applicants more likely to be offered a place if they can show some interest in shipping and freight management. Students without such experience are accepted if arrangements can be made for industrial training. **Manadon (RNEC)** At present the only formally recognised Access course in Naval Studies held at BRNC Dartmouth.

> **Examples of interview questions:** Why do you want to study this subject? Have you any family or other connections with the sea?

GAP YEAR ADVICE

Institutions accepting a Gap Year: Cardiff.

Institutions willing to defer entry after A-levels (see Ch 5): Newcastle.

GRADUATE EMPLOYMENT

New Graduates' destinations (percentages) 1991:
Permanent employment: P 75.
Unemployment: P 0.
Further studies (all types): P 60.

MARKETING

Special subject requirements: English and mathematics at GCSE (grade A-C); occasionally a language.

NB Institutions may raise or lower the level of published offers depending either on the quality or otherwise of individual applications or the numbers of applications received; grades/points offered may be adjusted downwards after A-level results. The level of an offer is not indicative of the quality of a course.

24pts.	**Aston** - BBB-BBC (Man/Admin)
	Lancaster - BBB (Mktg; Art/Mktg; ML Mktg(Fr))
22pts.	**Stirling** - BBC (Mktg and joint courses)
20pts.	**Aberystwyth** - 20 pts (BSc Econ)
	Lancaster - BCC (ML Mktg(Ger))
	Manchester Met - BCC (Retail Mark)
18pts.	**Guildhall London** - CCC/DD (Bus St)
16pts.	**Central Lancashire** - CCD (Comb St)
	Glamorgan - 16-14 pts (Mark) (BTEC 2-3D+Ms)
	Greenwich - CCD/CC (IM/Fr; IM/Ger; IM/Sp)
	Plymouth - CCD/AB-BB (Mark)
	Strathclyde - CCD (Arts Soc St)
14pts.	**Bournemouth** - 14 pts (Int Market; Leis/Mark) (6 AS)
	Cranfield (Silsoe) - CDD/CC (Food Mar/Dis) (BTEC 75%, 4 subjects)
	Huddersfield - 14 pts minimum (Mark)
	Paisley - BC (Mark)
12pts.	**Harper Adams (CAg)** - DDD/CC (Food/Mktg)
	Humberside - 12 pts (Eur Mark)
10pts.	**and below**
	De Montfort - (Comb St)

> **Derby** – (Modular) (4 AS)
> **East London** – (Biomark Man)
> **Northumbria** – (Art Foundation; Fashion Mark)
> **Roehampton (IHE)** – (Mark/Fr/Sp) (BTEC 3M)
> **Sheffield Hallam** – 10 pts (Food Market)

Offers for Foundation, Certificate and Diploma courses (see Ch 5):

Higher National Diploma courses (in Business Studies):
8 pts.   **and below** Anglia (Poly Univ); Blackburn (Coll); Bolton (IHE); Bournemouth; Bristol UWE, Central Lancashire; Coventry; De Montfort; Derby; Farnborough (CT); Glamorgan; Guildford (CT); Gwent (CHE); Hammersmith & West London (Coll); Harper Adams (CAg) 4 pts; Huddersfield; Humberside; Liverpool John Moores; London Inst (Coll Printing & Distributive Trades); Luton (CHE); Nene (CHE); North East Wales (IHE); Northumbria; North Worcestershire (Coll); Norwich City (CHFE); Oxford Brookes; Plymouth; Salford (Univ Coll); Sandwell (CHFE); Sheffield Hallam; South Bank; Southampton (IHE); Staffordshire; Stockport (CT); Suffolk (CFHE); Sunderland; Swansea (IHE); Teesside; West Herts (Coll).

Alternative offers:

IB offers: **Bournemouth** 26 pts; **Cranfield (Silsoe)** 26 pts; **Greenwich** 25 pts; **Lancaster** 32 pts; **Plymouth** H554.

SCE offers: **Lancaster** AABBB; **Paisley** BBBC.

CHOOSING YOUR COURSE (See also Ch 1)

> **Course information:** These are very popular courses and applications should include some evidence of work experience or shadowing. This is a subject also covered by most business studies courses and by specialist (and equally relevant) courses such as textile marketing and food marketing for which lower offers are often made. Most courses offer the same subject content.

Course highlights: Bournemouth Courses offered in Leisure Marketing and International Marketing, the latter has a language input. NOW CHECK PROSPECTUSES FOR ALL COURSES.

Study opportunities abroad: Bournemouth (E) FR G NL SP.

ADMISSIONS INFORMATION

Number of applicants per place (approx): Bournemouth 6; **Cranfield (Silsoe)** 2; **Huddersfield** 3; **Lancaster** 28, (ML/Mktg(Fr)) 18; **Sheffield Hallam** 9.

General Studies acceptable: East London; Harper Adams (CAg); Lancaster.

Admissions Tutors' advice: Bournemouth Conditions of offer must be met exactly. **Lancaster** (ML/Mktg/Fr/Ger/Sp) This is a popular course and only a small proportion of candidates can be interviewed. GCSE maths grade A or B essential. We do our best to consider candidates with unorthodox backgrounds but the pressure of applications makes this difficult.

> **Examples of interview questions:** What is marketing? Why do you want to take a degree in Marketing? Is sales pressure justified? How would you feel if you had to market a product which you considered to be inferior?

GAP YEAR ADVICE

Institutions accepting a Gap Year: Most institutions; **Greenwich** Improve your command of language (French/German/Spanish) and widen your business expertise. **Harper Adams (CAg)** Pre-college experience on a farm recommended.

Institutions willing to defer entry after A-levels (see Ch 5): Glamorgan (No); Humberside; Lancaster (No); Plymouth; Roehampton (IHE).

AFTER A-LEVELS ADVICE

Institutions with vacancies in Aug/Sept 1992 (see Ch 5): East London; Glamorgan 14 pts; Harper Adams (CAg) 8 pts; Roehampton (IHE).

Summary of vacancies in Aug/Sept 1992: There was a good choice of courses and institutions with vacancies.

GRADUATE EMPLOYMENT

New Graduates' destinations (percentages) 1991:
Permanent employment: P 82.
Unemployment: P 9.
Further studies (all types): P 6.

MATERIALS SCIENCE/METALLURGY

Special subject requirements: 2-3 A-levels in mathematics/science subjects. Mathematics occasionally required at A-level and with science subjects frequently at GCSE (grade A-C).

NB Institutions may raise or lower the level of published offers depending either on the quality or otherwise of individual applications or the numbers of applications received; grades/points offered may be adjusted downwards after A-level results. The level of an offer is not indicative of the quality of a course.

30 pts.	**Cambridge** (Nat Sci)/**Oxford** (Metal) - AAA potential recommended
22 pts.	**Newcastle** - BBC/AB (Mat Des Eng)
20 pts.	**Liverpool** - BCC-CCC/BB (Metal; Mat Sci; Mat/Micro Eng) (4 AS)
	Nottingham - BCC-CCD (Elect Mat)
18 pts.	**Aston** - CCC/AB (Comb Hons) (BTEC 5D+5M)
	Birmingham - CCC (Met/Mat Eng; Mat Sc/Eng) (BTEC 3M)
	Brunel - CCC-DDD/CC-DD (Mats/Man; Metal; Materials) (6 AS) (BTEC 3M)
	Durham - CCC (Phys/Chem)
	Loughborough - (Mats/Bus 3 & 4) (Contact Admissions Tutor)
	Newcastle - CCC/BB (Mat Des Man; Metall/Phys)
	Nottingham - CCC (Mat/Chem)
	Sheffield - CCC/BB (Materials; Metals; Ceramics; Glasses; Polymers; Mat/Phys) (4 AS) (BTEC 3M)
	Strathclyde - CCC (2nd yr entry) (Eng Mats)
	Surrey - CCC/BC (All courses except under 12 pts)
	Swansea - CCC/BB (All courses)
16 pts.	**Bath** - CCD (Mat Sci courses) (2 AS - physics AS acceptable) (BTEC Ms)
	Leeds - CCD (Mats Sci; Met; Cer Sci Eng)
	London (Imp) - CCD/BB (Mat Sci/Eng) (4 AS)
	Manchester - 16 pts approx (All courses)
	Manchester Met - 16-10 pts (Comb St)
	UMIST - CCD (All courses) (BTEC 3M)

14 pts.   **London (QMW)** - CDD (Mat Sci/Eng)
12 pts.   **Surrey** - CC (Arts A-levels) (Foundation)
 8 pts.   **and below**
        Bell (CT) - (Eng Mat)
        Coventry - DD (Mat Sci; Mat Eng/Man) (4 AS)
        Greenwich - EE (Mat Sci; EEM; Met/Mat Eng) (6 AS) (BTEC 3M)
        North East Wales (IHE) - (Mat Sci; Mat Sci/Mat Eng) (1 A-level pass from maths, phys, or chem)
        Sheffield Hallam - DD (Mat Eng) (BTEC 3M)
        Staffordshire - (Comb St)
        Sunderland - DEE/DD (All courses)

Offers for Foundation, Certificate and Diploma courses (see Ch 5):

Higher National Diploma courses:
  4 pts.   **and below** Bell (CT); Chesterfield (CT) (Cast Metals); Greenwich (Fab/Welding); Manchester Met; Sheffield Hallam; Sandwell (CHFE) (Cast Metals); Staffordshire (Ceramics); Sunderland.

Alternative offers:

EB offers: **Newcastle** 70%.

IB offers: **Bath** 30-28 pts inc H555; **Birmingham** 30 pts inc H655; **Brunel** Pass, average 65-60%; **Manchester** 26 pts; **Newcastle** 26 pts, 5 maths, 5 phys or chem; **Surrey** 30 pts; **UMIST** 26 pts inc H666/665.

Irish offers: **Greenwich** CCCCC; **Liverpool** BBCCC; **Swansea** CCCCC; **UMIST** ABBBBC.

SCE offers: **Sheffield** BBBCC; **Strathclyde** BBBB; **UMIST** BBBBB.

Overseas applicants: Swansea Foundation course essential. **Bath** English course available. **Newcastle, Coventry** Foundation courses available.

CHOOSING YOUR COURSE (See also Ch 1)

> **Subject information:** This is a subject which covers physics, chemistry and engineering at one and the same time! From its origins in metallurgy, materials science has now moved into the processing, structure and properties of materials - ceramics, polymers, composites and electrical materials. Materials science and metallurgy are perhaps the most misunderstood of all careers. Thus applications for degree courses are low and offers very reasonable. As with other careers in which there is a shortfall of applicants, graduate employment and future prospects are good.

Course highlights: Bath Multi-disciplinary degree course with complete spectrum of subjects. Sandwich year available for BEng and BEng/MEng candidates. Currently two million pounds of research grants and high research rating by national research committee (grade 4). Now offering a course which includes a language and study abroad. **Birmingham** Strong research opportunities involving aerospace materials, ceramics, superconductors and biomaterials. **Brunel** Sandwich placements in all three years mean early qualification to Chartered Engineer (CEng) status. French/German options - placements abroad. **London (Imp)** Some transfers in year 2 to the Materials in Europe course which has language options (French, German, Spanish) with year 3 spent at academic or industrial institutions in Europe. **Manchester Met** Language study possible. **Newcastle** Course in Materials Design/ Manufacture is common in years 1 and 2 with Materials Design/Engineering. **Surrey** 25% of students are female (student branch of Women's Engineering Society). Bridging studies in first year for students with poor A-levels or non-traditional subjects. **Swansea** Recently refurbished laboratories. Scholarships up to £500. Specialist topics including polymer engineering, biomedical materials and microelectronics materials technology. **UMIST** £500 scholarships available. NOW CHECK PROSPECTUSES FOR ALL COURSES.

Study opportunities abroad: London (Imp) EUR; **Sheffield** (E); **Swansea** (E).

Work opportunities abroad: Bath FR G USA CAN; **Birmingham** AUS NZ USA EUR; **Brunel** FR D G NL B USA AUS AF; **Swansea** B C USA AUS.

ADMISSIONS INFORMATION

Number of applicants per place (approx): Bath 4; **Birmingham** 4; **Brunel** 10; **Coventry** 4; **Greenwich** 6; **Leeds** 4; **Liverpool** 3; **London (Imp)** 3; **Manchester Met** 7; **Newcastle** 4; **Sheffield Hallam** 5; **Strathclyde** 5; **Sunderland** 2; **Surrey** 4; **Swansea** 3; **UMIST** 4.

General Studies acceptable: Birmingham; Coventry; Greenwich (2); Liverpool.

Selection interviews: Bath; Birmingham; Brunel; Cambridge; Greenwich; Leeds; Liverpool; Newcastle (some); Oxford; Sheffield; Sunderland (some); Surrey; Swansea; UMIST.

Offers to applicants repeating A-levels: Higher Strathclyde, Swansea; **Possibly higher** Coventry; **Same** Birmingham, Brunel, Greenwich, Leeds, Liverpool, Manchester Met, Surrey.

Admissions Tutors' advice: Bath (Materials Science) Candidates without physics at A-level will be accepted if they have good grades in mathematics and chemistry and one other relevant subject. Enthusiasm for subject at interview is important. Good GCSE grades preferred in English, maths, physics, chemistry.

> **Examples of interview questions:** Why did you choose Materials Science? What do you think of your A-level subjects? Which did you find the most difficult and why? Which did you find easy? How would you make each part of this table lamp (on the interviewer's desk)? Identify this piece of material. How was it manufactured? How has it been treated? (Questions related to metal and polymer samples.) What were your parents' reactions when you told them you were applying for this course? What would you consider the major growth area in materials science?

GAP YEAR ADVICE

Institutions accepting a Gap Year: Most institutions; **Bath** See the world and try to get some industrial experience; **Surrey** Take time to plan a gap year and use it constructively.

Institutions willing to defer entry after A-levels (see Ch 5): Aston; Brunel; Leeds; Swansea; UMIST.

AFTER A-LEVELS ADVICE

Institutions which may accept the same points score after A-levels: Bath; Birmingham; Brunel; Coventry; Greenwich; Leeds; Liverpool; Sheffield Hallam; Strathclyde; Sunderland; UMIST.

Institutions demanding the actual grades offered after A-levels: London Guildhall.

Institutions which may accept under-achieving applicants after A-levels: Bath; Coventry; Greenwich; Leeds; Newcastle; Strathclyde; Surrey; Swansea.

Institutions with vacancies in Aug/Sept 1992 (see Ch 5): Greenwich 3 pts; Leeds 14 pts; Surrey 16–12 pts; UMIST 10 pts.

GRADUATE EMPLOYMENT

New Graduates' destinations (percentages) 1991:
Permanent employment: U 79.
Unemployment: U 12; P 38.
Further studies (all types): U 14; P 17.

Surrey (Materials Technology) Five graduates entered subject-related occupations with British Aerospace, Vauxhall Motors, Pirelli and GEC. There was also one graduate who entered insurance, one in marketing and saleswork, one who trained as an air transport pilot and one who became an entertainments officer. Four are training for the teaching profession and one went on to study for a PhD.

MATHEMATICS (including Applied Mathematics)

Special subject requirements: usually 2 A-levels, mathematics essential, physics occasionally 'required' or 'preferred'.

NB Institutions may raise or lower the level of published offers depending either on the quality or otherwise of individual applications or the numbers of applications received; grades/points offered may be adjusted downwards after A-level results. The level of an offer is not indicative of the quality of a course.

30 pts.	**Cambridge/Oxford** - AAA potential recommended (Maths)
28 pts.	**Nottingham** - AAB-ABC/AA (Maths Sci)
26 pts.	**Warwick** - ABB (A in maths) (All Maths courses except under **24 pts**)
24 pts.	**Durham** - ABC (All courses)
	Edinburgh - BBB (Maths/Bus)
	Lancaster - BBB (Maths USA)
	Nottingham - ABC-ACC/AB-BB (Maths/Comp)
	Nottingham - ABC-ACC (Mathl/Phys)
	St Andrews - BBB (Maths Arts) (4 AS)
	Warwick - ABC (A in maths) (MORSE; Maths Phys; Maths Stats)
	York - ABC (Maths) (4 AS) (BTEC Ds+Ms)
22 pts.	**Aberdeen** - BBC (Maths Arts)
	Aston - BBC (Comb Hons) (2 AS inc a science or tech subject)
	Bath - ACC (Maths; Math Sc; Stat; Maths/Eur) (BTEC 1D+3M)
	Birmingham - BBC-BCD (All Maths courses)
	Bristol - ACC (Maths; Maths/Stats)
	Edinburgh - BBC (Maths; Maths/Phil)
	Exeter - ACC-BCC/AB (Maths) (BTEC Ds+Ms)
	Glasgow - BBC (Maths Arts) (BTEC 3M)
	Heriot-Watt - BBC (Act Maths)
	Hull - BBC-BCC/BB (Maths/MS) (BTEC Ms)
	Lancaster - BBC (Acc/Maths; Econ/Maths)
	Leeds - BBC/BB (Maths/Music; Man St/Maths)
	London (Imp) - BBC (Maths)
	London (King's) - BBC approx (Maths)
	London (RH) - BBC-BCC/BB (All Maths courses) (4 AS) (BTEC 1D maths +2M)
	Loughborough - BBC-BCC-BCD/AB (Maths) (See also under **16/12 pts**)
	Manchester - 22 pts approx (Maths)
	Salford - ACC-BCD/AB-BB (Maths)
	Southampton - BBC (Maths courses)
	Strathclyde - BBC (Maths/Acc)
	Swansea - BBC/AB (Maths/Man)
	UMIST - BBC-BCC/BB (All Maths courses)
	York - ACC (Maths in Germany)
	York - BBC (Maths combinations) (4 AS)
20 pts.	**Belfast** - BCC (Maths Sci; Maths/Arts)
	Bristol - BCC (Eng Maths)
	Brunel - BCC-BCD/BB (All Maths courses)
	Cardiff - BCC-CCC/BB (Maths courses) (BTEC 3D+Ms)
	Dundee - BCC (Maths - MA)
	East Anglia - BCC/BC (All Maths courses except under **16 pts**) (BTEC 3M)

Essex - 20 pts C in maths (Maths/Acc)
Exeter - BCC (Maths/OR) (BTEC Ds+Ms)
Keele - BCC-CCC/BB-BC (All courses except under **18 pts**) (4 AS)
Kent - BCC approx (Maths courses)
Lancaster - BCC (Approx offer for all Maths courses except **22 pts**)
Leeds - BCC (All courses)
Leicester - 20-16 pts (Maths/Ast; Maths Sci; Maths/Comp)
Leicester - BCC/BB (Sci Comb)
Liverpool - BCC (All Maths courses except under **14 pts**) (4-5 AS)
London (LSE) - BCC approx (Maths)
London (QMW) - BCC/BB (All Maths courses)
London (UC) - 20 pts approx (Maths courses)
Loughborough - BCC (Indust Maths 4)
Reading - BCC (Maths)
Salford - BCC-CCD (Joint Hons)
Sheffield - BCC/BB (Maths) (4 AS)
Strathclyde - BCC/BB (Maths - Bus Sch)
Surrey - BCC/BC (Maths; Maths/Stats; Maths/Comp)
Sussex - BCC-CCC/BB (Maths)
Ulster - BCC-BCD (Maths)

18 pts.
Aberdeen - CCC-CCD/BC (Maths Sci)
Bradford - BCD/BB (B in maths) (Maths Sci; Maths/Stats; Maths/Phil) (BTEC Ds)
Bristol - AB (Maths/Physics)
Coventry - 18-14 pts (Maths) (BTEC 5Ms inc maths)
Edinburgh - CCC/BB (All BSc courses except under **22/24 pts**)
Essex - BCD (Maths; MCC; M Stats; MORE; Maths/Op Res; Maths/Mus)
Glasgow - CCC-CCD/BC (Maths Sci) (BTEC 3M)
Hull - BCD (Maths Sci; Maths; Maths/Fr; Maths/Sp; Maths Stats; Maths/Ger) (4 AS)
Keele - CCC (Maths/Mus)
Leicester - 18 pts approx (Maths)
Loughborough - BCD-BDD (Math Eng 3 and 4; Maths/Econ 3 and 4)
Newcastle - BBE/18-16 pts (Maths; Maths/Stats; Math Sci) (4 AS)
Nottingham - BCD-CCD (Maths/Eng)
Reading - BBE (Pure Maths)
St Andrews - CCC (Maths - BSc)
Sheffield - BCD/BB (Dual Honours courses) (4 AS)
Stirling - CCC/BC (Maths)
Swansea - BCD/BB (Maths/Phys)

16 pts.
Aberystwyth - CCD/BC (All Maths courses)
City - BDD (All courses)
East Anglia - BDD/BC (Maths/Phys)
Glasgow Caledonian - CCD/CD (Maths/Bus Anal) (6 AS)
Hull - BDD/BB-BC (Maths/Phil)
Manchester Met - 16-10 pts (Ap Maths; Comb St)
Manchester Met - 16-12 pts (Quant St)
Middlesex - 16-12 pts (Quant St)

14 pts.
Bangor - 14-12 pts (All courses)
Cambridge (Hom) - BC-CC (Maths/Ed) (4 AS) (See also **Education**)
Coventry - 14 pts (All Maths courses except under **16 pts**) (BTEC Ms)
Dundee - CDD (All courses except under **20 pts**)
Heriot-Watt - CCE/BC (All Maths courses)
Liverpool - CDD/BC (Maths/Phys) (4 AS)
Robert Gordon - CDD/CC (Maths/Comp) (4 AS)
Strathclyde - CDD/BB-AC (Maths - BSc)

12 pts.
Anglia (Poly Univ) - CC-DD (MS courses) (BTEC 4M)
Brighton - 12-8 pts (Joint/Modular) (4 AS) (BTEC 3M)
Central Lancashire - CC (Comb St)
Dundee (IT) - DDD/CD (App Maths) (3 AS)
London (Gold) - CC (Maths courses)

Loughborough - CDE/CC (Maths/Educ)
South Bank - DDD/CD (Maths/Comp/Man)
Staffordshire - 12 pts (Maths/Comp) (6 AS)

10 pts. **Hertfordshire** - DDE/DE (Dec Sci)
Hertfordshire - CEE/CD (Maths; Maths/Comp)
Manchester Met - DDE/CD (Comb St)
Newcastle - CD-DD-CE (Maths - 4 yr course)
Oxford Brookes - CD (Modular)
Portsmouth - 10-8 pts (Maths Sci)
Sheffield Hallam - DDE (Comp Maths)
Warwick - CD (BA(QTS))
Westminster - CD (Maths courses)

8 pts. **and below**
Bath (CHE) - (Comb St)
Bolton (IHE) - (All Maths courses)
Canterbury Christ Church (CHE) - (Comb St)
Cheltenham & Glos (CHE) - (Maths modular)
Chester (CHE) - (Comb Hons)
De Montfort - DD (Comb St; Maths) (6 AS)
Derby - (Modular) (4 AS)
Dundee (IT) - (Maths/Comp)
East London - (Maths/Comp; Stats/Maths; Maths/Euro) (BTEC Ms)
Glamorgan - 8 pts (Maths/Comp; Maths)
Greenwich - (Maths/Stat/Comp; Comp Maths)
Guildhall London - DD (Maths - modular) (BTEC 4M)
Kingston - DEE/DD-EE (Maths St; Maths joint courses) (4 AS)
Liverpool (IHE) - (Comb St)
Manchester Met - 8 pts (App Maths - part-time)
Manchester Met - DD (Measure/Ins)
Middlesex - CE (Quantitative St; Comb St; Maths Bus) (2 AS - maths might be acceptable)
Napier - (Maths Eng Tech)
Nene (CHE) - (Comb St)
North London - EE (Maths courses) (4 AS)
Northumbria - (Maths) (4 AS) (BTEC Ms)
Nottingham Trent - DD (Maths/Phys; Maths/Info Tech) (4 AS)
Paisley - (Maths Sci)
Plymouth - (Maths St)
Portsmouth - (Maths/Comp; MFM; Maths) (6 AS) (BTEC Ms)
Ripon & York St John (CHE) - (Modular)
Robert Gordon - (Maths Sci)
Roehampton (IHE) - 4 pts (Comb St)
Sheffield Hallam - (Comp Maths) (4 AS)
South Bank - DD (Maths St)
Southampton (IHE) - (Maths Stud)
Staffordshire - (STORM)
St Mary's (CHE) - (Comb St)
Sunderland - (MCC; Maths/Phys)
Teesside - (Maths)
Trinity & All Saints (CHE) - 8 pts (Maths/BMA)

Diploma of Higher Education courses:
4 pts. Bath (CHE); East London; Hertfordshire; Manchester Met; Westminster (CHE).

Offers for Foundation, Certificate and Diploma courses (see Ch 5):

Higher National Diploma courses (England and Wales):
  8 pts.   and below Blackburn (Coll); Brighton; Bristol UWE; Central Lancashire; Cheltenham & Glos (CHE); Coventry; De Montfort; Glamorgan (Comp Maths); Hertfordshire; Leeds Met (Maths St); Greenwich; Manchester Met; North London; Portsmouth; Sheffield Hallam; Teesside.

Higher Diploma courses (Scotland):
  8 pts.   and below or equivalent Bell (CT); Napier EE.

Alternative offers:

EB offers: **Brunel** 70%; **Sheffield** 70%.

IB offers: **Aberdeen** (Arts) 30 pts; (Sci) 26 pts; **Anglia (Poly Univ)** (MS) 28 pts; **Belfast** H666; **Brighton** 24 pts inc 12 pts Highers; **Bristol** 30-28 pts inc H766; **Brunel** 30-27 pts; **Cardiff** 28 pts; **East Anglia** 32 pts; **Essex** 28 pts; **Exeter** 33-30 pts; **Glasgow** H555; **Heriot-Watt** H554; **Kent** 27 pts, H 12 pts; **Lancaster** 30 pts; **Leeds** 28 pts maths H6; **Leicester** 28 pts; **Liverpool** H655/555; **London (RH)** 28 pts; **Newcastle** 28 pts, 24 pts for 4 yr courses; **Portsmouth** 24 pts; **St Andrews** 30 pts; **Sheffield** H6 (maths) 55 or 555; **South Bank** 24 pts; **Surrey** 30 pts; **Sussex** 15 pts Highers; **York** 30 pts H6 maths.

Irish offers: **Aberdeen** (Arts) BBBB, (Sci) BCCCC; **Aberystwyth** ABBBC; **Bangor** BBCCC; **Brunel** BBBCCC; **Coventry** BBB; **Glamorgan** CCCC; **Glasgow** BBB; **Guildhall London** CCCCC; **Keele** BBBCC; **Liverpool** BBCCC; **North London** BCCC; **Sheffield** BBBB; **South Bank** CCCC.

SCE offers: **Aberdeen** (Arts) BBBB, (Sci) BBBC; **Brunel** BBBB/BBBC; **Dundee** BBBC; **Edinburgh** BBBB; **Glasgow** BBBB; **Guildhall London** BCCCC; **Heriot-Watt** ABB; **Leeds** AAAA; **Newcastle** AAAB; **Sheffield** ABBB; **South Bank** CCC; **St Andrews** BBBB/BBB; **Stirling** BBCC; **Strathclyde** BBBB.

Overseas applicants: Coventry Fluency in oral and written English required. **Newcastle** Preliminary course available. **Sheffield** Foundation course available.

CHOOSING YOUR COURSE (See also Ch 1)

> **Subject information:** This is an extension of A-level mathematics covering pure and applied mathematics, statistics, computing, mathematical analysis and mathematical applications. Alternative courses such as Operational Research, Statistics, Accountancy, Management Science and Actuarial Studies could also be considered.

Course highlights: Bath Common first year for all degree titles. **Bangor** Broad flexible course leaving final choices between pure maths, applied maths and computing until year 3. **Bradford** The courses in Maths and Maths/Stats have a common first year with decision to specialise in year 2; option to spend year in work experience between years 2 and 3. **Bristol** Flexible course structure at every undergraduate stage. Transfer possible between various honours schools and from joint honours to single honours at end of first or second year. Student can spend one third of time on subjects outside department in either or both of second or third years. **Cardiff** Flexible degree scheme with considerable choice of subjects in second and third years. Very active statistics and operational research section. **Coventry** Cluster of nine related degrees offering an unusually extensive range of options; 80 sandwich placements in public and private organisations. **East Anglia** (Deferred course choice) Transfer to Physics/ Maths/Physics and Maths programme expected after first year. Department strong and active in maths and physics research. **Heriot-Watt** Decisions on choice between joint or single honours degree can be deferred until the end of second year. Considerable research strength; close monitoring of students' progress. **London (RH)** First year tutorials in groups of three. Wide range of options and a course unit system allows students considerable flexibility to follow their strengths and interests. **Loughborough** (Maths/Educ) Degree and Certificate of Education awarded separately; students can opt out of teacher training in latter part of course. **Napier** Strong practical bias using computing to integrate maths and engineering. **Newcastle** Teaching via small group tutorials and lectures. Assessment via formal exams and continuous assessment. **Northumbria** Decisions on choice between full-time or sandwich course delayed until year 2. **Robert Gordon** Group projects (with computers) carried out with local industry. **St Andrews** See under **Arts**. **Salford** Optional one year sandwich placement. Two years' accommodation guaranteed. **Surrey** Strong links with industry and commerce. **York** Flexibility in changing course options. High research ratings at **Cambridge, Oxford, Warwick, London (Imp), (LSE), (QMW), (UC), Bath, East Anglia, Leeds, Liverpool, Manchester, Newcastle, Surrey, Dundee.** NOW CHECK PROSPECTUSES FOR ALL COURSES.

Study opportunities abroad: Aberystwyth (E); **Bangor** (E) IRE; **Birmingham** (E); **Bristol** (E) FR G; **Brunel** (E) FR G; **Coventry** (E); **East Anglia** FR G; **Glamorgan; Hull** (E) G; **Lancaster** USA; **Leeds** (E) FR G NL IT D; **London (QMW)** (E); **Sheffield** (E); **Sussex** EUR; **UMIST** FR G; **York** (E) USA CAN G.

Work opportunities abroad: Aberystwyth EUR; **Coventry** FR G HK; **De Montfort** EUR; **Napier; Sheffield** USA FR G.

ADMISSIONS INFORMATION

Number of applicants per place (approx): Aberystwyth 13, 5 (App Maths); **Anglia (Poly Univ)** (MS) 6; **Bangor** 4; **Bath** 8; **Birmingham** 5; **Bradford** 3; **Brighton** 5; **Bristol** 4, (Maths/Stats) 4, (Other courses) 7; **Brunel** 5; **Cambridge (Hom)** 4 (All BEd courses); **City** 10; **Coventry** 10; **De Montfort** 12; **Dundee** 9; **Dundee (IT)** 2; **Durham** 5; **East Anglia** 8; **Edinburgh** 4; **Exeter** 8; **Glamorgan** 5; **Hertfordshire** 9; **Heriot-Watt** 5; **Hull** 6; **Kent** 8; **Lancaster** 12; **Leeds** 7; **Leicester** 8; **Liverpool** 8; **London (QMW)** 5, (RH) 4; **Loughborough** (Math Eng) 5; **Middlesex** 5; **Newcastle** 7; **Northumbria** 11; **Nottingham** (Maths) 9; **Oxford Brookes** 21; **Plymouth** 3; **Portsmouth** 9; **Robert Gordon** 2; **Roehampton (IHE)** 6; **Salford** 10; **Sheffield** 5; **South Bank** 3; **Strathclyde** 6; **Surrey** 6; **Swansea** 4; **Teesside** 4; **Trinity & all Saints (CHE)** 16; **UMIST** 6; **Warwick** (App Maths) 8; **Westminster** 3; **York** 9.

General Studies acceptable: Aberdeen; Aberystwyth; Anglia (Poly Univ) (MS) (2); Aston; Birmingham; Bradford (Maths/Phil); Brunel; Cardiff; Cheltenham & Glos (CHE); Coventry; Dundee (IT); Essex; Exeter; Glamorgan (2); Greenwich; Heriot-Watt; Hertfordshire (2); Hull (possibly); Lancaster; Liverpool (JMB, Oxford, Camb only); Loughborough (Math Eng) (as a third A-level to maths and physics); Northumbria; Oxford Brookes; Roehampton (IHE) (2); South Bank; Surrey (2); Swansea; Teesside; Trinity & All Saints (CHE); Westminster; York.

Selection interviews: Aberystwyth (some); Bath (65%); Birmingham; Brunel; Cambridge; City; Coventry; De Montfort; Durham; East Anglia; Essex (some); Exeter; Greenwich; Guildhall London (some); Kent; Lancaster (some); Leeds; Liverpool; Loughborough (some); Newcastle; Northumbria (some); Nottingham; Oxford; Portsmouth; Reading (some); Robert Gordon; Salford; Sheffield; South Bank (some); St Mary's (CHE); Sussex; Teesside; Trinity & All Saints (CHE); UMIST; Warwick (MORSE); York (some).

Offers to applicants repeating A-levels: Higher Birmingham (BBB-BBC), Brighton, Coventry, De Montfort, Essex, Leeds (1-2 pts), Liverpool, North London, Salford (2 pts), South Bank, Strathclyde, Swansea (BBC/AB), Surrey; **Possibly higher** Cambridge (Hom), Durham, Lancaster, Loughborough (Maths Eng), Newcastle, Sheffield; **Same** Aberystwyth, Aston, Bath, Brunel, East Anglia, Hull, London (RH), Loughborough (usually), Manchester Met, Nottingham, Oxford Brookes, South Bank, Ulster, UMIST, York.

Admissions Tutors' advice: Bath Standard offer may be reduced as a result of a good interview. **Brunel** Students should be keen to pursue a sandwich course. Most applicants invited for a fact-finding interview. Suitability for industrial placement is important. **Liverpool** Most candidates interviewed before an offer is made. Do not apply for more than one mathematics course at Liverpool. Transfer between courses is usually possible up to the date of arrival at the University. **Loughborough** Decisions made after consideration by two selectors. Applicants receiving offers invited for overnight visit. **Nottingham** Because of continuing pressure on places and need to keep to intake targets, selection procedures are constantly under review. For up-to-date information write to the department admissions tutor. Oxbridge applicants may not be processed until outcome of their application is known. **York** Standard offer is lower than average attainment of the intake.

Examples of interview questions: Questions asked on A-level syllabus. Why do you think that mathematics is unpopular in schools? What field of mathematics most interests you? How many ways are there of incorrectly setting up the back row of a chess board? A ladder on a rough floor leans against a smooth wall - describe the forces acting on the ladder and give the maximum angle of inclination possible. There are three particles connected by a string, the middle one is made to move - describe the subsequent motion of the particles. What mathematics books have you read outside your syllabus? Questions needing explanations of mathematical formulae. Why does a ball bounce? Discuss the work of any renowned mathematician. Can you remember failing anything? How did you cope with this failure?

GAP YEAR ADVICE

Institutions accepting a Gap Year: Most institutions; **Bath** Not a good idea but we allow it; **Brunel** Maintain your A-level maths knowledge; **Cheltenham & Glos (CHE)** Read Martin Gardner's books to widen view of maths; **Coventry** Maths knowledge could get rusty if the year off does not have a maths input. **Heriot-Watt** Review your A-level maths course before starting our course; **Leicester** Do some revision before taking up your place; **London (RH)** Revision probably will be needed; **Northumbria** Try to keep in touch with the subject; **Roehampton (IHE)** Give your reasons; **York** Revise your A-level syllabus before arriving at university.

Institutions willing to defer entry after A-levels (see Ch 5): Aston; Bath; Bradford; Bristol (Maths/Phys); Brunel; Cheltenham & Glos (CHE); Coventry; Dundee; East Anglia; Glamorgan; Heriot-Watt; Hull; Kingston; Leeds; London (RH) (No); Newcastle; Plymouth; Robert Gordon (No); Roehampton (IHE); South Bank (Prefer not); Swansea; Trinity & All Saints (CHE); Westminster; York.

AFTER A-LEVELS ADVICE

Institutions which may accept the same points score after A-levels: Aberystwyth; Aston; Bath (depends on distribution of points); Birmingham; Bristol; Brunel; Coventry; Durham; East Anglia (perhaps); Essex; Greenwich; Heriot-Watt; Hull; Lancaster (B in maths); Liverpool; London (RH); Loughborough (Math Eng); Newcastle; Northumbria; Plymouth; Portsmouth; Robert Gordon; Salford; Sheffield; South Bank; Strathclyde; Surrey; Swansea; Teesside; Trinity & All Saints (CHE); UMIST.

Institutions demanding the actual grades offered after A-levels: Brighton; City; Dundee; Glamorgan; Hertfordshire; Nottingham; Warwick; York.

Institutions which may accept under-achieving applicants after A-levels: Most institutions.

Institutions with vacancies in Aug/Sept 1992 (see Ch 5): Aberystwyth 14-12 pts; Aston BBC; Bradford; Bristol (Maths/Phys) 12 pts, (Maths) 20 pts; Brunel 12 pts; Cheltenham & Glos (CHE) 6 pts; Coventry 10 pts; East Anglia 16-14 pts; Essex; Glamorgan 6 pts; Greenwich 4 pts; Heriot-Watt 14 pts; Hull (Maths/MS) 20pts; Kingston; Leeds 18 pts; London (RH) 16 pts; Newcastle 16 pts; Robert Gordon; Roehampton (IHE) 6 pts; Sheffield Hallam; South Bank EE; Swansea 14 pts; UMIST; Westminster; York 16 pts and most other institutions.

ADVICE FOR MATURE STUDENTS

Academic ability is important for all courses. Mature students account for approximately 10% of the student intake.

GRADUATE EMPLOYMENT

New Graduates' destinations (percentages) 1991:
Permanent employment: U 74; P 58.
Unemployment: U 20; P 30.
Further studies (all types): U 38; P 26.
Main career destinations (approx): Financial (Univ) 54, (Poly) 21; Computing (Univ) 25, (Poly) 52; Business/Admin (Univ & Poly) 14.

Surrey Accountancy, statistics, operational research, actuarial work, software engineering, retail management and teaching were among the destinations of graduates.

Teesside Graduates entered full-time employment as research assistants, management trainees and computer programmers.

York (1986-91) Out of 259 graduates from the department who entered employment, 137 went into careers in finance, 37% into one of the most challenging careers – actuarial work, 41% chose scientific and engineering careers and 33 into management services (21 into computing); 15 went into management – retail training and 5 into social work (care assistants and voluntary church and pastoral work). Teaching English as a foreign language, editorial work, the armed forces and a variety of other positions from management training in a night club to nursing accounted for the remainder.

MEDIA STUDIES

Special subject requirements: 2 A-levels from English, history, sociology or psychology.

NB Institutions may raise or lower the level of published offers depending either on the quality or otherwise of individual applications or the numbers of applications received; grades/points offered may be adjusted downwards after A-level results. The level of an offer is not indicative of the quality of a course.

26 pts.	**Leeds** - ABB (Broadcast St)
	Stirling - ABB (Film Media)
24 pts.	**Sussex** - BBB (Med St courses)
22 pts.	**Birmingham** - BBC (Media)
	Bournemouth - BBC-CCC (Media Prod) (6 AS)
	Bradford - BBC-CCC/BB-BC (Elec Med - lower offers for H6PL)
	Canterbury Christ Church (CHE) - BBC-DDD/AA-CC (Radio Film TV)
	De Montfort - BBC/AB (Media St)
	East Anglia - BBC/BB (Media/Lang)
	London (RH) - BBC (Media)
20 pts.	**Bristol UWE** - (Hum)
18 pts.	**Bournemouth** - 18-16 pts (Multi-Media Journ)
	City - CCC minimum (Journ/Soc; Journ/Econ; Journ/Soc Sci; Journ/Psy)
	Stirling - CCC/BB (Media; Media/Hist)
16 pts.	**Lancaster** - CCD (Hum)
	Ulster - CCD/BC (Media Stud)
14 pts.	**North Cheshire (CHE)** - 14 pts average (Media Bus; Con Media Pr)
	Nottingham Trent - BC (BJourn)
	Westminster - BC (Media St)
12 pts.	**Central Lancashire** - CC (Pre-Entry Certificate Newspaper Journalism)
	Trinity & All Saints (CHE) - CC-DD (Media St)
10 pts.	**and below**
	Bristol UWE - (Time Based Media)
	Buckingham (CHE) - 4 pts (Arts media Culture)
	Central Lancashire - (Audio Visual Media Studies - 1 A-level + Art Foundation course)

Derby - (Media Prod)
East London - 10 pts approx (Med/Film)
Edge Hill (CHE) - (Comm Inf Media - contact Admissions Tutor)
Kent (Inst) - (Comm Media - entry via ADAR)
Humberside - (Euro Audio Vis Prod - Good pass French or Spanish)
Liverpool John Moores - 10 pts (Media/Cul St)
Liverpool John Moores - (Int Credit Scheme) (6 AS)
London Inst (CP) - (Comm Med; Journalism)
Luton (CHE) - (Media Stud)
Northumbria - (Media Production)
Plymouth - (Med Lab Arts) (BTEC Ds+Ms)
Salford (UC) - (TV/Radio)
Sheffield Hallam - (Media Stud - contact Admissions Tutor)
St Mark & St John (CHE) - (Media PR)
Southampton (IHE) - (Media Communication - subject to approval)
Staffordshire - (Film/TV/Radio - contact Admissions Tutor)
Swansea (IHE) - (Arts/Media - contact Admissions Tutor)
Thames Valley London - (Des/Media - contact Admissions Tutor)
West Surrey (CA) - (Media St)
Westminster - 10 pts min (Con Media Practice)

Diploma of Higher Education courses:
Liverpool John Moores (Media/Cul St).

Offers for Foundation, Certificate and Diploma courses (see Ch 5):

Higher National Diploma courses (with Business Studies):
4 pts.   and below Salford (UC) (Media Performance; Media Prod); Thames Valley London (Media Studs).

Higher Diploma (Scotland):
Napier - EE (Journalism).

One-year Journalism courses: Central Lancashire; Darlington (CT); Harlow (Coll); Highbury (Coll, Portsmouth) (also Radio Journalism); London (Inst) (Periodical Journalism); Stradbroke (Coll, Sheffield).

Alternative offers:

IB offers: **Birmingham** 30 pts; **De Montfort** H666 S555.

SCE offers: **Westminster** AAA-BBB.

Overseas applicants: Bournemouth Fluency in written and spoken English required.

CHOOSING YOUR COURSE (See also Ch 1)

> **Subject information:** Intending applicants need to check course details carefully since this subject area can involve graphic design, illustration and other art courses as well as the media in the fields of TV, radio and journalism. See also **Communications Studies** and **Film and Video Studies.**

Course highlights: Birmingham The course focuses on critical understanding of social issues; it is not a practical media degree. **Bournemouth** In addition to Advertising degree courses, the University offers (subject to approval) a course in Multi-media Journalism. This covers studio skills in audio/video, photography, graphics and scriptwriting with specialist options in sport, crime, business, local affairs, politics and the arts. Placements in journalism are part of the course. **Bradford** A new course is offered in Electronic Imaging and Media Communications. **Bristol UWE** (Time Based Media) Radio, TV, animation and computer graphics. **City** Close links with media. Joint courses with Journalism. **Humberside** Four-year degree; three years spent in France or Spain. Aims to produce TV producers for the EC. **London (RH)** A new course emphasising the arts. The course covers three main areas – media practice, film, TV and video studies, cultural theory. **North Cheshire (CHE)** Practical/ academic study of media work. Experience in industry. **West Surrey (CA)** Emphasis on analysis of visual culture. NOW CHECK PROSPECTUSES FOR ALL COURSES.

Study opportunities abroad: City (E) FR NL D G.

Work opportunities abroad: Bournemouth EUR USA AUS; **City** FR SP G.

ADMISSIONS INFORMATION

Number of applicants per place (approx): Birmingham 37; **Bournemouth** 11; **Bradford** 6; **Bristol UWE** 2; **Canterbury Christ Church (CHE)** 23; **City (Poly)** 23; **De Montfort** 18; **Northumbria** 14; **North Cheshire (CHE)** 10; **Westminster** 44;üWest Surrey (CA) 3.

General Studies acceptable: West Surrey (CA).

Admissions Tutors' advice: Kent (IAD) Offers are based on a personal interview through ADAR. **London Inst (CP)** Portfolio important. Foundation course not necessary. **Northumbria** Entry to course based on an interview and student's portfolio and is via ADAR scheme. **Westminster** Applicants must show interest in the practical use of mass media (print, journalism, radio and television), with critical interest in the social role of media and in cultural value of their output. Those interested only in the practical side of course (which makes up only one third) should be discouraged from applying. Applicants should show some evidence of an interest and involvement in the field (for example school magazines, drama). We do not make a standard offer. We interview promising candidates and set them short test on the day of interview.

Examples of interview questions: Which newspapers do you read? Discuss the main differences between the national daily newspapers. Which radio programmes do you listen to each day? Which television programmes do you watch? Why do you think that ITV needs to spend two million pounds advertising itself? Should the BBC broadcast advertisments? What do you think are the reasons for the popularity of East Enders? (See also under **Admissions Tutors' advice**.)

GAP YEAR ADVICE

Institutions accepting a Gap Year: Most institutions; **Bournemouth** (Journ) Try to get work experience. **City** Travel and improve your language skills. **North Cheshire (CHE)** Must have relevant experience. **Westminster** We cannot hold places for students: we only offer places for the current academic year.

Institutions willing to defer entry after A-levels (see Ch 5): Bournemouth; De Montfort; Leeds; North Cheshire (CHE); Northumbria (No); Westminster (Con Media Practice).

AFTER A-LEVELS ADVICE

Institutions with vacancies in Aug/Sept 1992 (see Ch 5): De Montfort 20-18 pts; Humberside 14 pts; North Cheshire (CHE).

GRADUATE EMPLOYMENT

New Graduates' destinations (percentages) 1991:
Permanent employment: P 75; C 73.
Unemployment: P 17; C 20.
Further studies (all types): P 8; C 11.

MEDICINE

Special subject requirements: usually 3 A-levels from mathematics, physics, chemistry, physical science, engineering sciences, biology, zoology.

NB Institutions may raise or lower the level of published offers depending either on the quality or otherwise of individual applications or the numbers of applications received; grades/points offered may be adjusted downwards after A-level results. The level of an offer is not indicative of the quality of a course.

30 pts.	**Cambridge/Oxford** - AAA potential recommended (Med Sci) (Medicine)
28 pts.	**Edinburgh** - AAB (for students not offering biology) - ABB (Medicine) (2 AS with 2 A-levels, 5 AS without A-levels)
	Manchester - 28-24 pts approx (Medicine)
26 pts.	**Belfast** - ABB/26 pts (Medicine)
24 pts.	**Aberdeen** - BBB (Medicine)
	Birmingham - BBB/BB ask for details (Medicine) (For BMed Sci course see **Science**)
	Bristol - BBB or BB + BB AS-levels (2:1 for graduates) (Medicine) (For 2nd MB entry 2 AS, 1 in a science) (BTEC HND Ds+Ms)
	Cardiff (UWCM) - BBB (Medicine) AS - Contact Admissions Tutor)
	Glasgow - BBB (Medicine)
	Leeds - BBB (Medicine) (2 AS: 1 in phys/biol/maths if not at A-level + any other AS)
	Leicester - BBB (Medicine)
	Liverpool - BBB-BBC (Medicine)
	London (King's College (SMD)) - BBB (Medicine)
	London (HMC) - BBB-BCC (Medicine)
	London (Royal Free) - BBB (Medicine)
	London (St Bartholomew's HMC) - BBB (Medicine)
	Newcastle - BBB (Medicine) (2 AS maths/phys/biol preferred)
	Nottingham - BBB minimum (Medicine)
	St Andrews - BBB (Med) (4 AS)
	Sheffield - BBB-BB + 2 AS (Medicine) (BTEC Ds+Ms)
	Southampton - BBB (Medicine)
22 pts.	**Dundee** - BBC (Medicine)
	Leeds - BBC-BCC (Med Sci)
	London (Charing Cross/Westminster MS) - BBC (Medicine)
	London (St George's HMS) - BBC (Medicine) (See **Admissions Tutors' advice**)
	London (UMDS) - BBC at first sitting (Medicine) (See **Admissions Tutors' advice**)
20 pts.	**London (St Mary's HMS)** - BCC (Medicine)
18 pts.	**London (University College/Middlesex SM)** - CCC (Medicine)

Alternative offers:

EB offers: **Glasgow** 80%; **Sheffield** 80%.

IB offers: **Aberdeen** Average of 6 at Higher and Subsid; **Belfast** H766 S555; **Birmingham** 28 pts; **Bristol** 32 pts inc H666; **Dundee** H665; **Cardiff (UWCM)** H666; **Edinburgh** 35 pts inc H766; **Glasgow** Average of grade 6 but not less than 6 in chem; **Leeds** 30 pts inc H666; **Leicester** 30 pts inc H666; **Liverpool** H666; **London (Barts)** H666; **London (Ch Cross/West)** H665; **London (HMC)** H666; **London (King's)** H666; **London (Royal Free)** H666; **London (St George's)** H665; **London (St Mary's)** chem H6+55 S555; **London (UC/Middlesex)** chem H6+55; **London (UMDS)** H666 at first sitting; **Newcastle** H666; **Nottingham** H666; **St Andrews** 30 pts; **Sheffield** H666 S555; **Southampton** 30 pts.

Irish offers: **Glasgow** AAABBB; **St Andrews** AAABB; **Sheffield** AAAABB.

SCE offers: **Aberdeen** AAABB; **Bristol** AAAA; **Dundee** AAABB; **Edinburgh** AAABB; **Glasgow** AAABB or for repeating applicants ABBBB at the first sitting followed by B in SYS and A's in new Highers; **St Andrews** AAABB; **Sheffield** AABBB.

Overseas applicants: London (St George's) Distinct preferences for candidates from countries with inadequate facilities for training in Medicine.

CHOOSING YOUR COURSE (See also Ch 1)

Subject information: All courses will offer the same components leading to a career in medicine. For outstanding students without science A-levels, some pre-medical courses are available. Thereafter for all, a period of pre-clinical studies leads on to clinical studies. Intercalated courses of one year leading to a BSc are also offered and elective periods abroad in the final years can sometimes be taken. All courses are very similar in course content.

Deans of medical schools have decided unanimously to adopt a policy of 'no detriment' for applicants to Medicine who list one non-medical course on the UCAS application. However, applicants should know that if they receive four rejections for Medicine and an offer for a non-medical course, they are not allowed to change their decision and attempt to reopen negotiations with medical schools if they achieve higher A-level grades than expected. When selecting applicants, admissions tutors first look for evidence of academic excellence, not just for its own sake but because a medical course is long and demanding, and the ability to apply oneself and to survive are extremely important. Secondly, a long-standing interest in medicine is always an advantage, together with evidence that the applicant has a well-rounded personality, a wide range of interests, imagination, research potential and is socially aware. A year out is also becoming an asset with some medical schools. A history of mental illness - even the mildest form - can be a bar to entry, and students' physical and mental stability is often under review. The confidential report from the applicant's school is very important. In addition to A-level applicants, most medical schools have a small annual intake (4 to 8) of graduates (usually dental or science). Early applications are advantageous and very serious consideration is given to the overall GCSE grades achieved. The fact that applicants have five choices does not mean that they will receive equal consideration from all the institutions named on their UCAS application. In Medicine this is especially so: applicants receiving one or two offers often will be rejected by other medical schools. Therefore medical applicants receiving even one offer and four rejections have little cause for concern since any other offer they might have received would have de manded the same, or a very similar, high level of attainment. Letters have been received from medical schools indicating that they continue to receive applications from candidates who are not predicted by their schools to achieve grades above DDD. They stress the futility of such applications. See also **Admissions Tutors' advice**.

Course highlights: Birmingham Continuous assessment. **Cardiff (UWCM)** Clinical attachments throughout Wales, usually one student per firm in district general hospitals. **Dundee** Increasing number of options. Elective periods in fourth and fifth years. **Leeds** (Med Sci) New science course mirrors pre-clinical studies. **Leicester** Course orientated to the 'patient in society'. Very strong science base. Small-group teaching. **London (King's)** Pre-clinical course based in multi-faculty environment. **London (St George's)** Systematic teaching courses in pre-clinical years rather than compartmentalised basic medical sciences. Final written exams at beginning of fifth year allowing students to spend last nine months perfecting clinical skills. **London (Royal Free)** Increasing integration of pre-clinical and clinical stages; medical school and hospital are on one site. **Nottingham** MB awarded at end of third year spent in one department. **St Andrews** Unique two-part course. Pre-clinical at St Andrews followed by guaranteed place at Manchester. **Sheffield** Intercalated degree courses widely available. **Southampton** Integrated curriculum; early patient contact. High research ratings at **Cambridge, Oxford, Newcastle, Wales, Edinburgh, Glasgow, London (UC/Middlesex)**. NOW CHECK PROSPECTUSES FOR ALL COURSES.

Study opportunities abroad: Bristol (E); short elective periods abroad are available in most medical schools.

Work opportunities abroad: Bristol European Community Training Scheme; **Edinburgh** USA FE EUR AUS AF. **London (Royal Free)** All students have an elective period in the final clinical year which the majority spend abroad.

ADMISSIONS INFORMATION

Attitudes towards overseas (non-EC) applicants: Aberdeen 12 places available; **Glasgow** Limited number of places, BBB or higher required; **London (Barts)** 3 places available; **London (King's)** 4 places available; **London (Royal Free)** 4 places available; **London (St George's)** 6 places available; **London (St Mary's)** 5 places available. Preferences given to those from countries unable to offer a medical education; **London (UMDS)** 7 places available but applicants must meet normal entry requirements and be available for interview in UK; **Nottingham** 15 places available; **Southampton** 12 places available; **Aberdeen, Cardiff (UWCM), Glasgow, Nottingham** Preference given to applicants from countries unable to provide a medical training.

Attitudes towards EC applicants: All medical schools consider applicants from EC countries, all of whom must be able to attend for interview before offers are made. **London (UMDS)** Considered as 'Home' students but must offer A-levels or IB.

Number of applicants per place (approx): Aberdeen (Home) 10, (Overseas) 15; **Belfast** 3; **Birmingham** 15; **Bristol** 11; **Cardiff (UWCM)** 12; **Dundee** 11; **Edinburgh** 13; **Glasgow** 7; **Leeds** 20; **Leicester** 14; **London (Barts)** 11, **(Ch Cross/West)** 14, **(King's)** 10, **(Royal Free)** 17, **(St George's)** 10, **(St Mary's)** 20, **(UMDS)** 7; **Newcastle** 11; **Nottingham** 17; **St Andrews** 9; **Sheffield** 13; **Southampton** 12.

Selection interviews: Belfast (only borderline and mature students); Birmingham; Bristol; Cambridge; Cardiff (UWCM); Leeds; Liverpool; London Medical Schools except (St George's) 30%, (St Mary's) 25%, (UMDS) 50%; Newcastle; Nottingham (one in five applicants are interviewed); Oxford; St Andrews (some); Sheffield 30%.

No selection interviews: Aberdeen (rarely); Dundee (not usually); Edinburgh; St Andrews (seldom).

Under 18 age range not favoured: Cambridge; London (King's), (London HMC), (Royal Free), (St Mary's), (UC/Middlesex), (UMDS).

Grades required for second attempt: Belfast AAB; Birmingham AAA; Bristol BBB; Cardiff (UWCM) ABB for applicants with BCC/CCC at first attempt; Glasgow ABB for applicants with CCC at the first sitting; Leeds usually higher offers; Leicester ABB (if they applied to Leicester first time); London (Barts) applications from resit candidates are discouraged, London (Ch Cross/West) ABB-BBB, London (HMC) BBB, London (King's) offers not made; London (Royal Free) ABB, London (St George's) ABB, London (St Mary's) ABB, London (UC/Middlesex) BBB-BCC, London (UMDS) resit candidates considered only in cases of serious mitigating circumstances eg, illness, bereavement; Newcastle ABB; Nottingham AAB or ABB; St Andrews ABB; Sheffield ABB.

Commitment to medicine: Opinions differ among medical schools regarding commitment shown by a candidate who applies for five medical courses. The following are 'not particularly worried': Belfast; Dundee; Glasgow; Leeds; London (Ch Cross/West), (UC/Middlesex); St Andrews. All other medical schools consider commitment an asset, but see **Author's note** above.

Motivation: All institutions will seek some evidence of motivation in candidates applying for medical training. The following medical schools, say that they make a conscious effort to assess this quality, and in some cases, will 'test' it: Aberdeen; Birmingham; Bristol; Cambridge; Edinburgh; Glasgow; Leeds; Liverpool, London (Barts), (Ch Cross/West), (King's), (Royal Free), (St George's), (St Mary's), (UC/Middlesex), UMDS; Newcastle; Nottingham; Oxford; Sheffield.

Admissions Tutors' advice: Aberdeen Deferred entry exceptional. **Birmingham** Academic achievement is not sole factor. Performance at interview considered extremely important. **Bristol** Minimum GCSE requirement 5-6 grades A-C for interview and possible conditional offer. All candidates seriously considered for offers are interviewed; 12 students are admitted annually to the pre-medical course. **Cardiff (UWCM)** Requires sound science background; great emphasis placed on evidence of a caring nature - of exposure to the hospital/medical environment (eg, voluntary work in hospitals, homes etc). If not offered at A-level, biology or physics must be offered at GCSE (grade A-C) or AS-levels. There is a 10% intake of mature students each year aged 21 years and over, who are either graduates or have worked in hospitals. Considers applicants who have pursued 2 science A-levels (inc chemistry) and 1 other A-level provided they have good science background at GCSE or AS-level. **Glasgow** It is sometimes assumed that all candidates must meet the 'going rate' at the first attempt. In fact if a candidate just misses, he/she may be allowed to come on the basis of re-sits, although he/she would be expected to pass at the 'going rate'. English candidates wrongly assume that Glasgow is biased against anyone not from the West of Scotland. **Leeds** Consider your motivation carefully - we do. We look for evidence of it, broadly-ranging interests and academic capacity. Overseas students resitting are not usually accepted. **Liverpool** A few applicants are interviewed and those re-applying for the second time can only be considered if younger than normal. **London (Barts)** Candidates should be capable of achieving BBB minimum grades at A-level at the first attempt. Prefers all first-year students to live in college accommodation and guarantees a place in college hall for all first and final year students. Applicants strongly advised to obtain some first hand experience of medical work through voluntary work in a hospital or with a GP. If not possible, some form of social work is useful. Overseas student quota 3 places; resits not acceptable. **London (Ch Cross/West)** Looks for suitability for a medical career in terms of personal qualities and motivation, academic ability, ability to fit into student community and good health. UCCA applications to be sent as early as possible after 1 September to increase chances of being shortlisted for interview. **London (King's)** Clinical course based in residential area with no shortage of patients. School looks for suitability for medical career in terms of academic ability, determination, stamina and mental health. If a candidate achieves AAA and wants to apply for a place at Oxbridge next year but is already placed with us, he/she should contact us by phone immediately after A-level results are known; his/her case will be treated sympathetically and appropriate advice given. If a candidate does not want to take up his/her place they should inform us by the end of August so that the place can be filled. Great importance is attached to the interview. Most students invited for interview will have grades A or B in their GCSEs. **London (Royal Free)** Applicants preferably should be studying a biological subject to A-level. Those who are not must have at least a B grade in GCSE biology or human biology. An Open Day is usually held for sixth formers and careers staff early in July. **London (St George's)** Applicants may offer chemistry at A-level plus 1 approved science A-level plus 2 arts AS-levels OR chemistry A-level plus 2 science AS-levels plus 1 arts A-level, provided that in each case any missing science or maths subject is passed at grade A or B in GCSE. A score of 20 pts is sought at GCSE on the basis of A=3 pts, B=2 pts, C=1 pt if a candidate is to be considered seriously. Resit candidates expected to achieve an aggregate of ABB over the two attempts. **London (St Mary's)** Applicants are expected to have good GCSE passes in mathematics and individual sciences. Looks for resourceful men and women with wide interests and accomplishments, practical concern for others, and those who will make contribution to the life of School and hospital. Academic ability, motivation, character and depth of interests are all assessed. **London (United Medical and Dental Schools of Guys/St Thomas's)** Operates equal opportunities policy for student admissions and welcomes applications from enterprising and well-motivated candidates from a wide variety of backgrounds. Academic ability, personal qualities, interests and accomplishments all taken into account when selecting candidates for interview. Prospective students very welcome to attend annual UMDS Open Days in May. UMDS admits the largest number of medical and dental students in London, and its innovative courses emphasise wherever possible development of communication skills, early contact with patients, flexibility of study and self-directed learning. **Newcastle** This medical school has never encouraged applicants to think in terms of the same points score. This and other terms of the conditional offer are made clear in the offer letter. Most of our intake have achieved substantially higher than the three grade B offer made to first time applicants. The pre-medical course is intended for the following categories of applicant: candidates from schools with arts A-level subjects (and not candidates who have taken science A-levels, but not chemistry); Scottish candidates offering Highers (Scottish candidates offering CSYS in chemistry and a CSYS in one other subject will be considered for the five-year course provided they offer biology, physics and mathematics at GCSE (grade A-C)); arts graduates and mature students with an arts A-level background. The curriculum is integrated with teaching on a systematic basis and early clinical exposure with regular clinical demonstrations, clinical tutorials and family visits. Applicants with any queries should contact the administrative assistant (Admissions) at the medical school. five to ten students are admitted to the pre-medical course. **Nottingham** Candidates should familiarise themselves with course details. **Sheffield** Students without A or AS physics take short course in medical physics in first year.

Examples of interview questions: Should doctors be allowed to test patients for AIDS without their consent? What can you do with a brick? Why do you want to study Medicine? What qualities are needed to be a good doctor? What qualities would your friends say that you possess? What area of medicine is of special interest to you? What are your views on vivisection? Have you any relatives in the medical profession? Why should we offer you a place rather than giving it to another candidate? What do you think of the present nuclear arms position? What are your Christian beliefs? What are your views on private and NHS medicine? Questions on the medical advances made in the last 20 years. How is rejection prevented in transplants? How do they choose a transplant donor? Are heart transplants worth the money? What advance in medicine has impressed you the most? What does an ECG measure? How does the heart work? Are doctors paid well? Should nurses go on strike? Should mongol babies be put to sleep at birth? What satisfaction do you think a GP gets from his/her work? What outside activity interests you the most? Would you give it up to concentrate on your medical studies? Do you think your life-style will be affected by the course? What do you know about cystic fibrosis? What will you do if you fail to get into Medicine?

GAP YEAR ADVICE

Institutions willing to defer entry after A-levels (see Ch 5): Dundee (No).

Attitude towards a year out: *Acceptable:* Bristol; Cambridge; Cardiff (UWCM); Edinburgh; Liverpool; London (Ch Cross/West), (King's), (St Mary's), (UMDS); Newcastle; Oxford. *Acceptable for positive reasons:* Leeds; London (UC/Middlesex), (Royal Free) Use it wisely. *Not encouraged, but deferred applications seriously considered:* Check with Manchester. *If the candidate has sound academic background* and plans to make good use of the year: Glasgow, London (Barts), (St George's), (UMDS). *Not discouraged:* Sheffield.

AFTER A-LEVELS ADVICE

Medical Schools which may accept the same points score after A-levels: Birmingham; Cardiff (UWCM); Edinburgh (perhaps); Leicester (in special circumstances); Liverpool; London (Barts) (every candidate failing to meet exact offer automatically reconsidered to see if strengths likely to balance weaknesses. No use is made of points system), (Ch Cross/West), (Royal Free), (St George's) (ABD only), (St Mary's) (E grades not acceptable); Sheffield, Southampton.

Medical Schools demanding the actual grades offered after A-levels: Aberdeen; Bristol; Glasgow; Leeds; London (King's), (Lond HMC), (UC/Middlesex), (Royal Free); Newcastle (usually); Nottingham (usually).

Medical Schools which may accept under-achieving applicants after A-levels: Birmingham; Cardiff (UWCM) for very good interviewees if place available; Edinburgh (in special circumstances); Glasgow; Leeds and Leicester (Rarely); London (Barts), (HMC), (King's) very few, (St George's) only in exceptional non-academic circumstances, (Royal Free) very few, (UMDS); St Andrews; Sheffield and Southampton (only in special circumstances).

Attitudes towards applicants repeating A-levels (check with the Medical School before applying): *Acceptable but higher A-levels will be demanded:* Aberdeen; Cardiff (UWCM); Edinburgh; Leeds (probably); Liverpool; London (Ch Cross/West), (St George's); Newcastle; Sheffield. *Acceptable but few offers made:* Nottingham (Candidates considered on individual merit; grades A and B expected). *Rarely considered:* Aberdeen (2nd attempts); Birmingham. *Only if extenuating circumstances* for low grades at first attempt (eg illness) or in some cases a mature applicant who had taken A-levels several years ago: Bristol, Dundee, Edinburgh, Leeds, London (King's), Southampton. *Grades of at least CCC should have been achieved at the first attempt:* Glasgow. *Only in extremely unusual circumstances:* London (UMDS). *In some cases:* London (HMC). *Only in exceptional circumstances:* London (King's), (UC/Middlesex). *Rarely:* We discourage applications from re-sit candidates: London (Barts). *Depending on the initial A-level grades obtained:* London (Royal Free).

Attitudes towards second applications to the same Medical Schools (check with Medical School before applying): *Providing rejection was made before A-levels* had been taken and at A-level the candidate had achieved grades of BBB or higher: Birmingham; Bristol; Edinburgh; Glasgow; London (Barts), (King's). *In exceptional circumstances:* Leeds; London (UC/Middlesex). *Acceptable:* Dundee; London (HMC), Sheffield; Southampton. *Acceptable unless rejected after interview first time:* Cardiff (UWCM), London (Ch Cross/West), (Royal Free). *Only if the candidate did not achieve full potential at first attempt:* London (St Mary's). *If BBB grades or better had been achieved at first attempt:* Manchester.

Summary of vacancies in Aug/Sept 1992: Only one medical school declared vacancies at 26 pts.

ADVICE FOR MATURE STUDENTS

Medical schools usually accept a small number of mature students each year. However, several, if not the majority, reject applicants over 30 years of age. Some medical schools accept non-graduates although A-level passes at high grades usually would be stipulated. The majority of applicants accepted will be graduates with a first or 2:1 degree.

MICROBIOLOGY

Special subject requirements: 2-3 A-levels in science and mathematics subjects. Chemistry sometimes required. GCSE (grade A-C) mathematics important.

NB Institutions may raise or lower the level of published offers depending either on the quality or otherwise of individual applications or the numbers of applications received; grades/points offered may be adjusted downwards after A-level results. The level of an offer is not indicative of the quality of a course.

20 pts.	**Bristol** – BCC-CCD/BB-BC (Microbiol) (AS in biol when not at A-level or GCSE grade A-C)
	Kent – BCC-CCC/BB (Microbiol)
	London (Imp) – BCC (Microbiol; Biol/Microb)
18 pts.	**Aberdeen** – CCC-CCD/BC (Microbiol)
	Aberystwyth – 18-16 pts (Micro; Env Micro; Micro/Zoo) (BTEC 3M)
	Belfast – CCC/BB (Microbiol; App Micro)
	Birmingham – CCC (Micro/Vir; Micro/Tech)
	Cardiff – BCD/AB (Microb)
	East Anglia – BCD/BB (Microbiol)
	Edinburgh – CCC/BB (Microbiol) (4 AS)
	Glasgow – CCC-CCD/BC (Microbiol) (BTEC 3M)
	Heriot-Watt – CCC (Microbiol)
	Leicester – BCD (Biol Sci)
	London (QMW) – CCC-CCD (Microbiol)
	Manchester – 18 pts (Microbiol)
	Newcastle – CCC-CCD/BB (All courses) (2 AS) (BTEC M chem)
	Nottingham – CCC average (All courses)
	Reading – CCC-BCD (Microbiol)
	Sheffield – CCC (Micro) (BTEC Ms)
	Strathclyde – CCC-BCD (2nd yr entry) (App Microb)
	Surrey – CCC/BC (All courses) (4 AS A-levels biol/chem + AS phys/ maths ideal) (BTEC 5M)
	Swansea – CCC/BB (Microb) (BTEC 1D+Ms)
	Warwick – CCC (Micro Tech; Micro Virol; Biotech)
16 pts.	**Bradford** – CCD/BB (Microbiol) (BTEC 3M)
	Leeds – CCD (Minimum) (Microb; Microb) (2 AS in science subjects except chem)
	Liverpool – CCD (Microb) (5 AS)

	London (King's) – 16 pts approx (Microbiol)
	London (UC) – CCD (Micro Biol)
14pts.	**Dundee** – CDD/BC (Microbiol)
12pts.	**Heriot-Watt** – DDD (1st yr entry) (Microbiol) (CCC 2nd yr entry)
	Hertfordshire – 12-8 pts (App Biol Micro)
10pts.	**Liverpool John Moores** – DDE/DD (Ap Micro)
8pts.	**and below**
	East London – (Microbiol)
	Westminster – (Bioch/Micro)

Alternative offers:

EB offers: **Bradford** 65%; **East Anglia** 70%.

IB offers: **Aberdeen** 26 pts; **Aberystwyth** 28 pts and above; **Bradford** 24 pts; **Bristol** 30 pts with 5 or 6 in relevant subjects; **Glasgow** H555; **Heriot-Watt** 28 pts; **Hertfordshire** 24 pts; **Leeds** H555 S333; **Liverpool** 30 pts inc H555; **Newcastle** 28-25 pts inc 5 chem; **Surrey** H55 biol/chem; **Swansea** 28 pts.

Irish offers: **Aberdeen** BBCC/BCCCC; **Aberystwyth** BBBCC; **Bradford** BBBB; **East Anglia** BBBCCC; **Glasgow** BBB; **Liverpool** BBCCC.

SCE offers: **Aberdeen** BBBC; **Bradford** BBBB; **Dundee** BBCC; **Edinburgh** BBBB; **Glasgow** BBBB; **Heriot-Watt** BBBB; **Liverpool** AABB; **Newcastle** BBBB; **Sheffield** BBBB; **Strathclyde** ABBC/BBBB.

CHOOSING YOUR COURSE (See also Ch 1)

> **Subject information:** This is a branch of biological science specialising in a study of micro-organisms – bacteria, viruses and fungi. The subject covers the relationship between these organisms and disease and such industrial applications as food and drug production, waste-water treatment as well as future biochemical uses.

Course highlights: Aberystwyth Course decisions can be delayed until start of year 2. **Belfast** Strong final year emphasis on food and agriculture. **Bradford** Broad-based course in years 1 and 2 in subjects allied to medicine. Optional year out in industry. **Bristol** Broad course with flexible options. Strong research areas in genetics and virology. Close co-operation with Pathology with shared options and possibility of transfer. **East London** Remedial tutorials in year 1. **Heriot-Watt** Transfer between courses possible. Specialist options from other related biological areas. **Hertfordshire** Common first year, then seven pathways in agricultural biology, biochemistry, biotechnology, microbiology, molecular biology, physiology and pharmacology. **Newcastle** Six half-units taken in first year subjects chosen for entry to year 2. **Swansea** Specialisation possible in aquatic microbiology, genetic engineering of micro-organisms, biotechnology and immunology. **Surrey** Broad course which includes environmental aspects; carefully selected and monitored places for students' industrial placements with over 30 companies; sponsorship of selected students. NOW CHECK PROSPECTUSES FOR ALL COURSES.

Study opportunities abroad: Heriot-Watt FR; **Kent**; **Surrey** (E); **Swansea** (E).

Work opportunities abroad: East London GR SW; **Hertfordshire** B NL SZ; **Surrey** SZ SP.

ADMISSIONS INFORMATION

Number of applicants per place (approx): Aberystwyth 11; **Bradford** 10; **Bristol** 7; **Hertfordshire** 10; **Leeds** 7; **Liverpool** 3; **Newcastle** 9; **Strathclyde** 8; **Surrey** 6; **Swansea** 5.

General Studies acceptable: Aberystwyth; Bristol; Leeds; Newcastle (2).

Selection interviews: Bristol; Newcastle; Surrey; Swansea.

Offers to applicants repeating A-levels: Higher Bristol, Strathclyde, Swansea; **Possibly higher** Aberystwyth, East Anglia, Leeds, Newcastle; **Same** Bradford, Leeds, Liverpool.

Admissions Tutors' advice: Aberystwyth GCSE English and mathematics grade A-C required. **Leeds** Maths and English language required at GCSE. Offers made on basis of referee's report with A-level predictions of about 14 points.

Examples of interview questions: Is money spent on the arts a waste? How much does the country spend on research and on the armed forces? Discuss reproduction in bacteria. What do you particularly like about your study of biology? What would you like to do after your degree? Predict the grades you think you will get. Do you have any strong views on vivisection? Discuss the differences between the courses you have applied for. What important advances have been made in the biological field recently? How would you describe microbiology? Do you know anything about the diseases caused by micro-organisms? What symptoms would be caused by which particular organisms?

GAP YEAR ADVICE

Institutions accepting a Gap Year: Most institutions; **Aberystwyth** Apply before taking year out so that you can visit the universities of your choice. **Bristol** Consider carefully before you interrupt your studies. **East London** A year out is built into the course already. **Surrey** Have a positive reason: don't just take a break.

Institutions willing to defer entry after A-levels (see Ch 5): Aberystwyth (Contact Admissions Tutor); Bristol; Heriot-Watt; Swansea (Discouraged).

AFTER A-LEVELS ADVICE

Institutions which may accept the same points score after A-levels: Aberystwyth; Bradford; East Anglia; Leeds; Liverpool; Liverpool John Moores; Newcastle; Strathclyde; Swansea; Surrey.

Institutions which may accept under-achieving applicants after A-levels: Aberystwyth; Bradford; Bristol; East Anglia; Liverpool; Liverpool John Moores; Newcastle; Strathclyde; Surrey; Swansea.

Institutions with vacancies in Aug/Sept 1992 (see Ch 5): Aberdeen; Aberystwyth 14 pts; Anglia (Poly Univ); Bristol 16 pts; Dundee; East London; Heriot-Watt 12 pts; Kent; Leeds; Surrey CDD; Swansea 16-14 pts; most institutions are likely to have vacancies in 1993.

GRADUATE EMPLOYMENT

New Graduates' destinations (percentages) 1991:
Permanent employment: U 74.
Unemployment: U 18.
Further studies (all types): U 45.
Main career destinations (approx): Scientific 55; Admin 15; Financial 11; Business 10; Computing 2; Secretarial 3.

Surrey Those graduates who entered subject-related occupations were involved in research work in food and drink, virology, the Blood Transfusion Service and in sales work as medical representatives. Others went into accountancy and several went on to study for PhDs in molecular cell biology, genetics, pharmacology and toxicology.

See also under **Science.**

MICRO-ELECTRONICS

Special subject requirements: 2-3 A-levels in mathematics/science subjects.

NB Institutions may raise or lower the level of published offers depending either on the quality or otherwise of individual applications or the numbers of applications received; grades/points offered may be adjusted downwards after A-level results. The level of an offer is not indicative of the quality of a course.

22 pts.	**Brunel** - BBC/BB (Micro S Des) (BTEC 1D+4M)
	Newcastle - BBC/BB (Microelect)
	UMIST - BBC/AB (Micro Electronics courses) (BTEC Ds+Ms)
20 pts.	**Cardiff** - BCC (Micro/Man Sys)
	Newcastle - BCC/AB (Micro/Soft) (MEng)
18 pts.	**Edinburgh** - CCC (Micro)
	Hull - BCD/BB (Comp Eng) (4 AS)
	Newcastle - CCC/BB (Micro/Soft H616)
16 pts.	**Newcastle** - CCD/BC (Micro/Soft H617)
14 pts.	**Nottingham Trent** - CCE (Micro)
12 pts.	**Middlesex** - 12 pts (Micro Eng)
10 pts.	**Staffordshire** - (Micro) (BTEC 3M)
8 pts.	**and below**
	Anglia (Poly Univ) - (Micro Elect)
	Central Lancashire - (Comb Hons)
	Derby - (Modular) (4 AS)
	Oxford Brookes - DD (Modular) (4 AS)
	Paisley - (Phys Sci)
	Salford (UC) - (Micro Con Eng)

Alternative offers:

IB offers: **UMIST** H666.

CHOOSING YOUR COURSE (See also Ch 1)

> **Subject information:** These courses usually overlap those specialising in computing and electronic engineering. Applicants should check course details for their preferences.

Course highlights: Brunel French/German options. Course recognised by IEE. Placements in Europe. **UMIST** Equal content of hardware and software. NOW CHECK PROSPECTUSES FOR ALL COURSES.

Work opportunities abroad: Aston (E); **Brunel** (E).

ADMISSIONS INFORMATION

Number of applicants per place (approx): Brunel 3; **Newcastle** (Microelect) 2; **Oxford Brookes** 6; **UMIST** 3.

Selection interviews: Newcastle (some).

Offers to applicants repeating A-levels: Higher Newcastle (Microelect) (ABC-BBB) (Micro/Soft – unlikely to offer).

Admissions Tutors' advice: Newcastle (Micro/Soft) Industrial sponsorship normally required.

> **Examples of interview questions:** See under **Electrical/Electronic Engineering**.

GAP YEAR ADVICE

Institutions accepting a Gap Year: Most institutions; **Anglia (Poly Univ)** Apply for place before taking gap year; **Brunel** Follow some engineering activity if possible.

Institutions willing to defer entry after A-levels (see Ch 5): Brunel; UMIST.

AFTER A-LEVELS ADVICE

Institutions which may accept the same points score after A-levels: UMIST.

Institutions demanding the actual grades offered after A-levels: Newcastle.

Institutions with vacancies in Aug/Sept 1992 (see Ch 5): Brunel 18 pts and a large number of vacancies down to 4 pts.

MODERN LANGUAGES (See also **Language** and specific language subject tables)

Special subject requirements: A-level in chosen languages. GCSE (grade A-C) Latin for some courses.

NB Institutions may raise or lower the level of published offers depending either on the quality or otherwise of individual applications or the numbers of applications received; grades/points offered may be adjusted downwards after A-level results. The level of an offer is not indicative of the quality of a course.

30 pts. **Cambridge/Oxford** - AAA potential recommended (Mod/M Lang) (Mod Lang)
24 pts. **Aston** - BBB/AA (See subject tables)
Bath - ABC-BBC (All Europ courses)
Bristol - BBB (See subject tables) BBC (For combinations with Russian)
Durham - BBB (Mod Lang; Russ/Pol)
Leeds - BBB/AB (Fr/Ger; Fr/Sp)
Salford - BBB/BB (M Lang/Mark)
St Andrews - BBB (Mod Lang)
22 pts. **Birmingham** - BBC (Comb Hons and Mod Lang)
Cardiff - BBC (Int Scheme/3 Lang)
Durham - BBC (Mod Lang except under **24 pts**)
East Anglia - BBC-BCC/BB (Standard BCC) (Mod Lang/Eur Hist) (See also **20 pts**)
Exeter - BBC-BCC (Comb courses - approx offer)
Heriot-Watt - BBC (B in two languages)/AA (in languages) (All language courses)
Hull - BBC (Comb Lang)
Leeds - BBC/AB (Fr/Hist; Fr/Ital; Fr/Rus)
Newcastle - BBC/AB (French; Fr/Ger; Fr/Sp; Fr/Port; Fr/Comp Sc)
Nottingham - BBC (Mod Langs)
Salford - BBC-BCC (Mod Lang; Mod Lang/Acc)
Sheffield - BBC (Mod Lang); Mod Lang/Ed) (4 AS)
Swansea - BBC/BB-BC (Most Mod Lang/Bus St Courses)
20 pts. **Aberystwyth** - BCC (Mod Lang/Bus)
East Anglia - BCC/CC (Programmes with Scand St)
Essex - BCC/BB (Mod Lang courses)
Hull - BCC (Mod Lang)

	Lancaster – BCC (Fr/Ger; Fr/Ital; Germ/Ital)
	Sheffield – BCC (M Langs)
	York – BCC/BB (Language)
18 pts.	**Leicester** – BCD-CCC/BC (Mod Langs)
	Northumbria – CCC (Mod Lang/Bus Fin/Mark/PM)
	Strathclyde – CCC (BBD 2nd yr entry) (Mod Lang)
16 pts.	**Bristol UWE** – CCD/CC (Fr/Ger; Fr/Sp; Ger/Sp)
	St David's – CCD/CC (Mod Lang)
14 pts.	**Bristol UWE** – BC (FGIS; FSIS; GSIS)
	Liverpool John Moores – 14 pts (Mod Lang St)
	Southampton – BC (Mod Lang/Comp – 4 yr course)
12 pts.	**Kingston** – DDD/CC (Fr/Econ/Pol; Ger/Econ/Pol; Sp/Econ/Pol) (2 AS)
	Leeds Met – CC (Eur Lang Bus)
	Westminster – CC (Mod Lang)
	Wolverhampton – CC (Mod Lang)
10 pts.	**Anglia (Poly Univ)** – CD (Mod Lang in French, German, Italian and Spanish)
	Coventry – CD (Fr/Ger; Fr/Sp; Ger/Sp) (A-levels in languages)
	La Sainte Union (CHE) – DDE/DD (Mod Lang/Eur St)
	Manchester Met – CEE/CD (Mod Lang/Lit)
	Oxford Brookes – CD (Lang Bus)
8 pts.	**and below**
	South Bank – DD (MLIS)
	Thames Valley London – (App Lang St)

Offers for Foundation, Certificate and Diploma courses (see Ch 5):

Higher National Diploma courses:
> **Glamorgan** – (Euro Lang/Bus St)

For other **DipHE** and **HND** courses see under separate language tables.

Alternative offers:

EB offers: Leeds 60%.

IB offers: **Bath** 32-30 pts; **Birmingham** 30 pts; **Bristol** 32 pts inc H665; **Bristol UWE** 26 pts; **Exeter** 30 pts; **Lancaster** 30-28 pts; **Leeds** 28 pts H66; **Manchester Met** 28 pts 7 subjects 24 pts 6 subjects; **Northumbria** 30 pts; **Sheffield** 32 pts; **Swansea** 28-26 pts.

Irish offers: **Heriot-Watt** AABB.

SCE offers: **Bristol UWE** ABB; **Heriot-Watt** AABB + interview; **Lancaster** BBBB; **Leeds** AAABB; **Newcastle** BBB; **St Andrews** BBBB; **Strathclyde** ABBC.

CHOOSING YOUR COURSE (See also Ch 1)

> **Subject information:** These courses usually offer three main options: a single subject degree often based on literature and language; a European Studies courses; or two-language subjects which can often include languages different from those available at school eg, Scandinavian Studies, Russian and the languages of Eastern Europe, the Middle and Far East.

Course highlights: Aston French and German offered – a high level of language proficiency needed for options in Japanese, Spanish; Russian taken from scratch. Heavy investment in electronic media (audio, video, satellite, computer-assisted language learning). **Bradford** Emphasis in translating and interpreting. Will accept students without A-level German for combined courses in German; students must have a good A-level in the other language. **Bristol** Flexibility through increasing number of options in successive years. Major/minor or joint combinations after year 1. **Cardiff** (Int Scheme) Some flexibility after year 1 to drop one language. Many options eg, European politics, culture. Emphasis on present-day language and technical translation (a tough demanding course only for committed linguists). **East Anglia** French, German, Danish, Norwegian and Swedish offered. Intensive teaching in seminar groups covering literary, linguistic, cultural and historical subjects. Year abroad spent equally in both countries whose languages are studied. **Heriot-Watt** French, German, Russian and Spanish offered with an emphasis on translating and interpreting. **Liverpool John Moores** Students can choose which language to follow at end of second year, equally weighted or major/minor with a year abroad in one country or split residence. Many students combine languages with business modules. **Northumbria** Two languages and international marketing or Business finance or politics. **Salford** Concentration on language work and culture of countries concerned. Options in linguistics, history, politics, literature, liaison interpreting. **St David's** Opportunity to take two languages equally or in major/minor combination. Wide range of courses from literary to vocational (eg, business French, sub-titling in German). Strong emphasis on communicative competence. **Sheffield** High proportion of practical language work. **York** The 'language for all' programme allows any York first year students to follow a language course. NOW CHECK PROSPECTUSES FOR ALL COURSES.

Study opportunities abroad: Aston (E); **Birmingham** (E); **Bristol UWE** (E); **Cardiff** (E); **Coventry** (E); **Lampeter** (E); **Liverpool John Moores** (E); **Salford** (E)FR G IT SP; **Sheffield** (E) FR G SP USSR LA CAN; **St David's** (E); **Wolverhampton** (E); also other institutions offering four-year courses.

Work opportunities abroad: Bristol EUR; **Bristol UWE** FR S SP; **Salford** FR G IT SP; **South Bank** FR G SP; **Wolverhampton** EUR USSR.

ADMISSIONS INFORMATION

Number of applicants per place (approx): Anglia (Poly Univ) 5; **Aston** 6; **Birmingham** 19; **Bristol** 11; **Bristol UWE** 22; **Cardiff** 6; **Coventry** 10; **Durham** 8; **East Anglia** 15; **Lancaster** 10; **Liverpool John Moores** 12; **Manchester Met** 18; **Newcastle** 22; **Northumbria** 24; **Salford** 8; **St David's** 6; **Wolverhampton** 10.

General Studies acceptable: Aston; Birmingham; Coventry; La Sainte Union (CHE); Liverpool John Moores; Manchester Met; Newcastle; Northumbria; St David's; Salford (2); South Bank; Wolverhampton (2).

Selection interviews: Anglia (Poly Univ); Aston; Cambridge; East Anglia; Heriot-Watt; La Sainte Union (CHE) (T); Oxford.

Offers to applicants repeating A-levels: Higher Bristol UWE; **Possibly higher** Aston; **Same** Birmingham, Bristol, Leeds, Newcastle (BBC-BCC).

Examples of interview questions: See under specific language subject tables.

GAP YEAR ADVICE

Institutions accepting a Gap Year: Most institutions; **Birmingham** Always welcomes deferred entry applicants; **Bristol** Gap year should have some elements of language experience; **Liverpool John Moores** Essential to get abroad; **Northumbria** Maintain contact with your languages; **Salford** Spend year abroad using languages; apply in last year in school; **Wolverhampton** Spend part of year in countries whose languages were studied at A-level.

Institutions willing to defer entry after A-levels (see Ch 5): East Anglia; Leeds; Salford; Swansea.

AFTER A-LEVELS ADVICE

Institutions which may accept the same points score after A-levels: Anglia (Poly Univ); Aston; Birmingham (in some cases); Bristol UWE; Coventry; Leeds; Liverpool John Moores; Manchester Met; Newcastle; Northumbria; South Bank.

Institutions demanding the actual grades offered after A-levels: Bristol.

Institutions which may accept under-achieving applicants after A-levels: Birmingham (a few); Coventry; Exeter; Newcastle; Wolverhampton.

Institutions with vacancies in Aug/Sept 1992 (see Ch 5): Essex 20 pts; Leeds 22 pts; Salford 18 pts; Swansea (Some language combinations) 22-20 pts. There was a reasonable choice of applied and other language courses including languages with business with vacancies in the new universities.

ADVICE FOR MATURE STUDENTS

See under separate language tables.

GRADUATE EMPLOYMENT

New Graduates' destinations (percentages) 1991:
Main career destinations (approx): Business 27; Admin 22; Secretarial 10; Teaching 3; Social Work 7; Creative 4; Legal 12; Financial (Univ) 25, (Poly) 12, (Coll) 4.

MODERN STUDIES

Special subject requirements: At Staffordshire A-levels preferred in appropriate languages or GCSE (grade A-C) language.

NB Institutions may raise or lower the level of published offers depending either on the quality or otherwise of individual applications or the numbers of applications received; grades/points offered may be adjusted downwards after A-level results. The level of an offer is not indicative of the quality of a course.

16 pts.	**Staffordshire** - 16-12 pts (Mod St) (BTEC 3D+1M)
12 pts.	**Coventry** - BD (Mod St)
	Humberside - 12 pts (Euro Con St) (4-6 AS)
8 pts.	**Hertfordshire** - (Contem)

Diploma of Higher Education courses:
4 pts.	Crewe & Alsager (CHE).

CHOOSING YOUR COURSE (See also Ch 1)

> **Subject information:** This course title refers to interdisciplinary courses involving the study of a language but also covering other related topics such as geography, literature, philosophy, politics and sociology.

Course highlights: Humberside Teaching strengths in housing, welfare, health and environmental studies. NOW CHECK PROSPECTUSES FOR ALL COURSES.

Study opportunities abroad: Humberside; Staffordshire (E) FR G.

Work opportunities abroad: Humberside.

ADMISSIONS INFORMATION

Number of applicants per place (approx): Coventry 17; **Hertfordshire** 2; **Staffordshire** 30.

General Studies acceptable: Coventry.

Selection interviews: Staffordshire.

Offers to applicants repeating A-levels: Same Coventry.

> **Examples of interview questions:** Questions generally based on topics covered in syllabus.

GAP YEAR ADVICE

Institutions accepting a Gap Year: Staffordshire.

Institutions willing to defer entry after A-levels (see Ch 5): Staffordshire.

AFTER A-LEVELS ADVICE

Institutions demanding the actual grades offered after A-levels: Coventry.

Institutions with vacancies in Aug/Sept 1992 (see Ch 5): Staffordshire 14 pts.

MUSIC

Special subject requirements: A-level music 'required' or 'preferred' in most cases. Very occasionally English language is required at GCSE (grade A-C).

NB Institutions may raise or lower the level of published offers depending either on the quality or otherwise of individual applications or the numbers of applications received; grades/points offered may be adjusted downwards after A-level results. The level of an offer is not indicative of the quality of a course.

30 pts. **Cambridge/Oxford** - AAA potential recommended (Music)
26 pts. **Surrey** - ABB-BBC (Mus/Snd Rec) (BTEC Ds)
24 pts. **Durham** - ABC (Eng/Mus)
      Hull - BBB-BBC/BB-BC (Eng/Mus)
      Lancaster - BBB-BCC/BB-BC (Music)
      York - BBB/BB (Music Tech) (BTEC mainly Ds)
22 pts. **Bristol** - BBC/BB (Mod Lang/Mus)
      Cardiff - BBC (Joint courses) BCC (BA) CCC (BMus)/BB
      City - BBC-BCC/AA-AB (Music) (4 AS)
      Durham - BBC (Lat/Mus; Mod Lang/Mus)
      Glasgow - 22 pts (Music - variable offer dependent on entrance test)
      Hull - BBC-BBD (Drama/Mus; Fr/Mus)
      Leeds - BBC/AB (Comp/Mus)
      London (RH) - BBC-BCC/BB-BC (Music)
      Reading - BBC-BCC inc grade VIII in practical music (Music; Mus/Ital; Mus/Germ; Mus/Hist Art)
      Sheffield - BBC-CCC (Music and dual courses)
      Surrey - BBC-CCC (average BCC) (Music) (BTEC Ds)
      York - BBC-BCC/BB-BC (Music; Mus/Ed)
20 pts. **Birmingham** - BCC/BB (Music)
      Bristol - BCC/BB (Music)
      Durham - 20 pts inc B or C in music (Music) (2 AS music preferred at A-level)
      Exeter - BCC/BB varies (B in music) (Music) (4 AS)
      Leeds - BCC (Mus/Phil; Mus/Rel St; Mus/Theol; Maths/Mus)
      London (King's) - 20-18 pts (Music)
      Reading - BBD (Mus/Eng; Mus/Fr)
      Sussex - BCC/BC (Music/CCS)
18 pts. **Belfast** - CCC/BB (Music; Ethnomus)

        Keele - BCD-CCD/BB-BC (Joint courses) (4 AS)

        Leeds - BCD (Music)

        Liverpool - BCD/BC (Music)

        Manchester - 18 pts approx (Music)

        Newcastle - BCD/BB (Music) (See **Admissions Tutors' advice**) (BTEC Ds)

        Southampton - 18-16 pts (B in music)(Approx offer for all courses)

        Ulster - CCC/BC (Music)

16 pts. **Bangor** - CCD/BC (Music; Music Arts) (BTEC 3M)

        London (SOAS) - BB-BC (Music plus one other subject) (See also under **Japanese**)

        Middlesex - 16-12 pts (Music)

        Nottingham - BCE/BB (Music - no standard offer)

        Ulster - CCD/BC (Music)

14 pts. **East Anglia** - BC (Music)

        Edinburgh - BC (Music)

        London (Gold) - BC (Music)

        London (RH) - BC-CE (Music)

        Newcastle - BC (Comb St)

        Warwick - CDD/CD (BA (QTS))

        West Sussex (IHE) - CDD/CC (Joint and Comb Hons)

12 pts. **Cambridge (Hom)** - CC + Grade VIII on main inst (BEd)

        Canterbury Christ Church (CHE) - CC-EE (Comb St)

        Glasgow (Jordanhill) - DDD (Music BEd)

        Glasgow (RSAMD) - DDD/CC (Music St)

        Guildhall London - 12 pts approx (Music Tech)

10 pts. **and below**

        Anglia (Poly Univ) - CD (C in music) (Music)

        Bath (CHE) - CD (C in music) (Music)

        Birmingham (Poly Cons) - 4 pts (Music) (6 AS)

        Bretton Hall (CHE) - CD (Pop Music St; Music) (4 AS)

        Cardiff (Welsh CMus) - (Music; Perf Arts - grade VIII main instrument) (Apply direct)

        Colchester (Inst) - (Music) (4 AS)

        Dartington (CA) - CD (C in music) (Music; Perf Arts)

        Derby - (Modular) (4 AS)

        Hertfordshire - (Hum)

        Huddersfield - (C in Music) (Music)

        Kingston - CD (C in music) (Music - grade VIII main instrument)

        Liverpool (IHE) - (Comb St)

        London Guildhall (Sch Mus Dr) - (BMus)

        London (RAcMus) - BC possibly lower (Music)

        London (RCMus) - grades irrelevant (Music; GLCM)

        London (Tr CMus) - no specific grades (Music)

        Manchester (RNCM) - (G Mus)

        Nene (CHE) - (Comb St)

        Northern (Coll Ab) - (BEd Hons)

        Northumbria - (Music)

        Nottingham Trent - (Hum)

        Oxford Brookes - DD (Music Modular) (4 AS)

        Ripon & York St John (CHE) - (Modular)

        Roehampton (IHE) - (Comb St)

        Salford - (Band Music)

        Salford (UC) - 2 passes + Grade VIII (Pop Music/Rec)

        West London (IHE) - (Joint)

        West Sussex (IHE) - (Mus)

        Worcester (CHE) - Comb St)

Diploma of Higher Education courses:

  4 pts. Bath (CHE); Crewe & Alsager (CHE); Edge Hill (CHE); Middlesex; Nene (CHE); Oxford Brookes; Ripon & York St John (CHE).

Offers for Foundation, Certificate and Diploma courses (see Ch 5):

Higher National Diploma courses:
8pts.   and below Guildhall London (Musical Instr Tech); Salford (UC) (Pop Music/ Recording).

Diploma courses (England and Wales):
4pts.   and below Anglia (Poly Univ); Bangor (Graduate Diploma - Computer- based Electronic Music and Recording Techniques); Birmingham (Poly Cons); Cardiff (Welsh CMus); Chichester (CT); Colchester (Inst) (Graduate Dip CNAA); Guildhall London (Music tech); Huddersfield; Leeds (CM); Liverpool (Mabel Fletcher); London (RAcMus), (Guildhall Sch Mus Dr), (RCMus) Performers Dip; Graduate Dip, (Tr CMus); Manchester (RNCM); Newcastle (CAT); Salford (UC); Welsh (CMus).

Diplomas (Post Graduate):
Leeds - (Jazz and Contemporary Music)

College Diplomas (Scotland):
4pts.   and below or equivalent Glasgow (RASMD); Napier EE.

Alternative offers:

EB offers: **Bath (CHE)** 60%; **London (RH)** 75%; **Oxford Brookes** 60%.

IB offers: **Bangor** 28 pts; **Bath (CHE)** 24 pts; **Belfast** H655 28-27 pts overall; **Birmingham** 30 pts; **Cardiff** 28 pts H5 in music; **Durham** 30 pts; **Edinburgh** 30 pts; **Exeter** 30 pts; **Hull** 28 pts; **Keele** 28-24 pts H55; **Liverpool** 30 pts; **London (Gold)** mus H6 + 1 other H5; **Newcastle** 29 pts H6 music; **Surrey** 30 pts; **Sussex** H67; **York** 28 pts H6 music.

Irish offers: **Aberystwyth** BBBC; **Bangor** BBCCC; **Birmingham (Poly Cons)** CCCCC; **Keele** BBBCC; **London (RH)** BBBCC; **Oxford Brookes** CCCCC.

SCE offers: **Edinburgh** BBC; **Glasgow** BBBB (MA), CCC (Mus St); **Huddersfield** CCC; **Lancaster** BBBB; **Newcastle** ABBB inc music.

Overseas applicants: Recent written work and casette tape acceptable in lieu of interview in most cases.

CHOOSING YOUR COURSE (See also Ch 1)

> **Subject information:** Theory and practice are combined in most of these courses to a greater or lesser extent. The menu of options is varied - choose with care!

Course highlights: Anglia (Poly Univ) Study of many types of music - jazz, electronics, ethnic and classical. **Bath (CHE)** Work placement. Sound and Image course available. **Bangor** Five main study areas: performance and interpretation, technology composition, composition, ethnomusicology, history and analysis. **Belfast** Modular course structure. Strong on historical musicology and electro-acoustics studies. **Birmingham** Early music to 20th century electro-acoustic music. Continual assessment in first year. **Birmingham (Poly Cons)** Practical and theoretical studies specialising in one from performance, composition, conducting and thesis/project. **Bretton Hall (CHE)** Mixture of practical work and academic study. **Cambridge (Hom)** Initially emphasis on free composition, performance and historical studies. Close relationship with Cambridge University music scene - choirs, orchestras etc. **Cardiff** Balance between theory and practice. Free instrumental tuition. **Durham** Modular course structure; many performing opportunities. **Exeter** Very flexible course; options available after first year. **East Anglia** Western music (Middle Ages to present day). Personal contacts with employers in most branches of music profession. Options in performance, composition and conducting. **Edinburgh** Unusual breadth of syllabus with study of acoustics. Significant portion of faculty's work - practical, historical and scientific - is focused on the Russell Collection of Early Keyboard Instruments and the

University's collection of historical musical instruments. **Glasgow** One-year foundation course followed by second and third year of options eg, computer music, performance, early music. **Kingston** Broadly-based musical training including music and technology and world music. **Lancaster** Opportunity to delay course decisions; large amount of course assessment; 25% instrumental tuition free. Combined majors with many other subjects including languages. **Leeds** Balance between practical and academic approaches. **Liverpool** Balance between practical and academic studies. **London (RH)** Entrance scholarships in Music: one organ scholarship, three choral scholarships, three instrumental scholarships. **Manchester (RNCM)** Strong emphasis on performance. **Newcastle** Recent option includes arts administration, conducting, jazz, aesthetics and criticism. **Royal Scottish Academy** Emphasis on performance and practical studies. **Salford (UC)** (Pop Music/Recording) Popular music emphasis on music technology (recording, synthesis, electro-acoustics, video-composition, performance), experience and talent important. (Band Musicianship) Brass, wind, big-band ensembles, composition, conducting, electro-acoustics. **Southampton** Highly flexible curriculum. Music computing, ensemble performance options. Most extensive series of concerts promoted by a UK university. **Surrey** Subject options in second and third year. Specialisation in third year from performance, conducting, composition, dissertation. Broad core of subjects taken with a wide range of options (Conducting can be studied as an option). Courses are assessed by a mixture of formal exams, one week 'take away' papers and coursework. Electro-acoustics facilities. (Tonmeister) A unique combination of recording techniques audio-engineering and practical and academic music. **Warwick** Offer up to 10 music scholarships. (BA(QTS)) Research in electro-acoustic music and education. Good balance between practical and academic studies. Instrumental tuition. **Ulster** Two instruments compulsory in first year; options in popular American music and jazz. **Welsh (CMus)** Strong pracitical emphasis. **York** (Music Tech) Strong collaboration between the departments of music and electronics. Twentieth-century music features on a number of courses as at **Bangor** and **Nottingham**, and Music and Sound Recording (Tonmeister) at **Surrey**. Electro-acoustics has now appeared on number of courses as at **Birmingham, City** and **Newcastle**. NOW CHECK PROSPECTUSES FOR ALL COURSES.

Study opportunities abroad: Birmingham (Poly Cons) FR IS; **Lancaster** USA; **London (RH)** (E) FR G IT NL B IRE P CZ PL HG Y.

Work opportunities abroad: Bristol; Hull; Leeds FR G IT; **Surrey** USA (exchange scheme for a few students).

ADMISSIONS INFORMATION

Number of applicants per place (approx): Aberystwyth 5; **Anglia (Poly Univ)** 16; **Bangor** (BA) 6; **Bath (CHE)** 12; **Belfast** 6; **Birmingham (Poly Cons)** 5; **Bretton Hall (CHE)** 8; **Bristol** (Music) 15, (Music/Lang) 2; **Cambridge (Hom)** 4 (All BEd courses); **Cardiff** 8; **Durham** 5; **East Anglia** 12; **Exeter** 8; **Glasgow (RSAMD)** 6; **Glasgow (Jordanhill)** 4; **Huddersfield** 18; **Kingston** 18; **Hull** 10; **Lancaster** 8; **Leeds** 12; **Liverpool** 9; **London (Gold)** 6, **(RH)** 10, **(RCMus)** 15, **(Tr CMus)** 4; **Manchester (RNCM)** 8; **Middlesex** 23; **Newcastle** 13; **Nottingham** 20; **Oxford Brookes** 12; **Salford (Univ Coll)** 5; **Sheffield** 12; **Southampton** 12; **Surrey** (Music) 12, (Mus/Snd Rec) 11, (Music) 11; **Ulster** 8; **Warwick** (BA(QTS)) 4; **West London (IHE)** 7; **West Sussex (IHE)** 3; **York** (Music) 13,(Music/Ed) 15.

General Studies acceptable: Anglia (Poly Univ); Bangor; Belfast; Birmingham (JMB, Oxford Local, Cambridge Local, London); Birmingham (Poly Cons); Cardiff; Colchester (IHE); East Anglia; Exeter (2); Glasgow; Huddersfield; Kingston; Lancaster; Leeds; Liverpool; London (Gold) (2), (RCollMus) (2), (Tr Coll); Manchester (RNCM); Nene (CHE); Oxford Brookes; Surrey (Music); Ulster (2).

Selection interviews: In all cases except **Bath (CHE)** (some) and **Oxford Brookes** (Modular) see also under **Admissions Tutors' advice.**

Interview requirements:

Key:				
	P	Performance	A	Aural
	K	Keyboard Tests	H	Harmony & Counterpoint (Written)
	E	Essay	X	Extracts for analysis or 'guessing
	S	Sight-Singing		composer, date' etc.

Bath (CHE)	PKXA
Birmingham	PSKHXA
Bretton Hall (CHE)	PX
Bristol	PSKHEXA
Cambridge (Hom)	PKE (bring example)
Cardiff	PH
City	PASK
Colchester (Inst)	PKSX
Durham	KX (also ear tests)
East Anglia	PKHEXA
Edinburgh	PKHEA
Glasgow	PK (optional) EXH (portfolio)
Huddersfield	PEH
Hull	PSKX
Kingston	PSK
Lancaster	PAH
Liverpool	PK
Liverpool (IHE) (BEd)	PKH
London (Gold)	PS
London (RH)	PHEXA
London (RAcMus)	PKHX
London (RCollMus)	PKEXH
Manchester (RNCM)	PAX
Newcastle	PHXA
Nottingham	PKH
Salford (Univ Coll)	PKEH
Southampton	P
Surrey	PH or X
Ulster	P
Warwick (BA(QTS))	PS
York	PEKHX

Offers to applicants repeating A-levels: Higher Aberystwyth; **Possibly higher** Cambridge (Hom); **Same** Anglia (Poly Univ), Bath (CHE), Bristol, City, Colchester (Inst), Durham, East Anglia, Exeter, Hull, Kingston, Leeds, London (RAcMus), (RH Bed), Nottingham, Surrey, West London (IHE), York.

Admissions Tutors' advice: Anglia (Poly Univ) In addition to A-levels we also require Grade VII, good pass, first study, plus Grade V minimum keyboard standard. **Bangor** Grade A or B in music at GCSE. Offer depends on proven ability in historical or compositional fields plus acceptable performance standard. **Bath (CHE)** Some candidates interviewed required to perform and sight-read on main instrument, and given aural and critical listening tests. **Birmingham (Poly Cons)** A-level music plus a good Grade VIII pass in principal practical study with equivalent of Grade V in second practical study. Piano or organ should be presented as first or second study. The importance of a very high standard of performance in the principal practical study needs to be stressed. **Bretton Hall (CHE)** Great weight placed on achievement at very thorough practical interview/audition. There is also subsidiary interview for Dance Dramatic Presentation, English or Inter Arts. Good musicianship plus sound academic background required. Ethnic minority candidates welcomed. **Cambridge (Hom)** Tests will also include busking accompaniments to children's songs on keyboard. Questions on stylistic features of piece performed. **Canterbury Christ Church (CHE)** AEB examinations in two instruments (or one instrument and voice); keyboard competence essential particularly for the BEd course. **Dartington (CA)** Students with appropriate musical ability and interest but without qualifications in music may apply. Qualities required include a sensitive and discriminating ear, instrumental or vocal facility, a good musical memory, commitment to music, sufficient musical literacy and background to keep up with course demands. **Durham** We also require Grade VI piano (Assoc Board) and a foreign language (GCSE (grade A-C). A-level music not accepted. **East Anglia** Only unusual and mature candidates are interviewed. Applicants expected to perform music with insight and show genuine intellectual curiosity about music and its cultural background. At interview, candidates will be asked to perform on their principal instrument. Those who play orchestral instruments or sing will also be expected to play simple music on the piano. At interview we look for applicants with proficiency in instrumental or vocal performance (preferably at Grade VIII standard or above), range of experience of music of many types and an intelligent attitude towards discussion. **Exeter** Candidates cannot be accepted without interview, which is adapted to individuals. Entrants need not be good keyboard players but must be able to read easy music at the piano. **Glasgow** The BA (Music Education) course is for students aiming at a career in school music and is largely keyboard-orientated. The BA (Music Performance) course is for those wanting a career in professional performance (Instrument and Voice). Scholarships and prizes are available. **Hull** Good instrumental grades can improve chances of an offer and of confirmation in August. **Kingston** Associated Board Grade VIII on main instrument is required, with at least Grade IV on a keyboard instrument (where this is not the main instrument). Audition and interview may be required. **Lancaster** Grade VIII Associated Board required on an instrument or voice and some keyboard proficiency (grade VI) usually expected. We do not accept candidates without interview. **Leeds** Intending students should follow an academic rather than practical-orientated A-level course. The University is experimenting with abandoning the formal interview in favour of small group open days for those holding offers made on the UCAS information, which focus on a practical exchange of information relevant to the applicant's decision to accept or reject the offer. Grade VIII Associated Board on an instrument is a normal expectation. **Liverpool** At interview each candidate is required to take a piano sight-reading test (Associated Board Grade VI) and a series of simple aural tests. They will be asked to play a prepared piece on the piano or on their main instrument (required standard (approx) Grade VIII), and to enter into a musical discussion on a topic of interest to them. Great importance is attached to performing and composing achievement prior to interview and to potential for future development (intellect, motivation and enthusiasm). **London (Gold)** The interview will include an aural discussion of music and the personal interests of the applicant. **London (Royal Academy of Music)** All candidates are called for audition and those who are successful are called for a further interview; places are offered later, subject to the minimum GCSE requirements being achieved. **London (Royal College of Music)** All candidates are required to attend for audition in person, and are required to perform prepared work on first study and second study as well as undertaking sight-reading, aural tests, paperwork and (for BMus and GRSM courses) keyboard harmony tests. There is also an interview. Candidates showing scholarship potential continue to further auditions on the same day. Places on the BMus (Hons) and GRSM (Hons) courses require a minimum of 2 A-levels, including music. There is no minimum educational requirement for the Performers; diploma course. Acceptance for all courses is primarily based on the musical quality of applicants including advanced performing standard and evidence of performing experience. As a guideline, grade VIII should have been secured with distinction by those aspiring to places at the College. Overseas candidates may audition by tape but can only be considered for the Performers' course in the first instance. **London (RH)** Candidates are tested with an aural test, a harmony-counterpoint test, a conceptual essay, and a viva at which they are asked questions and asked to perform. On the basis of the results in these tests we make offers. For strong candidates we offer a place with a C in music and E in another A-level. For weaker candidates we offer a place with a B in music and a C in another A-level. There is a tradition caring for each individual and we strive to give each applicant a fair hearing. Musicality, a good intellect and real enthusiasm are the qualities we look for. **London (SOAS)** Candidates are judged on individual merits. Applicants are expected to have substantial practical experience of musical performance, but not necessarily Western Music. **London (Trinity College of Music)** Applicants for the B Mus degree must attend an audition and show that they have attained a certain level of competence in their principal and second studies, musical subjects and in musical theory. Grade VIII practical and theory can count as one A-level, but not if the second A-level is in music. Overseas applicants may submit a tape recording in the first instance when a place may be offered for one year. Thereafter they will have to undergo a further test. They must also show evidence of good aural perception in musical techniques and musical analysis. **Manchester (RNCM)** All applicants are called for audition. Successful auditionees proceed to an academic interview which will include aural tests and questions on music theory and history. **Newcastle** We expect a reasonable background knowledge of musical history, basic harmony and counterpoint and keyboard skills of approximately Grade VIII standard: if the main instrument is not piano or organ - Grade V. While practical skills are important, academic ability is the primary requisite. **Nottingham** A high standard of aural ability is expected. Interviewees take two short written papers, intellectual enquiry and attainment is looked for, together with a good range of knowledge and sense of enterprise. No places are offered without interview - each offer is 'tailored' to the student at interview. **Nottingham Trent** Music students require Grade VI on two instruments. **Surrey** (Music) Applicants may expect to be questioned in the interview about their musical experience, enthusiasm and any particular compositions they have studied. They will also be asked to perform on their first instrument. (Music/Sound/Recording) Applicants can expect to be questioned about their recording interests and motivation and show an ability to relate A-level scientific knowledge to simple recording equipment. They may be asked to perform on their first instrument. **Warwick** (BA(QTS)) Teaching motivation important.

Examples of interview questions: See under **Admissions Tutors' advice.**

GAP YEAR ADVICE

Institutions accepting a Gap Year: Most institutions; Cardiff, East Anglia, Durham, Exeter, Nene (CHE), Southampton Listen critically to as much serious music as possible plus performing experience. **Cambridge (Hom), Glasgow, London (Gold), Warwick** Apply as soon as possible stating preference for delayed entry. **Belfast, London (RCMus), Salford (UC)** We prefer singers to be slightly older than most undergraduates, otherwise please advise us. It might be necessary to reaudition since performance standard may diminish. **Lancaster** Apply in last year at school, not in gap year. **Royal Scottish Academy, Glasgow, Welsh (CMus)** Maintain performance skills.

Institutions willing to defer entry after A-levels (see Ch 5): Bangor (No); Glasgow (RSAMD); Kingston; Leeds; London (RH) (No); Manchester (RNCM) (No); Newcastle; Northern (Coll Ab) (No); Northumbria; Surrey (Prefer not); Welsh (CMus); York.

AFTER A-LEVELS ADVICE

Institutions which may accept the same points score after A-levels: Aberystwyth; Bangor; Birmingham (MUS DD); Bristol; City; Colchester (IHE); Durham; East Anglia; Huddersfield; Hull; Lancaster; Leeds; Liverpool; London (RH) (perhaps); Newcastle; Nottingham; Surrey; Ulster; York.

Institutions demanding the actual grades offered after A-levels: Bath (CHE); London (Gold).

Institutions which may accept under-achieving applicants after A-levels: Bangor; Belfast; Bretton Hall (CHE); Bristol; Cambridge (Hom); Colchester (Inst); East Anglia; Exeter; Hull; Leeds; Liverpool; London (RH); Newcastle; Nottingham; Oxford; Sheffield; Surrey; West Sussex (IHE); Ulster; York.

Institutions with vacancies in Aug/Sept 1992 (see Ch 5): Bangor 10 pts; Bristol 16 pts; Dartington (CA); London (RH) 20 pts; Newcastle 16 pts; Northern (Coll Ab); Northumbria EE; Welsh (CMus); in addition to a number of popular universities declared vacancies on their courses for applicants with scores from 20 to 14 pts. Other institutions, particularly those with teaching courses, were asking for grades/points scores down to 4 pts.

ADVICE FOR MATURE STUDENTS

Mature students account for approximately 5% of the intake on many courses. The Royal College of Music stipulate 'an extremely high standard of performance commensurate with the candidate's age'. Many other universities and colleges seek an A-level in music and/or recent study experience and appropriate practical skills.

GRADUATE EMPLOYMENT

New Graduates' destinations (percentages) 1991:
Permanent employment: U 72; P 69; C 80.
Unemployment: U 16; P 13; C 10.
Further studies (all types): U 51; P 48; C 49.

Surrey Teaching and retail sales work represented some of the graduate destinations from the Music degree course. Students completing the Music and Sound Recording course all entered the industry as sound assistants and engineers, tape editors, recording engineers and there was one who became a record department manager in a large retail outlet.

York (1986-91) Composer in Residence, public administration (London Sinfonietta) and the Royal Academy of Music, freelance musicians, copywriter (music publisher), opera house manager, theatre pianist, repetiteur (English National Opera), and freelance music teaching were the careers related to music entered by graduates. Two other students entered secretarial work with the Royal Schools of Music and the Incorporated Society of Musicians and others chose tax inspection and accountancy; 45% went on to further study, 18 on to advanced performers' courses, 6 for music diplomas and 24 into teacher training.

NATURAL SCIENCES

Special subject requirements: science A-levels.

NB Institutions may raise or lower the level of published offers depending either on the quality or otherwise of individual applications or the numbers of applications received; grades/points offered may be adjusted downwards after A-level results. The level of an offer is not indicative of the quality of a course.

30 pts.	**Cambridge** - AAA potential recommended (Nat Sci)
24 pts.	**Durham** - BBB (Nat Sci) (2 AS - complementary subjects may be requested - check with Admissions Tutor)
12 pts.	**Brunel** - DDD-CDE/CC (Nat Sci/Ed) (BTEC 3M, sci subjects)
10 pts.	**Brunel** - CD (Nat Sci) (BTEC 3M, sci subjects)
	Hertfordshire - CD/DD (Chem) (BTEC 3M)

Alternative offers:

IB offers: **Brunel** 25 pts; **Cambridge** H777 S777; **Durham** 30 pts.

CHOOSING YOUR COURSE (See also Ch 1)

> **Subject information:** This is a broad-based study covering the main science subjects with options to specialise at a later stage.

Course highlights: Brunel (Nat Sci/Ed) Course taught jointly by Faculties of Science and Education; 70% of time spent on science. NOW CHECK PROSPECTUSES FOR ALL COURSES.

ADMISSIONS INFORMATION

Number of applicants per place (approx): Durham 5; Hertforshire 2.

General Studies acceptable: Brunel; Hertfordshire.

> **Examples of interview questions: Cambridge** (Dependent on subject choices and studies at A-level.) Discuss the setting up of a chemical engineering plant and the probabilities of failure of various components. Questions on the basic principles of physical chemistry, protein structure and functions and physiology. Engineering problems. Questions on biological specimens. How would your friends describe you? Comment on the theory of evolution and the story of the Creation in Genesis. What are your weaknesses? Questions on electro-micrographs. Discuss these skulls. Discuss these shells. How would you write a detective novel? What would you do if you were Prime Minister for a day? What do you talk about with your friends? How would you benefit from a university education? What scientific magazines do you read? Questions on atoms, types of bonding and structures. What are the problems of being tall? What are the problems of introducing new technology? What are the differences between metals and non-metals? Why does graphite conduct? Questions on quantum physics and wave mechanics. How could you contribute to life here? What do you see yourself doing in five years' time? Was the Second World War justified? If it is common public belief that today's problems, for example industrial pollution, are caused by scientists, why do you wish to become one? Questions on the gyroscopic motion of cycle wheels, the forces on a cycle in motion and the design of mountain bikes. What do you consider will be the most startling scientific development in the future? What do you estimate is the mass of air in this room?

GAP YEAR ADVICE

Institutions accepting a Gap Year: Brunel Try to broaden your science base. (Nat Sci/Ed) Work with young people, not necessarily in an educational setting.

Institutions willing to defer entry after A-levels (see Ch 5): Brunel.

AFTER A-LEVELS ADVICE

Institutions with vacancies in Aug/Sept 1992 (see Ch 5): Brunel 10-8 pts.

NAVAL ARCHITECTURE (See also Maritime Studies)

Special subject requirements: 2-3 A-levels from mathematics/science subjects. GCSE (grade A-C) in mathematics, physics, chemistry if not at A-level.

NB Institutions may raise or lower the level of published offers depending either on the quality or otherwise of individual applications or the numbers of applications received; grades/points offered may be adjusted downwards after A-level results. NB The level of an offer is not indicative of the quality of a course.

20 pts.	**London (UC)** - BCC (Naval Arch)
	Strathclyde - BCC (2nd yr entry) (Naval Arch)
16 pts.	**Southampton** - 16 pts (Ship Sci)
14 pts.	**Newcastle** - CDD/CC (Naval Arch) (4 AS)
12 pts.	**Glasgow** - CC (Naval Arch)
8 pts.	**and below**
	Southampton (IHE) - (Small Craft Design)

Offers for Foundation, Certificate and Diploma courses (see Ch 5):

College Diploma:
   4 pts.   **and below** Southampton (IHE) (Yacht/Boat Design).

Alternative offers:

EB offers: **Newcastle** 70%.

IB offers: **Newcastle** H555; **Southampton** H665.

SCE offers: **Glasgow** BBBB; **Strathclyde** BBBB.

CHOOSING YOUR COURSE (See also Ch 1)

> **Subject information:** There is a shortage of applicants for these courses which can also form an option at **Newcastle** in the Marine Technology course. Studies involve marine structures, transport and operations, design and propulsion and mathematics.

Course highlights: Southampton (IHE) 20 years' experience in small craft design; world-wide reputation. **Strathclyde** Course includes business skills. NOW CHECK PROSPECTUSES FOR ALL COURSES.

ADMISSIONS INFORMATION

Number of applicants per place (approx): Glasgow 7; **Newcastle** 5; **Strathclyde** 18.

Selection interviews: Newcastle (some).

Offers to applicants repeating A-levels: Higher Newcastle.

Admissions Tutors' advice: Newcastle Prospective students are advised to write to the Department for the booklet detailing courses, grades required and employment opportunities, scholarships etc. There is a shortage of *well-qualified* naval architects.

> **Examples of interview questions:** What are the objectives in the design of a frigate, an oil tanker and a lifeboat, and how are they achieved?

AFTER A-LEVELS ADVICE

Institutions which may accept the same points score after A-levels: Newcastle; Strathclyde.

Institutions with vacancies in Aug/Sept 1992 (see Ch 5): Three courses advertised vacancies for scores of 20 pts and lower.

NEAR AND MIDDLE EAST STUDIES (See also under Arabic, Hebrew)

Special subject requirements: language at GCSE (grade A-C).

NB Institutions may raise or lower the level of published offers depending either on the quality or otherwise of individual applications or the numbers of applications received; grades/points offered may be adjusted downwards after A-level results. The level of an offer is not indicative of the quality of a course.

30 pts.	**Cambridge** – AAA potential recommended (Oriental)
24 pts.	**St Andrews** – BBB (Mid East) (4 AS)
22 pts.	**Bristol** – BBC-BCC/BC (Anc Med St)
	Edinburgh – BBC (All courses)
	Manchester – 22 pts approx (Mid East)
20 pts.	**Birmingham** – BCC (E Med)
16 pts.	**London (SOAS)** – BB-BC (Persian: Turkish; Semitic Langs)

Alternative offers:

IB offers: **St Andrews** 30 pts.

SCE offers: **Edinburgh** BBBB; **Glasgow** BBBB; **St Andrews** BBBB.

CHOOSING YOUR COURSE (See also Ch 1)

> **Subject information:** These courses cover the major language cultures of the Middle East such as Arabic, Hebrew, Akkadian, Persian and Turkish.

ADMISSIONS INFORMATION

Number of applicants per place (approx): Bristol 8; **London (SOAS)** (Persian) 2.

General Studies acceptable: London (SOAS).

> **Examples of interview questions:** Applicants will be questioned on the reasons for choosing this subject. Strong interest in the Near and Middle East must be shown at interview.

AFTER A-LEVELS ADVICE

Institutions with vacancies in Aug/Sept 1992 (see Ch 5): Three universities declared vacancies for scores of 20-12 pts. Bristol 20 pts.

NURSING (See also Life Sciences and Community Studies)

Applications for degree courses: Through UCAS.

Applications to Schools of Nursing: For training courses leading to RGN, RMN, RNMH, RGN/RMN, EN(G), EN(M), and EN(MH) qualifications, applications go through the Nurses' Central Clearing House (NCCH), PO Box 346, Bristol BS99 7FB. Candidates may apply up to 2 years before the starting date. Students cannot start training until they are 17½ and cannot submit applications until they are 16½. Further information from: Resources and Careers Services Department, PO Box 356, Sheffield S8 0SF.

Special subject requirements: varies depending on the School of Nursing. 2-3 A-levels; chemistry and biology are important for some courses and five GCSE (grade A-C) subjects, including English, maths and a science, are often required for non-degree courses.

NB Institutions may raise or lower the level of published offers depending either on the quality or otherwise of individual applications or the numbers of applications received; grades/points offered may be adjusted downwards after A-level results. The level of an offer is not indicative of the quality of a course.

20 pts.	**Bangor** - BCC/BB (Joint Hons – Modular)
	City and St Bartholomew's HMC - BCC-CCC/BB (Nurs)
	Edinburgh - BCC (Nursing)
18 pts.	**Birmingham** - CCC (Nursing)
	Cardiff (UWCM) - CCC (Nursing) (2 AS)
	Central England - CCC/CC (Nursing)
	Essex - 18 pts approx (Nurs St – Contact Admissions Tutor)
	Glasgow - CCC (Nursing) (BTEC Ms)
	Hull - CCC/BC-CC (Nursing; Nurs St) (4 AS)
	Liverpool - CCC (approx) (Nursing)
	London (King's) - CCC approx (Nursing)
	Manchester - 18 pts approx (Nursing)
	Northumbria - CCC/BC (Midwife) (BTEC 4D+1M)
	Nottingham - CCC minimum (Nursing)
	Southampton - CCC (Nursing)
	Strathclyde - CCC-BCD (Health)
	Surrey - CCC/BB (Nurse) (BTEC 3D+2M)
	Ulster - CCC/BB (Nurs) (AS from chem/maths/biol/phys/mod lang)
16 pts.	**Aberdeen** - CCD/BC (Health Sciences)
	Bradford - CCD/BB (Midwif) (BTEC 1D+3M)
	De Montfort - 16 pts (Nursing) (BTEC Ms overall)
	Dundee (IT) - CCD/BC (Nursing) (3 AS)
	Middlesex - 16-12 pts (Nursing)
	Oxford Brookes - (Midwifery)
	Queen Margaret (Coll) - 16 pts (Nursing)
14 pts.	**Bournemouth** - 14-12 pts (Clin Nurs; Midwife) (BTEC Ms overall)
	Hertfordshire - CDD (Nursing)
	S Martins (CHE) - 14 pts (Nursing)
	West Sussex (IHE) - CDD/CC (Health)
12 pts.	**Bristol UWE** - CDE/CC (Nursing)
	Central Lancashire - CC (Nursing St; Comb St)
	Glasgow Caledonian - DDD (Nurse St)

Leeds Met - CC (Nursing; Health Sci)
London (Gold) - CC (Soc Admin/Nurs)
North London - 12 pts (Health St)
Sheffield Hallam - CC and below (Nursing) (4 AS)
South Bank - CC (Nursing)

10 pts. **Bournemouth** - 10 pts (Health Comm St)
Oxford Brookes - CD (Nursing)

8 pts. **Chester (CHE)** - 8 pts (Health and Community St)
Coventry - (Health Sciences - course designed for applicants with a health care professional qualification)
King Alfred's (CHE) - (Nursing St)

4 pts. **and below**
Anglia (Poly Univ) - (Nursing St)
Cardiff (UWCM) - (Midwife - mature students)
Derby - (Midwif; Nursing)
Manchester Met - (Health Studies)
North East Surrey (CT) - (Nursing St) (See **Admissions Tutors' advice**)
North East Wales (IHE) - (Nursing)
Roehampton (IHE) - (Health Comb)
Wolverhampton - (Nursing Studies BSc for registered nurses)

Diploma of Higher Education courses:

Bournemouth; Bristol UWE; Buckingham (CHE); Canterbury Christ Church (CHE); Central England; De Montfort; Greenwich; King Alfred's (CHE); Leeds Met (Playwork); Liverpool John Moores; Luton (CHE); Suffolf (CFHE); Thames Valley London.

Alternative offers:

IB offers: **Hull** 30-26 pts; **Surrey** 28 pts (5 in chem and biol); **Ulster** H555 S44; **Wales (UWCM)** H555.

Irish offers: **Bristol UWE** BBCC; **Surrey** BBBB.

SCE offers: **Aberdeen** BBBB; **Bristol UWE** BBB; **City/Barts** AABB; **Edinburgh** BBBB; **Glasgow** BBBC; **Glasgow Caledonian** BBC; **Hull** BBBC; **Wales (UWCM)** BBBC.

Overseas applicants: North East Wales (IHE) No foundation courses. **Surrey** EFL course available.

CHOOSING YOUR COURSE (See also Ch 1)

> **Subject information:** These courses, usually covering the social sciences and biological and medical studies, lead to state registration. Alternative course choices could include Environmental Health, Community Studies and the para-medical courses and careers of Occupational or Speech Therapy, Physiotherapy or Radiography.

Course highlights: Aberdeen Health Sciences course shared between Medical, Science and Social Science faculties; leads to health-related occupations. **Anglia (Poly Univ)** The course leads to registration in adult, children's and mental handicap nursing. **Bangor** Emphasis on health promotion within education with complementary strands of information technology and counselling. Mature students particularly welcome. **Bournemouth** Strong clinical bias, 50% in practice (Project 2000 structure). **Bristol UWE** Intensive academic study plus nursing skills. **Cardiff (UWCM)** Four-year degree follows Project 2000 format. Years 1 and 2 share a common foundation, specialising in adult, child or mental health nursing. Three-year degree available for registered nurses. **City** Students gain RGN (Registered General Nurse) qualifications and BSc degree at end of course. **De Montfort** Adult or mental health nurse options. **Glasgow** Course has a science orientation and is based in the Medical Faculty. **Hertfordshire** New degree scheme linked with registration. **Hull** Unseen exams and continuous assessment. **Leeds Met** Clinical nursing studies plus biological and social studies. (Health

Sciences) Modular degree including health care service which embraces certain aspects of complementary medicine eg, homeopathy. **Manchester Met** Broadly-based and diagnostic first year. Choice of specialist area delayed until year 3. **North East Wales (IHE)** Department research-based and degree course operates in partnership with University of Wales College of Medicine; Clinically based course with students spending much of their time on supervised clinical practice. **North London** Close links with NHS, College of Nursing, community health programmes and related voluntary organisations. **Queen Margaret (Coll)** Health and Nursing a growing dynamic department offering wide variety of pre- and post-registration courses for nurses. **Roehampton (IHE)** Links with nursing schools and London School of Osteopathy. **South Bank** Community experience in Lambeth and Southwark; hospital experience at St Thomas's and Guy's. **Surrey** Integrated teaching of nursing and applied sciences with a final year choice of nursing courses. **West Sussex (IHE)** preparation for working in health and social, para-medical and leisure services. Options to choose career interests within course. NOW CHECK PROSPECTUSES FOR ALL COURSES.

Study opportunities abroad: Sheffield Hallam AUS USA IS EUR JAP PH IN IC.

Work opportunities abroad: North London (Health St) USA.

ADMISSIONS INFORMATION

Number of applicants per place (approx): Anglia (Poly Univ) 10; **Birmingham** 11; **Bristol UWE** 27; **Cardiff (UWCM)** 6; **Central England** 31; **Chester (CHE)** 3; **City** 21; **De Montfort** 1; **Dundee (IT)** 8; **Glasgow Caledonian** 12; **Hull** 17; **Leeds Met** 20; **Manchester Met** 6; **North East Surrey (CT)** 12; **North East Wales (IHE)** 4; **Northumbria** 12; **S Martins (CHE)** 8; **Sheffield Hallam** 22; **South Bank** 16; **Surrey** 3; **West Sussex (IHE)** 5.

General Studies acceptable: Central England; Hertfordshire; Hull; Manchester Met; Northumbria; S Martins (CHE) (2); Sheffield Hallam; South Bank (No); Surrey; West Sussex (IHE).

Selection interviews: City (T); Sheffield Hallam (T). Most institutions interview for this subject since personal qualities and motivation are particularly important.

Offers to applicants repeating A-levels: Higher Bristol UWE, Cardiff (UWCM) (BBB), Hull; **Same** Leeds Met, South Bank, Surrey.

Admissions Tutors' advice: Cardiff (UWCM) Emphasis placed on evidence of caring attitude in candidate, demonstrated eg, by community service, voluntary work, in caring institution. Informal interviews held. **Leeds Met** At interview we look for emotional stability, outgoing personality, physical fitness and a humane approach to the general public. **Sheffield Hallam** Applicants are advised to have some experience with elderly handicapped people. **Surrey** Voluntary nursing experience important together with communication skills and motivation. Applicants must be medically fit. Course strongly biased towards biological sciences. **North East Surrey (CT)** Three-year day-release course with final full-time year.

> **Examples of interview questions:** Why do you want to be a nurse? What experience have you had in nursing? What do you think of the nurse's pay situation? Should nurses go on strike? What are your views on abortion? What branch of nursing most interests you? How would you communicate with an Indian woman who can't speak English? What is the nurse's role in the community? How should a nurse react in an emergency? How would you cope with telling a patient's relative that the patient was dying?

GAP YEAR ADVICE

Institutions accepting a Gap Year: Most institutions; **Bournemouth** Not applicable; offers have to be limited because of clinical placement contracts with NHS Trusts. Offers have to be made subject to occupational health clearance which must be close to the start date. **De Montfort** Voluntary or paid work relating to an aspect of health care preferred; **Northumbria** No; **Surrey** Undertake work in a hospital/nursing home/community which will provide an insight into nursing.

Institutions willing to defer entry after A-levels (see Ch 5): Bradford; Hull; Sheffield Hallam; South Bank (Prefer not); Surrey.

AFTER A-LEVELS ADVICE

Institutions which may accept the same points score after A-levels: Bristol UWE; Cardiff (UWCM); City; Glasgow Caledonian; Hull; Leeds Met; North East Wales (IHE); Queen Margaret (Coll); Sheffield Hallam; Surrey.

Institutions demanding the actual grades offered after A-levels: South Bank.

Institutions which may accept under-achieving applicants after A-levels: Cardiff (UWCM); Chester (CHE); Glasgow Caledonian; Hull; North East Wales (IHE); Queen Margaret (Coll); Sheffield Hallam; Surrey.

Institutions with vacancies in Aug/Sept 1992 (see Ch 5): De Montfort 12 pts; Queen Margaret (Coll) 16 pts; Sheffield Hallam CC; South Bank CD; Surrey 12 pts+.

ADVICE FOR MATURE STUDENTS

Mature applicants should be aware that although most institutions will set an upper age limit for their courses. mature students are always welcome and on some courses represent up to 25% of the intake. Many such applicants are already registered nurses; however, other applicants should have an academic background in science subjects.

GRADUATE EMPLOYMENT

New Graduates' destinations (percentages) 1991:
Permanent employment: U 96; P 93; C 100.
Unemployment: U 2; P 4; C 0.
Further studies (all types): U 3; P 1; C 0.

Surrey All graduates entered hospitals throughout the UK as staff nurses, except one who became vice-president of the University's student union.

NUTRITION

Special subject requirements: 2-3 A-levels in science subjects. GCSE (grade A-C) in mathematics, physics, chemistry.

NB Institutions may raise or lower the level of published offers depending either on the quality or otherwise of individual applications or the numbers of applications received; grades/points offered may be adjusted downwards after A-level results. The level of an offer is not indicative of the quality of a course.

22 pts.	**Southampton** - BBC-BCC (All courses)
18 pts.	**London (King's)** - 18 pts approx (Nutrition)
	Surrey - CCC-CCD/BB-BC (All courses) (BTEC 4M)
	Ulster - BCD/BB (Hum Nut) (6 AS)
16 pts.	**Bradford** - CCD/BB (Nut/Food Pol) (BTEC 3M)
	Leeds Met - CCD/CC (Ap Hum Nutr) (4 AS)
14 pts.	**Cardiff (IHE)** - CDD/BC (Human Nutr/Diet)
	Newcastle - CDD/CC (Food/Hum Nut) (BTEC 3M)
	Nottingham - CDD/CC (Nutrition; Nutr Bioch; Nutr/Eur)
12 pts.	**Glasgow Caledonian** - 12 pts (Diet/Soc Nutr)
10 pts.	**Central Lancashire** - CC (Nutr)
	North London - 10 pts (Nutr/Biol)

8 pts.   and below
  Huddersfield - (Cate/Ap N)
  North London - (Comb Sci)
  Oxford Brookes - (Nut/Food Sci)
  Queen Margaret (Coll) - 4 pts (App Hum Nut)
  Robert Gordon - (Dietetics; Hum Nutr)
  South Bank - DD (Food Sci/Nut) (BTEC 3M)

Diploma of Higher Education courses:
  4 pts.   Oxford Brookes.

Alternative offers:

IB offers: **Bradford** 24 pts; **Nottingham** 28 pts 7 subjects 24 pts 6 subjects; **South Bank** 24 pts; **Surrey** 28 pts overall.

Irish offers: **South Bank** CCCC.

SCE offers: **Robert Gordon** BBCC; **South Bank** CCC.

CHOOSING YOUR COURSE (See also Ch 1)

> **Subject information:** This is a study of nutrition in health and disease combined with related subjects such as food science, biochemistry, microbiology and related medical subjects.

Course highlights: Bradford Optional year in industry. Final year options: biochemistry, cellular pathology, nutrition and food policy, pharmacology. **Glasgow Caledonian** Two routes: one to state registration, the other to employment in food industry and government agencies. **Huddersfield** The course covers the basic chemical and biological sciences leading to the study of metabolism, nutrition and food science, as well as catering technology and management. **Oxford** All students take courses in biochemistry, physiology, food chemistry and microbiology. Options include human and clinical nutrition, food science and technology, food microbiology and fermentation and dairy science. **Robert Gordon** Emphasis on applied nutrition, computer applications and management. Course decision can be delayed until end of second year. Course contains elements of business studies. **Surrey** Modular degree programme gives students opportunity to follow interests within discipline. NOW CHECK PROSPECTUSES FOR ALL COURSES.

Work opportunities abroad: Glasgow Caledonian NL; **Robert Gordon** HK USA CAN FR; **Ulster** EUR USA AF.

ADMISSIONS INFORMATION

Number of applicants per place (approx): Bradford 9; **Cardiff (IHE)** 5; **Glasgow Caledonian** 8; **Newcastle** 5; **North London** 9; **Robert Gordon** 4; **South Bank** 5; **Surrey** 10.

General Studies acceptable: Glasgow Caledonian; North London; Robert Gordon; South Bank (No).

Selection interviews: North London; Robert Gordon; South Bank.

Offers to applicants repeating A-levels: Higher Nottingham (CCD); **Same** Surrey.

> **Examples of interview questions:** Questions asked on scientific A-level subjects being studied – syllabuses and aspects of subjects enjoyed by the applicants. Questions then arise from these answers. Extensive knowledge of nutrition as a career expected and candidates should have talked to people involved in this type of work, for example, dietitians. They will also be expected to discuss wider

problems such as food supplies in developing countries and nutritional problems resulting from famine.

GAP YEAR ADVICE

Institutions accepting a Gap Year: Bradford We prefer that part of the year should be involved with experience relevant to the course.

Institutions willing to defer entry after A-levels (see Ch 5): Queen Margaret (Coll); Robert Gordon; Surrey (No preferences; most students change direction as a result of a gap year).

AFTER A-LEVELS ADVICE

Institutions which may accept the same points score after A-levels: Cardiff (IHE); Newcastle; North London; Nottingham; South Bank.

Institutions demanding the actual grades offered after A-levels: Robert Gordon; Surrey.

Institutions with vacancies in Aug/Sept 1992 (see Ch 5): Robert Gordon; South Bank 6 pts; Surrey CDD.

GRADUATE EMPLOYMENT

New Graduates' destinations (percentages) 1991:
Permanent employment: P 73; C 100.
Unemployment: P 16; C 0.
Further studies (all types): P 9; C 0.

Surrey Most graduates entered the hospital service as basic grade dietitians. Those who had taken Food Science courses entered the food industry (Dairy Crest, United Biscuits etc) as food technologists.

OCCUPATIONAL HYGIENE

Special subject requirements: chemistry or biology plus one other science at A-level.

NB Institutions may raise or lower the level of published offers depending either on the quality or otherwise of individual applications or the numbers of applications received; grades/points offered may be adjusted downwards after A-level results. The level of an offer is not indicative of the quality of a course.

12 pts.   **Greenwich** - CC (Occ Health Safe) (BTEC Ms)
8 pts.   **South Bank** - DD (Occ Hea Saf; Occ Env Hyg; PSE) (BTEC 2M)

CHOOSING YOUR COURSE (See also Ch 1)

Subject information: This course covers occupational and environmental diseases, psychology, occupational safety and organisational behaviour.

ADMISSIONS INFORMATION

Thirty places on the **South Bank** (Occ Health Safe) course with about 60 applicants each year. General Studies acceptable. Course is concerned with identifying possible health hazards in industrial environment and demands knowledge of science, medicine and social sciences. Study arrangements abroad through ERASMUS include France and Greece. Overseas students must submit an essay on why they wish to follow this course. A gap year is acceptable and South bank is willing to defer entry after A-levels.

> **Examples of interview questions:** Applicants expected to justify their choice of Occupational Hygiene and to be fully aware of the nature of the course and relevant careers.

AFTER A-LEVELS ADVICE

Institutions with vacancies in Aug/Sept 1992 (see Ch 5): There were vacancies at **South Bank** for Occupational and Environmental Hygiene at 6 pts.

ADVICE FOR MATURE STUDENTS

Mature students with industrial experience are particularly welcome; 30% on course at present. A significant proportion come with non-standard qualifications such as those for nursing (RGN).

OCCUPATIONAL THERAPY

Special subject requirements: 5 GCSEs, 2 at A- or AS-level equivalent. Or 5 SCE subjects, 3 at Higher Grade or equivalent. BTEC National Diplomas and Certificates acceptable as part-equivalent. Entry also possible for mature students through approved Access courses. Reference is recommended to individual schools for advice on additional individual requirements.

NB Institutions may raise or lower the level of published offers depending either on the quality or otherwise of individual applications or the numbers of applications received; grades/points offered may be adjusted downwards after A-level results. The level of an offer is not indicative of the quality of a course.

As from September 1992 all full-time 3/4 year pre-registration courses in the UK are at degree level.

24 pts.	**Ulster** - BBB (Occ Ther)
20 pts.	**Canterbury Christ Church (CHE)** - 20-12 pts (Occ Ther)
	East Anglia - BCC/BB (Occ Ther) (BTEC 4D + 3M)
	Liverpool - 20-16 pts approx (Occ Ther)
	Southampton - BCC (Occ Ther)
18 pts.	**Ripon & York St John (CHE)** - CCC/BB (Occ Ther) (BTEC Ms)
	West London (IHE) - (Occ Ther) (BTEC 5D)
12 pts.	**Coventry** - 12 pts (Occ Ther)
	London (HMC) - CC minimum (Occ Ther)
	Northumbria - 12 pts (Occ Ther) (BTEC in Health St or Social care 1D + 3M)
	Oxford Brookes - CDE/CD (Occ Ther)
	Queen Margaret (Coll) - 12 pts (Occ Ther)
	Sheffield Hallam - CC (Occ Ther)
10 pts.	**Derby** - (Occ Ther)
	Glasgow Caledonian - (Occ Ther)
8 pts.	and below approx
	Cardiff (Welsh SOT) - (Occ Ther) (Cardiff Univ)
	Exeter (St Loyes) - (Occ Ther)
	Northampton (St Andrews) - (Occ Ther)
	Robert Gordon - (Occ Ther)
	Salford (UC) - 8 pts (Occ Ther)
	South Bank - DD (Occ Ther) (BTEC 3M)

Offers for Foundation, Certificate and Diploma courses (see Ch 5):

Diploma courses:
Essex (SOT) (See **Admissions Tutors' advice**)

Alternative offers:

IB offers: **East Anglia** 32 pts; **Oxford Brookes** 24 pts.

CHOOSING YOUR COURSE (See also Ch 1)

> **Subject information:** This is not an art career although art and craftwork may be involved as a theraputic exercise. Occupational therapists (who mostly work in hospital departments) are involved in the rehabilitation of those who have required medical treatment and involve the young, aged and the mentally handicapped. Most courses include psychology, sociology and psychiatry.

Course highlights: Coventry The course covers biological, medical and behavioural sciences and occupational therapy in year 1. Clinical placements in blocks. **East Anglia** Combined Occupational Therapy and Physiotherapy department. **Essex (SOT)** Witham, Essex CM8 2TT. Four-year in-service course is also available (1½ days per week) and a two-year accredited graduate entry course available part-time. **Northumbria** Student-centred learning encouraged. **Oxford Brookes** Full-time or part-time course. Students progress relates to credits obtained. **Queen Margaret (Coll)** Placements (30 week) in hospital and community sectors. NOW CHECK PROSPECTUSES FOR ALL COURSES.

Number of applicants per place (approx): Canterbury Christ Church (CHE) 5; **Coventry** 2; **East Anglia** 150; **Glasgow Caledonian** 6; 6; **Northampton (St Andrew's)** 4; **Northumbria** 4; **Oxford Brookes** 5; **Robert Gordon** 6; **Salford (UC)** 3; **Ulster** 13.

Admissions Tutors' advice: Usually all candidates are interviewed at a School before acceptance. Selectors look for maturity, initiative, enterprise, tact, sound judgement, organising ability and a genuine interest in medical-social problems.

> **Examples of interview questions:** What is occupational therapy? What types of patients do you expect to treat? What experience of occupational therapy have you? What is the difference between an occupational therapist and a physiotherapist? What qualities are important in an occupational therapist?

GAP YEAR ADVICE

Institutions accepting a Gap Year: Most institutions; Northumbria (No); Queen Margaret (Coll); South Bank.

Institutions willing to defer entry after A-levels (see Ch 5): Queen Margaret (Coll); Ripon & york St John (CHE) (No); Robert Gordon; South Bank.

AFTER A-LEVELS ADVICE

Institutions which may accept the same points score after A-levels: East Anglia (in principle); Oxford Brookes; South Bank.

Institutions which may accept under-achieving applicants after A-levels: East Anglia (in principle); Oxford Brookes; South Bank.

Institutions with vacancies in Aug/Sept 1992 (see Ch 5): Northumbria.

ADVICE FOR MATURE STUDENTS

Most courses require some evidence of recent academic study eg A-levels, Access courses, Open University. A large number of mature applicants apply for these courses and represent up to 50% of the intake in some institutions. An upper age limit applies for most courses although this may vary between institutions.

OCEANOGRAPHY (including Marine Sciences) (See also MARITIME STUDIES)

Special subject requirements: 2-3 A-levels in science/mathematics subjects.

NB Institutions may raise or lower the level of published offers depending either on the quality or otherwise of individual applications or the numbers of applications received; grades/points offered may be adjusted downwards after A-level results. The level of an offer is not indicative of the quality of a course.

20 pts.   **Southampton** - BCC (Geog/Ocean)
18 pts.   **Bangor** - CCC/BB (Geol Oc; Mar Biol)
          Liverpool - CCC/BB (Mar Biol; Chem/Ocean) (4 AS)
          Southampton - BCD-CCC (All courses inc Mar Sci except under **20 pts**)
16 pts.   **Bangor** - CCD/BC (Ocean Sci) (4 AS)
14 pts.   **Bangor** - 14-12 pts (Phys Ocean/Maths; Mar Chem)
10 pts.   **and below**
          Plymouth - 10 pts (Ocean Sci; Marine St) (4 AS)

Diploma of Higher Education courses:
4 pts.   Plymouth.

Alternative offers:

IB offers: **Bangor** 30 pts; **Liverpool** H555.

SCE offers: **Bangor** BBBB; **Liverpool** BBBB.

CHOOSING YOUR COURSE (See also Ch 1)

> **Subject information:** Oceanography includes the dynamics and mathematical modelling of ocean circulation, waves, tides and turbulence; problems of ocean engineering related to oil and gas exploration are covered, together with studies of pollution, marine food production and aquaculture.

Course highlights: Aberdeen A mix of geography and zoology for those interested in coastal and marine fisheries. NOW CHECK PROSPECTUSES FOR ALL COURSES.

ADMISSIONS INFORMATION

Number of applicants per place (approx): Bangor (Geol Oc) 3, (Mar Biol) 3, (Phys Oc/Maths) 2, (Mar Chem) 1; **Liverpool** 3.

Selection interviews: Bangor (some); Liverpool (some).

Admissions Tutors' advice: Bangor There are many applicants each year and evidence of motivation in Marine Science is important. If you are very keen but not invited for an interview, continue to pester us irrespective of your grades or points!

> **Examples of interview questions:** Questions asked on applicant's reasons for choosing Oceanography or Marine Sciences and on A-level science subjects studied. Be prepared to be asked on the aspects of the A-level subjects you enjoy since questions will arise from this.

AFTER A-LEVELS ADVICE

Institutions with vacancies in Aug/Sept 1992 (see Ch 5): Bangor.

OPERATIONAL RESEARCH

Special subject requirements: A-level mathematics at Leeds. GCSE (grade A-C) mathematics at Lancaster.

NB Institutions may raise or lower the level of published offers depending either on the quality or otherwise of individual applications or the numbers of applications received; grades/points offered may be adjusted downwards after A-level results. The level of an offer is not indicative of the quality of a course.

24 pts.	**Swansea** - ABC-BBD/AA (Op Res)
20 pts.	**Lancaster** - BCC (OR; MS/OR; Comb courses)
	Leeds - BCC/BB (All Comb St courses)
16 pts.	**Essex** - CCD/BB-BC (MORE)
8 pts.	**Coventry** - (Modular)
	Plymouth - (Comb Sci/Soc)

Alternative offers:

IB offers: **Lancaster** 30 pts.

SCE offers: **Lancaster** BBBBB.

CHOOSING YOUR COURSE (See also Ch 1)

> **Subject information:** This study involves mathematical programming, management and statistics leading to applications in production, marketing, distribution and information systems. NOW CHECK PROSPECTUSES FOR ALL COURSES.

Study opportunities abroad: Lancaster USA.

ADMISSIONS INFORMATION

Number of applicants per place (approx): Lancaster 7; **Leeds** 8; **Swansea** 20.

Admissions Tutors' advice: Leeds The ability to think logically and communicate, together with mathematical ability at A-level, are all sought at interview.

> **Examples of interview questions:** How would you describe operational research? Can you give an example of operational research in practice?

AFTER A-LEVELS ADVICE

Institutions with vacancies in Aug/Sept 1992 (see Ch 5): Several universities offered places for scores of 16 pts or lower.

OPHTHALMIC OPTICS (OPTOMETRY)

Special subject requirements: 2-3 A-levels in mathematics/science subjects. GCSE (grade A-C) in mathematics/biology/physics.

NB Institutions may raise or lower the level of published offers depending either on the quality or otherwise of individual applications or the numbers of applications received; grades/points offered may be adjusted downwards after A-level results. The level of an offer is not indicative of the quality of a course.

22 pts.	**Aston** - BBC-BCC (Oph Opt)
	Bradford - BBC/AB (Optom) (2 AS inc 1 science)
	Cardiff - BBC (Optics)
20 pts.	**City** - BCC/BB (Optom) (BTEC Ms)
	UMIST - BCC/BB (Optics) (BTEC 3M)
18 pts.	**Glasgow Caledonian** - CCC/BB (Ophth/Optics)

Alternative offers:

IB offers: **Cardiff** H655 + 14 pts; **City** H655.

SCE offers: **Cardiff** AAAB; **UMIST** AAAAA.

CHOOSING YOUR COURSE (See also Ch 1)

> **Subject information:** This is a career leading to qualification as an ophthalmic optician now called an optometrist. Courses provides training in detecting defects and diseases in the eye and prescribing treatment with, eg spectacles, contact lenses and other appliances to correct or improve vision.

Course highlights: Aston Two week period of hospital experience. **Bradford** Students have opportunity to work in four eye hospitals on this very clinically orientated course. **City** Tuition in small groups. Modular course in second and third years. Attendance at Moorfields Eye Hospital as part of course. **UMIST** Optometry can be studied with business management, optical instrumentation or clinical neuroscience. NOW CHECK PROSPECTUSES FOR ALL COURSES.

ADMISSIONS INFORMATION

Number of applicants per place (approx): Aston 9; **Bradford** 13; **City** 6; **Glasgow Caledonian** 15; **UMIST** 12.

General Studies acceptable: Aston.

Selection interviews: Aston; City; Glasgow Caledonian; UMIST.

Offers to applicants repeating A-levels: Higher City; **Same** Aston, UMIST.

GAP YEAR ADVICE

Institutions accepting a Gap Year: City.

Institutions willing to defer entry after A-levels (see Ch 5): City (Submit request in writing); UMIST.

AFTER A-LEVELS ADVICE

Institutions which may accept the same points score after A-levels: Aston; Cardiff; City; Glasgow Caledonian; UMIST.

Institutions which may accept under-achieving applicants after A-levels: City; UMIST.

Institutions with vacancies in Aug/Sept 1992 (see Ch 5): Three universities (**Aston, Liverpool** and **UMIST**) declared vacancies for 16, 15 and 12 pts respectively.

GRADUATE EMPLOYMENT

New Graduates' destinations (percentages) 1991:
Permanent employment: U 100.
Unemployment: U 0.
Further studies (all types): U 0.

ORTHOPTICS

Special subject requirements: GCSE (grade A-C) English and mathematics plus two A-levels.

20 pts.	**Sheffield** - BCC (Orthoptics)
18 pts.	**Liverpool** - CCC (Orthoptics)
10 pts.	**and below**
	Glasgow Caledonian - (Orthoptics)

Alternative offers:

SCE offers: **Sheffield** BBBB.

CHOOSING YOUR COURSE (See also Ch 1)

> **Subject information:** This is a study of general anatomy, physiology and normal child developments. The main body of degree courses covers the study of the eye, the use of diagnostic and measuring equipment and treatment of eye abnormalities. **Note** From 1992 all Orthoptics courses must lead to degrees.

ADMISSIONS INFORMATION

Number of applicants per place (approx): Glasgow Caledonian 6.

> **Examples of interview questions:** All applicants should have spent some time observing an orthoptist at work in a hospital, school, clinic etc. Questions at interview most likely will test this experience.

OSTEOPATHY

(College Diploma course)

Special subject requirements: A-level in science subjects.

16pts. **British School of Osteopathy** - CCD

CHOOSING YOUR COURSE (See also Ch 1)

> **Subject information:** This course leads to qualification as an osteopath and focuses on the treatment of muscular and skeletal problems by means of manipulative techniques. The British School of Osteopathy is a private foundation and local authorities are unlikely to award grants to students. (Check with your local education office.) Full details concerning the course are available from the British School of Osteopathy, 1-4 Suffolk Street, London SW1Y 4HG.

> **Examples of interview questions:** It is very important that applicants should have discussed this career with a practising osteopath. Interview questions are likely to arise from this and will test the applicant's understanding of osteopathy, including the differences between the work of osteopaths and physiotherapists.

PACKAGING TECHNOLOGY

Special subject requirements: one A-level science subject.

NB Institutions may raise or lower the level of published offers depending either on the quality or otherwise of individual applications or the numbers of applications received; grades/points offered may be adjusted downwards after A-level results. The level of an offer is not indicative of the quality of a course.

4pts. **Sheffield Hallam** - Application through ADAR + portfolio (Packaging and Design Promotion)
West Herts (Coll) - EE (All PPT courses) (4 AS)

Offers for Foundation, Certificate and Diploma courses (see Ch 5):

HND courses:

2pts. **Sheffield Hallam** - (Packaging Design)
Swindon (Coll) - (Packaging Design)
West Herts (Coll) - (PPP)

CHOOSING YOUR COURSE (See also Ch 1)

> **Subject information:** This unusual subject would be of particular interest to students interested in graphic art and three dimensional design; sponsorships are available.

Course highlights: Sheffield Hallam Two routes to the degree - either three years' study or HND followed by a further year of study. A year out is possible after year 2 of the HND course. NOW CHECK PROSPECTUSES FOR ALL COURSES.

ADMISSIONS INFORMATION

Admissions Tutors' advice: There is a business and management studies component on the **West Herts (Coll)** course. There are 24 places on this course with 40 (approx) applicants.

> **Examples of interview questions:** Applicants need to be fully aware of the course and of related careers involved.

AFTER A-LEVELS ADVICE

Institutions with vacancies in Aug/Sept 1992 (see Ch 5): Sheffield Hallam.

PAPER SCIENCE

Special subject requirements: A-levels in mathematics and a physical science subject.

NB Institutions may raise or lower the level of published offers depending either on the quality or otherwise of individual applications or the numbers of applications received; grades/points offered may be adjusted downwards after A-level results. The level of an offer is not indicative of the quality of a course.

16 pts. **UMIST** - CCD/CC + 2 AS at CC (All Paper Science courses) (2 AS preferably inc 1 science)

Offers for Foundation, Certificate and Diploma courses (see Ch 5):

Higher National Diploma courses:
  2 pts. London (Inst - Camberwell) (Paper Conservation)

Alternative offers:

Irish offers: **UMIST** BBBBBC.

SCE offers: **UMIST** BBBC.

CHOOSING YOUR COURSE (See also Ch 1)

> **Subject information:** This is a specialised course in applied science. There is only one degree course in the UK, at UMIST, which has a broad base of general science and provides all graduates for the paper industry. It is well worth considering by all those interested in sciences. There is a considerable shortage of applicants. Of the 22 students on this course, 50% are sponsored by industry.

Study opportunities abroad: UMIST.

Work opportunities abroad: UMIST.

ADMISSIONS INFORMATION

Admissions Tutors' advice: UMIST The annual intake is 20 with about 30 applicants each year. Offers to applicants re-sitting A-levels would be the same. All students are interviewed. Scholarships and sponsorships available (five British paper companies sponsor students). About 30% of students receive sponsorship. Eight per cent of those on the course are mature students (over 21 years of age). A-levels are preferred and there were vacancies after A-levels last summer (10 pts).

> **Examples of interview questions:** Applicants should be fully familiar with the content of the course and with the career opportunities in this field.

PATHOLOGY

Special subject requirements: 3 A-levels in mathematics/science subjects; GCSE (grade A-C) in mathematics.

NB Institutions may raise or lower the level of published offers depending either on the quality or otherwise of individual applications or the numbers of applications received; grades/points offered may be adjusted downwards after A-level results. The level of an offer is not indicative of the quality of a course.

30 pts. **Cambridge** - AAA potential recommended (Pathol)
20 pts. **Bristol** - BCC/BB (Path) (BTEC 1D+Ms)
         St Andrews - BCC-CCC (Pathology; Path Bioch) (4 AS)
16 pts. **Bradford** - CCD/BB (Cell Path) (BTEC 3M)
         Glasgow - CCD/BC (Pathology)

Alternative offers:

IB offers: **Bradford** 24 pts; **Bristol** 34 pts; **St Andrews** 28 pts.

CHOOSING YOUR COURSE (See also Ch 1)

> **Subject information:** This subject is concerned with the study of disease processes and their underlying cellular and molecular mechanisms. Most courses are research-based and students normally undertake their own final year original research projects.

Course highlights: Bradford See under **Nutrition**. **Bristol** Emphasis on cancer biology; immunology and virology at cellular and molecular level. **St Andrews** See under **Arts**. NOW CHECK PROSPECTUSES FOR ALL COURSES.

ADMISSIONS INFORMATION

Admissions Tutors' advice: Bristol There are nine applicants for each place. Higher offers (ABB-BBB) are made to repeaters. This is a strong science-based course with emphasis on research.

> **Examples of interview questions:** Applicants are likely to be tested on their motivation in choosing a degree course in Pathology. Questions are often asked about their A-level syllabuses, particularly on work relating to the biological sciences.

PEACE STUDIES

Special subject requirements: 2 A-levels, any subjects.

NB Institutions may raise or lower the level of published offers depending either on the quality or otherwise of individual applications or the numbers of applications received; grades/points offered may be adjusted downwards after A-level results. The level of an offer is not indicative of the quality of a course.

20 pts.	**Bradford** - BCC/BB (Pax Stud; Def/Sec; Conflict) (BTEC 2D + Ms)
16 pts.	**Ulster** - CCD/BC (Pax/Conf Stud)
12 pts.	**Bolton (IHE)** - DDD/CD (Comb St)

Diploma of Higher Education courses:
   4 pts.   East London.

Alternative offers:

IB offers: **Bradford** 28 pts.

CHOOSING YOUR COURSE (See also Ch 1)

> **Subject information:** This is a very specialised subject which can be described as a joint study of politics and sociology covering international relations, conflict, democracy, Third World politics, peace and security.

Course highlights: Bradford Focus on contemporary issues of peace, conflict and conflict resolution. Specialisms include conflict, international relations, defence and security. Part-time evening courses available. NOW CHECK PROSPECTUSES FOR ALL COURSES.

Work opportunities abroad: Ulster.

ADMISSIONS INFORMATION

General Studies acceptable: Bradford.

Admissions Tutors' advice: Bradford Great importance normally is attached to the interview; the intake is 40 with about 400 applicants. About one third of each annual intake is made up of mature students.

> **Examples of interview questions:** Applicants should be fully aware of the course content. They should also have read widely outside the subject and be familiar with national, international, social and political problems relating to it.

GAP YEAR ADVICE

Institutions accepting a Gap Year: Most institutions; **Bradford** Contact the admissions tutor if unavailable for an interview during your year out.

PHARMACOLOGY

Special subject requirements: 2-3 A-levels in mathematics/science subjects. Chemistry normally 'required' or 'preferred'. GCSE (grade A-C) in mathematics/science subjects.

NB Institutions may raise or lower the level of published offers depending either on the quality or otherwise of individual applications or the numbers of applications received; grades/points offered may be adjusted downwards after A-level results. The level of an offer is not indicative of the quality of a course.

30 pts.	**Cambridge** - AAA potential recommended (Nat Sci)
22 pts.	**Southampton** - BBC-BCC (Combined courses)
20 pts.	**Bath** - BCC (Pharmacol) (2 AS: if chem and biol at A-level then arts AS acceptable) (See **Admissions Tutors' advice**) (BTEC Ds+Ms)
	Birmingham - BCC (2 from biol/phys/chem) (Med Sci)
	Bristol - BCC (Pharmacol)
	Cardiff - BCC/BC + 2 AS-levels at grade C (Pharmacol)
	Liverpool - BCC (Pharmacol) (5 AS)
18 pts.	**Aberdeen** - CCC-CCD/BC (Pharmacol)
	Edinburgh - CCC (Pharmacol)
	Glasgow - CCC-CCD/BC (Pharmacol) (BTEC 3M)
	Leeds - BCD (Pharmacol; Combined courses) (2 AS - not chem)
	London (King's) - 18 pts approx (Pharmacol)
	London (UC) - CCC (Pharmacol)
	Manchester - 18 pts approx (Pharmacol)
	Portsmouth 18 pts (Pharmacol) (BTEC 3M)
	Sheffield - CCC/BB (Pharm/Chem; Pharm) (6 AS) (See **Admissions Tutors' advice**) (BTEC Ds+Ms)
	Strathclyde - 18 pts (Pharmacol) (BTEC Ms)
16 pts.	**Bradford** - CCD/BB (Pharm) (BTEC 3M)
14 pts.	**Dundee** - CDD/BC (Pharmacol)
12 pts.	**Central Lancashire** - CC (Comb Hons)
	Hertfordshire - 12-8 pts (App Biol Pharm)
10 pts.	**and below**
	East London - EEE/EE (Pharmacol) (BTEC 3M)
	Greenwich - 10 pts (Pharm Sciences)
	Sunderland - CD (Pharmacol)

Alternative offers:

EB offers: **Bradford** 65%.

IB offers: **Aberdeen** 26 pts; **Bath** 30 pts; **Bradford** 24 pts; **Bristol** 30 pts; **Glasgow** H555; **Leeds** 30 pts inc H555; **Liverpool** 30 pts H555; **Portsmouth** H555; **Sheffield** 28 pts inc H6 chem.

Irish offers: **Aberdeen** BBCC/BCCCC; **Bradford** BBBB; **Glasgow** BBB; **Liverpool** BBCCC; **Sheffield** BBBBC inc chemistry.

SCE offers: **Aberdeen** BBBC; **Dundee** BBCC; **Edinburgh** BBBB; **Glasgow** BBB; **Liverpool** AABB; **Strathclyde** BBB.

CHOOSING YOUR COURSE (See also Ch 1)

Subject information: This is the study of drugs and medicine in which courses focus on physiology, biochemistry, toxicology, immunology, microbiology and chemotherapy. Pharmacologists are not qualified to work as pharmacists.

Course highlights: Bath Majority of students follow sandwich courses. Department has strong links with pharmaceutical industry. **Birmingham** Options in anatomy, pharmacology, physiology. **Bradford** Broad-based course with subjects allied to medicine (see **Nutrition**). **Bristol** Research interests in pain/analgesia, schizophrenia and epilepsy. **Cardiff** Specialist services (clinical trials unit, poisons information and adverse drug reaction) allow for a broad-based course and provide excellent individual research projects in final year. **Dundee** During the third year, two courses are taken: pharmacology of systems and pharmacology of drug action. **East London** Second year students take pharmacology, human physiology and biochemistry. Fourth year students take pharmacology and toxicology. **Edinburgh** Biology and physiology are taken by all students specialising in Pharmacology. **Leeds** Pharmacology is taken with physiology and biochemistry in the first year. **Sheffield** Close contacts with two pharmaceutical companies, one giving financial support to Department; paid vacation employment arranged with this company. One-year placement possible for students aiming for a research career. **Bristol, Cambridge, Liverpool, Oxford, London (UC), Aberdeen, Edinburgh, Strathclyde** - all high research ratings. NOW CHECK PROSPECTUSES FOR ALL COURSES.

Work opportunities abroad: Hertfordshire SZ B NL.

Study opportunities abroad: Greenwich (E).

ADMISSIONS INFORMATION

Number of applicants per place (approx): Bath 8; **Bradford** 10; **Bristol** 8; **Cardiff** 6; **East London** 4; **Hertfordshire** 10; **Leeds** 10; **Liverpool** 8; **Portsmouth** 19; **Sheffield** 12; **Sunderland** 12.

General Studies acceptable: East London.

Selection interviews: Bath; Sheffield; Sunderland (some).

Offers to applicants repeating A-levels: Higher Bristol (BBB or ABB), Leeds; **Possibly higher** Bath, Sheffield; **Same** Bradford, Portsmouth.

Admissions Tutors' advice: Bath English, maths and biology (GCSE (grade A-C) required if not at A-level. **Sheffield** GCSE (grade A-C) in English and mathematics required.

Examples of interview questions: Why do you want to do Pharmacology? Why not Pharmacy? Why not Chemistry? How are pharmacologists employed in industry? What are the issues raised by anti-vivisectionists on animal experimentation? Questions relating to the A-level syllabus in chemistry and biology.

GAP YEAR ADVICE

Institutions accepting a Gap Year: Most institutions; **East London** No advantage - a year out is built into the course.

AFTER A-LEVELS ADVICE

Institutions which may accept the same points score after A-levels: Bath; Bradford; Bristol; Leeds; Liverpool; Portsmouth; Sheffield (C in chem); Sunderland.

Institutions with vacancies in Aug/Sept 1992 (see Ch 5): A good choice of institutions declared vacancies from 18 pts downwards. Bath 18 pts; East London.

GRADUATE EMPLOYMENT

New Graduates' destinations (percentages) 1991:
Permanent employment: U 71.
Unemployment: U 26.

Further studies (all types): U 60.

PHARMACY

Special subject requirements: 2-3 A-levels in science/mathematics subjects. Chemistry always required. GCSE (grade A-C) mathematics, physics and biology usually required.

NB Institutions may raise or lower the level of published offers depending either on the quality or otherwise of individual applications or the numbers of applications received; grades/points offered may be adjusted downwards after A-level results. The level of an offer is not indicative of the quality of a course.

26 pts.	**Belfast** - ABB (Pharm)
24 pts.	**Aston** - BBB-BBC (Pharmacy) (See **Admissions Tutors' advice**)
	Bath - BBB/BBC (Minimum BBC, B in chem) (Pharm) (2 AS inc 1 in a complementary subject)
	Brighton - BBB-CCC/18 pts (Pharmacy) (BTEC Ms)
	Nottingham - BBB-BBC (Pharmacy)
	Strathclyde - BBB (Pharmacy)
22 pts.	**Cardiff** - BBC-BCC (Pharm)
20 pts.	**Bradford** - BCC/AB (Pharm)
	De Montfort - BCC (Pharmacy; Pharm Cos Sci)
	Liverpool John Moores - BCC/exceptionally BB (Pharmacy) (BTEC Ms)
	London (King's) - 20 pts approx (Pharmacy)
	London (Sch Pharm) - BCC (Pharmacy)
	Manchester - 20 pts approx (Pharmacy)
	Sunderland - BCC (Pharmacy) (BTEC Ms)
	Portsmouth - BCC (1st attempt) (Pharmacy) (4 AS) (BTEC 2D+3M)
18 pts.	**Robert Gordon** - CCC (Pharmacy) (4 AS)
16 pts.	**De Montfort** - (Pharm/Cosmetic Sciences)
14 pts.	**Bradford** - 14 pts (Pharm Man) (BTEC Ms)

Offers for Foundation, Certificate and Diploma courses (see Ch 5):

Higher National Diploma courses:
   4 pts. **and below** De Montfort (Med/Cos Prod); Sheffield Hallam (Physio/Pharm).

Alternative offers:

IB offers: **Aston** 32 pts; **Bath** 30 pts; **Belfast** H766; **Cardiff** H6 chem H5 biol + H5.

SCE offers: **Robert Gordon** BCCC; **Strathclyde** BBBB.

Overseas applicants: De Montfort Introductory courses available. **Robert Gordon** No foundation course.

CHOOSING YOUR COURSE (See also Ch 1)

> **Subject information:** All courses are very similar and lead to qualification as a pharmacist who may then work in hospitals or private practice. Alternative courses include Biochemistry, Biological Sciences, Chemistry or Pharmacology.

Course highlights: Aston Introductory courses available for those without A-levels in maths and biology. Continuous assessment throughout the course. **Bath** Final year compulsory courses in infectious diseases, chemotherapy, medicinal chemistry, the practice of pharmacy, computer-aided learning, clinical pharmacy and therapeutics. Students taught by practising pharmacists. Assistance and encouragement given in obtaining vacation employment and pre-registration placements. **Bradford** (Pharm Man) The course covers pharmaceutical science, management and a language but is not a qualification as a pharmacist. (Pharm) Unique sandwich course. **Brighton** Very active science research group, internationally recognised; teacher-practitioners provide professional experience. **De Montfort** 'Outstanding Quality' rating. Relevance of course to current practice guaranteed by participation of team of teacher-practitioners. Some teaching carried out within local hospitals. (Pharm Cos Sci) 100% sandwich placements and graduate employment. The only course of its kind in EC. **Aston, Nottingham, Manchester** - high research ratings. **Aston, Bradford** Offer sandwich courses. NOW CHECK PROSPECTUSES FOR ALL COURSES.

ADMISSIONS INFORMATION

Number of applicants per place (approx): Aston 21; Bath 19; Bradford 12; Brighton 21; De Montfort 25; **Liverpool John Moores** 38; **London (Sch Pharm)** 16; **Nottingham** 25; **Portsmouth** 57; **Robert Gordon** 8; **Strathclyde** 11; **Sunderland** 20.

Selection interviews: Aston; Bath (50%); Brighton (some); De Montfort (some); Liverpool John Moores (some); Nottingham; Robert Gordon; Strathclyde; Sunderland (occasionally).

Offers to applicants repeating A-levels: Higher Bath (depending upon various factors), Belfast, Cardiff, De Montfort, Liverpool John Moores, Nottingham (offers rarely made), Strathclyde, Sunderland (CCD); **Possibly higher** Aston; **Same** Brighton.

Admissions Tutors' advice: Aston The department has a flexible admissions policy and welcomes applications from candidates with unorthodox combinations of subjects. Two science A-levels are required together with grade B in GCSE chemistry and biology if those subjects are not offered at A-level. **Bath** We would hope to attract applicants of good scientific potential, well motivated to the career and who can make a contribution to the course, the Department and the University. **Brighton** Apply early and always attend open days everywhere! **Nottingham** Pressure for places is very high. All candidates called for interview will have a prediction of at least about BBB. **London (Sch Pharm)** Contact registrar for up-to-date information.

> **Examples of interview questions:** Why do you want to study Pharmacy? What types of work do pharmacists do? Do you know any pharmacists? Have you visited any pharmacies (other than as a customer)? What interests you about the Pharmacy course? What branch of pharmacy do you want to enter? Name a drug - what do you know about it (formula, use etc)? Name a drug from a natural source and its use. Can you think of another way of extracting a drug? Why do fungi destroy bacteria? What is an antibiotic? Can you name one and say how it was discovered? What is insulin? What is its source and function? What is diabetes? What type of insulin is used in its treatment? What is a hormone? What drugs are available over the counter without prescription? What is the formula of asprin?

GAP YEAR ADVICE

Institutions accepting a Gap Year: Most institutions; **De Montfort** Apply during gap year. **Liverpool John Moores** Applicants must confirm in writing their intention to join the course at least 6 weeks before the course starts.

Institutions willing to defer entry after A-levels (see Ch 5): Aston; Bath; Bradford; De Montfort (No); Robert Gordon.

AFTER A-LEVELS ADVICE

Institutions which may accept the same points score after A-levels: Aston; Bath; Brighton; De Montfort; Portsmouth; Robert Gordon; Strathclyde; Sunderland.

Institutions demanding the actual grades offered after A-levels: Liverpool John Moores.

Institutions with vacancies in Aug/Sept 1992 (see Ch 5): Bath 24 pts; Bradford 22 pts; Brighton 18 pts; De Montfort (16 pts required).

ADVICE FOR MATURE STUDENTS

Only a limited number of places are available for mature students, who are usually required to have a good academic record prior to entry, in a number of cases BBB at A-level.

GRADUATE EMPLOYMENT

New Graduates' destinations (percentages) 1991:
Permanent employment: U 100; P 97.
Unemployment: U 0; P 2.
Further studies (all types): U 0; P 4.

PHILOSOPHY

Special subject requirements: GCSE (grade A-C) mathematics, and a language in some cases.

NB Institutions may raise or lower the level of published offers depending either on the quality or otherwise of individual applications or the numbers of applications received; grades/points offered may be adjusted downwards after A-level results. NB Thelevel of an offer is not indicative of the quality of a course.

30 pts.	**Cambridge/Oxford** - AAA potential recommended (All courses)
26 pts.	**Bristol** - ABB/AB (Phil/Maths)
24 pts.	**Durham** - BBB (Phil/Pol)
	Durham - ABC (Eng/Phil)
	Edinburgh - BBB (Phil/Pol; Phil/Psy)
	Sheffield - BBB (Philosophy)
	St Andrews - BBB (Phil) (4 AS)
	Warwick - BBB-BBC (Phil/Comp; Phil Pol; Psy Phil)
	York - BBB/AB (PPE; Econ/Phil EQ; Phil/Pol) (See **Admissions Tutors' advice**)
22 pts.	**Aberdeen** - BBC (Phil)
	Bristol - BBC/BB (Philosophy; all courses except under **26 pts**)
	Cardiff - BBC/AB (Phil courses)
	Durham - BBC (Phil/Psy; Phil/Theol)
	East Anglia - BBC/BB (Phil) (Average offer)
	Edinburgh - BBC (Philosophy)
	Glasgow - BBC (Philosophy)
	Hull - BBC-BCC (Phil/Sp) (4 AS)
	Leeds - BBC-BCC (All Comb courses)
	Manchester - 22-20 pts approx (Phil)
	Nottingham - BBC-BCC (All courses)
	Reading - BBC (Phil/Eng)
	Warwick - BBC (Phil Lit; Phil; Phil/Ed; Psy Phil; Phil Class Civ) (2 AS except gen stds)
	York - BBC/BB (Phil/Ling)
20 pts.	**Birmingham** - BCC/BC (All courses)
	Bradford - BCC/BB (Phil)
	Dundee - BCC (Phil)
	Durham - BCC (Gk/Phil)
	Essex - BCC/BB-BC (Philosophy courses)
	Keele - BCC-BCD/BB-BC (Joint courses) (4 AS)
	Lancaster - BCC-BCD (All courses)
	Liverpool - BCC-CCC/BC-CC (Philosophy)

Reading - BCC (Philosophy and joint courses except under **22** and **16 pts**)
Southampton - BCC-BCD/BB-BC (All courses except **14 pts**)
Sussex - BCC/BB (Average offer all courses)
Swansea - BCC/BB (All courses) (BTEC 2D+Ms)
Warwick - BCC/BC (Phil/Ed)
York - BCC (Phil/Soc EQ) (See **Admission Tutors' advice**)

18 pts. **Belfast** - CCC/BB (Phil courses)
City - CCC/BB (Joint courses)
Hull - BCD/BB (All courses except **22 pts**) (4 AS)
Kent - CCC/BC-CC (All courses)
Liverpool - CCC (Phil/Pol)
London (King's) - CCC/BC approx (Philosophy)
Stirling - CCC/BB (All courses)

16 pts. **Middlesex** - 16-12 pts (Phil; Phil/Sp)
Reading - CCD (Phil/Class)
St David's - 16 pts (All courses) (4 AS)
Ulster - CCD/BC (Phil; Hum Comb)

14 pts. **Manchester Met** - CDD/CC-CD (Hum/Soc St)

12 pts. **Kingston** - CC (Hist of Ideas)
London (Hey) - CC (Phil/Theol)

10 pts. **North London** - CD (Phil)

8 pts. **and below**
Bolton (IHE) - (Comb St)
Glamorgan - (Hum)
Greenwich - (Hum)
Hertfordshire - (Hum; Comb St)
Huddersfield - DD (Hum)
London (UC) - EE (Phil)
Staffordshire - (Mod St)
Sunderland - (All courses)
Teesside - (Hum)

Diploma of Higher Education courses:
4 pts. Crewe & Alsager (CHE); Middlesex.

Alternative offers:

EB offers: **Keele** 60%; **Sheffield** 65%.

IB offers: **Aberdeen** 30 pts; **East Anglia** 30 pts; **Essex** 28 pts inc 10 pts in 2 Highers; **Kent** 25 pts, H 11 pts; **Lancaster** 30 pts; **Leeds** 30 pts; **St Andrews** 30 pts; **St David's** 28 pts; **York** 27 pts.

Irish offers: **Aberdeen** BBBB; **East Anglia** CCCCC; **Keele** BBBCC.

SCE offers: **Aberdeen** BBBB; **Bangor** BBB; **City** AABBC; **Dundee** BBBC; **Edinburgh** BBBB; **Essex** BBBB; **Glasgow** BBBB; **Hull** BBBCC; **Lancaster** BBBBB; **Nottingham** BBB; **St Andrews** BBBB; **Stirling** BBCC.

Overseas applicants: East Anglia Pre-sessional courses in English and study skills.

CHOOSING YOUR COURSE (See also Ch 1)

Subject information: Contemporary philosophy covers political, educational, psychological, linguistic, aesthetic and religious issues. Some reading of the works of the leading philosophers is recommended prior to applying for these courses.

Course highlights: Birmingham Central areas of philosophy including ethics, logic, political philosophy and the philosophy of the mind are studied in the first year. **Bristol** Language option offered. **Cardiff** No previous knowledge of philosophy is required by the student who is introduced to the practical relevance of political and moral philosophy and the theory of knowledge in part I. **Hull** The first two terms introduce the subject: its history, methods and problems. Over the next six terms courses are taken in epistemology (theory of knowledge), moral philosophy and metaphysics. **Lancaster** Two philosophy options are taken in the first year. These include logic and metaphysics, the history of philosophy, philosophy, politics and society. **Leeds** Emphasis on the development of study skills and organisational technique. **Sheffield** Year I is organised round six basic topics: ethics, knowledge, religious belief, free will and determination, liberty and logic. **York** Advanced options are also offered in certain specialised areas (classical philosophy, modern European philosophy, political philosophy, the philosophy of science and the philosophy of religion). (Phil/Ling) Language options. NOW CHECK PROSPECTUSES FOR ALL COURSES.

Study opportunities abroad: Bristol (E); **Dundee** FR; **Hull** (E) SP B; **Lancaster** USA; **Warwick** USA.

Work opportunities abroad: Bristol FR USA SZ.

ADMISSIONS INFORMATION

Number of applicants per place (approx): Birmingham 7; **Bristol** 10, (Phil/Econ) 6; **Durham** 14 (all courses); **East Anglia** 6; **Hull** 41; **Kent** 9; **Lancaster** 9; **Leeds** 7; **Liverpool** 5; **Middlesex** 8; **North London** 3; **Nottingham** 9; **St David's** 8; **Sheffield** 6; **Swansea** 5; **York** 12.

General Studies acceptable: Aberdeen; Birmingham (2); Essex; Hull (2); Kent; Lancaster; Leeds; Liverpool; Newcastle; Nottingham; St David's; Teesside; York (2).

Selection interviews: Bangor; Birmingham; Bristol (some); Cambridge; City (some); Durham (relaxed); East Anglia (some); Hull (some); Lancaster (some); Leeds (some); Liverpool (some); Newcastle; Oxford; St David's (50%); Swansea; Warwick (T); York.

Offers to applicants repeating A-levels: Higher Bristol (Phil/Econ), City, Essex, Nottingham (in some cases); **Same** Bangor, Birmingham, Bristol, Hull, Leeds, Newcastle, Nottingham (for previous applicants), Swansea, Ulster, York.

Admissions Tutors' advice: Birmingham We attach importance to interview and the motivation of the applicant to acquaint him/herself with books and information on philosophy. **Durham** Do well in GCSE, especially in mathematics and a language (Greek is best)! When you complete the UCAS application write neatly and in decent English. Do not list your good works - it only prejudices me against you. Academic work is, and should be seen to be, your primary concern. **East Anglia** Our standard offer may be modified to take into account potential performance and personal circumstances as indicated by the UCAS referee's report. We usually look for one grade B (not in general studies). **Leeds** We seek some understanding of what Philosophy at university involves - both as an object of study and as an activity in thinking and discussion. Interviewees should be ready to give an account of their choice of Philosophy and to discuss a topic of their own choosing. Lower offers are sometimes made after interview. A-level general studies may be an advantage. Mature applicants without A-levels are especially welcomed. **Liverpool** We look for a combination of imagination and logical rigour. It is possible to read Philosophy with a wide range of subjects. **St David's** We interview more than half our applicants and actively encourage applications from mature students. Few of our applicants have a formal philosophy background. **York** (2 AS-levels) If three A-levels are taken together with one AS-level the offer will be CCC for A-levels and D at AS-level; if 2 A-levels are taken together with one AS-level the offer will be BC for A-levels and D at AS-level. Applications from mature students with non-standard qualifications welcomed.

Examples of interview questions: Is there a difference between being tactless and being insensitive? Can you be tactless and thick-skinned? Define the difference between knowledge and belief. Was the vertical distortion of El Greco's paintings a product of a vision defect? What is the point of studying philosophy? What books on philosophy have you read? What is a philosophical novel? Who has the right to decide your future – yourself or another? What do you want to do with your life? What is a philosophical question? John is your husband, and if John is your husband then necessarily you must be his wife; if you are necessarily his wife then it is not possible that you could not be his wife; so it was impossible for you not to have married him – you were destined for each other. Discuss. What is the difference between a man's entitlements, his desserts and his attributes? What are morals? A thorough understanding of philosophy is needed for entry to degree courses, and applicants are expected to demonstrate this if they are called to interview. As one admissions tutor stated, 'If you find Bertrand Russell's *Problems of Philosophy* unreadable – don't apply!'

GAP YEAR ADVICE

Institutions accepting a Gap Year: Most institutions.

Institutions willing to defer entry after A-levels (see Ch 5): Dundee; East Anglia; Lancaster; Leeds; St David's; Swansea; York.

AFTER A-LEVELS ADVICE

Institutions which may accept the same points score after A-levels: Birmingham; Bristol (except for joint courses); City; Essex; Hull; Kent; Lancaster; Leeds; Liverpool; Newcastle; Nottingham; Swansea; York.

Institutions demanding the actual grades offered after A-levels: Dundee; Leicester; Stirling.

Institutions which may accept under-achieving applicants after A-levels: Essex; Kent; Leeds; Liverpool; Newcastle; North London; Nottingham; Swansea; York.

Institutions with vacancies in Aug/Sept 1992 (see Ch 5): Essex 20 pts; Leeds 24 pts; St David's 12 pts; Swansea 18 pts. An average of 16 pts would secure a place on courses at the more popular universities and there were vacancies at other institutions also.

ADVICE FOR MATURE STUDENTS

This is a popular subject for mature students for which no formal qualifications are required. A special entrance exam, however, may be set and evidence of ability to follow an academic course is also important.

GRADUATE EMPLOYMENT

New Graduates' destinations (percentages) 1991:
Permanent employment: U 51; P 57.
Unemployment: U 38; P 14.
Further studies (all types): U 55; P 50.
Main career destinations (approx): Administration/Management 15; Financial 14; Business 16; Social/Welfare 16; Secretarial 12; Creative 5; Computing 9; Legal 8.

York (1988-91) The destinations of the 60 graduates who went into employment were almost equally divided between education, finance, law, information and library work and social work. A small number went into journalism (3), editorial work, media planning and press relations, administration, publishing, retail management and advertising.

PHOTOGRAPHY

Special subject requirements: none.

NB Institutions may raise or lower the level of published offers depending either on the quality or otherwise of individual applications or the numbers of applications received; grades/points offered may be adjusted downwards after A-level results. The level of an offer is not indicative of the quality of a course.

12 pts.   **Westminster** - CC-CD (Photo)
10 pts.   **Nottingham Trent** - 10 pts (Photography)
8 pts.   **Napier** - 8 pts (Photo St)
6 pts.   **Westminster** - DE (Photo Sci)
       Westminster - EEE/DD (Photo)
4 pts.   **Brighton** - (Editorial Photo)
       Derby - (Modular) (4 AS)
       Gwent (CHE) - EE (Dip course - Doc/Film/Animation)
       Humberside - (Doc Comm)
       London Inst (CP) - No standard offer (Photography) (See **Admissions Tutors' advice**)
       West Surrey (CA) - EE (Photo/Film/Video)

Degree courses applied for through ADAR: (Lens-based Media)
       Bristol UWE; Derby; Kent (IAD); Manchester Met; Northumbria; Portsmouth; Staffordshire; West Surrey (CA).

Offers for Foundation, Certificate and Diploma courses (see Ch 5):

Higher National Diploma course (England and Wales):

4 pts.   **and below** Blackpool & Fylde (Coll); Bournemouth (Coll); Bradford & Ilkley (CmC); Cheltenham & Glos (CHE) (Adv Photo); Cleveland (CA); Dewsbury (Coll); Gwent (CHE); Kent (IAD); Newcastle (Coll); Plymouth (Coll); Salisbury (CAD); Sandwell (Coll); Swansea (IHE).

Higher Diploma courses (Scotland):
4 pts.   **and below or equivalent** Glasgow (CB); Napier (HNC).

College awards:
2 pts.   Manchester Met (Prtg/Photo); Salisbury (CAD).

Overseas applicants: Derby Fluency in written and spoken English important. Portfolio of work essential.

CHOOSING YOUR COURSE (See also Ch 1)

> **Subject information:** These courses offer a range of specialised studies involving commercial, industrial and still photography, portraiture and film and video work. **West Surrey (CA)** 70% practice, 30% theory. NOW CHECK PROSPECTUSES FOR ALL COURSES.

ADMISSIONS INFORMATION

Number of applicants per place (approx): Derby 8; **Gwent (CHE)** 2; **London Inst (CP)** 10; **Napier** 20; **Nottingham Trent** 23; **West Surrey (CA)** 8.

General Studies acceptable: London Inst (CP); Nottingham Trent; West Surrey (CA).

Admissions Tutors' advice: Westminster (Photo Sci) We look for a serious interest in photographic materials and experience in handling them (black and white only) and a background in science and mathematics. The course is one of science and technology – not an artistic one. **West Surrey (CA)** The preferred route for entry is a Foundation course.

> **Examples of interview questions:** Questions relate to the applicant's portfolio of work, which for these courses is of prime importance.

AFTER A-LEVELS ADVICE

Institutions which may accept the same points score after A-levels: Nottingham Trent; Westminster.

Institutions demanding the actual grades offered after A-levels: Derby.

Institutions with vacancies in Aug/Sept 1992 (see Ch 5): A small number of institutions declared vacancies.

ADVICE FOR MATURE STUDENTS

Up to 30% of mature students are admitted to some courses, for which the entrance requirement will be a good portfolio of work or experience, and evidence that the applicant has motivation and will benefit from the course.

PHYSICAL EDUCATION (See also Human Movement Studies and Sports Studies)

Special subject requirements: GCSE (grade A-C) English and mathematics for some courses.

NB Institutions may raise or lower the level of published offers depending either on the quality or otherwise of individual applications or the numbers of applications received; grades/points offered may be adjusted downwards after A-level results. The level of an offer is not indicative of the quality of a course.

22 pts.	**Loughborough** - BBC-BCC/BB (All courses) (2 AS)
20 pts.	**Bangor** - 20-18 pts (PE Joint Hons; SHAPE)
	Warwick - BCC (Phys Ed)
18 pts.	**Ripon & York St John (CHE)** - CCC/BB (PE/Dr/TV; PE/App Soc Sci; PE/Geog)
	Trinity & All Saints (CHE) - (PER/PM; PER/BMA)
16 pts.	**London (Gold)** - CCD/CC (BEd)
14 pts.	**Trinity & All Saints (CHE)** - 14 pts (PER/Pr)
	West London (IHE) - 14 pts (Sp St; BEd/PE)
12 pts.	**Brighton** - 12-10 pts (Sports Sci; Exercise Sci)
	Crewe & Alsager (CHE) - 12 pts (Sports Sci)
	Exeter - DDD/BC (Sec PE)
	Leeds Met - 12 pts (Hum Mov St)
	Liverpool John Moores - 12 pts (Sports Sci)
	West Sussex (IHE) - DDD/CC (BEd)
10 pts.	**Cheltenham & Glos (CHE)** - (BEd PE Pr/Sec)
8 pts.	**and below**
	Brighton - (PE Spec)
	Canterbury Christ Church (CHE) - (Sports Sci)
	Cardiff (IHE) - (SHMS; BEd PE)
	Cheltenham & Glos (CHE) - (Sports Sci)
	Chester (CHE) - (Comb Hons; BEd)

De Montfort: Bedford – 8-6 pts (Modular (Sports); BEd/Phy Ed) (4 AS) (See **Admissions Tutors' advice**) (BTEC 4-5M)
Edge Hill (CHE) – (BEd)
Heriot-Watt/Moray House – (BEd PE)
Liverpool (IHE) - (Comb St; BEd))
Nene (CHE) – (BEd Mov)
Newman & Westhill (CHE) – (BEd)
Roehampton (IHE) – (Comb St; BA (QTS))
Sheffield Hallam – (Rec Man; BEd)
St Mark & St John (CHE) - (BEd)
St Mary's (CHE) – (BA QTS)
Trinity & All Saints (CHE) – 8 pts (PE/Ed)
Trinity Carmarthen (CHE) – (Hum)
Wolverhampton – (Comb St)
Worcester (CHE) – (BEd)

Diploma of Higher Education courses:
4 pts.   Edge Hill (CHE).

Alternative offers:

IB offers: **Bangor** 28-24 pts; **De Montfort: Bedford** 26 pts; **Exeter** 30 pts; **Liverpool** 30 pts H655 (6 in biol); **Loughborough** 30-29 pts; **Ripon & York St John (CHE)** 30 pts.

SCE offers: **Loughborough** BBBB.

Overseas applicants: Loughborough 3 week pre-sessional course.

CHOOSING YOUR COURSE (See also Ch 1)

> **Subject information:** These are very popular courses and unfortunately restricted in number. Ability in gymnastics and involvement in sport are obviously important factors. Refer also to courses in **Sports Studies**.

Course highlights: Bangor Part II (years 2 and 3) include sports psychology, human development and health promotion and students will pursue sporting excellence in their own field. **Loughborough** In the first year all students take introductory courses in anatomy, biology of physical activity, biomechanics, skill acquisition and psychology plus two other subjects including English, maths, geography as well as sports technology (games/sports). NOW CHECK PROSPECTUSES FOR ALL COURSES.

ADMISSIONS INFORMATION

Number of applicants per place (approx): Bangor 8; **Brighton** 9; **De Montfort: Bedford** 7; **Exeter** 14; **Heriot-Watt/Moray House** 4; **Liverpool John Moores** 9; **St Mary's (CHE)** 9; **Trinity & All Saints (CHE)** 33; **West London (IHE)** 7.

General Studies acceptable: Bangor; Brighton; St Mary's (CHE).

Selection interviews: Bangor (some); De Montfort: Bedford.

Offers to applicants repeating A-levels: Possibly higher Heriot-Watt/Moray House; **Same** Loughborough.

Admissions Tutors' advice: De Montfort: Bedford Candidates take part in PE practical tests (games, dance, gymnastics) and have two interviews. **Heriot-Watt/Moray House** This course is taken by all trainee physical education teachers in Scotland. **Leeds (Tr/All Sts)** Primary BEd students should have some experience of working with young children. **Loughborough** A high level of sporting achievement is required. Two A-levels are not normally accepted.

Examples of interview questions: Questions on sportsmanship, refereeing and umpiring. What qualities should a good netball goal defence possess? How could you encourage a group of children into believing that sport is fun? Do you think that physical education should be compulsory in schools?

GAP YEAR ADVICE

Institutions accepting a Gap Year: Most institutions; De Montfort: Bedford.

Institutions willing to defer entry after A-levels (see Ch 5): Brighton (No); De Montfort: Bedford; Ripon & York St John (CHE) (No); Trinity & All Saints (CHE).

AFTER A-LEVELS ADVICE

Institutions which may accept the same points score after A-levels: Bangor; Brighton.

Institutions demanding the actual grades offered after A-levels: Loughborough.

Institutions which may accept under-achieving applicants after A-levels: Bangor; De Montfort: Bedford; Exeter; Trinity & All Saints (CHE).

Institutions with vacancies in Aug/Sept 1992 (see Ch 5): Brighton; Trinity & All Saints (CHE) (PER/Pr) 12 pts.

ADVICE FOR MATURE STUDENTS

In some courses mature students represent up to 15% of the student intake. An upper age limit of 40 may apply for some courses.

GRADUATE EMPLOYMENT

New Graduates' destinations (percentages) 1991: See under **Education.**

PHYSICS (including **Applied Physics**)

Special subject requirements: 2-3 A-levels in mathematics/physics subjects.

NB Institutions may raise or lower the level of published offers depending either on the quality or otherwise of individual applications or the numbers of applications received; grades/points offered may be adjusted downwards after A-level results. The level of an offer is not indicative of the quality of a course.

30 pts.	**Cambridge** (Nat Sci)/**Oxford** (Physics) - AAA-AAB potential recommended
26 pts.	**East Anglia** - ABB (UTEX) (4 AS)
24 pts.	**Bristol** - ABC (Maths/Phys)
	Durham - ABC (Maths/Phys)
	Southampton - BBB-BBC/BB-CC (Physics courses)
	Warwick - ABC (Maths/Phys)
22 pts.	**Aberdeen** - BBC (Maths/Phys - MA)
	Bristol - BBC (Chem Phys)
	Edinburgh - BBC (Maths/Phys)
	Lancaster - BBC (Phys USA)
	London (Imp) - BBC/BB-CC (Physics courses)

Manchester - 22-20 pts (Physics courses

Nottingham - BBC-CCD (All courses except under **14 pts**)

UMIST - BBC/BB (Math Phys)

20 pts. **Aston** - BCC (Ap Phys/Elec)

Birmingham - BCC/BB (All courses)

Durham - BCC (Physics; App/Phy)

East Anglia - BCC/BC (Phys; M Phys)

Exeter - BCC (Phys/Maths)

Keele - BCC (All courses)

Kent - BCC (Econ/Phys)

Liverpool - BCC/AB-BB (Maths/Physics group) (4 AS)

London (QMW) - BCC/BC (Phys/Comp)

London (RH) - BCC-BCD/BC (Phys/Cryst; Phys/Astro; Theor/Phys) (BTEC 3M)

London (RH) - BCC/BB (Physics) (BTEC Ds+Ms)

Newcastle - BCC (Phys 4 yr; Theor Phys)

Sheffield - BCC (Chem Phys)

Strathclyde - BCC (All courses except Maths Phys)

Swansea - BCC/BB (Phys/Man Sci)

Warwick - BCC (All courses except under **24 pts**)

18 pts. **Aberdeen** - CCC-CCD/BC (Maths/Phys - BSc)

Bath - BCD-CCC/BC-CC (All course) (4 AS) (BTEC Ds+Ms)

Belfast - CCC/BB-BC (All courses)

Brunel - CCC/CC (Physics; Phys/Comp; Phys/Ad Inst)

Cardiff - CCC/CC (All courses except under **12 pts**) (BTEC 75% overall)

Durham - CCC (Phys/Chem)

East Anglia - CCC (Chem Phys; Phys/Electron; App Phys; Theor Phys; Phys BSc; Phys Bus)

East Anglia - BB (Phys/Euro; Phys/USA)

Edinburgh - CCC/BB (All courses except under **22/16 pts**) (4 AS)

Exeter - CCC (Phys/Chem)

Kent - BCD-CCD/BB (All courses except under **20 pts**)

Lancaster - CCC (Geophys Sci) (BTEC Ds+Ms)

Leeds - CCC/BC (All courses) (6 AS)

Leicester - CCC (All courses)

Liverpool - CCC/BB (All courses except under **20 pts**) (4 AS; AS maths and physics considered) (BTEC 3M)

London (King's) - CCC approx (Physics)

London (QMW) - CCC-CCD/CC (All courses except under **20 pts**)

London (UC) - CCC/BC (All courses)

Loughborough - BCD/BB (All Physics courses) (BTEC Ds+Ms)

Newcastle - CCC/BC (Phys; Geoph Planet; Phys Med Appl)

Reading - BCD/BC-CC (Physics/Met)

St Andrews - CCC (Physics courses)

Sheffield - BCD/BB (Physics courses except under **20 pts**) (4 AS) (BTEC Ms)

Surrey - CCC/CC (All courses except under **12 pts**) (BTEC 3M)

Sussex - CCC (Physics courses)

Swansea - CCC/BC (Physics)

UMIST - BCD (All courses except under **22 pts**)

York - BCD/BC (Physics; Theor Phys; Comp Phys courses; Phys (Major) Phil (Minor)) (BTEC Ds)

16 pts. **Edinburgh** - CCD/BB (All courses except under **22 pts**) (4 AS)

Glasgow - CCD/BC (Physics)

Hull - CCD-CDD/CC (All courses)

Lancaster - BCE (All courses except under **22/18 pts**)

London (RH) - CCD/CC (Ap Phys/Ap Phys/Elect)

Manchester Met - 16-10 pts (Ap Phys)

Sheffield - BCE/BB (All courses - except **20/18 pts**) (4 AS)

Southampton - BB (Physics courses except under **24 pts**)

York - CCD/CD (BSc courses except under **18 pts**) (BTEC Ds)

14 pts.	**Aberystwyth** – CDD/CC (All courses)
	Bristol – BC (All courses except under **22/24 pts**)
	De Montfort – 14 pts (Phys/Bus) (4 AS)
	Dundee – CDD/BC (Phys/Maths; Phys Comp; Phys/Phil; Phys/Man)
	East Anglia – 14-12 pts (All course except under **18/20/26 pts**) (4 AS)
	Essex – CDD/CC (Physics courses)
	Nottingham – BC (Phys/Phil)
	Salford – CDD/CC (Physics courses) (BTEC 3M)
12 pts.	**Brighton** – 12-8 pts (Joint/Modular) (4 AS) (BTEC 3M)
	Cambridge (Hom) – CC-CD (Phys/Ed) (Any 4 AS)
	Cardiff – CC (Phys; Astrophys; Phys/Astro; Phys/Med; Phys/Electro; Theor Phys)
	Central Lancashire – CC (Comb Hons)
	Exeter – CC (All courses except under **20/18 pts**) (4 AS)
	Heriot-Watt – CC-DD (1st yr entry) BBE (2nd yr entry)(All courses)
	Oxford Brookes – CC (App Phys)
	Reading – CC (Physics)
	Surrey – CC (Foundation courses)
	Swansea – CC (All courses except under **18/20 pts**)
10 pts.	**Strathclyde** – CD (BBB 2nd yr entry) (Physics; Phys/Laser; App Phys)
8 pts.	**and below**
	Bangor – DD (App Phys/Elec) (BTEC 3M)
	Central Lancashire – DD (App Phys/Env)
	Coventry – DD (Med Inst and all Physics courses) (BTEC 3M)
	De Montfort – (Comb St; Phys/Bus extended)
	Dundee – DD (Phys/D Micro; Phys; Phys Elect)
	Glasgow Caledonian – DEE/DD (Ins/App Phys)
	Greenwich – (Phys/Elect; Phys/Comp) (BTEC 3M)
	Hertfordshire – (Comb St)
	Kingston – (All courses) (4 AS)
	Liverpool John Moores – (Ap Phys; Phys/Germ) (4 AS)
	Manchester Met – DD (Physics courses)
	Napier – (App Phys courses)
	North East Wales (IHE) – 6 pts (Physics)
	North London – (All courses)
	Northumbria – DD (Ap Phys Micro) (4 AS)
	Oxford Brookes – (Modular; Phys Sci) (4 AS)
	Oxford Brookes – DD (Phys)
	Paisley – (Physics) (4 AS)
	Portsmouth – 4 pts (All courses)
	Robert Gordon – (Physics)
	Sheffield Hallam – DD-EE (Eng Phys; Phys/Man) (BTEC 3M)
	South Bank – (Phys/Comp) (BTEC 3M)
	Staffordshire – (Comb St)
	Wolverhampton – (All courses)

Diploma of Higher Education courses:
8 pts.   Glamorgan; Hertfordshire.

Offers for Foundation, Certificate and Diploma courses (see Ch 5):

Higher National Diploma courses (England and Wales):
4 pts.   **and below** Central Lancashire (App Phys); Coventry; De Montfort; Kingston (App Phys); Middlesex; Portsmouth; Sheffield Hallam; Staffordshire; Suffolk (CFHE) (Radiation St).

Higher Diploma courses (Scotland):
4 pts.   **and below or equivalent** Bell (CT); Dundee (IT); Glasgow Caledonian; Napier EE; Robert Gordon.

Alternative offers:

EB offers: **East Anglia** 60%; **Keele** 60%; **London (RH)** 75%; **Salford** 60%; **UMIST** 65%, (Phys/Fr; Comp Phys) 70%.

IB offers: **Aberystwyth** 24 pts H6 phys H5 maths; **Bangor** H555; **Bath** 30-28 pts Gr 5 Phys/Maths; **Birmingham** H655; **Bristol** 30 pts inc H666; **Cardiff** H555 + 13 pts; **Durham** H555; **East Anglia** 30 pts inc 5 phys and maths; **Essex** 28 pts; **Exeter** 30 pts; **Glasgow** H555; **Hull** 28 pts; **Kent** 25 pts, H 11 pts; **Lancaster** 28 pts inc maths and physics H; **Leeds** 30 pts inc maths H5 phys H6; **Liverpool** 30 pts; **London (RH)** 30 pts; **Loughborough** H555 30 pts total; **Newcastle** H655; **St Andrews** 30 pts; **Salford** 28 pts; **South Bank** 24 pts; **Surrey** 28 pts; **Swansea** 26 pts; **UMIST** 27 pts; **York** 28 pts H55 phys maths.

Irish offers: **East Anglia** (Chem Phys/USA) ABBBB; **Glasgow** BBB; **Keele** BBCCC; **Liverpool** BBCCC; **London (RH)** BBBCC; **Loughborough** BBCCC; **Salford** BBCCC; **South Bank** CCCC; **UMIST** AABBC.

SCE offers: **Aberdeen** BBBB; **Bangor** BBBC; **Bath** ABBB; **Dundee** BBCC/BBB; **Durham** ABB; **Edinburgh** BBBB; **Glasgow** BBB; **Heriot-Watt** ABBB; **Keele** BBCC; **Lancaster** BBBBB; **Leeds** AAAB; **Liverpool** AABB; **Salford** AABB; **Sheffield Hallam** BCC; **Sheffield** BBBB; **St Andrews** BBCC; **Strathclyde** BBBB; **Sussex** ABBB.

Overseas applicants: Coventry Induction courses and support language classes. **Durham** Interview essential. **East Anglia, York** English language courses. **Loughborough** A pre-sessional course of 3 weeks is offered. **UMIST** Foundation courses.

CHOOSING YOUR COURSE (See also Ch 1)

> **Subject information:** There is a considerable shortage of applicants for this subject. Many courses have flexible arrangements to enable students to follow their own interests and specialisations eg, circuit design microwave devices, cosmology, medical physics, solid state electronics. Possible alternative courses include Astronomy, Astrophysics, Computing, Engineering, Geophysics.

Course highlights: Aberystwyth Foreign language option. **Bath** The final year allows for a choice of specialisms between geophysics, microelectronics, computing or applied physics. **Bristol** Core of subjects studied in first and second years; students' own choice of specialisms follow in third year. Easy transfers to Chemical Physics, Maths/Physics or Physics/ Philosophy. (Chem/Phys) Option to change to Single Honours Physics or Chemistry at end of first year. **Brunel** Broad-based course covering maths, computing and electronics. Three courses have common first year; transfers possible in second year. **Coventry** Opportunity to spend a year abroad having studied the appropriate language modules. **Durham** Second and third year courses develop and allow for specialisation in subjects which include astrophysics and planetary physics, modern optics and nuclear physics. **East Anglia** Lectures backed by tutorials and seminars. Options to transfer to other Physics courses. (Phys/Electron) 25% electronics. (Phys/Ed) Teaching training done in parallel with the Physics course, not end on. Strong research activity in condensed matter physics. **Hull** Flexible transfer arrangements between courses. Specialisms in electronics, laser technology, medical technology, optoelctronics. **Keele** In the third year options allow for specialisation in, eg acoustics, astrophysics, lasers and wave optics. A subsidiary course is offered in astronomy. **Lancaster** In the third year students also choose four options which include circuit design, microwave devices, cosmology, medical physics and the physics of stars. **Leeds** Optional subjects include low temperature physics, polymer and theoretical physics, astrophysics, geophysics and computing. **London (Imp)** Options include astrophysics, space physics, electronics and computing, languages; 10 students each year do research in France, Germany and Italy. **London (RH)** Wide range of third year options; great flexibility to change degree option (eg, physics to Physics/Astrophysics or Management). **Newcastle** Physics students cover such topics as optics, nuclear physics, thermodynamics, solid state physics, astrophysics and geophysics. **Oxford** In the final year there is a choice of two from: statistical mechanics and solid state physics, atomic physics, nuclear physics, modern optics and laser physics, electronics, physics of the atmosphere, ocean and earth, astrophysics, mathematical physics. **Swansea** Three and four-year courses; modular courses in medical physics, microelectronics, laser physics and computing physics. High research ratings also at **Cambridge, Liverpool, Manchester, Nottingham, Oxford, London (Imp), (UC)**. NOW CHECK PROSPECTUSES FOR ALL COURSES.

Study opportunities abroad: Brunel USA; **Exeter** (E); **Kent** EUR; **Lancaster** USA; **Leeds** (E); **London (Imp)** EUR, **(QMW)** (E) FR G IT; **Newcastle; Reading** FR; **Sheffield** (E) FR; **South Bank** EUR; **Surrey** (E); **Sussex** EUR; **UMIST** FR G.

Work opportunities abroad: Bath FR G SZ USA; **Birmingham** G FR; **Coventry** FR G; **Loughborough** FR G N; **Northumbria** FR; **Surrey** EUR CAN.

ADMISSIONS INFORMATION

Number of applicants per place (approx): Bath 4; **Birmingham** 6; **Bristol** 5; **Cambridge (Hom)** 3 (All BEd courses); **Coventry** 10; **Durham** 2; **East Anglia** 5; **Edinburgh** 9; **Exeter** 5; **Heriot-Watt** 4; **Hull** 6; **Kent** 8; **Lancaster** 8; **Leeds** 7; **Leicester** 10; **Liverpool** 4; **London (Imp)** 3, **(QMW)** 6, **(RH)** 5; **Loughborough** 5; **Manchester Met** 13; **Newcastle** 4; **Nottingham** 6; **Portsmouth** 6; **Salford** 5; **South Bank** 5; **Strathclyde** 8, (Phys/Laser) 5, (App Phys) 7; **Surrey** 4; **Swansea** 0.5; **UMIST** 8; **York** 9.

General Studies acceptable: Aston; Bath; Birmingham (not AEB); Essex; Exeter; Heriot-Watt; Hull; Leeds; Liverpool (JMB, Oxford, Cambridge only); Liverpool John Moores; Newcastle; Salford; South Bank (No); Wolverhampton; York.

Selection interviews: Aston; Bath 70%; Birmingham; Brunel; Cambridge; Durham; East Anglia; Essex; Heriot-Watt (some); Hull (some); Lancaster; Liverpool; London (RH); Newcastle; Nottingham (some); Oxford; Portsmouth; Salford; Sheffield; South Bank; Swansea (some); UMIST; York.

Offers to applicants repeating A-levels: Higher UMIST; **Possibly higher** Aberystwyth, Cambridge (Hom), Essex (interview important), Hull, Leeds, Loughborough (BBC), Newcastle, York (BCC/BCE/BC); **Same** Bath, Birmingham, Coventry, East Anglia, Lancaster, Leicester, Liverpool, Salford, South Bank, Swansea.

Admissions Tutors' advice: Aberystwyth We like people to visit us before we make an offer, but if this is not possible they are given equal consideration. **Durham** Always apply if you think you have a potential of CCC including physics and maths, if you are keen on physics and on Durham. (App Phys) Try us. We are seeking to expand our intake in the next three years. Potential ability to cope is our only criterion. **Leicester** On receiving an offer applicants should make every effort to visit us and see our facilities. Grade C in maths preferred. Good GCSE results in arts as well as science subjects are an advantage. Offers usually made after interview. **Leeds** Good mathematics background at GCSE required. **London (RH)** Majority of applicants invited for interview; we look for strong motivation and genuine interest in the subject. **Loughborough** Students are made an offer and invited to visit the university. Technical work experience is desirable. **York** All applicants who seem likely to achieve our normal offer are invited for an interview. Normally at least B grades in GCSE maths and physics are required.

> **Examples of interview questions:** Questions asked on the A-level syllabus. What parts of the Physics course interest you most? (Questions are often based on the answer to this question.) Why do you want to study Physics? What career do you hope to follow when you graduate?

GAP YEAR ADVICE

Institutions accepting a Gap Year: Most institutions; **Bath** Try to work in a related field; **Birmingham** Indicate your intentions on the UCAS application; **Coventry** Maintain your mathematical competence; **Newcastle** It is difficult to resume a study of mathematics after a year out.

Institutions willing to defer entry after A-levels (see Ch 5): Aberystwyth; Aston; Bath; Bristol; Brunel; Coventry; East Anglia; Heriot-Watt; Kingston; Lancaster; Leeds; London (RH); Loughborough; Newcastle; Portsmouth; Robert Gordon; Salford; South Bank; Swansea; Surrey; UMIST.

AFTER A-LEVELS ADVICE

Institutions which may accept the same points score after A-levels: Bath (perhaps); Birmingham; Brunel; Durham (App Phys); Essex; East Anglia (perhaps); Hull; Kent; Lancaster; Leeds; Leicester; Liverpool; London (RH); Newcastle; Northumbria; Nottingham; Portsmouth; Salford; Strathclyde; Swansea; York; most institutions.

Institutions demanding the actual grades offered after A-levels: Aberystwyth; Belfast; Bristol; Durham; Exeter; Loughborough.

Institutions which may accept under-achieving applicants after A-levels: Aston; Bath; Birmingham; Brunel; Cambridge (Hom); Durham; East Anglia (not Phys/Eur); Essex; Exeter; Kent; Lancaster; Leeds; Liverpool; London (RH); Loughborough; Newcastle; Northumbria; Portsmouth; Nottingham; Salford; York.

Institutions with vacancies in Aug/Sept 1992 (see Ch 5): Almost every institution offering this subject declared vacancies. Even the most popular universities would accept a Grade C in physics - or lower. Aberystwyth DD (maths + phys + interview); Aston 18 pts; Bangor 4 pts; Bath 8 pts; Bristol (Chem/Phys) 18 pts; Brunel 10 pts; Coventry; East Anglia 14-10 pts; Essex 8-6 pts; Heriot-Watt 10 pts; Kingston 6 pts; Lancaster 14 pts; Leeds 14 pts; London (RH) 14 pts (higher in 1993); Loughborough 14 pts; Newcastle; Portsmouth 4 pts; Robert Gordon 4 pts; Salford 8 pts; South Bank 6 pts; Swansea; UMIST 16 pts; York 14-12 pts.

ADVICE FOR MATURE STUDENTS

Only a small proportion of mature students are accepted on these courses often because formal academic qualifications are required. With the introduction of Foundation courses, however, applicants with prior experience should not be afraid to apply. **Loughborough** prefers technical work experience.

GRADUATE EMPLOYMENT

New Graduates' destinations (percentages) 1991:
Permanent employment: U 66; P 71.
Unemployment: U 24; P 24.
Further studies (all types): U 51; P 27.
Main career destinations (approx): Scientific (Univ) 48, (Poly) 75; Computing (Univ) 16, (Poly) 10; Financial (Univ) 15, (Poly) 3; Business (Univ) 15, (Poly) 20.

Surrey Acoustics, the aerospace industry and British Nuclear Fuels attracted some of the 1990/91 cohort as research physicists, technical engineers, radiation effects engineers and health physicists. Several students went on to study for MSc or PhD degrees.

York (1987-91) 96 graduates went into employment, 53 of whom entered scientific and engineering careers, 17 chose financial occupations whilst others chose a variety of destinations including computing, the police (2), marketing and pilot (British Airways). 43% of graduates went on to higher degrees, diplomas and certificates.

See also under **Science**.

PHYSIOLOGY

Special subject requirements: usually 3 A-level passes in science/mathematics subjects. Chemistry often required. Similar subjects required at GCSE (grade A-C).

NB Institutions may raise or lower the level of published offers depending either on the quality or otherwise of individual applications or the numbers of applications received; grades/points offered may be adjusted downwards after A-level results. The level of an offer is not indicative of the quality of a course.

30 pts.	**Cambridge/Oxford** – AAA potential recommended (Nat Sci; Physiol; PPP)
22 pts.	**Leeds** – BBC-BCC (Phys/Sports Sci)
	Southampton – BBC-BCC (All courses)
20 pts.	**Birmingham** – BCC (2 from biol/chem/phys) (Med Sci)
	Cardiff – 20 pts (Bioch/Phys) (BTEC 3M)
	Leeds – BCC/BB (All Comb St courses)
	St Andrews – BCC-CCC (Physiol) (4 AS)
	York – BCC-CCC (Physiol)
18 pts.	**Aberdeen** – CCC-CCD/BC (Physiol)
	Belfast – CCC/BB (Physiol)
	Birmingham – BCD (Biol Sci)
	Bristol – BCD (Physiol)
	Cardiff – CCC/BB (Approx offer for all courses – except **20 pts**)
	Edinburgh – CCC (Physiol)
	Glasgow – CCC-CCD/BC (Physiol) (BTEC 3M)
	Leeds – CCC (Physiol) (BTEC 3M)
	Leicester – BCD (Biol Sci)
	Liverpool – CCC (Physiol) (5 AS)
	London (King's) – CCC approx (Physiol)
	London (QMW) – CCC-CCD/BB-BC (Physiol)
	Manchester – 18 pts approx (Physiol)
	Newcastle – CCC (Physiol) (4 AS)
	Sheffield – 18 pts (Physiol courses) (BTEC Ms)
16 pts.	**London (UC)** – CCD (Physiol)
14 pts.	**Dundee** – CDD/BC (Physiology)
12 pts.	**Central Lancashire** – CC (Comb Hons)
	Hertfordshire – 12-8 pts (Ap Biol (Phys))
8 pts.	**and below**
	East London – (Hum Physiol)
	Sunderland – (Joint St)
	Westminster – DD (Sci Life Modular) (BTEC 3M)

Diploma of Higher Education courses:
4 pts.   East London.

Alternative offers:

IB offers: **Aberdeen** 26 pts; **Bristol** 28-26 pts; **Cardiff** 24 pts, H 15 pts; **Liverpool** 30 pts + H55; **St Andrews** 30 pts.

Irish offers: **Aberdeen** BBCC/BCCCC; **Dundee** BBCC; **Edinburgh** BBBB; **Glasgow** BBB; **Liverpool** BBCCC; **Sheffield** AABB.

SCE offers: **Aberdeen** BBBC; **Belfast** BBBB-BBBC; **Dundee** BBBB/BBBCC; **Glasgow** BBB; **Liverpool** AABB; **St Andrews** BBBC; **Sheffield** BBBB.

Overseas applicants: Leeds Foundation courses offered.

CHOOSING YOUR COURSE (See also Ch 1)

> **Subject information:** This is a study of body function and courses in this wide-ranging subject will cover the central nervous system, special senses and neuro-muscular mechanisms, and body regulating systems such as exercise, stress and temperature regulation. See also **Anatomy** and **Medicine.**

Course highlights: Birmingham (Med Sci) Options in anatomy, pharmacology, physiology. **Bristol** Course primarily related to mammalian physiology. Options include anatomy, psychology, pharmacology, zoology etc. **Cardiff** Emphasis in neurophysiology with a sound background of human physiology. Transfers possible to Physiology, Biochemistry, Pharmacology or joint honours courses. **Leeds** (Phys/Sports Sci) Rigorous science course plus psychology of sport; can lead to National Coaching Federation certificate. **Newcastle** Possibility to change to one of six other biological science subjects at end of first year. Components of physiological biochemistry and biophysics integrated into physiology. **St Andrews** See under **Science. Sheffield** Modular course. The subject is taught within School of Biological Sciences and offers 24 courses. Flexible first year enables students to change course at end of the year. **Hertfordshire** See under **Microbiology.** NOW CHECK PROSPECTUSES FOR ALL COURSES.

Work opportunities abroad: Bristol FR; **York** USA (for some students).

ADMISSIONS INFORMATION

Number of applicants per place (approx): Bristol 3; **Cardiff** 3; **Leeds** 6; **Liverpool** 10; **Newcastle** 11; **Sheffield** 25.

General Studies acceptable: Dundee (2); East London; Westminster.

Selection interviews: Birmingham; Bristol; Cambridge; Cardiff; Leeds (some); Oxford; Sheffield.

Offers to applicants repeating A-levels: Higher Bristol, Leeds (BCC), Liverpool, Newcastle (Grade B in resit subjects), Sheffield, York.

Admissions Tutors' advice: Edinburgh GCSE grades A-C in physics required. **Leeds** Look critically at the final year syllabus – this is where the major differences lie. Offers may rise to BCC. **Newcastle** Many complex factors are involved in the selection of applicants. Students should read the departmental brochure carefully. All those given conditional or firm offers are invited to visit. Visits can also be organised before the UCAS application is completed. At **Newcastle** Students on the Biological Sciences deferred choice course may change course to Physiological Sciences at the end of the first year. Emphasis on human and mammalian physiology.

> **Examples of interview questions:** What made you decide to do Physiology? What experimental work have you done connected with physiology? What future career do you have in mind? What is physiology? Why not choose Medicine instead? What practicals do you do at school?

GAP YEAR ADVICE

Institutions accepting a Gap Year: Most institutions; **Newcastle** Indicate on UCAS application how gap year will be spent.

Institutions willing to defer entry after A-levels (see Ch 5): Leeds; Newcastle (No); Westminster.

AFTER A-LEVELS ADVICE

Institutions which may accept the same points score after A-levels: Bristol; Cardiff; Leeds; Liverpool; Newcastle; Sheffield; York.

Institutions with vacancies in Aug/Sept 1992 (see Ch 5): Many vacancies were declared. An average of 14 pts would secure a place at the more popular universities. Leeds 16 pts; Newcastle 16 pts; Westminster.

GRADUATE EMPLOYMENT

See also under **Science**.

PHYSIOTHERAPY

Special subject requirements: five good GCSEs (grade A-C) and two A-levels or four Scottish H grades. GCSEs (grade A-C) must include English and at least two science subjects, passed at one sitting. Physics and/or chemistry, or physics with chemistry, and biology recommended and in some cases required.

NB Institutions may raise or lower the level of published offers depending either on the quality or otherwise of individual applications or the numbers of applications received; grades/points offered may be adjusted downwards after A-level results. The level of an offer is not indicative of the quality of a course.

Degree courses:
24 pts. **East Anglia** - BBB/AB (Physio) (BTEC 4D+3M)
     Ulster - BBB/AA (Physio)
22 pts. **Manchester** - BBC-BCC (Physio)
     Nottingham - BBC-BCC (Physio)
20 pts. **Birmingham** - BCC (Physio)
     Bradford - BCC (Physio) (BTEC 4D+Ms)
     Bristol (Avon Coll of Health) - BBC (See **Admissions Tutors' advice**)
     Coventry - BCC/BB or 20 pts (Physio) (BTEC 4M)
     Keele - BCC (Physio)
     Leeds Met - BCC (Physio)
     Liverpool - BCC (Physio)
     London (King's) - BCC approx (Physio)
     London (UC) - BCC (Physio)
     Queen Margaret (Coll) - BCC (Physio)
     Robert Gordon - BCC (Physio)
     Southampton - BCC (Physio)
     Teesside - BCC (Physio)
18 pts. **Bath** - CCC/AB (Physio)
     Cardiff (IHCS) - CCC (Physio)
     Northumbria - CCC/AB (Physio)
     Sheffield Hallam - CCC (Physio)
     Wolverhampton - CCC (Physio)
16 pts. **Brighton** - 16 pts (Physio)
     East London - 16 pts (Physio - contact Admissions Tutor)
     North London (SP) - CCD/CC (Physio - RNIB) (See **Admissions Tutors' advice**)
     West London (IHE) - C (biol) CC (Physio) (BTEC 5D+3M)
14 pts. **Salford (UC)** - 14 pts approx (Physio)
12 pts. **Glasgow Caledonian** - CC (Physio)
     Westminster - (Physio)
8 pts. **Hertfordshire** - (Ap Bio Phys)

Alternative offers:

IB offers: **East Anglia** 35 pts.

Irish offers: **Ulster** AABBBB.

SCE offers: **Glasgow Caledonian** BBCC; **Liverpool** BCC; **Queen Margaret (Coll)** BBCC; **Sheffield Hallam** BBBB.

Overseas applicants: Places for students from overseas are limited, and applicants must be able to read, speak and write English fluently. Information on the minimum educational qualifications required by overseas students and details concerning grants and funding are available from the Chartered Society of Physiotherapy. **Glasgow Caledonian, West London (IHE)** Proficiency in English essential. **Queen Margaret (Coll)** Several overseas students recruited each year. **Ulster** Exams and continuous assessment.

CHOOSING YOUR COURSE (See also Ch 1)

> **Subject information:** All courses lead to full qualification as Physiotherapists. The course content is similar in all cases. Competition is intense for the limited number of places available each year for physiotherapists and only one applicant in four is successful. Good work experience or work shadowing is necessary prior to application. Guidelines for mature students and careers information is available from: The Chartered Society of Physiotherapy, 14 Bedford Row, London WC1R 4ED.

Applications for degree courses are made through UCAS.

Course highlights: East London Mature students welcome. **North London** Course designed to benefit the visually impaired and blind candidates. **Northumbria** Emphasis on small group teaching. **Nottingham** Very practical course with 1200 hours of clinical placement. **Queen Margaret (Coll)** Strong research background; range of teaching methods; laboratory-based teaching; research into the investigation of human performance. Strong liaison with the NHS. **Robert Gordon** Clinical placements in second and third years. **Sheffield Hallam** Ten per cent shortfall in physiotherapists nationally. Employment prospects excellent. **Teesside** Most staff are qualified physiotherapists. **West London (IHE)** The subject is taught within the Department of Health and Paramedical Professions. NOW CHECK PROSPECTUSES FOR ALL COURSES.

Work opportunities abroad: Northumbria USA CAN; **Queen Margaret (Coll)** CAN; **Wolverhampton** SLC K USA.

ADMISSIONS INFORMATION

Number of applicants per place (approx): Bath 5; **Bradford** 17; **Brighton** 25; **Bristol** 4; **Cardiff** 3; **East London** 11; **Glasgow Caledonian** 10 (200 1st choice); **Newcastle** 8; **Nottingham** 65; **Queen Margaret (Coll)** 8; **Sheffield Hallam** 60; **Teesside** 23; **Ulster** 12; **West London (IHE)** 5; **Wolverhampton** 6.

General Studies acceptable: Bradford.

Selection interviews: Brighton (all); North London (all); Nottingham (some).

Offers to applicants repeating A-levels: Higher East London (CCC), Glasgow Caledonian, Teesside, Wolverhampton.

Admissions Tutors' advice: Brighton Six places available for overseas candidates. All applicants interviewed. **Bristol (Avon Coll of Health)** Biology must be one of three A-levels offered. Physics at GCSE or an integrated science course containing physics must also be offered. Candidates who do not show evidence of work experience/visit to a physiotherapy department on their application form will not be selected for interview, and normally no candidates are selected without an interview. **East Anglia** Combined Occupational Therapy and Physiotherapy departments. **Glasgow Caledonian** Applicants must demonstrate knowledge of the career and have observed physiotherapy in a hospital setting. **North London (SP)** The course is specifically designed for students with little or no sight. Applications are made direct to the principal. **Nottingham** Candidates will normally be expected to have a good GCSE history. Applicants are advised not to apply to Nottingham School of Physiotherapy if they are applying for other subjects at universities since they will not be considered for the Physiotherapy course. **Queen Margaret (Coll)** Grade C GCSE in physics required (physics emphasis on course). **Salford (UC)** Grades are not specified but the majority of students obtained two, three or four A-levels. There are also some graduates on the course. **Wolverhampton** 'I do not usually interview candidates who have previously failed A-levels. An offer may be made to a candidate who has previously been made an offer but a 'two grade' improvement would be expected. We may accept the equivalent points score in August.'

Examples of interview questions: What cases have you seen in hospital? How were they being treated? Is religion important to you? How would you deal with a difficult patient? Is medicine preferable to physiotherapy as a treatment?

GAP YEAR ADVICE

Institutions accepting a Gap Year: Most institutions; **Birmingham** It needs to be for a very good reason; **West London (IHE)** Not acceptable.

Institutions willing to defer entry after A-levels (see Ch 5): Bradford; Brighton (No); Queen Margaret (Coll); Robert Gordon; Sheffield Hallam (No); West London (IHE) (No).

AFTER A-LEVELS ADVICE

Institutions which may accept the same points score after A-levels: Brighton; East London; Nottingham.

Institutions which may accept under-achieving applicants after A-levels: Brighton (if candidate improved at interview); Bristol; East Anglia (perhaps); East London (some); North London (SP); Northumbria; Nottingham; Queen Margaret (Coll); Teesside; Ulster; West London (IHE).

Institutions with vacancies in Aug/Sept 1992 (see Ch 5): Brighton 18-16 pts; Coventry; Sheffield Hallam. 20 to 24 pts were asked for places at London University. A slightly lower points score was acceptable at Hertfordshire and Wolverhampton.

ADVICE FOR MATURE STUDENTS

This is a popular subject for mature students who often represent up to 30% of the student intake. An upper age limit of 35-40 may apply and formal qualifications are often important. Full details can be obtained from the Chartered Society of Physiotherapy, 14 Bedford Row, London WC1R 4ED.

PODIATRY (CHIROPODY)

These courses lead to membership of the Society of Chiropodists and State Registration.

Special subject requirements: Five GCSE (grades A-C) inc English and one science subject (min) with two passes (preferably sciences) at A-level.

NB Institutions may raise or lower the level of published offers depending either on the quality or otherwise of individual applications or the numbers of applications received; grades/points offered may be adjusted downwards after A-level results. The level of an offer is not indicative of the quality of a course.

16 pts.	**Central England** - CCDCC (Pod) (BTEC Ms)
14 pts.	**London (UC)** - 14 pts (Pod)
12 pts.	**Belfast** - CC (Pod) (BTEC Ms)
8 pts.	**Huddersfield** - 8 pts (Podiatry)
	La Sainte Union (CHE) - 8-6 pts (Chiropody Dip)
	Nene (CHE) - 8 pts (Pod)
	Salford (UC) - 8 pts (Podiatry)
	Sunderland/Durham (New Coll) - (Podiatric Medicine)
4 pts.	**and below**
	Brighton - (Podiatry)
	Cardiff (IHE) - (Podiatric Medicine Dip)
	Durham (New Coll) - (Pod) (BTEC Ms)
	London (Foot Hosp) - (Chiropody)
	London (Paddington) - (Chiropody)
	Plymouth - (Pod)
	Queen Margaret (Coll) - (BSc - Podiatry)
	Salford (UC) - (Podiatric Med)
	Westminster - (Pod Med)

CHOOSING YOUR COURSE (See also Ch 1)

> **Subject information:** Podiatry is the new term for Chiropody. Courses lead to state registration. Some work shadowing prior to application is preferred by admissions tutors. In addition to the courses listed above a private Podiatry/Chiropody course is offered by Scholl leading to a Certificate or Diploma. Details are available from Scholl, 40 Upper Street, London N1 0PM.

Course highlights: Cardiff (IHE) School is a self-contained unit with clinics, operating theatre suite, orthotics laboratory. **Central England** Health-related course experience; clinical placements. **Nene (CHE)** Clinical experience includes sports injuries, orthopaedics, paediatrics. **Queen Margaret (Coll)** Placement in wide variety of clinical settings. NOW CHECK PROSPECTUSES FOR ALL COURSES.

ADMISSIONS INFORMATION

Number of applicants per place (approx): Brighton 6; **Cardiff (IHE)** 2; **Central England** 8; **London (Foot Hosp)** 16; **Plymouth** 4; **Salford (UC)** 5.

General Studies acceptable: Brighton; Cardiff (IHE); Central England; Plymouth.

Admissions Tutors' advice: Visit a podiatrist's practice (either private or Community Health). **Westminster** All applicants are interviewed.

Examples of interview questions: Have you visited a chiropodist's surgery? What do your friends think about your choice of career? Do you think that being a chiropodist could cause any physical strain? What groups of people do chiropodists come into contact with?

GAP YEAR ADVICE

Institutions accepting a Gap Year: Brighton (Advise us); Queen Margaret (Coll) (Apply year of entry).

Institutions willing to defer entry after A-levels (see Ch 5): Brighton; Cardiff (IHE); Central England; Durham (New Coll); Nene (CHE) (No); Salford (UC); Westminster.

AFTER A-LEVELS ADVICE

Institutions with vacancies in Aug/Sept 1992 (see Ch 5): Belfast 12 pts; Brighton; Cardiff (IHE); Central England 10 pts; La Sainte Union (CHE); Westminster 2 pts.

ADVICE FOR MATURE STUDENTS

Nene (CHE) accepts students between the ages of 23 and 36. Some students have degrees in other subjects. A-level passes are preferable for many courses.

POLITICS (See also GOVERNMENT)

Special subject requirements: 2-3 A-levels; GCSE (grade A-C) mathematics.

NB Institutions may raise or lower the level of published offers depending either on the quality or otherwise of individual applications or the numbers of applications received; grades/points offered may be adjusted downwards after A-level results. The level of an offer is not indicative of the quality of a course.

30 pts.	**Cambridge/Oxford** - AAA potential recommended (PPE)
28 pts.	**Bristol** - AAB-BBC (Pol; Econ/Pol; Phil/Pol; Soc A/Pol)
	Newcastle - AAB-BBB/AA-AB (Pol/EAS)
26 pts.	**Durham** - ABB (Law/Pol)
24 pts.	**Birmingham** - BBB (Law/Politics)
	Durham - ABC-BBB (All courses except **26 pts**)
	Edinburgh - BBB (Pol - MA (Arts))
	Exeter - BBB-BBC/AB (Politics; Pol/Socy) (BTEC Ds+Ms)
	Hull - BBB (PPE) (BTEC Ds+Ms)
	Leeds - BBB (All courses) (4 AS)
	Newcastle - BBB-BBC/AA-AB (Pol; Pol/Hist; Pol/Econ) (6 AS) (See **Admissions Tutors' advice**)
	Nottingham - BBB-BBC (All courses)
	Sheffield - BBB (Politics) (BTEC 3D)
	Warwick - BBB (Politics; Pol Fr; Pol Int; Econ Pol; Hist Pol)
	Warwick - BBB-BBC (Pol Soc; Phil Pol)
	York - BBB (PPE; Pol/Phil; Econ/Pol) (BTEC Ds)
22 pts.	**Aberdeen** - BBC (Pol St)
	Cardiff - BBC-BCC (Politics and joint courses)
	East Anglia - BBC (Pol; PPE)
	Edinburgh - BBC (Pol- MA Soc Sci)
	Glasgow - BBC (All courses)
	Hull - BBC/BB (Politics; Pol Leg) (4 AS)
	Keele - BBC-BCD/BB-BC (All courses)
	Kent - BBC/BC (Am St)

        Lancaster - BBC (Econ/Pol; Hist/Pol)
        Liverpool - BBC-BCC (M Hist/Pol)
        London (QMW) - BBC/AB (Pol/Econ)
        London (RH) - 22 pts (Hist/Pol)
        Manchester - 22 pts approx (All Politics courses)
        Sheffield - BBC (Soc Pol Stud) (6 AS)
        Southampton - BBC (Pol/Law; Pol; Pol/Int; Pol/Ec Hist; Com Int Pol)
        Stirling - BBC (Pol)
        Warwick - BBC-BCC (Ger Pol)
        York - BBC (All courses except under **24 pts**) (Ref CCC)

20 pts.   **Aberystwyth** - BCC/BB (Pol/Law; Int Pol; Pol; Pol/Mod Hist)
        Birmingham - BCC/BB (Int Stds; Int Std Econ)
        Bradford - BCC/BB (Pol/Soc) (BTEC 1D+3M)
        Bristol - BCC/AB (Pol/Sociol)
        Dundee - BCC (Pol)
        Essex - BCC/BC (GS Com; GSS)
        Kent - BCC/BB (All courses unless combined with a subject having a higher offer) (See
          22 pts)
        Lancaster - BCC (All courses except **22 pts**) (BTEC Ms)
        Leicester - BCC (Politics; Pol/Ec Hist)
        Liverpool - BCC/BB (Politics)
        London (QMW) - BCC/AB (Politics)
        London (QMW) - BCC/BB (Pol/Ger)
        Newcastle - BCC/BB (Pol/Soc Pol; PEAS + Korean)
        Reading - BCC (Pol/Int Rel; Pol/Econ; Pol)
        Southampton - BCC-CCC (Pol/Soc; Pol/Soc Ad)
        Strathclyde - BCC/BB (Pol - Bus Sch)
        Sussex - BCC/BB (All courses)
        Swansea - BCC (Politics; Eur Pol/Fr; Eur Pol/Ger)

18 pts.   **Belfast** - CCC/BB (Pol/Sc)
        Bradford - CCC/BB (Pol/Hist) (BTEC 1D+3M)
        Brunel - 18 pts (Pol/Mod Hist)
        Essex - CCC (WEP)
        Liverpool - CCC (Phil/Pol)
        London (RH) - CCC (Hist/Pol)
        Loughborough - CCC-BCD/BB-BC (Pol) (4 AS)
        Oxford Brookes - CCC (Pol - single field)
        Salford - 18 pts (Pol/Soc) (BTEC Ds)
        Southampton - BCD-CCC (Pol/Span)
        Strathclyde - CCC/BC (Pol; BA Arts Soc St)

16 pts.   **Buckingham** - CCD/BB (Pol/Law)
        Central Lancashire - CCD (Comb Hons)
        London (SOAS) - BB (All courses)
        Portsmouth - CCD/CC (Pol) (4 AS)

14 pts.   **Bristol UWE** - CDD/BC (BTEC 2D+2M)
        Coventry - 14 pts (Int St Bus St) (BTEC Ds)
        Guildhall London - BC (Pol/Govt) (BTEC 4M)
        Manchester Met - CDD/CC-CD (Hum/Soc St; Pol)

12 pts.   **Buckingham** - DDD/CC (All Politics courses except under **16 pts**)
        Leicester - CC (Fr/Pol)
        North London - 12 pts (Ap Soc Sci) (BTEC Ds+Ms)
        Salford - CC (Pol/Hist)

10 pts.   **Bristol UWE** - (Soc Sci)
        Central England - (Govt)
        Coventry - CD-DD (Mod St)
        Liverpool John Moores - 12 pts (Integrated Scheme)
        Middlesex - (Modular)
        Plymouth - 10 pts (Pol)
        South Bank - CD (Pol) (6 AS) (BTEC M overall)

8 pts. and below
      Staffordshire – (Mod St)
      Sunderland – (All courses; Soc Sci)
      Teesside – (Hum)
      Westminster – (Soc Sci)
      Wolverhampton – (Soc Sc)
0 pts. Salford – (Pol/Hist) (Open entry subject to interview/essay for mature students)

Diploma of Higher Education courses:
4 pts.   Bradford & Ilkley (CmC); Guildhall London; La Sainte Union (CHE); Oxford Brookes; Plymouth; Wolverhampton.

Alternative offers:

EB offers: **Brunel** 70%; **Keele** 65%; **Lancaster** 70%; **Liverpool** 60%; **Newcastle** 75%.

IB offers: **Aberdeen** 30 pts; **Aberystwyth** 30 pts; **Birmingham** H16 pts S16 pts; **Bradford** 28 pts; **Buckingham** 28 pts; **Durham** H666; **East Anglia** 30 pts; **Essex** 28 pts; **Exeter** 32 pts; **Hull** (PPE) 30 pts; **Kent** 29 pts; **Lancaster** 30 pts; **Liverpool** 28 pts; **London (SOAS)** 32 pts; **Newcastle** (Pol/Econ) 30 pts, (Pol/Hist) 33 pts H7 hist; **Swansea** 30-28 pts; **York** 28 pts.

Irish offers: **Aberdeen** BBBC; **Brunel** BBCCC; **East Anglia** CCCCC; **Guildhall London** CCCCC; **Keele** BBBCC; **Newcastle** ABBBB.

SCE offers: **Aberdeen** BBBB; **Aberystwyth** ABBB; **Birmingham** AAAB; **Dundee** BBBC; **Edinburgh** AAB-BBBB; **Essex** BBBB; **Glasgow** ABBB/BBBB; **Guildhall London** BBCCC; **Keele** BBBC; **Lancaster** BBBBB; **Newcastle** BBBB; **Sheffield** BBBBB; **Stirling** BBBC; **Strathclyde** BBBB; **Sussex** AABB; **York** BBBBB.

Overseas applicants: East Anglia Pre-sessional courses available in English and study skills. **Hull** Living costs 30% lower than in London.

CHOOSING YOUR COURSE (See also Ch 1)

> **Subject information:** These courses have become increasingly popular in recent years and usually cover the politics and government of the major powers. Through the degree courses on offer it is possible to study the politics of almost any country in the world. See also under **Peace Studies.**

Course highlights: Aberystwyth Second largest department in UK. Wide choice of options include strategic studies, political studies in international relations. **Birmingham** In the second and third years students take either political theory or political analysis, with either a choice of options from British, European, American, Latin-American, Soviet or African politics. **Brunel** Course options from other departments eg, law, electronics, sociology, psychology. All students take word-processing. **Durham** Optional subjects include political activity in the USA, the former Soviet Union and Eastern Europe, Western Europe, the Middle East and Southern Africa as well as British government, local government and public administration. **Leeds** Second year subjects cover foreign governments and comparative government in the USA, the former Soviet Union, France, China, India and Pakistan, modern political doctrines and political and social history. **Loughborough** There is a western Europe emphasis with French/German available as minor subjects; possibility to transfer within Social Sciences in second year. **Newcastle** Government and European Community Studies students have one year in Europe; a year in the Far East for Politics and East Asian Studies students. There is an emphasis on British politics, parties and policy making and also coverage of European Community and Caribbean politics. **Portsmouth** In the first year politics is studied alongside economics, modern history, political thought and current politics. **York** A wide spectrum of subjects include the major governmental systems of Britain, Western Europe, America, China, Japan and the former Soviet Union. Subject strengths include Third World and British politics and political philosophy. NOW CHECK PROSPECTUSES FOR ALL COURSES.

Study opportunities abroad: Aberystwyth (E) USA; **Bradford** (E) FR B IRE GR SZ SW; **Cardiff** (E) IT G SP FR; **Dundee** FR; **Guildhall London** (E) G IT; **Lancaster** USA; **Leeds** USA; **Sheffield** FN.

Work opportunities abroad: Brunel USA; **Leeds** USA CAN SP.

ADMISSIONS INFORMATION

Number of applicants per place (approx): Birmingham 10; **Bradford** 10; **Bristol** 12; **Buckingham** 2; **Cardiff** 14; **Durham** 16 (all courses); **East Anglia** 15; **Exeter** 8; **Guildhall London** 5; **Hull** (PPE) 20; **Kent** 14; **Lancaster** 14; **Leeds** 18; **Liverpool** 9; **London (QMW)** 10, **(SOAS)** 8; **Loughborough** 7; **Newcastle** 17; **Nottingham** 12; **Portsmouth** 19; **Swansea** 8; **York** 13.

General Studies acceptable: Aberdeen; Birmingham; Bradford; Essex; Exeter (2); Guildhall London; Hull; Kent (JMB only); Lancaster; Leeds; Newcastle (2); Oxford Brookes; Swansea; York.

Selection interviews: Birmingham; Brunel; Cambridge; Durham (challenging, informal and relaxed); East Anglia (some); Exeter; Guildhall London (some); Hull; Leeds (Pol/Parl St); Liverpool (some); London (SOAS); Loughborough (some); Newcastle (some); Nottingham (some); Oxford; Portsmouth (some); Sheffield; South Bank; Swansea; Warwick (some); York (some).

Offers to applicants repeating A-levels: Higher East Anglia, Essex, Leeds, Newcastle, Nottingham; **Possibly higher** Durham, Hull, Lancaster, Oxford Brookes, Swansea; **Same** Birmingham, Bristol, Guildhall London, Lancaster, London (SOAS), Loughborough (Pol/Soc Sci), Portsmouth, South Bank, Sussex, York.

Admissions Tutors' advice: Buckingham As the economics component involves some elementary mathematics we are looking for some maths/science background, at least to GCSE (grade A-C) in addition to normal A-level requirements. Students who interview well may be offered places even though their A-levels results may not be outstanding. **East Anglia** Our standard offer may be modified to take into account potential performance and personal circumstances. **Hull** Candidates who are invited to open days and decline without reason or similarly fail to accept invitation to interview, are rejected. **Loughborough** Special consideration is given to mature applicants. Interviews are made prior to offer. **Newcastle** For Politics our offers vary substantially, depending on the applicant. With a school's consent we are willing to make offers as low as EE to good candidates who interview well. **Nottingham** All sections of the UCAS application are taken into account. **York** We welcome mature applicants.

Examples of interview questions: What constitutes a 'great power'? What is happening at present in the Labour Party? Define capitalism. Define Thatcherism? What is a political decision? How do opinion polls detract from democracy? Why has Welsh nationalism lost its impetus? Is the European Community a good idea? Why? What is the Maastricht Agreement? Why did the Danes say No?

GAP YEAR ADVICE

Institutions accepting a Gap Year: Most institutions; **Bradford** Contact admissions tutor if unavailable for interview during year out; **Brunel** Deferred entry welcome; **York** We welcome those hoping/wishing to take a year off between school and university.

Institutions willing to defer entry after A-levels (see Ch 5): Aberystwyth; Bristol UWE; Brunel (No); Buckingham; Dundee; Hull; Newcastle (No); Plymouth; South Bank (Prefer not); Swansea; York.

AFTER A-LEVELS ADVICE

Institutions which may accept the same points score after A-levels: Birmingham; Durham; East Anglia; Essex; Guildhall London; Hull; Kent; Liverpool; London (SOAS); Loughborough; Oxford Brookes; Newcastle; Portsmouth; South Bank; Swansea.

Institutions demanding the actual grades offered after A-levels: Bristol; Lancaster; Leeds; Newcastle (Pol/EAS); Nottingham; Stirling; York (preferably).

Institutions which may accept under-achieving applicants after A-levels: Aberystwyth; Birmingham; Buckingham (Univ); East Anglia; Essex; Exeter; Hull (Overseas applicants 18-16 pts); London (SOAS); Portsmouth; South Bank; Swansea; York.

Institutions with vacancies in Aug/Sept 1992 (see Ch 5): Aberystwyth 18 pts; Bristol UWE; Brunel 16 pts; Buckingham 12 pts; Coventry (Int St Bus St) 14 pts; North London 12 pts; Plymouth 14 pts; Salford (Pol/Hist) 18 pts; South Bank CD.

ADVICE FOR MATURE STUDENTS

This is a popular subject for mature students who represent up to 20% of the student intake on some courses. Formal entry qualifications may not be required.

GRADUATE EMPLOYMENT

New Graduates' destinations (percentages) 1991:
Permanent employment: U 61; P 60.
Unemployment: U 26; P 26.
Further studies (all types): U 32; P 14.
Main career destinations (approx): Admin 23; Financial 21; Business 16; Secretarial 13; Social/Welfare 13; Creative 6; Legal 4; Teaching 1.

York (1988-91) Choice of careers was fairly equally divided between law, social/welfare, management services, journalism and editorial work, advertising, sales and marketing, accountancy, public sector administration and education. 20% went on to further study (teacher training (15), law (solicitor 12), journalism (3) and further research (16).

POLYMER SCIENCE (See also **Materials Science**)

Special subject requirements: 2-3 A-levels; chemistry usually 'required'.

NB Institutions may raise or lower the level of published offers depending either on the quality or otherwise of individual applications or the numbers of applications received; grades/points offered may be adjusted downwards after A-level results. The level of an offer is not indicative of the quality of a course.

18 pts.	**Sheffield** - CCC (Polymers) (BTEC 3M)
	Sussex - CCC/BC (CPS/Mols)
16 pts.	**Lancaster** - CCD (Chem/Polymer)
	Manchester - CCD (Polymer)
	UMIST - CCD (Polymer TC)
14 pts.	**London (QMW)** - CDD/BC-CC (Poly Sci/Eng)
	Loughborough - CCE (Chem/Poly 3 and 4)
8 pts.	**and below**
	Manchester Met - 8 pts (Polymer S/T) (4 AS) (BTEC 3M)

Offers for Foundation, Certificate and Diploma courses (see Ch 5):

Higher National Diploma courses:
   4 pts.   and below North London.

Alternative offers:

IB offers: **Manchester Met** 24 pts; **UMIST** 26 pts.

SCE offers: **Sheffield** BBBC.

CHOOSING YOUR COURSE (See also Ch 1)

> **Subject information:** This is often studied in conjunction with Chemistry and covers such topics as polymer properties and processing relating to industrial applications with plastics, natural and synthetic rubbers, paints, adhesives, space technology, agriculture and medicine.

Course highlights: Manchester Met Transfer to Combined Studies possible. Sponsorships often available. NOW CHECK PROSPECTUSES FOR ALL COURSES.

Work opportunities abroad: Manchester Met NL F.

ADMISSIONS INFORMATION

Number of applicants per place (approx): Manchester Met 2; **UMIST** 3.

General Studies acceptable: Manchester Met.

Selection interviews: Manchester Met; Sussex; UMIST (after offer).

Offers to applicants repeating A-levels: Same Manchester Met, UMIST.

Admissions Tutors' advice: UMIST Motivation and interest are considered alongside academic record.

> **Examples of interview questions:** Applicants questioned on their A-level work, particularly in chemistry, and aspects of study which interest them. Their knowledge of polymers and industrial applications will also be tested.

GAP YEAR ADVICE

Institutions accepting a Gap Year: Manchester Met Experience in the industry useful.

Institutions willing to defer entry after A-levels (see Ch 5): Manchester Met; UMIST.

AFTER A-LEVELS ADVICE

Institutions which may accept the same points score after A-levels: Manchester Met; UMIST.

Institutions which may accept under-achieving applicants after A-levels: Manchester Met.

Institutions with vacancies in Aug/Sept 1992 (see Ch 5): Manchester Met 2 pts; UMIST 10 pts.

PORTUGUESE (See also Spanish/Hispanic Studies and Modern Languages)

Special subject requirements: 2-3 A-levels. Spanish sometimes 'required'.

NB Institutions may raise or lower the level of published offers depending either on the quality or otherwise of individual applications or the numbers of applications received; grades/points offered may be adjusted downwards after A-level results. The level of an offer is not indicative of the quality of a course.

30 pts.	**Cambridge** – AAA potential recommended (Mod/M Lang)
20 pts.	**Cardiff** – BCC (Joint Hons)
	Leeds – BCC (Port/Rus; Port/Sp)
	London (King's) – BCC approx (Port)
18 pts.	**Southampton** – CCC (Span/Port)

CHOOSING YOUR COURSE (See also Ch 1)

> **Subject information:** This may be studied as a language in its own right, but more often is a combined study with another language, or part of a course in Hispanic Studies.

ADMISSIONS INFORMATION

Selection interviews: Cambridge.

> **Examples of interview questions:** Why Portuguese? Have you been to Portugal? What career are you aiming for at the end of the course? (It is important for applicants to be informed about Portugal and its people.)

PRINTING and PUBLISHING

Special subject requirements: A science subject at A-level.

NB Institutions may raise or lower the level of published offers depending either on the quality or otherwise of individual applications or the numbers of applications received; grades/points offered may be adjusted downwards after A-level results. The level of an offer is not indicative of the quality of a course.

14 pts.	**Oxford Brookes** – CDD/BC (Pub Modular) (4 AS)
10 pts.	**Manchester Met** – 10 pts (Prin Phot)
	Napier – CEE (Publishing)
6 pts.	and below
	Hertfordshire/West Herts (Coll) – EE (PPT/BM; PPT Pub) (4 AS)
	London Inst (CP) – (Prtg Man)
	Robert Gordon – (Pub Stud)
	Thames Valley London – (Inf Man)

Diploma of Higher Education courses:
4 pts.   Oxford Brookes.

Offers for Foundation, Certificate and Diploma courses (see Ch 5):

Higher National Diploma courses (Printing) (England and Wales):
    4 pts.   **and below** London Inst (CP) (with Bus St); Manchester Met; Nottingham Trent; West Herts (Coll) (PPP).

Higher National Diploma courses (Publishing) (England and Wales):
    4 pts.   **and below** London Inst (CP) (with Bus St)

Higher Diploma courses (Scotland):
    4 pts.   **and below or equivalent** Glasgow (CP); Napier EE.

CHOOSING YOUR COURSE (See also Ch 1)

> **Subject information:** An undersubscribed area for applications, yet this is a vast industry requiring graduates to work at all levels.

Course highlights: London Inst (CP) (Prtg Man) Mature students with practical experience but limited academic qualifications are welcome. (HND Bus St) Options in publishing, marketing and advertising. **Manchester Met** (Prin Phot) Sandwich course. Strong links with employers. Course combines 50% business and management with 50% practical workshop experience, with hands-on experience of printing and allied processes etc, desk top publishing on Apple Mac machines and practical printing exercises. **West Herts (Coll)** Research at MSc, MPhil and PhD levels. Company consultancy work; strong employer contacts. NOW CHECK PROSPECTUSES FOR ALL COURSES.

Study opportunities abroad: West Herts (Coll) (E).

Work opportunities abroad: West Herts (Coll) FR G FN.

ADMISSIONS INFORMATION

Number of applicants per place (approx): Glasgow (CP) 3; **Hertfordshire/ West Herts (Coll)** 2 (Interviews held); **Oxford Brookes** 16.

> **Examples of interview questions:** Applicants should have knowledge of methods of printing and of printing and publishing industry. This should come from personal contact with printers and publishers, especially the latter since many applicants think that publishing editors devote most of their time to enjoying a good meal!

GAP YEAR ADVICE

Institutions willing to defer entry after A-levels (see Ch 5): Hertfordshire/West Herts (Coll).

AFTER A-LEVELS ADVICE

Institutions with vacancies in Aug/Sept 1992 (see Ch 5): A number of course vacancies were advertised.

PSYCHOLOGY

Special subject requirements: 2-3 A-levels; GCSE (grade A-C) mathematics.

NB Institutions may raise or lower the level of published offers depending either on the quality or otherwise of individual applications or the numbers of applications received; grades/points offered may be adjusted downwards after A-level results. The level of an offer is not indicative of the quality of a course.

30 pts.	**Cambridge/Oxford** - AAA potential recommended (PPP)
26 pts.	**Nottingham** - ABB-BBB (All courses)
	St Andrews - ABB (Psy - MA) (4 AS)
24 pts.	**Birmingham** - BBB-BBC (Psy Sc; Psy/Sport)
	Bristol - BBB (Psy Soc Sci; Psy/Zoo - BSc)
	Cardiff - BBB-BBC (Joint courses)
	Edinburgh - BBB (Psy - MA)
	Exeter - BBB-BBC/AB (Psy Soc St) (6 AS) (BTEC Ds+Ms)
	Hull - BBB-BBC/AB (Phil/Psy; Psy/Soc; Psy/Clin) (4 AS) (BTEC 4D)
	Manchester - 24-22 pts approx (Psy)
	Newcastle - ABC-BBB (Psy Arts) (BTEC 4M)
	Oxford Brookes - BBB (Modular Psy)
	St Andrews - BBB-CCC (Psy - BSc)
	Sheffield - BBB (Psy) (BTEC 3D+3M)
	Warwick - BBB-BBC (Psy; Psy Phil)
	York - BBB (Psy)
22 pts.	**Aberdeen** - BBC (Psy - MA)
	Aston - BBC/AB (Hum Psy; Psy/Man)
	Durham - BBC (All courses)
	Essex - BBC (Psych) (BTEC 3D+Ms)
	Exeter - BBC (Psy Sci - BSc) (6 AS)
	Glasgow - BBC (Psy - MA)
	Hull - BBC/AA-BB (Psy; Psy/Occ Psy) (BTEC 2D+2M)
	Lancaster - BBC (Psy; Comb courses) (4 AS) (BTEC Ds+Ms)
	Leeds - BBC-CCC (Psy/Soc)
	Leeds - BBC/BB (Comp/Psy)
	London (LSE) - 22 pts approx (Soc/Psy)
	London (RH) - BBC/BB (All courses) (BTEC Ms)
	London (UC) - BBC-CCC/BB (Psy Sci)
	Loughborough - 22 pts flexible/BB for mature students only (Soc Psy)
	Oxford Brookes - BBC-CDD (Psych) (See **Admissions Tutors' advice**)
	Plymouth - BBC/AB (Psy) (BTEC 2D+3M)
	Southampton - BBXC (Psy; Psy/Physio)
	Stirling - BBC (Psy - BA/BSc)
	Surrey - BBC (Psy)
	Sussex - BBC (Psy courses)
	Swansea - BBC/BB (Psy Arts; Psy/Phil; Psy/Soc Anth; Psy/Soc; Psy/Econ)
20 pts.	**Aberdeen** - BCC (Psy - BSc)
	Aston - BCC/BB (Psy Comb Hons) (BTEC 5D+5M)
	Bangor - BCC/AB (Psy Arts; Psy Sci; Psy/Health Psy)
	Bath - BCC (Soc/Psy)
	Belfast - BCC/BB (Psy Sci; Psy Soc Sc; Psy Arts)
	Bradford - BCC (Psy)
	Brunel - BCC (Psy; SA/Psy) (BTEC 5M)
	Dundee - BCC (Psy - MA)
	Exeter - BCC (Psych/Euro) (4 AS) (BTEC Ds+Ms)
	Keele - BCC-CCC/BB-BC (All courses)
	Kent - BCC (Approx offer for most courses except below)
	Kent - BCC/BB (Soc Psych; App Soc Psy; Soc Psy/Phil; Psych; Soc/Clin Psy)

Lancaster - BCC (Hum Comm)
Leeds - BCC/AB (Psy) (4 AS)
Leicester - BCC/BB (Psy Sci; Psy Arts)
Liverpool - BCC (Psy Arts; Psy Sci; Psycol Comb) (5 AS)
London (Gold) - BCC (Psych)
Loughborough - 20-18 pts (Hum Psy)
Oxford Brookes - BCC (Modular) (4 AS)
Reading - BCC (Psy Arts and all Psy Arts joint courses)
Sheffield - BCC-CCC (Psy/Soc)
Strathclyde - BCC/BB (Psy- Bus Sch)
Swansea - BCC/BB-BC (Psy Sci; Psy/Soc Stat; Psy/Biol; Psy/Comp)

18 pts.
Bradford - CCC/BB (Soc/Psy)
Bristol UWE - 18 pts (Psy/Health St) (See **Admissions Tutors' advice**)
City - CCC/BB (All courses) (BTEC 4D+Ms)
Edinburgh - CCC (Psy - BSc)
Glasgow - CCC-CCD/BB (Psy - BSc)
Hertfordshire - 18-16 pts (Psy) (4 AS) (BTEC 1D+4M)
Manchester Met - CCC/BB (Psych)
Newcastle - CCC (Psy Sci) (BTEC 4M)
Northumbria - CCC/AB (Psych) (4 AS) (BTEC 4D+1M)
Portsmouth - CCC (Psy)
St Andrews - CCC (Psy/Comp; Psy/Econ)
Sheffield Hallam - CCC (Psych)
Staffordshire - 18 pts (BTEC 2D+Ms)
Strathclyde - CCC/BC (BBD 2nd yr entry) (Psy - BA)
Sunderland - CCC/BC (Psy)
Trinity & All Saints (CHE) - CCC/BB (Psy/PM; Psy/BMA)

16 pts.
Bournemouth - 16-14 pts (Psy Com Comp) (BTEC 3D)
Central Lancashire - CCD (Psych) (4 AS)
Dundee - CCD (Psychology)
Leicester - CCD (Sci Comb)
Liverpool John Moores - 14 pts (Psychology courses)
Middlesex - 16-12 pts (Soc Sci) (4 AS)
Plymouth - BB minimum (Sci/Soc) (4 AS)
Reading - CCD (Psy Sci; Psy/Cyb; Psy/Zool)
Teesside - 16 pts (19 pts if A-level psychology is inc)/CE (Psych)
Ulster - CCD/BC (Comb Soc Bhv - all courses)

14 pts.
Ulster - CDD/CC (Hum Comm)

12 pts.
Bolton (IHE) - CC (Psych; Comb St) (4 AS)
Buckingham - 12 pts (Psychology courses) (BTEC 3M)
Central Lancashire - CC (App Psy)
Guildhall London - CC (Psych)
Huddersfield - CC (Bhv Sci)
Humberside - 12 pts (Psy) (4 AS)
Middlesex - CC (Psych)
Nene (CHE) - CDE/CC or CD (Comb St)
Roehampton (IHE) - CC (Psy Coun; Comb) (BTEC Ds+Ms)
Thames Valley London - 12 pts (Psy/Comm)
Trinity & All Saints (CHE) - CC (Psy)
Worcester (CHE) - 12 pts approx (Psy)

10 pts.
Cheltenham & Glos (CHE) - 10 pts (Psyc; Modular)

8 pts. and below
Cardiff (IHE) - (Psy Comm)
Chester (CHE) - (Comb Hons)
East London - (Psych Sci)
Greenwich - (Psy - new courses, contact Admissions Tutor)
Hertfordshire - (Comb St; Hum)
Liverpool John Moores - (Integrated Credit Scheme)
Liverpool (IHE) - (Comb St)

South Bank - EE (Psy)
Westminster - (Soc Sci; Psy Sci; Psy; Modular) (BTEC 3M)
Wolverhampton - (All courses)

Diploma of Higher Education courses:
4 pts.   East London; Guildhall London; Middlesex; Oxford Brookes; Wolverhampton; Worcester
(CHE).

Alternative offers:

EB offers: **Keele** 70%; **Plymouth** 68%; **Sheffield** 70%.

IB offers: **Aberdeen** 30 pts; **Aston** 31 pts overall; **Birmingham** 30 pts; **Bradford** 32-30 pts; **Bristol** 33-30 pts; **Brunel** 28 pts; **Buckingham** 24 pts; **Cardiff** H555 + 13 pts; **City** 28 pts overall H655 S444; **Dundee** H544; **Essex** 28 pts; **Exeter** 32 pts; **Glasgow** H555 (BSc); **Hull** 30 pts inc scores of 6; **Kent** 27 pts, H 12 pts; **Lancaster** 32-30 pts; **Leicester** 28 pts; **Liverpool** 30 pts H65; **London (RH)** 30 pts; **Loughborough** 28 pts inc H6; **Plymouth** 24 pts; **Portsmouth** 24 pts; **St Andrews** 30 pts; **Sheffield** H666; **South Bank** 24 pts; **Staffordshire** 24 pts; **Surrey** 30 pts; **Swansea** 28 pts; **York** H555 S555.

Irish offers: **Aberdeen** BBBB; **Brunel** BBBCCC; **Glasgow** BBB (BSc); **Keele** BBBCC; **Liverpool** BBCCC; **Plymouth** BBCC; **Sheffield** ABBBB; **South Bank** CCCC.

SCE offers: **Aberdeen** BBBBB; **Bristol** ABBBC; **Brunel** BBBC; **Dundee** BBBC; **Edinburgh** BBBBB/ BBBB; **Glasgow** BBB (BSc), ABBB (Soc Sci), BBBB (Arts); **Keele** BBCC; **Lancaster** BBBBB; **Liverpool** AABB; **Loughborough** AABB; **Newcastle** BBBB; **Sheffield** AABBB; **South Bank** CCC; **Stirling** BBBC; **Strathclyde** BBBB (Arts), AABB (Bus Sch); **Surrey** AABB-ABBB.

Overseas applicants: Bangor English language courses available. **Manchester Met, Northumbria** Fluency in English required. **Oxford Brookes** Access courses available.

CHOOSING YOUR COURSE (See also Ch 1)

Subject information: This is an ever popular course covering studies in development, perception, learning, personality as well as social and abnormal psychology. Applications for degree courses increased by more than 10% in 1992/3. (It is not a training to enable you to psycho-analyse your friends!) All courses approved for future training as psychologists are listed in the publications of the British Psychological Society, St Andrews, 48 Princess Road East, Leicester LE1 7DR.

Course highlights: Aston The course's emphasis is on human psychology, and is provided either as a full-time or as a sandwich course; decision is made in the second year. **Bangor** Child and health psychology bias. Applied mental health option in second year covering schizophrenia, child abuse, depression, Aids, addictive behaviour; growing, vigorous department. (Health Psy) A unique course in the UK; gives BPS recognition. **Bradford** Strong bias towards physiological and pharmacological aspects of behaviour – emphasis on experimental work. **Bristol** Emphasis on both human and animal behaviour; no practical work on animals. **Cardiff** In Part II (years 2 and 3) core courses and options are taken including social and occupational psychology, abnormal psychology and applied biology. **City** The course involves cognitive and social psychology, learning, clinical and abnormal psychology. Emphasis on health and organisational psychology. **Durham** In the third year three options are chosen from a list which includes developmental, medical, social and animal psychology. **Hertfordshire** Attention is given to computer applications and artificial intelligence. Language options (French, German, Spanish) can be taken at minor levels. One month work placement between years 2 and 3. **Hull** Comprehensive course covering clinical and occupational areas. **Humberside** The course includes child psychology, occupational psychology, research into health and illness. **Kent** In Part II there is an emphasis on practical work and such topics as clinical psychology, psychology and law, occupational psychology. **Leeds** In the first year core topics deal with behaviour through studies of social and child psychology, perception, learning and biological psychology. Two subsidiary subjects are also taken. **London (RH)** Topics include psychometrics, psychopathology, social and developmental psychology, animal behaviour, individual differences and occupational psychology. **Manchester Met** Emphasis on applied psychology as a vocational preparation at a later stage in the course. **Northumbria** Specialised areas include social psychology, artificial intelligence, behaviour, health and illness, dyslexia and word recognition (no animal experiments). **Roehampton (IHE)** Psychology and Counselling course is first of its kind in the country. **Sheffield** In the first year lectures fall into four groups: psychobiology, personality, social psychology and psychological disorders, cognition and developmental psychology. **Stirling** Part II covers psychological methods, animal behaviour, social psychology, perception and performance, clinical and counselling psychology and occupational psychology. **Surrey** This is a four-year sandwich course in which the third year is spent in professional placement. These placements are in hospitals and clinical schools, social survey companies, personnel and occupational guidance services, industry and commerce. **Thames Valley London** Bias towards social welfare aspects of applied psychology. **Warwick** Core courses in second year cover personality, psychopathology, perception, action, memory and language. **Cambridge, Exeter, Nottingham, Oxford, Sheffield, York, St Andrews, Birmingham, Lancaster, Surrey, Cardiff** – high research ratings. NOW CHECK PROSPECTUSES FOR ALL COURSES.

Study opportunities abroad: Brunel (E); **Cardiff** (E); **Exeter** (E); **Lancaster** USA EUR; **Portsmouth** (E); **Manchester Met** (E); **Newcastle** (E); **Oxford Brookes** (E); **Plymouth** USA NL F G GR.

Work opportunities abroad: Brunel USA EUR; **Plymouth** USA NL F G GR; **Surrey** USA.

ADMISSIONS INFORMATION

Number of applicants per place (approx): Bangor 11; **Birmingham** 14; **Bolton (IHE)** 4; **Bradford** 14; **Bristol** 22; **Bristol UWE** 2; **Brunel** 12; **Cardiff** 12; **Cardiff (IHE)** 10; **Central Lancashire** 16; **City** 23; **Dundee** 27; **Durham** 17; **Exeter** 12; **Hertfordshire** 27; **Hull** 17; **Kent** (Soc Psych) 14; **Lancaster** 20; **Leicester** 17; **Liverpool** 19; **Liverpool John Moores** 20; **London (RH)** 11; **Loughborough** 26; **Manchester Met** 43; **Nene (CHE)** 13; **Newcastle** 20; **Northumbria** 53; **Nottingham** (Psy Sci) 15, (Psy Soc) 16; **Portsmouth** 40; **Sheffield** 14; **Surrey** (Psy) 12, (App Psy/Soc) 7; **Swansea** 10; **Teesside** 11; **Trinity & All Saints (CHE)** 13; **Westminster** 6; **York** 14.

General Studies acceptable: Aberdeen; Aston; Birmingham; Bradford; Brunel; Central Lancashire; Durham; Essex; Guildhall London (2); Hull; Lancaster; Loughborough; Manchester Met; Oxford Brookes; South Bank; Thames Valley London; Worcester (CHE); York.

Selection interviews: Aston; Bangor (some); Birmingham (JMB); Bolton (IHE) (T); Brunel (T) (maths test if no maths at GCSE (grade A-C)); Durham; Guildhall London (some); Hull (some); Liverpool; London (RH); Newcastle (some); Nottingham (some); Oxford; Oxford Brookes (some); Plymouth; Portsmouth; South Bank (some); Swansea; Trinity & All Saints (CHE); Warwick (some); most other colleges.

Offers to applicants repeating A-levels: Higher Aston, Bangor, Birmingham, City, Loughborough, Newcastle, Portsmouth, Swansea, York (BBB); **Possibly higher** Aston (Hum Psy), Nene (CHE); **Same** Aston (Comb Hons), Bolton (IHE), Brunel, Huddersfield, Hull, London (RH), Manchester Met, Nottingham, Oxford Brookes, South Bank, Surrey, Ulster.

Admissions Tutors' advice: Bristol UWE (Psy/Health St) Course not eligible as yet for graduate membership of BPS. **Durham** Performance at interview and other factors are of less significance than A-level grades in selection. A good GCSE (grade A-C) in maths or statistics is required. **Guildhall London** It is possible to major or specialise in Psychology or combine it with other disciplines. **Loughborough** Mature students with good academic records welcomed. **Manchester Met** All suitable applicants are sent a questionnaire and asked to write an essay on their choice of Psychology. Selection is based on their answers. **Nottingham** Good GCSE maths welcomed (grades A or B). **Oxford Brookes** Offers can range from BBC-CDD depending on the other chosen field. **Surrey** We prefer A-levels to include science or quantitative subjects. **Swansea** We are looking for a good spread of arts and science subjects at GCSE and welcome this mixture at A-level. Deferred entry applicants also welcomed. **York** Candidates are expected to have a good GCSE (grade A–C) in mathematics or statistics in addition to the required A-levels.

> **Examples of interview questions:** What have you read in relation to psychology? What do you expect to gain by studying psychology? What are your parents' and teachers' views on your choice of subject? Are you interested in any particular branch of the subject? Do you think you are well suited to this course? Why? Do you think it is possible that if we learn enough about the functioning of the brain that we can artificially create a computer which is functionally the same? What are your views on child psychology?

GAP YEAR ADVICE

Institutions accepting a Gap Year: Most institutions; **Bristol** Work experience or employment abroad or time spent caring for people recommended; **Hull** Apply for deferred entry stating reasons; **Liverpool John Moores** Early application for year in which entry is required; **Loughborough** Deferred entries welcome; **Oxford Brookes** Apply early for deferred entry; **Portsmouth** Apply after your A-level results are known; **Thames Valley London** Apply early.

Institutions willing to defer entry after A-levels (see Ch 5): Aston; Bangor; Bradford; Bristol; Brunel; Buckingham; City (No); Hull; Lancaster; London (RH); Newcastle; Northumbria; Portsmouth; Plymouth; Roehampton (IHE); Sheffield Hallam; South Bank; Staffordshire (No); Sunderland; Trinity & All Saints (CHE) (Prefer not); Westminster; York (No).

AFTER A-LEVELS ADVICE

Institutions which may accept the same points score after A-levels: Aston; Bangor; Birmingham; Bolton (IHE); Bradford; Brunel; Cardiff; Central Lancashire; City; Huddersfield; Hull; Humberside; Liverpool; London (RH); Loughborough (some); Manchester Met; Nene (CHE); Newcastle (BA); Northumbria; Plymouth (perhaps); Portsmouth; Sheffield; Surrey; Swansea; Trinity & All Saints (CHE); York (varies).

Institutions demanding the actual grades offered after A-levels: Dundee; Durham; Lancaster; Loughborough (Soc Psy); Newcastle (BSc); Nottingham; Portsmouth; Stirling.

Institutions which may accept under-achieving applicants after A-levels: Aston; Bangor; Bolton (IHE); Bradford; Brunel; City; Essex; Exeter; Hertfordshire; Hull; Humberside; Kent; Liverpool; London (RH); Manchester Met; Newcastle; Northumbria; Portsmouth; Sheffield; Surrey; Trinity & All Saints (CHE).

Institutions with vacancies in Aug/Sept 1992 (see Ch 5): Bradford BBC; Buckingham 12-10 pts; Essex 22 pts; London (RH) 20 pts; Northumbria 16-14 pts; Sheffield Hallam 16 pts; South Bank EE; Sunderland 18 pts; Trinity & All Saints (CHE) (Psy/PM) 16 pts; Westminster 8 pts.

ADVICE FOR MATURE STUDENTS

This subject attracts a large number of applications from mature students who represent up to 30% of the student intake on some courses. A-levels are preferred by some universities although alternative qualifications (including nursing qualifications) are considered appropriate. Apply early.

GRADUATE EMPLOYMENT

New Graduates' destinations (percentages) 1991:
Permanent employment: U 70; P 55; C 50.
Unemployment: U 18; P 21; C 35.
Further studies (all types): U 35; P 26; C 37.
Main career destinations (approx): Medical/Social 39; Business 17; Admin 12; Financial 8; Secretarial 6; Teaching (Univ/Poly) 5.

Surrey (Applied Psychology/Sociology) Graduates moved towards careers in psychology (Health Authority work or industrial research) whilst two joined the police force. Other students followed postgraduate courses in teaching (aiming for work as educational psychologists) or in counselling.

(Psychology) Live-in warden at a home for the disabled, residential social worker, assistant psychologist, self-employed therapist were some of the posts occupied by graduates in 1990. Three went into computer programming, insurance and accountancy and three went on to do post-graduate studies in HIV/Aids, Clinical Psychology and Cognitive Psychology.

York (1989-91) 63 graduates went into employment, 25 going into subject-related work (residential social work, counselling, voluntary social work, probation work, welfare, clinical psychology, nursing and occupational therapy); 13 went on to teacher training (a required route for those aiming to be educational psychologists). Other destinations followed the usual graduate pattern and covered accountancy, management training, advertising and management services.

PUBLIC ADMINISTRATION

Special subject requirements: GCSE (grade A-C) mathematics.

NB Institutions may raise or lower the level of published offers depending either on the quality or otherwise of individual applications or the numbers of applications received; grades/points offered may be adjusted downwards after A-level results. The level of an offer is not indicative of the quality of a course.

20 pts.	**Aston** - BCC/AA (Pub Pol/Man) (BTEC 5D+5M)
	Birmingham - BCC/BB (PMA) (See **Admissions Tutors' advice**)
	London (RH) - BCC/BB (Econ/Pub Admin)
	Newcastle - BCC/BC (Pub Pol - new course)
	Southampton - BCC (PS/Admin)
18 pts.	**Durham** - CCC (SP/Admin)
	Kent - CCC/BB (PAM)
14 pts.	**Brighton** - CDD/CC (Pub Pol/Ad)
	Glamorgan - CDD/CD (Pub Pol; Pub Man - subject to approval)
	Glasgow Caledonian - CDD (PA)
	Sheffield Hallam - CDD/CC (Pub Admin; Pub Sec Man) (BTEC Ms)
12 pts.	**Bournemouth** - 12 pts (Public Rel)
	De Montfort - 12-10 pts (P Admin) (4 AS)
	Manchester Met - 12 pts at least 1 grade C (P Admin) (4 AS) (BTEC 5M)
	Nottingham Trent - 12 pts (Pub Admin) (4 AS)
	Teesside - CDE/CD (Pub Admin)
10 pts.	**Glamorgan** - CD (Pub Admin) (4 AS)
6 pts.	**Robert Gordon** - EEE (P Admin)
4 pts.	and below
	Bradford & Ilkley (CmC) - (Comm St)
	Humberside - (Public Sec)

Offers for Foundation, Certificate and Diploma courses (see Ch 5):

Higher National Diploma courses (with Business Studies):
4 pts.   and below Brighton; Central Lancashire; De Montfort; Glamorgan; Humberside; Luton (CHE); Sheffield Hallam also HNC; South Bank; Southampton (IHE); Stockport (CT); Teesside; Wolverhampton.

Alternative offers:

IB offers: **Birmingham** 33 pts inc 17 pts Highers; **London (RH)** 30 pts.

SCE offers: **Manchester Met** BBBB.

Overseas applicants: Central Lancashire English tuition available. **Sheffield Hallam** Orientation programme and languages tuition.

CHOOSING YOUR COURSE (See also Ch 1)

> **Subject information:** This is a vocational course for those interested in administrative work for agencies providing public services such as the NHS, the Civil Service, local authorities, public corporations and housing associations.

Course highlights: Birmingham National and international reputation of Department of Local Government Studies. Work placement in third year. **De Montfort** All students go on salaried placements. **Glamorgan** Many students obtain sponsorship through sandwich placement year. **Manchester Met** Contacts with employers strong and good employment prospects in both private and public sectors. Opportunity to study a modern language and for placements in a Western European university through the ERASMUS scheme. **Nottingham Trent** Course focuses on politics and economics. **Robert Gordon** Foreign language options. **Teesside** Modular course gives students wider choice of options in placement year. NOW CHECK PROSPECTUSES FOR ALL COURSES.

Study opportunities abroad: De Montfort SP; **Glamorgan** (E); **Manchester Met** (E) IT FR D G; **Teesside** (E) NL IRE.

ADMISSIONS INFORMATION

Number of applicants per place (approx): Birmingham 8; **De Montfort** 9; **Glamorgan** 3; **Glasgow Caledonian** 15; **Kent** 12; **Manchester Met** 7; **Nottingham Trent** 13; **Robert Gordon** 4; **Sheffield Hallam** 11; **Teesside** 4.

General Studies acceptable: Birmingham (2); Manchester Met; Sheffield Hallam.

Offers to applicants repeating A-levels: Higher Teesside; **Same** Manchester Met.

Admissions Tutors' advice: Birmingham The above information relating to the standard offer is intended only as a rough guide. Normally students will not be offered a place until after a visit and a short personal interview which will help determine the precise offer made. **De Montfort** In support of their application students are invited to send copies of any additional information from their current Records of Achievement (up to a maximum of 2 sides of A4) direct to the Admissions Tutor quoting their UCAS number.

> **Examples of interview questions:** It is important for applicants to have made the effort to discuss this career with management staff in town halls, hospitals etc. Questions will arise from these contacts.

GAP YEAR ADVICE

Institutions accepting a Gap Year: Most institutions; **Birmingham** Very beneficial, particularly with experience in public sector work; **Teesside** Inform course leader before gap year.

Institutions willing to defer entry after A-levels (see Ch 5): Aston; Brighton; De Montfort; London (RH).

AFTER A-LEVELS ADVICE

Institutions which may accept the same points score after A-levels: Montfort; Glamorgan; Kent; Manchester Met; Nottingham Trent.

Institutions demanding the actual grades offered after A-levels: Sheffield Hallam.

Institutions with vacancies in Aug/Sept 1992 (see Ch 5): Aston BBC; De Montfort 12 pts; London (RH) 20-18 pts; Robert Gordon.

QUANTITY SURVEYING

Special subject requirements: 2 A-levels from mathematic/physics subjects. GCSE (grade A-C) in English and mathematics.

NB Institutions may raise or lower the level of published offers depending either on the quality or otherwise of individual applications or the numbers of applications received; grades/points offered may be adjusted downwards after A-level results. The level of an offer is not indicative of the quality of a course.

22 pts.	**Reading** - BBC/AB (Quant Surv)
20 pts.	**Loughborough** - 20 pts (Man/Quant Surv)
	Salford - BCC-CCC/BB (Quant Surv)
	UMIST - 20 pts (Comm Man/QS) (BTEC 2D + 2M)
18 pts.	**Brighton** - CCC/BC (Quant Surv) (BTEC Ds + Ms)
	Heriot-Watt - CCC (Build Ec/QS)
	Ulster - CCC/BB (Quant Surv)
16 pts.	**Glasgow Caledonian** - CCD/EE (Quant Surv)
14 pts.	**Greenwich** - 14-12 pts (Quant Surv) (4 AS) (BTEC Ds + Ms)
	Leeds Met - BC-CC (Quant Surv) (4 AS) (BTEC 5M)
	Liverpool John Moores - 14 pts (Quant Surv) (4 AS) (BTEC 6M)
	Northumbria - 14 pts or CC (Quant Surv) (4 AS) (BTEC 4M)
	Nottingham Trent - 14 pts (Quant Surv) (4 AS)
	Westminster - 14 pts (Quant Surv) (4 AS) (BTEC 4M)
12 pts.	**Bristol UWE** - 12-10 pts (Quant Surv)
	Central England - 12 pts (Quant Surv) (BTEC 5M)
	Central Lancashire - 12 pts (Quant Surv)
	Portsmouth - 12 pts (Quant Surv) (4 AS) (BTEC 6M)
	Robert Gordon - DDD/CC (Quant Surv) (4 AS)
	Sheffield Hallam - CC (Quant Surv)
	Staffordshire - 12 pts (Quant Surv) (BTEC 4-5M)
	Stoke on Trent (CT) - 12 pts (Quant Surv) (BTEC 4-5M)
10 pts.	**Dundee (IT)** - DDE/DD (Quant Surv)
	Glamorgan - 10 pts (Quant Surv) (4 AS) (BTEC 3-5M)
	Kingston - 10 pts/CD (Quant Surv) (4 AS)
	Wolverhampton - 10 pts minimum (Quant Surv) (BTEC 5M)
8 pts.	**and below**
	Anglia (Poly Univ) - EE (Quant Surv - part-time)
	Glamorgan - DE (Quant Surv - part-time) (BTEC 5M)
	Napier - (Quant Surv)
	North East Wales (IHE) - (Quant Surv)
	South Bank - DD (Quant Surv)

Offers for Foundation, Certificate and Diploma courses (see Ch 5):

Higher National Diploma courses:
8 pts.   **and below** Nene (CHE); Nottingham Trent (with Building).

Higher National Diploma courses in Scotland:
6 pts.   **and below** Robert Gordon.

College Diploma courses:
  4 pts.   and below Cauldon (CFHE).

Alternative offers:

IB offers: **South Bank** 24 pts.

Irish offers: **South Bank** CCCC.

SCE offers: **Glasgow Caledonian** BBBB; **Heriot-Watt** BBBC.

Overseas applicants: Northumbria, Westminster Competence in English required.

CHOOSING YOUR COURSE (See also Ch 1)

Subject information: This is a specialised field of surveying which focuses on the costing of the built environment. Students are introduced to construction studies, measurement cost studies, economics and law. This work is similar in some aspects to the work of an accountant and requires the same attention to detail. See also **Building** and **Surveying** courses.

Course highlights: Heriot-Watt In the first two years building technology, mathematics, economics and legal and business studies are included. **Liverpool John Moores** Increasing emphasis on computer-aided techniques. **Loughborough** All students sponsored by industry. **Nottingham Trent** This four-year sandwich course has a particular emphasis on building economics and control of costs of buildings. **Portsmouth** Financial management is an important feature of course. **Reading** The course has a common first two tears with Building Construction and Management and Building Surveying. **Robert Gordon** Year 1 common with Building Surveying. **Staffordshire** After a common first year with Valuation Surveying, specialist studies cover the analysis, construction and documentation techniques needed by the quantity surveyor. **Westminster** The course has a modular structure, gives students flexibility of choice, but they are required to study construction, economics, management and law. Other modules include languages, design and sociology. **Wolverhampton** Studies include construction technology and economics, contract procedures, measurement and costing, law, the use of computers and foreign language options. NOW CHECK PROSPECTUSES FOR ALL COURSES.

Study opportunities abroad: Wolverhampton (E).

Work opportunities abroad: Central Lancashire FR G; **South Bank** USA AUS G M HK WI; **Wolverhampton** G.

ADMISSIONS INFORMATION

Number of applicants per place (approx): Anglia (Poly Univ) 2; **Bristol UWE** 15; **Central England** 14; **Dundee (IT)** 5; **Glamorgan** 7; **Glasgow Caledonian** 13; **Greenwich** 11; **Kingston** 13; **Leeds Met** 11; **Liverpool John Moores** 10; **Loughborough** 9; **Napier** 2; **Northumbria** 11; **Nottingham Trent** 9; **Portsmouth** 16; **Robert Gordon** 5; **Salford** 12; **Staffordshire** 5; **Wolverhampton** 6.

General Studies acceptable: Anglia (Poly Univ); Glamorgan; Liverpool John Moores (in some cases); Portsmouth; Robert Gordon (2); Salford; Wolverhampton.

Selection interviews: Anglia (Poly Univ); Bristol UWE (T); Central England (some); Dundee (IT); Glasgow Caledonian; Glamorgan (T); Greenwich (usually); Leeds Met; Liverpool John Moores; South Bank; Ulster.

Offers to applicants repeating A-levels: Higher Bristol UWE, Nottingham Trent; **Possibly higher** Glamorgan, Liverpool John Moores; **Same** Leeds Met, South Bank.

Admissions Tutors' advice: Greenwich Motivation and desire to learn are important. **Liverpool John Moores** Good knowledge of quantity surveying necessary, obtained by visiting quantity surveyor's practice.

> **Examples of interview questions:** What is quantity surveying? What is the scope of the work? How do you qualify to do this work? Have you spoken to a quantity surveyor or spent any time in a quantity surveyor's office?

GAP YEAR ADVICE

Institutions accepting a Gap Year: Most institutions; **Portsmouth** Gain experience and maturity dealing with people of all ages; **Salford** Students must inform the department and liaise during the gap year.

Institutions willing to defer entry after A-levels (see Ch 5): Brighton; Glamorgan; Heriot-Watt; Kingston; Loughborough; Portsmouth; Robert Gordon; South Bank; Staffordshire (No); Stoke on Trent (CT); UMIST (No – because of the need to obtain sponsorship applications).

AFTER A-LEVELS ADVICE

Institutions which may accept the same points score after A-levels: Bristol UWE; Central England; Central Lancashire; Glamorgan; Glasgow Caledonian; Greenwich; Liverpool John Moores; Nottingham Trent; Portsmouth; Salford; Ulster.

Institutions demanding the actual grades offered after A-levels: Anglia (Poly Univ); Leeds Met.

Institutions which may accept under-achieving applicants after A-levels: Central England; Central Lancashire; Glamorgan; Liverpool John Moores; Nottingham Trent; Salford.

Institutions with vacancies in Aug/Sept 1992 (see Ch 5): Glamorgan 6 pts; Heriot-Watt 18 pts; Kingston; Robert Gordon 10 pts; Stoke on Trent (CT) 10-8 pts; Staffordshire 10-8 pts.

ADVICE FOR MATURE STUDENTS

A small number of mature students apply for these courses each year for which recent study experience is preferred. Work experience is also advantageous.

QUARRYING

(Not a degree course)

Special subject requirements: Four subjects at GCSE (grade A-C), and mathematics or physics at A-level.

NB Institutions may raise or lower the level of published offers depending either on the quality or otherwise of individual applications or the numbers of applications received; grades/points offered may be adjusted downwards after A-level results. The level of an offer is not indicative of the quality of a course.

Offers for Foundation, Certificate and Diploma courses (see Ch 5):

Higher National Diploma courses (England):
    2 pts. Doncaster (Coll).

Higher Diploma courses (Scotland):
   4 pts.   **and below or equivalent** Kirkcaldy (CT).

CHOOSING YOUR COURSE (See also Ch 1)

> **Subject information:** This is a very specialised vocational course of interest to those with a background in physical geography or an interest in geology.

ADMISSIONS INFORMATION

> **Examples of interview questions:** Applicants questioned on why they have chosen quarrying as a career. Good knowledge of work, and quarry visits are important.

RADIOGRAPHY

Special subject requirements: Science at A-level.

NB Institutions may raise or lower the level of published offers depending either on the quality or otherwise of individual applications or the numbers of applications received; grades/points offered may be adjusted downwards after A-level results. The level of an offer is not indicative of the quality of a course.

20 pts.   **Keele** - BCC (Radiog)
18 pts.   **Bradford** - CCC/BB (Radiog) (BTEC 1D+3M)
        Liverpool - CCC (Radiog)
        London (King's) - CCC (Radio)
        Southampton - CCC (Both Radiography courses)
        Ulster - CCC (Radiog)
14 pts.   **Cardiff (IHCS)** - CCD (Diag Radiog) (See **Admissions Tutors' advice**)
12 pts.   **Canterbury Christ Church (CHE)** - CC (Radiog)
        Cranfield - CC (Radiog)
        Portsmouth - 12 pts (Radiog)
        Sheffield Hallam - CC (Radiog)
10 pts.   **S Martins (CHE)** - 10 pts (Radiog)
8 pts.   **Anglia (Poly Univ)** - DD (Radiog)
        Bangor - (Radiog)
        Derby - 8 pts (Radiog)
        Edinburgh - 4 pts (Radiog)
        Glasgow Caledonian - (Radiog)
        Humberside - 8 pts minimum (Radiog - diploma)
        Kingston - 8 pts (Radiog)
        Leeds (SR) - DD approx (Radiog)
        London Guy's/South Bank - 8 pts (Radiog)
        London (St Thomas's) - 8 pts (Radiog)
        Robert Gordon - (Radiog)
        Salford (UC) - DD (Contact Admissions Tutor)
        South Bank - DD (Radiog) (BTEC 3M)

Details of entry requirements should be obtained from these institutions. Information on courses is available from the College of Radiographers, 14 Upper Wimpole Street, London W1M 8BN.

Alternative offers;

IB offers: **South Bank** 24 pts; **Southampton** 28 pts.

Irish offers: **South Bank** CCCC.

CHOOSING YOUR COURSE (See also Ch 1)

> **Subject information:** Radiographers work under the direction of doctors and operate X-Ray equipment for the diagnosis of medical conditions in addition to providing treatment by way of radiotherapy.

Course highlights: Anglia (Poly Univ) Therapeutic and diagnostic radiography; 60% practical studies in hospital. School located at Addenbrookes Hospital, Cambridge. **Cranfield (Shrivenham)** Course leads to State registration. **London (Guy's)/South Bank** Fifteen places for Diagnostic Radiography and 12 for Therapeutic Radiography. **Portsmouth** Academic teaching takes place in new centre at St Mary's Hospital with clinical placements in hospitals of Portsmouth Health Authority. Degree course is offered in Eire. **Salford (UC)** Centre for degrees in paramedic courses. **Southampton** Links with the University medical school. **Ulster** Course has close links with employers throughout Europe and North America. NOW CHECK PROSPECTUSES FOR ALL COURSES.

ADMISSIONS INFORMATION

Number of applicants per place (approx): Anglia (Poly Univ) 10; **Bradford** 10; **Glasgow Caledonian** 7; **Humberside** 6; **Leeds (SR)** 6; **Liverpool** 13; **London (Guy's)/South Bank** 17, **(St Thomas's)** 9; **Portsmouth** 10; **Salford (UC)** 3; **Southampton** 5.

General Studies acceptable: Leeds (SR); London (Guy's)/South Bank; Southampton.

Admissions Tutors' advice: Cardiff No applicants are considered who fail to achieve the grades or points scores required. Half the applicants are interviewed. **Cranfield (Shrivenham)** Normally one science subject preferred. **Portsmouth** Gain work experience or visit an imaging department close to home before applying for the course. **Salford (UC)** Offers will depend on the quality of the applicant. All students interviewed.

> **Examples of interview questions:** All applicants should have discussed this career with a radiographer and visited a hospital department. Questions follow from these contacts.

GAP YEAR ADVICE

Institutions accepting a Gap Year: Most institutions; **London (Guy's)/South Bank** Apply before gap year. **London (King's), (St Thomas's)** Plans must be discussed with Principal. **Portsmouth** Gain experience of working with a wide range of people of different age groups.

Institutions willing to defer entry after A-levels (see Ch 5): Bradford (No); Cranfield (Shrivenham); Sheffield Hallam; South Bank.

AFTER A-LEVELS ADVICE

Institutions with vacancies in Aug/Sept 1992 (see Ch 5): Bradford 10 pts; Cranfield (Shrivenham) 10 pts; Portsmouth 10 pts if science based.

ADVICE FOR MATURE STUDENTS

This subject attracts a large number of mature students each year. On some courses they represent up to 40% of the student intake. **Liverpool** Must show evidence of recent study – Access course in science/technology.

RELIGIOUS STUDIES (including Biblical Studies, Theology and Divinity)

Special subjects requirements: GCSE (grade A-C) language in some cases.

NB Institutions may raise or lower the level of published offers depending either on the quality or otherwise of individual applications or the numbers of applications received; grades/points offered may be adjusted downwards after A-level results. The level of an offer is not indicative of the quality of a course.

30 pts. **Cambridge** (Theol/Rel St)/**Oxford** (Theol) – AAA potential recommended.

24 pts. **Bristol** – BBB/AB (Theol/Pol)

22 pts. **Aberdeen** – BBC (MA)
Durham – BBC (Theol; Phil/Theol)
Glasgow – BBC (MA)
Lancaster – BBC-BCC (Eng/Rel; Theatre/Rel)

20 pts. **Birmingham** – BCC-CCC average (Theology)
Bristol – BCC/BB (All courses except under **24 pts**)
Cardiff – BCC/AA (Rel St – all courses)
Edinburgh – BCC/BB (MA/BA/BD)
Lancaster – BCC (Phil/Rel; Pol/Rel) (4 AS)

18 pts. **Exeter** – CCC/BB (Theol St) (6 AS)
Kent – CCC/BC-CC (Theology)
Lancaster – BCD (Rel St; most Comb courses except **22/20 pts**)(4 AS)
London (Heythrop) – CCC (Theology; Phil/Theol; Bib Studs)
London (Jews' Coll) – CCC (Jewish Studies)
London (King's) – 18 pts approx (Rel Studs)
Manchester – 18 pts approx (Rel St)
Newcastle – BCD/AB (Rel Studs)
Nottingham – CCC (Theology)
Ripon & York St John (CHE) – CCC (Theol/Women's St; Theol/App Soc Sci; Theol/Hist)
St Andrews – CCC (BD)
Sheffield – CCC/CC (All Bib St courses) (4 AS)
St Andrews – CCC (MA)
Stirling – CCC/BC (Rel Stud)

16 pts. **Bangor** – CCD/BC (Theol; Rel St; Bib Studs)
Belfast – CCD/BC-CC-CD (Theol; Bib Studs)
Hull – CCD/BC (All courses)
Leeds – BCE (Theol/Rel St) (4 AS)
London (SOAS) - BB (All Rel St courses)
Middlesex – 16-12 pts (RS)
Warwick – CCD/CC (BA (QTS) Rel St)

14 pts. **Cambridge (Hom)** – BC-CC (Relig/Ed) (See also **Education**)
Glasgow – CDD/BC (BD)
London (Oak Hill) – CDD/CC-DD (Theol/Past St)
St David's – CDD/BC (Theol; Rel St; Rel Eth)

12 pts. **Aberdeen** – CC (BD)
Aberystwyth – CC (BD - V800)
Bath (CHE) – 12 pts (Comb St)
Canterbury Christ Church (CHE) – CC-EE (Comb St)
S Martins (CHE) – CDE/CC (Rel St)
St David's – CC (Divinity)
Trinity & All Saints (CHE) – CD (Theol/BMA; Theol/PM)

10 pts. **Cheltenham & Glos (CHE)** – 10 pts (Rel St)
La Sainte Union (CHE) – 10-8 pts (Theology)
London (Bible Coll) – CD (Theol; Chr Life/Min)

8 pts. **and below**
      Bristol (Tr Coll) - (Theol)
      Cheltenham & Glos (CHE) - (Modular)
      Chester (CHE) - (Comb Hons)
      Derby - (Modular) (4 AS)
      Glamorgan - (Hum)
      Greenwich - DD (Theol St)
      Gwent (CHE) - (Cul St)
      Liverpool (IHE) - DD-EE (Comb St) (4 AS)
      London (Spur) - (Theol)
      Newman & Westhill (CHE) - DD (App Theol - BEd)
      Roehampton (IHE) - (Comb St)
      St Mark & St John (CHE) - (Rel St; Comb St)
      St Mary's (CHE) - (Comb St)
      Sunderland - (Rel St/Psych; Rel St/Soc)
      Trinity & All Saints (CHE) - DD (Theol)
      Trinity Carmarthen (CHE) - (Hum)
      West London (IHE) - (Modular)
      Westminster (CHE) - Offer decided at interview (Theology)
      West Sussex (IHE) - (RS)

Diploma of Higher Education courses:
  4 pts.   Bath (CHE); Crewe & Alsager (CHE); Edge Hill (CHE); Middlesex; Ripon & York St John (CHE); Westminster (CHE).

Alternative offers:

IB offers: **Exeter** 30 pts; **Kent** 25 pts, H 11 pts; **Lancaster** 28 pts; **St Andrews** 27 pts; **St David's** 28 pts.

Irish offers: **St Andrews** BBBB.

SCE offers: **Aberdeen** BBBB-BBB; **Durham** ABB-ABC; **Edinburgh** BCCC-BBC; **Glasgow** BBBB (MA), BBCC (BD); **Lancaster** BBBB; **Sheffield** BBBCC; **St Andrews** BBB (BD), BBBB (MA); **Stirling** BBCC.

CHOOSING YOUR COURSE (See also Ch 1)

> **Subject information:** Religious Studies courses cover four degree course subjects, namely Religious Studies, Divinity, Theology and Biblical Studies. The subject content of these courses varies and students should check prospectuses carefully. They are not intended as training courses for the church ministry; an adherance to a particular religious persuasion is not a necessary qualification for entry. (A-level religious studies is an acceptable second or third A-level for any non-scientific degree course.)

Course highlights: Bristol Emphasis on biblical studies. **Cardiff** Three-subject first year allows for delay in decisions. Strengths in biblical languages, Indian religions, pastoral studies, feminist theology. **Durham** In the second and third years students choose between three options: biblical studies; systematic theology, philosophy and the Christian religion; special study of selected parts of the history of Christian tradition. **Glasgow** Opportunities to study theological subjects in both breadth and depth in a stimulating environment. **Greenwich** Origins and contemporary experiences of Christianity. Attention given to relationship between religious belief, values and social structures. **Hull** Common first year followed by free choice of courses in second and third years; Indian religions a departmental speciality. Second and third years are 'free option' years (students plan own courses). **Leeds** Equal grounding in biblical studies, Christian history, theology and religious studies. **Liverpool (IHE)** Options to transfer to BA (Comb St) at end of first year. **London (Oak Hill)** Wide range of pastoral subjects on offer. **Newcastle** A broad first year including biblical studies, Christianity, Hinduism, Islam and contemporary issues. Years two and three are flexible with many options assessed by written work.

Greek, Hebrew and Sanskrit are optional languages. **St Andrews** Small group teaching emphasised. **St David's** The course provides a very wide range of options including Greek and Roman religion and new religious movements. NOW CHECK PROSPECTUSES FOR ALL COURSES.

Study opportunities abroad: Lancaster USA G; **London (Oak Hill)** USA; **Sheffield** (E) EUR USA.

ADMISSIONS INFORMATION

Number of applicants per place (approx): Bangor 4; **Birmingham** 7; **Cambridge (Hom)** 4 (All BEd courses); **Durham** 4; **Edinburgh** 4; **Exeter** 29; **Glasgow** 4; **Greenwich** 10; **Kent** 13; **Lancaster** 6; **La Sainte Union (CHE)** 2; **Leeds** (Theol/Rel St) 6; **Liverpool (IHE)** 6; **London (Bible Coll)** 1; **London (Oak Hill)** 2; **Newcastle** 8; **St David's** 5; **Sheffield** 7; **Trinity & All Saints (CHE)** 4; **West London (IHE)** 8; **West Sussex (IHE)** 6.

General Studies acceptable: Bangor; Birmingham; Cheltenham & Glos (CHE); Exeter (2); Glasgow; Greenwich; Lancaster; Leeds; Liverpool (IHE); London (Bible Coll); London (Oak Hill); Nottingham; S Martins (CHE) (2); Sheffield; Southampton (LSU); Trinity & All Saints (CHE) (2); West Sussex (IHE).

Selection interviews: Aberystwyth (some); Birmingham; Cambridge; Cardiff; Durham (important); Edinburgh; Glasgow (some); Hull (some); Kent (frequently); Lancaster; Leeds; Liverpool (IHE); London (Bible Coll) (T); London (Oak Hill); Newcastle; Nottingham; St David's; Trinity & All Saints (CHE); most colleges.

Offers to applicants repeating A-levels: Higher Durham (BCD), Hull, Manchester (BCD), St David's; **Possibly higher** Cambridge (Hom); **Same** Bangor, Birmingham, Glasgow, Greenwich, Lancaster, La Sainte Union (CHE), Leeds, London (Bible Coll), London (Oak Hill), Nottingham, Sheffield.

Admissions Tutors' advice: Bangor Be prepared to be interviewed. The interview is the prime means of determining those whom we really want. **Birmingham** All students study the history of religion, Israelite religion, the life and teaching of Jesus, New Testament Greek and theological thinking. **Greenwich** Selection is made on the basis of academic achievement and potential of experience of work in a relevant field, of personal and intellectual integrity. **Leeds** General Studies acceptable and any other indication of a breadth of interest. **London (Bible Coll)** Evidence of personal suitability to study at LBC important. **London (Oak Hill)** Most students are accepted for the ministry in the Church of England or another Church. Many entrants are mature students. The interview is of great importance. **London (Jews College)** A good knowledge of Hebrew required. Ability to handle biblical/rabbinical texts (normally gained after spending a minimum of one year in Israeli Rabbinical Seminary). **Nottingham** In Part II (years 2 and 3) the three compulsory courses cover the social anthropology of religion, biblical theology and systematic theology. Assessment of potential for higher education through testimonials and interview is reckoned of more importance than the attainment of particular A-level grades. **St David's** If taking religious studies, a C pass is expected. Two new entrants' conferences are held annually and play a large part in the decision of the candidates who choose this University.

Examples of interview questions: Why do you want to study Theology/ Biblical Studies/ Religious Studies? What do you hope to do after obtaining your degree? Questions relating to the A-level syllabus. Questions relating to current theological topics. Do you have any strong religious convictions? Do you think that your religious beliefs will be changed at the end of the course? Why did you choose Religious Studies rather than Biblical Studies? How would you explain the miracles to a ten-year old? (BEd course). How would you teach scripture to children with Muslim or Jewish backgrounds?

GAP YEAR ADVICE

Institutions accepting a Gap Year: Most institutions; **Cardiff** Contact department well before your month of proposed entry to confirm your intentions; **Glasgow** Make it useful in a general educational sense; **Greenwich** Early application advised. (BEd courses): Some teaching in schools preferred and general reading in theology. **London (Jews College)** We encourage at least a year of prior-degree experience. **Newcastle** Do something interesting, demanding and useful.

Institutions willing to defer entry after A-levels (see Ch 5): Bristol (No); Glagow; Hull; London (Jew's Coll); Newcastle; Newman & Westhill (CHE); Ripon & York St John (CHE) (No); Roehampton (IHE); St Andrews; St David's; Trinity & All Saints (CHE); Westminster (CHE).

AFTER A-LEVELS ADVICE

Institutions which may accept the same points score after A-levels: Bangor; Birmingham; Durham; Edinburgh; Exeter; Glasgow; Greenwich; Hull; Kent; Lancaster; Leeds; London (Oak Hill); Newcastle; Nottingham; St Andrews; Sheffield.

Institutions demanding the actual grades offered after A-levels: London (Bible Coll); Stirling.

Institutions which may accept under-achieving applicants after A-levels: Bangor; Birmingham; Cambridge (Hom); Durham; Edinburgh; Exeter; Glasgow; Kent; Lancaster; Leeds; London (Bible Coll); London (Oak Hill); Newcastle; St Andrews; Sheffield; Trinity & All Saints (CHE); most institutions.

Institutions with vacancies in Aug/Sept 1992 (see Ch 5): Cheltenham & Glos (CHE); Hull 15 pts; Roehampton (IHE) 4 pts; St Andrews 18 pts; St David's 12 pts; West Sussex (IHE) 4 pts; Westminster (CHE) 8 pts.

ADVICE FOR MATURE STUDENTS

This subject attracts a large number of mature applicants each year. On some courses they represent up to 60% of the student intake. In almost all cases some formal qualification or previous study experience will be sought.

GRADUATE EMPLOYMENT

New Graduates' destinations (percentages) 1991:
Permanent employment: U 78; P 55; C 60.
Unemployment: U 14; P 45; C 35.
Further studies (all types): U 47; P 48; C 44.

There is a considerable shortage of RE specialists in schools.

RUSSIAN

Special subject requirements: 2-3 A-levels. Russian and a second language sometimes 'required' or 'preferred'.

NB Institutions may raise or lower the level of published offers depending either on the quality or otherwise of individual applications or the numbers of applications received; grades/points offered may be adjusted downwards after A-level results. The level of an offer is not indicative of the quality of a course.

30 pts.	**Cambridge/Oxford** - AAA potential recommended (Mod/M Lang;Mod Lang)
24 pts.	**Bath** - ABC (Mod Lang/Europ)
	Bristol - BBB-BBC/BB (Fr/Russ)
	Durham - BBB (Russ/Pol)
	St Andrews - BBB (Russ) (4 AS)
22 pts.	**Edinburgh** - BBC (Russ St)
	Glasgow - BBC (Russian)
	Heriot-Watt - BBC (Joint Hons)
	Leeds - BBC-BCD (Joint courses)
	London (SSEES) - BBC-BCC (Russian)
	Newcastle - BBC (Euro Studs)
	Nottingham - BBC (Sov/Euro)
	Sheffield - BBC-BCC (Russian)
20 pts.	**Birmingham** - BCC (Sov St)
	Bradford - BCC (Russ/Sp; Fr/Russ; Ger/Russ)
	Bristol - BCC (Russ; Russ/Pols; Russ/Phil; Ger/Russ; Ital/Russ; Span/Russ)
	Essex - BCC/BB (All courses)
	Keele - BCC-CCC/BB-BC (All joint courses) (4 AS)
	Surrey - BCC-CCC/BB (Joint courses) (4 AS)
18 pts.	**Bangor** - CCC/CC (All courses)
	Belfast - CCC/BB (Russ)
	Exeter - CCC/BB (Russian) (6 AS)
	Leeds - CCC/BC (Russian) (6 AS)
	London (SSEES) - CCC/CC (All courses except under **22 pts**)
	Manchester - 18 pts approx (Russian courses)
	Strathclyde - CCC/BC (BBD 2nd yr entry) (Russian)
	Sussex - CCC/BC (Soviet/Euro and all Russian courses)
	Swansea - CCC/BC (Russian)
	Swansea - CCC-CCD (Joint Hons)
16 pts.	**Birmingham** - CCD (Russian)
	Durham - BB (Russian)
12 pts.	**Northumbria** - CDE/CC (Rus/Ger; Rus/Sp)
	Nottingham - CC (All courses except **22 pts**)
	Portsmouth - 12-10 pts (Russ/Ger St; Rus/Sov St) (4 AS inc any foreign lang preferred) (BTEC Ms)
10 pts.	**Westminster** - CC-CD (Russian courses)
8 pts.	**and below**
	Thames Valley London - (All Ap Lang St courses)
	Wolverhampton - (Mod Lang)

Offers for Foundation, Certificate and Diploma courses (see Ch 5):

Higher National Diploma courses (with Bus St):
   4 pts.   **and below** Northumbria.

Alternative offers:

EB offers: **Keele** 60%.

IB offers: **Bristol** 30-28 pts; **Essex** 28 pts inc 10 pts in 2 Highers; **Exeter** 30 pts; **Newcastle** 32-30 pts; **St Andrews** 30 pts; **Swansea** 28 pts H55.

SCE offers: **Edinburgh** BBBB; **Essex** BBBB; **Glasgow** ABBB/BBBB; **Heriot-Watt** AABB; **Keele** BBCC; **Sheffield** BBBB; **St Andrews** BBBB; **Strathclyde** BBBB.

Overseas applicants: Surrey, Leeds Fluent English important.

CHOOSING YOUR COURSE (See also Ch 1)

Subject information: Studies in Russian language and literature are the main features of most courses.

Course highlights: Bath See under **European Studies. Birmingham** Assessment by course work and examination. For students without A-level Russian, preliminary year is unusually intensive and effective. Many options. Computer-assisted learning. **Bristol** Subsidiary subject must be taken in first and second years from 11 options; 19th and 20th century literature. Fluency in language emphasised. Czech options in third year. **Exeter** Course covers language, literature and history of Russia. **Leeds** The Department's interest is in language teaching. **Surrey** Beginners in Russian accepted; two periods of 3 months in Russia. **Swansea** Options include business Russian, politics, economics and history. Three subjects taken in first year; final course choice can be delayed until end of first year. NOW CHECK PROSPECTUSES FOR ALL COURSES.

Study opportunities abroad: Birmingham (E); **Sheffield** (E); Most institutions have contacts in Russia.

ADMISSIONS INFORMATION

Number of applicants per place (approx): Birmingham 12; **Bristol** 4; **Durham** 7; **Exeter** 4; **Leeds** 5; **Portsmouth** (Rus/Ger St) 10, (Rus/Sov St) 5; **Surrey** 5; **Swansea** 7.

General Studies acceptable: Birmingham; Bristol; Durham (for single hons); Essex; Exeter (2); Hull; Leeds; Portsmouth; Surrey (2); Swansea.

Selection interviews: Bangor (some); Bristol (some); Cambridge; Durham; Essex; Exeter; Leeds (T); London (SSEES); Nottingham (some); Oxford; Portsmouth; Swansea (some).

Offers to applicants repeating A-levels: Higher Bradford, Essex, Surrey (if candidate is re-sitting 2 A-levels), Swansea; **Possibly higher** Portsmouth; **Same** Birmingham, Bristol, Durham, Leeds.

Admissions Tutors' advice: Birmingham Russian can be taken with commerce. **Bristol** Selectors look for linguistic ability; no rigid adherence to standard offer. **Leeds** Wide-ranging course offering many options based on initial central body of literary, historical and linguistic study; an entry for able linguists to begin Russian. **Nottingham** All applications considered equally. Open days held for applicants; mature students welcomed. **Portsmouth** Evidence of interest in the former USSR and current developments. Good GCSE grades (A-B) in any foreign language and A-level pass in any foreign language preferred but not essential. **Surrey** We look for candidates with a sound knowledge of at least one foreign language (not necessarily Russian, as we have a course for complete beginnners in addition to our post A-level course). We are guided primarily by examination results and the report from the school. The interview is useful too: we regard it as being as much for the candidate to find about the course and the University as for us to find out about the candidate.

Examples of interview questions: Since many applicants will not have taken Russian at A-level, questions often focus on the reasons for choosing a Russian degree, and the candidate's knowledge and interest in Russia. Those taking A-level Russian will be questioned on the course and on any reading done outside A-level work.

GAP YEAR ADVICE

Institutions accepting a Gap Year: Most institutions; **Birmingham** Apply before gap year for deferred entry; **Surrey** Experience involving Russian an asset.

Institutions willing to defer entry after A-levels (see Ch 5): Bradford; Leeds; Newcastle; Portsmouth; Swansea.

AFTER A-LEVELS ADVICE

Institutions which may accept the same points score after A-levels: Bristol; Durham; Essex; Hull; Leeds; Portsmouth; Swansea.

Institutions demanding the actual grades offered after A-levels: Birmingham; Bradford; Nottingham.

Institutions which may accept under-achieving applicants after A-levels: Bristol; Essex; Exeter; Leeds; Swansea.

Institutions with vacancies in Aug/Sept 1992 (see Ch 5): Bradford 20 pts; Essex 20 pts; Leeds; London (SSEES) 20 pts; Portsmouth 10 pts with a good reference from school; Surrey CCC; Swansea 16 pts.

GRADUATE EMPLOYMENT

New Graduates' destinations (percentages) 1991:
Permanent employment: U 69; P 40.
Unemployment: U 18; P 40.
Further studies (all types): U 36; C 44.

Surrey Graduates became tour consultants, interpreters/translators and teachers whilst others followed post-graduate courses in Information Technology, Law and Publishing.

SCANDINAVIAN STUDIES

Special subject requirements: none.

NB Institutions may raise or lower the level of published offers depending either on the quality or otherwise of individual applications or the numbers of applications received; grades/points offered may be adjusted downwards after A-level results. The level of an offer is not indicative of the quality of a course.

24 pts.	**Edinburgh** - BBC (Scan Stud)
22 pts.	**East Anglia** - BCC-CCC/BC-CC (Scand courses)
	Hull - ABD-CCD (Joint courses) (BTEC Ds+Ms)
	St David's - BCC (Joint courses)
	York - BCC/BB (Ling/Swed)
18 pts.	**Hull** - CCC/BB (Sp Scand) (6 AS) (BTEC Ds+Ms)
16 pts.	**St David's** - CCD/CC (Swed; Joint courses)
4 pts.	**London (UC)** - EE (To strong candidates only) (Scand)

Alternative offers:

IB offers: **Edinburgh** H665; **Hull** 28 pts.

SCE offers: **Edinburgh** BBBB.

CHOOSING YOUR COURSE (See also Ch 1)

> **Subject information:** These are usually offered as an option on modern language courses and provide a useful second language for linguists looking towards careers abroad.

Course highlights: Hull Wide range of courses in Nordic history, philosophy and literature. Danish or Swedish can be taken as specialist languages. **St David's** Staff strengths in translating and options for those interested in publishing and journalism careers. NOW CHECK PROSPECTUSES FOR ALL COURSES.

Study opportunities abroad: Hull (E).

ADMISSIONS INFORMATION

Number of applicants per place (approx): East Anglia 5.

General Studies acceptable: Hull; St David's.

Admissions Tutors' advice: East Anglia Students interested in Scandinavian can opt for a more literature-based course, or for one with a stronger language component, or for a combined language/literature/history course. In all cases students specialise in one Scandinavian language (Danish, Norwegian or Swedish) but acquire a working knowledge of the other two. **St David's** (Swedish) Modern language background preferred. Applicants should have a special interest in Scandinavia. There may be vacancies after the A-level results.

> **Examples of interview questions:** Applicants questioned on why they have chosen this subject area, on any visits to Scandinavia and on their knowledge of the country/countries and their people. Future career plans are likely to be discussed.

SCIENCE (including Combined and General Science; see also Biological Sciences)

Special subject requirements: 2-3 A-levels and GCSE (grade A-C) in science/mathematics subjects.

NB Institutions may raise or lower the level of published offers depending either on the quality or otherwise of individual applications or the numbers of applications received; grades/points offered may be adjusted downwards after A-level results. The level of an offer is not indicative of the quality of a course.

30 pts.	**Cambridge** - AAA potential recommended (Nat Sci)
22 pts.	**Aston** - BBC-BCC (Comb Hons; Comb Sci) (BTEC 5D+5M)
	Leeds - BBC/BB (Comb Hons - Science 55 combinations)
20 pts.	**Birmingham** - BCC (B Med Sci)
	Edinburgh - BCC (Sci)
	London (QMW) - BCC (Comb Hons Science and Technology courses)
	St Andrews - BCC-CCC average (Fac of Sci) (4 AS)
	Sussex - BCC (Hum S)
18 pts.	**Leeds** - BCD/BC (HST/Soc; HST/Rel St; HST/Theol)
	Leicester - CCC/BB (Sci Comb)
	Loughborough - 18 pts (Ergon; Inf Tech 3)
	Newcastle - BCD/BB (Sci Gen and joint courses)
	Salford - CCC/BC (Joint Hons Sci) (BTEC 4D+1M maths)
	Sheffield - BCD (Sci/Tech)
	Sheffield - CCC (Courses in Ceramics/Glasses/Materials/Polymers)

16 pts.	**Brunel** - CCD/CC (Des Tech Ed)
	East Anglia - CCD approx (Sci)
	Glasgow - CCD/CC (Science) (BTEC 3M)
	Lancaster - CCD/BC (Comb Sci) (BTEC Ms)
	Middlesex - 16-12 pts (Mod)
	Reading - CCD (Cyb Sci)
	Ripon & York St John (CHE) - CCD-DDD/BB-CC (Joint Sci)
14 pts.	**Aberdeen** - CDD/BC (Fac of Science)
	Cranfield (Shrivenham) - CCE/BC (App Sci) (4 AS) (BTEC Ms)
	Dundee - CDD (Fac of Sci)
	Newcastle - CDD/CC (Nat Res)
	Strathclyde - 14 pts approx (Sci St)
12 pts.	**Brighton** - 12-8 pts (Mod) (4 AS) (BTEC 3M)
	Dundee (IT) - DDD/CD (Sci)
	Hertfordshire - CC-DD (Comb St) (4 AS) (BTEC 5M)
	Humberside - 12 pts (Comb St) (4 AS)
	Sunderland - 12 pts (BSc)
	Wolverhampton - 12 pts (Comb Stud)
10 pts.	**Bath (CHE)** - CD (Comb St)
	Belfast - CD (Comb Sci)
	Cheltenham & Glos (CHE) - 10 pts (BEd Primary) (BTEC Ms)
	Chester (CHE) - 10 pts D in selected subject (Comb Hons) (BTEC 3M)
	De Montfort - CD-DD (Sci/Env; Comb Sci) (BTEC 5M)
	Kingston - DDE-DEE/CD-DD (Res/Env; Env St) (4 AS)
	Manchester Met - 10 pts (Comb St)
	Westminster - CD (All courses)
	Worcester (CHE) - 10 pts approx inc Access (Comb St) (4 AS)
8 pts.	**and below**
	Aberystwyth - (BSc Ord)
	Anglia (Poly Univ) - (Modular)
	Bishop Grosseteste (CHE) - (Ed/Sci)
	Bristol UWE - (Comb Sci)
	Canterbury Christ Church (CHE) - (Comb St)
	Charlotte Mason/Lancaster - (Ed/Sci)
	Coventry - DD-DE (Comb Sci; Phys Sci) (BTEC 3M)
	Derby - (Modular) (4 AS)
	East Anglia - (Sci Gen) (Open entry scheme for non-scientists)
	East London - (Sci)
	Glamorgan - DD (Comb Sci) (4 AS)
	Greenwich - (Ap Sci) (4 AS)
	Liverpool (IHE) - 8 pts (BSc Comb St) (4 AS)
	Loughborough - DD (Science Foundation course)
	Luton (CHE) - (BSc Science)
	Middlesex - (Sci/Tech/Soc)
	Napier - (Sci Ind St; Sci Man)
	Nene (CHE) - DD (Sci)
	North London - (Modular)
	Nottingham Trent - (Comb St) (4 AS)
	Oxford Brookes - DD (Modular)
	Paisley - (Sci) (4 AS)
	Plymouth - (Sci/Marine)
	Ripon & York St John (CHE) - (BA; BSc Hons) (4 AS)
	Robert Gordon - (App Sci) (4 AS)
	Roehampton (IHE) - EE (Comb Hons)
	Sheffield Hallam - (Comb St Sci)
	South Bank - DD (Sci)
	Staffordshire - DEE/DD (App Sci)
	St Mark & St John (CHE) - (Ed/Sci)
	St Mary's (CHE) - DD-EE (Comb Hons)

Trinity & All Saints (CHE) - EE (Sci/Ed)
Wolverhampton - DE (Ap Sci Combinations)

Diploma of Higher Education courses:
4pts. East London; Manchester Met; Middlesex; Oxford Brookes.

Offers for Foundation, Certificate and Diploma courses (see Ch 5):

Higher National Diploma courses:
4pts. and below Bristol UWE; Cardiff (IHE); Coventry; South Bank.

Higher National Diploma courses in Scotland:
Robert Gordon.

Foundation or Extended Science courses for those without the normal A-level or equivalent qualifications are available as follows: Bristol UWE; Coventry; De Montfort; East London; Glamorgan; Manchester Met; North London; Northumbria; Oxford Brookes; Portsmouth; South Bank; Teesside.

Alternative offers:

EB offers: **Keele** 60%; **Lancaster** 65%; **Newcastle** 70-65%; **St Andrews** 65%.

IB offers: **Aberdeen** 26 pts; **Aston** 32 pts; **Birmingham** 28 pts; **Brunel** 25 pts; **Cheltenham & Glos (CHE)** 27 pts; **Glasgow** 36-30 pts; **Lancaster** 28 pts; **Leeds** H655; **Leicester** 28 pts; **Loughborough** 28 pts; **Newcastle** 29 pts inc H5 in relevant subject; **Salford** 35 pts; **St Andrews** 28 pts; **South Bank** 24 pts; **Staffordshire** 24 pts.

Irish offers: **Aberdeen** BBCC/BCCCC; **Brighton** CCC; **Glamorgan** CCCCC; **Glasgow** BBB; **Keele** BBCCC; **Lancaster** BBBB; **Leeds** BBBCC; **Newcastle** AABB; **Nottingham Trent** CCCCC; **North London** CCCC; **South Bank** CCCC; **Westminster** BBB.

SCE offers: **Aberdeen** BBBC; **Dundee** BBBB; **Edinburgh** BBBB; **Glasgow** BBB; **Lancaster** BBBB; **St Andrews** BBBB/BBCC.

Overseas applicants: St Andrews Pre-sessional English course available.

CHOOSING YOUR COURSE (See also Ch 1)

> **Subject information:** These courses cover various scientific subjects in combination. There is a considerable shortage of applicants. For studies in the history and philosophy of sciences, A-levels in science subjects are not always required.

Course highlights: Anglia (Poly Univ) Broad science course emphasising chemistry and biology. **Birmingham** (Medical Science) Many departments within the Medical School offer subject options for this course. **Brighton** Two sciences taken from biology, chemistry, computing, energy studies, geography, maths, physics, statistics. **Bristol UWE** (Comb Sci) Options in applied biology, applied chemistry, information technology, environmental studies, psychology. **Chester (CHE)** Final choice of degree programme made during 2nd term. **Cranfield (Shrivenham)** (App Sci) Broad course in applied maths, physics and materials science; specialism in two of these three after first year. **De Montfort** (Science/Environment) In second year students opt for biotechnology or applied biosciences. **Durham** (Natural Sciences) Broad, demanding course - wide choice of subject combinations available. **Glasgow** Faculty entry, with flexibility of subject choice, and honours decisions made at end of second year are all features of this course. **Greenwich** Two science subjects taken from a choice of ten. **Humberside** Modular degree allowing students to build their own scheme. **Lancaster** Exchange programme with USA possible in year 2. **Nene (CHE)** See under **Arts**. **Newcastle** (Nat Res) Modular course with subjects ranging across physical, biological, economic and social sciences. **Salford** Study of two subjects gives greater breadth of knowledge. Final combinations decided at end of first year. Optional industrial year. **Robert Gordon** Options in chemistry, physics and biology. **Sheffield Hallam** See under **Arts**. **Worcester (CHE)** See under **Arts**. NOW CHECK PROSPECTUSES FOR ALL COURSES.

Study opportunities abroad: Glasgow EUR USA; **Leicester** (E).

Work opportunities abroad: Middlesex; Wolverhampton EUR IRE.

ADMISSIONS INFORMATION

Number of applicants per place (approx): Anglia (Poly Univ) 11; **Aston** (All Comb Hons courses) 10; **Brighton** 6; **Chester (CHE)** 4; **Coventry** 2; **De Montfort** 3; **Durham** 50; **East London** 8; **Glamorgan** 9; **Greenwich** 7; **Hertfordshire** 14; **Kingston** 4; **Lancaster** 7; **Leeds** 10; **Leicester** 8; **Liverpool (IHE)** 10; **Luton (CHE)** 4; **Loughborough** (Ergon 4) 4; **Napier** 4; **Newcastle** (Nat Res) 2; **Nottingham Trent** 9; **Paisley** 4; **Ripon & York St John (CHE)** 7; **Roehampton (IHE)** 1; **Salford** 3; **Staffordshire** 6; **Westminster** 7; **Worcester (CHE)** 5.

General Studies acceptable: Aston; Bristol UWE; Chester (CHE); Leeds; Liverpool John Moores; Luton (CHE); Newcastle (Nat Res); Ripon & York St John (CHE); Roehampton (IHE); St Mary's (CHE); Sunderland; Wolverhampton; Worcester (CHE) (2).

Selection interviews: Anglia (Poly Univ); Westminster (some).

Offers to applicants repeating A-levels: Higher Hertfordshire, Leeds, Newcastle; **Possibly higher** Coventry, Roehampton (IHE); **Same** Anglia (Poly Univ), Aston, De Montfort, Glasgow, North London, Ulster, Wolverhampton.

Admissions Tutors' advice: Anglia (Poly Univ) Offers are made on individual merit and are not always dependent on academic criteria, eg in the case of mature students. **Cheltenham & Glos (CHE)** Post-GCSE science study strongly recommended. **Cranfield (Shrivenham)** Grade C at A-level in sciences. **Kingston** Considerable weight is attached to the interview and reference. **Nottingham Trent** We are more likely to make lower offers to those who have applied early and who attend for interview.

Examples of interview questions: Applicants likely to be questioned on their A-level work and aspects they particularly enjoy. They could well be tested on this!

GAP YEAR ADVICE

Institutions accepting a Gap Year: Most institutions; **Loughborough** Enjoy yourselves!

Institutions willing to defer entry after A-levels (see Ch 5): Aston; Bristol UWE; Cheltenham & Glos (CHE); Cranfield (Shrivenham); Glamorgan; Glasgow (Only for good academic reason); Heriot-Watt; Lancaster; Salford; South Bank; Sunderland; Trinity & All Saints (CHE).

AFTER A-LEVELS ADVICE

Institutions which may accept the same points score after A-levels: Aston; Bristol UWE; Coventry; Glamorgan; Glasgow; Leeds; Luton (CHE); Newcastle; Robert Gordon; St Mary's (CHE); Sunderland; Westminster; Wolverhampton.

Institutions which may accept under-achieving applicants after A-levels: Anglia (Poly Univ); Coventry; Hertfordshire; Humberside; Glasgow; Leeds; Worcester (CHE).

Institutions with vacancies in Aug/Sept 1992 (see Ch 5): A large number of these courses had vacancies for quite moderate A-level scores including Aston BBC-BCC; Cranfield (Shrivenham) 12 pts; Glasgow CCD approx; Greenwich 4 pts; Heriot-Watt 8 pts; Salford 12-10 pts; Trinity & All Saints (CHE).

ADVICE FOR MATURE STUDENTS

In all cases evidence of academic study is important. Mature students represent about 10% of the intake.

GRADUATE EMPLOYMENT

New Graduates' destinations (percentages) 1991:
Permanent employment: P 56; C 67.
Unemployment: P 31; C 22.
Further studies (all types): P 28; C 33.
Main career destinations (approx): Admin 20; Science 19; Financial 8; Computing 12; Business 15; Secretarial/Clerical 12.

The following institutions are perceived as being above average in producing graduates for employment in all science subjects: Birmingham; Bristol; Brunel; Cambridge; Durham; Leeds; Loughborough; Manchester; Nottingham; Oxford; Reading; Southampton; UMIST; Warwick. (See PIP reference in Chapter 5.)

SCIENTIFIC ILLUSTRATION

Special subject requirements: GCSE (grade A-C) in English, maths and a science plus either 2 A-level passes or a Foundation Art course.

Institutions may raise or lower the level of published offers depending either on the quality or otherwise of individual applications or the numbers of applications received; grades/points offered may be adjusted downwards after A-level results.

  4pts.   **Cornwall CFHE (Falmouth)** – (Sci/Tech Graph)

Offers for Foundation, Certificate and Diploma courses (see Ch 5):

Higher National Diploma courses:
  2pts.   Blackpool (CFHE); Birmingham (Bourneville CA); Bournemouth/Poole (CA); Portsmouth (CA); Sunderland; Swansea (IHE).

CHOOSING YOUR COURSE (See also Ch 1)

> **Subject information:** These are very specialised art courses which may require foundation studies or at least an impressive portfolio of A-level art work.

ADMISSIONS INFORMATION

> **Examples of interview questions:** This is an art course and the interview will largely focus on the applicant's portfolio of work.

SECRETARIAL ADMINISTRATION

Special subject requirements: none.

NB Institutions may raise or lower the level of published offers depending either on the quality or otherwise of individual applications or the numbers of applications received; grades/points offered may be adjusted downwards after A-level results. The level of an offer is not indicative of the quality of a course.

16 pts.   **Northumbria** - 16-12 pts (Sec/Bus Admin - Fr/Ger/Pr)
12 pts.   **Chichester (CT)** - DDD (RSA Dip Pers Ass)
8 pts.   **Humberside** - DD (Off Sys Man)

Offers for Foundation, Certificate and Diploma courses (see Ch 5):

Higher National Diploma courses (with Bus St) (England and Wales):
8 pts.   **and below** Anglia (Poly Univ); Bradford & Ilkley (CmC); Central Lancashire; Derby; Humberside; Llandrillo (Coll); Loughborough (CT); Nene (CHE); Northumbria; Norwich City (CFHE); Swansea (IHE); Teesside; Thames Valley London; West Herts (Coll); Westminster.

Higher Diploma courses (Scotland):
8 pts.   **and below or equivalent** Aberdeen (CC); Angus (CT); Banff & Buchan (Coll); Bell (CT); Clackmannan (Coll); Dumfries & Galloway (Coll); Dundee (IT); Falkirk (CT); Glasgow Caledonian; Inverness (Coll); Kirkcaldy (Coll); Lews Castle (Coll); Moray (Coll); Napier EE (Sec St with Lang); Reid Kerr (Coll); Perth (Coll); Scottish (CText).

Bilingual Secretarial courses (England):

2 pts.   Buckinghamshire (Coll); Central Lancashire; Loughborough (CT); Luton (CHE); Salford (UC).

CHOOSING YOUR COURSE (See also Ch 1)

Subject information: These are not to be confused with secretarial or personal assistant courses. Students with skills in office administration, as well as wide-ranging clerical aptitudes and languages, are increasingly sought after by employers.

Course highlights: Northumbria Year 1 covers secretarial studies, business information and organisation; year 2 options include public relations or post A-level French or German. NOW CHECK PROSPECTUSES FOR ALL COURSES.

ADMISSIONS INFORMATION

Number of applicants per place (approx): Northumbria 7.

General Studies acceptable: Central Lancashire.

Admissions Tutors' advice: Central Lancashire Mature students must be able to demonstrate fluency in one of the languages. **Northumbria** French or *ab initio* Spanish or German can be taken with this course and also business studies, information technology and public relations.

Examples of interview questions: What do you hope to do after completing this course? What makes you think you would be a competent secretary? How is an office organised? What priorities do you think a managing director would look for in choosing a secretary? What is the difference between a secretary and a personal assistant?

AFTER A-LEVELS ADVICE

Institutions with vacancies in Aug/Sept 1992 (see Ch 5): Vacancies still existed after the A-level results were declared. Northumbria 10 pts.

SOCIAL ADMINISTRATION (See also **Social Policy**)

Special subject requirements: GCSE (grade (A-C) in mathematics usually required.

NB Institutions may raise or lower the level of published offers depending either on the quality or otherwise of individual applications or the numbers of applications received; grades/points offered may be adjusted downwards after A-level results. The level of an offer is not indicative of the quality of a course.

24 pts.	**Durham** – BBB (SP/Admin)
22 pts.	**Lancaster** - BBC-BCC (Soc Admin; SW)
20 pts.	**Bath** - BCC (Pub Pol)
	Birmingham – BCC/BB (Soc Wk; PSPM)
	Bristol - BCC/BB (Soc A/Pol)
	Glasgow – BCC (MA Soc Sci CQSW)
	London (LSE) – 20 pts approx (Soc Admin)
	Nottingham - BCC (SPA)
	York – BCC/BB-BC (Soc Admin)
18 pts.	**Bangor** – CCC/BC (All courses)
	Bristol - CCC/BC (Soc A/Sociol; Soc Admin)
	Hull - BCD (Soc Pol Admin)
	Kent - CCC (SPA)
	Lancaster – CCC (Soc Admin courses) (4 AS)
	Leeds - BCD (Soc Pol/Ad)
	Loughborough – CCC/BB (Soc Admin) (BTEC 5M)
16 pts.	**Middlesex** - 16-12 pts (Soc Pol)
14 pts.	**Portsmouth** - 14-12 pts (Soc Pol Admin)
	Southampton - BC (PS/Admin)
12 pts.	**Brighton** - CC (Soc Admin) (4 AS)
	Manchester Met - CC (Soc Admin) (4 AS)
	North London – 12 pts (Policy St) (4 AS)
10 pts.	**and below**
	Plymouth - CD (Soc Pol/Admin; SP/Admin/CQSW)
	Roehampton (IHE) - (Comb St) (BTEC 3M)
	Teesside - (Soc St)

Alternative offers:

IB offers: **Bangor** 30-28 pts; **Birmingham** 32 pts inc 16 pts Highers; **Durham** H666 S555; **Lancaster** 32-30 pts; **Loughborough** 28 pts.

Irish offers: **Loughborough** BBCCC.

SCE offers: **Birmingham** AABB; **Bristol** BBBB; **Glasgow** ABBB; **Lancaster** ABBBB; **Loughborough** BBCC.

Overseas applicants: Loughborough Proficiency in English important.

CHOOSING YOUR COURSE (See also Ch 1)

Subject information: These courses are a good vocational preparation for careers in the Social Services. A wide range of topics are covered eg, housing policy, health services, mental illness, the family and prisons. See also under **Social Policy** and **Social Work**.

Course highlights: Bangor Close links with Sociology which can be taken with one other subject in first year; placements in second year. **Brighton** Three main areas – core studies in social policy and admin, social sciences (economics, law, psychology, sociology), specialist studies in health services, housing or personal social services. **Lancaster** In the first year social administration is taken with two other courses, for example, English, law, philosophy, psychology. In years two and three compulsory and optional courses are taken including welfare and urban environment, education, understanding youth, social policy and social work for young people, criminology and the psychology of sex and gender. **Loughborough** The first year includes a study of anthropology, sociology and options from world politics, economics and psychology. NOW CHECK PROSPECTUSES FOR ALL COURSES.

ADMISSIONS INFORMATION

Number of applicants per place (approx): Bangor 8; **Birmingham** 15; **Bristol** (Soc Admin) 7, (Soc A/Sociol) 5; **Lancaster** 12; **Loughborough** 13; **Manchester Met** 20; **Middlesex** 12; **North London** 8; **Nottingham** 11.

General Studies acceptable: Birmingham; Brighton; Lancaster; Loughborough; Manchester Met.

Selection interviews: Birmingham; Bristol (some); Cardiff (some); Lancaster (some); Loughborough; North London; Nottingham (informal); Portsmouth (some).

Offers to applicants repeating A-levels: Same Birmingham, Brighton, Bristol, Loughborough, North London, Ulster.

Admissions Tutors' advice: Birmingham (Soc Wk) Preference given to students with experience or at least a year between school and university. Offers made only after interview. (PSPM) Most applicants not interviewed. **Brighton** In addition to A-level entrants, the course welcomes applications from older candidates with relevant experience – these usually comprise 25% of the intake. **Lancaster** Competition for places is intense and is not reflected in the offer made. Mature students are given some preference. **Loughborough** We like to see candidates who have some previous experience in youth work, welfare, etc. We also welcome mature students with similar experience. **Manchester Met** GCSE (grade A–C) mathematics required. **Nottingham** The Department particularly welcomes applications from those not coming straight from school, whether they have had a 'year off' or a gap of several years between school and university.

Examples of interview questions: What relevance has history to social administration? What qualities are needed to be a social worker? What use do you think you will be to society as a social worker? Why should money be spent on prison offenders? Your younger brother is playing truant, and mixing with bad company. Your parents don't know. What would you do? What do you understand by 'public policy'? What advantage do you think studying Social Science provides for working in policy fields? How could the image of public management of services be improved?

GAP YEAR ADVICE

Institutions willing to defer entry after A-levels (see Ch 5): Roehampton (IHE).

AFTER A-LEVELS ADVICE

Institutions which may accept the same points score after A-levels: Birmingham; Brighton; Bristol; Loughborough; Manchester Met; North London.

Institutions demanding the actual grades offered after A-levels: Nottingham.

Institutions with vacancies in Aug/Sept 1992 (see Ch 5): There were some vacancies in the new universities.

ADVICE FOR MATURE STUDENTS

Mature students are generally welcomed on these courses which often lead to careers in Social Work. The mature student intake on these courses can be as high as 25 to 30%.

SOCIAL ANTHROPOLOGY

Special subject requirements: GCSE (grade A-C) mathematics may be required.

NB Institutions may raise or lower the level of published offers depending either on the quality or otherwise of individual applications or the numbers of applications received; grades/points offered may be adjusted downwards after A-level results. The level of an offer is not indicative of the quality of a course.

24 pts.	**St Andrews** - BBB (Soc Anthr) (4 AS)
22 pts.	**Edinburgh** - BBC (Soc Anthr)
20 pts.	**Brunel** - BCC/BB ((SA/Soc; SA/Psy) (4 AS)
	Durham - BCC (Ant/Soc)
	Kent - BCC (All courses)
	Manchester - 20 pts approx (Anthrop)
	Sussex - BCC/BC (All courses)
18 pts.	**Belfast** - CCC/BB (Anth Soc Sc)
	Hull - CCC/BC (Soc/S Ant)
	Swansea - CCC-CCD/BB-BC (Dev St/S Anth; Soc Anth/Sociol)
16 pts.	**London (SOAS)** - BB (All courses)
	Swansea - CCD/BC (Soc Anth)

Alternative offers:

IB offers: **East Anglia** 30 pts; **St Andrews** 30 pts.

CHOOSING YOUR COURSE (See also Ch 1)

Subject information: This subject is concerned with the study of the institutions and cultures of the world and each course will offer a range of subject specialisms. See also under **Anthropology**. NOW CHECK PROSPECTUSES FOR ALL COURSES.

ADMISSIONS INFORMATION

Examples of interview questions: Applicants usually questioned on what social anthropology involves and, since it is not an A-level subject, they will be expected to have read extensively about it.

GRADUATE EMPLOYMENT

New Graduates' destinations (percentages) 1991:

See under **Anthropology**.

SOCIAL POLICY (See also Social Administration)

Special subject requirements: GCSE (grade A-C) mathematics in some cases.

NB Institutions may raise or lower the level of published offers depending either on the quality or otherwise of individual applications or the numbers of applications received; grades/points offered may be adjusted downwards after A-level results. The level of an offer is not indicative of the quality of a course.

22 pts. **Hull** - BBC/AB (Soc Pol Crim) (BTEC Ds+Ms)
Sheffield - BBC (Soc P/Soc)
20 pts. **Birmingham** - BCC (PMA)
Bristol - BCC (Soc A/Pol)
Dundee - BCC (Soc Pol)
Durham - BCC (Soc/SP)
Edinburgh - BCC (Soc Pol)
Essex - BCC/BB (PMA)
Kent - BCC-CCC (SPA; SPA/Comp)
Leeds - BCC (All courses) (NMI)
London (RH) - BCC/BB (Soc Pol; Soc/Soc Pol)
Manchester - 20 pts approx (Soc Pol)
Nottingham - BCC (SPA)
Sussex - BCC (Soc Pol)
Swansea - BCC/BB (Soc Pol joint hons)
York - BCC/BC-CC (Soc Admin)
18 pts. **Bangor** - CCC/BB-BC (Soc Pol) (4 AS)
Bradford - CCC/AB (App Soc, see under **Social Studies** for details)
Bristol - CCC/BB (Soc Pol/Pl) (BTEC 3D/M)
Cardiff - CCC/BC (Soc Pol)
Durham - CCC/BC (Soc/Sp)
Exeter - CCC/BB (SSP) (6 AS) (BTEC Ms)
Hull - BCD/BB (Soc Pol Admin; Soc Wk) (BTEC 4-5D+Ms)
London (Gold) - CCC (Soc Pol)
Newcastle - BCD/BB-BC (Social Pol; Public Pol) (6 AS)
Stirling - CCC/BC (Soc Pol)
York - CCC (Soc Pol)
16 pts. **Central Lancashire** - 16 pts (Comb St)
Middlesex - 16-12 pts (Soc Pol)
14 pts. **Guildhall London** - CDD/CC (Soc Pol/Man)
Staffordshire - 14-10 pts (Int Pol/Admin) (BTEC 4M)
12 pts. **Anglia (Poly Univ)** - DDD/CD (Euro Soc Pol)
Brighton - CC (Soc Admin)
Leeds Met - CC (Soc Pol/Admin)
North London - CC (Policy St; Soc Res) (4 AS)
Portsmouth - 12 pts (Soc Pol Admin)
10 pts. **and below**
Bradford & Ilkley (CmC) - (Comm St)
Plymouth - CD (Soc Pol/Admin) (4 AS)
Teesside - DEE/DD (Soc Pol)

Alternative offers:

IB offers: **Bangor** 30 pts; **Bristol** 30-28 pts; **Exeter** 30 pts; **London (RH)** 26 pts; **York** 28 pts.

Irish offers: **Bangor** BBBBB.

SCE offers: **Dundee** BBBC; **Edinburgh** BBBB; **Leeds** BBB; **Newcastle** BBBB; **Stirling** BBCC.

Overseas applicants: Hull Living costs 30% lower than in London; **Leeds** English language package available; **Plymouth** Fluency in English important - no EFL facilities.

CHOOSING YOUR COURSE (See also Ch 1)

> **Subject information:** These courses overlap with those in Social Administration.

Course highlights: Anglia (Poly Univ) (Euro Soc Pol) Chance to live and study abroad, with English as the language of instruction and to spend time working in/observing European health and welfare agencies. **Bristol** Strength in international social policy and planning, gender and social policy, poverty and health. **Cardiff** Students must take six first year courses: social welfare and social change, and social welfare in Britain, as well as four options in the social sciences. Later studies cover poverty, housing, crime, the care of the elderly, health and welfare agencies. **Hull** Option courses include health, education, crime and housing - 10-week placement in second year. **Leeds** Year three options include labour markets, social security, housing, sociology of medicine, race relations and the family. **Nottingham** In the third year three optional subjects are taken from options covering social work, criminology, childhood and society, social change and manpower planning. **Swansea** Strengths in community care, mental health services, social policy and political parties. See also under **Social Administration.** NOW CHECK PROSPECTUSES FOR ALL COURSES.

Study opportunities abroad: Anglia (Poly Univ) (E) NL; **Bristol** (E); **London (RH)** IT G.

Work opportunities abroad: Leeds Met G FR; **Plymouth** USA; **Teesside** USA.

ADMISSIONS INFORMATION

Number of applicants per place (approx): Bristol 10; **Durham** 8; **Exeter** 7; **Leeds** 10; **Leeds Met** 9; **London (RH)** 5; **Newcastle** 8; **North London** 8; **Plymouth** 10; **York** 14.

General Studies acceptable: Durham; Essex; Exeter (2); Leeds; Newcastle; Swansea (2); Teesside (2); York.

Selection interviews: Durham (some); Newcastle (some); York (some).

Offers to applicants repeating A-levels: Higher East Anglia, Leeds Met, Newcastle; **Possibly higher** Leeds; **Same** Durham, York.

Admissions Tutors' advice: Hull We are keen to make offers to applicants not taking the traditional three A-level route. There is a strong professional emphasis on our **Policy** courses. **Newcastle** Applications from mature students, including those without formal qualifications, are welcome. **York** Mature applicants are encouraged to apply - they usually comprise one quarter of the intake. Offers depend on individual circumstances.

> **Examples of interview questions:** Applicants should be fully aware of the content and the differences between all the courses on offer, why they want to study the subject and their career objectives.

GAP YEAR ADVICE

Institutions accepting a Gap Year: Most institutions; **Guildhall London** Apply a year in advance. Work experience in management, welfare or social care an advantage; **London (RH)** The year should not be wasted; plan it carefully.

Institutions willing to defer entry after A-levels (see Ch 5): Bristol; London (RH); Plymouth.

AFTER A-LEVELS ADVICE

Institutions which may accept the same points score after A-levels: Essex; Kent; London (RH); Newcastle; North London; Plymouth; York.

Institutions demanding the actual grades offered after A-levels: Durham; Leeds; Leeds Met.

Institutions which may accept under-achieving applicants after A-levels: Durham; Essex; Kent; Hull (overseas applicants 18-16 pts); London (RH); Newcastle; North London; Plymouth; York.

Institutions with vacancies in Aug/Sept 1992 (see Ch 5): Quite a large number of institutions advertised vacancies, including London (RH) 20-18 pts; Staffordshire 14 pts.

ADVICE FOR MATURE STUDENTS

See under **Social Administration**.

GRADUATE EMPLOYMENT

New Graduates' destinations (percentages) 1991:
Permanent employment: U 70; P 68.
Unemployment: U 19; P 19.
Further studies (all types): U 28; P 17.

York (1989-91) 26 students entered full-time employment, 10 going into social and welfare occupations (residential social work, AIDS counselling, youth work and community work). Others found employment with Age Concern, hospital administration services, nursing and insurance; 21 students went on to further training (housing (3), teaching (3), industrial relations (1), business studies (1) and social work (1)) and further research.

SOCIAL STUDIES/SCIENCE (including **Applied Social Studies**) (See also under chosen subjects in the Social Science category)

Special subject requirements: GCSE (grade A-C) in English, mathematics and a science subject in some cases.

NB Institutions may raise or lower the level of published offers depending either on the quality or otherwise of individual applications or the numbers of applications received; grades/points offered may be adjusted downwards after A-level results. The level of an offer is not indicative of the quality of a course.

30 pts.	**Cambridge** - AAA potential recommended (Soc Pol Sci)
26 pts.	**Edinburgh** - ABB-BCC (Fac of Soc Sci)
24 pts.	**Brunel** - BBB (Comb)
	Durham - ABC (Soc Comb)
	Salford - BBB (Social Sciences/USA)
22 pts.	**East Anglia** - BBC (Soc St) (BTEC 3D+3M)
	Glasgow - BBC (Fac of Soc Sci)
	Lancaster - BBC-BCC (Women's Studies; Combined degrees)
	Leeds - BCC approx (Women's Studies - contact Admissions Tutor)
	Sheffield - BBC (Soc Pol Stud)
20 pts.	**Aberdeen** - BCC (Fac of Soc Sci)
	Aston - BCC/AA (Soc St) (BTEC 5D+5M)
	Bristol UWE - 20 pts (Women's St/Hum)
	Dundee - BCC/BB (Fac of Soc Sci)

Lancaster - BCC (App Soc Sci with Dip SW)
Liverpool - BCC/BB (Social Comb) (4 AS)
London (Gold) - BCC (Soc Sci)
Nottingham - BCC (Soc Cult)
Ripon & York St John (CHE) - BCC (Ap Soc Sci/Eng)
Swansea - BCC-CCC/BB (Econ Soc Stats - deferred choice)

18 pts. **Belfast** - CCC/BC (Soc Sc Comb)
Bradford - CCC/BB (App Soc) (BTEC 3M)
City - CCC/BB (Soc Sci)
Essex - CCC/BC (Def)
Lancaster - CCC (App Soc Sci) (BTEC Ds+Ms)
Newcastle - CCC-CDD/BC-CC (Soc Studs)
Reading - BCD (Comb Soc Sci)
Ripon & York St John (CHE) - CCC/BB (Ap Soc Sci/Theol; Ap Soc Sci/Dr/TV; Ap Soc Sci/Eng St; Ap Soc Sci/Women's St)
Salford - CCC (Soc Sci)
Strathclyde - CCC (Soc St)

16 pts. **Birmingham** - CCD/BB (Soc Afric)
Central Lancashire - CCD/CC (Ap Soc St; Women's St)
Kingston - 16-14 pts (Ap Soc Sci) (4 AS)
Middlesex - 16-12 pts (Modular - Women's St)
Nottingham Trent - 16 pts approx (Soc Sci; Ap Soc St) (Contact Admissions Tutor)

14 pts. **Bristol UWE** - 14 pts (Soc Sci; Soc Sci/IS)
Glasgow Caledonian - CDD/BC (Soc Sci) (6 AS)
Hertfordshire - 14-10 pts (Soc Sci)
Humberside - 14-12 pts/12-10 pts (App Soc Sci; Con St)
North London - CDD (Women's St; Irish St)
Sheffield Hallam - CDD/CC (Ap Soc St) (BTEC 5M)
Sunderland - 14 pts (Soc Sci)
Thames Valley London - 14-10 pts (Soc Sci)
Wolverhampton - 14-12 pts (Soc Sci) (6 AS)

12 pts. **Bretton Hall (CHE)** - CC-EE (Soc St/Eng)
Buckinghamshire (CHE) - DDD/DD (Soc/App Soc St)
Coventry - CC (Ap Soc Sci) (4 AS)
Crewe & Alsager (CHE) - 12 pts (Ind St)
Derby - 12 pts (Soc Pol Modular)
East London - CDE/CC (Sociol/Prof St)
Glamorgan - CC (Women's Studies) (BTEC 5M)
Liverpool John Moores - DDD/CC (Modular)
Luton (CHE) - 12 pts (Comm Man)
Manchester Met - CC (Soc Sci)
North London - 12-10 pts (Ap Soc Sci courses)
Paisley - DDD/CC (Ap Soc St)
Plymouth - 12 pts (Sci Soc)
S Martins (CHE) - CDE/CC (Soc Eth) (4 AS) (BTEC 3M)
Teesside - 12-10 pts (Soc St)
Thames Valley London - 12 pts (Cont Soc St)
Westminster - CC (Soc Sci)

10 pts. **East London** - (Soc Sci)
Hertfordshire - CD (Ap Soc St/CQSW)
Humberside - 12 pts (Soc Sci; Soc/Prof St) (4 AS)
South Bank - CD (Soc Sci) (4 AS) (BTEC 2D+2M)
Southampton (IHE) - 10 pts (App Soc St - subject to approval)
Worcester (CHE) - 10 pts approx inc Access (Soc Sci) (4 AS)

8 pts. **and below**
Anglia (Poly Univ) - (Hum/Soc St)
Cheltenham & Glos (CHE) - EE (Women St - non-traditional entry for mature students))
Edge Hill (CHE) - (App Soc Sci)

King Alfred's (CHE) - 4 pts (Soc Prof St) (BTEC 3M)
North Riding (Coll) - (Ap Soc Sci)
Robert Gordon - DEE/DD (Ap Soc St)
Roehampton (IHE) - (Women's St)
Salford (UC) - (Soc Sci)
St Mary's (CHE) - (Irish St)
Southampton (IHE) - (Soc Sci) (4 AS)
Swansea (IHE) - (Comb St)

Diploma of Higher Education courses:
  4 pts.   Crewe & Alsager (CHE); East London; Edge Hill (CHE); Manchester Met; Nottingham Trent; Wolverhampton.

Alternative offers:

IB offers: **Aberdeen** 30 pts; **City** H655 S655; **East Anglia** 30 pts; **Edinburgh** 32-30 pts; **Reading** 31 pts; **Sheffield Hallam** 24 pts.

Irish offers: **Aberdeen** BBBB; **Bristol UWE** CCCC; **East Anglia** CCCCC; **Humberside** CCCC; **Nottingham Trent** BBCCC; **Sheffield Hallam** BBCC.

SCE offers: **Aberdeen** BBBB; **Central Lancashire** BBB; **Dundee** BBBB; **Durham** BBB; **Edinburgh** AAAA-BBBB; **Essex** BBBB; **Glasgow** BBBB/AAB; **Keele** BBCC; **Newcastle** BBCC; **Paisley** BBCC/BBB.

Overseas applicants: East Anglia Pre-sessional courses in English and study skills. **Robert Gordon** High standard of English required.

CHOOSING YOUR COURSE (See also Ch 1)

> **Subject information:** Most courses will take a broad-brush view of aspects of society eg, economics, politics, history, social psychology and urban studies. Applied Social Studies usually focuses on practical and theoretical preparation for a career in social work.

Course highlights: Bradford Final choice of specialist subject deferred until end of year 1. Specialist areas include politics and history. (App Soc) This is a four-year course in which academic work and practical experience are combined in the third and fourth years. **Coventry** Combination of major subject choice between sociology, social work and psychology. **East Anglia** Course covers economics, politics, sociology, philosophy. **East London** After a common first year students choose pathways in Sociology, Psychological Studies, Social Policy Research, Social Work with Sociology, Sociology with European Studies. **Hertfordshire** Common foundation year followed by a choice covering political economy, public policy, European studies (subject to approval) and law. **Humberside** Employer contacts in social work, housing, youth and community work, health etc. **Leeds** (Women's Studies) New course; single or joint combination with subjects from areas of economics, politics and social studies; explores gender issues in a wide variety of courses from arts, literature and social issues. **Newcastle** Course covers sociology, anthropology, politics, economics and psychology. **North London** Broad first year with cores and options in law, psychology, sociology, information science, economics, politics, social history and social policy. **Nottingham Trent** (Ap Soc St) Professional training in social work. **Robert Gordon** A four-year course with nine-month placements with social work agencies followed by the Diploma in Social Work. **Sheffield Hallam** (Ap Soc St) Course covers sociology, psychology, social work, health studies, equal opportunities; career related options in year three. Social work qualification in year four. **South Bank** Social policy, sociology, economics, psychology. **Swansea** Six subjects in year one with delayed choice until end of first year in choice of two subjects. NOW CHECK PROSPECTUSES FOR ALL COURSES.

Study opportunities abroad: Bristol UWE USA; **Central Lancashire** (E); **Edinburgh** (E) USA EUR; **Hertfordshire**; **Lancaster** USA; **Manchester Met** (E); **Salford** USA; **Westminster** EUR.

Work opportunities abroad: Manchester Met USA; **Salford** USA.

ADMISSIONS INFORMATION

Number of applicants per place (approx): Bradford 12; **Bristol UWE** 12; **Central Lancashire** 11; **City** 9; **Coventry** 14; **Durham** 3; **East London** 6; **Glasgow Caledonian** 9; **Hertfordshire** 6; **Kingston** 5; **Liverpool** 13; **Manchester Met** 23; **Nottingham Trent** 17, (Ap Soc St) 15; **Paisley** 5; **S Martins (CHE)** 4; **Salford** 12; **Sheffield Hallam** 20; **South Bank** 5; **Sunderland** 11; **Swansea** 8; **Westminster** 14.

General Studies acceptable: Aberdeen; Bradford (2); Bristol UWE; Central Lancashire; Coventry (2); Derby; East Anglia; Edge Hill (CHE); Humberside; Keele; Liverpool; Liverpool John Moores; Manchester Met; North London; S Martins (CHE) (2); Salford (2); South Bank; Sunderland; Thames Valley London (2); Wolverhampton; Worcester (CHE) (2).

Selection interviews: Anglia (Poly Univ); Birmingham; Bradford (occasionally); Bristol UWE (some); Coventry; Edge Hill (CHE) (some); Essex; Glasgow Caledonian; Hull (some); Kingston (T); Newcastle (some); S Martins (CHE); Salford (some); South Bank (some); Westminster (some).

Offers to applicants repeating A-levels: Higher Bristol UWE, City, Essex, Salford (possibly), Swansea; **Same** Anglia (Poly Univ), Bath, Bradford, Durham, Liverpool, Manchester Met, Nottingham Trent, S Martins (CHE), South Bank.

Admissions Tutors' advice: Bretton Hall As part of the College's equal opportunities policy, applications from ethnic minority students are welcomed. **Durham** Candidates must state the choice of subjects on their UCAS application. Any A-level subjects (science or arts) acceptable; motivation important. **Liverpool** (Social Comb) Mature applicants welcome with appropriate social science background. **Manchester Met** Long established department. Applicants are strongly advised to apply as soon as possible. Mature students are welcomed. **North London** Must show evidence of interest in current affairs, policy issues. Applications from ethnic minorities particularly welcome. Candidates for Social Work must be over 21. **South Bank** Open and flexible about entry requirements. We look for students with a strong interest and curiosity about the social world.

> **Examples of interview questions:** How do you think religion should be presented to people? Define democracy. What is the role of the Church in nationalistic aspirations? Does today's government listen to its subjects? Questions on current affairs. How would you change the running of your school? What are the faults of the Labour Party? What are your views on nuclear disarmament?

GAP YEAR ADVICE

Institutions accepting a Gap Year: Most institutions; **Kingston** Not recommended; **Manchester Met** Not encouraged; **Swansea** Consult us first.

Institutions willing to defer entry after A-levels (see Ch 5): Aston; Bradford; Bristol UWE; King Alfred's (CHE); Kingston; Lancaster; Ripon & York St John (CHE) (No); Robert Gordon; Roehampton (IHE); Sheffield Hallam; South Bank (Prefer not); Sunderland; Swansea.

AFTER A-LEVELS ADVICE

Institutions which may accept the same points score after A-levels: Bradford; Bristol UWE; Central Lancashire; Coventry; Durham; Essex; Humberside; Kingston; Liverpool; Manchester Met; Newcastle; North London; Sheffield Hallam (perhaps); South Bank; Sunderland; Westminster; most institutions.

Institutions demanding the actual grades offered after A-levels: Anglia (Poly Univ); Dundee; Hull; Kent; Liverpool John Moores; Nottingham Trent.

Institutions which may accept under-achieving applicants after A-levels: Bristol UWE; Durham (2 pts); Humberside; Sheffield Hallam (perhaps).

Institutions with vacancies in Aug/Sept 1992 (see Ch 5): Vacancies were plentiful after A-levels at scores from 20 pts and lower. Aston BBC; Bristol UWE; East London; Kingston 12-10 pts; South Bank 8 pts; Swansea CCC.

ADVICE FOR MATURE STUDENTS

Literacy and numeracy are important but each applicant will be judged individually for these courses, among the most popular with mature students. **South Bank** We are particularly interested in students from all backgrounds.

GRADUATE EMPLOYMENT

New Graduates' destinations (percentages) 1991:
Permanent employment: U 93; P 68; C 58.
Unemployment: U 3; P 21; C 22.
Further studies (all types): U 5; P 14; C 21.
Main career destinations (approx): Social/Medical (Poly) 39, (Coll) 4; Business (Poly) 14, (Coll) 22; Creative 11; Financial 6; Teaching 2; Clerical 14.

Teesside About 60% of students went into full-time employment in a variety of occupations. These included computing, residential care, management training, housing, the police and the prison service.

SOCIAL WORK (See also Social Administration)

Special subject requirements: none.

NB Institutions may raise or lower the level of published offers depending either on the quality or otherwise of individual applications or the numbers of applications received; grades/points offered may be adjusted downwards after A-level results. The level of an offer is not indicative of the quality of a course.

20 pts.	**Glasgow** - BCC (MA Soc Sci with qual in Social Work)
	Lancaster - BCC (SW) (2 AS)
18 pts.	**Hull** - BCD/BB (Soc Wk)
	Reading - 18 pts approx (Social Work) (Contact Admissions Tutor)
16 pts.	**Ulster** - CCD/BC (Comb Soc Bhv)
14 pts.	**Sheffield Hallam** - 14 pts (Ap Soc St)
12 pts.	**Central Lancashire** - 12 pts (Comb St)
	Coventry - CC-BD (Soc Wk/Dip SW)
	Middlesex - 12 pts (Soc Work) (4 AS)
	North London - CC (Soc Work) (4 AS)
	South Bank - (See under **Nursing**)

Offers for Foundation, Certificate and Diploma courses (see Ch 5):

Diploma courses (England):
Bretton Hall (CHE).

Diploma of Higher Education courses:
Birmingham; Suffolk (CFHE).

Diploma courses (Scotland):
Heriot-Watt/Moray House.

CHOOSING YOUR COURSE (See also Ch 1)

Subject information: These courses overlap those in Applied Social Studies and lead to careers in social work. Full details of all qualifying Social Work courses and the new method of application through The Social Work Admissions System (SWAS) can be obtained from UCAS, Fulton House, Jessop Avenue, Cheltenham, Glos GL50 3SH (which will be operating the system) and from the Central Council for Education and Training in Social Work at the addresses below:

CCETSW Information Service
Central Office
St Chad's Street
London WC1H 8AD
Tel 071 278 2455

CCETSW Information Service
78/80 George Street
Edinburgh EH2 3BU
Scotland
031 220 0093

CCETSW Information Service
6 Malone Road
Belfast BT9 5BN
Northern Ireland Tel 0232 665390

CCETSW Information Service
West Wing
St David's House
Wood Street
Cardiff CF1 1ES
Wales
Tel 0222 226257

ADMISSIONS INFORMATION

Examples of interview questions: See under **Social Administration**.

GAP YEAR ADVICE

Institutions accepting a Gap Year: Since qualified social workers are not able to practise until they are 22, institutions actively encourage a year out. **Coventry** Gain social work experience.

AFTER A-LEVELS ADVICE

Institutions with vacancies in Aug/Sept 1992 (see Ch 5): Hull 18 pts.

ADVICE FOR MATURE STUDENTS

See also **Social Studies**.

GRADUATE EMPLOYMENT

New Graduates' destinations (percentages) 1991:

See under **Social Policy**.

SOCIOLOGY

Special subject requirements: GCSE (grade A-C) mathematics usually required.

NB Institutions may raise or lower the level of published offers depending either on the quality or otherwise of individual applications or the numbers of applications received; grades/points offered may be adjusted downwards after A-level results. The level of an offer is not indicative of the quality of a course.

26 pts.   **Durham** - ABB (Law/Soc)

24 pts.   **Bristol** - BBB-BCC (All courses)
         Durham - ABC (Soc/Hist; Econ/Soc)
         Durham - BBB (Pol/Soc)
         Leeds - BBB (Psy/Soc)

22 pts.   **Aberdeen** - BBC (Soc)
         Bath - BBC/AA (Soc/Psy)
         Cardiff - BBC/AB (Soc/Ind Rel; Soc/Econ; Soc/Law) (BTEC 3M)
         Durham - BBC (Anth/Soc; Psy/Soc)
         East Anglia - BBC/BB (Soc/Scand; Soc; Soc/Fr; Soc/Ger) (BTEC 3D+3M)
         Edinburgh - BBC (Sociol)
         Glasgow - BBC (Soc)
         Hull - BBC-BCC (Soc/Soc An) (BTEC 2D+4M)
         Keele - BBC-BCD-CCC/BB-BC (Joint Hons) (4 AS)
         Lancaster - BBC-BCC (Soc Comb courses) (BTEC Ds+Ms)
         Leeds - BBC (Econ/Soc; Geog/Soc)
         Liverpool - BBC-BCC/AB-BB (Sociology) (4 AS)
         Nottingham - BBC (Psy/Soc)
         Sheffield - BBC-BCC (Sociology courses) (6 AS) (BTEC 3D)

20 pts.   **Aston** - BCC/BB (Soc St Comb Hons)
         Bath - 20 pts (Soc Ind R; Sociology; Soc/Soc Wk)
         Bradford - BCC/BB (Sociol)
         Brunel - BCC/AB (Soc; Soc/Psy; Soc/Soc Anth; Soc/Comm) (4 AS)
         Cardiff - BCC/BB (Soc/Psy; Soc/Educ) (BTEC 3M)
         City - BCC/BB (Soc/Media St) (BTEC 4D+3M)
         Durham - BCC (Soc)
         East Anglia - BCC (All Sociology courses except **22 pts**)
         Essex - BCC/BB (Sociology courses)
         Kent - BCC-CCC (All courses)
         Lancaster - 20 pts/BB (Soc) (BTEC mainly Ds)
         Leeds - BCC/BB (Dat Pro Soc)
         Leicester - BCC/BB (Sociology; Ap Sociology) (BTEC 1D+Ms or M overall)
         London (LSE) - 20 pts approx (Sociol)
         London (RH) - BCC/BB (Soc/Soc P; Soc/Econ)
         Manchester - 20-18 pts approx (Sociol)
         Nottingham - BCC (All courses except **22 pts**)
         Oxford Brookes - BCC (Modular)
         Salford - BCC-CCD/AB (Soc)
         Southampton - BCC-CCC (Sociology courses)
         Surrey - BCC/AB (Econ/Soc) (6 AS)
         Sussex - BCC/BB (All courses)
         Swansea - BCC/BB (Sociol and joint courses) (BTEC Ds+Ms)
         Warwick - BCC (Sociol)
         York - BCC/BB (Soc; Soc/E Hist EQ; Soc/Soc Pol) (BTEC Ds)

18 pts.   **Bangor** - CCC/BC (Sociol; Soc/Soc Pol) (4 AS)
         Bradford - CCC/BB (Soc/Psy) (BTEC 3M)
         Cardiff - CCC/BC (Soc; Soc/Soc Pol) (BTEC 3M)
         City - CCC/BB (All Sociology courses except under **20 pts**) (BTEC 4D+3M)
         Exeter - CCC/BB (Sociology) (BTEC Ms)

           Hull - CCC/BC (Soc Pol/Crim)
           Leeds - CCC/BB (Sociology; Soc/Theol)
           Loughborough - CCC/BB (Sociol with a minor subject) (4 AS) (BTEC 4-8M)
           Reading - CCC (Sociology courses)
           Stirling - CCC/BB (Soc)
           Strathclyde - CCC (BBD 2nd yr entry) (Arts/Soc St)
           Surrey - CCC/BB (Socio) (6 AS) (BTEC 3D+4M)
           Warwick - CCC (Soc/S Policy; Ed Soc)
           York - CCC/BC (Soc/Educ) (BTEC Ds)

16pts. **Belfast** - CCD (Sociol)
           Middlesex - 16-12 pts (Soc)
           Nottingham - CCD/BC (Sociology)
           Trinity & All Saints (CHE) - CCD/CC (Soc/BMA; Soc/PM)
           Ulster - CCD/BC (Comb Soc Bhv)

14pts. **Bristol UWE** - CDD/BC (Sociol) (BTEC 2D+2M)
           Kingston - 14 pts/BB (Soc)
           Liverpool John Moores - 14-12 pts (Integrated Credit Scheme - Soc/Women's St)
           London (Gold) - BC (Soc)
           Northumbria - BC (Soc)
           Plymouth - 14 pts (Soc) (6 AS) (BTEC 3-5M)
           Staffordshire - 14 pts (Soc) (BTEC 6M)

12pts. **Anglia (Poly Univ)** - 12 pts (Sociol)
           Bath (CHE) - (Comb St)
           Central Lancashire - (Comb St)
           East London - CDE/CC (Soc/Pro St)
           Greenwich - 12 pts (Soc) (BTEC 4M)
           Liverpool John Moores - 12 pts (Modular)
           Manchester Met - DDD/CC (Hum Soc/St)
           Northumbria - CC (All courses except under **14 pts**) (2 AS)
           Portsmouth - DDD/DD (Soc)
           Teesside - 12-10 pts (Sociol)

10pts. **Central England** - DDE/DE (Soc)
           Greenwich - CD (Soc) (3 AS)
           Guildhall London - CD (Sociology)
           Plymouth - 10 pts (Sci/Soc) (BTEC 3-5M)

 8pts. **and below**
           Bath (CHE) - Soc Sci new course - contact Admissions Tutor)
           Bedford (CHE) - (Comb St)
           Bristol UWE - (Soc Sci)
           Buckinghamshire (CHE) - no standard offers (Soc/Ap Soc St)
           Cheltenham & Glos (CHE) - (Mod)
           Liverpool (IHE) - (Comb St)
           Manchester Met - no standard offer (Hum Soc St)
           Middlesex - (Modular)
           Nene (CHE) - (Comb St)
           North London - (Soc Res; Soc Work)
           Roehampton (IHE) - (Women's St; Comb St)
           Staffordshire - (Mod St)
           St Mary's (CHE) - (Comb St)
           Sunderland - (Comb St; Soc Sci)
           Teesside - (Hum)
           Westminster - (Soc Sci)
           Wolverhampton - (Sociology)
           Worcester (CHE) - (Comb St)

Diploma of Higher Education courses:
  4pts. Bath (CHE); East London; Greenwich; Guildhall London; Middlesex; Oxford Brookes; Plymouth; Worcester (CHE).

Alternative offers:

EB offers: **Liverpool** 60%.

IB offers: **Aberdeen** 30 pts; **Aberystwyth** 30 pts; **Bangor** 30 pts; **Bath** H665; **Bradford** 28 pts; **Bristol** 28 pts inc 15 pts Highers; **Cardiff** 30 pts; **City** H655 S655; **East Anglia** 30 pts; **Essex** 28 pts inc 10 pts in 2 Highers; **Exeter** 30 pts; **Hull** 27 pts inc H65; **Kent** H554; **Lancaster** 30 pts; **Leicester** 28 pts; **Liverpool** 28 pts; **Loughborough** 28 pts; **Nottingham** H554; **Sheffield** H665 inc English or H665 + S6 English; **Surrey** 30 pts; **Swansea** 28 pts; **York** 28 pts.

Irish offers: **Aberdeen** BBBB; **Bangor** BBB; **Bath** BBBB; **Brunel** BBBCC; **East Anglia** CCCCC; **Guildhall London** CCCCC; **Keele** BBBCC; **Liverpool** BBCCC.

SCE offers: **Aberdeen** BBBB; **Aberystwyth** BBBB; **Bath** BBBB; **Bristol** ABBCC; **Brunel** ABB; **City** AABB; **East Anglia** BBB; **Edinburgh** BBBBB-BBBC; **Essex** BBBB; **Glasgow** ABBB-BBBB; **Guildhall London** BBCCC; **Lancaster** BBBBB; **Liverpool** BBCC; **Newcastle** BBBB/BBB; **Sheffield** ABBB; **Stirling** BBCC; **Strathclyde** BBBCC; **York** BBBC.

Overseas applicants: East Anglia Pre-sessional study skills and English courses available. **Northumbria** Fluency in English required.

CHOOSING YOUR COURSE (See also Ch 1)

Subject information: This is the study of societies in general, both in Britain and abroad. Elective subjects offered will include industrial behaviour, crime and deviance, health and illness.

Course highlights: Bangor Course covers criminology and penology, law and social policy, health services, community studies, Northern Ireland and gender. **Bath** Subsidiary subjects include psychology, history, politics, philosophy and economics, with elective subjects covering social work, industrial relations and sociology of health, illness, crime, deviance and education. **Central England** Options in research, social action or social work. **City** The course includes applied sociology, race and society, mass communications, the sociology of work and industrial relations. **Greenwich** Comparative focus on different societies eg, the former Soviet Union, USA, China, Middle East. **Hull** (Soc Pol/Crim) Health policy and administration, criminology and criminal justice social work. **Lancaster** In year one the introductory course includes two options from the sociology of class and gender, criminal law, culture and the media. In years two and three subjects include deviance and social control, education and society, health and illness, the sociology of sport, popular culture and race. **Leeds** Sociological theory, sociology of modern Britain and the developing countries. **Newcastle** Teaching strengths in contemporary culture, analysis, feminism and equal opportunities. Research strengths in criminal justice system, trade union studies. Six-month placement arranged for those taking Social Research (four-year degree). **Portsmouth** Options include psychology, criminology and criminal justice, race and society, social work and society. **Staffordshire** Multidisciplinary department with teaching staff covering sociology, psychology and social work. **Swansea** Broad Part I course. Dissertation may be offered to replace one exam out of eight. **Teesside** Course covers ageing, culture, lifestyle and gender. NOW CHECK PROSPECTUSES FOR ALL COURSES.

Study opportunities abroad: East Anglia USA; **Greenwich** (E); **Lancaster** USA; **Leeds** (E) SP P BR; **Salford** (E) IT SP G; **Staffordshire** (E) FR G GR SP B; **Surrey** (E).

Work opportunities abroad: Brunel USA EUR.

ADMISSIONS INFORMATION

Number of applicants per place (approx): Bangor 9; **Bath** 12; **Bath (CHE)** 4; **Birmingham** 10; **Bradford** 20; **Bristol** 12; **Brunel** 11; **Cardiff** 5; **Central England** 10; **City** 11; **Durham** 8; **East Anglia** 15; **East London** 8; **Exeter** 5; **Greenwich** 5; **Kent** 15; **Kingston** 9; **Lancaster** 12; **Leicester** 10; **Liverpool** 9; **Loughborough** 10; **Northumbria** 18; **Nottingham** 13; **Portsmouth**

12; **Salford** 8; **Staffordshire** 8; **Surrey** 3; **Swansea** 10; **Trinity & All Saints (CHE)** 5; **York** 11.

General Studies acceptable: Aberdeen; Aberystwyth; Aston; Bath (mature students only); Bedford (CHE); Bradford; Bristol; Brunel; Durham; East Anglia; Essex; Exeter (2); Greenwich; Kent; Lancaster; Leeds; Leicester (2); Liverpool; Loughborough; Newcastle; Nottingham; Oxford Brookes; Plymouth (2); Portsmouth; Salford; Surrey; Swansea; Trinity & All Saints (CHE); York.

Selection interviews: Aston; Bath; Bristol; Brunel; City; Durham; East Anglia (some); East London; Hull (some); Lancaster (some); Leeds (some); Liverpool (some); Liverpool (IHE); Loughborough; Newcastle (some); Nottingham (some); Portsmouth; Salford; St Mary's (CHE); Trinity & All Saints (CHE); York.

Offers to applicants repeating A-levels: Higher Brunel, East London, Essex, Guildhall London, Hull, Newcastle, Swansea; **Possibly Higher** Aston, Leeds, Liverpool, Portsmouth, Salford, York; **Same** Bangor, Bath, Bristol, Central England, Durham, Kingston, Lancaster, London (RH), Loughborough, Northumbria.

Admissions Tutors' advice: Bath GCSE English and maths (grade A–C); nursing, Open University, banking qualifications etc also accepted. **East Anglia** Our standard offer may be modified to take into account potential performance and personal circumstances as indicated by the UCAS referee's report. We usually look for at least one B grade, but do not accept general studies as that B grade. **Guildhall London** It is possible to major or specialise in this subject or to combine it with other disciplines. **Kingston** Emphasis is given to interviewing and enrolling mature unqualified applicants. **Lancaster** We welcome applications from mature students and those with unorthodox educational backgrounds but we do expect these applicants to have some awareness of the nature of sociological inquiry. **Loughborough** A strong emphasis is placed on the interview in our selection procedure, rather than on A-level grades alone. **Salford** The department seeks a balance between school and further education leavers and mature students.

> **Examples of interview questions:** Why do you want to study Sociology? What books have you read on the subject? Why? How do you see the role of women changing in the next 20 years?

GAP YEAR ADVICE

Institutions accepting a Gap Year: Most institutions; **Bristol** Inform us when you apply; **Cardiff** Apply before departure asking for deferred entry; **Greenwich** Maintain reading; **Kingston** Contact admissions tutor; **Salford** Try to maintain some contact with academic work; **Surrey** Do not apply for deferred entry.

Institutions willing to defer entry after A-levels (see Ch 5): Bangor; Bristol UWE; Brunel; Greenwich; Humberside; Kingston (contact Admissions Tutor); Lancaster; Northumbria; Plymouth; Salford; Swansea; Trinity & All Saints (CHE).

AFTER A-LEVELS ADVICE

Institutions which may accept the same points score after A-levels; Aberystwyth; Aston; Bangor; Bath; Bradford; Bristol; Birmingham; Brunel; Central England; City; East Anglia; East London; Essex; Greenwich; Hull; Kent; Lancaster; Liverpool; Loughborough; Newcastle; Nottingham; Portsmouth; Salford; Sheffield; York.

Institutions demanding the actual grades offered after A-levels: Durham; Guildhall London; Kingston; Stirling.

Institutions which may accept under-achieving applicants after A-levels: Bangor; Birmingham; Bristol; Brunel; City; Durham; Essex; Exeter; Liverpool; London (RH); Nottingham; Salford; Swansea; Trinity & All Saints (CHE); York; most new universities.

Institutions with vacancies in Aug/Sept 1992 (see Ch 5): Bangor 18 pts; Bristol UWE; Brunel BCC; Essex 20 pts; Greenwich 10 pts; Humberside 10 pts; Kingston 14 pts; Lancaster 18 pts; Salford 18 pts; Surrey 16 pts; Swansea 18 pts; Trinity & All Saints (CHE) CDD.

ADVICE FOR MATURE STUDENTS

See under **Social Studies**.

GRADUATE EMPLOYMENT

New Graduates' destinations (percentages) 1991:
Permanent employment: U 64; P 60; C 100.
Unemployment: U 25; P 25; C 0.
Further studies (all types): U 31; P 22; C 0.
Main career destinations (approx): Medical/Social (Univ/Poly) 38, (Coll) 54; Admin 15; Business 14; Clerical 12; Financial 7; Legal 5; Teaching 5.

York (1989-91) Social and welfare occupations accounted for the majority of destinations in probation work (4), childcare (3), residential social work, Oxfam, drug rehabilitation and welfare work. Six students went on to train as nurses and one as an occupational therapist. Retail management and personnel work attracted five graduates and the same number went into finance careers. Legal work, secretarial work and education also attracted a number of graduates.

SOIL SCIENCE

Special subject requirements: 2-3 A-levels, at least 1 from science subjects with science/mathematics at GCSE (grade A-C).

NB Institutions may raise or lower the level of published offers depending either on the quality or otherwise of individual applications or the numbers of applications received; grades/points offered may be adjusted downwards after A-level results. The level of an offer is not indicative of the quality of a course.

18 pts.	**Aberdeen** - CCC-CCD/BC (Soil Sci)
	Edinburgh - CCC (Crop Sci)
14 pts.	**Bangor** - CDD/CC (All courses)
	Newcastle - CDD/BC (Agric Env; Soil Sci) (BTEC Ms)
	Reading - CDD/CC (Soil Sci)

Alternative offers:

IB offers: **Aberdeen** 26 pts; **Newcastle** 28 pts inc 15 pts Highers.

CHOOSING YOUR COURSE (See also Ch 1)

> **Subject information:** Soil Science influences agricultural production and plant nutrition and the quality of drinking water. It is also involved in mineralogy, microbiology, medical applications and the use of fertilisers and pesticides. See also under **Agriculture**.

Course highlights: Aberdeen The course includes studies of water quality, environmental pollution and soil erosion. **Bangor** Joint Honours with four other subjects. Chemically based course with emphasis on environmental aspects. **Newcastle** Broad studies covering biological, chemical and physical processes, and includes laboratory and field work in agricultural and natural environments. NOW CHECK PROSPECTUSES FOR ALL COURSES.

ADMISSIONS INFORMATION

Number of applicants per place (approx): Bangor 4; **Newcastle** 3.

Admissions Tutors' advice: Newcastle Variety of AS-levels accepted, but not general studies as third A-level. Open University credits and GCSE (grade A-C) qualifications also considered.

> **Examples of interview questions:** Applicants tested on their knowledge of soil science and reasons for choosing it.

GAP YEAR ADVICE

Institutions accepting a Gap Year: Newcastle.

Institutions willing to defer entry after A-levels (see Ch 5): Newcastle.

AFTER A-LEVELS ADVICE

Institutions which may accept the same points score after A-levels: Bangor; Newcastle.

Offers to applicants repeating A-levels: Higher Newcastle (by 2 pts).

Institutions with vacancies in Aug/Sept 1992 (see Ch 5): Newcastle 8 pts.

SOUTH ASIAN STUDIES or INDOLOGY (Includes SOUTH EAST ASIAN STUDIES)

Special subject requirements: a language at GCSE (grade A-C).

NB Institutions may raise or lower the level of published offers depending either on the quality or otherwise of individual applications or the numbers of applications received; grades/points offered may be adjusted downwards after A-level results. The level of an offer is not indicative of the quality of a course.

22 pts.	**London (SOAS)** - BBC/BC (Vietn Studies)
20 pts.	**York** - BCC/BB (Chin/Ling; Hind/Ling)
16 pts.	**London (SOAS)** - BB (Sanskrit; SAS; Indon St; Burm St)
	London (SOAS) - BB-BC (Urdu St and second subject; Tamil St and second subject; Hindi St and second subject; Soc A/Lang (Nep); Thai St)
	London (SOAS) - CCD/CC (Two-subject degree including a South Asian language - Bengali/Gujarati/Marathi/Tamil/Urdu)
12 pts.	**Hull** - CC (SEA Studs; SEAS Lang)
	North London - CC-CD (SEA) (4 AS)

Alternative offers:

IB offers: **York** H665.

Overseas applicants: Hull Living costs 30% lower than in London.

CHOOSING YOUR COURSE (See also Ch 1)

> **Subject information:** These courses focus on the study of the cultures and the languages of this region of the world, such as Burmese, Sanskrit, Vietnamese, Bengali, Marathi, Tamil and Urdu. NOW CHECK PROSPECTUSES FOR ALL COURSES.

ADMISSIONS INFORMATION

Number of applicants per place (approx): Hull (SEA Studs) 6; **London (SOAS)** (Thai St) 2, (Burm St) 1.

Admissions Tutors' advice: London (SOAS) For Vietnamese Studies a good reading knowledge of French is required.

> **Examples of interview questions:** General questions are usually asked which relate to applicants' reasons for choosing a degree course in this subject area, and to a background knowledge of the various cultures.

GAP YEAR ADVICE

Institutions accepting a Gap Year: Most institutions.

Institutions willing to defer entry after A-levels (see Ch 5): Hull.

AFTER A-LEVELS ADVICE

London (SOAS) Actual grades are required after A-levels and interviews are held.

Institutions which may accept under-achieving applicants after A-levels: Hull (overseas applicants 14-12 pts).

SPANISH

Special subject requirements: Spanish A-level preferred or required in most cases.

NB Institutions may raise or lower the level of published offers depending either on the quality or otherwise of individual applications or the numbers of applications received; grades/points offered may be adjusted downwards after A-level results. The level of an offer is not indicative of the quality of a course.

30 pts.	**Cambridge/Oxford** - AAA potential recommended (Mod/M Lang; Mod Lang)
26 pts.	**Bristol** - ABB-BBB/AB (Span/Ital; Span/Fr; Span/Ger)
24 pts.	**Hull** - BBB-BCC/AA (Sp - special/joint) (BTEC 4M)
	Newcastle - BBB/BB (Sp/Lat Amer; Sp Major with a Minor Subject)
	St Andrews - BBB (Span)
22 pts.	**Aberdeen** - BBC (Hisp St) (6 AS)
	Edinburgh - BBC (Span; Span/Port)
	Glasgow - BBC (Hisp St)
	Heriot-Watt - BBC (Span)
	Leeds - BBC/AB (Spanish; Iber/Amer St)
	Manchester - 22 pts approx (Hisp St)
	Nottingham - BBC (Spanish and combined courses)
	Sheffield - BBC-BCC/BB (All courses) (Single Hons 4 AS, Dual Hons 6 AS)
	Swansea - BBC-BCD/BB-BC (Spanish/BS)
20 pts.	**Birmingham** - BCC-CCC (Hisp St)
	Bradford - BCC/BC (All courses)
	Bristol - BCC (Spanish; Hisp St)
	Cardiff - BCC/BB (Span; Sp/Port; Hisp St) (BTEC 2D+3M)
	Essex - BCC (Span)
	Exeter - BCC-CCC/BB (Spanish courses)
	London (King's) - 20 pts approx (Span)
	Salford - 20 pts approx (Joint courses)

	Trinity & All Saints (CHE) - BCC (Sp/BMA; Sp/PM)
18pts.	**Aberystwyth** - CCC (Sp; Joint Hons)
	Belfast - CCC/BB (Span)
	Hull - CCC/AB (Span) (BTEC 3M)
	Liverpool - CCC/BC-CC (Approx offer for Hispanic Studies courses)
	London (Gold) - BCD/BC (Sp/Lat Am)
	London (QMW) - 18-14 pts (Hispanic St; Hisp Eur St)
	Southampton - CCC-BCD (C in languages) (All courses)
	Stirling - CCC/BC (Sp)
	Strathclyde - CCC/BC (BBD 2nd yr entry) (Arts/Soc St)
	Swansea - CCC/BC (Approx offer for Joint Hons except under **22 pts**)
16pts.	**Durham** - BB (Spanish; Mod/Lang)
	Middlesex - 16-12 pts (Modular)
12pts.	**Bristol UWE** - DDD/CC (FGIS; FSIS; GSIS)
	London (UC) - CC (MILARS)
	North London - CC-CD (Sp/Lat Am; Hum Comb) (4 AS)
	Northumbria - CC-EE (Sp/Ger; Sp/Rus)
	Portsmouth - CC-CD (Sp St; His/Fr St; Sp/Area St)
	Wolverhampton - CC (All courses)
10pts.	**Kingston** - 10 pts (Sp/Econ/Pol)
	Manchester Met - CD-DD (Sp/Ger)
8pts.	**and below**
	Anglia (Poly Univ) - (Fr/Sp; Ger/Sp; Comb St)
	Coventry - (Fr/Sp; Ger/Sp)
	Hertfordshire - (Hum)
	Leeds Met - (ELI/Sp)
	Liverpool John Moores - (Fr/Sp; Ger/Sp)
	Portsmouth - CE (Sp/Lat Am St)
	South Bank - 8 pts (Joint courses) (BTEC D in lang)
	Thames Valley London - (EFL/Sp)

Diploma of Higher Education courses:
   4pts.   Leeds Met (Euro Bus Comm); Middlesex.

Offers for Foundation, Certificate and Diploma courses (see Ch 5):

Higher National Diploma courses (with Bus St):
   8pts.   **and below** Northumbria; Sheffield Hallam; Southampton (IHE); Thames Valley London.

Polytechnic and College awards:
   4pts.   **and below** Anglia (Poly Univ); Central England; Glamorgan; Leeds Met; Oxford
            Brookes.

Alternative offers:

IB offers: **Aberdeen** 30 pts; **Aberystwyth** 32 pts; **Bradford** 24 pts; **Bristol** 32 pts; **Cardiff** 30 pts, H 15 pts; **Edinburgh** H655; **Exeter** 30 pts; **Hull** 27 pts; **Leeds** 30-28 pts Span H6; **Liverpool** 28 pts inc 15 pts Highers; **Portsmouth** 25 pts; **Sheffield** H665; **Swansea** 28 pts.

SCE offers: **Aberdeen** BBBB; **Edinburgh** BBBB; **Glasgow** BBBB; **Heriot-Watt** AABB; **Liverpool** BBBB; **Newcastle** BBB; **St Andrews** BBBB; **Stirling** BBCC; **Strathclyde** BBBB.

CHOOSING YOUR COURSE (See also Ch 1)

Subject information: This subject can be studied focusing on the language and literature of Spain although broader courses in Hispanic Studies also include Portuguese and Latin American studies.

Course highlights: Aberystwyth Wide range of topics covered including language of business and current affairs. **Bristol** Opportunity to learn three languages - Spanish, Portuguese and Catalan. Department ranked as outstanding in recent national assessment on research. Numerous contacts established with law firms, banks, insurance companies, travel companies, broadcasting, teaching, industry and commerce where graduates now employed. **Cardiff** Spanish and Portuguese fully integrated in School of European Studies also offering politics, culture and society. **Leeds** Innovative approaches to language teaching. Integrated area studies course, comprising study of language, culture, history or geography of Iberian Peninsula and Latin America including Portuguese-speaking countries. **Sheffield** Emphasis on communication skills and contemporary Spanish and South American affairs. Wide range of options. Small group teaching. **Swansea** (Spanish/BS) The business element occupies one third of the degree. NOW CHECK PROSPECTUSES FOR ALL COURSES.

Study opportunities abroad: Aberystwyth (E) SP SPA; **Central England** (E) B NL; **Bradford** (E) SP; **Hull** (E); **London (QMW)** (E); **Portsmouth** (E); **Sheffield** (E); **Trinity & All Saints (CHE)** (E); most institutions in Spain or Spanish-speaking countries.

Work opportunities abroad: Most universities and colleges offering four-year courses.

ADMISSIONS INFORMATION

Number of applicants per place (approx): Birmingham 14; **Bradford** 5; **Cardiff** 6; **Durham** 5; **Exeter** 5; **Hull** 14; **Liverpool** 6; **London (QMW)** 5; **Middlesex** 2; **Newcastle** 20; **Nottingham** 16; **Trinity & All Saints (CHE)** 2.

General Studies acceptable: Aberdeen; Bradford; Durham; Exeter (2); Hull (2); Leeds; Liverpool; London (QMW) (2); Newcastle; Portsmouth; Trinity & All Saints (CHE) (2).

Selection interviews: Cambridge; Durham (usually); Hull (some); Leeds; Liverpool; Newcastle (some); Nottingham (some); Oxford; Portsmouth (50%); South Bank; Swansea (some); Trinity & All Saints (CHE).

Offer to applicants repeating A-levels: Same Durham, Hull, Leeds (grade C Spanish required), Newcastle, Nottingham, Swansea.

Admissions Tutors' advice: Bristol Applicants without a Spanish qualification may be admitted to single Spanish. They should have one other language and some experience in a Spanish-speaking country (work or residence). **Durham** There is a special pre-Honours course available for Single Honours candidates only without previous knowledge of Spanish. Combined Studies courses are also available for beginners. **Newcastle** Department is flexible in its admissions policy. We give sympathetic consideration to applications from mature students. **Portsmouth** All applications are considered on merit.

Examples of interview questions: Candidates offering A-level Spanish questioned on their A-level work, their reasons for wanting to take the subject and on their knowledge of Spain and its people. Interest in Spain important for all applicants. **Durham** looks especially for evidence of wide reading (outside the syllabus), curiosity and intellectual initiative.

GAP YEAR ADVICE

Institutions accepting a Gap Year: Most institutions; **Bradford** Special tutorial assistance for deferred entry students; **Bristol** Students may go abroad but must find and propose the placement concerned which is subject to departmental approval; **Cardiff** Spend some time in Spain or Portugal; **Hull** If possible visit Spain or Spanish America; **Portsmouth** We look more favourably on applicants who use the year to enhance their knowledge of Spanish life and language.

Institutions willing to defer entry after A-levels (see Ch 5): Bradford; Bristol (No); Hull; London (Gold); Portsmouth; South Bank (Prefer not); Swansea.

AFTER A-LEVELS ADVICE

Institutions which may accept the same points score after A-levels: Aberdeen; Aberystwyth; Durham; Hull; Leeds; Liverpool; Portsmouth; Sheffield; Strathclyde; Swansea.

Institutions demanding the actual grades offered after A-levels: Newcastle; Nottingham; South Bank; Stirling.

Institutions which may accept under-achieving applicants after A-levels: Aberystwyth; Durham; Exeter; Liverpool; Newcastle.

Institutions with vacancies in Aug/Sept 1992 (see Ch 5): Vacancies existed on a large number of joint courses. Bradford (Beginners Spanish) 20 pts; Essex 20 pts; London (Gold) 18 pts; Portsmouth CDE/12 pts; South Bank DE; Swansea (Very few) 22-18 pts.

GRADUATE EMPLOYMENT

New Graduates' destinations (percentages) 1991:
Permanent employment: U 73; P 56.
Unemployment: Average in producing graduates for employment: 19; P 33.
Further studies (all types): U 37; P 25.

SPEECH PATHOLOGY/SCIENCES/THERAPY

Special subject requirements: 2-3 A-levels, chemistry or biology preferred; GCSE (grade A-C) in mathematics and science subjects (biology preferred) and a language.

NB Institutions may raise or lower the level of published offers depending either on the quality or otherwise of individual applications or the numbers of applications received; grades/points offered may be adjusted downwards after A-level results. The level of an offer is not indicative of the quality of a course.

22 pts.	**Manchester** – 22-20 pts approx (Speech)
	Reading – BBC/CC (Ling/Lang P)
	Sheffield – BBC (Sp Sci) (4 AS) (BTEC 3D)
20 pts.	**City** – BCC/AA (Cl Comm St)
	De Montfort – 20-18 pts (SPT) (4 AS) (BTEC 4M)
	London (UC) – BCC-CCC (Sp Sci)
	Newcastle – BCC (BSc (Sp); Sp/Psy)
18 pts.	**London (Nat Hosp Coll of Sp Sci)** – CCC/BC (Speech Sci)
	London (Central Sch Sp Dr) – CCC/BC (SLP)
	Ulster – CCC/BB (Sp Ther)
16 pts.	**Central England** – 16 pts (SLPT)
	Manchester Met – CCD/BB (SPT) (4 AS)
14 pts.	**Leeds Met** – CCE/BC (CLS)
12 pts.	**and below**
	Cardiff (IHE) – 12 pts approx (Speech Therapy)
	Queen Margaret (Coll) – CC (Sp Th/Path) (4 AS)
	Strathclyde/Jordanhill – EE (Speech Path)

Alternative offers:

IB offers: **City** H655 S555; **Manchester Met** 28 pts inc biol.

Irish offers: **Manchester Met** BBBBB.

SCE offers: **Manchester Met** BBBB; **Newcastle** BBBB; **Queen Margaret (Coll)** BBB; **Sheffield** BBBB.

Overseas applicants: Manchester Met Good English required because of placement periods.

CHOOSING YOUR COURSE (See also Ch 1)

> **Subject information:** This is the study of speech defects which may be caused by accident, disease or psychological trauma. Courses lead to qualification as a speech therapist.

Course highlights: Central England Knowledge of processes underlying speech and language behaviour in both normal and pathological states. **Cardiff (IHE)** Strong emphasis on practical work. **City** Specialisation possible in counselling, computer studies, cerebral palsy, working with the deaf. **London (Central Sch Sp Dr)** New modular degree in Psychology and Speech Therapy (subject to approval) with clinical and non-clinical pathways; qualified teacher option. **London (Nat Hosp Coll)** Excellent teaching facilities. Strong contacts with NHS and local health authorities. **Manchester Met** Integration of theory with clinical practice; Collaboration of psychologists with speech therapists. Extensive employer contact. On-site speech therapy clinic and speech laboratory. Ethnic minority applicants particularly welcomed. **Newcastle** Multidisciplinary department, substantial clinical practice, active in research, some medical school teaching. **Queen Margaret (Coll)** Clinical placements and research projects. Course covers clinical education, linguistics, disordered speech and language, severe learning difficulties, cerebral palsy, stroke. NOW CHECK PROSPECTUSES FOR ALL COURSES.

Work opportunities abroad: Queen Margaret (Coll) WI IRE USA CAN; **Sheffield** (E).

ADMISSIONS INFORMATION

Number of applicants per place (approx): Birmingham 21; **Cardiff (IHE)** 10; **City** 12; **De Montfort** 27; **Leeds Met** 27; **London (Central Sch Sp Dr)** 7; **Manchester Met** 28; **Newcastle** 15.

General Studies acceptable: City; London (Central Sch Sp Dr); Manchester Met.

Selection interviews: All institutions. These interviews often include an ear test (test of listening ability).

Offers to applicants repeating A-levels: Higher Central England, Leeds Met, London (Central Sch Sp Dr); **Possibly higher** Manchester Met; **Same** City, London (Nat Hosp Coll), Newcastle, Ulster.

Admissions Tutors' advice: Birmingham We look for a mix of GCSEs (at least five with A-B grades). **City** We are very interested in mature students and in achieving a better balance of male entrants into the profession. **Leeds Met** No applicant with a speech or hearing defect can be considered. **Manchester Met** Modern language or music, English and a biological subject are required at GCSE (grade A-C). Applicants must have observed a speech therapist at work with children and adults.

> **Examples of interview questions:** Have you visited a speech therapy clinic? What made you want to become a speech therapist? What type of speech problems are there? What type of person would make a good speech therapist?

GAP YEAR ADVICE

Institutions accepting a Gap Year: Most institutions; **London (Central Sch Sp Dr)** Travel; work in health care, social services, speech therapy settings useful.

Institutions willing to defer entry after A-levels (see Ch 5): De Montfort; Queen Margaret (Coll).

AFTER A-LEVELS ADVICE

Institutions which may accept the same points score after A-levels: Central England; City; De Montfort; London (Nat Hosp Coll); Manchester Met; Ulster.

Institutions demanding the actual grades offered after A-levels: Leeds Met; Newcastle.

Institutions which may accept under-achieving applicants after A-levels: Central England; City; Leeds Met; London (Central Sch Sp Dr); Manchester Met; Sheffield.

Institutions with vacancies in Aug/Sept 1992 (see Ch 5): Very few vacancies were advertised.

ADVICE FOR MATURE STUDENTS

This course attracts a number of mature students (up to 30% of the student intake on some courses). Entry requirements vary but a social science background is always an advantage.

SPORTS STUDIES (including Sport and Recreation Studies, Sports Science)

Special subject requirements: 2 A-levels; science subjects preferred.

NB Institutions may raise or lower the level of published offers depending either on the quality or otherwise of individual applications or the numbers of applications received; grades/points offered may be adjusted downwards after A-level results. The level of an offer is not indicative of the quality of a course.

22 pts.	**Birmingham** - BBC-BCC (Sports courses)
	Loughborough - BBC-BCC/BB (PE)
20 pts.	**Bangor** - BCC/BB (Shape)
18 pts.	**Canterbury Christ Church (CHE)** - CCC-BCC/BB-CC (Sp Sci)
	Ulster - CCC (Sp Leis)
16 pts.	**Bedford (CHE)** - 16-14 pts (Modular)
	Glasgow - CCD/BC (Physio/Sports)
	Northumbria - 16 pts (Sport St)
	Staffordshire - CCD/BC (Sport/Rec St) (BTEC 2D+2M)
	West London (IHE) - 16 pts (Joint)
14 pts.	**Brighton** - BC (Sport Sci; Exercise Sci) (BTEC 3M)
	Liverpool John Moores - BC (Sport Sci)
	Manchester Met - 14 pts (Sport Sci)
12 pts.	**Cardiff (IHE)** - 12 pts minimum (SHMS)
	Nottingham Trent - 12 pts (Sport Sci/Admin) (4 AS)
	Sunderland - CC (Sports St)
	West Sussex (IHE) - 12 pts minimum (Sport St) (BTEC 6M)
10 pts.	**Bradford & Ilkley (CmC)** - CD (Comm St)
	Cheltenham & Glos (CHE) - (Sports Sci - Modular minor route)
	Chester (CHE) - (Comb St)
	Roehampton (IHE) - CD (Comb) (BTEC 2D+2M)
	Strathclyde/Jordanhill - (Sport)
	Wolverhampton - (Modular - SR)
8 pts.	and below
	North Cheshire (CHE) - (LRBM)

Sheffield Hallam – (Comb St)
St Mary's (CHE) – (Comb)
West Glamorgan (IHE) – (Comb St)

Diploma of Higher Education courses:
 4pts.   Crewe & Alsager (CHE).

Higher National Diploma courses (with Bus St):
 8pts.   and below Crewe & Alsager (CHE).

Alternative offers:

IB offers: **Birmingham** 30-28 pts; **Staffordshire** 28 pts.

Irish offers: **Liverpool John Moores** CCCCC.

SCE offers: **Glasgow** BBB; **Liverpool John Moores** CCC; **Nottingham Trent** BBB.

CHOOSING YOUR COURSE (See also Ch 1)

> **Subject information:** In addition to the theory and practice of many different sporting activities, students will also cover the psychological aspects of sport and business administration. The geography, economics and sociology of recreation may also be included.

Course highlights: Bedford (CHE) Long-standing reputation for sport and PE studies. **Birmingham** The course covers detailed studies of physical performance and of the role of physical education and sport in society. Practical studies give experience in team and racquet games, swimming, athletics, dance and outdoor pursuits. **Cardiff (IHE)** Practical and theoretical studies well integrated with concern for sporting excellence. Expanding research area with students receiving Dissertation of the Year awards from the Sports Council and National Coaching Federation. Excellent employment record especially in the fields of leisure and recreation, the media, teaching, sport, the armed forces, personnel management, sports administration and coaching. **Crewe & Alsager (CHE)** Recognised strength in sport and exercise science. Strong links with the British Association of Sports Science, Sports Council and other bodies. **Glasgow** (Physio Sports) First year students take courses in biology, chemistry, physics and psychology before concentrating on physiology, biomechanics, neurophysiology and sports psychology. **Liverpool John Moores** Modular degree offers routes in coaching and applied sports science, health sciences and recreation management science. Organisers of international events and conferences. Emphasis on practical sport. European placements. **Loughborough** In year 1 all students take introductory courses in anatomy, biology of physical activity, biomechanics, skill acquisition and psychology plus two other subjects including English, maths, geography as well as sports technology (games/sports). **Staffordshire** Keen sporting tradition, particularly athletics. Options in exercise science or planning and management. **West Sussex (IHE)** Specialisation in sports studies, sports science or recreation management possible. NOW CHECK PROSPECTUSES FOR ALL COURSES.

Study opportunities abroad: Cardiff (IHE) USA NZ G; **Crewe & Alsager (CHE)** (E); **Northumbria** (E); **Nottingham** USA.

Work opportunities abroad: Brighton CAN.

ADMISSIONS INFORMATION

Number of applicants per place (approx): Bangor 15; **Bedford (CHE)** 11; **Birmingham** 25; **Brighton** 26; **Canterbury Christ Church (CHE)** 30; **Cardiff (IHE)** 10; **Crewe & Alsager (CHE)** 10; **Liverpool John Moores** 33; **Northumbria** 40; **Nottingham Trent** 33; **Staffordshire** 30; **West London (IHE)** 7; **West Sussex (IHE)** 30.

General Studies acceptable: Bedford (CHE); Brighton; Cardiff (IHE) (2); Cheltenham & Glos (CHE); Northumbria (2); Staffordshire (2); West Sussex (IHE).

Admissions Tutors' advice: Brighton Strong commitment to sport needed but assessment based on academic results. **Nottingham Trent** Grades A-C in GCSE maths, English and a science subject required.

> **Examples of interview questions:** Applicants' interests in sport and their sporting activities discussed at length. (A high level of sporting achievement is expected at **Loughborough**.)

GAP YEAR ADVICE

Institutions accepting a Gap Year: Most institutions; **Crewe & Alsager (CHE)** Gain relevant experience to strengthen your application; **Liverpool John Moores** Preliminary reading required during year out; **West Sussex (IHE)** Apply before taking a gap year.

Institutions willing to defer entry after A-levels (see Ch 5): Brighton (No); Crewe & Alsager (CHE); Staffordshire (No).

AFTER A-LEVELS ADVICE

Institutions which may accept the same points score after A-levels: Brighton; Cardiff (IHE); Crewe & Alsager (CHE); Northumbria; Nottingham Trent; Sunderland; West Sussex (IHE).

Institutions which may accept under-achieving applicants after A-levels: Liverpool John Moores; Staffordshire.

Institutions with vacancies in Aug/Sept 1992 (see Ch 5): Brighton 14 pts; Manchester Met BC. Some vacancies were declared by a number of colleges of higher education.

ADVICE FOR MATURE STUDENTS

Applicants should demonstrate considerable motivation. A science background is required by some universities and colleges.

STATISTICS

Special subject requirements: 2-3 A-levels with at least one in a mathematical subject.

NB Institutions may raise or lower the level of published offers depending either on the quality or otherwise of individual applications or the numbers of applications received; grades/points offered may be adjusted downwards after A-level results. The level of an offer is not indicative of the quality of a course.

28 pts.	**Warwick** - AAB-ABC (AM Stat)
24 pts.	**Bristol** - ABC (Maths/Stats)
	St Andrews - BBB (Stats - MA)
22 pts.	**Bath** - ACC (Stat)
	Edinburgh - BBC (Econ Stats - MA)
	Glasgow - 22 pts approx (Stats - MA, Soc Sci)
	Heriot-Watt - BBC/AB (Stats) (6 AS)
	London (LSE) - BBC-CCC (Stats)
	London (UC) - BBC-CCC/BB (Statistics; SCORE; Stats/Comp)
	St Andrews - 22 pts approx (Stats Arts)
20 pts.	**Aberystwyth** - BCC/BB (Stats)
	Brunel - BCC-BCD/BB (Stats/Maths) (BTEC Ds+Ms)

Cardiff - BCC/BB (Stats/Man Sci)
Exeter - BCC/BB (Stats/OR)
Keele - BCC-CCC/BB-CC (Joint Hons) (4 AS)
Kent - BCC (CORS)
Lancaster - BCC (Maths/Stats)
Leeds - BCC/BB (All Comb St courses)
Leicester - BCC/BB (Sci Comb)
Liverpool - BCC/AB (Mathl Stats; Maths/Stats; Maths Stats Arts; Stat Comb)
Reading - BCC (Stats)
Sheffield - BCC/AA (Prob Stats) (4 AS)
Sussex - BCC (All Maths/Stats courses)
Swansea - BCC/BB (Stats)
UMIST - BCC/BB (Stats/OR)

18 pts.   **Aberdeen** - CCC-CCD/BC (Stats - BSc)
City - CCC (Stats) (BTEC 4M)
Edinburgh - CCC (Stats)
Glasgow - CCC-CCD/BC (Stats - BSc)
Newcastle - 18-16 pts inc B in maths (Stats; Stats/Comp)
St Andrews - CCC (Stats - BSc)

16 pts.   **Central Lancashire** - 16 pts (Comb St)
Coventry - 16 pts (Stats/Bus St)
London (QMW) - 16 pts approx (Stats)
Strathclyde - CCD/AC-BB (Stats; Stats/Comp) (4 AS)

14 pts.   **Aberdeen** - CDD/BC (Stats)
Bristol UWE - 14-10 pts (Ap Stats)

12 pts.   **Belfast** - CC (Maths/Stats)
Coventry - 12 pts (Stats/Comp; Stats/Geog; Stats/Econ; Stats/Biol)
Dundee - 12 pts (Joint Hons)

10 pts.   **Coventry** - 10 pts (Stats/OR)
Hertfordshire - CD-DD (Comb St)
Liverpool John Moores - 10 pts (Ap Stat/Comp) (4 AS)
Northumbria - 10 pts (App Stats Bl)
Oxford Brookes - CD (Ap Stats - Modular)
Plymouth - (Comb Sci)
Sheffield Hallam - 10 pts (Ap Stat) (4 AS)
Westminster - (Stats OR)

8 pts.   **and below**
East London - (Stats/Maths; Stats/Comp)
Greenwich - (App Stats courses)
Guildhall London - DD (Stats - Modular)
North London - (Stats/Comp; Comb Sci) (4 AS)
Staffordshire - (Comb St)
Westminster - (Soc Sci)

Offers for Foundation, Certificate and Diploma courses (see Ch 5):

Higher National Diploma courses (England and Wales):
4 pts.   **and below** Blackburn (Coll); Bristol UWE; Central Lancashire; Cheltenham & Glos (CHE); Coventry; De Montfort; Glamorgan; Hertfordshire; Leeds Met; Manchester Met; North London; Portsmouth; Sheffield Hallam; Teesside.

College awards (Scotland):
4 pts.   **and below or equivalent** Aberdeen (CC) (Inst of Stats).

Alternative offers:

IB offers: **Aberdeen** (Arts) 30 pts, (Sci) 26 pts; **Brunel** 29 pts; **Exeter** 30 pts; **Glasgow** H555; **Kent** 27 pts, H 12 pts; **Lancaster** 30 pts; **Liverpool** H555; **Newcastle** 28 pts; **St Andrews** 30 pts.

Irish offers: **Aberdeen** (Arts) BBBB, (Sci) BCCCC; **Brunel** BBCCC; **Guildhall London** CCCCC; **Heriot-Watt** BBBBC; **Keele** BBBCC; **Sheffield Hallam** BBBBB.

SCE offers: **Aberdeen** (Arts) BBBB, (Sci) BBBC; **Cardiff** ABBB; **Dundee** ABB/BBBC; **Edinburgh** BBBB/BBBBB; **Glasgow** BBBB (Arts), ABBB (Soc Sci), BBB (BSc); **Guildhall London** BBCCC; **Heriot-Watt** AABB; **Liverpool** ABBB; **Newcastle** AAAB; **St Andrews** BBBB; **Strathclyde** BBBB.

Overseas applicants: Sheffield Hallam English language programme possible.

CHOOSING YOUR COURSE (See also Ch 1)

> **Subject information:** This is a challenging branch of mathematics currently with a shortage of applicants.

Course highlights: Heriot-Watt Common first year with Actuarial Maths and Stats; opportunity to change course at end of second year. **Liverpool John Moores** Course covers computing, operational research and business information systems. **Newcastle** See under **Mathematics. Northumbria** Integration between statistics and industry, particularly communication and business; course particularly suitable for mature students. **St Andrews** See under Arts. **Sheffield Hallam** Experimental design, surveys, applied probability covered in course. Active links with public and private sectors via the final year student project programme. **Strathclyde** Strong in computer technology. NOW CHECK PROSPECTUSES FOR ALL COURSES.

Study opportunities abroad: Swansea (E) FR G IT SP GR P D NL.

ADMISSIONS INFORMATION

Number of applicants per place (approx): Brunel 3; **Coventry** 3; **East London** 3; **Exeter** 5; **Lancaster** 11; **Liverpool John Moores** 6; **Newcastle** 7; **Northumbria** 3; **Sheffield Hallam** 6; **UMIST** 2; **York** 5.

Selection interviews: Birmingham (some); Brunel; Liverpool; Liverpool John Moores (some); Newcastle; Sheffield; Sheffield Hallam; Sussex; UMIST.

General Studies acceptable: Aberdeen; Bristol UWE; Coventry; East London; Exeter; Heriot-Watt; Kent; Lancaster; Liverpool; Liverpool John Moores; North London; Northumbria (2).

Offers to applicants repeating A-levels: Higher Kent, Liverpool, Liverpool John Moores, Newcastle, Swansea; **Same** Birmingham, Brunel.

Admissions Tutors' advice: Liverpool John Moores A sound knowledge of basic mathematical techniques is required. In all cases acceptable evidence of competence in written English is sought.

> **Examples of interview questions:** The A-level syllabus (particularly in mathematics) is discussed and applicant's knowledge of statistics and his/her interest in the subject tested.

GAP YEAR ADVICE

Institutions accepting a Gap Year: Most institutions; **Brunel** Keep A-level maths knowledge up to standard; **Newcastle** Try to keep in touch with the subject.

Institutions willing to defer entry after A-levels (see Ch 5): Bristol UWE; Brunel; Coventry; Newcastle (Not if A-level performance was weak); Plymouth.

AFTER A-LEVELS ADVICE

Institutions which may accept the same points score after A-levels: Birmingham; Brunel; Central Lancashire; Greenwich; Liverpool; Liverpool John Moores; Newcastle; North London; Northumbria; Sheffield Hallam; Ulster; UMIST.

Institutions demanding the actual grades offered after A-levels: Kent.

Institutions which may accept under-achieving applicants after A-levels: Birmingham; Brunel; Exeter.

Institutions with vacancies in Aug/Sept 1992 (see Ch 5): Most institutions including Bristol UWE; Brunel 12 pts; Coventry 6-2 pts; Greenwich 4 pts; Newcastle 16 pts; Northumbria 8-6 pts; Plymouth.

GRADUATE EMPLOYMENT

New Graduates' destinations (percentages) 1991:
Permanent employment: U 77; P 74.
Unemployment: U 19; P 15.
Further studies (all types): U 30; P 4.

SURVEYING (See also Housing and Quantity Surveying)

Special subject requirements: 2 A-levels (mathematics required at Heriot-Watt); English and mathematics at GCSE (grade A-C).

NB Institutions may raise or lower the level of published offers depending either on the quality or otherwise of individual applications or the numbers of applications received; grades/points offered may be adjusted downwards after A-level results. The level of an offer is not indicative of the quality of a course.

30 pts.	**Cambridge** - AAA potential recommended (Land Econ)
24 pts.	**Aberdeen** - BBB (Land Economy)
	Reading - BBB-BCC (Land Man)
22 pts.	**City** - BBC/AA (Prop Val/Fin)
	Reading - BBC (Rur Land Man; Build Surv)
20 pts.	**Salford** - BCC (Build Surv; Prop Dev Man)
18 pts.	**Cranfield (Silsoe)** - CCC (Rur Env Man)
	Heriot-Watt - CCC (Est Man; Build Surv)
	London (Wye) - CCC (Country Man)
	Newcastle - CCC-CCD/BB-BC (Country Man)
	Ulster - CCC/BB (Est Man)
16 pts.	**Liverpool John Moores** - 16 pts (Urb St)
	Northumbria - 16-14 pts (Est Man) (BTEC 2D+3M)
	Nottingham Trent - 16 pts (Urb Est Surv) (4 AS)
	Oxford Brookes - 16 pts inc B (Est Man) (BTEC 5M)
	Sheffield Hallam - 16 pts (Urb Land Econ; Min Est Man) (BTEC 3M)
	Westminster - 16-12 pts (Urb Est Man) (4 AS)
14 pts.	**Brighton** - CDD/CC (Build Surv) (BTEC 4M)
	Central England - 14-12 pts (Build Surv)
	De Montfort (MK) - 14-10 pts (Land Man) (4 AS) (BTEC 1D minimum + 5M/P)
	De Montfort - 14 pts (Building Surv) (4 AS)
	Glasgow Claedonian - 14 pts (Build Surv)
	Greenwich - 14 pts (Est Man) (4 AS) (BTEC 5M)
	Harper Adams (CAg) - CDD/BC (RELM) (BTEC Ds+Ms)
	Kingston - 14 pts (Urb Est Man) (BTEC 5M)

Newcastle - CDD/CC (Surv/Mapp Sci) (BTEC Ds+Ms)
Portsmouth - 14-12 pts (Land man) (4 AS) (BTEC 6M)
12pts. **Bristol UWE** - 12 pts (Build Surv)
Central England - CC (Est Man)
Cirencester (RAC) - CC (Rur Land Man)
East London - CC/12 pts (Land Admin; Surv/Map Sci)
Glamorgan - CC (Urb Est Man) (4 AS) (BTEC 5M)
Liverpool John Moores - 12 pts (Count Mgt; Build Surv) (BTEC 4M)
Paisley - 12 pts (Land Econ)
Plymouth/Seale Hayne (CAg) - DDD/CC (Rur Est Man) (BTEC 3M)
Reading - DDD/CD (Est Man for external students)
South Bank - 12 pts (Est Man) (Also part-time course) (6 AS)
Staffordshire - 12 pts (Val Surv) (BTEC 4-5M)
Stoke on Trent (CT) - 12 pts (Val Surv) (BTEC 4-5M)
10pts. **Sheffield Hallam** - 10 pts (Min Est Man) (4 AS)
8pts. **Bristol UWE** - 8 pts (Val/Est Man)
4pts. **Glamorgan** - (Surv/RD) (BTEC 4M)
Robert Gordon - (Build Surv) (4 AS)
Trinity Carmarthen (CHE) - EE (Rural Env)

Offers for Foundation, Certificate and Diploma courses (see Ch 5):

Higher National Diploma courses:
10pts. Cirencester (RAC).
8pts. **and below** Bristol UWE (Real Estate); De Montfort; Doncaster (Coll) Min Surv; East London; Exeter (CSM); Glamorgan (Min Surv); Hertfordshire; Luton (CHE); North East Wales (IHE); Northumbria; Nottingham Trent); Sheffield Hallam (Land Admin); Sheffield (Shirecliffe Coll); Southampton (IHE); Stoke on Trent (CT).

Higher Diploma courses (Scotland):
Robert Gordon (Build Surv).

Other Diploma courses:
Cirencester (RAC) (Rural Est Man).

Alternative offers:

IB offers: **Newcastle** 30 pts.

SCE offers: **Aberdeen** ABBB; **Heriot-Watt** BBBC.

Overseas applicants: Newcastle List of alumni available. **Oxford Brookes** Written and spoken English must be good. **Sheffield Hallam** (Min Est Surv) Induction and language course available.

CHOOSING YOUR COURSE (See also Ch 1)

Subject information: This is a very broad subject (and career) which includes several specialisms eg, building, surveying, quantity surveying and land and valuation surveying.

Course highlights: Bristol UWE Transfer to Quantity Surveying possible in first year. **Central England** Main emphasis on legal aspects of property valuation, property development and management. **Cirencester (RAC)** Both courses above give RICS exemptions. Very strong links with rural surveying profession; wide range of options. **De Montfort** Unique planning and development option in third year. (Build Surv) Continuous assessment. **Glamorgan** Twenty-five years of contacts with employers. All subjects covered including computer applications; third year sandwich placement counts towards professional practice. **Newcastle** High research standing. Subject of interest to students interested in mapping, engineering, geography and computing. (Surv/Mapp Sci) The course covers land surveying and mapping. First year maths course necessary without A-level maths (see **Admissions Tutors'**

advice). Course relies on computer technology but includes fieldwork, map appreciation and management. **Northumbria** Common first year course with Quantity and Building Surveying. Full-time or sandwich course choice made in second year. Options in conservation, European property studies management. Emphasis on live project work. **Oxford Brookes** Research programmes in property valuation, management of property assets, 1992, property market and property law. **Plymouth** Course covers agriculture and other land use. **Portsmouth** Strong management and property development emphasis. **Sheffield Hallam** (Min Est Surv) Minerals surveying and extraction - unique course in UK. **Westminster** Practical approach to study and projects, simulations and role-playing. NOW CHECK PROSPECTUSES FOR ALL COURSES.

ADMISSIONS INFORMATION

Number of applicants per place (approx): Bristol UWE 11; **Central England** 28; **Cirencester (RAC)** 3; **City** 20; **De Montfort** 20 (Build Surv) 10; **Glamorgan** 6; **Greenwich** 9; **Kingston** 22; **Liverpool John Moores** 15; **Newcastle** 6; **Northumbria** 17; **Nottingham Trent** 17; **Portsmouth** 16; **Sheffield Hallam** 10; **Westminster** 10.

General Studies acceptable: Aberdeen; Cirencester (RAC); Glamorgan; Liverpool John Moores; Portsmouth; Sheffield Hallam; South Bank; Westminster (JMB).

Selection interviews: Bristol UWE (T); Cambridge; East London (some); Glamorgan; Greenwich; Heriot-Watt; Liverpool John Moores; Newcastle.

Admissions Tutors' advice: Cirencester (RAC) Apply at least two years in advance. **City** Candidates are expected to show some mathematical ability (preferably A-level or GCSE (grade A-C) maths). Economics, geography and maths are ideal A-levels. **Greenwich** Motivation towards Surveying necessary. **Newcastle** (Surv/Mapp Sci) Interviewees will be questioned about the course; minimum maths requirement is GCSE Grade B. The course covers land surveying only and motivation is paramount. **Westminster** Highly qualified applicants may find places available in September. Applicants should make an effort to find out about estate management careers.

> **Examples of interview questions:** Why have you chosen Estate Management? What does the career involve? If you asked your friends about your personality, what would they say? Are you motivated? What are the qualities needed to be a successful surveyor? What appeals to you about the course? What do you think about the current housing situation?

GAP YEAR ADVICE

Institutions accepting a Gap Year: Most institutions; **De Montfort** (Build Surv) Gain work experience if possible; **Liverpool John Moores** No. **Westminster** A year in a surveyor's office is highly desirable.

Institutions willing to defer entry after A-levels (see Ch 5): Bristol UWE; Glamorgan; Harper Adams (CAg); Kingston; Newcastle (Surv/Mapp Sci) Prefers applications after A-level results known; Northumbria; Oxford Brookes (No); Portsmouth; Sheffield Hallam; Staffordshire (No); Stoke on Trent (CT).

AFTER A-LEVELS ADVICE

Institutions which may accept the same points score after A-levels: Bristol UWE; Central England; City; De Montfort; East London; Greenwich; Liverpool John Moores; Newcastle (Surv/Mapp Sci); Northumbria; Nottingham Trent; Plymouth; Portsmouth; Sheffield Hallam; South Bank; Ulster; Westminster.

Institutions with vacancies in Aug/Sept 1992 (see Ch 5): Bristol UWE; Glamorgan; Greenwich; Kingston; Newcastle (Surv/Mapp Sci) 10 pts; Sheffield Hallam 16 pts; Staffordshire 10-8 pts; Stoke on Trent (CT) 10-8 pts.

ADVICE FOR MATURE STUDENTS

Practical experience in the profession is an advantage to mature students.

GRADUATE EMPLOYMENT

New Graduates' destinations (percentages) 1991:
Permanent employment: U 78; P 71.
Unemployment: U 19; P 22.
Further studies (all types): U 11; P 7.

TECHNOLOGY (See also Science)

Special subject requirements: A-levels in mathematics and science subjects.

Institutions may raise or lower the level of published offers depending either on the quality or otherwise of individual applications or the numbers of applications received; grades/points offered may be adjusted downwards after A-level results.

NB The level of an offer is not indicative of the quality of a course.

20 pts.	**Brunel** - BCC/AA (Man/Tech)
18 pts.	**Bradford** - CCC/BB (Tech/Man) (BTEC 3M)
14 pts.	**Brunel** - CDD/CC (Des/Tech/Ed) (6 AS)
	Glamorgan - 14 pts (En/Env Tech) (BTEC 3M)
	Strathclyde - BC (BBC 2nd yr entry) (TBS courses)
12 pts.	**and below**
	Anglia (Poly Univ) - (ETMM)
	Glasgow Caledonian - (Tech Inst)
	Glamorgan - 12 pts (Tech/Bus) (4 AS)
	Heriot-Watt/Moray House - (Technology - BEd)
	Humberside - 10 pts (All courses) (BTEC 5M)
	Napier - (Tech; Tech Ind St)
	Oxford Brookes - (Tech/Man)
	Paisley - (Tech Mgt)
	Plymouth - 8 pts (TEC) (4 AS)
	Robert Gordon - EEE (Tech/Bus) (4 AS)
	Sheffield Hallam - (Biomed Tech)
	South Bank - DD (Proc Tech/Mgt; Tech Man) (4 AS) (BTEC 3M)
	Staffordshire - DD (Tech Man) (BTEC 3M)
	Strathclyde/Jordanhill - (Tech/Ed)
	Sunderland - (Tech Man; Env Tech)
	Swansea (IHE) - (Tech Man)
	Wolverhampton - (All courses)

Diploma of Higher Education courses:
4 pts.   Doncaster (Coll) (Tech and Society); Manchester Met; Swansea (IHE) (High Tech Man)

Alternative offers:

IB offers: **Bradford** 24 pts; **Brunel** 28-25 pts; **South Bank** 24 pts; **Staffordshire** 27 pts

Irish offers: **South Bank** CCCC.

CHOOSING YOUR COURSE (See also Ch 1)

> **Subject information:** These are broad courses covering various aspects of technology and will overlap into manufacturing and production engineering.

Course highlights: Glamorgan Language and sandwich options available. **Staffordshire** Course taught in School of Computing. NOW CHECK PROSPECTUSES FOR ALL COURSES.

Study opportunities abroad: Anglia (Poly Univ) (E); **Robert Gordon** (E).

ADMISSIONS INFORMATION

Admissions Tutors' advice: Glamorgan Applicants must be prepared for a numerical and analytical course.

> **Examples of interview questions:** Applicants should be fully aware of the breadth of this subject and familiar with the different courses on offer. (See also under the various **Engineering** subject tables.)

GAP YEAR ADVICE

Institutions accepting a Gap Year: Most institutions; South Bank; Staffordshire; Swansea IHE) (No).

Institutions willing to defer entry after A-levels (see Ch 5): Humberside; Robert Gordon; South Bank; Staffordshire; Swansea (IHE).

AFTER A-LEVELS ADVICE

Institutions with vacancies in Aug/Sept 1992 (see Ch 5): Most institutions; Glamorgan 12 pts; Humberside 12-8 pts; Robert Gordon; Staffordshire 8-6 pts.

TEXTILE COURSES (Design/Management/Marketing/ Technology (See also Textile Fashion))

Special subject requirements: A-level art required in some cases or at GCSE (grade A-C) for Design courses. Mathematics/science A-levels appropriate for Technology courses. Mathematics A-level or GCSE (grade A-C) for Management/Marketing courses.

NB Institutions may raise or lower the level of published offers depending either on the quality or otherwise of individual applications or the numbers of applications received; grades/points offered may be adjusted downwards after A-level results. The level of an offer is not indicative of the quality of a course.

20 pts.	**UMIST** - BCC (MMT; Tex Sci/Tech; Courses with languages) (BTEC 6M)
18 pts.	**Leeds** - CCC (Tex St; Tex Chem; Tex Des; Tex Man) (BTEC 6M)
	UMIST - CCC/BB (All courses except under **20 pts**) (BTEC 5M)
16 pts.	**Plymouth** - CCD (Des Arts)
14 pts.	**De Montfort** - 14-12 pts (TK Tech)
	Manchester Met - 14-12 pts (Fash Des/Tech) (BTEC Ds+Ms)
12 pts.	**Bretton Hall (CHE)** - CC-EE (Fashion) (4 AS)
	Kidderminster (Coll) - CC (Floor Covering Design)
	Manchester Met - 12 pts (Cloth Man/Tech; Cloth Eng)
	Nottingham Trent - 12 pts approx (Cloth/Tex)
10 pts.	**Heriot-Watt** - CD (Man Comp St; Qual Man; Ind Des)

8 pts. **Manchester Met** - (App Cons St)
Robert Gordon - (Food/Tex/Con St)
4 pts. **Bolton (IHE)** - EE (Text) (Associateship of the Textile Institute) (4 AS)
Bradford & Ilkley (CmC) - (Euro Text St)
Huddersfield - (Tex Manu)
London (Inst) - (Clothing)
Heriot-Watt/Scottish (CText) - EE (Text Cloth; Clothing; Comb St; Tex Mark)

Diploma of Higher Education courses:
4 pts.   Bath (CHE) (Text Design).

Offers for Foundation, Certificate and Diploma courses (see Ch 5):

Higher National Diploma courses:
4 pts.   **and below** Bolton (IHE); Cleveland (CA); De Montfort; Derby; Jacob Kramer (Coll) (Clothing); Kent (IAD) (Cloth Tech); London (Chelsea), (CDT), (Inst) (Fashion; Fashion Management); Manchester Met; Nottingham Trent; Stockport (CT); West Sussex (CD).

Alternative offers:

Irish offers: **De Montfort** CCCCC; **UMIST** ABBBBC.

SCE offers: **Heriot-Watt** CCC.

CHOOSING YOUR COURSE (See also Ch 1)

> **Subject information:** Textile technologists and managers are in short supply and these courses offer those students interested in applied science or management an opportunity to gain the necessary skills and knowledge. Low grades are usually acceptable.

Course highlights: Bolton (IHE) Recognised centre of excellence for textiles. Close ties with national employers who frequently sponsor students. Foundation and bridging course for those without the necessary qualifications. **Huddersfield** and **Leeds** Textile design and technology. **Leeds** All courses have very strong industrial contacts. **Manchester Met** (Cloth Eng/Man) Joint course with UMIST. Large circle of contacts and very good employment prospects. Teaching combines experience and expertise of the two faculties – Textile and Fashion, and Clothing Design and Technology – and ranges from innovative design to applied technology and business studies. (App Cons St) Options in clothing, housing or food. **Plymouth** (Des Arts) Two streams, textile or environmental arts. **Wolverhampton** Marketing, management and carpet technology. NOW CHECK PROSPECTUSES FOR ALL COURSES.

Study opportunities abroad: Bolton (IHE) (E); **De Montfort** (E) HK SA G; **Heriot-Watt** HK NZ NL; **Manchester Met** (E).

Work opportunities abroad: Huddersfield FR G; **Manchester Met** FR AUS HK G P.

ADMISSIONS INFORMATION

Number of applicants per place (approx): Bolton (IHE) 2; **De Montfort** 6; **Heriot-Watt** 2; **Huddersfield** 7; **Kidderminster (Coll)** 3; **Leeds** (Tex Design) 6, (Tex Man) 8, (Tex Chem) 5; **Manchester Met** (Cloth Eng Man) 10; **UMIST** (Cloth Man) 4, (Ind Des (Tex) 6.

General Studies acceptable: Heriot-Watt; Huddersfield (JMB); Kidderminster (Coll); Leeds; Manchester Met; UMIST.

Offers to applicants repeating A-levels: Same Heriot-Watt, Leeds (Tex Design; Tex Man).

Admissions Tutors' advice: Manchester Met Course in Clothing Engineering offered in conjunction with UMIST.

> **Examples of interview questions:** Applicants should be very familiar with the content of each textile course and be able to discuss reasons for their choices and their career interests. Questions on properties of different fabrics.

GAP YEAR ADVICE

Institutions accepting a Gap Year: Most institutions; **Heriot-Watt** Work in textiles useful. **Kidderminster (Coll)** Keep up the drawing. **Manchester Met** (Fash Des/Tech) A foundation course in art and design would be useful but not essential. **UMIST** Talk to Admissions Tutor first.

Institutions willing to defer entry after A-levels (see Ch 5): Heriot-Watt/Scottish (CText); Manchester Met (Fash Des/Tech); UMIST (Prefer not).

AFTER A-LEVELS ADVICE

Institutions which may accept the same points score after A-levels: Bolton (IHE); Leeds (all courses); Manchester Met; UMIST.

Institutions with vacancies in Aug/Sept 1992 (see Ch 5): Heriot-Watt/ Scottish (CText) 4 pts; Manchester Met (Fash Des/Tech) 10 pts; UMIST 16-14 pts.

GRADUATE EMPLOYMENT

New Graduates' destinations (percentages) 1991:
Permanent employment: P 79; C 86.
Unemployment: P 16; C 9.
Further studies (all types): P 28; C 19.

TEXTILE FASHION (See also Textile courses)

Special subject requirements: none (Entry is with A-levels, a Foundation Art course or BTEC National Diploma. Only about eight per cent of candidates enter with A-levels only.

Applications are normally submitted through the Art and Design Admissions Registry (ADAR) scheme. (See Chapter 3.)

This subject area covers woven and printed textiles, fashion, embroidery or contour fashion.

Institutions may raise or lower the level of published offers depending either on the quality or otherwise of individual applications or the numbers of applications received; grades/points offered may be adjusted downwards after A-level results. The level of an offer is not indicative of the quality of a course.

Institutions offering courses: Bretton Hall (CHE); Brighton; Bristol UWE; Buckinghamshire (Coll); Central England; Central Lancashire (Fashion; Fashion Promotion); Cheltenham & Glos (CHE); De Montfort (Knitwear Des/Prod); East London (Fashion Design with Marketing); Kent (IAD) (European Fashion Prod Dev); Kidderminster (Coll) (Carpet Design); Kingston; Liverpool John Moores; London (Inst - Camberwell CA), (Central St Martin's SA); Loughborough (CA); Manchester Met; Middlesex; Northumbria (Fashion Marketing); Nottingham Trent; Plymouth; Ravensbourne (CDC); Salford (UC) (Des Practice); Somerset (CT); West Surrey (CAD) (Textiles); Westminster; Winchester (SA).

Higher National Diploma courses:
4 pts.   and below Berkshire (CA); Bournemouth; Bristol UWE; Buckinghamshire (CHE); Cheltenham & Glos (CHE); Chichester (CT) (Beauty Therapy); Cleveland (CA); Derbyshire (CHE); Dewsbury & Batley (CA); Epsom (SA); Huddersfield; Kent (IAD); London (Inst - Chelsea), (CFash); South Manchester (Coll) (Beauty Therapy); Southampton (IHE); Worthing (Northbrook CD).

CHOOSING YOUR COURSE (See also Ch 1)

> **Subject information:** These specialised degree courses almost always follow Foundation Art courses.

Course highlights: Westminster Good contacts with fashion industry through placements, competitions, projects, visiting lecturers from industry. Subsidiary subjects include business studies, fashion jewellery and knitwear design. International contacts with Italy. Industrial sponsorhips. **Ravensbourne (CDC)** 100 first choice applicants for 34 places. Places cannot be held open for students taking a gap year. NOW CHECK PROSPECTUSES FOR ALL COURSES.

Work opportunities abroad: Brighton; Central Lancashire EUR; **Liverpool John Moores** USA FR; **Nottingham Trent** (Knitwear); **Ravensbourne (CDC)** IT; **Westminster** IT.

ADMISSIONS INFORMATION

Number of applicants per place (approx): 12; **Brighton** 6; **Central England** 12; **Central Lancashire** 4; **Cheltenham & Glos (CHE)** 7; **De Montfort** 5; **Heriot-Watt/Scottish (CText)** 6; **Huddersfield** 4; **Loughborough (CA)** 7; **Manchester Met** 3; **Middlesex** 5; **Northumbria** 8; **West Surrey (CAD)** 8; **Winchester (SA)** 3; **Wolverhampton** 2.

Selection interviews: All institutions; East London (T).

> **Examples of interview questions:** Questions largely originate from student's portfolio.

GRADUATE EMPLOYMENT

New Graduates' destinations (percentages) 1991: See under **Art (Design)**.

THREE DIMENSIONAL DESIGN

Special subject requirements: none. Entry via Foundation Art course. Selection by interview and scrutiny of portfolio of student's work.

Applications should be made to the Art and Design Admissions Registry (ADAR). (See Chapter 2)

Institutions may raise or lower the level of published offers depending either on the quality or otherwise of individual applications or the numbers of applications received; grades/points offered may be adjusted downwards after A-level results.

Institutions offering courses:

Silversmithing: Central England; De Montfort; Guildhall London; Loughborough (CA); Sheffield Hallam.

Silver/Metal Jewellery: Buckinghamshire (CHE); Central England; Guildhall London; London (Inst - Camberwell SA, Central St Martin's SA); Loughborough (CA); Manchester Met; Wimbledon (SA).

Footwear Design: De Montfort.

Three Dimensional and/or Industrial Design (Engineering): Cardiff (IHE); Central England; De Montfort; Humberside; Kent (IAD) (Model Making); Leeds Met; London (Inst - Central St Martin's SA); Manchester Met; Plymouth; Ravensbourne (CDC) Product Design; Salford (UC); Sheffield Hallam (Packaging Design/Promotion; Prod Des); Teesside.

Furniture: Buckinghamshire (Coll); Central England; De Montfort; Kingston; Leeds Met; Loughborough (CA); Middlesex; Nottingham Trent; Ravensbourne (CDC).

Ceramics/Glass: Bath (CHE); Bristol UWE; Buckinghamshire (CHE); Cardiff (IHE); Central England; De Montfort; London (Inst - Camberwell SA, Central St Martin's SA); Loughborough (CA); Middlesex; Sunderland; West Surrey (CA); Wolverhampton.

Interior Design: Brighton; Buckinghamshire (CHE); Cardiff (IHE); Central England; De Montfort; Kingston; Leeds Met; Manchester Met; Middlesex; North London; Ravensbourne (CDC); Teesside.

Wood/Metal/Ceramics/Plastics: Brighton; Bristol UWE; Manchester Met; Northumbria; Wolverhampton.

Theatre: Central England; London (Inst - Central St Martin's SA); Nottingham Trent; Wimbledon (SA).

Glass: Stourbridge (CT).

Courses with A-level entry:
 12pts.   **Napier** - CC (Ind des Tech)

Offers for Foundation, Certificate and Diploma courses (see Ch 5):

Higher National Diploma courses:
 4pts.   **and below**

Ceramics: Cornwall (CFE); Croydon (Coll); Staffordshire; Swansea (IHE); Westminster Harrow (Coll).

Silversmithing: Kent (IAD).

Multi-Disciplinary Design: Cardiff (IHE); Portsmouth (CA); Stockport (CT); West Sussex (CD).

Design Crafts: Carmarthenshire (CT); Central England; Crewe & Alsager (IHE); Cumbria (CA); Derbyshire (CHE); Epsom (SA); Hertfordshire (CD); Medway (CD); North East Wales (IHE); Swansea (IHE) (Architectural Stained Glass).

Spatial Design: Berkshire (CA); Bournemouth/Poole (CA); Central Lancashire; Dewsbury & Batley (CT); Hastings (CA) Exhibition Des; Humberside; Kent (IAD); London (Inst - Chelsea), Guildhall London/CFurn; Medway (CD); Newcastle-upon-Tyne (CT); Salford (UC); Sheffield Hallam; Suffolk (CFHE).

Theatre Design: Croydon (Coll); Liverpool (Mabel Fletcher CT); London/Guildhall.

CHOOSING YOUR COURSE (See also Ch 1)

Subject information: Foundation art courses are required prior to specialised studies in this wide-ranging field of design which can range from architectural stained glass and stage design to silverware and jewellery.

Course highlights: Bournemouth The course in European Business Development includes design elements. NOW CHECK PROSPECTUSES FOR ALL COURSES.

Study opportunities abroad: Middlesex (Jewellery/Ceramics) EUR.

ADMISSIONS INFORMATION

Number of applicants per place (approx): Bath (CHE) (Ceramics) 4; **Brighton** (Interior) 4, (Wood) 3; **Bristol UWE** (Cer) 3; **De Montfort** 3; **Leeds Met** (3D Design) 5; **London (Inst - Camberwell SA)** 2, (Ceramics) 3, **(Central St Martin's SA)** (Ceramics) 2, (Jewellery) 2; **Loughborough** (Furn) 1, (Cer) 4, (Silver) 3; **Manchester Met** 5; **Middlesex** (3D Design) 4, (Jewellery) 4, (Int Des) 4; **Nottingham Trent** (Theatre Des) 5 - ADAR first choice; **Ravensbourne (CDC)** Furniture 110 first choice applicants; **Wolverhampton** (Wood/Metal/ Plastics) 4.

Admissions Tutors' advice: Napier An ability in art and design is sought.

> **Examples of interview questions:** Questions focus on the art work presented in the student's portfolio.

GRADUATE EMPLOYMENT

New Graduates' destinations (percentages) 1991: See under **Art (Design).**

TIMBER TECHNOLOGY

Special subject requirements: an A-level in a science or technology subject; GCSE (grade A-C) English and mathematics.

Institutions may raise or lower the level of published offers depending either on the quality or otherwise of individual applications or the numbers of applications received; grades/points offered may be adjusted downwards after A-level results. The level of an offer is not indicative of the quality of a course.

12 pts.   **Buckinghamshire (CHE)** - DDD (Wood Tech)
4 pts.   **Buckinghamshire (CHE)** - EE minimum preferred (FPT)

One science subject is required for the FPT - Forest Products Technology (formerly Timber Technology) course with an annual intake of 30 from 150 applicants. Candidates are interviewed. Offers are made on the basis of individuals rather than points.

CHOOSING YOUR COURSE (See also Ch 1)

> **Subject information:** This subject is now referred to as Forest Products Technology at Buckinghamshire (CHE) and provides a study of timber, its uses and the associated technology.

Course highlights: Buckinghamshire (CHE) Sponsorship offered by leading companies to undergraduates.

Study opportunities abroad: Buckinghamshire (CHE) (E) G FR P SP F SW IRE.

ADMISSIONS INFORMATION

Admissions Tutors' advice: Buckinghamshire (CHE) (FPT) Candidates must show a genuine interest for this unusual course and be fairly outgoing in character. A blend of interest, both business and scientific, is important. Try to get to know the timber-using industries. Careers teachers generally overstate the forestry or craft element of the course. The subject is not covered at school except in a minimal way in A-level woodwork. (Wood Tech) Covers engineering, preservation and processing.

> **Examples of interview questions:** Applicants should be fully aware of the content of the course (note **Admissions Tutors' advice**)

TOPOGRAPHIC SCIENCE

Special subject requirements: mathematics at GCSE (grade A-C), mathematics or physics at A-level.

Institutions may raise or lower the level of published offers depending either on the quality or otherwise of individual applications or the numbers of applications received; grades/points offered may be adjusted downwards after A-level results. The level of an offer is not indicative of the quality of a course.

| 20 pts. | **Swansea** - BCC-CCC/AB (All joint courses) |
| 16 pts. | **Glasgow** - CCD/BC (Topog Sci) |

CHOOSING YOUR COURSE (See also Ch 1)

> **Subject information:** This very specialised area focuses on mapping and geography.

> **Examples of interview questions:** Questions often asked on content of all courses in this subject. Applicants must be able to give sound reasons for their course choice.

TOWN AND COUNTRY PLANNING (See also Environmental Science/Studies and Development Studies)

Special subject requirements: 2-3 A-levels; mathematics at GCSE (grade A-C).

NB Institutions may raise or lower the level of published offers depending either on the quality or otherwise of individual applications or the numbers of applications received; grades/points offered may be adjusted downwards after A-level results. The level of an offer is not indicative of the quality of a course.

22 pts.	**East Anglia** - BBC-BCC/BB (All Development Studies Courses)
20 pts.	**Aston** - BCC (Public Policy) (Comb Hons)
	Belfast - BCC/BB (Env Plan)
	London (UC) - BCC (Planning)
	Newcastle - BCC-BCD/BB (Town Plan) (BTEC Ms)
	Strathclyde - BCC (Planning)
18 pts.	**Cardiff** - BCD/AB (City Plan) (BTEC 4M)
	Manchester - 18 pts approx (Town Plan)
	Sheffield - CCC (Urb Studs)
16 pts.	**Liverpool John Moores** - 16 pts (Urban Plan)
14 pts.	**Dundee** - CDD (Plan)
	Sheffield Hallam - (TCP) (BTEC 4M)
12 pts.	**Bristol UWE** - DDD/BC (TC Plan; Env Q/RM)
	Heriot-Watt - CC (Town Plan)

Leeds Met - CC (Urb Dev)
Oxford Brookes - DDD/CC (Plan St courses – Modular) (4 AS) (BTEC 4M)
Westminster - CDE/CD (Urb Plan St)
10 pts. **Central England** - 10 pts (Env/Plan)
Cheltenham & Glos (CHE) - 10 pts (Countryside) (6 AS) (BTEC 2D+2M)
8 pts. **and below**
Coventry - (Plan/Rec; Rec Country; Plan/LED)
Middlesex - (Mod) (4 AS)
South Bank - EEE/DD (Town Plan) (DD part-time course) (BTEC 3M)
Worcester (CHE) - (Comb - URB)

Offers for Foundation, Certificate and Diploma courses (see Ch 5):

Higher National Diploma courses:
4 pts. **and below** Sheffield Hallam (Land Admin).

Alternative offers:

EB offers: **Newcastle** 60%.

IB offers: **Belfast** H655 S555; **Cardiff** 26 ptsl; **Newcastle** 30 pts; **South Bank** 24 pts; **Sheffield Hallam** 30-25 pts.

Irish offers: **Bristol UWE** CCCC; **Dundee** CCCCC; **Newcastle** CCCCC; **Sheffield** CCCCC; **South Bank** CCCC; **Westminster** CCCCC.

SCE offers: **Belfast** ABBB; **Bristol UWE** BBC; **Cardiff** BBCC; **Dundee** BBBC; **Heriot-Watt** BBB + interview; **Newcastle** CCCC; **Strathclyde** BBBC.

Overseas applicants: Oxford Brookes, **South Bank** Good spoken English essential.

CHOOSING YOUR COURSE (See also Ch 1)

Subject information: These courses, which are all very similar, lead to qualification as a member of the Royal Town Planning Institute. Courses usually include a year out. This is an ideal course for the geographer. The change in employment prospects for graduate planners has undergone a remarkable transformation in recent years. There is now a considerable shortage of planners in view of the increased demand by the local authorities and private sector. Increasingly consultants, developers and other property-related organisations such as major retailers, are employing qualified planning graduates and the net result is that demand is far out-stripping supply. In response, the planning schools have increased their intakes but there would appear to be a significant shortage for the foreseeable future.

It also may be worth mentioning that the new 3 + 1 format of courses provides an opportunity for students who are well trained in environmental matters to leave such courses after three years with an honours degree, but without the necessity of completing the BTP for professional qualification. There are also increasing job opportunities for such students. See also **Urban Studies**.

Course highlights: Cardiff Largest university planning school in UK with widest range of specialist options eg, housing, developing countries, transport, information systems. **Cheltenham & Glos (CHE)** Balance between social, economic and environmental aspects of countryside. **Coventry** Foreign language options available. **Dundee** Final year options include housing policy, minerals planning employment, agriculture and forestry, countryside planning and urban design. **Liverpool John Moores** (Urban Plan) Urban renewal, housing and transport options. **Newcastle** Options include housing, landscape, European property development. Employer contact in project work. Professional practice placements. 100% employment record over 15 years. **Sheffield** The three major subjects studied in the first year are urban studies, the design of urban areas and one from economics, social history, geography, politics or sociology and social policy. **South Bank** Options in the fourth year include computing, transport, housing, urban design, rural land management. **Westminster** Four main themes of this three-year course cover the environment and society, public intervention, policy and skills for planning. Later studies include social, housing, housing and transport policy. NOW CHECK PROSPECTUSES FOR ALL COURSES.

Study opportunities abroad: Dundee (E); **Heriot-Watt** (E); **Newcastle** (E) FR G IT.

Work opportunities abroad: Heriot-Watt.

ADMISSIONS INFORMATION

Number of applicants per place (approx): Bristol UWE 6; **Cardiff** 4; **Central England** 8; **Cheltenham & Glos (CHE)** 4; **Dundee** 6; **Heriot-Watt** 9; **Middlesex** 4; **Newcastle** 9.

General Studies acceptable: Aston; Bristol UWE; Central England; Cheltenham & Glos (CHE) (2); Heriot-Watt; Leeds Met; Newcastle (2) Sheffield Hallam (2).

Selection interviews: Aston; Bristol UWE; Dundee (borderline cases only); Heriot-Watt; Leeds Met; Newcastle (T); South Bank; Swansea (some).

Offers to applicants repeating A-levels: Higher Bristol UWE, Central England, East Anglia, Newcastle; **Same** Leeds Met, Oxford Brookes, South Bank.

Admissions Tutors' advice: Central England Because this is not an A-level subject, we have discovered that A-level grades are not a good guide to potential. Interviews are therefore important – also motivation, knowledge of the subject and environmental awareness. **Westminster** Less strong candidates may be made a higher offer.

> **Examples of interview questions:** If you were replanning your home county for the future, what points would you consider? How are statistics used in urban planning? How do you think the problem of inner cities can be solved? Have you visited the local planning office? What problems are they facing at present?

GAP YEAR ADVICE

Institutions accepting a Gap Year: Most institutions; **Cardiff** Work experience in a planning office valuable; **Heriot-Watt** Work experience useful; **Sheffield Hallam, Oxford Brookes** Not with two-year deferred entry.

Institutions willing to defer entry after A-levels (see Ch 5): Cheltenham & Glos (CHE) (Prefer not); Heriot-Watt; Newcastle (No); Oxford Brookes; Sheffield Hallam; South Bank.

AFTER A-LEVELS ADVICE

Institutions which may accept the same points score after A-levels: Bristol UWE; Cardiff; Cheltenham & Glos (CHE); Newcastle; South Bank.

Institutions demanding the actual grades offered after A-levels: Dundee.

Institutions which may accept under-achieving applicants after A-levels: Bristol UWE; Cheltenham & Glos (CHE); Newcastle; South Bank.

Institutions with vacancies in Aug/Sept 1992 (see Ch 5): Cheltenham & Glos (CHE) 8 pts; Dundee 12 pts; Heriot-Watt 14 pts.

ADVICE FOR MATURE STUDENTS

Previous academic study is important and also experience in the profession.

518 – TOWN AND COUNTRY PLANNING

GRADUATE EMPLOYMENT

New Graduates' destinations (percentages) 1991:
Permanent employment: U 76; P 68; C 66.
Unemployment: U 18; P 19; C 13.
Further studies (all types): U 34; P 30; C 8.

TOXICOLOGY

Special subject requirements: Chemistry and at least one other science at A-level.

Institutions may raise or lower the level of published offers depending either on the quality or otherwise of individual applications or the numbers of applications received; grades/points offered may be adjusted downwards after A-level results. The level of an offer is not indicative of the quality of a course.

18pts.   London (Sch Pharm) - CCC (Tox/Pharm)

Other courses containing a major component of Toxicology are as follows:
        Aberdeen - (Pharmacology - option in Toxicology)
        East London - (Pharmacology)
        Hull - (Chemistry with Analytical Bio-Organic Chemistry and Toxicology)
        South Bank - (Occupational Hygiene)
        Surrey - (Biochemistry)

CHOOSING YOUR COURSE (See also Ch 1)

> **Subject information:** This is the study of the adverse effects of chemicals on living systems.

Course highlights: London (Sch Pharm) Well equipped, good research department. Four-year sandwich course with placements in UK or Europe. Job prospects excellent. NOW CHECK PROSPECTUSES FOR ALL COURSES.

ADMISSIONS INFORMATION

Number of applicants per place (approx): London (Sch Pharm) 5.

GAP YEAR ADVICE

Institutions accepting a Gap Year: London (Sch Pharm)

TRANSPORT MANAGEMENT AND PLANNING

Special subject requirements: 2 A-levels and GCSE (grade A-C) mathematics.

NB Institutions may raise or lower the level of published offers depending either on the quality or otherwise of individual applications or the numbers of applications received; grades/points offered may be adjusted downwards after A-level results. The level of an offer is not indicative of the quality of a course.

20 pts.	**Cardiff** - BCC–CCC/BB (Int Tran) (BTEC Ds+Ms)
18 pts.	**Aston** - CCC/AB (Tran Man)
	Guildhall London - CCC/DD (Bus St)
16 pts.	**Loughborough** - CCD/CC (Trans/Man 3 and 4)
	Ulster - CCD/BC (Trans) (AS des tech/maths/phys/biol/chem/ mod lang)
14 pts.	**Huddersfield** - CDD/CC (Trans/Dist)
10 pts.	**Plymouth** - 10 pts (Transport) (4 AS)
8 pts.	**South Bank** - (Highway Engineering - see under **Engineering (Civil)**)
4 pts.	**Coventry** - (Trans Design)
	Napier - (Trans Eng) (See **Admissions Tutors' advice**)
	Southampton (IHE) - (Int Trans)
	Swansea (IHE) - (Trans Man)

Diploma of Higher Education courses:
    4 pts.   Plymouth.

Offers for Foundation, Certificate and Diploma courses (see Ch 5):

Higher National Diploma courses (in Business Studies):
    4 pts.   **and below** Bournemouth; Glamorgan; Northumbria (Transport and Physical Distribution); North Worcestershire (Coll); Plymouth; Swansea (IHE) (Transport).

Alternative offers:

IB offers: **Cardiff** 28 pts.

CHOOSING YOUR COURSE (See also Ch 1)

Subject information: This is a specialised branch of business studies with many applications on land, sea and air. It is not as popular as the less specialised business studies courses but just as relevant and will provide the student with an excellent introduction to management and its problems.

Course highlights: Aston Course covers road, rail, air, maritime transport, inland waterways, pipeline (ie passenger and freight movements). **Huddersfield** Emphasis on road freight transport and distribution. NOW CHECK PROSPECTUSES FOR ALL COURSES.

Study opportunities abroad: Aston (E).

ADMISSIONS INFORMATION

Number of applicants per place (approx): Aston 4; **Cardiff** 8; **Huddersfield** 4; **Loughborough** 11.

General Studies acceptable: Aston (2); Cardiff; Huddersfield.

Selection interviews: Loughborough (some).

Offers to applicants repeating A-levels: Higher Cardiff; **Same** Aston.

Admissions Tutors' advice: Huddersfield While the course is aimed at students looking for a career in private sector freight transport management, a career in public sector and passenger transport is possible. **Napier** Transportation Engineering is one of the main activities of civil engineering covering planning, design, construction of roads and airports. (See also under **Engineering (Civil)**).

Examples of interview questions: A sound knowledge of the transport industry (land, sea and air) is likely to be important at interview. Reading round the subject is also important, as are any contacts with management staff in the industries.

GAP YEAR ADVICE

Institutions accepting a Gap Year: Plymouth.

Institutions willing to defer entry after A-levels (see Ch 5): Plymouth.

AFTER A-LEVELS ADVICE

Institutions which may accept the same points score after A-levels: Aston.

Institutions with vacancies in Aug/Sept 1992 (see Ch 5): Plymouth.

GRADUATE EMPLOYMENT

New Graduates' destinations (percentages) 1991:
Permanent employment: P 76.
Unemployment: P 15.
Further studies (all types): P 12.

URBAN STUDIES (See also **Town and Country Planning** and **Development Studies**)

Special subject requirements: GCSE (grade A-C) mathematics.

NB Institutions may raise or lower the level of published offers depending either on the quality or otherwise of individual applications or the numbers of applications received; grades/points offered may be adjusted downwards after A-level results. The level of an offer is not indicative of the quality of a course.

18 pts.	**Kent** - CCC/BC (Urb Studs)
	Nottingham - CCC (Urb Plan Man)
	Sheffield - CCC (Urb Studs) (BTEC 4M)
	Sussex - CCC/BC (Urban/CCS)
16 pts.	**Liverpool John Moores** - 16 pts (Urb Plan)
	Middlesex - 16-12 pts (Urb St)
14 pts.	**Sheffield Hallam** - 14 pts (URP) (BTEC 4M)
12 pts.	**Bolton (IHE)** - DDD/CD (Comb St)
	Leeds Met - 12 pts (Urb Dev)
	Westminster - CDE/CD (Urb Plan St) (4 AS)
8 pts.	and below
	Anglia (Poly Univ) - (RDHS)
	Edge Hill (CHE) - (UPPR)
	North London - (Urban St)
	Swansea (IHE) - (Comb St)
	Worcester (CHE) - (Comb St)

Alternative offers:

IB offers: **Sheffield Hallam** 30-25 pts.

CHOOSING YOUR COURSE (See also Ch 1)

> **Subject information:** This is a broad study of the social, economic and political processes underlying contemporary problems in towns and cities. See also **Town Planning**.

Course highlights: Sheffield Periods of work experience spent in local authority planning departments. **Liverpool John Moores** See **Town and Country Planning. Westminster** Focus on policy-making and planning in an urban setting. NOW CHECK PROSPECTUSES FOR ALL COURSES.

Study opportunities abroad: Sheffield (E).

ADMISSIONS INFORMATION

Number of applicants per place (approx): Liverpool John Moores 10; **Middlesex** 2; **Sheffield** 8; **Swansea (IHE)** 2; **Westminster** 5.

General Studies acceptable: Aston; Liverpool John Moores; Sheffield Hallam (2); Westminster (2).

Offers to applicants repeating A-levels: Same Aston.

> **Examples of interview questions:** See under **Town and Country Planning**.

GAP YEAR ADVICE

Institutions accepting a Gap Year: Sheffield Hallam.

Institutions willing to defer entry after A-levels (see Ch 5): Sheffield Hallam.

AFTER A-LEVELS ADVICE

Institutions accepting the same points score after A-levels: Aston.

Institutions with vacancies in Aug/Sept 1992 (see Ch 5): A large number of vacancies were declared with some popular universities asking 14 pts.

VETERINARY SCIENCE

Special subject requirements: 3 A-levels in mathematics/science subjects. Chemistry or physical science 'required'.

NB Institutions may raise or lower the level of published offers depending either on the quality or otherwise of individual applications or the numbers of applications received; grades/points offered may be adjusted downwards after A-level results. The level of an offer is not indicative of the quality of a course.

30 pts.	**Cambridge** - AAA potential recommended (Vet Med)
28 pts.	**Bristol** - AAB (Vet Sci) (2 AS maths/phys/comp + 1 other) (BTEC Ds)
	Edinburgh - AAB (Vet Med) (2 AS – chem + a science at A-level + another science at AS)

Glasgow - AAB (Vet Sci) (Or 2 A-levels + 2 AS-levels in approved subjects)
Liverpool - AAB (Vet Sci) (Ref AAB but not most important factor) (2 AS - non-science acceptable)
London (RVC) - AAB (Vet Sci)

Alternative offers:

IB offers: **Bristol** 32 pts inc H766; **Edinburgh** 34 pts inc 6/7 in science subjs; **Glasgow** H766; **Liverpool** H666; **London (RVC)** H777-H666.

SCE offers: **Edinburgh** AAABB; **Glasgow** AAABB (Minimum).

Author's note: This is the most intensely competitive course and, as in the case of Medicine, one or two offers and three rejections are not uncommon. As a result of this a newsletter on the *Selection of Veterinary Students* was published by the Royal College of Veterinary Surgeons. In this a number of points are raised which are still relevant to applicants and advisers:

(a) Every candidate for a veterinary degree course should be advised to spend a suitable period with a veterinarian in practice.

(b) A period spent in veterinary work may reveal a hitherto unsuspected allergy or sensitivity following contact with various animals.

(c) Potential applicants should be under no illusions about the difficulty of the tasks they have set themselves... five applicants for every available place... with no likelihood of places being increased at the present time.

(d) There are so many candidates who can produce the necessary level of scholastic attainment that other considerations have to be taken into account in making the choice. This is current practice. Headteachers' reports and details of applicants' interests, activities and background are very relevant and are taken fully into consideration... applicants are reminded to include details of periods of time spent with veterinary surgeons.

(e) Any applicant who has not received an offer but who achieves the grades required for admission ought to write as soon as the results are known to the schools and enquire about the prospects of entry at the clearing stage.

CHOOSING YOUR COURSE (See also Ch 1)

Subject information: These are very popular and academically demanding courses for which some work experience prior to application is obligatory. All courses have much the same content, but check with prospectuses for all courses.

ADMISSIONS INFORMATION

Number of applicants per place (approx): Bristol 15; **Edinburgh** 15; **Glasgow** 15; **Liverpool** 17; **London (RVC)** 12.

Selection interviews: Edinburgh; Glasgow.

Offers to applicants repeating A-levels: Higher London (RVC) (AAA); **Unlikely** Liverpool; **Not acceptable** Edinburgh, Glasgow.

Admissions Tutors' advice: Bristol Get plenty of vet experience. Course heavily oversubscribed and good applicants MUST show motivation and experience. A gap year on a farm is useful. **Glasgow** Offers are made on grades, not points. Grades A or B in physics GCSE required. **Liverpool** Courses in Veterinary Science are heavily oversubscribed. Competition between many able and worthy candidates for a limited number of places rather than between the universities for the able and worthy candidates. Do not hesitate to write to veterinary schools on any matter affecting an application. Practical experience with livestock and in veterinary practice is essential.

Examples of interview questions: Questions asked on the A-level science syllabus. Why do you want to be a vet? Have you visited a veterinary practice? What did you see? Do you think there should be a Vet National Health Service? What are your views on vivisection? What are your views on intensive factory farming? How can you justify thousands of pounds of taxpayers' money being spent on training you to be a vet when it could be used to train a civil engineer? When would you feel it your responsibility to tell battery hen farmers that they were being cruel to their livestock? What are your views on vegetarians? How does aspirin stop pain? Why does it only work for a certain length of time?

GAP YEAR ADVICE

Institutions willing to defer entry after A-levels (see Ch 5): Bristol.

AFTER A-LEVELS ADVICE

Institutions which may accept the same points score after A-levels: Bristol; Edinburgh; Glasgow; Liverpool; London (RVC).

GRADUATE EMPLOYMENT

New Graduates' destinations (percentages) 1991:
Permanent employment: U 92.
Unemployment: U 6.
Further studies (all types): U 4.

VISUAL COMMUNICATIONS STUDIES (See also Photography, Film, TV)

Special subject requirements: art/design emphasis.

Institutions may raise or lower the level of published offers depending either on the quality or otherwise of individual applications or the numbers of applications received; grades/points offered may be adjusted downwards after A-level results. The level of an offer is not indicative of the quality of a course.

14pts.   **Oxford Brookes** - CDD/CD (Vis Studs - Modular)
4pts.   **London Inst (CP)** - EE (G Des)

CHOOSING YOUR COURSE (See also Ch 1)

Subject information: These courses normally require a Foundation art course prior to entry and focus on graphic design and communication. NOW CHECK PROSPECTUSES FOR ALL COURSES.

ADMISSIONS INFORMATION

Number of applicants per place (approx): London Inst (CP) 7.

Examples of interview questions: Applicants usually expected to show evidence of interest in art and design in their portfolio of work and will be questioned on their interests and future career aims.

WOOD SCIENCE (See also **Timber Technology**)

Special subject requirements: 3 A-levels, 2 from mathematics/science subjects.

Institutions may raise or lower the level of published offers depending either on the quality or otherwise of individual applications or the numbers of applications received; grades/points offered may be adjusted downwards after A-level results. The level of an offer is not indicative of the quality of a course.

14pts. **Bangor** – (Wood Sci Wood Sci Joint) (2AS)

There are 20 places on the course with 20 (approx) applicants. The same points score is acceptable after A-levels.

CHOOSING YOUR COURSE (See also Ch 1)

> **Subject information:** This is a unique course offered by Bangor University offering a study of wood as an industrial raw material, how it is processed, marketed and used.

Course highlights: Bangor Strong links with industry involving sponsorships and sandwich placements. Three subjects taken in first year; transfers possible between subjects in second year. Job prospects good.

ADMISSIONS INFORMATION

Admissions Tutors' advice: Bangor We offer interviews to all suitable candidates. Our main interest is in candidates studying A/AS-level chemistry, physics, biology, economics. design and technology, maths. The course covers the materials science of wood, wood processing technologies, economic and marketing aspects of the wood-based industries. Forestry can be studied in the first two years.

> **Examples of interview questions:** The interview will assess the applicant's knowledge of and interest in Wood Science. (See also under **Forestry** and **Timber Technology**)

ZOOLOGY

Special subject requirements: 2-3 A-levels, mathematics/science subjects at A and/or GCSE (grade A-C).

NB Institutions may raise or lower the level of published offers depending either on the quality or otherwise of individual applications or the numbers of applications received; grades/points offered may be adjusted downwards after A-level results. The level of an offer is not indicative of the quality of a course.

30pts. **Cambridge/Oxford** – AAA potential recommended (Nat Sci; Zool)
20pts. **Bristol** – BCC/BB (Zoology) (AS in biol if not biol/zool at A-level)
        Leeds – BCC/BB (Zoo; Comb courses) (BTEC 5M)
        Southampton – BCC-BCD (Zool)
18pts. **Aberdeen** – CCC-CCD/BC (Zool)
        Aberystwyth – CCC-CCD/BB-BC (Zoology courses) (BTEC 3M)
        Belfast – CCC/BB (Zoology)
        Birmingham – BCD (Biol Sci)
        Cardiff – BCD/AB (Zool)
        Edinburgh – CCC (Zoology)
        Leicester – BCD (Biol Sci)
        Liverpool – CCC (Zoo; Zoo Comb)

          London (Imp) - BCD-CCC (Zool)
          London (King's) - CCC approx (Zool)
          London (RH) - BCD/BC (Zoology; Zoo Physiol) (4 AS)
          Manchester - 18 pts approx (Zoology)
          Newcastle - BCD (Zool)
          Nottingham - CCC-CCD (Zoology)
          Reading - CCC (Zoology; Appl Zool)
          Sheffield - CCC (Zoology) (4 AS) (BTEC Ms)
          Swansea - CCC/BB (Zoology) (BTEC 1D+Ms)
16 pts. **Bangor** - CCD/BC (App Zoo joint degrees; Zoo M Zoo) (4 AS)(BTEC 4M)
          Glasgow - CCD/BC (Zool) (BTEC 3M)
          London (QMW) - CCD/BC (Zoology)
          London (UC) - CCD (Zoology)
14 pts. **Dundee** - CDD/BC (Zool)
          Newcastle - CDD/BC (Ag/Env/Zool)
 8 pts. **and below**
          Westminster - DD (Modular)

Alternative offers:

EB offers: **Bangor** 65%; **London (RH)** 70%; **Newcastle** 65%.

IB offers: **Aberdeen** 26 pts; **Aberystwyth** 28 pts and above; **Bangor** 28 pts H655 S555; **Bristol** 30 pts inc H655/S555; **Glasgow** H555; **Leeds** 30-28 pts; **Liverpool** 30 pts; **London (RH)** 27 pts; **Newcastle** 24 pts from 5 subjs inc H666; **Swansea** 28 pts.

Irish offers: **Aberdeen** BBBC; **Aberystwyth** BBBCC; **Bangor** BBCCC; **Dundee** BBCC; **Edinburgh** BBBB; **Glasgow** BBB; **Liverpool** BBCC; **London (RH)** BBBCC; **Newcastle** BBCC.

SCE offers: **Aberdeen** BBBC; **Glasgow** BBB; **Sheffield** BBBB.

Overseas applicants: Newcastle English language courses offered.

CHOOSING YOUR COURSE (See also Ch 1)

> **Subject information:** These courses have a biological science foundation and could cover animal ecology, marine and fisheries biology, animal population development and behaviour and on some courses wildlife management and fisheries. There is a shortage of applicants. Refer also to **Biological Sciences**.

Course highlights: Aberdeen All students take a marine biology field course and options in freshwater and marine studies. **Aberystwyth** Opportunity to change courses at start of second year. Optional one year employment scheme. **Bangor** Modular course structure now established in all three years of the course. Broad coverage of pure and applied biology. Excellent location. **Bristol** Three subjects taken in first year with final choice made at end of the year. Emphasis on animal behaviour, reproduction, neurobiology and parasitology. **Cardiff** For single honours students the theme of the course is the animal in its environment and they study the behaviour, physiology and ecology of animals and special topics on cell and marine biology. **Leeds** Six degree schemes (including Zoology) and transfer between most is possible at end of first year. A very large school of biology; transfer between departments and between single and joint honours also possible. **Liverpool** Zoology courses include animal diversity, ecology, freshwater biology and animal behaviour. **London (RH)** Course includes small mammal ecology, parasitology, fresh water ecology, neurobiology. Good contacts with employers eg, London Zoo, Metropolitan Water Board, Kew Gardens, London hospitals (physiology). **Newcastle** Degree based on ecology and behaviour. Flexible first year; course based on ecology and neurobiology. New psychology modules in each year of course. **Swansea** Modular course. Variety of marine and terrestrial habitats. See also under **Agriculture** and **Biology**. NOW CHECK PROSPECTUSES FOR ALL COURSES.

Work opportunities abroad: Bangor USA B IT FR P; **Swansea** (E) IT FR SP G P IRE.

ADMISSIONS INFORMATION

Number of applicants per place (approx): Aberystwyth 8 all Biol Sci; **Bangor** 6; **Bristol** 3; **Leeds** 11; **London (RH)** 6; **Newcastle** 10; **Nottingham** 7; **Swansea** 6.

General studies acceptable: Aberdeen; Aberystwyth; Exeter; Liverpool (JMB, Oxford, Camb only).

Selection interviews: Aberystwyth (some); Cambridge; Hull; Leeds (some); Liverpool; London (RH); Nottingham.

Offers to applicants repeating A-levels: Higher Aberystwyth; Bristol, Hull, Leeds (CCC), Swansea (2 pts); **Same** Durham, Liverpool, London (RH Bed).

Admission Tutors' advice: Aberystwyth Applicants with BTEC qualifications are considered for entry into the first year and in some cases the second year. GCSE (grade A-C) English and mathematics are required. **Leeds** (Agric Zool) All candidates are invited for interview. Offers are rarely made to those candidates not attending. Biology is the most important subject – a good grade is expected. (Zoology) A good performance in general studies may be taken into account. **Nottingham** Every application is considered in detail.

> **Examples of interview questions:** Specimens may be given to identify. Why do you want to study Zoology? What career do you hope to follow on graduation? Questions asked on the A-level syllabuses.

GAP YEAR ADVICE

Institutions accepting a Gap Year: Most institutions; **Newcastle** Use the year wisely. A year wasted is not impressive. Try to gain experience in the biological field.

Institutions willing to defer entry after A-levels (see Ch 5): Aberystwyth (Contact Admissions Tutor); Bangor; Bristol; Leeds; Newcastle (No); Swansea (Discouraged).

AFTER A-LEVELS ADVICE

Institutions which may accept the same points score after A-levels: Bangor; Bristol; Hull; Leeds; Liverpool; Southampton; Swansea.

Institutions demanding the actual grades offered after A-levels: London (RH Bed); Nottingham.

Institutions which may accept under-achieving applicants after A-levels: Aberystwyth; Bangor; Bristol; Leeds; Liverpool; London (RH); Swansea.

Institutions with vacancies in Aug/Sept 1992 (see Ch 5): Aberystwyth 14 pts; Bangor CCD; Leeds (App Z) 16 pts; Swansea 16 pts.

GRADUATE EMPLOYMENT

New Graduates' destinations (percentages) 1991:
Permanent employment: U 51.
Unemployment: U 31.
Further studies (all types): U 40.
Main career destinations (approx): Scientific 25; Business 17; Admin 14; Finance 13; Clerical 10; Medical/Social 9; Legal 5; Computing 4; Teaching 2.

BOOKLIST

Standard Reference Books

Compendium of Advanced Courses in Colleges of Further and Higher Education 1993/94 Regional Advisory Council for Technological Education, Tavistock House South, Tavistock Square, London WC1H 9LR. A list of degree and diploma courses outside the university sector. Published annually.

Handbook of Degree and Advanced Courses in Institutes of Higher Education 1994 Linneys ESL, 121 Newgate Lane, Mansfield, Notts NG18 2PA. A list of courses. Published annually.

The UCAS Handbook - 1994 Entry The Universities and Colleges Admissions System (UCAS), PO Box 28, Cheltenham, Glos GL50 3SA. Published annually.

University and College Entrance - The Official Guide Available from Sheed and Ward Ltd, 2 Creechurch Lane, London EC3A 5AQ. The official list of all degree and diploma courses, giving details of general entry requirements and average offers. Published annually.

The Scottish Universities Entrance Guide (for courses in the Scottish universities, obtainable from the Scottish Universities Council on Entrance, Kinnessburn, Kennedy Gardens, St Andrews, Fife).

Books for Career Choice

An A-Z of Careers and Jobs Kogan Page Ltd, 120 Pentonville Road, London N1 9JN.

Career Choice Pan Books Ltd, 18 Cavaye Place, London SW10.

Careers Encyclopaedia Cassell & Co Ltd, Villiers House, 41-47 Strand, London WC2N 5JE.

Careers Guide 1993/94 CASCAID Unit, County Hall, Glenfield, Leicester LE3 8RF.

Equal Opportunities - A Careers Guide Ruth Miller and Anna Alston. Penguin Books Ltd, Harmondsworth, Middlesex.

Jobfile 93 Hodder & Stoughton, Mill Road, Dunton Green, Sevenoaks, Kent TN13 2TG.

Opportunities '93 Careers and Occupational Information Centre, Moorfoot, Sheffield S1 4PQ.

The Job Book Hobsons Press, Bateman Street, Cambridge CB2 1LZ.

Getting into Higher Education

CRAC Degree Course Guides Hobsons Press, Bateman Street, Cambridge CB2 1LZ.

Getting into University and College Trotman and Company Ltd, 12 Hill Rise, Richmond, Surrey TW10 6UA.

Getting into Oxford & Cambridge Trotman and Company Ltd, 12 Hill Rise, Richmond, Surrey TW10 6UA.

Higher Education in the European Community edited by Brigitte Mohr and Innes Liebig. Office for Official Publications of the European Communities/Kogan Page, 120 Pentonville Road, London N1 9JN.

How to Choose Your Degree Course Brian Heap. Trotman and Company Ltd, 12 Hill Rise, Richmond, Surrey TW10 6UA.

How to Complete Your UCAS Form Stephen Lamley & Tony Higgins. Trotman and Company Ltd, 12 Hill Rise, Richmond, Surrey TW10 6UA.

Mature Students University Degree Courses UCAS, PO Box 28, Cheltenham, Glos GL50 1HY.

Sponsorships Careers and Occupational Information Centre, Moorfoot, Sheffield S1 4PQ.

The Sixth Former's Guide to Visits and Open Days ISCO, 12a Princes Street, Camberley, Surrey GU15 3SP.

The Student Book 1994 edited by Boehm and Wellings. Macmillan Books Ltd, 4 Little Essex Street, London WC2R 3LF.

A Two-Way Success Preparation for Higher Education Interviews. Trotman and Company Ltd, 12 Hill Rise, Richmond, Surrey TW10 6UA.

Other Useful Publications

A Survey of Access Courses in England Lucas and Ward. School of Education, The University, Lancaster, LA1 4YW.

Discretionary Awards Survey and *Welfare Manual* (Both are published by the National Union of Students and can be consulted in Student Union offices in universities and colleges.)

Grants to Students Department for Education, Sanctuary Buildings, Great Smith Street, London SW1P 5BT.

Mature Students' Handbook Iris Rosier and Lynn Earnshaw. Trotman and Company Ltd, 12 Hill Rise, Richmond, Surrey TW10 6UA.

The Kogan Page Mature Students Handbook - Make a Fresh Start Margaret Korving. Kogan Page Ltd, 120 Pentonville Road, London N1 9JN.

The Potter Guide to Higher Education Dalebank Books, 4-8 Bank Lane, Derby Dale, Huddersfield, West Yorkshire HD8 8QP.

Staying the Course: How to Survive Higher Education edited by John K Gilbert. Kogan Page, 120 Pentonville Road, London N1 9JN.

Students' Money Matters Trotman and Company Ltd, 12 Hill Rise, Richmond, Surrey TW10 6UA.

Taking a Year Off Val Butcher. Trotman and Company Ltd, 12 Hill Rise, Richmond, Surrey TW10 6UA.

Way In - After A-levels Way In - Law Way In - Business Studies Way In - Accountancy

The *Way In* series - Brian Heap. Holborn Press, 200 Greyhound Road, London W14 9RY.

Which Subject? Which Career? ed. Alan Jamieson. CRAC Publications, Bateman Street, Cambridge CB2 1LZ.

COURSE INDEX